# STANDARD PRICE GUIDE TO
# U.S. SCOUTING COLLECTIBLES

## GEORGE CUHAJ

Bookplate by Louise Cadwalader, Cincinnati,
OH, 1915.

Published by

**krause
publications**

700 E. State Street • Iola, WI  54990-0001
Telephone: 715/445-2214

**www.krause.com**

Please call or write for our free catalog.
Our toll-free number to place an order or obtain a free catalog is 800-258-0929
or please use our regular business telephone 715-445-2214
for editorial comment and further information.

Library of Congress Catalog Number: 97-80596
ISBN: 0-87341-520-5

Printed in the United States of America

Illustration on next page by Mel Kishner (1915–1991), who was a Milwaukee native and graduate of North Division High School and the Milwaukee State Teachers College (now University of Wisconsin - Milwaukee.) Professionally, he started working for *The Journal* in 1940, and in 1970 was appointed art director for *The Journal and Milwaukee Sentinel*. He retired in 1978. In his private life, his painting earned national awards, and he served four terms as president of the Wisconsin Painters and Sculptors organization. The father of four children, his widow, Jane, kindly granted permission to use this illustration in the catalog.

# TABLE OF CONTENTS

# DEDICATION

When one spends 30 years in the scout program there are opportunities to meet council executives, chief scout executives, mayors, crown princes, and presidents; however, it is really the people who bring scouting to the boy on a weekly basis that leave the lasting impression and to whom this book is dedicated.

For John Williamson, who grew up in the program as a cub and scout, and was eventually Assistant Scoutmaster of Troop 201 in Gateway District, Queens Council. A fellow advisor in the Tatanta Chapter of Suanhacky Lodge #49, whose life was cut short in October 1993 when killed in the line of duty as a New York City Housing Police Officer. Fond memories of collecting and camping remain with me.

A scout has influences, be they mother, Eileen, who as others' Den Mother and later Cub-

George Cuhaj and John Williamson on a Suanhacky Lodge Honors Weekend. Photo by Robert Petrillo.

master, enjoys working with neighborhood youth and saw the benefits of scouting in the life of her son. To the troop leaders of my scout years, Joseph Chvatal, Andrew Paraschuk, and Robert Ohrablo, who gave up their time for us kids.

For my father, George, who as a stamp collector got me interested in collecting. Realizing that my stamp collection would never be equal to his, I got going on a lifetime interest in coins, tokens, and medals. Dad enjoyed scouting through stamps, along with John Kubat, Jack Knoops, and Joe O'Hare. All four are now gone and are missed.

To my fellow scout leaders of the Gateway District and Suanhacky Lodge of Queens Council, NY, who gave me opportunities for leadership on training courses and adventure on touring camps ranging in location from Vermont to the Florida Keys and westward to Yellowstone and the Grand Canyon. Thanks Ralph, John, Bruce, Bro. Hugh, Fr. Barry, Kevin, Franco, Reidan, Rob, Frank, Dennis, Mitch, Ina, Leona, Joan, Johann…and the rest.

My first experiences of collecting scouting stuff came from working with three 50-year volunteer members of the B.S.A.: Julius Yavarkovsky "Julie Y," John "Jack" Kohler, and John Kubat. They, as all collectors do, reveled in sharing their collections of books, neckerchiefs, stories, patches, and stamps with one beginning in the hobby. I also thank Rudy Dioszegi whose interest in scout tokens brought me into involvement with his book project.

Finally to the leaders of my home since 1993, the Twin Lakes District of The Bay Lakes Council in central Wisconsin, where I currently do my scouting.

— George Cuhaj

# ACKNOWLEDGMENTS AND THANKS

There are probably hundreds of people who have assisted in this project, by offering items for sale either by printed list, at a trade-o-ree, or on the Internet.

This author would like to single out the following authors and collectors for their assistance with the use of their published works:

Doug Bearce

Rudy Dioszegi

Fred Duersch

Chuck Fisk

Terry Groves

Jane Kishner

John Pleasants

Jim and Bea Stevenson

John Vacca

# INTRODUCTION

Welcome to this first edition of the *Standard Price Guide to U.S. Scouting Collectibles* brought to you by Krause Publications. The author's goal was to list items most commonly encountered by the casual collector and to include adequate descriptions and helpful photographs for one to use this guide as a means of identification and price information.

Special highlights in this guide are extensive specialized listings in the Boy Scout section including knives, merit badge pamphlets and merit badges, medallions (which are known as coins to some), postcards and greeting cards, seals, War Service Awards, National and World Jamboree items, calendars, handbooks, and series and fiction books. Listings of Council Shoulder Patches or O.A. Lodge Flaps are not included in this book because they are covered in very large specialized publications which are already standards in their own right. To have included them here would be to have made this work too large.

Should you require more information on a collecting specialty—books, rank patches, medallions, or any of the others—please consider purchasing the specialty volume for the area of interest. Titles of a number of quality resources are listed in the Reference Books section.

I come to author this book from a scouting background of 30 years, growing up in the program from a Cub through Eagle Scout, and attending Philmont and the 1977 Jamboree along the way. Staying with the troop I was in as a youth, I served as Scoutmaster for 13 years, had an opportunity to be a summer camp staff member at Camp Aquehonga, Ten Mile River Scout Camps, and a member of the Brooklyn Diocese Catholic Committee on Scouting. Later I was awarded the Silver Beaver Award by the Queens Council and the Vigil Honor by Suanhacky Lodge #49. I organized and staffed the Coin Collecting Merit Badge Booths at the National Jamborees of 1981, 1985, 1989, 1993, and 1997. Upon relocating to central Wisconsin, I have remained active as an Assistant Scoutmaster and am now Troop Committee Chairman, and have started to work on District Training staff and with the Catholic Committee of the Green Bay Diocese.

Professionally, I have been employed by the American Numismatic Society as its computer systems operator, Chief Usher at St. Patrick's Cathedral, Catalog Production Manager for Stack's Rare Coins, and most recently Numismatic and Philatelic Catalog Production Manager for Krause Publications, Iola, WI. So, collecting, cataloging, and publishing have been both a profession and an avocation, mainly due to exposure through scouting's Merit Badge Program.

I am sorry for any omissions. Should you have information which you would like to see considered for future editions, please contact the author.

George S. Cuhaj
P.O. Box 433
Iola, WI 54945
cuhajg@krause.com

THE BOY SCOUT

COPYRIGHT, 1912, R. HILL

A popular print for framing from 1914, value $20.00 - $30.00.

# HOW TO USE THIS BOOK

Each major chapter starts on its own page, usually with a very short introduction and historical perspective. The chapters are organized first by the program group (Cub Scout, Boy Scout, Sea Scout, etc.). The second breakdown is to type of material (handbooks, rank badges, medallions, pinbacks, etc.). There are nearly 35 different groupings, with most sections having a miscellaneous listing area.

The specific listing titles are large and bold for the major identification, and the variety identifications appear following in a smaller typeface. On the line of the variety identification appear a years-of-use range, and then a reference and range of price.

# A WORD ABOUT THE CROSS REFERENCES

In the past 15 years specialists have developed detailed publications on specialized areas of scouting collectibles. These specialists have assigned numbers to specific identifiable items. These numbering systems have become a standard identification within the hobby, in auctions, and trade listings. These systems are used in this book and referenced at the beginning of each section when used.

For example:

### Handbook for Scoutmasters

| | | |
|---|---|---|
| Proof editions (3). 203 or | | |
| 161 pgs.1912-1912 | F.SM.1.1-3 | 150.00 - 200.00 |
| 1st Edition. 344, 352, or | | |
| 404 pgs. plus ads. | | |
| 9 printings. 1913-1919 | F.SM.2.4-10 | 125.00 - 175.00 |
| 2nd Edition. 1st printing. | | |
| 608 pgs.1920-1920 | F.SM.3.11 | 100.00 - 135.00 |

In this example, the "F" stands for the Bearce and Fisk book, *Collecting Boy Scout Literature.* The "SM" designation stands for Scoutmaster Handbooks. The numbers that follow are Bearce and Fisk variety numbers. Similar listings can be found for medallions, eagle medals, rank badges and Lone Scout items.

# THE PRICE RANGE

In general, the prices are for items in good condition. Square merit badges cut to round will be worth less than half the low price, while square merit badges with lots of space, and never sewn on a sash, could be worth double the high price. The range is for items in a condition commonly encountered. In the open market, and over time, you may be able to purchase items at less than the catalog range, more than the catalog range, and maybe within the catalog range. Supply, demand, and venue all play a part in the equation.

The best thing on an 8th Birthday—a Cub Scout Uniform!

# Cub Scouts

The Cub Scout program went nationwide to join the Boy Scout program in 1930, but many troops had unofficial Junior Scouts or troop mascots—even the national supply division sold the English Wolf Cub's Handbook in the late 1920s. The Cub program is divided into age groups. When the program first began, a boy joined at nine, advancing to Wolf the first year. At ten he became a Bear and at eleven a Lion. The Cubs wore knickers or shorts until 1947, when long pants were introduced. In 1949, when the Boy Scouts lowered the joining age to eleven, the Cub program lowered its to eight. In 1969, Webelos replaced Lion, and in 1982 a Tiger Cub program was introduced for seven-year-olds. Each group of eight or so Cubs was organized into dens, with a Den Mother (more recently Den Leader) in charge. A group of dens is organized into a Cub Pack, with a Cubmaster as the unit leader.

## RANK BADGES

### Arrow of Light

| | | |
|---|---|---|
| Blue bordered yellow arrow on khaki fine twill cut edge border. | 1965-1973 | 3.00 - 5.00 |
| Blue bordered yellow arrow on khaki rough twill cut edge border. | 1940-1965 | 3.00 - 5.00 |
| Blue bordered yellow arrow on khaki twill. Plastic back. | 1973 | 1.00 - 2.00 |

### Arrow Point

| | | |
|---|---|---|
| Gold, cloth back. | 1930-1970 | 1.00 - 2.00 |
| Gold, plastic back. | 1970 | 0.25 - 0.50 |
| Silver, cloth back. | 1930-1970 | 1.00 - 2.00 |
| Silver, plastic back. | 1970 | 0.25 - 0.50 |

### Bear Patch

| | | |
|---|---|---|
| Felt. | 1930-1940 | 3.00 - 5.00 |
| Twill, cloth back. | 1940-1975 | 1.00 - 2.00 |
| Twill, plastic back. | 1975 | 0.50 - 1.00 |

### Bobcat Patch

| | | |
|---|---|---|
| Twill, plastic back. | 1975 | 0.50 - 1.00 |

### Bobcat Pin

| | | |
|---|---|---|
| Clutch back. | 1965 | 1.00 - 2.00 |
| Safety pin back. | 1957-1965 | 2.00 - 3.00 |

### Lion Patch

| | | |
|---|---|---|
| Felt. | 1930-1940 | 3.00 - 5.00 |
| Twill, cloth back. | 1930-1940 | 1.00 - 2.00 |

## Sports Belt Loop

| | | |
|---|---|---|
| Archery | 1985 | 0.25 - 0.50 |
| Art | 1985 | 0.25 - 0.50 |
| Badminton | 1985 | 0.25 - 0.50 |
| Baseball | 1985 | 0.25 - 0.50 |
| Basketball | 1985 | 0.25 - 0.50 |
| BB Shooting | 1985 | 0.25 - 0.50 |
| Bicycling | 1985 | 0.25 - 0.50 |
| Bowling | 1985 | 0.25 - 0.50 |
| Citizenship | 1985 | 0.25 - 0.50 |
| Communicating | 1985 | 0.25 - 0.50 |
| Fishing | 1985 | 0.25 - 0.50 |
| Geography | 1985 | 0.25 - 0.50 |
| Golf | 1985 | 0.25 - 0.50 |
| Gymnastics | 1985 | 0.25 - 0.50 |
| Heritages | 1985 | 0.25 - 0.50 |
| Marbles | 1985 | 0.25 - 0.50 |
| Mathematics | 1985 | 0.25 - 0.50 |
| Music | 1985 | 0.25 - 0.50 |
| Physical Fitness | 1985 | 0.25 - 0.50 |
| Science | 1985 | 0.25 - 0.50 |
| Skating | 1985 | 0.25 - 0.50 |
| Skiing | 1985 | 0.25 - 0.50 |
| Soccer | 1985 | 0.25 - 0.50 |
| Softball | 1985 | 0.25 - 0.50 |
| Swimming | 1985 | 0.25 - 0.50 |
| Table Tennis | 1985 | 0.25 - 0.50 |
| Tennis | 1985 | 0.25 - 0.50 |
| Ultimate | 1985 | 0.25 - 0.50 |
| Volleyball | 1985 | 0.25 - 0.50 |

## Webelos Activity Badge

| | | |
|---|---|---|
| Aquanaut. Enameled pin. | 1990 | 0.50 - 0.75 |
| Aquanaut. Nickel pin. | 1970 | 1.00 - 2.00 |
| Artist. Enameled pin. | 1990 | 0.50 - 0.75 |

| | | |
|---|---|---|
| Artist. Nickel pin. | 1970 | 1.00 - 2.00 |
| Athlete. Enameled pin. | 1990 | 0.50 - 0.75 |
| Athlete. Nickel pin. | 1970 | 1.00 - 2.00 |
| Citizen. Enameled pin. | 1990 | 0.50 - 0.75 |
| Citizen. Nickel pin. | 1970 | 1.00 - 2.00 |
| Communicator. Enameled pin. | 1990 | 0.50 - 0.75 |
| Craftsman. Enameled pin. | 1990 | 0.50 - 0.75 |
| Craftsman. Nickel pin. | 1970 | 1.00 - 2.00 |
| Engineer. Enameled pin. | 1990 | 0.50 - 0.75 |
| Engineer. Nickel pin. | 1970 | 1.00 - 2.00 |
| Family Member. Enameled pin. | 1990 | 0.50 - 0.75 |
| Fitness. Enameled pin. | 1990 | 0.50 - 0.75 |
| Forester. Enameled pin. | 1990 | 0.50 - 0.75 |
| Forester. Nickel pin. | 1970 | 1.00 - 2.00 |
| Geologist. Enameled pin. | 1990 | 0.50 - 0.75 |
| Geologist. Nickel pin. | 1970 | 1.00 - 2.00 |
| Handyman. Enameled pin. | 1990 | 0.50 - 0.75 |
| Naturalist. Enameled pin. | 1990 | 0.50 - 0.75 |
| Naturalist. Nickel pin. | 1970 | 1.00 - 2.00 |
| Outdoorsman. Enameled pin. | 1990 | 0.50 - 0.75 |
| Outdoorsman. Nickel pin. | 1970 | 1.00 - 2.00 |
| Readyman. Enameled pin. | 1990 | 0.50 - 0.75 |
| Scholar. Enameled pin. | 1990 | 0.50 - 0.75 |
| Scholar. Nickel pin. | 1970 | 1.00 - 2.00 |
| Scientist. Enameled pin. | 1990 | 0.50 - 0.75 |
| Scientist. Nickel pin. | 1970 | 1.00 - 2.00 |
| Showman. Enameled pin. | 1990 | 0.50 - 0.75 |
| Showman. Nickel pin. | 1970 | 1.00 - 2.00 |
| Sportsman. Enameled pin. | 1990 | 0.50 - 0.75 |
| Sportsman. Nickel pin. | 1970 | 1.00 - 2.00 |
| Traveler. Enameled pin. | 1990 | 0.50 - 0.75 |
| Traveler. Nickel pin. | 1970 | 1.00 - 2.00 |

### Webelos compass points emblem and devices
| | 1985 | 1.00 - 2.00 |
|---|---|---|

### Webelos Patch
| | | |
|---|---|---|
| W, cloth patch. | 1965 - 1969 | 2.00 - 3.00 |
| Twill, cloth back. | 1969 - 1975 | 1.00 - 2.00 |
| Twill, plastic back. | 1975 | 0.50 - 1.00 |

### Webelos Tri-color
| | | |
|---|---|---|
| Locking pin. | 1970 | 2.00 - 3.00 |
| Pin, clutch back. | 1990 | 1.00 - 2.00 |

### Wolf Patch
| | | |
|---|---|---|
| Felt. | 1930-1940 | 3.00 - 5.00 |
| Twill, cloth back. | 1940-1975 | 1.00 - 2.00 |
| Twill, plastic back. | 1975 | 0.50 - 1.00 |

# POSITION BADGES

### Assistant Denner
| | | |
|---|---|---|
| 1 gold bar on blue twill cut cloth. | 1930-1955 | 10.00 - 15.00 |
| 1 gold bar on blue twill cut edge. | 1955-1964 | 8.00 - 10.00 |
| 1 gold bar on blue twill rolled edge, cloth back. | 1965-1975 | 3.00 - 5.00 |
| 1 gold bar on blue twill rolled edge, plastic back. | 1975 | 1.00 - 2.00 |

### Denner
| | | |
|---|---|---|
| 2 gold bars on blue twill cut cloth. | 1930-1955 | 10.00 - 15.00 |
| 2 gold bars on blue twill cut edge. | 1955-1964 | 8.00 - 10.00 |
| 2 gold bars on blue twill rolled edge, cloth back. | 1965-1975 | 3.00 - 5.00 |
| 2 gold bars on blue twill rolled edge, plastic back. | 1975 | 1.00 - 2.00 |

# HANDBOOKS

### The Boy's Cubbook Vol. 1, Wolf
Drawing of Indian on board cover.
| 7 printings. | 1930-1935 | 15.00 - 25.00 |
|---|---|---|

### The Wolf Cubbook
| Wolf and cub on card cover. 8 printings. | 1936-1942 | 10.00 - 15.00 |
|---|---|---|
| Wolf and cub on card cover. 7 printings, w/ color plates. | 1943-1946 | 10.00 - 15.00 |

### Wolf Book
| | | |
|---|---|---|
| Red cover. 8 printings. | 1947-1954 | 5.00 - 10.00 |
| 13 printings. | 1954-1965 | 4.00 - 6.00 |
| 24 printings. | 1967-1979 | 2.00 - 3.00 |

### The Boy's Cubbook Vol. 2, Bear
Drawing of Indian on board cover.
| 9 printings. | 1930-1937 | 15.00 - 25.00 |
|---|---|---|

### The Bear Cubbook
| Bear and cub on card cover. 9 printings. | 1937-1942 | 10.00 - 15.00 |
|---|---|---|

### The Bear Cubbook, w/ color plates
| Bear and cub on card cover. 7 printings w/ color plates. | 1943-1947 | 10.00 - 15.00 |
|---|---|---|

### Bear Book
| | | |
|---|---|---|
| Blue cover. 7 printings. | 1948-1953 | 5.00 - 10.00 |
| 13 printings. | 1954-1965 | 4.00 - 6.00 |
| 24 printings. | 1967-1979 | 2.00 - 3.00 |

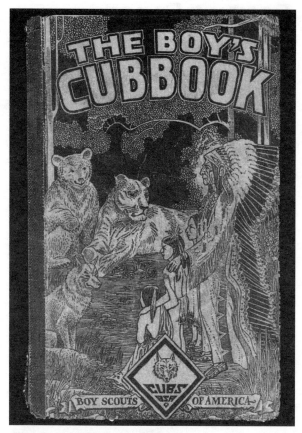

The Boy's Cubbook, 1930-35

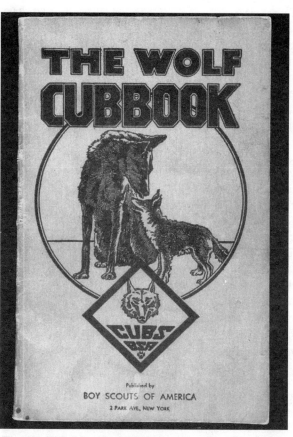

The Wolf Cubbook, 1936-42

Wolf Cub Scout Book, 1947-54

Wolf Cub Scout Book, 1954-65

 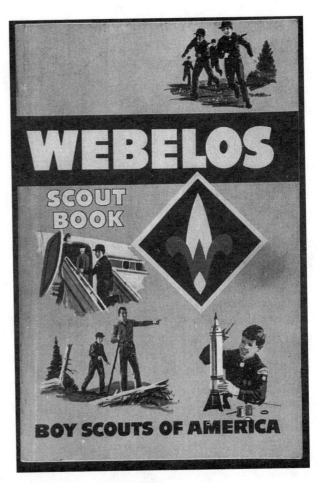

At left is the Lion-Webelos Book (1954-65); the Webelos Book at right was used from 1967-79.

## The Boy's Cubbook Vol. 3, Lion
Drawing of Indian on board cover.
8 printings.                          1930-1937  15.00 - 25.00

## The Lion Cubbook
Lion and cub on card cover. 7 printings.   1938-1942  10.00 - 15.00
Lion and cub on card cover. 4 printings,
w/ color plates.                           1943-1946  10.00 - 15.00

## Lion Book
Black cover. 9 printings.              1947-1953  5.00 - 10.00

## Lion-Webelos Book
15 printings.                         1954-1965  4.00 - 6.00

## Webelos Book
26 printings including 1 in Spanish.  1967-1979  2.00 - 3.00

# AWARD MEDALS

## Pinewood Derby Medal
Race car in red, white, or blue enamel disc
  hanging from red-white-blue ribbon.  1981       2.00 - 3.00
Race car in relief. Copper, silvered, or
  gilt pendant.                        1970-1980  3.00 - 5.00

## Regatta Medal
Ship in red, white, or blue enamel disc
  hanging from red-white-blue ribbon.  1981       2.00 - 3.00
Ship in relief. Copper, silvered, or
  gilt pendant.                        1970-1980  3.00 - 5.00

## Space Derby Medal
Space craft in red, white, or blue
  enamel disc hanging from
  red-white-blue ribbon.               1981       2.00 - 3.00
Space craft in relief. Copper,
  silvered, or gilt pendant.           1970-1980  3.00 - 5.00

## Summertime Pack Award Pin
                                       1981       0.50 - 1.00

The CUBS BSA program strip above the left shirt pocket identifies a uniform shirt from the early 1930s.

# UNIFORMS

### Assistant Denner
Shoulder Cord. 1 yellow cord and tab.
    Safety pin back.                          1970        5.00 - 7.50

### Cub Hat
Blue baseball style w/ yellow front section. 1970        3.00 - 6.00
Blue w/ yellow stripes, CUB SCOUTS BSA
    on patch emblem.                       1940-1970   10.00 - 15.00
Blue w/ yellow stripes, CUBS BSA on
    patch emblem.                          1930-1940   15.00 - 20.00

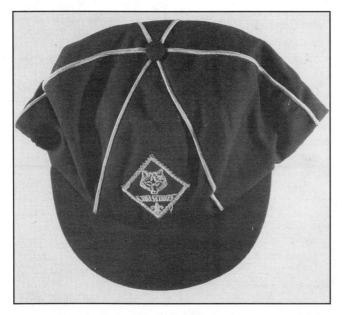

The familiar hat from the 1940s through the 1960s was a rounded and striped small-billed item.

### Denner
Shoulder Cord. 2 yellow cords and tab.
    Safety pin back.                          1970        5.00 - 7.50

### Knee Socks
Blue w/ yellow tops.                          1975        4.00 - 7.50
Blue w/ elastic garters and yellow tabs.   1930-1975   10.00 - 15.00

### Knickers
Buckle below knee.                         1930-1947   15.00 - 25.00

### Long Paints
W/ button down flap on pocket.             1947-1970   10.00 - 15.00

### Long Sleeve Shirt
Plain front pockets.                       1970-1990    5.00 - 10.00
Pleated pockets.                           1947-1970    7.50 - 10.00

### Neckerchief
Webelos plaid w/ patch sewn on.            1970-1980    5.00 - 7.50
Yellow, w/ CUB SCOUTS BSA on emblem.
    Triangle.                              1940-1970    7.50 - 10.00
Yellow, w/ CUBS BSA on emblem.
    Full square.                           1930-1940   15.00 - 20.00
Yellow, w/ CUBS BSA on emblem.
    Triangle.                              1930-1940   12.50 - 17.50

### Service Star
Gold star w/ tenure number, clutch back pin.
    Yellow plastic disc.                      1956        0.50 - 1.00

### Short Sleeve Shirt
Plain front pockets.                       1970-1990    5.00 - 10.00
Pleated pockets.                           1947-1970   10.00 - 15.00

### Shorts                                  1930-1947   10.00 - 15.00

### Unit Number
Blue twill w/ yellow embroidery.              1950        1.00 - 1.50
Yellow felt rectangle w/ blue embroidery.  1930-1950    3.00 - 5.00

### Web belt
CUB SCOUTS BSA on buckle emblem.           1940-1970    2.50 - 7.50
CUBS BSA on buckle emblem.                 1930-1940   10.00 - 15.00

### Webelos Hat
Blue baseball style w/ Webelos patch.         1970        3.00 - 6.00

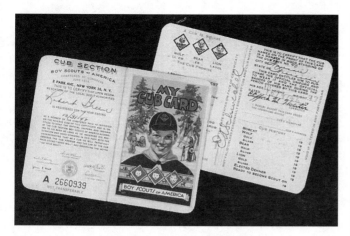

Early Cub membership cards were colorful.

Advancement cards from the late 1940s.

# ADVANCEMENT CARDS

## Arrow of Light Card
Colored patch on yellow background. 1972-1989 0.50 - 1.00

## Bear Cub Card
CUBS BSA at bottom of diamond-shaped
card. 1930-1950 5.00 - 7.50
CUBS BSA on patch design flanked by
orange color bar. 1945-1953 3.00 - 5.00
CUB SCOUTS BSA on patch design. 1953-1965 2.00 - 4.00
Colored patch on blue background. 1972-1989 0.50 - 1.00

## Bobcat Cub Card
CUBS BSA on patch design flanked by
orange color bar. 1945-1953 3.00 - 5.00
CUB SCOUTS BSA on patch design. 1953-1965 2.00 - 4.00
Colored patch on blue background. 1972-1989 0.50 - 1.00

## Lion Cub Card
CUBS BSA at bottom of diamond-shaped
card. 1930-1950 5.00 - 7.50
CUBS BSA on patch design flanked by
orange color bar. 1945-1953 3.00 - 5.00
CUB SCOUTS BSA on patch design. 1953-1965 2.00 - 4.00

## Webelos Card
Arrow of Light patch design flanked by
orange color bar. 1945-1953 3.00 - 5.00
Arrow of Light design. 1953-1965 2.00 - 4.00
Webelos badge patch on gray background. 1972-1989 0.50 - 1.00

## Wolf Cub Card
CUBS BSA at bottom of diamond-shaped
card. 1930-1950 5.00 - 7.50
CUBS BSA on patch design flanked by
orange color bar. 1945-1953 3.00 - 5.00
CUB SCOUTS BSA on patch design. 1953-1965 2.00 - 4.00
Colored patch on blue background. 1972-1989 0.50 - 1.00

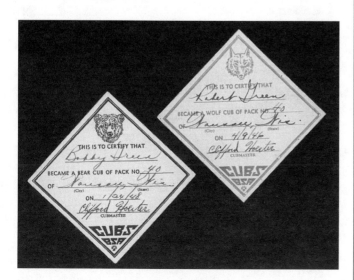

Some early advancement cards were privately printed.

Advancement cards from the 1970s.

# PINBACK BUTTONS

## Cub Scout Facing

| | | |
|---|---|---|
| On red-white-blue. 7/8". | 1940-1946 | 3.00 - 5.00 |
| On red-white-blue. 1-1/4". | 1940-1946 | 7.50 - 10.00 |

# MEDALLIONS

Medallions are referenced to Rudy Diozegi's book *Scouting Exonumnia Worldwide.*

## Audubon District Cub Scouts, New Orleans, LA, Mardi Gras

| | | | |
|---|---|---|---|
| 39mm, bronze. | 1969 | Dio.1969.13.d | 1.00 - 2.00 |
| 39mm, aluminum. | 1969 | Dio.1969.13a | 1.00 - 2.00 |
| 39mm, aluminum, blue color. | 1969 | Dio.1969.13b | 1.00 - 2.00 |
| 39mm, aluminum, golden color. | 1969 | Dio.1969.13c | 1.00 - 2.00 |
| 39mm, .999 fine silver. | 1969 | Dio.1969.13e | 20.00 - 25.00 |

## Audubon District Cub Scouts, New Orleans, LA

| | | | |
|---|---|---|---|
| 39mm, aluminum, 5 rotation or edge varieties. | 1971 | Dio.1971.9a | 1.00 - 2.00 |
| 39mm, aluminum, blue color. | 1971 | Dio.1971.9b | 1.00 - 2.00 |
| 39mm, oxidized bronze. | 1971 | Dio.1971.9c | 1.00 - 2.00 |
| 39mm, bronze. | 1971 | Dio.1971.9d | 1.00 - 2.00 |
| 39mm, .999 fine silver. | 1971 | Dio.1971.9e | 20.00 - 25.00 |
| 39mm, aluminum. | 1972 | Dio.1972.13a | 1.00 - 2.00 |
| 39mm, aluminum, blue color. | 1972 | Dio.1972.13b | 1.00 - 2.00 |
| 39mm, bronze. | 1972 | Dio.1972.13b | 1.00 - 2.00 |
| 39mm, aluminum. | 1973 | Dio.1973.13a | 1.00 - 2.00 |
| 39mm, aluminum, blue color. | 1973 | Dio.1973.13b | 1.00 - 2.00 |
| 39mm, oxidized bronze. | 1973 | Dio.1973.13c | 1.00 - 2.00 |
| 39mm, bright bronze. | 1973 | Dio.1973.13d | 1.00 - 2.00 |

## Audubon District, New Orleans, LA, Cub Scouts

| | | | |
|---|---|---|---|
| 39mm, aluminum. | 1968 | Dio.1968.6a | 1.00 - 2.00 |
| 39mm, aluminum, blue color. | 1968 | Dio.1968.6b | 1.00 - 2.00 |
| 39mm, bronze. | 1968 | Dio.1968.6c | 1.00 - 2.00 |
| 39mm, .999 fine silver. | 1968 | Dio.1968.6d | 20.00 - 25.00 |

## Cub Scout Pack #73, Mater Dolorosa School, New Orleans, LA

| | | | |
|---|---|---|---|
| 40mm, .999 fine silver. | 1969 | Dio.1969.14.d | 20.00 - 25.00 |
| 40mm, aluminum. | 1969 | Dio.1969.14a | 1.00 - 2.00 |
| 40mm, aluminum, blue color. | 1969 | Dio.1969.14b | 1.00 - 2.00 |
| 40mm, bronze. | 1969 | Dio.1969.14c | 1.00 - 2.00 |
| 40mm, oxidized bronze. | 1969 | Dio.1969.14e | 1.00 - 2.00 |

## Cub Scout Pack #73, Mater Dolorosa School, New Orleans

| | | | |
|---|---|---|---|
| 40mm, aluminum. | 1968 | Dio.1968.7a | 1.00 - 2.00 |
| 40mm, aluminum, golden color. | 1968 | Dio.1968.7b | 1.00 - 2.00 |
| 40mm, bronze. | 1968 | Dio.1968.7c | 1.00 - 2.00 |
| 40mm, .999 fine silver. | 1968 | Dio.1968.7d | 20.00 - 25.00 |
| 40mm, aluminum, blue color. | 1968 | Dio.1968.7e | 1.00 - 2.00 |

## Cub Scout Promise Official Medal

| | | | |
|---|---|---|---|
| 32mm, bronze, square. | 1992 | Dio.1992.6 | 2.00 - 3.00 |

## Cub Scouts, 50th Anniversary, Cub Promise reverse

| | | | |
|---|---|---|---|
| 33mm, brass, square. | 1980 | Dio.1980.2 | 2.00 - 3.00 |

## Cub Scouts, BSA, Cub Promise

| | | | |
|---|---|---|---|
| 32mm, bronze. Correct quotes. | 1970 | Dio.1970.1a | 1.00 - 2.00 |
| 32mm, bronze. Inverted quotes. | 1970 | Dio.1970.1a1 | 1.00 - 2.00 |
| 32mm, bronze. Paw filled in. | 1970 | Dio.1970.1b | 1.00 - 2.00 |

## Cub Scouts, BSA, Cub Promise Key Chain

| | | | |
|---|---|---|---|
| Wolf w/ full ears, 31mm, brass. | 1950 | Dio.1950.11a | 3.00 - 4.00 |
| Wolf w/ full ears, double thickness. 32mm, brass. | 1950 | Dio.1950.11b | 3.00 - 4.00 |
| Wolf w/ pointed ears, 32mm, brass. | 1950 | Dio.1950.11c | 3.00 - 4.00 |

## Cub Scouts, Cub Promise

| | | | |
|---|---|---|---|
| Comma after "People" on reverse. 32mm, bronze, square, not holed. | 1972 | Dio.1972.18a | 1.00 - 2.00 |
| No comma after "People" on reverse. 32mm, bronze, square, not holed. | 1972 | Dio.1972.18b | 1.00 - 2.00 |

## Cubs BSA Pocket Piece

| | | | |
|---|---|---|---|
| 31mm, bright bronze, holed. | 1935 | Dio.1935.2 | 4.00 - 5.00 |

## Ei Cuhaj, Gateway District, Queens Council, NY, Personal Token

| | | | |
|---|---|---|---|
| 42mm, blue plastic, gold letting. 1985 | | Dio.1985.4 | 1.00 - 2.00 |

## Johnny Appleseed Council, OH, Catch that Pepsi Spirit

| | | | |
|---|---|---|---|
| Bobcat Badge. 38mm, bronze, cast. | 1982 | Dio.1982.4 | 8.00 - 15.00 |
| Wolf Badge. 38mm, bronze, cast. | 1982 | Dio.1982.5 | 8.00 - 15.00 |
| Bear Badge. 38mm, bronze, cast. | 1982 | Dio.1982.6 | 8.00 - 15.00 |
| Webelos Badge. 38mm, bronze, cast. | 1982 | Dio.1982.7 | 8.00 - 15.00 |
| Arrow of Light Award. 38mm, bronze, cast. | 1982 | Dio.1982.9 | 8.00 - 15.00 |

## New Orleans Area Council, LA, Pow Wow

| | | | |
|---|---|---|---|
| 39mm, aluminum. | 1975 | Dio.1975.9a | 1.00 - 2.00 |
| 39mm, aluminum, golden color. | 1975 | Dio.1975.9b | 1.00 - 2.00 |
| 39mm, aluminum, purple. | 1975 | Dio.1975.9c | 1.00 - 2.00 |

## New Orleans Area Council, Pow Wow

| | | | |
|---|---|---|---|
| 39mm, aluminum, bronze color. | 1973 | Dio.1973.16a | 1.00 - 2.00 |
| 39mm, aluminum. | 1973 | Dio.1973.16b | 1.00 - 2.00 |
| 39mm, blue aluminum. | 1977 | Dio.1977.5a | 1.00 - 2.00 |
| 39mm, red aluminum. | 1977 | Dio.1977.5b | 1.00 - 2.00 |
| 39mm, aluminum. | 1977 | Dio.1977.5c | 1.00 - 2.00 |

## New Orleans Council, LA, Pow Wow

| | | | |
|---|---|---|---|
| 39mm, aluminum. | 1967 | Dio.1967.8a | 1.00 - 2.00 |
| 39mm, aluminum, blue color. | 1967 | Dio.1967.8b | 1.00 - 2.00 |
| 39mm, bronze. | 1967 | Dio.1967.8c | 1.00 - 2.00 |
| 39mm, oxidized bronze. | 1967 | Dio.1967.8d | 1.00 - 2.00 |
| 39mm, bronze. | 1968 | Dio.1968.8a | 1.00 - 2.00 |
| 39mm, aluminum. | 1968 | Dio.1968.8b | 1.00 - 2.00 |
| 39mm, .999 fine silver. | 1968 | Dio.1968.8c | 20.00 - 25.00 |
| 39mm, aluminum, blue color. | 1969 | Dio.1969.15a | 1.00 - 2.00 |
| 39mm, aluminum, golden color. | 1969 | Dio.1969.15b | 1.00 - 2.00 |
| 39mm, bronze. | 1969 | Dio.1969.15c | 1.00 - 2.00 |
| 39mm, aluminum, green color. | 1969 | Dio.1969.15d | 1.00 - 2.00 |
| 39mm, aluminum. | 1971 | Dio.1971.10a | 1.00 - 2.00 |
| 39mm, aluminum, green color. | 1971 | Dio.1971.10b | 20.00 - 25.00 |
| 39mm, aluminum, red color. | 1971 | Dio.1971.10c | 1.00 - 2.00 |
| 39mm, oxidized bronze. | 1971 | Dio.1971.10d | 1.00 - 2.00 |
| 39mm, aluminum. | 1972 | Dio.1972.15a | 1.00 - 2.00 |
| 39mm, aluminum, purple color. | 1972 | Dio.1972.15b | 1.00 - 2.00 |
| 39mm, aluminum, copper color. | 1972 | Dio.1972.15c | 1.00 - 2.00 |
| 39mm, oxidized bronze. | 1972 | Dio.1972.15d | 1.00 - 2.00 |

## Tiger Cubs, Official, Program Emblem, Search, Discover and Share

| | | | |
|---|---|---|---|
| 31mm, bronze, square. | 1992 | Dio.1992.5 | 2.00 - 3.00 |

# RELIGIOUS AWARDS - YOUTH

### Aleph
| | | |
|---|---|---|
| Jewish. Lamp on open scroll. | 1980 | 7.50 - 12.50 |

### Bismillah
| | | |
|---|---|---|
| Islamic. Arabic calligraphy. | 1980 | 7.50 - 12.50 |

### Chi Rho
| | | |
|---|---|---|
| Eastern Orthodox. White cross w/ red orthodox cross within. | 1980 | 7.50 - 12.50 |

### Dharma
| | | |
|---|---|---|
| Hindu. Legend on diamond pendant. | 1980 | 7.50 - 12.50 |

### Faith in God
| | | |
|---|---|---|
| Church of Jesus Christ of Latter-day Saints (Mormon). Father, mother, and son before Salt Lake Temple. | 1980 | 7.50 - 12.50 |

### Friends, That of God
| | | |
|---|---|---|
| Religious Society of Friends (Quakers). The Light Shines on in the Dark legend around compass. | 1980 | 7.50 - 12.50 |

### God and Country, God and Family
| | | |
|---|---|---|
| Episcopal. Red cross on white field, stars in blue 1st quadrant. | 1980 | 7.50 - 12.50 |
| Protestant. Red cross on white field. | 1980 | 7.50 - 12.50 |

### God and Country, God and Me
| | | |
|---|---|---|
| Protestant. Red cross on white field. | 1980 | 7.50 - 12.50 |

### God and Country
| | | |
|---|---|---|
| First Church of Christ Scientist. Red cross on white field. | 1980 | 7.50 - 12.50 |

### God and Family
| | | |
|---|---|---|
| The Salvation Army. Army emblem. | 1980 | 7.50 - 12.50 |

### God and Life
| | | |
|---|---|---|
| The Salvation Army. Army emblem. | 1980 | 7.50 - 12.50 |

### Joyful Servant
| | | |
|---|---|---|
| Churches of Christ. Cross and 4 hearts within white field. | 1980 | 7.50 - 12.50 |

### Light of Christ
| | | |
|---|---|---|
| Roman Catholic. Youth w/ candle. | 1980 | 7.50 - 12.50 |

## Love and Help
Unitarian Universalist. Flame on pedestal,
    church steeple in background.        1980        7.50 - 12.50

## Love for God
Meher Baba. Pendant w/ Mastery in
    Service legend.        1980        7.50 - 12.50

## Love of God
Polish National Catholic Church. Open book
    and cross in oval within cross.        1980        7.50 - 12.50

## Lutheran, God and Family
Red cross on white field.        1980        7.50 - 12.50

## Maccabee
Jewish. Flame and Star of David in menorah.1980        7.50 - 12.50

## Metta
Buddhist. Ship wheel.        1980        7.50 - 12.50

## Parvuli Dei
Roman Catholic. Mary, Jesus, and Joseph,
    Holy Spirit above.        1980        7.50 - 12.50

## Saint George
Eastern Orthodox. Saint on horseback.        1980        7.50 - 12.50

## Silver Crest
The Salvation Army. Pendant and red-
    orange-blue ribbon bar.        1980        7.50 - 12.50

## St. Gregory
Eastern Diocese of the Armenian
    Church of America. Church.        1980        7.50 - 12.50

## Unity of Mankind
Baha'l. Globe.        1980        7.50 - 12.50

## Unity, God in Me
Association of Unity Churches. Flower bud. 1980        7.50 - 12.50

# POSITION BADGES - LEADERS

## Assistant Cubmaster

| | | |
|---|---|---|
| Gold on blue twill. CUBS BSA below emblem. Diamond-shaped patch. | 1930-1940 | 15.00 - 20.00 |
| Gold on blue twill. CUB SCOUTS BSA below emblem. Diamond-shaped cut edged patch. | 1940-1964 | 10.00 - 15.00 |
| Gold on blue twill. CUB SCOUTS BSA below emblem. Diamond-shaped rolled edged patch. | 1965-1970 | 5.00 - 7.50 |
| Fully embroidered Mylar thread (Trained Leader). | 1972-1989 | 3.00 - 5.00 |
| On blue background. | 1972-1989 | 2.00 - 3.00 |

## Assistant Den Leader

| | | |
|---|---|---|
| Fully embroidered Mylar thread (Trained Leader). | 1972-1989 | 3.00 - 5.00 |
| On blue background. | 1972-1989 | 2.00 - 3.00 |

## Assistant Den Mother

| | | |
|---|---|---|
| On blue background. | 1972-1989 | 2.00 - 3.00 |

## Assistant Webelos Den Leader

| | | |
|---|---|---|
| On blue background. | 1972-1989 | 2.00 - 3.00 |

Cub Leader position badges of the 1970s Mylar design.

## Assistant Webelos Leader

Fully embroidered, Mylar thread
   (Trained Leader).          1972-1989   3.00 - 5.00

## Cubmaster

Silver on blue twill. CUBS BSA below emblem.
   Diamond-shaped patch.      1930-1940 15.00 - 20.00
Silver on blue twill. CUB SCOUTS BSA
   below emblem. Diamond-shaped
   cut edged patch.        1940-1964 10.00 - 15.00
Silver on blue twill. CUB SCOUTS BSA
   below emblem. Diamond-shaped
   rolled edged patch.     1965-1970  5.00 - 7.50
Fully embroidered, Mylar thread
   (Trained Leader).          1972-1989   3.00 - 5.00
On blue background.          1972-1989   2.00 - 3.00

## Den Leader Coach

Fully embroidered Mylar thread
   (Trained Leader).          1972-1989   3.00 - 5.00
On blue background.          1972-1989   2.00 - 3.00

## Den Leader

Fully embroidered, Mylar thread
   (Trained Leader).          1972-1989   3.00 - 5.00
On blue background.          1972-1989   2.00 - 3.00

## Den Mother

On blue background.          1972-1989   2.00 - 3.00

## Pack Committee Chairman

Silver on green twill. CUBS BSA below
   emblem. Diamond-shaped cut
   edge patch.           1930-1955 15.00 - 20.00
Silver on green twill. CUB SCOUTS BSA
   below emblem. Diamond-shaped cut
   edge patch.           1955-1964 10.00 - 15.00
Silver on green twill. CUB SCOUTS BSA
   below emblem. Diamond-shaped rolled
   edge patch.           1965-1970  5.00 - 7.50

## Pack Committee

Gold on green twill. CUBS BSA below
   emblem. Diamond-shaped patch. 1930-1940 15.00 - 20.00
Gold on green twill. CUB SCOUTS BSA
   below emblem. Diamond-shaped cut
   edged patch.          1940-1964 10.00 - 15.00
Gold on green twill. CUB SCOUTS BSA
   below emblem. Diamond-shaped rolled
   edged patch.         1965-1970  5.00 - 7.50
On blue background.          1972-1989   2.00 - 3.00

## Tiger Cub Coach

On orange background.         1989        1.00 - 1.50

## Webelos Den Leader

Fully embroidered, Mylar thread.
   (Trained Leader)           1972-1989   3.00 - 5.00
On blue background.          1972-1989   2.00 - 3.00

# UNIFORMS - LEADERS

## Blazer, bullion-embroidered program emblem

Cub Scout.                 1971      10.00 - 17.50

# ADULT RECOGNITIONS

## Cub Scouter Award

Gold ribbon w/ blue stripe.     1985      7.50 - 10.00

## Cubmaster Award

Gold ribbon w/ 2 blue stripes.   1985      7.50 - 10.00

## Den Leader Award

Blue ribbon w/ gold stripe.     1985      7.50 - 10.00

## Den Leader Coach Award

Blue ribbon.               1985      7.50 - 10.00

## Den Leader Coach Training Award

Tenderfoot emblem on diamond-shaped
   background. 10 kt. GF on white ribbon
   w/ 2 thin green stripes.     1960-1970 10.00 - 15.00
Tenderfoot emblem on diamond-shaped
   background. Gilt pendant on white ribbon
   w/ 2 thin green stripes.     1960-1970  5.00 - 7.50

## Den Mother's Training Award

Tenderfoot emblem on diamond-shaped
   background. 10 kt. GF pendant on white
   ribbon w/ 1 thin green stripe.  1960-1970 10.00 - 15.00
Tenderfoot emblem on diamond-shaped
   background. Gilt pendant, white ribbon
   w/ 1 thin green stripe.      1960-1970  5.00 - 7.50

## Tiger Cub Coach Award

Orange ribbon w/ black stripe.  1985      7.50 - 10.00

## Webelos Den Leader Award

Gold ribbon.               1985      7.50 - 10.00

# RESOURCE BOOKS

### Cub Master's Pack Book

| | | |
|---|---|---|
| 1st edition, 5 printings. | 1932-1939 | 10.00 - 15.00 |
| 2nd edition, 13 printings. | 1943-1954 | 10.00 - 15.00 |
| 3rd edition, 13 printings. | 1954-1966 | 7.50 - 12.50 |
| 4th edition, 15 printings. | 1967-1981 | 5.00 - 8.00 |

### Cub Scout Leader Book

| | | |
|---|---|---|
| 10 printings. 3-ring binder format. | 1982-1990 | 5.00 - 7.50 |

### Cub Scout Songbook

| | | |
|---|---|---|
| 12 printings. | 1947-1969 | 5.00 - 7.50 |

### Cub Scout Sport Book

| | | |
|---|---|---|
| Archery | 1985 | 1.00 - 2.00 |
| Badminton | 1985 | 1.00 - 2.00 |
| Baseball | 1985 | 1.00 - 2.00 |
| Basketball | 1985 | 1.00 - 2.00 |
| Bicycling | 1985 | 1.00 - 2.00 |
| Bowling | 1985 | 1.00 - 2.00 |
| Golf | 1985 | 1.00 - 2.00 |
| Marbles | 1985 | 1.00 - 2.00 |
| Physical Fitness | 1985 | 1.00 - 2.00 |
| Skating | 1985 | 1.00 - 2.00 |
| Skiing | 1985 | 1.00 - 2.00 |
| Soccer | 1985 | 1.00 - 2.00 |
| Softball | 1985 | 1.00 - 2.00 |
| Swimming | 1985 | 1.00 - 2.00 |
| Table Tennis | 1985 | 1.00 - 2.00 |
| Ultimate | 1985 | 1.00 - 2.00 |
| Volleyball | 1985 | 1.00 - 2.00 |

### Den Chief's Den Book

| | | |
|---|---|---|
| 1st edition, 12 printings. | 1932-1941 | 5.00 - 7.50 |
| Revised edition, 25 printings. | 1942-1962 | 4.00 - 6.00 |
| Revised edition, 28 printings. | 1965-1990 | 4.00 - 6.00 |

### Den Leader Coach Book

| | | |
|---|---|---|
| 2 printings. | 1967-1968 | 5.00 - 7.50 |

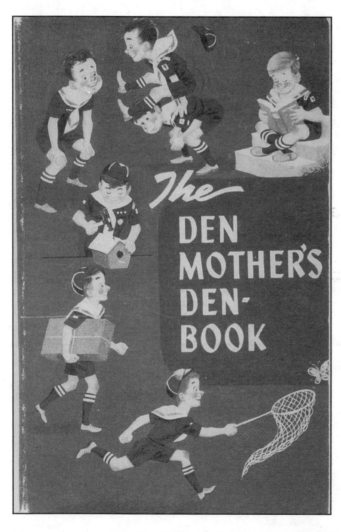

Two examples of the Den Mother's Den-Book: 1937-50 (left) and 1951-66.

Den Leader's Book, 1970-88

## Den Leader's Book

19 printings.                      1970-1988    4.00 - 6.00

## Den Mother's Den Book

| | | |
|---|---|---|
| 1st edition, 18 printings. | 1937-1950 | 5.00 - 7.50 |
| 2nd edition, 16 printings. | 1951-1966 | 5.00 - 7.50 |
| 3rd edition, 3 printings. | 1967-1969 | 5.00 - 7.50 |

## How Book of Cub Scouting

Heavy fabric hardcover w/ red question mark.
    16 printings.                  1951-1966    5.00 - 7.50

## How Book of Cubbing

Golden hardcover w/ large question mark.
    5 printings.                   1938-1942    10.00 - 15.00
Heavy fabric hardcover w/ green question
    mark. 1 printing.              1950         15.00 - 20.00
Yellow hardcover w/ large question mark.
    7 printings.                   1943-1949    10.00 - 15.00

## Staging Den and Pack Ceremonies

26 printings.                      1953-1987    4.00 - 5.00

## Webelos Den Leader's Book

15 printings.                      1967-1981    5.00 - 7.50

# SERIES BOOKS

## The Dan Carter Series, Cupples & Leon

| | | |
|---|---|---|
| Dan Carter - Cub Scout. Wirt, Mildred A. | 1949 | 5.00 - 10.00 |
| Dan Carter and the Cub Honor. Wirt, Mildred A. | 1953 | 5.00 - 10.00 |

## Whitman Tell-a-Tale Series

| | | |
|---|---|---|
| Lassie and the Cub Scout. Michelson, Florence, Western Publishing Co. | 1966 | 3.00 - 7.50 |

# FICTION BOOKS

## Boyton, Fr. Neil, S.J.

Ex-Cub Fitzie.                     1950         5.00 - 10.00

## Disney, Walt

Donald and Mickey, Cub Scouts,
    Whitman Publishing Co.         1950         15.00 - 20.00

## Felsen, Henry Gregor

| | | |
|---|---|---|
| Anyone for Cub Scouts? Charles Scribners' Sons | 1954 | 7.50 - 12.50 |
| Cub Scout at Last. Charles Scribners' Sons. | 1952 | 10.00 - 15.00 |
| Cub Scout at Last. Charles Scribners' Sons, paperback reprint. | 1952 | 7.50 - 12.50 |

## Friend, Russell and Esther

Easy Cub Scout Plays. Baker's Plays.   1948     10.00 - 15.00

## Gardner, Lillian Soskin

| | | |
|---|---|---|
| Bill Martin, Cub Scout, From Bobcat to Wolf. Franklin Watts, Inc. reprint of Den Seven title. | 1952 | 5.00 - 10.00 |
| From Bobcat to Wolf: The Story of Den Seven, Pack Four. Franklin Watts, Inc. | 1952 | 5.00 - 10.00 |

## Guy, Ann

Cub Scout Donny. Abingdon Press.   1958         5.00 - 10.00

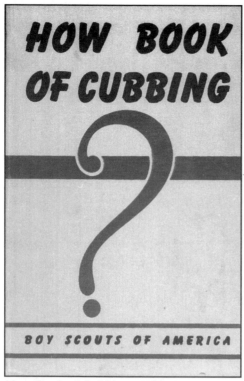

How Book of Cubbing, 1938-42

Rand McNally Cub Scout book, 1964

Cubmaster's Pack Book, 1943-54

Den Chief's Denbook, 1942-62

## Kohler, Julilly H.
Daniel in the Cub Scout Den. Aladdin Books,
    American Book Co.    1951    5.00 - 10.00

## Martin, Patricia Miles
Calvin and the Cub Scouts.
    G.P. Putnam's Sons.    1964    5.00 - 10.00
Calvin and the Cub Scouts. Scholastic
    Book Services paperback.    1971    5.00 - 10.00

## Sterling, Dorothy
The Cub Scout Mystery.
    Doubleday & Co., Inc.    1952    5.00 - 10.00

## Tousey, Sanford
Cub Scout. Ariel.    1952    5.00 - 10.00

## Watts, Mabel
Cub Scout. Giant Books,
    Rand McNally & Co.    1964    5.00 - 10.00
Cub Scout. A Tip-Top Elf Book reprint.    1964    5.00 - 10.00

## Young Lantern Press Editors
Young Reader's Cub Scout Stories.    1930    5.00 - 10.00

# COMIC BOOKS

## American Dental Association
The Friendly Cub Scout Casper, His Den
    and Dentist Fight the Tooth Demons.
    Harvey Publications.    1974    4.00 - 5.00

## Harvey Publications, Inc.
Casper: Cub Scout of Den Five.    1974    2.00 - 3.00
The Friendly Ghost, Casper and
    Cub Scout Stories. 1974.    1974    2.00 - 3.00
The Friendly Ghost, Casper,
    Cub Scouts Den O' Fun.    1975    2.00 - 3.00

# MISCELLANEOUS STUFF

## Avon Brush and Comb
Plastic, blue. Looks like pocket knife.    1975    7.50 - 12.50

## Cake Top Figures
Cub Scout seated, legs crossed in front.
    Plastic.    1955-1965    7.50 - 12.50
Cub Scout standing, hands at side.
    Painted plaster.    1955-1965    3.00 - 5.00

## Charms
Silvered bracelet, Charms for Bobcat,
    Bear, Wolf, Webelo, Arrow of Light.    1975    10.00 - 15.00

## Den Flag - Webelos
Webelos emblem on blue background.    1970    5.00 - 7.50

## Den Flag
Yellow number and diamond.
    Blue background.    1940    5.00 - 7.50

## Flag Pole Top
Wolf head within open diamond.
    CUBS BSA below.    1930-1940  40.00 - 60.00
Wolf head within open diamond.
    CUB SCOUTS BSA below.    1940    15.00 - 25.00
Special Cub Scout 50th Anniversary Logo.    1980    25.00 - 40.00

## Game
The Game of Cub Scouting. Cadaco Div.,
    Rapid Mounting & Finishing Co.    1987    10.00 - 15.00

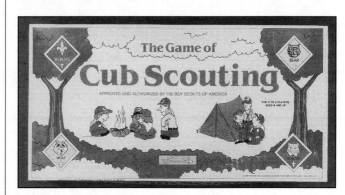

## Greeting Cards
Like a Good Cub Scout, Do your Best!    1965    2.00 - 3.00
To a Great Cub Scout. Cub helping little
    girl across street.    1965    2.00 - 3.00

## Handkerchief

Blue and yellow. Cub activities displayed.    1960-1975    3.00 - 5.00

## Kenner Doll

Cub Scout uniform on blond boy.    1974    20.00 - 30.00

Central design of a Pack Flag.

## Pack Flag

Wool. Yellow top, blue bottom.
    CUBS BSA on red diamond in ctr.    1930-1940    40.00 - 60.00
Wool. Yellow top, blue bottom. CUB
    SCOUTS BSA on red diamond in ctr.    1940-1955    25.00 - 40.00
Cotton. Yellow top, blue bottom. CUB
    SCOUTS BSA on red diamond in ctr.    1955-1970    20.00 - 40.00
Nylon. Yellow top, blue bottom. CUB
    SCOUTS BSA on red diamond in ctr.    1970    15.00 - 25.00

## Pinewood Derby Car

Thin body, detachable axles,
    solid thin wheels.    1955-1980    10.00 - 15.00
Thick body, fat wheels, cut-out for driver.    1980-1993    5.00 - 7.50
Thick body, fat wheels, no cut-out for driver.    1993    4.00 - 6.00

## Pressed Wood Plaques

A Cub is Square. CUBS BSA
    on diamond patch.    1930-1950    10.00 - 15.00
Cub Law. CUBS BSA on diamond patch.    1930-1950    15.00 - 20.00
Cub Promise, CUBS BSA
    on diamond patch.    1930-1950    15.00 - 20.00
A Cub is Square. CUB SCOUTS BSA
    on diamond patch.    1950-1975    7.50 - 12.50
Cub Law. CUB SCOUTS on diamond patch.    1950-1975    7.50 - 12.50
Cub Scout Promise. CUB SCOUTS
    on diamond patch.    1950-1975    7.50 - 12.50

A Cub Scout is Helpful. CUB SCOUTS
    BSA on diamond patch.    1975-1985    7.50 - 12.50

## Ring

CUBS BSA in diamond. Sterling.    1930-1945    15.00 - 20.00
CUB SCOUTS BSA in diamond. Sterling.    1950-1975    7.50 - 12.50

## Sweater Chain

Cub Scout emblem on white enamel
    background. Gilt chain.    1965-1975    7.50 - 10.00

## Tie Bar

Gilt w/ Cub Scout emblem in square
    at end.    1970    2.00 - 3.00

## Watch

Timex. Blue plastic band, white dial.    1975    7.50 - 10.00

Scouts of Wauwatosa, WI, attending Indian Mound Scout Reservation in 1928—quite handsome in full uniforms!

# BOY SCOUTS

The Boy Scouts of America was founded in February 1910, based on the programs of Englishman Robert Baden-Powell's Boy Scouts, Ernest Thompson Seaton's Woodcraft Indians (1902), and Daniel Carter Beard's Society of the Sons of Daniel Boone—later called Boy Pioneers (1905). William D. Boyce, a newspaper publisher from Chicago, financed the organization's beginnings, and with assistance from YMCA executive Edgar M. Robinson's New York office, scout troops were being formed throughout the nation. Seaton and Beard were brought into the fold of the new organization, and by the fall of 1910, James E. West was hired for what was to be a 32-year run as the B.S.A.'s Chief Scout Executive. The headquarters moved out of the YMCA offices on 28th Street and took up home at 200 Fifth Avenue, New York City.

Early scouting opportunities for the "good turn" came available with a service corps at the 50th Anniversary Reunion of the Battle of Gettysburg and selling of Liberty Loan Bonds during World War I. By this time the scouting movement was a hit, because it educated youth in outdoor skills and leadership, and youth were exposed to many worthwhile professions due to the merit badge program. In the 1930s the National Office moved to 2 Park Avenue, and in 1953 to North Brunswick, New Jersey.

The scouting movement was at its height in the 1950s and early 1960s, with the advent of the baby boomers. The war in Vietnam affected scout membership, and the revision of the program in 1971 seemed to set it back even more. It took nearly 10 years, until the 1979 handbook revision by the master William "Green Bar Bill" Hillcourt, to set the program back on track. At this time the National Office moved to its current location in Irving, Texas.

Scouting has become a major part in the fabric of youth, and there are countless political leaders, sports and entertainment figures, CEOs, astronauts, and a former president of these United States (Gerald Ford) who have progressed through scouting to attain the Eagle Scout Award. Even for those who did not earn the Eagle Award, though, scouting has had a positive affect on the character of its members, and most can look back on good times and experiences when they were scouts. Scouts in the United States have had opportunities to become involved in a great number of programs to help them expand their horizons and learn that they are not alone in enjoying things that are special to the Boy Scout movement, including High Adventure opportunities like the Philmont Scout Ranch, the Charles M. Sommers Canoe Base, the Florida Sea Base, and National Jamborees.

# RANK BADGES

References in the Rank Badges section are to Paul Meyer's book *Collecting Boy Scout Rank Badges*.

Rank patches have different backs which are collectible. The top two are both cut khaki cloth, one with a glue back and the second with a gauze backing. The bottom row illustrates twill cut edge badges with glue, gauze, and plastic backs.

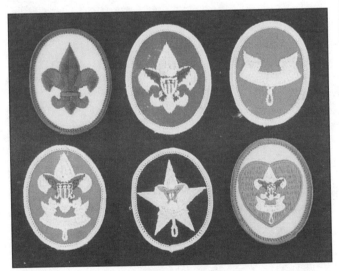

A group of 1972 oval badges: l. to r. (from top): Scout, Tenderfoot, Second Class, First Class, Star, and Life.

## Scout

| | | | |
|---|---|---|---|
| Oval R/E, brown on orange or gold background. | 1972-1989 | PM.1.1-3 | 1.00 - 2.00 |
| Oval R/E, brown on tan background. | 1989 | PM.1.4 | 1.00 - 1.50 |

## Tenderfoot

| | | | |
|---|---|---|---|
| Tan cloth, no ctr. line in short crown. | 1921-1936 | PM.2.1-2 | 30.00 - 40.00 |
| Tan cloth, no ctr. line in tall crown. | 1936-1937 | PM.2.3 | 30.00 - 40.00 |
| Tan cloth, ctr. line in tall crown. | 1938-1942 | PM.2.4-5A | 20.00 - 30.00 |
| Sand twill, ctr. line in tall crown. | 1942-1945 | PM.2.5B | 20.00 - 30.00 |
| Khaki cloth, ctr. line in tall crown. | 1946-1954 | PM.2.5c-6 | 10.00 - 15.00 |
| Khaki C/E, coarse twill. | 1955-1964 | PM.2.7A, 8A | 5.00 - 7.50 |
| Khaki C/E, fine twill. | 1965-1971 | PM.2.7B, 8B | 3.00 - 7.50 |
| Oval R/E, brown background. | 1972-1989 | PM.2.9-11 | 1.00 - 2.00 |
| Oval R/E, tan background. | 1989 | PM.2.12 | 1.00 - 1.50 |

## Second Class

Second Class badges: Top row are fine tan twill with low and high scrolls; the bottom two are a cut khaki cloth and a cut edge khaki twill.

| | | | |
|---|---|---|---|
| Tan cloth, high scroll. | 1913-1936 | PM.3.1-4 | 30.00 - 40.00 |
| Tan cloth, low scroll. | 1937-1942 | PM.3.5A | 30.00 - 40.00 |
| Sand twill, low scroll. | 1942-1945 | PM.3.5B | 20.00 - 30.00 |
| Khaki cloth. | 1946-1954 | PM.3.5C, 6 | 15.00 - 25.00 |
| Khaki C/E, coarse twill. | 1955-1964 | PM.3.7A | 5.00 - 10.00 |
| Khaki C/E, fine twill. | 1965-1971 | PM.3.7B | 3.00 - 5.00 |
| Oval R/E, green background. | 1972-1989 | PM.3.8-10 | 1.00 - 2.00 |
| Oval C/E, tan background. | 1989 | PM.3.11 | 1.00 - 1.50 |

## First Class

| | | | |
|---|---|---|---|
| Tan cloth, short crown. | 1913-1936 | PM.4.1-3 | 50.00 - 75.00 |

| | | | |
|---|---|---|---|
| Tan cloth, ctr. line in tall crown. | 1937-1942 | PM.4.4, 5A | 40.00 - 60.00 |
| Sand twill, ctr. line in tall crown. | 1942-1945 | PM.4.5B | 40.00 - 60.00 |
| Khaki cloth, ctr. line in tall crown. | 1946-1954 | PM.4.5C, 6 | 20.00 - 30.00 |
| Khaki C/E, coarse twill. | 1955-1964 | PM.4.7A, 8A | 5.00 - 7.50 |
| Khaki C/E, fine twill. | 1965-1971 | PM.4.7B, 8B | 2.00 - 5.00 |
| Oval R/E, red background. | 1972-1989 | PM.4.9AB, 10 | 1.00 - 2.00 |
| Oval R/E, tan background. | 1989 | PM.4.11 | 1.00 - 1.50 |

## Star Scout

Star badges of short crown and tall crown varieties of sand twill (top row); bottom row of cut khaki cloth and cut edge khaki.

| | | | |
|---|---|---|---|
| Tan cloth, eagle head right, w/o hanging knot. | 1913-1924 | PM.5.1,3 | 60.00 - 80.00 |
| Tan cloth, eagle head right, w/ hanging knot. | 1913-1924 | PM.5.2,4 | 50.00 - 60.00 |
| Tan cloth, eagle head left. | 1925-1942 | PM.5A, 6A, 7A | 40.00 - 60.00 |
| Sand twill. | 1942-1945 | PM.5.7D | 20.00 - 30.00 |
| Khaki cloth. | 1946-1954 | PM.5.7E | 15.00 - 20.00 |
| Khaki C/E, coarse twill. | 1955-1964 | PM.5.8A | 7.50 - 10.00 |
| Khaki C/E, fine twill. | 1965-1971 | PM.5.8B | 5.00 - 7.50 |
| Oval R/E, purple background. | 1972-1989 | PM.5.9-11A | 1.00 - 2.00 |
| Oval R/E, tan background. | 1989 | PM.5.12 | 1.00 - 1.50 |

## Life Scout

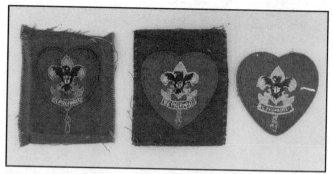

Life Scout badges. From left: a sand twill with the knot outside the heart, a khaki cut square, and a rolled edge heart.

| | | | |
|---|---|---|---|
| Tan cloth, eagle head right, knot inside heart. | 1913-1924 | PM.6.1-2 | 60.00 - 80.00 |
| Tan cloth, eagle head right, red hanging knot. | 1913-1924 | PM.6.3A, B.C.D, 4 | 80.00 - 100.00 |
| Tan cloth, eagle head left, gold hanging knot. | 1925-1940 | PM.6.5A | 80.00 - 100.00 |
| Tan cloth, no hanging knot. | 1941-1942 | PM.6.6A, 7A | 40.00 - 60.00 |
| Sand twill. | 1942-1945 | PM.6.7D | 30.00 - 40.00 |
| Khaki cloth. | 1946-1954 | PM.6.7E | 20.00 - 30.00 |
| Cut to heart shape. | 1955-1971 | PM.8A, 8B. | 5.00 - 7.50 |
| Oval R/E, orange background. | 1972-1989 | PM.6.9A-B | 1.00 - 2.00 |
| Oval R/E, tan background. | 1989 | PM.6.10 | 1.00 - 1.50 |

## Eagle Scout

Eagle Scout badges show (top) a khaki cut square, a 1960s rolled edge, and the 1973 no name oval, and (bottom) late 1970s silver thread rolled edge (with and without a Mylar edge), and a 1985 Mylar thread.

| | | | |
|---|---|---|---|
| Cut edge, tan or coffee cloth, scroll outline extends beyond oval. | 1924-1932 | PM9.1A1 | 60.00 - 80.00 |

**THE SCOUT OATH**

*"On my honor I will do my best:
To do my duty to God and my Country,
And to obey the Scout Law;
To help other people at all times;
To keep myself physically strong, men-
tally awake, and morally straight."*

The Scout Oath, as pictured in a 1936 Official Souvenir Book.

Eagle patch, first type, scroll extends into oval.

Cut edge, tan or coffee cloth, scroll outline inside oval, no knot beneath scroll.    1924-1932    PM.9.1A2    250.00 - 300.00

Cut edge, tan or coffee cloth, complete lettering, cotton or silk threads.    1932-1955    PM.9.2A    40.00 - 75.00

Cut edge sand (tan) twill cloth, fine weave, complete lettering around, cotton threads.    1933-1955    PM.9.2D    60.00 - 80.00

Cut edge khaki cloth, complete lettering around oval border, cotton threads.    1933-1955    PM.9.2E    40.00 - 60.00

Oval red cloth, gray rolled edge, complete lettering. Small head, closed beak on eagle, thin knot, white gauze back.    1956-1972    PM.9.3A    10.00 - 20.00

Oval red cloth, gray rolled edge, complete lettering. Thick neck, closed beak on eagle, knot is thick circle, starched gauze back.    1956-1972    PM.9.3B    10.00 - 15.00

Oval red cloth, gray rolled edge, complete lettering. Open beak on eagle, white gauze or plastic back.    1956-1972    PM.9.3C    10.00 - 20.00

Oval fully embroidered background, gray rolled edge, no lettering. Eagle w/ 32mm wingspan, tail feathers visible below perch, plain cloth or plastic back.    1972-1975    PM.9.4A    10.00 - 15.00

Oval fully embroidered gray rolled edge, no lettering. Eagle w/ 29mm wingspan, no tail feathers visible, plain embroidered back.    1972-1975    PM.9.4B    10.00 - 15.00

Red cloth, white (silver) rolled edge, gray eagle and EAGLE SCOUT legend. Plastic back w/ or w/o gauze beneath. 3 or more minor varieties.    1975-1985    PM.9.5A-C    5.00 - 10.00

Oval red cloth, silver Mylar rolled edge, eagle and complete lettering. Small eagle, flat scroll base.    1985-1986    PM.9.6    5.00 - 10.00

Oval red cloth, silver Mylar edge, dark gray or silver gray eagle. Scroll curved, larger motto letters.    1987-1988    PM.9.7A-B    5.00 - 10.00

Oval red cloth, silver gray rolled edge, dark gray eagle.    1988    PM.9.8    5.00 - 10.00

## Achievement Award #1
Gold legend on purple background.    1923-1950    15.00 - 25.00
Gold legend on red background.    1923-1950    15.00 - 25.00

## Achievement Award #2
Gold legend on red background.    1923-1950    15.00 - 25.00
Gold lettering on purple background.    1923-1950    15.00 - 25.00

## Achievement Tenderfoot
Gold lettering on purple background.    1937-1950    20.00 - 30.00
Gold lettering on red background.    1937-1950    20.00 - 30.00

# Scouting for the Handicapped Program

Small patches are added to the exterior of an oval rank patch in the Scouting for the Handicapped Program.

| | | |
|---|---|---|
| 12 Ideals badges. | 1972 | 10.00 - 15.00 |
| Camping badge. | 1972 | 1.00 - 1.50 |
| Citizenship badge. | 1972 | 1.00 - 1.50 |
| Cooking badge. | 1972 | 1.00 - 1.50 |
| First Aid badge. | 1972 | 1.00 - 1.50 |
| Flag badge. | 1972 | 1.00 - 1.50 |
| Hiking badge. | 1972 | 1.00 - 1.50 |
| Knot Tying badge. | 1972 | 1.00 - 1.50 |
| Swimming badge. | 1972 | 1.00 - 1.50 |
| Symbols badge. | 1972 | 1.00 - 1.50 |

# RANK & POSITION BADGES

## Tenderfoot

Tenderfoot Scribe and Tenderfoot Bugler.

| | | | |
|---|---|---|---|
| Scribe. Tenderfoot badge, gold thread crossed quills on tan cloth. | 1916-1925 | PMR.1.1 | 200.00 - 250.00 |
| Bugler. Tenderfoot badge, gold thread bugle on tan cloth. | 1917-1925 | PMR.1.2 | 250.00 - 300.00 |
| Patrol Leader. Silver thread Tenderfoot badge on tan cloth. | 1921-1925 | PMR.1.3 | 250.00 - 300.00 |
| Patrol Leader Scribe. Silver thread Tenderfoot badge and crossed quills on tan cloth. | 1916-1925 | PMR.1.4 | 250.00 - 300.00 |
| Patrol Leader Bugler. Silver thread Tenderfoot badge and bugle on tan cloth. | 1917-1925 | PMR.1.5 | 300.00 - 400.00 |

## Second Class

| | | | |
|---|---|---|---|
| Scribe. Second Class badge, gold thread crossed quills on tan cloth. | 1916-1925 | PMR.2.1 | 200.00 - 250.00 |
| Bugler. Second Class badge, gold thread bugle on tan cloth. | 1917-1925 | PMR.2.2 | 250.00 - 300.00 |

Second Class Scribe and Second Class Bugler.

| | | | |
|---|---|---|---|
| Patrol Leader. Silver thread Second Class badge on tan cloth. | 1915-1925 | PMR.2.3 | 250.00 - 300.00 |
| Patrol Leader Scribe. Silver thread Second Class badge and crossed quills on tan cloth. | 1916-1925 | PMR.2.4 | 350.00 - 400.00 |
| Patrol Leader Bugler. Silver thread Second Class badge and bugle on tan cloth. | 1917-1925 | PMR.2.5 | 350.00 - 400.00 |

## First Class

First Class Scribe and First Class Bugler.

| | | | |
|---|---|---|---|
| Scribe. Green First Class badge, gold thread crossed quills on tan cloth. | 1916-1925 | PMR.3.1 | 250.00 - 300.00 |
| Bugler. Green First Class badge, gold thread bugle on tan cloth. | 1917-1925 | PMR.3.2 | 250.00 - 300.00 |

Patrol Leader. Silver thread
   First Class badge on
   tan cloth.                1915-1925  PMR.3.3    350.00 - 400.00
Patrol Leader Scribe.
   Silver First Class
   badge, silver thread
   crossed quills
   on tan cloth.             1916-1925  PMR.3.4    350.00 - 400.00
Patrol Leader Bugler.
   Silver First Class badge,
   silver thread bugle
   on tan cloth.             1917-1925  PMR.3.5    400.00 - 450.00

# EAGLE SCOUT AWARD

Eagle Medals are referenced to Terry Grove's book *A Comprehensive Guide to the Eagle Scout Award.*

## T.H. Foley, maker

                            1912-1915  TG.1.1-4   200.00 - 275.00

T.H. Foley

## Dieges & Clust, maker

                            1916-1920  TG.2.1-3   150.00 - 200.00

Dieges & Clust

## Robbins Co., maker

Closed beak, deep notch
   on back where body
   tail feathers meet.      1920-1925  TG.3.1A    100.00 - 150.00

TG.3.1A                            TG.3.1B

Eagle Scout with merit badge sash, late 1920s.

Closed beak, where body
    and tail feathers meet
    on back form "W."    1925-1926  TG.3.1B    175.00 - 225.00

Closed beak, no BSA,
    flat back.    1955-1969  TG.3.4    60.00 - 85.00
Closed beak, BSA, feathered
    but flatter back.    1970-1978  TG.3.5    60.00 - 85.00

TG.3.1C                        TG.3.1D

TG.3.3                        TG.3.4

Open beak, flat line notch
    on back where body meets
    tail feathers.    1926-1930  TG.3.1C-D    100.00 - 150.00
Closed beak, BSA is high,
    A hangs over edge.    1930    TG.3.1E    150.00 - 200.00
Finely engraved feathers,
    centered BSA. Back feathers
    form a body-ridge as V
    or a smooth transition.  1930-1933  TG.3.2A-B    100.00 - 150.00

TG.3.5

TG.3.E                    TG.3.2A

Closed beak, no BSA,
    full back.    1933-1954  TG.3.3    60.00 - 100.00

# Stange Co., maker

TG.4.1

TG.4.2

| Description | Years | ID | Value |
|---|---|---|---|
| Closed beak, no BSA, flat back. | 1968-1971 | TG.4.1 | 100.00 - 125.00 |
| Closed beak, BSA, feathered but flatter back. | 1971-1974 | TG.4.2 | 60.00 - 85.00 |
| Closed, thin beak, "mechanical deco" look to the feathers. Usually a very long ribbon. | 1974-1978 | TG.4.3 | 75.00 - 100.00 |
| Short, closed beak, BSA, feathered but flatter back. White stitched edge to ribbon. | 1978-1980 | TG.4.4 | 60.00 - 85.00 |

TG.4.3

TG.4.4

| Description | Years | ID | Value |
|---|---|---|---|
| Silver-plated copper or sterling silver on special order. Short, closed beak, BSA, feathered but flatter back. White stitched edge to ribbon. | 1980-1983 | TG.4.5A | 50.00 - 75.00 |
| Silver-plated copper or sterling silver on special order. Short, closed beak, BSA, modified feather back. White stitched edge to ribbon. | 1983-1986 | TG.4.5B | 50.00 - 75.00 |
| Silver-plated copper or sterling silver on special order. Closed beak, BSA. S is not struck well and appears wider than B and A. | 1986-1989 | TG.4.5C | 50.00 - 75.00 |

TG.4.5A

TG.4.5B

TG.4.5C                    TG.4.5D

Silver-plated copper or sterling silver
on special order. Closed beak, BSA
of even thickness, feathered
but flatter back.          1990       TG.4.5D       50.00 - 75.00

# POSITION BADGES

## Junior Assistant Scoutmaster

| | | |
|---|---|---|
| Tan cloth, 3 green felt bars. | 1926-1933 | 40.00 - 60.00 |
| Tan cloth, 3 green felt bars, gold First Class w/ short crown. | 1934-1936 | 35.00 - 55.00 |
| Tan cloth, 3 green bars, gold First Class w/ tall crown. | 1936-1942 | 30.00 - 45.00 |
| Sand twill. | 1942-1945 | 30.00 - 45.00 |
| Khaki cloth. | 1946 | 15.00 - 25.00 |
| Round C/E, brown design w/o legend. | 1947-1951 | 7.50 - 15.00 |
| Round C/E, brown and gold design w/o legend. | 1952-1958 | 5.00 - 10.00 |
| Round C/E, brown and gold design w/ legend. | 1959-1966 | 5.00 - 10.00 |
| Round R/E, brown and gold design, First Class w/ legend. | 1967-1969 | 5.00 - 10.00 |
| Round R/E, brown and gold design, Tenderfoot w/ legend JR. ASST. | 1970-1971 | 5.00 - 10.00 |
| Round R/E, green background, Tenderfoot w/ legend JUNIOR ASSISTANT. | 1972-1989 | 2.00 - 3.00 |
| Round R/E, tan background, Tenderfoot. | 1989 | 1.00 - 2.00 |

Senior Patrol Leader patch, cut
khaki cloth.

## Senior Patrol Leader

| | | |
|---|---|---|
| Tan cloth, 2-1/2 white felt bars. | 1910-1914 | 60.00 - 80.00 |
| Tan cloth, 2-1/2 green felt bars. | 1915-1933 | 50.00 - 75.00 |
| Tan cloth, 2-1/2 green bars, First Class w/ short crown. | 1934-1936 | 50.00 - 75.00 |
| Tan cloth, 2-1/2 green bars, gold First Class w/ tall crown. | 1936-1942 | 40.00 - 65.00 |
| Sand Twill. | 1942-1945 | 30.00 - 45.00 |
| Khaki cloth. | 1946-1954 | 20.00 - 30.00 |
| Khaki C/E, coarse twill. | 1955-1964 | 7.50 - 10.00 |
| Khaki C/E, fine twill. | 1965-1971 | 5.00 - 7.50 |
| Round R/E, Tenderfoot on green background, 3 bars and legend. | 1972-1989 | 2.00 - 3.00 |
| Round R/E, First Class on tan background, 3 bars and legend. | 1989 | 1.00 - 2.00 |

## Assistant Senior Patrol Leader

| | | |
|---|---|---|
| Khaki C/E, coarse twill, gold First Class, 2 green bars. | 1959-1964 | 3.00 - 5.00 |
| Khaki C/E, fine twill. | 1965-1971 | 3.00 - 5.00 |
| Round R/E, Tenderfoot on green background, 2-1/2 bars and legend. | 1972-1989 | 2.00 - 3.00 |
| Round R/E, First Class on tan background, 2-1/2 bars and legend. | 1989 | 1.00 - 2.00 |

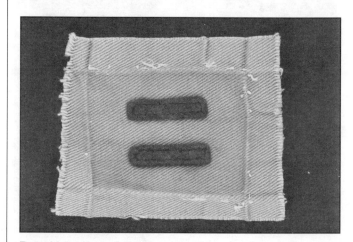

Patrol Leader in felt sewn on cut square tan cloth.

Patrol Leader patches in cut square khaki (l.), cut edge twill, coarse (top r.), and fine twill (bottom r.) varieties.

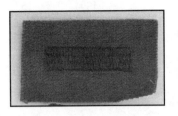

Assistant Patrol Leader patches in cut square khaki (l.), cut edge twill, coarse (top r.), and fine twill (bottom r.) varieties.

## Assistant Patrol Leader

| | | |
|---|---|---|
| 1 white bar. | 1910-1914 | 40.00 - 60.00 |
| Tan cloth, 1 green felt bar. | 1914-1933 | 20.00 - 30.00 |
| Tan cloth, 1 green bar. | 1934-1942 | 15.00 - 25.00 |
| Sand twill. | 1942-1945 | 7.50 - 15.00 |
| Khaki cloth. | 1946-1954 | 5.00 - 10.00 |
| Khaki C/E, coarse twill. | 1955-1964 | 3.00 - 5.00 |
| Khaki cloth, fine twill. | 1965-1971 | 3.00 - 5.00 |
| Round R/E, green background. Tenderfoot w/ 1 bar and legend. | 1972-1989 | 2.00 - 3.00 |
| Round R/E, tan background. FDL w/ 1 bar and legend. | 1989 | 1.00 - 2.00 |

## Patrol Leader

| | | |
|---|---|---|
| 2 white bars. | 1910-1914 | 40.00 - 60.00 |
| Tan cloth, 2 green felt bars. | 1914-1933 | 30.00 - 40.00 |
| Tan cloth, 2 green bars. | 1934-1942 | 20.00 - 30.00 |
| Sand twill. | 1942-1945 | 20.00 - 30.00 |
| Khaki cloth. | 1946-1954 | 10.00 - 15.00 |
| Khaki C/E, coarse twill, 2 green bars. | 1955-1964 | 3.00 - 5.00 |
| Khaki C/E, fine twill, 2 green bars. | 1965-1971 | 3.00 - 5.00 |
| Round R/E. Tenderfoot on green background, 2 bars and legend. | 1972-1989 | 2.00 - 3.00 |
| Round R/E, FDL on tan background, 2 bars and legend. | 1989 | 1.00 - 2.00 |

## Bugler

| | | |
|---|---|---|
| Tan cloth, gold bugle. | 1926-1942 | 20.00 - 30.00 |

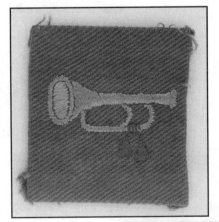

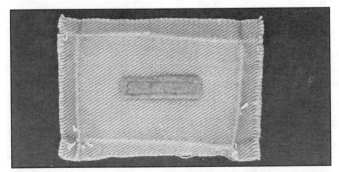

Assistant Patrol Leader patch in felt sewn on cut square tan cloth.

Bugler patches in cut square sand twill (top) and cut edge twill (bottom).

| | | |
|---|---|---|
| Sand twill. | 1942-1945 | 15.00 - 25.00 |
| Khaki cloth. | 1946-1954 | 10.00 - 15.00 |
| Khaki C/E, coarse twill. | 1955-1964 | 5.00 - 7.50 |
| Khaki C/E, fine twill. | 1965-1971 | 5.00 - 7.50 |
| Round R/E, green background, yellow border, gold bugle. | 1972-1989 | 2.00 - 3.00 |
| Round R/E, green background, red border, gold bugle. Error. | 1980 | 5.00 - 7.50 |
| Round R/E, tan background. FDL and bugle. | 1989 | 1.00 - 2.00 |

## Chaplain Aide

| | | |
|---|---|---|
| Round R/E, green background, crozier. | 1976-1989 | 2.00 - 3.00 |
| Round R/E, tan background. | 1989 | 1.00 - 2.00 |

## Den Chief

| | | |
|---|---|---|
| Round R/E, green background. | 1972-1989 | 2.00 - 3.00 |
| Round R/E, tan background. | 1989 | 1.00 - 2.00 |

## Historian

| | | |
|---|---|---|
| Round R/E, green background, FDL, and open book. | 1972-1989 | 2.00 - 3.00 |
| Round R/E, tan background. | 1989 | 1.00 - 2.00 |

## Instructor

| | | |
|---|---|---|
| Round R/E, khaki background, brown border, Tenderfoot emblem at ctr. | 1962-1971 | 5.00 - 7.50 |
| Round R/E, green background, yellow border. | 1972-1989 | 3.00 - 5.00 |
| Round R/E, tan background. | 1989 | 1.00 - 2.00 |

## Interpreter Strip

| | | |
|---|---|---|
| White lettering on tan cut edge cloth. "I Speak" German, French, Spanish, Italian | 1932-1935 | 50.00 - 75.00 |
| Red lettering on tan cut cloth. "I Speak" German, French, Spanish, Italian. | 1936-1946 | 20.00 - 30.00 |
| Red Lettering on khaki cut edge twill. "I Speak" German, French, Spanish, Italian, Hebrew. | 1946-1956 | 10.00 - 15.00 |
| White lettering on red cut edge twill. Language name in vernacular only. | 1957-1988 | 2.00 - 5.00 |
| Red lettering on tan cut edge twill, plastic back. Language name in vernacular only. | 1989 | 1.00 - 2.00 |

## Leadership Corps

| | | |
|---|---|---|
| Tall keystone, R/E, red twill background, lamp of knowledge. | 1972-1982 | 2.00 - 3.00 |

## Librarian

| | | |
|---|---|---|
| Tan cloth, Tenderfoot emblem and open book. | 1936-1942 | 30.00 - 45.00 |
| Sand twill. | 1942-1945 | 30.00 - 45.00 |
| Khaki cloth. | 1946-1954 | 10.00 - 20.00 |
| Khaki C/E, coarse twill. | 1955-1964 | 5.00 - 10.00 |

| | | |
|---|---|---|
| Khaki C/E, fine twill. | 1965-1971 | 5.00 - 10.00 |
| Round R/E, green background, 3 books. | 1972-1989 | 2.00 -3.00 |
| Round R/E, tan background, FDL, and 3 books. | 1989 | 1.00 - 2.00 |

## Musician

| | | |
|---|---|---|
| Tan cloth. Short crown Tenderfoot on lyre. | 1923-1936 | 40.00 - 60.00 |
| Tan cloth. Tall crown Tenderfoot on lyre. | 1937-1942 | 40.00 - 60.00 |
| Round R/E dark green twill (for regional and national bands). | 1938-1951 | 75.00-100.00 |
| Sand twill. | 1942-1945 | 30.00 - 45.00 |
| Khaki cloth. | 1946-1954 | 20.00 - 30.00 |
| Khaki C/E, coarse twill. | 1955-1964 | 5.00 - 10.00 |
| Khaki C/E, fine twill. | 1965-1971 | 5.00 - 10.00 |
| Round R/E, green background, red border, music notes. | 1972-1989 | 2.00 - 3.00 |
| Round R/E, tan background. FDL and music note. | 1989 | 1.00 - 2.00 |

## Quartermaster

| | | |
|---|---|---|
| Tan cloth, key and wagon wheel. | 1923-1942 | 30.00 - 40.00 |
| Sand twill. | 1942-1945 | 25.00 - 35.00 |
| Khaki cloth. | 1946-1954 | 20.00 - 30.00 |
| Khaki C/E, coarse twill. | 1955-1964 | 5.00 - 10.00 |
| Khaki C/E, fine background. | 1965-1971 | 5.00 - 10.00 |
| Round R/E, green background, backpack. | 1972-1989 | 2.00 - 3.00 |

Quartermaster patches in cut square khaki (top) and cut edge twill.

| Round R/E, tan background. FDL and backpack. | 1989 | 1.00 - 2.00 |
|---|---|---|

| Round R/E, tan background, FDL w/ 1 quill and legend. | 1989 | 1.00 - 2.00 |
|---|---|---|

## Scribe

| Tan cloth, 2 gold crossed quills. | 1926-1942 | 35.00 - 45.00 |
|---|---|---|
| Sand twill. | 1942-1945 | 30.00 - 40.00 |
| Khaki cloth. | 1946-1951 | 20.00 - 30.00 |
| Khaki cloth. Tenderfoot emblem w/ 2 crossed quills. | 1952-1954 | 20.00 - 30.00 |
| Khaki C/E, coarse twill. | 1955-1964 | 5.00 - 10.00 |
| Khaki C/E, fine twill. | 1965-1971 | 5.00 - 10.00 |
| Round C/E, green background, 1 quill and legend. | 1972-1989 | 2.00 - 3.00 |

## Troop Guide

| Round R/E, red background. First Class w/ GUIDE. | 1988-1989 | 2.00 - 3.00 |
|---|---|---|
| Round R/E, tan background. First Class w/ TROOP GUIDE. | 1989 | 1.00 - 2.00 |

## Venture Crew Chief

| Tan rolled edge. | 1989 | 1.00 - 2.00 |
|---|---|---|

# HANDBOOKS

Handbooks are referenced to Doug Bearce and Chuck Fisk's book, *Collecting Boy Scout Literature: A Collector's Guide to Boy Scout Fiction and Non-Fiction.* When used in these descriptions "BSA" is spelled out on book titles.

William "Green Bar Bill" Hillcourt, author of the first Patrol Leader Handbook and several editions of the Scout Handbook and Fieldbook. In the 1980s he was very popular on the autograph circuit.

## BSA, Official Handbook, Baden-Powell and Seaton, authors.

192 pgs. Tan-yellow
    w/ brown imprint or green
    w/ light green imprint.    1910    F1-5    100.00 - 250.00
192 pgs. Red leather-bound,
    gilt imprint.    1910    F.6    500.00 - 600.00

## BSA, Official Manual or Handbook, Seaton, author

192 pgs. Cloth cover.    1910    F.7-9    75.00 - 200.00

## BSA, Handbook for Boys, scout striding, raising hat in air

320 or 400 pages.
    Olive-drab or maroon
    cover. Proof Copy,
    First Edition.    1911    F.10-12    75.00 - 125.00
404 pgs. Olive-drab or
    maroon cover. Second
    Edition, 1-5 printing.
    Some marked
    Fourth Edition.    1911-1913    F.13-19    75.00 - 125.00
416 pgs. Maroon cover.
    Fourth Edition.    1913-1914    F.20-21    75.00 - 125.00
440 pgs. Maroon cover.    1914    F.22-23    75.00 - 125.00

## BSA, Handbook for Boys

472 pgs. Light gray cover.
    Morse Code Signal Flags
    (square ctr.) no knot
    on First Class badge.
    Eleventh-Twelfth Edition.    1914-1915    F.24-25    75.00 - 125.00
464 pgs. Light gray cover.
    Morse Code Signal Flags
    (square ctr.) no knot
    on First Class badge.
    Thirteenth Edition.    1915-1916    F.26-27    75.00 - 125.00
498 pgs. Red or green cover.
    Scout signals letter "L,"
    knot on First Class badge.
    Fourteenth-Eighteenth
    Edition.    1916-1918    F.28-32    40.00 - 75.00
496 pgs. Pale green cover.
    Eighteenth Edition
    Reprint-Nineteenth
    Edition.    1918    F.32-33    40.00 - 75.00
496 pgs. Pale green cover.
    Twentieth-Twenty-first
    Edition.    1919    F.34-35    40.00 - 75.00
492 pgs. Pale green cover.
    Twenty-second Edition.    1920    F.36    40.00 - 75.00
488 pgs. Pale green cover.
    Twenty-third Edition.    1921    F.37    40.00 - 75.00

1921 cover

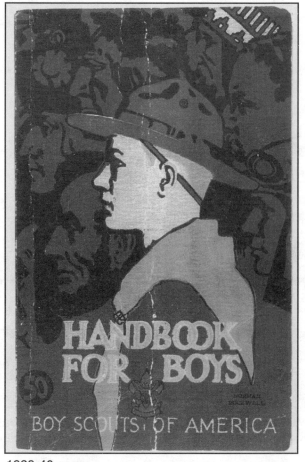

1928-40 cover

1940-46 cover

488 pgs. Pale green cover.
  Signal flags corrected to
  Semaphore type. Updated
  uniforms. Twenty-fourth
  Edition.           1921      F.38        40.00 - 75.00
512 pgs. Olive-green cover.
  Twenty-fifth to
  Thirty-seventh Edition.   1922-1927  F.3, 9-51   40.00 - 75.00

## Handbook for Boys, BSA

Conquistador at far right.
  636 pgs.          1927      F.52        15.00 - 25.00
Conquistador at left.
  638 pgs.          1927-1928  F.53-57    15.00 - 25.00
Lindbergh profile at far right.
  646 pgs.          1928-1930  F.58-64    10.00 - 25.00
650 pgs.            1930-1931  F.65-66    10.00 - 25.00
646 pgs.            1931      F.67        10.00 - 25.00
650 pgs.            1932      F.68-69     10.00 - 25.00
658 pgs.            1933-1935  F.70-75    10.00 - 25.00
660 pgs.            1936      F.76-77     10.00 - 25.00
668 pgs.            1936-1938  F.78-82    10.00 - 25.00
676 pgs.            1938-1940  F.83-85    10.00 - 25.00

## Handbook for Boys, BSA

680 pgs. Some printings w/
  8- or 16-page
  color insert.     1940-1943  F.86-89    12.50 - 30.00
570 pgs. plus 6 in b/w.
  Size reduction.   1944-1946  F.90-92    10.00 - 20.00

## Handbook for Boys, BSA

566 pgs. Fifth Edition.
  1-2 printing.       1948-1949  F.93-94    10.00 - 20.00

1948-49 cover

## Handbook for Boys, BSA

564 pgs. Fifth Edition.
  3-4 printing.       1950-1951  F.95-96    7.50 - 15.00
568 pgs. Fifth Edition.
  5-12 printing. Some tenth
  editions have special
  4-pg. commemorative
  for 15-millionth Handbook
  copy.               1952-1958  F.97-104   7.50 - 15.00

1950-58 cover

## Boy Scout Handbook, BSA

480 pgs. Sixth Edition.

| | | | |
|---|---|---|---|
| 1-6 printing. | 1959-1963 | F.105-110 | 7.50 - 15.00 |
| 439 pgs. Special printing for use in Ryuku Islands and Okinawa. | 1963 | F.109a | 5.00 - 10.00 |
| 470 pgs. Ads replaced w/ 24-pg. supplement of revised requirements. | 1965 | F.111 | 5.00 - 10.00 |

## Boy Scout Handbook, BSA

448 pgs. Seventh Edition.

| | | | |
|---|---|---|---|
| 1-7 printing. | 1965-1971 | F.112-118 | 2.50 - 7.50 |
| Features "orientalized" for use in Ryuku Islands. | 1966 | F.113a | 2.50 - 7.50 |

## Scout Handbook, BSA

480 pgs. Eighth Edition.

| | | | |
|---|---|---|---|
| 1-3 printing. | 1972-1975 | F.119-121 | 2.00 - 5.00 |

1940-46 cover

1959-65 cover

1972-75 cover

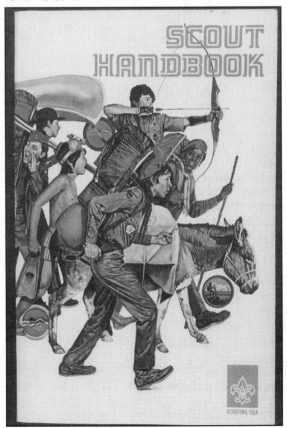

1976-77 cover

## Scout Handbook, BSA

480 pgs. Eighth Edition.
4-5 printing.                    1976-1977  F.122-123      2.50 - 7.50

## Official Boy Scout Handbook

576 pgs. Ninth Edition.
1-12 printings. 1st and
2nd printings have
either a black or blue
and red cover title.
2nd printing also
includes some
w/ Simon and Schuster
name on spine.           1979-1989  F.124-135      2.50 - 5.00

## Boy Scout Handbook, BSA

662 pgs. Tenth edition.
1-7 printings. Black
or green Child Abuse
Parents Guide
tear-out in front.       1990-1997  F.136-143      2.50 - 5.00

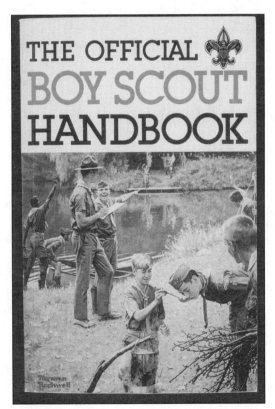

1979-89 cover

1990-97 cover

# AWARD MEDALS

## Contest Medal, octagonal pendant, regular ribbon and drape behind

Plain ctr., laurel wreath. Red-white-blue ribbon,
pendant in gold, silver, or bronze.    1914-1920   75.00 - 100.00

## Contest Medal, octagonal pendant, regular ribbon

Plain ctr., laurel wreath. Red-white-blue ribbon,
pendant in gold, silver, or bronze.    1921-1928   60.00 - 80.00

## Contest Medal, scalloped pendant, regular ribbon and drape behind

Female striding, facing forward,
outstretched arms. Solid ribbon,
pendant in gold, silver, or bronze.    1914-1920   75.00-100.00
First Aid. Female seated.
W/ eagle and shield,
white enamel cross.
Red-white-blue ribbon,
pendant in gold, silver, or bronze.    1914-1920   75.00-100.00
Plain ctr., laurel wreath.
Red-white-blue ribbon,
pendant in gold, silver, or bronze.    1914-1920   75.00-100.00
Signal flags within wreath.
Red-white-blue ribbon,
pendant in gold, silver, or bronze.    1914-1920   75.00-100.00

Swimming. Red-white-blue ribbon,
pendant in gold, silver, or bronze.    1914-1920   75.00-100.00
Tenderfoot emblem in ctr.
Red-white-blue ribbon,
pendant in gold, silver, or bronze.    1914-1920   75.00-100.00
Track runner at start.
Red-white-blue ribbon,
pendant in gold, silver, or bronze.    1914-1920   75.00-100.00
Track runner w/ palm branch.
Red-white-blue ribbon,
pendant in gold, silver, or bronze.    1914-1920   75.00-100.00
Tug of war contest.
Red-white-blue ribbon,
pendant in gold, silver, or bronze.    1914-1920   75.00-100.00

## Contest Medal, scalloped pendant, regular ribbon

Early Contest Medal,
First Aid. 1921-28 type.

Female striding forward,
arms outstretched.
Red-white-blue ribbon,
pendant in gold, silver, or bronze.    1921-1928   60.00 - 80.00
First Aid. Female seated w/ eagle
and shield, enamel white cross.
Red-white-blue ribbon,
pendant in gold, silver, or bronze.    1921-1928   60.00 - 80.00
Plain ctr. laurel wreath.
Red-white-blue ribbon,
pendant in gold, silver, or bronze.    1921-1928   60.00 - 80.00
Signal flags within laurel wreath.
Red-white-blue ribbon,
pendant in gold, silver, or bronze.    1921-1928   60.00 - 80.00
Swimming. Red-white-blue ribbon,
pendant in gold, silver, or bronze.    1921-1928   60.00 - 80.00
Tenderfoot emblem.
Red-white-blue ribbon,
pendant in gold, silver, or bronze.    1921-1928   60.00 - 80.00
Track runner and laurel branch.
Red-white-blue ribbon,
pendant in gold, silver, or bronze.    1921-1928   60.00 - 80.00

Track runner at start.
   Red-white-blue ribbon,
   pendant in gold, silver, or bronze.   1921-1928 60.00 - 80.00
Tug of war contest.
   Red-white-blue ribbon,
   pendant in gold, silver, or bronze.   1921-1928 60.00 - 80.00

## Octagonal pendant in gold, silver, or bronze, regular red-white-blue ribbon

| | | |
|---|---|---|
| Archery. | 1928-1932 | 50.00 - 75.00 |
| Bridge Building. | 1928-1932 | 50.00 - 75.00 |
| Bugling. | 1928-1932 | 50.00 - 75.00 |
| Camping. | 1928-1932 | 50.00 - 75.00 |
| Canoeing. | 1928-1932 | 50.00 - 75.00 |
| Cooking. | 1928-1932 | 50.00 - 75.00 |
| Field. | 1928-1932 | 50.00 - 75.00 |
| Fire Making. | 1928-1932 | 50.00 - 75.00 |
| First Aid. | 1928-1932 | 50.00 - 75.00 |
| First Class emblem within wreath. | 1928-1932 | 50.00 - 75.00 |
| Handicraft. | 1928-1932 | 50.00 - 75.00 |
| Knife & Axe Work. | 1928-1932 | 50.00 - 75.00 |
| Knot Tying. | 1928-1932 | 50.00 - 75.00 |
| Plain within laurel wreath. | 1928-1932 | 50.00 - 75.00 |
| Signaling. | 1928-1932 | 50.00 - 75.00 |
| Tent Pitching. | 1928-1932 | 50.00 - 75.00 |
| Tower Building. | 1928-1932 | 50.00 - 75.00 |
| Track. | 1928-1932 | 50.00 - 75.00 |
| Wall Scaling. | 1928-1932 | 50.00 - 75.00 |

Contest Medals: Knot Tying (left) and Fire Building.

## Octagonal pendant in gold, silver, or bronze, regular solid blue ribbon

| | | |
|---|---|---|
| Archery. | 1933-1954 | 25.00 - 50.00 |
| Bridge Building. | 1933-1954 | 25.00 - 50.00 |
| Bugling. | 1933-1954 | 25.00 - 50.00 |
| Camping. | 1933-1954 | 25.00 - 50.00 |
| Canoeing. | 1933-1954 | 25.00 - 50.00 |

General Contest Medal, Tenderfoot emblem.

General Contest Medal, First Class emblem.

| | | |
|---|---|---|
| Cooking. | 1933-1954 | 25.00 - 50.00 |
| Field. | 1933-1954 | 25.00 - 50.00 |
| Fire Making. | 1933-1954 | 25.00 - 50.00 |
| First Aid. | 1933-1954 | 25.00 - 50.00 |
| First Class emblem within wreath. | 1933-1954 | 25.00 - 50.00 |
| Handicraft. | 1933-1954 | 25.00 - 50.00 |
| Knife & Axe Work. | 1933-1954 | 25.00 - 50.00 |
| Knot Tying. | 1933-1954 | 25.00 - 50.00 |
| Plain within wreath. | 1933-1954 | 25.00 - 50.00 |
| Signaling. | 1933-1954 | 25.00 - 50.00 |
| Swimming. | 1933-1954 | 25.00 - 50.00 |
| Tent Pitching. | 1933-1954 | 25.00 - 50.00 |
| Tower Building. | 1933-1954 | 25.00 - 50.00 |
| Track. | 1933-1954 | 25.00 - 50.00 |
| Wall Scaling. | 1933-1954 | 25.00 - 50.00 |

## Tenderfoot Emblem in ctr., in gold, silver, or bronze-plated base metal, on red-white ribbon

| | | |
|---|---|---|
| Locking clasp back, fine detail. | 1953-1975 | 5.00-10.00 |
| Locking clasp back, rough detail. | 1975-1985 | 3.00-7.50 |
| Open clasp back, rough detail. | 1985- | 2.00-5.00 |

Scout John Flory of Wauwatosa, WI, receives a Heroism Certificate in 1929.

# HEROISM MEDALS

Lifesaving Medal, 1910-1925.

## Lifesaving Gold Award

Maltese cross w/ First Class badge
   suspended from BE PREPARED
   scroll, blue ribbon drape.          1910-1925   3,000.00 - 4,000.00

## Lifesaving Silver Award

Maltese cross w/ First Class badge
   suspended from BE PREPARED
   scroll, white ribbon drape.         1910-1925   2,000.00 - 2,500.00

## Lifesaving Bronze Award

Maltese cross w/ First Class badge
   suspended from BE PREPARED
   scroll, red ribbon drape.           1910-1925   1,500.00 - 2,000.00

## Certificate For Heroism

Larch parchment.                       1910-1930     300.00 - 500.00

## Honor Medal w/ Crossed Palms

Type I. Gold w/ tri-colored enameled ctr.
   Red ribbon.                         1925         1,500.00 - 1,750.00
Type II. Gilt silver w/ tri-colored enameled ctr.
   Red ribbon.                         1950           300.00 - 500.00

Honor Medal, for Life
Saving.

## Honor Medal

Type I. Gold w/ tri-colored enameled ctr.
   Red ribbon.                         1925   1,250.00 - 1,500.00
Type II. Gilt silver w/ tri-colored
   enameled ctr.                       1950     500.00 - 750.00

## Heroism Award Medal

Type I reads "FOR MERITORIOUS ACTION."
   Gilt silver, red enamel.
   Red-white-red ribbon.          1979-1989  200.00 - 250.00
Type II reads "FOR HEROISM." Gilt silver,
   red enamel. Red-white-red ribbon.  1989     200.00 - 250.00

Medal of Merit

## Medal of Merit

| | | |
|---|---|---|
| Type I. Gilt silver w/ blue enamel, gold-blue-gold ribbon. | 1946-1989 | 300.00 - 500.00 |
| Type II. Gilt silver w/ red enamel, gold-blue-gold ribbon. | 1989 | 175.00 - 225.00 |

Queens Scout Salvatore Bonamico receives a Medal of Merit from NYC Mayor Edward Koch.

## Harmon Foundation Scholarship

| | | |
|---|---|---|
| Small Eagle on "H" in circle, lapel stud. | 1927-1931 | 400.00-600.00 |

## William T. Hornaday Award

| | | |
|---|---|---|
| Gold medal, green ribbon, no legend. | 1951-1975 | 2,500.00-3,000.00 |
| Gold pin bar. Legend: FOR SERVICE TO WILD LIFE. | 1914-1950 | 1,500.00-2,000.00 |
| Bronze medal, green ribbon, legend. | 1979 | 250.00 - 400.00 |
| Gold medal. | 1979 | 750.00-1,000.00 |
| Gold pin bar, no legend. | 1951-1975 | 750.00-1,000.00 |
| Silver medal, green ribbon, legend. | 1978 | 750.00-1,000.00 |
| Silver medal, green ribbon, no legend. | 1976-1977 | 750.00-1,000.00 |
| Silver pin bar, no legend. | 1976-1977 | 250.00 - 400.00 |

# UNIFORMS

Tenderfoot scout with 4 bellow pocket coat and belt, breeches, and Army duck leggings.

## Belt

| | | |
|---|---|---|
| Olive-drab web, black buckle, First Class emblem. | 1911-1930 | 10.00 - 15.00 |

## Breeches

| | | |
|---|---|---|
| Knee length, ties at ends. Heavy olive-drab material. | 1911-1930 | 40.00 - 60.00 |

Knee length, ties at ends.
 Light olive-drab material.          1911-1930  30.00 - 50.00

## Campaign Hat
Summer weight, olive-drab,
 leather reinforced brown band.      1911-1930  20.00 - 30.00
Thin olive-drab felt, leather or silk
 hat band. Various makers.           1911-1930  20.00 - 60.00

## Coat
Open collar, w/ rank, merit badges
 and troop insignia on sleeves.
 Inside pocket for membership card.  1923-1928  100.00-150.00
High collar, 4 bellow pockets,
 light olive-drab material.          1911-1930  50.00 - 75.00
High collar, 4 pockets, heavy
 olive-drab material.                1911-1930  50.00 - 75.00
Open collar, w/ rank, merit badges
 and troop insignia on sleeves.
 No inside pocket for
 membership card.                    1920-1923  100.00-150.00
Open collar, w/o insignia.           1928-1941  75.00-125.00

## Collar Brass
BSA, screw post or crude fold pins.  1912-1920  40.00 - 60.00
Unit numerals: 1, 2, 3, 4, 5, 6, 7, 8, 0.
 Screw post.                         1912-1920  20.00 - 30.00

1911-1920 BSA Copper Collar Monogram.

1911-1920 Unit Collar
Number.

Community and State Strips in khaki with red embroidery
or red with white embroidery. Council Shoulder Strip in
red with white embroidery.

## Community Strip
Khaki and red.
 Various town names.                 1945-1955  4.00 - 8.00
Red and white.                       1955-1972  1.00 - 2.00

## Council Strip
Khaki and red.
 New York City/(Any of the 5 Boroughs). 1945-1955 12.50 - 17.50
Red and white.                       1955-1972  3.00 - 4.00
Red and white, Trans Atlantic Service. 1955-1972  7.50 - 10.00

## Knickers
Knee length, buckles at ends.
 Olive-drab material.                1911-1930  40.00 - 60.00

## Leggings
Army duck.                           1911-1930  15.00 - 20.00

## Merit Badge Sash
False sleeve for coat.               1916-1925  40.00 - 60.00
Narrow tan (2 across).               1924-1945  5.00 - 10.00
Wide tan (3 across).                 1924-1945  5.00 - 10.00
Narrow khaki (2 across).             1946-1979  5.00 - 7.50
Wide khaki (3 across).               1946-1979  5.00 - 7.50
Wide dark green (3 across).          1972-1979  3.00 - 6.00
Wide olive (3 across).               1980       3.00 - 6.00

## Neckerchief Slide
Braided "Turk's head"
 14 colors available.                1918-1940  3.00 - 7.50
Braided "Turk's head"
 Blue-orange, NY World's Fair
 Scout Service Corps.                1939-1940  30.00 - 40.00
Metal stamped braided "Turk's head"
 2 thick back flaps.                 1945-1975  3.00 - 5.00
Metal stamped braided "Turk's head"
 thin 1-piece loop.                  1991       0.50 - 1.00

Top: Neckerchief, Full Square, with small National Headquarters emblem. Bottom: Full Square with BSA and
Tenderfoot emblem in contrasting colors.

## Neckerchief

Full Square. Solid color, 28",
   w/ Official Badge 11 x 6-1/2".
   8 colors available.                    1914-1915  20.00 - 25.00
Full Square. Solid color, Merceen,
   28", small Official Badge.
   18 colors available.                   1916-1918  15.00 - 25.00
Full Square. Solid color, Pongee,
   28 x 32", small Official Badge.
   16 colors available.                   1919-1920  15.00 - 20.00

Full Square. Solid color, Soisette,
   28 x 32", small Official Badge.
   16 colors available.                   1921-1926  10.00 - 15.00
Full Square. Combination of 2 colors,
   28 x 32", First Class Badge. 14 available. 1924-1926  7.50 - 12.50
Full Square. Solid color, 28 x 32",
   First Class Badge within circle.
   17 colors available.                   1926-1931  5.00 - 7.50
Full Square. Combination of 2 colors,
   28 x 32", First Class Badge within circle.
   14 available.                          1926-1931  5.00 - 7.50
Full Square. Solid color, 30 x 30",
   Tenderfoot Badge within diamond.
   13 colors available.                   1932       5.00 - 7.50
Full Square. Combination of 2 colors,
   30 x 30", Tenderfoot Badge within diamond.
   14 colors available.                   1932       5.00 - 7.50
Full Square. Solid color, 32 x 32",
   Tenderfoot Badge within diamond.
   15 colors available.                   1933-1947  4.00 - 7.50
Full Square. Combination of 2 colors,
   32 x 32", Tenderfoot Badge within diamond.
   16 colors available.                   1933-1947  4.00 - 7.50
Triangular. Solid color, Tenderfoot
   Badge within diamond.                  1947       2.00 - 5.00
Triangular. Combination of 2 colors,
   Tenderfoot Badge within diamond.       1947       2.00 - 5.00
Triangular. Embroidered Tenderfoot Badge. 1972      5.00 - 7.50

## Pants

Khaki long w/ red piping around
   front pocket flaps.                    1946-1971  5.00 - 7.50
Khaki long w/ regular pockets.            1972-1979  5.00 - 7.50
olive drab w/ cargo pockets.              1980-1989  5.00 - 7.50
olive drab w/ regular pockets.            1990       5.00 - 7.50

## Patrol Ribbons

5-1/2" long. 50 available.                1911-1916  5.00 - 10.00
5" long. 50 available.                    1917-1928  5.00 - 10.00
4-1/2" long. 50 available.                1926-1929  5.00 - 7.50

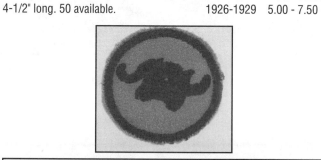

Patrol medallion varieties include a felt w/o BSA (top),
felt w/ BSA (bottom l.), and red twill (bottom r.).

First Class Scout Jon Flory of Wauwatosa, WI, 1929.

## Patrol Medallions

| | | |
|---|---|---|
| Red felt square, black image. | 1926 | 40.00 - 75.00 |
| Red felt circle, black image. | 1927-1933 | 10.00 - 25.00 |
| Red felt circle, black image w/ BSA below. | 1933-1952 | 3.00 - 7.50 |
| Red twill circle, gauze back. | 1953-1965 | 1.00 - 2.00 |
| Red twill circle, plastic back. | 1965-1972 | 1.00 - 2.00 |
| Colored. | 1972-1989 | .50 - 1.00 |

## Program Strip

| | | |
|---|---|---|
| BOY SCOUTS OF AMERICA in red on 1 line. Khaki cloth. | 1946-1971 | 3.00 - 5.00 |
| BOY SCOUTS OF AMERICA in red on 1 line. Tan cloth. | 1920-1921 | 50.00 - 75.00 |
| BOY SCOUTS OF AMERICA in red on 1 line. Tan cloth. | 1922-1945 | 10.00 - 15.00 |
| BOY SCOUTS OF AMERICA in red on 2 lines. Tan cloth. | 1918-1919 | 50.00 - 75.00 |
| BOY SCOUTS OF AMERICA in red. Tan khaki cloth. | 1980 | 3.00 - 5.00 |
| SCOUT B.S.A. in red. Dark green cloth. | 1972-1979 | 3.00 - 5.00 |
| SCOUT B.S.A. in red. Khaki cloth. | 1972-1979 | 3.00 - 5.00 |

## Puttees

| | | |
|---|---|---|
| Leather. | 1911-1930 | 20.00 - 25.00 |

## Service Star

| | | |
|---|---|---|
| Gold star screwback on gray felt (3 years). | 1932-1936 | 2.00 - 4.00 |
| Gold star screwback on green felt (1 year). | 1923-1946 | 2.00 - 4.00 |
| Gold star screwback on purple felt (10 years). | 1932-1946 | 2.00 - 4.00 |
| Gold star screwback on red felt (5 years). | 1932-1946 | 2.00 - 4.00 |
| Gold star w/ tenure number, screwback on green felt. | 1947-1955 | 2.00 - 4.00 |
| Gold star w/tenure number, clutch back on green plastic disc. | 1956 | 1.00 - 2.00 |
| Silver star screwback on red felt (5 years). | 1923-1931 | 2.00 - 4.00 |

## Service Stripe

| | | |
|---|---|---|
| Gold, 1/8" wide. (5 years). | 1921-1924 | 15.00 - 25.00 |
| Green, 1/8" wide (1 year). | 1920-1924 | 15.00 - 25.00 |
| Green, 3/8" wide (1 year). | 1913-1919 | 15.00 - 25.00 |
| Red, 1/8" wide (3 years). | 1920-1924 | 15.00 - 25.00 |
| Red, 3/8" wide (3 years). | 1913-1919 | 15.00 - 25.00 |

## Shirt

| | | |
|---|---|---|
| Heavy olive-drab material. Winter weight. | 1911-1930 | 20.00 - 30.00 |
| Heavy olive-drab material. Woolen. | 1911-1930 | 20.00 - 30.00 |
| Khaki long sleeves, pleated pocket. | 1946-1965 | 5.00 - 7.50 |
| Khaki short sleeves, pleated pocket. | 1946-1965 | 5.00 - 7.50 |
| Light olive-drab material. Summer weight. | 1911-1930 | 20.00 - 30.00 |
| Tan khaki long sleeves w/ epaulets. | 1980 | 5.00 - 10.00 |
| Tan khaki short sleeves w/ epaulets. | 1980 | 5.00 - 10.00 |

## Shorts

| | | |
|---|---|---|
| Heavy olive-drab material. | 1911-1930 | 20.00 - 35.00 |
| Heavy olive-drab material. Woolen. | 1911-1930 | 20.00 - 35.00 |
| Light olive-drab material. | 1911-1930 | 20.00 - 35.00 |

## State Strip, khaki and red

| | | |
|---|---|---|
| ALA. | 1945-1955 | 5.00 - 7.50 |
| ALASKA. | 1945-1955 | 30.00 - 40.00 |
| ARIZ. | 1945-1955 | 5.00 - 7.50 |
| ARK. | 1945-1955 | 7.50 - 12.50 |
| CALIF. | 1945-1955 | 5.00 - 7.50 |
| COLO. | 1945-1955 | 5.00 - 7.50 |
| CONN. | 1945-1955 | 5.00 - 7.50 |
| DEL. | 1945-1955 | 20.00 - 25.00 |
| FLA. | 1945-1955 | 5.00 - 7.50 |
| GA. | 1945-1955 | 5.00 - 7.50 |
| IDAHO. | 1945-1955 | 12.50 - 17.50 |
| ILL. | 1945-1955 | 5.00 - 7.50 |
| IND. | 1945-1955 | 5.00 - 7.50 |
| IOWA. | 1945-1955 | 5.00 - 7.50 |
| KANS. | 1945-1955 | 5.00 - 7.50 |
| KY. | 1945-1955 | 5.00 - 7.50 |
| LA. | 1945-1955 | 5.00 - 7.50 |
| MASS. | 1945-1955 | 5.00 - 7.50 |
| MD. | 1945-1955 | 5.00 - 7.50 |
| ME. | 1945-1955 | 50.00 - 75.00 |
| MICH. | 1945-1955 | 5.00 - 7.50 |
| MINN. | 1945-1955 | 5.00 - 7.50 |
| MISS. | 1945-1955 | 17.50 - 25.00 |
| MO. | 1945-1955 | 5.00 - 7.50 |
| MONT. | 1945-1955 | 30.00 - 40.00 |
| N. DAK. | 1945-1955 | 7.50 - 12.50 |
| N. MEX. | 1945-1955 | 7.50 - 12.50 |
| N.C. | 1945-1955 | 5.00 - 7.50 |
| N.H. | 1945-1955 | 17.50 - 25.00 |
| N.J. | 1945-1955 | 5.00 - 7.50 |
| N.Y. | 1945-1955 | 5.00 - 7.50 |
| N.Y.C. | 1945-1955 | 80.00 - 110.00 |
| NEB. | 1945-1955 | 5.00 - 7.50 |
| NEV. | 1945-1955 | 30.00 - 40.00 |
| OHIO. | 1945-1955 | 5.00 - 7.50 |
| OKLA. | 1945-1955 | 5.00 - 7.50 |
| ORE. | 1945-1955 | 5.00 - 7.50 |
| PA. | 1945-1955 | 5.00 - 7.50 |
| R.I. | 1945-1955 | 5.00 - 7.50 |
| S. DAK. | 1945-1955 | 7.50 - 12.50 |
| S.C. | 1945-1955 | 30.00 - 40.00 |
| T.H. (Territory of Hawaii). | 1945-1955 | 500.00 - 650.00 |
| TENN. | 1945-1955 | 5.00 - 7.50 |
| TEXAS. | 1945-1955 | 5.00 - 7.50 |
| UTAH. | 1945-1955 | 5.00 - 7.50 |
| VA. | 1945-1955 | 5.00 - 7.50 |
| VT. | 1945-1955 | 17.50 - 25.00 |
| W. VA. | 1945-1955 | 5.00 - 7.50 |
| WASH. | 1945-1955 | 5.00 - 7.50 |
| WIS. | 1945-1955 | 5.00 - 7.50 |
| WYO. | 1945-1955 | 10.00 - 15.00 |

## Stockings

| | | |
|---|---|---|
| Knee length green cotton. | 1911-1930 | 10.00 - 15.00 |

## Unit Number

| | | |
|---|---|---|
| Red square screen printed on white felt square, white numeral. | 1915-1926 | 20.00 - 25.00 |

| | | | |
|---|---|---|---|
| Red felt square, white embroidered numeral. | 1927-1952 | | 2.00 - 4.00 |
| Red square, white numeral, fully embroidered. | 1953-1992 | | 0.50 - 1.00 |
| Red cut edge, white embroidered numeral. | 1992 | | 0.25 - 0.35 |

Scout knives are identified by the shield on the handle. Shown are: Remington (acorn shield), Camillus Cutlery (shield; two examples), Ulster (round), and Imperial (stamped emblem).

## Camillus Cutlery Co.

| | | | |
|---|---|---|---|
| First Class emblem in shield-shaped shield. 3-5/8" black handle, two-piece can opener, line on bolsters. | 1946-1949 | CC.1 | 275.00 - 325.00 |
| First Class emblem in shield-shaped shield. 3-5/8" pearl handle, two-piece can opener, line on bolsters. | 1949-1953 | CC.1A | 150.00 - 200.00 |
| First Class emblem in shield-shaped shield, 3-5/8" black handle, one-piece can opener, line on bolsters. | 1950-1953 | CC.2 | 50.00 - 75.00 |
| First Class emblem in shield-shaped shield. 3-5/8" black handle, one-piece can opener, short screwdriver, line on bolsters. Removable shackle. | 1954 | CC.3 | 275.00 - 325.00 |
| First Class emblem in shield-shaped shield. 3-5/8" black handle, match nail nick. | 1947-1969 | CW.1 | 100.00 - 150.00 |
| First Class emblem in shield-shaped shield. 3-5/8" black handle, match nail nick. Removable shackle. | 1947-1969 | CW.1A | 100.00 - 150.00 |
| First Class emblem in shield-shaped shield. 3-5/8" brown handle, match nail nick. | 1947-1969 | CW.1B | 100.00 - 150.00 |
| Tenderfoot emblem in round shield, black handle. | 1965-1970 | CW.3 | 60.00 - 80.00 |
| Tenderfoot emblem in round shield, brown handle. | 1965-1970 | CW.3A | 40.00 - 60.00 |
| Tenderfoot emblem in round shield, brown handle. W/ shackle. | 1970-1979 | CW.3B | 25.00 - 40.00 |

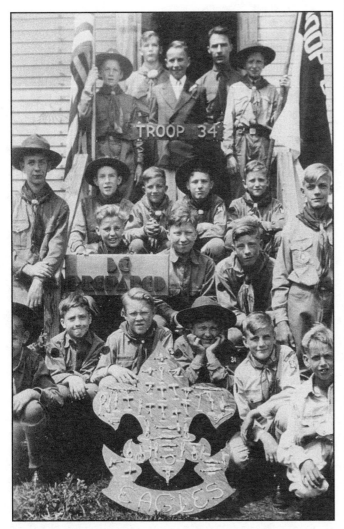

Troop 34, Waupaca, WI (ca. 1936).

# KNIVES

After the handbook and a uniform, most scouts want a knife. At first many think it is cool to have a knife, but use it before proper training and care for the tool can be instilled. Finger carving becomes one of the immediate projects, soon followed by realistic first aid. If one is scarred by scouting, this is the quickest way. A scout knife was intended to be used, therefore very few of the pre-1960 issues exist with clean blades and etching. Collector editions and premium knives did not come along until the mid-1980s with the 75th anniversary of the program. Those knives were never really intended for use, and always should be collected in the original box.

| Description | Years | No. | Price |
|---|---|---|---|
| Tenderfoot emblem in round shield. 3-5/8" stag handle. | 1985-1989 | CW.W3C | 25.00 - 40.00 |
| Tenderfoot emblem in round shield. 3-5/8" white handle. | 1980-1984 | CW.W3D | 20.00 - 35.00 |
| Eagle emblem on red-white-blue handle. 2-1/4", spear, file, and scissors. | 1987-1990 | E.1 | 25.00 - 40.00 |

## Cattaraugus Cutlery Co.

| Description | Years | No. | Price |
|---|---|---|---|
| First Class emblem in octagon shield. 3-7/16" bone handle, 4 blades. W/ shackle. | 1933-1940 | CAC.2 | 275.00 - 325.00 |
| First Class emblem in octagon shield. 3-7/16" bone handle, 3 blades. No shackle. | 1933-1940 | CAC.3 | 275.00 - 325.00 |
| First Class emblem in octagon shield. 3-7/16" bone handle, 3 blades. W/ shackle. | 1933-1940 | CAC.4 | 275.00 - 325.00 |
| First Class emblem in octagon shield. 3-7/16" bone handle, 4 blades. No shackle. | 1933-1940 | CAC.1 | 275.00 - 325.00 |

## Imperial Knife Co.

| Description | Years | No. | Price |
|---|---|---|---|
| First Class emblem on shield. 3-3/4" black handle, large can opener, long screwdriver. | 1949-1955 | I.1 | 40.00 - 75.00 |
| First Class emblem on shield. 3-3/4" pearl handle, large can opener, long screwdriver. | 1949-1955 | I.2 | 40.00 - 75.00 |
| First Class emblem in plastic shield. 3-3/4" black handle, large can opener, long screwdriver. | 1955-1958 | I.3 | 20.00 - 25.00 |
| First Class emblem in plastic shield. 3-3/4" black handle, can opener, short screwdriver. | 1958-1962 | I.3A | 20.00 - 25.00 |
| First Class emblem on shield. 3-1/2" rosewood handle, 5-blade deluxe. | 1952-1962 | I.4 | 20.00 - 25.00 |
| First Class emblem on shield. 3-1/2" pearl handle, 5-blade deluxe. | 1952-1962 | I.4A | 20.00 - 25.00 |
| First Class emblem on circle. 3-1/2" stag handle, 5-blade deluxe. | 1963-1970 | I.4B | 20.00 - 25.00 |
| First Class emblem on circle. 3-1/2" smooth plastic handle, simulated wood. | 1962-1963 | I.4C | 25.00 - 35.00 |
| First Class emblem carved. 3-3/4" reddish brown handle. | 1958-1962 | I.5 | 20.00 - 25.00 |
| Tenderfoot emblem stamped on black handle. 3-3/4", utility knife. | 1973-1979 | I.6 | 15.00 - 20.00 |
| Tenderfoot emblem stamped on white handle. 3-3/4", utility knife. | 1980-1981 | I.6A | 15.00 - 20.00 |
| Tenderfoot emblem stamped on brown handle. 3-3/4", utility knife. | 1982-1985 | I.6B | 15.00 - 20.00 |
| Tenderfoot emblem stamped on red handle. 3-3/4", utility knife. | 1986-1989 | I.6C | 15.00 - 20.00 |
| First Class emblem in plastic shield. 3-5/8" black handle, long puff on main blade. | 1963-1969 | IW.2 | 25.00 - 35.00 |

## Imperial Knife Co. - Frontier

| Description | Years | No. | Price |
|---|---|---|---|
| Tenderfoot emblem stamped on white handle. 2-7/8", blade etched, clip and pen on same end. | 1982-1985 | IF.1 | 17.50 - 22.50 |
| Tenderfoot emblem stamped on white handle. 2-7/8", blade not etched, clip and pen on opposite ends | 1981 | IF.1A | 17.50 - 22.50 |

## Imperial Knife Co. - Kingston

| Description | Years | No. | Price |
|---|---|---|---|
| No shield, stainless handle, main blade etched. Shackle stamped KINGSTON. | 1945-1947 | IK.2 | 45.00 - 60.00 |

## Keen Kutter Mfg. Co.

| Description | Years | No. | Price |
|---|---|---|---|
| Name etched on handle. 3-3/8", spear and pen blades. For Boy's Life subscriptions. | 1916-1921 | KK.1 | 300.00 - 350.00 |

## Landers, Frary and Clark

| Description | Years | No. | Price |
|---|---|---|---|
| First Class emblem in flat-top shield. 3-3/4" black composition handle, lines on bolster. | 1931-1939 | LFC.1 | 130.00 - 160.00 |
| First Class emblem in flat-top shield. 3-3/8" black composition handle, no lines on bolster. | 1931-1939 | LFC.2 | 130.00 - 160.00 |
| First Class emblem in flat-top shield. 3-3/8" black composition handle, spear and screwdriver/cap lifter. | 1931-1933 | LFC.3 | 130.00 - 160.00 |
| First Class emblem in flat-top shield. 3-3/8" black composition handle, 3 blades. No shackle. | 1934-1939 | LFC.4 | 130.00 - 160.00 |

## New York Knife Co.

| Description | Years | No. | Price |
|---|---|---|---|
| BE PREPARED on plaque. 3-5/8" bone handle, punch blade w/ pat. date of 6.10.02. Very large shackle. | 1911-1916 | NYK.1 | 225.00 - 275.00 |

| | | | |
|---|---|---|---|
| BE PREPARED on plaque. 3-5/8" bone handle, punch blade w/ pat. #. Removable shackle. | 1917-1922 | NYK.1A | 275.00 - 325.00 |
| BE PREPARED on plaque. 3-1/2" ebony handle, sheepfoot and pen blade. Very large shackle. | 1911-1916 | NYK.2 | 275.00 - 325.00 |
| BE PREPARED on plaque. 3-1/2" ebony handle, 2 blades. Removable shackle. | 1917-1922 | NYK.2A | 225.00 - 325.00 |
| First Class emblem in oval shield. 3-1/2" bone handle, 2 blades. Removable shackle. | 1917-1922 | NYK.2B | 275.00 - 325.00 |
| BE PREPARED on plaque. 3-5/8" bone handle, clip and implement blade. | 1920-1925 | NYK.3 | 275.00 - 325.00 |
| First Class emblem in oval shield. 3-5/8" bone handle, punch blade w/ pat. #. Removable shackle. | 1923-1926 | NYK.4 | 225.00 - 275.00 |
| First Class emblem in oval shield. 3-5/8" bone handle, screwdriver/wirescraper, can opener/caplifter, spiral punch w/ pat. #1,171,422. | 1926-1931 | NYK.5 | 225.00 - 275.00 |
| First Class emblem in oval shield. 3-5/8" bone handle, screwdriver/wirescraper, can opener/caplifter, spear. | 1926-1931 | NYK.5A | 225.00 - 275.00 |
| First Class emblem in oval shield. 3-5/8" pearl shell handle, screwdriver/wirescraper, can opener/caplifter, spiral punch w/ pat. #1,171,422. | 1926-1931 | NYK.5B | 450.00 - 550.00 |
| First Class emblem in oval shield. 3-3/8" bone handle, screwdriver/wirescraper, can opener/caplifter, spiral punch w/ pat. #1,171,422. | 1926-1931 | NYK.6 | 175.00 - 225.00 |
| First Class emblem in oval shield. 3-3/8" bone handle, screwdriver/wirescraper, can opener/caplifter, spear. | 1926-1931 | NYK.6A | 175.00 - 225.00 |
| First Class emblem in oval shield. 3-3/8" bone handle, clip and punch blade. | 1926-1931 | NYK.7 | 175.00 - 225.00 |

## PAL Blade Co.

| | | | |
|---|---|---|---|
| First Class emblem in circle. 3-3/4" bone handle, two-piece can opener. | 1940-1942 | PB.1 | 50.00 - 75.00 |
| First Class emblem in circle. 3-1/2" bone handle, No belt shackle. | 1940-1942 | PB.2 | 60.00 - 80.00 |
| First Class emblem in circle. 3-3/4" black plastic handle, one-piece can opener. | 1942 | PB.3 | 50.00 - 75.00 |

## Remington

| | | | |
|---|---|---|---|
| First Class emblem in Acorn shield. 3-3/4" bone handle, can opener/ stubby screwdriver. | 1923-1924 | R.1 | 275.00 - 325.00 |
| First Class emblem in Acorn shield. 3-3/4" bone handle, two-piece can opener w/ lift tab. | 1924-1926 | R.1A | 275.00 - 325.00 |
| First Class emblem in Acorn shield. 3-3/4" bone handle. Second shield engraved "The Remington Award for Heroism" | 1924-1932 | R.1B | 400.00 - 500.00 |
| First Class emblem in Acorn shield. 3-3/8" bone handle, can opener. | 1923-1924 | R.2 | 275.00 - 325.00 |
| First Class emblem in Acorn shield. 3-3/8" bone handle, two-piece can opener w/ lift tab. | 1924-1926 | R.2A | 275.00 - 325.00 |
| First Class emblem in cut out shield. 3-3/4" one handle, long screwdriver. | 1927 | R.3 | 275.00 - 325.00 |
| First Class emblem in round shield. 3-3/4" bone handle, long screwdriver, vertical lift tab on can opener. | 1929-1932 | R.4 | 150.00 - 200.00 |
| First Class emblem in round shield, 3-3/4" bone handle, long screwdriver, parallel lift tab on can opener. | 1933-1935 | R.4A | 150.00 - 200.00 |
| First Class emblem in round shield. 3-3/4" bone handle, parallel lift tab on can opener, plain bolster. | 1935-1939 | R.4B | 150.00 - 200.00 |
| First Class emblem in round shield. 3-3/8" bone handle, pinched bolster, vertical lift tab on can opener. | 1929-1932 | R.5 | 150.00 - 200.00 |
| First Class emblem in round shield. 3-3/8" bone handle, smooth bolster, parallel lift tab on can opener. | 1933-1939 | R.5A | 150.00 - 200.00 |
| First Class emblem in round shield. 3-3/8" bone handle, 3 blades. No shackle. | 1928-1932 | R.6 | 150.00 - 200.00 |

First Class emblem in round shield. 3-1/2" bone handle, 3 blades, screwdriver w/ main blade. Removable shackle.  1934-1939  R.7   250.00 - 300.00

First Class emblem in round shield. 3-1/2" bone handle, 3 blades, can opener w/ main blade. Removable shackle.  1934-1939  R.7A  250.00 - 300.00

## Schrade Co.

Tenderfoot emblem stamped on stainless handle. 2-7/8", spear and file blade.  1970-1978  S.2  17.50 - 22.50

Tenderfoot emblem in round shield. 3-5/8" Delrin stag handle, long pull.  1973  SW.4  17.50 - 22.50

## Schrade Walden

First Class emblem on oval shield. 2-3/4" Delrin stag handle, clip and pen blade.  1962-1972  S.1  17.50 - 22.50

## Ulster Knife Co.

First Class emblem in shield-shaped shield. 3-5/8" bone handle, short screwdriver, one-piece can opener, long nail nick.  1923-1926  U.1  20.00 - 30.00

First Class emblem in shield-shaped shield. 3-5/8" pearl shell handle, short screwdriver, one-piece can opener, long nail nick.  1926-1928  U.1A  17.50 - 22.50

First Class emblem in shield-shaped shield. 3-3/8" bone handle, short screwdriver, one-piece can opener, long nail nick.  1923-1926  U.2  17.50 - 22.50

First Class emblem in shield-shaped shield. 3-5/8" bone handle, long screwdriver, short nail nick, three-piece can opener.  1927-1940  U.3  17.50 - 22.50

First Class emblem in shield-shaped shield. 3-3/8" bone handle, long screwdriver, short nail nick, three-piece can opener.  1927-1940  U.4  10.00 - 17.50

First Class emblem in shield-shaped shield. 3-3/8" bone handle, long screwdriver, three-piece can opener.  1934-1940  U.5  10.00 - 17.50

First Class emblem in shield-shaped shield. 3-3/8" bone handle, long screwdriver, three-piece can opener. Removable shackle.  1934-1940  U.5A  10.00 - 17.50

First Class emblem in shield-shaped shield. 3-1/2" bone handle, spear and pen blades.  1923-1931  U.6  10.00 - 17.50

## Ulster, USA

Tenderfoot emblem in round shield. 3-3/4" brown handle.  1962-1979  U.1  60.00 - 80.00

Tenderfoot emblem in round shield. 3-3/4" white handle.  1962-1979  U.1A  17.50 - 22.50

Tenderfoot emblem in round shield. 3-3/4" stag handle.  1983-1985  U.1B  15.00 - 25.00

Tenderfoot emblem in round shield. 3-3/4" stag groved handle, stainless blades.  1966-1976  U.2  15.00 - 25.00

Tenderfoot emblem in round shield. 3-3/4" stag handle, 5-blade deluxe. No shackle.  1976-1979  U.3  15.00 - 25.00

Tenderfoot emblem in round shield. 3-3/4" ivory handle, 5-blade deluxe. No shackle.  1980-1981  U.3A  20.00 - 35.00

Tenderfoot emblem in round shield. 3-3/4" white handle, 5-blade deluxe. No shackle.  1982-1983  U.3B  20.00 - 30.00

Tenderfoot emblem in round shield. 3-3/4" smooth white handle, 5-blade deluxe. No shackle.  1984-1985  U.3C  20.00 - 30.00

Tenderfoot emblem in round shield. 3-3/4" black handle, 5-blade deluxe, stamped Camillus.  1986-1987  UC.4  20.00 - 30.00

## Victorinox

Tenderfoot and Swiss emblem stamped on red handle. 3-1/2", 14 tools (8 blades) Huntsman.  1987-1989  V.1  45.00 - 55.00

Tenderfoot and Swiss emblem stamped on red handle. 3-1/4", 12 tools (6 blades). Tinker.  1987-1989  V.2  25.00 - 35.00

Tenderfoot and Swiss emblem stamped on red handle. 2-1/4", 5 tools (3 blades). Classic.  1987-1989  V.3  20.00 - 25.00

# Boy Scout Stamps

| | | | | | |
|---|---|---|---|---|---|
| 3¢ 40th Anniversary | | 1950 | 22¢ 75th Anniversary | | 1985 |
| Mint single | .25 | | Mint single | | .50 |
| Plate Block of 4 | 1.00 | | Plate block of 4 | | 2.00 |
| Full sheet of 50 | 6.00 | | Full sheet of 50 | | 13.50 |
| 4¢ 50th Anniversary | | 1960 | 32¢ Part 2 of Centry Series | | 1997 |
| Mint single | .25 | | Mint single | | .50 |
| Plate block of 4 | 1.00 | | Full sheet of 15 | | 7.00 |
| Full sheet of 50 | 6.00 | | | | |

## Wenger

| | | | |
|---|---|---|---|
| Tenderfoot and Swiss emblem stamped on red handle. 3-3/8", 9 tools. Young Hunter. | 1982-1986 | W.1 | 30.00 - 40.00 |
| Tenderfoot and Swiss emblem stamped on red handle. 3-3/8", 7 tools. Scout Special. | 1982-1986 | W.2 | 25.00 - 35.00 |
| Tenderfoot and Swiss emblem stamped on red handle. 2-1/2", 5 tools. Viceroy. | 1982-1986 | W.3 | 15.00 - 20.00 |

# MEMBERSHIP CARDS

## Pocket Card. 4 page, rivet corner.

Square ctr. to flags. (Morse Code Flags)     1911-1918  30.00 - 50.00

The earliest style of membership cards were multiple pages held together by a corner grommet.

## Tri-fold Card

| | | |
|---|---|---|
| Scout signaling, 200 Fifth Avenue Address. Square ctr. morse code flags | 1919-1921 | 25.00-40.00 |
| Scout signaling diagonal semaphore flags, 200 Fifth Avenue address. Loyalty, Patriotism, Chivalry below flag, rope border to design scenes. | 1922-1927 | 20.00 - 30.00 |
| Scout signaling, 2 Park Avenue address. Loyalty, Patriotism, Service in gray bordered scenes. | 1928-1940 | 10.00 - 20.00 |
| Cub, Boy Scout, and Sea Scout walking left. Loyalty, Patriotism, Service in tan bordered scenes. | 1939-1943 | 10.00 - 20.00 |

Two membership cards: 1928-1927 (top) and 1928-1940.

The tri-fold membership cards came with three distinct graphics in the centerfold.

The third and final tri-fold card is a Rockwell design, which was changed into a bi-fold card format during World War II (shown here).

Membership cards from the 1950s and 1960s became single cards, some with nice graphics.

## Single Card

Scout Leader and boy within archway
on top. Olive-black color.                1942-1945   5.00 - 7.50

## Bi-fold Card

Cub, Boy Scout, and
Sea Scout walking left.              1944-1948  10.00 - 15.00

## Single Card

Cub, Boy Scout, and Sea Scout walking
left, red banner at bottom.                       1946-1949   5.00 - 7.50
Cub, Boy Scout, and Explorer walking
forward, Liberty Bell in background.
Forward on Liberty's Team legend.                 1952-1956   5.00 - 7.50
Leader and scout looking up at tablet
w/ Oath, Law, and Cub Promise.                    1955-1958   4.00 - 6.00
Scout Oath and Tenderfoot emblem on
blue background.                                  1959-1965   3.00 - 4.00
Cub, Explorer, and scout looking upward,
Washington in prayer in background.               1957-1960   4.00 - 6.00
Scout Oath and Tenderfoot emblem on
blue background. 50th Anniversary
emblem added.                                     1960        3.00 - 5.00
First Class emblem and patrol hiking.             1965-1972   2.00 - 4.00
Tenderfoot emblem on green background.            1972-1976   0.50 - 1.00
Bicentennial motif.                               1975-1977   0.50 - 1.00
Scouting's 70th, Cub Scouts'
50th Anniversaries.                               1979-1981   0.50 - 1.00
Scouting the Better Life slogan.                  1981-1983   0.50 - 1.00

## Bi-fold Card

Flag exterior. Cub, Tenderfoot, and
Explorer E emblems inside.                        1983-1984   0.50 - 1.00
Flag exterior. Diamond Jubilee
emblem inside.                                    1985-1986   0.50 - 1.00

## Single Card

Tenderfoot emblem on red background.              1986-1990   0.50 - 1.00
Modernized Tenderfoot emblem.                     1990        0.25 - 0.50

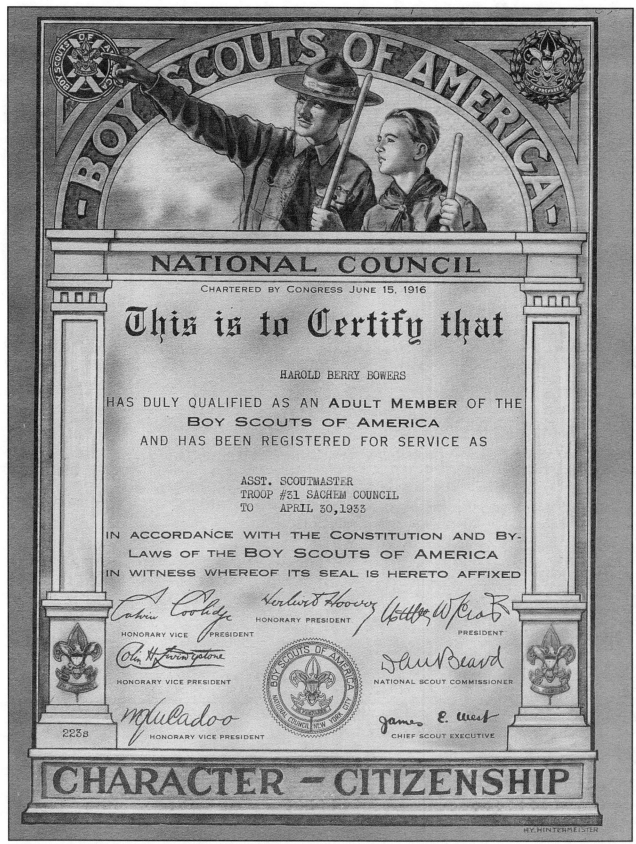

Using the same design as the membership card, an 8-1/2" x 10-1/2" certificate was available to adults for framing, value $5.00 - $10.00. This example is from 1933.

# ADVANCEMENT CARDS

Early style advancement cards. This group is from the late 1920s and early 1930s.

## Tenderfoot Card

| | | |
|---|---|---|
| 200 Fifth Avenue Address. | 1920-1930 | 5.00 - 7.50 |
| 2 Park Avenue Address. | 1930-1945 | 5.00 - 7.50 |
| Pocket size, National Council New York City seal. | 1945-1953 | 3.00 - 5.00 |
| Badge in circle, line flanking, National Council on seal. | 1953-1968 | 2.00 - 4.00 |
| Badge at top, National Council on yellow seal. | 1960-1968 | 1.00 - 2.00 |
| Badge at top, BE PREPARED on yellow seal. | 1968-1972 | 1.00 - 2.00 |
| Colored background patch, green border. | 1972-1989 | 0.50 - 1.00 |

## Second Class Card

| | | |
|---|---|---|
| 200 Fifth Avenue Address. | 1920-1930 | 5.00 - 7.50 |
| 2 Park Avenue Address. | 1930-1945 | 5.00 - 7.50 |
| Pocket size, National Council New York City seal. | 1945-1953 | 3.00 - 5.00 |
| Badge in circle, line flanking, National Council on seal. | 1953-1968 | 2.00 - 4.00 |
| Badge at top, National Council on yellow seal. | 1960-1968 | 1.00 - 2.00 |
| Badge at top, BE PREPARED on yellow seal. | 1968-1972 | 1.00 - 2.00 |
| Colored background patch, green border. | 1972-1989 | 0.50 - 1.00 |

## First Class Card

| | | |
|---|---|---|
| 200 Fifth Avenue Address. | 1920-1930 | 5.00 - 7.50 |
| 2 Park Avenue Address. | 1930-1945 | 5.00 - 7.50 |
| Pocket size, National Council New York City seal. | 1945-1953 | 3.00 - 5.00 |
| Badge in circle, line flanking, National Council on seal. | 1953-1968 | 2.00 - 4.00 |

| | | |
|---|---|---|
| Badge at top, National Council on yellow seal. | 1960-1968 | 1.00 - 2.00 |
| Badge at top, BE PREPARED on yellow seal. | 1968-1972 | 1.00 - 2.00 |
| Colored background patch, green border. | 1972-1989 | 0.50 - 1.00 |

Advancement cards of the 1960s.

Advancement cards of the 1970s.

## Star Scout Card

| | | |
|---|---|---|
| 200 Fifth Avenue Address. | 1920-1930 | 7.50 - 12.50 |
| 2 Park Avenue Address. | 1930-1945 | 7.50 - 12.50 |
| Pocket size, National Council New York City seal. | 1945-1953 | 5.00 - 7.50 |
| Badge in circle, line flanking, National Council on seal. | 1953-1968 | 2.00 - 4.00 |
| Badge at top, National Council on yellow seal. | 1960-1968 | 1.00 - 2.00 |
| Badge at top, BE PREPARED on yellow seal. | 1968-1972 | 1.00 - 2.00 |
| Colored background patch, green border. | 1972-1989 | 0.50 - 1.00 |

## Life Scout Card

| | | |
|---|---|---|
| 200 Fifth Avenue Address. | 1920-1930 | 7.50 - 12.50 |

| | | |
|---|---|---|
| 2 Park Avenue Address. | 1930-1945 | 7.50 - 12.50 |
| Pocket size, National Council New York City seal. | 1945-1953 | 5.00 - 7.50 |
| Badge in circle, line flanking, National Council on seal. | 1953-1968 | 2.00 - 4.00 |
| Badge at top, National Council on yellow seal. | 1960-1968 | 1.00 - 2.00 |
| Badge at top, BE PREPARED on yellow seal. | 1968-1972 | 1.00 - 2.00 |
| Colored background patch, green border. | 1972-1989 | 0.50 - 1.00 |

## Eagle Scout Card

| | | |
|---|---|---|
| 200 Fifth Avenue Address. | 1920-1930 | 10.00 - 15.00 |
| 2 Park Avenue Address. | 1930-1945 | 10.00 - 15.00 |
| Pocket size, National Council New York City seal. | 1945-1953 | 7.50 - 10.00 |
| Badge in circle, line flanking, National Council on seal. | 1953-1968 | 3.00 - 6.00 |
| Badge at top, National Council on yellow seal. | 1960-1968 | 4.00 - 6.00 |
| Badge at top, BE PREPARED on yellow seal. | 1968-1972 | 2.50 - 5.00 |
| Medal design w/ yellow seal. | 1972-1989 | 4.00 - 6.00 |

## Eagle Palm Card, bronze, silver, or gold

| | | |
|---|---|---|
| Pocket size, National Council New York City seal. | 1945-1953 | 7.50 - 10.00 |
| Badge in circle, line flanking, National Council on seal. | 1953-1968 | 3.00 - 6.00 |
| Badge at top, National Council on yellow seal. | 1960-1968 | 3.00 - 5.00 |
| Badge at top, BE PREPARED on yellow seal. | 1968-1972 | 2.50 - 5.00 |
| Medal design w/ yellow seal. | 1972-1989 | 4.00 - 6.00 |

## Merit Badge Card

| | | |
|---|---|---|
| 200 Fifth Avenue Address. | 1920-1930 | 5.00 - 7.50 |
| 2 Park Avenue Address. | 1930-1945 | 5.00 - 7.50 |
| Badge in circle, line flanking, National Council on seal. | 1953-1968 | 2.00 - 4.00 |
| Badge at top, National Council on yellow seal. | 1960-1968 | 1.00 - 2.00 |
| Badge at top, BE PREPARED on yellow seal. | 1968-1972 | 1.00 - 2.00 |
| Red stripes at top and bottom w/ rank badges in blue. | 1972-1989 | 0.50 - 1.00 |

# MERIT BADGE PAMPHLETS

Until 1915, when separate pamphlets made an appearance, merit badge requirements were printed in the Scout Handbook. There have been nine major types of covers with several minor varieties in the early types and numerous printing dates in the later issues of these pamphlets.

The first type is the "White Cover." The first variety (1a) and the interior were printed on the same weight paper stock.

Its title is "BE PREPARED for Merit Badge Examinations," and there is a line drawing of a scene, which includes the badge design and name. The second variety (1b) of the White Covers has an ornate frame design around the requirements and a line illustration below. Both "White Cover" varieties were issue concurrently, from roughly 1918–1922. Value 55.00 - 80.00 each.

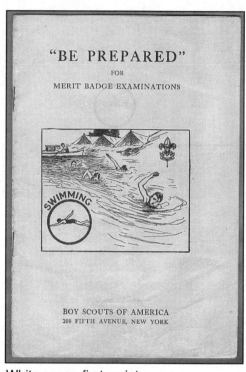

White cover, first variety

White cover, second variety

The second major type of pamphlet cover is the "Brown or Tan Cover." Above a large colored illustration there is the title of the badge, and below there is a First Class emblem, Merit Badge Series, and the National Office name and address. There are four varieties of the type, which are easy to distinguish by the phrasing of the national address. The first (2a) has "200 Fifth Ave. New York City" on two lines (1925–1928). The second variety (2b) has "Two Park/Avenue New York City" on two lines (1928–1939, but some into the mid-1940s); this is the most common brown-covered pamphlet. The third variety (2c) has "Two Park/Avenue New York, N.Y." on two lines (1936–1939); this is the hardest brown-covered pamphlet to find. The fourth variety (2d) has "Two Park Avenue, New York, N.Y." on one line (1937–1939). Value 5.00 - 17.50 each.

The third major type (3) of pamphlet is the "Standing Scout Cover." A uniformed scout (in color) stands to the left of a vertical red stripe. Sometimes this is called the "vertical red and white." It was in use from 1939–1944. Value 7.50 - 12.50 each.

The fourth type (4) is the "Red & White Cover." Used from 1944–1952, the design has the badge name and design in black on the white top half, and a red bottom area with the National Office information. There are two collectible varieties based on the thickness of the cover stock. A heavy cardboard stock was used in 1944 and 1945, then it was changed to a lighter weight and coated card stock. Value 3.00 - 7.50 each.

The fifth type (5) is the "Photo Red Covers," in use from 1949–1966. This is the most common of all pamphlet cover designs, due to its long use and use during scouting's membership peak. The top half has a photo of a scout doing something relating to the badge, and the lower portion remained red as in the fourth type. Changes appear in some photos in later printings. Value 2.00 - 5.00 each.

The sixth type (6) is the "Full Photo Cover" in use from 1966–1971. There is no red stripe, the badge name appears at the top, and a line drawing of the badge appears in a red circle in the lower right corner. Changes appear in some photos in later printings. Value 1.00 - 3.00 each.

The seventh type (7) is the "Green Stripe Top," which made its introduction with the "improved" scouting program of 1971–1979. The badge name in black outlined letters appears on a light green background above a full photo. Changes appear in some photos in later printings. Value .50 - 1.50 each.

The eighth type (8) is the "Red Stripe Top," which was introduced in 1980. It has the merit badge name within a red stripe at the top and a full photo. Changes appear in some photos in later printings. Value .50 - 1.00 each.

The ninth type (blue) is for Air Scout program and was introduced in 1940 and used until 1949. The covers are blue. Value 30.00 - 50.00 each.

Serious collectors of merit badge pamphlets wishing additional information should consider Joseph Price's detailed *Kahuna Katalog of Merit Badge Pamphlets.*

## Aerodynamics    blue.

## Aeronautics    blue.

Brown cover, first variety

**Agribusiness**    8.

**Agriculture**    1a, b; 2a, b, c, d; 3, 4, 5, 6, 7.

**Airplane Design**    blue, 4.

**Airplane Structure**    blue, 4.

**American Business**    6, 7, 8.

**American Cultures**    8.

**American Heritage**    7, 8.

**American Labor**    8.

**Angling**    1a, b; 2a, b, c, d; 3, 4.

**Animal Industry**    2a, b, c, d; 3, 4, 5, 6, 7.

**Animal Science**    7, 8.

**Archery**    1a, b; 2a, b, c, d; 3, 4, 5, 6, 7, 8.

**Architecture**    1a, b; 2a, b, c, d; 3, 4, 5, 6, 7, 8.

Brown cover, second variety

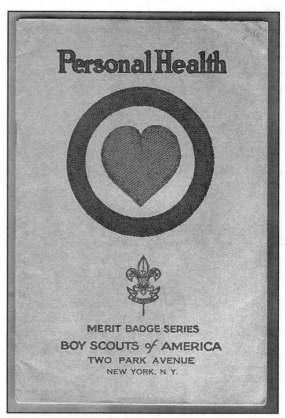

Brown cover, third variety

| | |
|---|---|
| **Art** | 1a, b; 2a, b, c, d; 3, 4, 5, 6, 7, 8. |
| **Astronomy** | 1a, b; 2a, b, c, d; 3, 4, 5, 6, 7, 8. |
| **Athletics** | 1a, b; 2a, b, c, d; 3, 4, 5, 6, 7, 8. |
| **Atomic Energy** | 5, 6, 7, 8, special yellow cover edition. |
| **Automobiling** | 1a, b; 2a, b, c, d; 3, 4, 5. |
| **Automotive Safety** | 5, 6, 7. |
| **Aviation** | 1a, b; 2a, b, c, d; 3, 5, 6, 7, 8. |
| **Backpacking** | 8. |
| **Basketry** | 2a, b, c, d; 3, 4, 5, 6, 7, 8. |
| **Bee Keeping** | 1, 2a, b, c, d; 4, 5, 6, 7, 8. |
| **Beef Production** | 2a, b, c, d; 4, 5, 6, 7. |
| **Bird Study (Ornithology)** | 1a, b; 2a, b, c, d; 3, 4, 5, 6, 7, 8. |

| | |
|---|---|
| **Blacksmithing** | 1a, b; 2a, b, c, d; 3, 4. |
| **Bookbinding** | 2a, b, c, d; 3, 4, 5, 6, 7, 8. |
| **Botany** | 1a, b; 2a, b, c, d; 3, 4, 5, 6, 7, 8. |
| **Business** | 1a, b; 2a, b, c, d; 3, 4, 5. |
| **Camping** | 1a, b; 2a, b, c, d; 3, 4, 5, 6, 7, 8. |
| **Canoeing** | 2a, b, c, d; 3, 4, 5, 6, 7, 8. |
| **Carpentry** | 1a, b; 2a, b, c, d; 3, 4. |
| **Cement Work** | 1a, b; 2a, b, c, d; 3, 4, 5. |
| **Chemistry** | 2a, b, c, d; 3, 4, 5, 6, 7, 8. |
| **Citizenship in the Home** | 6. |
| **Citizenship in the Community** | 7, 8. |
| **Citizenship in the Nation** | 7, 8. |

Brown cover, fourth variety

Red & white cover

**Citizenship in
the World**          7, 8.

**Citrus Fruit
Culture**            2a, b, c, d.

**Civics**           1a, b; 2a, b, c, d; 3, 4.

**Coin Collecting**  2a, b, c, d; 4, 5, 6, 7, 8.

**Colonial
Philadelphia**       Special council pamphlet.

**Communications**   6, 7, 8.

**Computers**        6, 7, 8.

**Conservation**     1a, b; 2, a, b, c, d; 3, 4.

**Conservation
of Natural
Resources**          6.

**Consumer
Buying**             7, 8.

**Cooking**          1a, b; 2a, b, c, d; 3, 4, 5, 6, 7, 8.

**Corn Farming**     2a, b, c, d; 3, 4, 5, 6, 7.

**Cotton Farming**   2a, b, c, d; 4, 5, 6, 7.

**Craftsmanship -
Basketry**           1, 2a, b, c, d.

**Craftsmanship -
Bookbinding**        1, 2a, b, c, d.

**Craftsmanship -
Cement**             1, 2a, b, c, d.

**Craftsmanship -
Leather**            1, 2a, b, c, d.

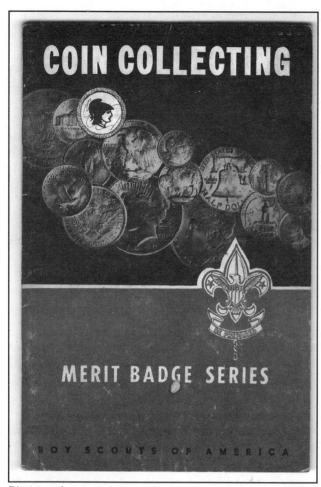

Photo red cover

Scout standing, red stripe cover

**Craftsmanship - Metal**      1, 2a, b, c, d.

**Craftsmanship - Pottery**      1, 2a, b, c, d.

**Craftsmanship - Wood**      1, 2a, b, c, d.

**Craftsmanship - Wood Carving**      1, 2a, b, c, d.

**Cycling**      1a, b; 2a, b, c, d; 3, 4, 5, 6, 7, 8.

**Dairying**      1a, b; 2a, b, c, d; 3, 4, 5, 6, 7.

**Dentistry**      7, 8.

**Dog Care**      2a, b, c, d; 3, 4, 5, 6, 7, 8.

**Drafting**      5, 6, 7, 8.

**Dramatics**      2a, b, c, d; 4, 5.

**Electricity**      1a, b; 2a, b, c, d; 3, 4, 5, 6, 7, 8.

**Electronics**      5, 6, 7, 8.

**Emergency Preparedness**      7, 8.

**Energy**      7, 8.

**Engineering**      6, 7, 8.

**Environmental Science**      7, 8.

**Farm & Ranch Management**      8.

**Farm Arrangements**      5, 6, 7.

Full photo cover

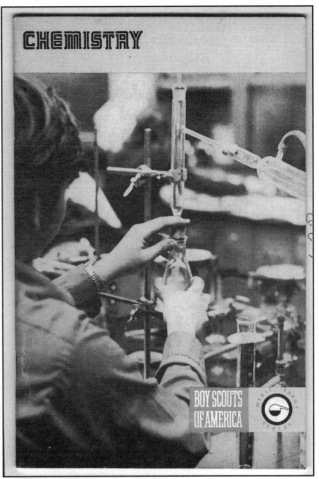

Green stripe cover

**Farm Home
and its Planning** 2a, b, c, d; 4.

**Farm Layout
and Building
Arrangement** 2a, b, c, d; 4, 5.

**Farm Mechanics** 2a, b, c, d; 4, 5, 6, 7, 8.

**Farm Records** 5, 6, 7.

**Farm Records &
Bookkeeping** 2a, b, c, d; 4, 5.

**Fingerprinting** 2a, b, c, d; 3, 4, 5, 6, 7, 8, special
Jamboree printing.

**Firemanship** 1a, b; 2a, b, c, d; 3, 4, 5, 6, 7, 8.

**First Aid** 1a, b; 2a, b, c, d; 3, 4, 5, 6, 7, 8.

**First Aid to
Animals** 1a, b; 2a, b, c, d; 3, 4, 5, 6.

**Fish & Wildlife
Management** 7, 8.

**Fishing** 4, 5, 6, 7, 8.

**Food Systems** 7, 8.

**Forage Crops** 5, 6, 7.

**Forestry** 1a, b; 2a, b, c, d; 3, 4, 5, 6, 7, 8.

**Foundry
Practice** 2a, b, c, d; 4.

**Fruit and
Nut Growing** 5, 6, 7.

**Fruit Culture** 2a, b, c, d; 4.

Red stripe cover

| | |
|---|---|
| **Gardening** | 1a, b; 2a, b, c, d; 3, 4, 5, 6, 7, 8. |
| **Genealogy** | 7, 8. |
| **General Science** | 7, 8. |
| **Geology** | 5, 6, 7, 8. |
| **Golf** | 7, 8. |
| **Graphic Arts** | 8. |
| **Grasses, Legumes & Forage Crops** | 2a, b, c, d; 4, 5. |
| **Handicapped Awareness** | 8. |
| **Handicraft** | 6, 7, 8. |
| **Hiking** | 1a, b; 2a, b, c, d; 3, 4, 5, 6, 7, 8. |
| **Hog & Pork Production** | 2a, b, c, d; 4, 5. |
| **Hog Production** | 5, 6, 7. |
| **Home Repairs** | 3, 4, 5, 6, 7, 8. |
| **Horsemanship** | 1a, b; 2a, b, c, d; 3, 4, 5, 6, 7, 8. |
| **Indian Lore** | 2a, b, c, d; 3, 4, 5, 6, 7, 8. |
| **Insect Life** | 2a, b, c, d; 4, 5, 6, 7, 8. |
| **Insect Study** | 8. |
| **Interpreting** | 1a, b; 2a, b, c, d; 4. |
| **Journalism** | 2a, b, c, d; 3, 4, 5, 6, 7, 8. |
| **Landscape Architecture** | 6, 7, 8. |
| **Landscape Gardening** | 2a, b, c, d; 3, 4, 5. |
| **Landscaping** | 5. |
| **Law** | 7, 8. |
| **Leathercraft** | 2a, b, c, d; 3, 4. |
| **Leatherwork** | 2a, b, c, d; 3, 4, 5, 6, 7, 8. |
| **Leatherworking** | 1a, b; 2a, b, c, d. |
| **Lifesaving** | 1a, b; 2a, b, c, d; 3, 4, 5, 6, 7, 8. |
| **Machinery** | 1a, b; 2a, b, c, d; 3, 4, 5, 6, 7, 8. |
| **Mammal Study** | 8. |
| **Mammals** | 6, 7, 8. |
| **Marksmanship** | 1a, b; 2a, b, c, d; 3, 4, 5. |
| **Masonry** | 1a, b; 2a, b, c, d; 3, 4, 5, 6, 7, 8. |

| | |
|---|---|
| **Mechanical Drawing** | 2a, b, c, d; 4, 5. |
| **Metal Work** | 1a, b; 2a, b, c, d; 3, 4, 5, 6, 7, 8. |
| **Metallurgy** | 6. |
| **Metals Engineering** | 7, 8. |
| **Mining** | 1a, b; 2a, b, c, d. |
| **Model Design & Building** | 5, 6, 7, 8. |
| **Motorboating** | 5, 6, 7, 8. |
| **Music & Bugling** | 1a, b; 2a, b, c, d; 3, 4, 5, 6, 7, 8. |
| **Nature** | 5, 6, 7, 8. |
| **Nut Culture** | 2a, b, c, d; 4. |
| **Oceanography** | 5, 6, 7, 8. |
| **Orienteering** | 7, 8. |
| **Painting** | 1a, b; 2a, b, c, d; 3, 4, 5, 6, 7, 8. |
| **Pathfinding** | 1a, b; 2a, b, c, d; 3, 4, 5. |
| **Personal Finances** | 5, 6. |
| **Personal Fitness** | 5, 6, 7, 8. |
| **Personal Health** | 1a, b; 2a, b, c, d; 3, 4. |
| **Personal Management** | 7, 8. |
| **Pets** | 5, 6, 7, 8. |
| **Photography** | 1a, b; 2a, b, c, d; 3, 4, 5, 6, 7, 8. |
| **Physical Development** | 1a, b; 2a, b, c, d; 3, 4. |
| **Pigeon Raising** | 2a, b, c, d; 3, 4, 5, 6, 7. |
| **Pioneering** | 1a, b; 2a, b, c, d; 3, 4, 5, 6, 7, 8. |
| **Plant Science** | 7, 8. |
| **Plumbing** | 1a, b; 2a, b, c, d; 3, 4, 5, 6, 7, 8. |
| **Pottery** | 2a, b, c, d; 3, 4, 5, 6, 7, 8. |
| **Poultry Keeping** | 1a, b; 2a, b, c, d; 3, 4, 5, 6, 7. |
| **Printing** | 1a, b; 2a, b, c, d; 3, 4, 5, 6, 7, 8. |
| **Printing Communication** | 8. |
| **Public Health** | 1a, b; 2a, b, c, d; 3, 4, 5, 6, 7, 8. |
| **Public Speaking** | 2a, b, c, d; 4, 5, 6, 7, 8. |
| **Pulp & Paper** | 7, 8. |
| **Rabbit Raising** | 4, 5, 6, 7, 8. |
| **Radio** | 1a, b; 2a, b, c, d; 3, 4, 5, 6, 7, 8. |
| **Railroading** | 5, 6, 7, 8, special AAR edition. |
| **Reading** | 2a, b, c, d; 3, 4, 5, 6, 7, 8. |
| **Reptile Study** | 2, b, c, d; 4, 5, 6, 7, 8. |
| **Rifle & Shotgun Shooting** | 6, 7, 8. |
| **Rifle Shooting** | 8. |
| **Rocks & Minerals** | 2a, b, c, d; 3, 4. |
| **Rowing** | 2a, b, c, d; 3, 4, 5, 6, 7, 8. |
| **Safety** | 2a, b, c, d; 3, 4, 5, 6, 7, 8. |
| **Safety First** | 1a, b; 2a, b, c, d. |
| **Salesmanship** | 2a, b, c, d; 4, 5, 6, 7, 8. |

Scouts of Troop 85 at the 1938 Cleveland Council Exposition.

| | |
|---|---|
| **Scholarship** | 1a, b; 2a, b, c, d, 3, 4, 5, 6, 7, 8. |
| **Sculpture** | 1a, b; 2a, b, c, d; 4, 5, 6, 7, 8. |
| **Seamanship** | 1a, b; 2a, b, c, d; 3, 4, 5. |
| **Sheep Farming** | 2a, b, c, d; 4, 5, 6, 7. |
| **Shotgun Shooting** | 8. |
| **Signaling** | 1a, b; 2a, b, c, d; 3, 4, 5, 6, 7, 8. |
| **Skating** | 7, 8. |
| **Skiing** | 2a, b, c, d; 3, 4, 5, 6, 7, 8. |

| | |
|---|---|
| **Small Boat Sailing** | 6, 7, 8. |
| **Small Grains** | 5, 6, 7. |
| **Small Grains & Cereal Foods** | 3, 4, 5. |
| **Soil & Water Conservation** | 5, 6, 7, 8. |
| **Soil Management** | 2a, b, c, d; 3, 4. |
| **Space Exploration** | 6, 7, 8. |
| **Sports** | 7, 8. |

| | | | |
|---|---|---|---|
| **Stalking** | 1a, b; 2a, b, c, d; 3, 4. | **Water Skiing** | 6, 7, 8. |
| **Stamp Collecting** | 2a, b, c, d; 3, 4, 5, 6, 7, 8. | **Weather** | 2a, b, c, d; 3, 4, 5, 6, 7, 8. |
| **Surveying** | 1a, b; 2a, b, c, d; 3, 4, 5, 6, 7, 8. | **Whitewater** | 8. |
| **Swimming** | 1a, b; 2a, b, c, d; 3, 4, 5, 6, 7, 8. | **Wilderness Survival** | 7, 8. |
| **Taxidermy** | 1a, b; 2a, b, c, d; 3, 4. | **Wildlife Management** | 5, 6, special 1953 Jamboree issue. |
| **Textiles** | 2a, b, c, d; 3, 4, 5, 6, 7, 8. | **Wireless** | 1a, b. |
| **Theater** | 6, 7, 8. | **Wood Turning** | 2a, b, c, d; 3, 4. |
| **Traffic Safety** | 7, 8. | **Wood Work** | 2a, b, c, d; 3, 4, 5, 6, 7, 8. |
| **Truck Transportation** | 7, 8. | **Woodcarving** | 2a, b, c, d; 3, 4, 5, 6, 7, 8. |
| **Veterinary Science** | 7, 8. | **Zoology** | 2a, b, c, d; 3, 4, 5, 6. |

The trek cart of Troop 25, Wauwatosa, WI, 1928.

A proud Scoutmaster and two Eagle Scouts wearing their sashes which include square cut merit badges and Indian Mound Reservation Patches of the late 1920s.

# MERIT BADGES

Merit badges come in nine major styles. Dating badges by their manufacture versus their dates of use has been a problematic item for some, and not of concern to others. The date of distribution at the council service center to a unit could be several years after a particular design was changed and in use in other areas of the country. This listings are based on those developed by Fred Duersch and John Pleasants and published in the Spring 1996 issue of the *Journal of the American Scouting Historical Society*, which holds the copyright.

The first is full square tan twill, in use from 1911–1933. The size varies from 1-1/2" to 3" square, with the larger size the scarcer. Some of these were sewn on the sash in a square format, others were tucked under, and still others were trimmed round and tucked under.

Full square

Second is a tan twill wide border crimped edge. This 1934–1935 type was the first circular design, with a 1/4" area from the exterior of the green ring to the material crimp (assisting in sewing the badge on a sash in a neat circle.) This is one of the most difficult types to find.

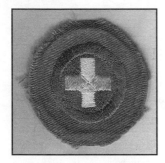

Wide Border Crimped

Third is a coarse tan twill narrow border crimped edge. This 1936–1942 type is a circular design with a 1/8" area from the exterior of the green ring to the material crimp.

Fourth is a fine tan twill narrow border crimped edge. This 1942–1946 type is probably the most difficult to find behind the second type. The material was changed from a coarse twill to fine twill due to the war effort.

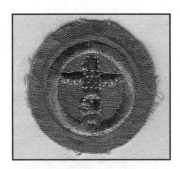

Fine Twill

Fifth is a khaki twill narrow border crimped edge. In use from 1947–1960, it is one of the more common varieties.

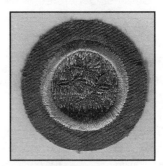

Khaki Narrow Border Crimped

Sixth is the khaki twill rolled edge. Issued from 1961–1968, these have a cloth (gauze) backing.

Khaki Rolled Edge

Seventh is a fully-embroidered cloth back, rolled edge of green or white. (1961–1971).

Eighth is a fully-embroidered plastic back, rolled edge of green or white (1972–present)

Plastic Back

Ninth is a computer generated design, plastic back (1993-present), which is distinguished by a wide or narrow tan circle on the back, usually larger in diameter than a rolled edge, which is flat. They are often issued in individual packages.

Computer Generated

### Aerodynamics
| | | |
|---|---|---|
| Tan rough twill, narrow crimped. | 1942-1946 | 300.00-500.00 |
| Khaki twill, narrow crimped. | 1947-1952 | 300.00-550.00 |

### Aeronautics
| | | |
|---|---|---|
| Tan rough twill, narrow crimped. | 1942-1946 | 60.00 - 90.00 |
| Khaki twill, narrow crimped. | 1947-1952 | 200.00-300.00 |

### Agribusiness
| | | |
|---|---|---|
| Fully embroidered, plastic back. | 1987 | 0.50 - 1.00 |

### Agriculture
| | | |
|---|---|---|
| Cut square. | 1912-1933 | 40.00 - 60.00 |
| Tan, wide crimped. | 1934-1935 | 25.00 - 40.00 |
| Tan rough twill, narrow crimped. | 1936-1942 | 7.50 - 12.50 |
| Tan fine twill, narrow crimped. | 1942-1946 | 300.00-400.00 |
| Khaki twill, narrow crimped. | 1947-1960 | 3.00 - 5.00 |
| Khaki twill, rolled edge. | 1961-1968 | 0.50 - 1.00 |
| Fully embroidered, cloth back. | 1969-1971 | 1.00 - 3.00 |
| Fully embroidered, plastic back. | 1972 | 0.50 - 1.00 |

### Airplane Design
| | | |
|---|---|---|
| Tan rough twill, narrow crimped. | 1942-1946 | 300.00-500.00 |
| Khaki twill, narrow crimped. | 1947-1952 | 300.00-550.00 |

### Airplane Structure
| | | |
|---|---|---|
| Tan fine twill, narrow crimped. | 1942-1946 | 90.00-125.00 |
| Tan rough twill, narrow crimped. | 1942-1946 | 300.00-500.00 |
| Khaki twill, narrow crimped. | 1947-1952 | 125.00-175.00 |

### American Business
| | | |
|---|---|---|
| Fully embroidered, cloth back. | 1967-1971 | 1.00 - 3.00 |
| Fully embroidered, plastic back. | 1972 | 0.50 - 1.00 |

### American Cultures
| | | |
|---|---|---|
| Fully embroidered, cloth back (error). | 1979 | 90.00-120.00 |
| Fully embroidered, plastic back. | 1979 | 0.50 - 1.00 |

### American Heritage
| | | |
|---|---|---|
| Fully embroidered, plastic back. | 1975 | 0.50 - 1.00 |
| Computer stitched, bagged. | 1993 | 0.50 - 1.00 |

### American Labor
| | | |
|---|---|---|
| Fully embroidered, plastic back. | 1987 | 0.50 - 1.00 |

### Angling
| | | |
|---|---|---|
| Cut square. | 1913-1933 | 40.00 - 60.00 |
| Tan, wide crimped. | 1934-1935 | 25.00 - 40.00 |
| Tan rough twill, narrow crimped. | 1936-1942 | 7.50 - 15.00 |
| Tan fine twill, narrow crimped. | 1942-1946 | 10.00 - 17.50 |

### Angling/Fishing
| | | |
|---|---|---|
| Khaki twill, narrow crimped. | 1947-1960 | 2.50 - 5.00 |

### Animal Industry
| | | |
|---|---|---|
| Cut square. | 1928-1933 | 20.00 - 30.00 |
| Tan, wide crimped. | 1934-1935 | 7.50 - 12.50 |
| Tan rough twill, narrow crimped. | 1936-1942 | 5.00 - 10.00 |
| Tan fine twill, narrow crimped. | 1942-1946 | 10.00 - 17.50 |
| Khaki twill, narrow crimped. | 1947-1960 | 3.00 - 7.50 |
| Khaki twill, rolled edge. | 1961-1968 | 0.50 - 1.00 |
| Fully embroidered, cloth back. | 1969-1971 | 1.00 - 3.00 |
| Fully embroidered, plastic back. | 1972-1975 | 0.50 - 1.00 |

### Animal Science
| | | |
|---|---|---|
| Fully embroidered, plastic back. | 1975-1992 | 0.50 - 1.00 |
| Computer stitched, bagged. | 1993 | 0.50 - 1.00 |

### Archaeology
| | | |
|---|---|---|
| Computer stitched, bagged. | 1993 | 0.50 - 1.00 |

### Archery
| | | |
|---|---|---|
| Cut square. | 1914-1933 | 80.00-120.00 |
| Tan, wide crimped. | 1934-1935 | 90.00-120.00 |
| Tan rough twill, narrow crimped. | 1936-1942 | 12.50 - 20.00 |
| Tan fine twill, narrow crimped. | 1942-1946 | 30.00 - 50.00 |
| Khaki twill, narrow crimped. | 1947-1960 | 2.50 - 5.00 |
| Khaki twill, rolled edge. | 1961-1968 | 0.50 - 1.00 |
| Fully embroidered, cloth back. | 1969-1971 | 1.00 - 3.00 |
| Fully embroidered, plastic back. | 1972 | 0.50 - 1.00 |

### Architecture
| | | |
|---|---|---|
| Cut square. | 1912-1933 | 80.00-120.00 |
| Tan, wide crimped. | 1934-1935 | 40.00 - 60.00 |
| Tan rough twill, narrow crimped. | 1936-1942 | 12.50 - 20.00 |
| Tan fine twill, narrow crimped. | 1942-1946 | 20.00 - 30.00 |
| Khaki twill, narrow crimped. | 1947-1960 | 3.00 - 7.50 |
| Khaki twill, rolled edge. | 1961-1968 | 0.50 - 1.00 |
| Fully embroidered, cloth back | 1969-1971 | 1.00 - 3.00 |
| Fully embroidered, plastic back. | 1972-1992 | 0.50 - 1.00 |
| Computer stitched, bagged. | 1993 | 0.50 - 1.00 |

## Art

| | | |
|---|---|---|
| Cut square. | 1911-1933 | 25.00 - 40.00 |
| Tan, wide crimped. | 1934-1935 | 20.00 - 30.00 |
| Tan rough twill, narrow crimped. | 1936-1942 | 5.00 - 10.00 |
| Tan fine twill, narrow crimped. | 1942-1946 | 20.00 - 40.00 |
| Khaki twill, narrow crimped. | 1947-1960 | 3.00 - 5.00 |
| Khaki twill, rolled edge. | 1961-1968 | 0.50 - 1.00 |
| Fully embroidered, cloth back. | 1969-1971 | 1.00 - 3.00 |
| Fully embroidered, plastic back. | 1972 | 0.50 - 1.00 |

## Astronomy

| | | |
|---|---|---|
| Cut square. | 1911-1933 | 80.00-120.00 |
| Tan rough twill, narrow crimped. | 1936-1942 | 12.50 - 20.00 |
| Tan fine twill, narrow crimped. | 1942-1946 | 15.00 - 25.00 |
| Khaki twill, narrow crimped (star). | 1947-1958 | 5.00 - 10.00 |
| Khaki twill, narrow crimped (saturn). | 1958-1960 | 5.00 - 10.00 |
| Fully embroidered, cloth back. | 1961-1971 | 1.00 - 3.00 |
| Fully embroidered, plastic back. | 1972 | 0.50 - 1.00 |

## Athletics

| | | |
|---|---|---|
| Cut square. | 1912-1933 | 5.00 - 12.50 |
| Tan, wide crimped. | 1934-1935 | 5.00 - 10.00 |
| Tan rough twill, narrow crimped. | 1936-1942 | 3.00 - 7.50 |
| Tan fine twill, narrow crimped. | 1942-1946 | 5.00 - 10.00 |
| Khaki twill, narrow crimped. | 1947-1960 | 1.00 - 3.00 |
| Khaki twill, rolled edge. | 1961-1968 | 0.50 - 1.00 |
| Fully embroidered, cloth back. | 1969-1971 | 1.00 - 3.00 |
| Fully embroidered, plastic back. | 1972 | 0.50 - 1.00 |

## Atomic Energy

| | | |
|---|---|---|
| Fully embroidered, cloth back (no nucleus). | 1964-1971 | 1.00 - 3.00 |
| Fully embroidered, cloth back (w/ nucleus). | 1964-1971 | 50.00 - 75.00 |
| Fully embroidered, plastic back. | 1972-1993 | 0.50 - 1.00 |
| Computer stitched, bagged. | 1993 | 0.50 - 1.00 |

## Auto Mechanics

| | | |
|---|---|---|
| Fully embroidered, plastic back. | 1991-1992 | 0.50 - 1.00 |
| Computer stitched, bagged. | 1993 | 0.50 - 1.00 |

## Automobiling

| | | |
|---|---|---|
| Cut square (12-spoke wheel). | 1912-1933 | 7.50 - 15.00 |
| Cut square (9-spoke wheel). | 1912-1933 | 7.50 - 15.00 |
| Tan, wide crimped. | 1934-1935 | 10.00 - 17.50 |
| Tan rough twill, narrow crimped (wheel). | 1936-1942 | 5.00 - 10.00 |
| Tan rough twill, narrow crimped (car). | 1943-1946 | 10.00 - 17.50 |

## Automotive Safety

| | | |
|---|---|---|
| Tan fine twill, narrow crimped. | 1942-1946 | 20.00 - 30.00 |
| Khaki twill, narrow crimped. | 1947-1960 | 3.00 - 5.00 |
| Khaki twill, rolled edge. | 1961-1968 | 0.50 - 1.00 |

## Automotive Safety/Traffic Safety

| | | |
|---|---|---|
| Fully embroidered, cloth back. | 1969-1971 | 1.00 - 3.00 |

## Aviation

| | | |
|---|---|---|
| Cut square (biplane). | 1912-1933 | 100.00-150.00 |
| Tan, wide crimped. | 1934-1935 | 90.00-120.00 |
| Tan rough twill, narrow crimped (biplane). | 1936-1939 | 100.00-150.00 |
| Tan rough twill, narrow crimped (propeller airplane). | 1940-1943 | 60.00 - 90.00 |
| Khaki twill, narrow crimped. | 1947-1960 | 7.50 - 15.00 |
| Khaki twill, rolled edge. | 1957-1960 | 7.50 - 15.00 |
| Fully embroidered, cloth back (no pilot in jet). | 1961-1971 | 1.00 - 3.00 |
| Fully embroidered, cloth back (pilot in jet). | 1961-1971 | 1.00 - 3.00 |
| Fully embroidered, plastic back. | 1972 | 0.50 - 1.00 |

## Backpacking

| | | |
|---|---|---|
| Fully embroidered, plastic back. | 1972 | 0.50 - 1.00 |

## Basketry

| | | |
|---|---|---|
| Cut square. | 1928-1933 | 20.00 - 35.00 |
| Tan, wide crimped. | 1934-1935 | 7.50 - 12.50 |
| Tan rough twill, narrow crimped. | 1936-1942 | 5.00 - 10.00 |
| Tan fine twill, narrow crimped. | 1942-1946 | 10.00 - 17.50 |
| Khaki twill, narrow crimped. | 1947-1960 | 1.00 - 3.00 |
| Khaki twill, rolled edge. | 1961-1968 | 0.50 - 1.00 |
| Fully embroidered, cloth back. | 1969-1971 | 1.00 - 3.00 |
| Fully embroidered, plastic back. | 1972 | 0.50 - 1.00 |

## Bee Keeping

| | | |
|---|---|---|
| Cut square. | 1912-1934 | 20.00 - 35.00 |
| Tan, wide crimped. | 1934-1935 | 60.00 - 90.00 |
| Tan rough twill, narrow crimped (black bee, 4 legs). | 1936-1939 | 25.00 - 40.00 |
| Tan rough twill, narrow crimped (black bee, 4 legs). | 1936-1939 | 10.00 - 20.00 |
| Tan rough twill, narrow crimped (black bee, 6 legs). | 1940-1946 | 10.00 - 20.00 |
| Tan fine twill, narrow crimped. | 1942-1946 | 20.00 - 30.00 |
| Khaki twill, narrow crimped (black bee, 6 legs). | 1947-1960 | 40.00 - 60.00 |
| Khaki twill, narrow crimped (top view bee). | 1952-1956 | 7.50 - 15.00 |
| Khaki twill, narrow crimped (side view bee). | 1957-1960 | 10.00 - 20.00 |
| Fully embroidered, cloth back. | 1961-1971 | 1.00 - 3.00 |
| Fully embroidered, cloth back, silver border (error). | 1969-1971 | 50.00 - 75.00 |
| Fully embroidered, plastic back. | 1972 | 0.50 - 1.00 |

## Beef Production

| | | |
|---|---|---|
| Cut square (white horns). | 1928-1929 | 150.00-200.00 |
| Cut square (brown and white horns). | 1929-1933 | 80.00-120.00 |
| Tan, wide crimped. | 1934-1935 | 40.00 - 60.00 |
| Tan rough twill, narrow crimped. | 1936-1942 | 10.00 - 20.00 |
| Tan fine twill, narrow crimped. | 1942-1946 | 15.00 - 25.00 |
| Khaki twill, narrow crimped. | 1947-1960 | 3.00 - 5.00 |

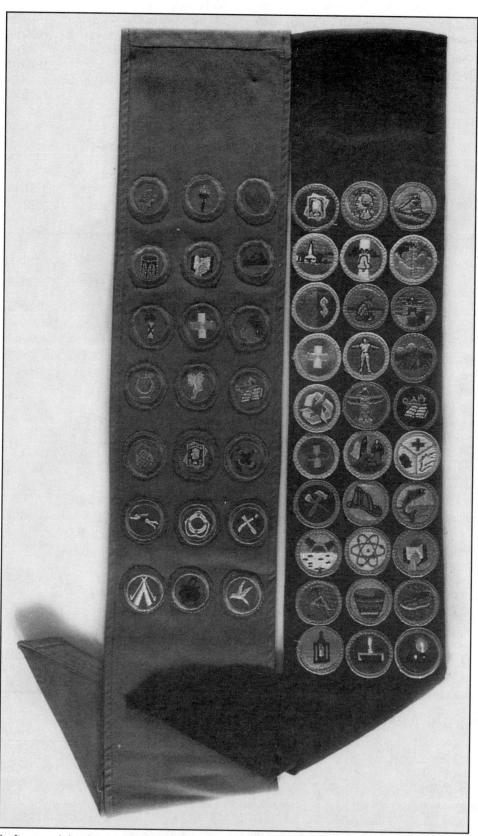

Left, a merit badge sash with narrow crimped edge khaki badges, ca. 1950. Right, a dark green leadership corps/explorer sash with plastic back badges from 1977.

| | | |
|---|---|---|
| Khaki twill, rolled edge. | 1961-1968 | 0.50 - 1.00 |
| Fully embroidered, cloth back. | 1969-1971 | 1.00 - 3.00 |
| Fully embroidered, plastic back. | 1972 | 0.50 - 1.00 |

## Bird Study/Ornithology

| | | |
|---|---|---|
| Cut square. | 1912-1933 | 3.00 - 10.00 |
| Tan, wide crimped. | 1934-1935 | 7.50 - 12.50 |
| Tan rough twill, narrow crimped. | 1936-1942 | 3.00 - 7.50 |
| Tan fine twill, narrow crimped. | 1942-1946 | 5.00 - 10.00 |
| Khaki twill, narrow crimped. | 1947-1960 | 1.00 - 3.00 |
| Khaki twill, rolled edge. | 1961-1968 | 0.50 - 1.00 |
| Fully embroidered, cloth back. | 1969-1971 | 1.00 - 3.00 |
| Fully embroidered, plastic back. | 1972 | 0.50 - 1.00 |

## Blacksmithing

| | | |
|---|---|---|
| Cut square. | 1913-1933 | 60.00 - 90.00 |
| Tan, wide crimped. | 1934-1935 | 40.00 - 60.00 |
| Tan rough twill, narrow crimped. | 1936-1942 | 40.00 - 60.00 |
| Tan fine twill, narrow crimped. | 1942-1946 | 30.00 - 45.00 |
| Khaki twill, narrow crimped. | 1947-1952 | 30.00 - 60.00 |

## Bookbinding

| | | |
|---|---|---|
| Cut square. | 1928-1933 | 5.00 - 12.50 |
| Tan, wide crimped. | 1934-1935 | 7.50 - 12.50 |
| Tan rough twill, narrow crimped. | 1936-1942 | 5.00 - 10.00 |
| Tan fine twill, narrow crimped. | 1942-1946 | 7.50 - 15.00 |
| Khaki twill, narrow crimped. | 1947-1960 | 3.00 - 5.00 |
| Khaki twill, rolled edge. | 1960-1969 | 2.00 - 4.00 |
| Khaki twill, rolled edge (no bookmark). | 1961-1968 | 0.50 - 1.00 |
| Khaki twill, rolled edge (w/ bookmark). | 1961-1968 | 3.00 - 7.50 |
| Fully embroidered, plastic back. | 1972-1987 | 0.50 - 1.00 |
| Fully embroidered, cloth back. | 19669-1971 | 1.00 - 3.00 |

## Botany

| | | |
|---|---|---|
| Cut square. | 1911-1933 | 30.00 - 50.00 |
| Tan, wide crimped. | 1934-1935 | 25.00 - 40.00 |
| Tan rough twill, narrow crimped. | 1936-1942 | 7.50 - 15.00 |
| Tan fine twill, narrow crimped. | 1942-1946 | 15.00 - 25.00 |
| Khaki twill, narrow crimped. | 1947-1960 | 5.00 - 10.00 |
| Khaki twill, rolled edge. | 1961-1968 | 0.50 - 1.00 |
| Fully embroidered, cloth back. | 1969-1971 | 1.00 - 3.00 |
| Fully embroidered, plastic back. | 1972 | 0.50 - 1.00 |

## Bugling

| | | |
|---|---|---|
| Cut square. | 1912-1933 | 40.00 - 60.00 |
| Tan, wide crimped. | 1934-1935 | 15.00 - 25.00 |
| Tan rough twill, narrow crimped. | 1936-1942 | 5.00 - 12.50 |
| Tan fine twill, narrow crimped. | 1942-1946 | 15.00 - 25.00 |
| Khaki twill, narrow crimped. | 1947-1960 | 3.00 - 5.00 |
| Khaki twill, rolled edge. | 1961-1968 | 0.50 - 1.00 |
| Fully embroidered, cloth back. | 1969-1971 | 1.00 - 3.00 |
| Fully embroidered, plastic back. | 1972 | 0.50 - 1.00 |

## Business

| | | |
|---|---|---|
| Cut square. | 1912-1933 | 50.00 - 75.00 |

| | | |
|---|---|---|
| Tan, wide crimped. | 1934-1935 | 25.00 - 40.00 |
| Tan rough twill, narrow crimped. | 1936-1942 | 12.50 - 20.00 |
| Tan fine twill, narrow crimped. | 1942-1946 | 15.00 - 25.00 |
| Khaki twill, narrow crimped. | 1947-1960 | 3.00 - 5.00 |
| Khaki twill, rolled edge. | 1961-1966 | 0.50 - 1.00 |

## Camping

| | | |
|---|---|---|
| Cut square. | 1911-1933 | 3.00 - 10.00 |
| Tan, wide crimped. | 1934-1935 | 7.50 - 12.50 |
| Tan rough twill, narrow crimped. | 1936-1942 | 3.00 - 7.50 |
| Tan fine twill, narrow crimped. | 1942-1946 | 5.00 - 10.00 |
| Khaki twill, narrow crimped. | 1947-1960 | 1.00 - 3.00 |
| Khaki twill, rolled edge. | 1961-1968 | 0.50 - 1.00 |
| Fully embroidered, cloth back, silver border. | 1969-1971 | 1.00 - 3.00 |
| Fully embroidered, plastic back, green border. | 1972 | 0.50 - 1.00 |
| Fully embroidered, plastic back, silver border. | 1972 | 0.50 - 1.00 |

## Canoeing

| | | |
|---|---|---|
| Cut square. | 1928-1933 | 40.00 - 60.00 |
| Tan, wide crimped. | 1934-1935 | 20.00 - 30.00 |
| Tan rough twill, narrow crimped. | 1936-1942 | 7.50 - 15.00 |
| Tan fine twill, narrow crimped. | 1942-1946 | 25.00 - 40.00 |
| Khaki twill, narrow crimped. | 1947-1960 | 3.00 - 5.00 |
| Khaki twill, rolled edge. | 1961-1968 | 0.50 - 1.00 |
| Fully embroidered, cloth back. | 1969-1971 | 1.00 - 3.00 |
| Fully embroidered, plastic back. | 1972 | 0.50 - 1.00 |

## Carpentry

| | | |
|---|---|---|
| Cut square (plane). | 1912-1933 | 3.00 - 10.00 |
| Tan, wide crimped. | 1934-1935 | 5.00 - 10.00 |
| Tan rough twill, narrow crimped. | 1936-1942 | 3.00 - 7.50 |
| Tan fine twill, narrow crimped. | 1942-1946 | 5.00 - 10.00 |
| Khaki twill, narrow crimped. | 1947-1952 | 1.00 - 3.00 |

## Cement Work

| | | |
|---|---|---|
| Cut square. | 1928-1933 | 60.00 - 80.00 |
| Tan, wide crimped. | 1934-1935 | 60.00 - 90.00 |
| Tan rough twill, narrow crimped. | 1936-1942 | 30.00 - 50.00 |
| Tan fine twill, narrow crimped. | 1942-1946 | 40.00 - 60.00 |
| Khaki twill, narrow crimped. | 1947-1952 | 20.00 - 45.00 |

## Chemistry

| | | |
|---|---|---|
| Cut square. | 1911-1933 | 20.00 - 30.00 |
| Tan, wide crimped. | 1934-1935 | 12.50 - 20.00 |
| Tan rough twill, narrow crimped. | 1936-1942 | 5.00 - 10.00 |
| Tan fine twill, narrow crimped. | 1942-1946 | 12.50 - 20.00 |
| Khaki twill, narrow crimped. | 1947-1960 | 3.00 - 5.00 |
| Khaki twill, rolled edge. | 1961-1968 | 0.50 - 1.00 |
| Fully embroidered, cloth back. | 1969-1971 | 1.00 - 3.00 |
| Fully embroidered, plastic back. | 1972-1992 | 0.50 - 1.00 |
| Computer stitched, bagged. | 1993 | 0.50 - 1.00 |

## Cinematography

| | | |
|---|---|---|
| Fully embroidered, plastic back. | 1989-1992 | 0.50 - 1.00 |
| Computer stitched, bagged. | 1993 | 0.50 - 1.00 |

## Citizenship in the Community

| | | |
|---|---|---|
| Khaki twill, narrow crimped. | 1952-1960 | 1.00 - 3.00 |
| Fully embroidered, cloth back, green border. | 1969-1971 | 1.00 - 3.00 |
| Fully embroidered, cloth back, silver border. | 1969-1971 | 1.00 - 3.00 |
| Fully embroidered, plastic back, silver border. | 1972 | 0.50 - 1.00 |

## Citizenship in the Home

| | | |
|---|---|---|
| Khaki twill, narrow crimped. | 1952-1960 | 1.00 - 3.00 |
| Fully embroidered, cloth back. | 1961-1971 | 1.00 - 3.00 |
| Fully embroidered, plastic back. | 1972-1972 | 0.50 - 1.00 |

## Citizenship in the Nation

| | | |
|---|---|---|
| Khaki twill, narrow crimped. | 1952-1960 | 1.00 - 3.00 |
| Fully embroidered, cloth back, blue-white-red stripes, green border. | 1961-1969 | 1.00 - 3.00 |
| Fully embroidered, cloth back, red-white-blue stripes, large bell, silver border. | 1961-1971 | 1.00 - 3.00 |
| Fully embroidered, cloth back, red-white-blue stripes, small bell, silver border. | 1961-1971 | 1.00 - 3.00 |
| Fully embroidered, cloth back, blue-white-red stripes, silver border. | 1969-1971 | 1.00 - 3.00 |
| Fully embroidered, plastic back, blue-white-red, silver border. | 1972-1975 | 0.50 - 1.00 |
| Fully embroidered, plastic back, red-white-blue, small bell, silver border. | 1976-1992 | 0.50 - 1.00 |
| Fully embroidered, plastic back, red-white-blue, large bell, silver border. | 1992 | 0.50 - 1.00 |

## Citizenship in the World

| | | |
|---|---|---|
| Fully embroidered, plastic back, silver border. | 1972 | 0.50 - 1.00 |

## Citrus Fruit Culture

| | | |
|---|---|---|
| Cut square. | 1931-1933 | 600.00-750.00 |
| Tan, wide crimped. | 1934-1935 | 125.00-175.00 |
| Tan rough twill, narrow crimped. | 1936-1942 | 90.00-120.00 |
| Tan fine twill, narrow crimped. | 1942-1946 | 150.00-225.00 |
| Khaki twill, narrow crimped. | 1947-1954 | 100.00-175.00 |

## Civics

| | | |
|---|---|---|
| Cut square. | 1911-1933 | 3.00 - 10.00 |
| Cut square (reversed colors). | 1911-1933 | 10.00 - 20.00 |

| | | |
|---|---|---|
| Tan, wide crimped. | 1934-1935 | 5.00 - 10.00 |
| Tan rough twill, narrow crimped. | 1936-1942 | 3.00 - 7.50 |
| Tan fine twill, narrow crimped. | 1942-1946 | 5.00 - 10.00 |
| Khaki twill, narrow crimped. | 1947-1952 | 1.00 - 3.00 |

## Climbing

| | | |
|---|---|---|
| Computer stitched, bagged. | 1993 | 0.50 - 1.00 |

## Coin Collecting

| | | |
|---|---|---|
| Tan rough twill, narrow crimped. | 1938-1942 | 15.00 - 25.00 |
| Tan fine twill, narrow crimped. | 1942-1946 | 20.00 - 30.00 |
| Khaki twill, narrow crimped. | 1947-1960 | 3.00 - 5.00 |
| Khaki twill, rolled edge. | 1961-1968 | 0.50 - 1.00 |
| Fully embroidered, cloth back. | 1969-1971 | 1.00 - 3.00 |
| Fully embroidered, cloth back (white letters). | 1969-1971 | 1.00 - 3.00 |
| Fully embroidered, plastic back, white letters. | 1972 | 75.00-100.00 |
| Fully embroidered, plastic back, black letters. | 1973-1992 | 0.50 - 1.00 |
| Fully embroidered, plastic back, black ring. | 1992 | 0.50 - 1.00 |

## Collections

| | | |
|---|---|---|
| Fully embroidered, plastic back. | 1991 | 0.50 - 1.00 |

## Colonial Philadelphia

| | | |
|---|---|---|
| Fully embroidered, cloth back (error). | 1974 | 75.00-100.00 |
| Fully embroidered, plastic back, green or yellow. | 1974 | 20.00 - 30.00 |

## Communications

| | | |
|---|---|---|
| Fully embroidered, cloth back. | 1966-1971 | 1.00 - 3.00 |
| Fully embroidered, plastic back, green border (satellite). | 1972 | 80.00-110.00 |
| Fully embroidered, plastic back, silver border (satellite). | 1972-1973 | 0.50 - 1.00 |
| Fully embroidered, plastic back, silver border (telephone). | 1973 | 75.00-100.00 |

## Computers

| | | |
|---|---|---|
| Fully embroidered, cloth back. | 1967-1971 | 1.00 - 3.00 |
| Fully embroidered, plastic back (punch card). | 1972-1984 | 0.50 - 1.00 |
| Fully embroidered, plastic back (personal computer). | 1984 | 0.50 - 1.00 |

## Conservation of Natural Resources

| | | |
|---|---|---|
| Fully embroidered, cloth back, green border. | 1966-1969 | 1.00 - 3.00 |
| Fully embroidered, cloth back, silver border. | 1969-1971 | 1.00 - 3.00 |
| Fully embroidered, plastic back, green border. | 1972 | 3.00 - 5.00 |

Fully embroidered, plastic back,
  silver border.                        1972-1973     3.00 - 5.00

## Conservation
Cut square.                             1911-1933     20.00 - 35.00
Tan, wide crimped.                      1934-1935     12.50 - 20.00
Tan rough twill, narrow crimped.        1936-1942     7.50 - 12.50
Tan fine twill, narrow crimped.         1942-1946     12.50 - 20.00
Khaki twill, narrow crimped.            1947-1952     3.00 - 5.00

## Consumer Buying
Fully embroidered, plastic back.        1975          0.50 - 1.00

## Cooking
Cut square.                             1911-1933     3.00 - 10.00
Tan, wide crimped.                      1934-1935     5.00 - 10.00
Tan rough twill, narrow crimped.        1936-1942     3.00 - 7.50
Tan fine twill, narrow crimped.         1942-1946     5.00 - 10.00
Khaki twill, narrow crimped.            1947-1960     1.00 - 3.00
Khaki twill, rolled edge.               1961-1968     0.50 - 1.00
Fully embroidered, cloth back,
  silver border.                        1969-1971     1.00 - 3.00
Fully embroidered, plastic back,
  green border.                         1972          0.50 - 1.00
Fully embroidered, plastic back,
  silver border.                        1972          0.50 - 1.00

## Corn Farming
Cut square.                             1928-1933     80.00 - 100.00
Tan, wide crimped.                      1934-1935     25.00 - 40.00
Tan rough twill, narrow crimped.        1936-1942     10.00 - 17.50
Tan fine twill, narrow crimped.         1942-1946     20.00 - 30.00
Khaki twill, narrow crimped.            1947-1960     5.00 - 10.00
Khaki twill, rolled edge.               1961-1968     0.50 - 1.00
Fully embroidered, cloth back.          1969-1971     1.00 - 3.00
Fully embroidered, plastic back.        1972-1975     0.50 - 1.00

## Cotton Farming
Cut square.                             1931-1933     300.00 - 450.00
Tan rough twill, narrow crimped.        1936-1942     25.00 - 40.00
Tan fine twill, narrow crimped.         1942-1946     60.00 - 90.00
Khaki twill, narrow crimped.            1947-1960     10.00 - 15.00
Khaki twill, rolled edge.               1961-1968     0.50 - 1.00
Fully embroidered, cloth back.          1969-1971     0.50 - 1.00
Fully embroidered, plastic back.        1972-1975     0.50 - 1.00

## Craftsmanship
Cut square.                             1911-1927     5.00 - 15.00

## Crime Prevention
Computer stitched, bagged.              1993          0.50 - 1.00

## Cycling
Cut square.                             1911-1933     3.00 - 10.00
Tan, wide crimped.                      1934-1935     12.50 - 20.00
Tan rough twill, narrow crimped.        1936-1942     5.00 - 10.00
Tan fine twill, narrow crimped.         1942-1946     10.00 - 15.00
Khaki twill, narrow crimped.            1947-1960     3.00 - 5.00
Khaki twill, rolled edge.               1961-1968     0.50 - 1.00
Fully embroidered, cloth back.          1969-1971     1.00 - 3.00
Fully embroidered, plastic back
  (bicycle).                            1972-1974     0.50 - 1.00
Fully embroidered, plastic back
  (bicycle within triangle).            1975          0.50 - 1.00

## Dairying
Cut square.                             1912-1933     40.00 - 60.00
Tan, wide crimped.                      1934-1935     25.00 - 40.00
Tan rough twill, narrow crimped.        1936-1942     7.50 - 12.50
Tan fine twill, narrow crimped.         1942-1946     20.00 - 30.00
Khaki twill, narrow crimped.            1947-1960     3.00 - 5.00
Khaki twill, rolled edge.               1961-1968     0.50 - 1.00
Fully embroidered, cloth back.          1969-1971     1.00 - 3.00
Fully embroidered, plastic back.        1972-1975     0.50 - 1.00

## Dentistry
Fully embroidered, plastic back.        1975-1992     0.50 - 1.00
Computer stitched, bagged.              1993          0.50 - 1.00

## Disability Awareness
Computer stitched, bagged.              1993          0.50 - 1.00

## Dog Care
Tan rough twill, narrow crimped.        1938-1942     7.50 - 12.50
Tan fine twill, narrow crimped.         1942-1946     20.00 - 30.00
Khaki twill, narrow crimped.            1947-1960     3.00 - 5.00
Khaki twill, rolled edge.               1961-1968     0.50 - 1.00
Fully embroidered, cloth back.          1969-1971     1.00 - 3.00
Fully embroidered, plastic back.        1972          0.50 - 1.00

## Drafting
Fully embroidered, cloth back.          1969-1971     1.00 - 3.00
Fully embroidered, plastic back.        1972          0.50 - 1.00

## Dramatics
Cut square.                             1932-1933     400.00 - 550.00
Tan, wide crimped.                      1934-1935     60.00 - 90.00
Tan rough twill, narrow crimped.        1936-1942     15.00 - 25.00
Tan fine twill, narrow crimped.         1942-1946     30.00 - 40.00
Khaki twill, narrow crimped.            1947-1960     5.00 - 10.00

## Dramatics/Theater
Fully embroidered, cloth back.          1961-1971     1.00 - 3.00

## Electricity
Cut square.                             1911-1933     3.00 - 12.50
Tan, wide crimped.                      1934-1935     7.50 - 12.50
Tan rough twill, narrow crimped.        1936-1942     3.00 - 7.50

| Description | Years | Price |
|---|---|---|
| Tan fine twill, narrow crimped. | 1942-1946 | 10.00 - 15.00 |
| Khaki twill, narrow crimped. | 1947-1960 | 1.00 - 3.00 |
| Khaki twill, rolled edge (hand as a blob). | 1961-1962 | 30.00 - 60.00 |
| Khaki twill, rolled edge (hand w/ fingers). | 1961-1962 | 30.00 - 60.00 |
| Fully embroidered, cloth back. | 1963-1971 | 1.00 - 3.00 |
| Fully embroidered, plastic back. | 1972 | 0.50 - 1.00 |

## Electronics

| Description | Years | Price |
|---|---|---|
| Fully embroidered, cloth back. | 1964-1971 | 1.00 - 3.00 |
| Fully embroidered, plastic back. | 1972 | 0.50 - 1.00 |
| Computer stitched, bagged. | 1993 | 0.50 - 1.00 |

## Emergency Preparedness

| Description | Years | Price |
|---|---|---|
| Fully embroidered, plastic back, red cross, silver border. | 1972-1979 | 0.50 - 1.00 |
| Fully embroidered, plastic back, green cross, silver border. | 1979 | 0.50 - 1.00 |

## Energy

| Description | Years | Price |
|---|---|---|
| Fully embroidered, plastic back. | 1976 | 0.50 - 1.00 |

## Engineering

| Description | Years | Price |
|---|---|---|
| Fully embroidered, cloth back. | 1962-1971 | 1.00 - 3.00 |
| Fully embroidered, plastic back. | 1972 | 0.50 - 1.00 |

## Entrepreneurship

| Description | Years | Price |
|---|---|---|
| Computer stitched, bagged. | 1993 | 0.50 - 1.00 |

## Environmental Science

| Description | Years | Price |
|---|---|---|
| Fully embroidered, plastic back, silver border. | 1972 | 0.50 - 1.00 |

## Family Life

| Description | Years | Price |
|---|---|---|
| Fully embroidered, plastic back, green border (error). | 1991 | 0.50 - 1.00 |
| Fully embroidered, plastic back, silver border. | 1991 | 0.50 - 1.00 |

## Farm Arrangement

| Description | Years | Price |
|---|---|---|
| Khaki twill, narrow crimped. | 1947-1960 | 7.50 - 12.50 |

## Farm Arrangements/Farm & Ranch Management

| Description | Years | Price |
|---|---|---|
| Fully embroidered, cloth back (small buildings). | 1961-1963 | 1.00 - 3.00 |
| Fully embroidered, cloth back (large buildings). | 1964-1971 | 1.00 - 3.00 |
| Fully embroidered, plastic back. | 1972-1987 | 0.50 - 1.00 |

## Farm Home & Its Planning

| Description | Years | Price |
|---|---|---|
| Cut square. | 1928-1933 | 40.00 - 60.00 |
| Tan, wide crimped. | 1934-1935 | 20.00 - 30.00 |

| Description | Years | Price |
|---|---|---|
| Tan rough twill, narrow crimped. | 1936-1942 | 7.50 - 15.00 |
| Tan fine twill, narrow crimped. | 1942-1946 | 15.00 - 25.00 |
| Khaki twill, narrow crimped. | 1947-1959 | 5.00 - 10.00 |

## Farm Layout & Building Arrangement

| Description | Years | Price |
|---|---|---|
| Cut square. | 1928-1933 | 50.00 - 75.00 |
| Tan, wide crimped. | 1934-1935 | 20.00 - 30.00 |
| Tan rough twill, narrow crimped. | 1936-1942 | 7.50 - 15.00 |
| Tan fine twill, narrow crimped. | 1942-1946 | 20.00 - 30.00 |
| Khaki twill, narrow crimped. | 1947-1959 | 5.00 - 10.00 |

## Farm Mechanics

| Description | Years | Price |
|---|---|---|
| Cut square. | 1928-1933 | 30.00 - 55.00 |
| Tan, wide crimped. | 1934-1935 | 20.00 - 40.00 |
| Tan rough twill, narrow crimped. | 1936-1942 | 5.00 - 12.50 |
| Tan fine twill, narrow crimped. | 1942-1946 | 20.00 - 30.00 |
| Khaki twill, narrow crimped. | 1947-1960 | 3.00 - 5.00 |
| Khaki twill, rolled edge. | 1961-1968 | 0.50 - 1.00 |
| Fully embroidered, cloth back. | 1969-1971 | 1.00 - 3.00 |
| Fully embroidered, plastic back. | 1972 | 0.50 - 1.00 |

## Farm Records & Bookkeeping/Farm Records

| Description | Years | Price |
|---|---|---|
| Cut square. | 1928-1933 | 80.00 - 100.00 |
| Tan, wide crimped. | 1934-1935 | 35.00 - 50.00 |
| Tan fine twill, narrow crimped. | 1942-1946 | 20.00 - 30.00 |
| Khaki twill, narrow crimped. | 1947-1960 | 5.00 - 10.00 |
| Khaki twill, rolled edge. | 1961-1968 | 0.50 - 1.00 |
| Fully embroidered, cloth back. | 1969-1971 | 1.00 - 3.00 |
| Fully embroidered, plastic back. | 1972-1978 | 0.50 - 1.00 |

## Fingerprinting

| Description | Years | Price |
|---|---|---|
| Tan rough twill, narrow crimped. | 1938-1942 | 10.00 - 15.00 |
| Tan fine twill, narrow crimped. | 1942-1946 | 20.00 - 30.00 |
| Khaki twill, narrow crimped. | 1947-1960 | 5.00 - 10.00 |
| Fully embroidered, cloth back. | 1961-1971 | 1.00 - 3.00 |
| Fully embroidered, plastic back. | 1972 | 0.50 - 1.00 |

## Firemanship

| Description | Years | Price |
|---|---|---|
| Cut square. | 1911-1933 | 3.00 - 12.50 |
| Tan, wide crimped. | 1934-1935 | 3.00 - 7.50 |
| Tan rough twill, narrow crimped. | 1936-1942 | 3.00 - 7.50 |
| Tan fine twill, narrow crimped. | 1942-1946 | 5.00 - 10.00 |
| Khaki twill, narrow crimped. | 1947-1960 | 1.00 - 3.00 |
| Khaki twill, rolled edge. | 1961-1968 | 0.50 - 1.00 |
| Fully embroidered, cloth back. | 1969-1971 | 1.00 - 3.00 |

## Firemanship/Fire Safety

| Description | Years | Price |
|---|---|---|
| Fully embroidered, plastic back. | 1972 | 0.50 - 1.00 |

## First Aid to Animals

| Description | Years | Price |
|---|---|---|
| Cut square. | 1912-1933 | 4.00 - 15.00 |
| Tan, wide crimped. | 1934-1935 | 5.00 - 10.00 |
| Tan rough twill, narrow crimped. | 1936-1942 | 5.00 - 10.00 |

Dining hall KP (kitchen patrol) of the 1940s.

| | | |
|---|---|---|
| Tan fine twill, narrow crimped. | 1942-1946 | 10.00 - 15.00 |
| Khaki twill, narrow crimped. | 1947-1960 | 3.00 - 5.00 |
| Khaki twill, rolled edge. | 1961-1968 | 0.50 - 1.00 |
| Fully embroidered, cloth back. | 1969-1971 | 1.00 - 3.00 |
| Fully embroidered, plastic back, green border. | 1972-1974 | 0.50 - 1.00 |
| Fully embroidered, plastic back, silver border (error). | 1972 | 1.00 - 3.00 |

## First Aid

| | | |
|---|---|---|
| Cut square. | 1911-1933 | 3.00 - 7.50 |
| Tan, wide crimped. | 1934-1935 | 3.00 - 7.50 |
| Tan rough twill, narrow crimped. | 1936-1942 | 3.00 - 7.50 |
| Tan fine twill, narrow crimped. | 1942-1946 | 5.00 - 10.00 |
| Khaki twill, narrow crimped. | 1947-1960 | 1.00 - 3.00 |
| Fully embroidered, cloth back, green border. | 1961-1969 | 1.00 - 3.00 |
| Fully embroidered, cloth back, silver border. | 1969-1971 | 1.00 - 3.00 |
| Fully embroidered, plastic back, silver border. | 1972 | 0.50 - 1.00 |

## Fishing

| | | |
|---|---|---|
| Fully embroidered, cloth back. | 1969-1971 | 1.00 - 3.00 |
| Khaki twill, rolled edge. | 1961-1968 | 0.50 - 1.00 |
| Fully embroidered, plastic back. | 1972 | 0.50 - 1.00 |

## Food Systems

| | | |
|---|---|---|
| Fully embroidered, cloth back. | 1961-1971 | 1.00 - 3.00 |
| Fully embroidered, plastic back. | 1978-1987 | 0.50 - 1.00 |

## Forestry

| | | |
|---|---|---|
| Cut square. | 1912-1933 | 40.00 - 65.00 |
| Tan, wide crimped. | 1934-1935 | 12.50 - 20.00 |
| Tan rough twill, narrow crimped. | 1936-1942 | 7.50 - 12.50 |
| Tan fine twill, narrow crimped. | 1942-1946 | 12.50 - 20.00 |
| Khaki twill, narrow crimped. | 1947-1960 | 3.00 - 5.00 |
| Khaki twill, rolled edge. | 1961-1968 | 0.50 - 1.00 |
| Fully embroidered, cloth back. | 1969-1971 | 1.00 - 3.00 |
| Fully embroidered, plastic back. | 1972 | 0.50 - 1.00 |

## Foundry Practice

| | | |
|---|---|---|
| Cut square. | 1923-1933 | 100.00-150.00 |
| Tan, wide crimped. | 1934-1935 | 100.00-150.00 |
| Tan rough twill, narrow crimped. | 1936-1942 | 60.00 - 90.00 |
| Tan fine twill, narrow crimped. | 1942-1946 | 60.00 - 90.00 |
| Khaki twill, narrow crimped. | 1947-1952 | 80.00-120.00 |

## Fruit & Nut Growing

| | | |
|---|---|---|
| Khaki twill, narrow crimped. | 1953-1960 | 10.00 - 20.00 |
| Fully embroidered, cloth back. | 1961-1971 | 1.00 - 3.00 |
| Fully embroidered, plastic back. | 1972-1975 | 0.50 - 1.00 |

## Fruit Culture

| | | |
|---|---|---|
| Cut square. | 1928-1933 | 200.00-300.00 |

| | | |
|---|---|---|
| Tan, wide crimped. | 1934-1935 | 100.00-150.00 |
| Tan rough twill, narrow crimped. | 1936-1942 | 90.00-120.00 |
| Tan fine twill, narrow crimped. | 1942-1946 | 100.00-150.00 |
| Khaki twill, narrow crimped. | 1947-1954 | 100.00-175.00 |

## Gardening

| | | |
|---|---|---|
| Cut square (tan corn). | 1912-1933 | 30.00 - 50.00 |
| Cut square (white corn). | 1912-1933 | 30.00 - 50.00 |
| Cut square (yellow corn). | 1912-1933 | 30.00 - 50.00 |
| Tan, wide crimped. | 1934-1935 | 20.00 - 30.00 |
| Tan rough twill, narrow crimped (vegetables). | 1936-1942 | 12.50 - 20.00 |
| Tan rough twill, narrow crimped (yellow corn). | 1936-1939 | 15.00 - 25.00 |
| Tan fine twill, narrow crimped. | 1940-1946 | 20.00 - 30.00 |
| Khaki twill, narrow crimped. | 1947-1960 | 5.00 - 10.00 |
| Fully embroidered, cloth back. | 1961-1971 | 1.00 - 3.00 |
| Khaki twill, rolled edge. | 1961-1968 | 0.50 - 1.00 |
| Fully embroidered, plastic back. | 1972-1992 | 0.50 - 1.00 |
| Computer stitched, bagged. | 1993 | 0.50 - 1.00 |

## Genealogy

| | | |
|---|---|---|
| Fully embroidered, plastic back. | 1972 | 0.50 - 1.00 |

## General Science

| | | |
|---|---|---|
| Fully embroidered, plastic back. | 1972-1992 | 0.50 - 1.00 |
| Computer stitched, bagged. | 1993 | 0.50 - 1.00 |

## Geology

| | | |
|---|---|---|
| Khaki twill, narrow crimped. | 1953-1960 | 5.00 - 10.00 |
| Fully embroidered, cloth back. | 1961-1971 | 1.00 - 3.00 |
| Fully embroidered, plastic back. | 1972 | 0.50 - 1.00 |

## Golf

| | | |
|---|---|---|
| Fully embroidered, plastic back. | 1972-1992 | 0.50 - 1.00 |
| Computer stitched, bagged. | 1993 | 0.50 - 1.00 |

## Graphic Arts

| | | |
|---|---|---|
| Fully embroidered, plastic back. | 1987 | 0.50 - 1.00 |

## Grasses, Legumes & Forage Crops/ Forage Crops

| | | |
|---|---|---|
| Tan rough twill, narrow crimped. | 1939-1942 | 25.00 - 40.00 |
| Tan fine twill, narrow crimped. | 1942-1946 | 35.00 - 50.00 |
| Khaki twill, narrow crimped. | 1947-1960 | 7.50 - 15.00 |
| Fully embroidered, cloth back. | 1961-1971 | 1.00 - 3.00 |
| Fully embroidered, plastic back. | 1972-1975 | 0.50 - 1.00 |

## Handicap Awareness/Disability Awareness

| | | |
|---|---|---|
| Fully embroidered, plastic back. | 1980 | 0.50 - 1.00 |

## Handicraft

| | | |
|---|---|---|
| Cut square. | 1911-1933 | 3.00 - 7.50 |

| | | |
|---|---|---|
| Tan, wide crimped. | 1934-1935 | 3.00 - 7.50 |
| Tan rough twill, narrow crimped. | 1936-1942 | 3.00 - 7.50 |
| Tan fine twill, narrow crimped. | 1942-1944 | 5.00 - 10.00 |

## Hiking
| | | |
|---|---|---|
| Cut square. | 1921-1933 | 20.00 - 30.00 |
| Tan, wide crimped. | 1934-1935 | 15.00 - 25.00 |
| Tan rough twill, narrow crimped. | 1936-1942 | 7.50 - 12.50 |
| Tan fine twill, narrow crimped. | 1942-1946 | 12.50 - 20.00 |
| Khaki twill, narrow crimped. | 1947-1960 | 1.00 - 3.00 |
| Khaki twill, rolled edge. | 1961-1968 | 0.50 - 1.00 |
| Fully embroidered, cloth back. | 1969-1971 | 1.00 - 3.00 |
| Fully embroidered, plastic back. | 1972 | 0.50 - 1.00 |

## Hog & Pork Production/Hog Production
| | | |
|---|---|---|
| Cut square. | 1928-1933 | 125.00-200.00 |
| Tan, wide crimped. | 1934-1935 | 25.00 - 40.00 |
| Tan rough twill, narrow crimped. | 1936-1942 | 12.50 - 20.00 |
| Tan fine twill, narrow crimped. | 1942-1946 | 20.00 - 30.00 |
| Khaki twill, narrow crimped. | 1947-1960 | 3.00 - 5.00 |
| Khaki twill, rolled edge. | 1961-1968 | 0.50 - 1.00 |
| Fully embroidered, cloth back. | 1969-1971 | 1.00 - 3.00 |
| Fully embroidered, plastic back. | 1972-1975 | 0.50 - 1.00 |

## Home Repairs
| | | |
|---|---|---|
| Tan rough twill, narrow crimped. | 1945-1946 | 1.00 - 3.00 |
| Khaki twill, narrow crimped. | 1947-1960 | 1.00 - 3.00 |
| Khaki twill, rolled edge. | 1961-1968 | 0.50 - 1.00 |
| Fully embroidered, cloth back. | 1969-1971 | 1.00 - 3.00 |
| Fully embroidered, plastic back. | 1972 | 0.50 - 1.00 |

## Horsemanship
| | | |
|---|---|---|
| Cut square. | 1912-1933 | 30.00 - 35.00 |
| Tan, wide crimped. | 1934-1935 | 25.00 - 40.00 |
| Tan rough twill, narrow crimped. | 1936-1942 | 7.50 - 12.50 |
| Tan fine twill, narrow crimped. | 1942-1946 | 15.00 - 25.00 |
| Khaki twill, narrow crimped. | 1947-1960 | 5.00 - 10.00 |
| Khaki twill, rolled edge. | 1961-1968 | 0.50 - 1.00 |
| Fully embroidered, cloth back. | 1969-1971 | 1.00 - 3.00 |
| Fully embroidered, plastic back. | 1972 | 0.50 - 1.00 |

## Indian Lore
| | | |
|---|---|---|
| Cut square. | 1911-1933 | 150.00-200.00 |
| Tan, wide crimped. | 1934-1935 | 60.00 - 90.00 |
| Tan rough twill, narrow crimped. | 1936-1942 | 10.00 - 15.00 |
| Tan fine twill, narrow crimped. | 1942-1946 | 20.00 - 30.00 |
| Khaki twill, narrow crimped. | 1947-1960 | 3.00 - 5.00 |
| Khaki twill, rolled edge. | 1961-1968 | 0.50 - 1.00 |
| Fully embroidered, cloth back. | 1969-1971 | 1.00 - 3.00 |
| Fully embroidered, plastic back. | 1972 | 0.50 - 1.00 |

## Insect Life
| | | |
|---|---|---|
| Cut square (spider). | 1923-1924 | 400.00-600.00 |
| Cut square (aphid). | 1924-1933 | 90.00-120.00 |

| | | |
|---|---|---|
| Tan, wide crimped. | 1934-1935 | 90.00-125.00 |
| Tan rough twill, narrow crimped. | 1936-1942 | 12.50 - 20.00 |
| Tan fine twill, narrow crimped. | 1942-1946 | 30.00 - 45.00 |
| Khaki twill, narrow crimped. | 1947-1960 | 3.00 - 5.00 |
| Khaki twill, rolled edge. | 1961-1968 | 0.50 - 1.00 |
| Fully embroidered, cloth back. | 1969-1971 | 1.00 - 3.00 |

## Insect Life/Insect Study
| | | |
|---|---|---|
| Fully embroidered, plastic back. | 1972 | 0.50 - 1.00 |

## Interpreting
| | | |
|---|---|---|
| Cut square. | 1911-1933 | 50.00 - 75.00 |
| Tan, wide crimped. | 1934-1935 | 40.00 - 60.00 |
| Tan rough twill, narrow crimped. | 1936-1942 | 25.00 - 40.00 |
| Tan fine twill, narrow crimped. | 1942-1946 | 60.00 - 90.00 |
| Khaki twill, narrow crimped. | 1947-1952 | 40.00 - 60.00 |

## Invention
| | | |
|---|---|---|
| Cut square. | 1913-1915 | none known |

## Journalism
| | | |
|---|---|---|
| Cut square. | 1927-1933 | 80.00-120.00 |
| Tan, wide crimped. | 1934-1935 | 40.00 - 60.00 |
| Tan rough twill, narrow crimped. | 1936-1942 | 7.50 - 12.50 |
| Tan fine twill, narrow crimped. | 1942-1946 | 15.00 - 25.00 |
| Khaki twill, narrow crimped. | 1947-1960 | 5.00 - 10.00 |
| Khaki twill, rolled edge. | 1961-1968 | 0.50 - 1.00 |
| Fully embroidered, cloth back (J-key). | 1969-1971 | 1.00 - 3.00 |
| Fully embroidered, plastic back (J-key). | 1972-1976 | 0.50 - 1.00 |
| Fully embroidered, cloth back (error) (microphone). | 1976 | 40.00 - 60.00 |
| Fully embroidered, plastic back (microphone). | 1976-1992 | 0.50 - 1.00 |
| Computer stitched, bagged. | 1993 | 0.50 - 1.00 |

## Landscape Gardening/Landscaping
| | | |
|---|---|---|
| Cut square. | 1930-1933 | 175.00-250.00 |

## Landscape Gardening/Landscaping/ Landscape Architecture
| | | |
|---|---|---|
| Tan, wide crimped. | 1934-1935 | 60.00 - 90.00 |
| Tan rough twill, narrow crimped. | 1936-1942 | 20.00 - 30.00 |
| Tan fine twill, narrow crimped. | 1942-1946 | 25.00 - 40.00 |
| Khaki twill, narrow crimped. | 1947-1960 | 5.00 - 10.00 |
| Fully embroidered, cloth back (sun dial). | 1961-1971 | 1.00 - 3.00 |

## Landscape Architecture
| | | |
|---|---|---|
| Fully embroidered, cloth back (pine tree). | 1961-1971 | 1.00 - 3.00 |
| Fully embroidered, plastic back. | 1972 | 0.50 - 1.00 |

## Landscape Gardening
| | | |
|---|---|---|
| Computer stitched, bagged. | 1993 | 0.50 - 1.00 |

# CURRENT MERIT BADGE DESIGNS

AMERICAN BUSINESS

AMERICAN CULTURES

AMERICAN HERITAGE

AMERICAN LABOR

ANIMAL SCIENCE

ARCHERY

ARCHITECTURE

ART

ASTRONOMY

# CURRENT MERIT BADGE DESIGNS

*ATHLETICS*

*ATOMIC ENERGY*

*AUTO MECHANICS*

*AVIATION*

*BACKPACKING*

*BASKETRY*

*BIRD STUDY*

*BUGLING*

*CAMPING*

*CANOEING*

*CHEMISTRY*

*CINEMATOGRAPHY*

# CURRENT MERIT BADGE DESIGNS

*CITIZENSHIP
IN THE COMMUNITY*

*CITIZENSHIP
IN THE NATION*

*CITIZENSHIP
IN THE WORLD*

*COIN COLLECTING*

*COLLECTIONS*

*COMMUNICATIONS*

*COMPUTERS*

*COOKING*

*CYCLING*

*DENTISTRY*

*DISABILITIES AWARENESS*

*DOG CARE*

# CURRNET MERIT BADGE DESIGNS

*DRAFTING*

*ELECTRICITY*

*ELECTRONICS*

*EMERGENCY
PREPAREDNESS*

*ENERGY*

*ENGINEERING*

*ENVIRONMENTAL
SCIENCE*

*FAMILY LIFE*

*FARM MECHANICS*

*FINGERPRINTING*

*FIRE SAFETY*

*FIRST AID*

# CURRENT MERIT BADGE DESIGNS

FISH AND WILDLIFE
MANAGEMENT

FISHING

FORESTRY

GARDENING

GENEALOGY

GEOLOGY

GOLF

GRAPHIC ARTS

HIKING

HOME REPAIRS

HORSEMANSHIP

INDIAN LORE

# CURRENT MERIT BADGE DESIGNS

*INSECT STUDY*

*JOURNALISM*

*LANDSCAPE ARCHITECTURE*

*LAW*

*LEATHERWORK*

*LIFESAVING*

*MAMMAL STUDY*

*MEDICINE*

*METAL WORK*

*MODEL DESIGN & BUILDING*

*MOTORBOATING*

*MUSIC*

# CURRENT MERIT BADGE DESIGNS

*NATURE*

*OCEANOGRAPHY*

*ORIENTEERING*

*PAINTING*

*PERSONAL FITNESS*

*PERSONAL MANAGEMENT*

*PETS*

*PHOTOGRAPHY*

*PIONEERING*

*PLANT SCIENCE*

*PLUMBING*

*POTTERY*

# CURRENT MERIT BADGE DESIGNS

PUBLIC HEALTH

PUBLIC SPEAKING

PULP & PAPER

RADIO

RAILROADING

READING

REPTILE AND
AMPHIBIAN STUDY

RIFLE SHOOTING

ROWING

SAFETY

SALESMANSHIP

SCHOLARSHIP

# CURRENT MERIT BADGE DESIGNS

*SCULPTURE*

*SHOTGUN SHOOTING*

*SKATING*

*SKIING*

*SMALL-BOAT SAILING*

*SOIL & WATER*

*SPACE EXPLORATION*

*SPORTS*

*STAMP COLLECTING*

*SURVEYING*

*SWIMMING*

*TEXTILE*

# CURRENT MERIT BADGE DESIGNS

THEATER

TRAFFIC SAFETY

TRUCK TRANSPORTATION

VETERINARY MEDICINE

WATER SKIING

WEATHER

WHITEWATER

WILDERNESS SURVIVAL

WOOD CARVING

WOODWORK

## Law
Fully embroidered, plastic back. | 1972 | 0.50 - 1.00

## Leathercraft
Cut square (shoe). | 1928-1933 | 3.00 - 7.50
Tan, wide crimped. | 1934-1935 | 7.50 - 12.50
Tan rough twill, narrow crimped. | 1936-1942 | 3.00 - 7.50
Tan fine twill, narrow crimped. | 1942-1946 | 10.00 - 15.00

## Leathercraft/Leatherwork
Khaki twill, narrow crimped (shoe). | 1953-1960 | 3.00 - 5.00

## Leatherwork
Fully embroidered, cloth back. | 1961-1971 | 1.00 - 3.00
Khaki twill, rolled edge. | 1961-1968 | 0.50 - 1.00
Fully embroidered, plastic back. | 1972 | 0.50 - 1.00

## Leatherworking
Cut square (awl). | 1911-1933 | 25.00 - 40.00

## Leatherworking/Leatherwork
Tan, wide crimped. | 1934-1935 | 15.00 - 25.00
Tan rough twill, narrow crimped. | 1936-1942 | 10.00 - 15.00
Tan fine twill, narrow crimped. | 1942-1946 | 12.50 - 17.50
Khaki twill, narrow crimped. | 1947-1952 | 3.00 - 5.00

## Lifesaving
Cut square (all white buoy). | 1911-1933 | 10.00 - 17.50
Cut square (white and green buoy). | 1911-1933 | 3.00 - 7.50
Tan, wide crimped. | 1934-1935 | 5.00 - 10.00
Tan rough twill, narrow crimped. | 1936-1942 | 3.00 - 7.50
Tan fine twill, narrow crimped. | 1942-1946 | 5.00 - 10.00
Khaki twill, narrow crimped. | 1947-1960 | 1.00 - 3.00
Khaki twill, rolled edge. | 1961-1968 | 0.50 - 1.00
Fully embroidered, cloth back, silver border. | 1969-1971 | 1.00 - 3.00
Fully embroidered, plastic back, silver border. | 1972 | 0.50 - 1.00

## Machinery
Cut square. | 1912-1933 | 20.00 - 30.00
Tan, wide crimped. | 1934-1935 | 12.50 - 20.00
Tan rough twill, narrow crimped. | 1936-1942 | 5.00 - 10.00
Tan fine twill, narrow crimped. | 1942-1946 | 10.00 - 15.00
Khaki twill, narrow crimped. | 1947-1960 | 3.00 - 5.00
Khaki twill, rolled edge. | 1961-1968 | 0.50 - 1.00
Fully embroidered, cloth back. | 1969-1971 | 1.00 - 3.00
Fully embroidered, plastic back. | 1972 | 0.50 - 1.00

## Mammals/Mammal Study
Fully embroidered, plastic back. | 1972 | 0.50 - 1.00

## Marksmanship
Cut square. | 1912-1933 | 20.00 - 35.00

Tan, wide crimped. | 1934-1935 | 12.50 - 20.00
Tan rough twill, narrow crimped. | 1936-1942 | 7.50 - 15.00
Tan fine twill, narrow crimped. | 1942-1946 | 12.50 - 20.00
Khaki twill, narrow crimped. | 1947-1960 | 3.00 - 5.00

## Marksmanship/Rifle & Shotgun Shooting
Fully embroidered, cloth back. | 1961-1971 | 1.00 - 3.00
Fully embroidered, plastic back. | 1972 | 0.50 - 1.00

## Masonry
Cut square. | 1912-1933 | 15.00 - 25.00
Tan, wide crimped. | 1934-1935 | 15.00 - 25.00
Tan rough twill, narrow crimped. | 1936-1942 | 5.00 - 12.50
Tan fine twill, narrow crimped. | 1942-1946 | 12.50 - 20.00
Khaki twill, narrow crimped. | 1947-1960 | 3.00 - 5.00
Khaki twill, rolled edge. | 1961-1968 | 0.50 - 1.00
Fully embroidered, cloth back. | 1969-1971 | 1.00 - 3.00
Fully embroidered, plastic back. | 1972 | 0.50 - 1.00

## Mechanical Drawing
Cut square. | 1933-1933 | 200.00-275.00
Khaki twill, rolled edge. | 1961-1968 | 0.50 - 1.00

## Mechanical Drawing/Drafting
Tan, wide crimped. | 1934-1935 | 20.00 - 35.00
Tan rough twill, narrow crimped. | 1936-1942 | 5.00 - 10.00
Tan fine twill, narrow crimped. | 1942-1946 | 10.00 - 15.00
Khaki twill, narrow crimped. | 1947-1960 | 3.00 - 5.00

## Medicine
Fully embroidered, plastic back. | 1991 | 0.50 - 1.00

## Metallurgy
Computer stitched, bagged. | 1993 | 0.50 - 1.00

## Metallurgy/Metals Engineering
Fully embroidered, cloth back. | 1965-1971 | 1.00 - 3.00

## Metals Engineering
Fully embroidered, plastic back. | 1972 | 0.50 - 1.00

## Metalwork
Cut square. | 1928-1933 | 10.00 - 17.50
Tan, wide crimped. | 1934-1935 | 7.50 - 12.50
Tan rough twill, narrow crimped. | 1936-1942 | 3.00 - 7.50
Tan fine twill, narrow crimped. | 1942-1946 | 7.50 - 12.50
Khaki twill, narrow crimped. | 1947-1960 | 1.00 - 3.00
Khaki twill, rolled edge. | 1961-1968 | 0.50 - 1.00
Fully embroidered, cloth back. | 1969-1971 | 1.00 - 3.00
Fully embroidered, plastic back. | 1972 | 0.50 - 1.00

## Mining
Cut square. | 1912-1933 | 100.00-175.00

| | | |
|---|---|---|
| Tan, wide crimped. | 1934-1935 | 90.00-125.00 |
| Tan rough twill, narrow crimped. | 1936-1947 | 80.00-120.00 |

## Model Design & Building
| | | |
|---|---|---|
| Fully embroidered, cloth back. | 1964-1971 | 1.00 - 3.00 |
| Fully embroidered, plastic back. | 1972 | 0.50 - 1.00 |

## Motorboating
| | | |
|---|---|---|
| Fully embroidered, cloth back. | 1961-1971 | 1.00 - 3.00 |
| Fully embroidered, plastic back. | 1972 | 0.50 - 1.00 |

## Music
| | | |
|---|---|---|
| Cut square. | 1911-1933 | 15.00 - 30.00 |
| Tan, wide crimped. | 1934-1935 | 7.50 - 12.50 |
| Tan rough twill, narrow crimped. | 1936-1942 | 2.50 - 7.50 |
| Tan fine twill, narrow crimped. | 1942-1946 | 7.50 - 12.50 |
| Khaki twill, narrow crimped. | 1947-1960 | 3.00 - 5.00 |
| Khaki twill, rolled edge. | 1961-1968 | 0.50 - 1.00 |
| Fully embroidered, cloth back. | 1969-1971 | 1.00 - 3.00 |
| Fully embroidered, plastic back. | 1972 | 0.50 - 1.00 |

## Nature
| | | |
|---|---|---|
| Khaki twill, narrow crimped. | 1953-1960 | 1.00 - 3.00 |
| Fully embroidered, cloth back, green border. | 1961-1969 | 1.00 - 3.00 |
| Fully embroidered, cloth back, silver border. | 1969-1971 | 1.00 - 3.00 |
| Fully embroidered, plastic back, green border. | 1972 | 0.50 - 1.00 |
| Fully embroidered, plastic back, silver border. | 1972 | 0.50 - 1.00 |

## Nut Culture
| | | |
|---|---|---|
| Cut square. | 1928-1933 | 15.00 - 30.00 |
| Tan, wide crimped. | 1934-1935 | 150.00-225.00 |
| Tan rough twill, narrow crimped. | 1936-1942 | 80.00-120.00 |
| Tan fine twill, narrow crimped. | 1942-1946 | 150.00-200.00 |
| Khaki twill, narrow crimped. | 1947-1954 | 125.00-175.00 |

## Oceanography
| | | |
|---|---|---|
| Fully embroidered, cloth back. | 1964-1971 | 1.00 - 3.00 |
| Fully embroidered, plastic back. | 1972 | 0.50 - 1.00 |

## Orienteering
| | | |
|---|---|---|
| Fully embroidered, plastic back. | 1972 | 0.50 - 1.00 |

## Painting
| | | |
|---|---|---|
| Cut square (narrow brush). | 1912-1933 | 15.00 - 25.00 |
| Cut square (wide brush). | 1912-1933 | 15.00 - 25.00 |
| Tan, wide crimped. | 1934-1935 | 12.50 - 20.00 |
| Tan rough twill, narrow crimped. | 1936-1942 | 5.00 - 10.00 |
| Tan fine twill, narrow crimped. | 1942-1946 | 12.50 - 17.50 |
| Khaki twill, narrow crimped. | 1947-1960 | 3.00 - 5.00 |
| Khaki twill, rolled edge. | 1961-1968 | 0.50 - 1.00 |

| | | |
|---|---|---|
| Fully embroidered, cloth back. | 1969-1971 | 1.00 - 3.00 |
| Fully embroidered, plastic back. | 1972 | 0.50 - 1.00 |

## Pathfinding
| | | |
|---|---|---|
| Cut square (4 feathers). | 1911-1933 | 3.00 - 10.00 |
| Cut square (5 feathers). | 1911-1933 | 3.00 - 10.00 |
| Cut square (6 feathers). | 1911-1933 | 3.00 - 10.00 |
| Tan, wide crimped. | 1934-1935 | 5.00 - 10.00 |
| Tan rough twill, narrow crimped. | 1936-1942 | 3.00 - 7.50 |
| Tan fine twill, narrow crimped. | 1942-1946 | 7.50 - 12.50 |
| Khaki twill, narrow crimped. | 1947-1952 | 1.00 - 3.00 |

## Personal Finances
| | | |
|---|---|---|
| Fully embroidered, cloth back. | 1963-1971 | 1.00 - 3.00 |
| Fully embroidered, plastic back. | 1972 | 0.50 - 1.00 |

## Personal Fitness
| | | |
|---|---|---|
| Fully embroidered, cloth back, silver border. | 1969-1971 | 1.00 - 3.00 |
| Fully embroidered, plastic back, silver border. | 1972 | 0.50 - 1.00 |

## Personal Health/Personal Fitness
| | | |
|---|---|---|
| Cut square. | 1911-1933 | 3.00 - 10.00 |
| Tan, wide crimped. | 1934-1935 | 3.00 - 7.50 |
| Tan rough twill, narrow crimped. | 1936-1942 | 3.00 - 7.50 |
| Tan fine twill, narrow crimped. | 1942-1946 | 5.00 - 10.00 |
| Khaki twill, narrow crimped. | 1947-1960 | 1.00 - 3.00 |
| Khaki twill, rolled edge. | 1961-1968 | 0.50 - 1.00 |

## Personal Management
| | | |
|---|---|---|
| Fully embroidered, plastic back, silver border. | 1972 | 0.50 - 1.00 |

## Pets
| | | |
|---|---|---|
| Khaki twill, narrow crimped. | 1958-1960 | 7.50 - 12.50 |
| Khaki twill, rolled edge. | 1961-1968 | 0.50 - 1.00 |
| Fully embroidered, cloth back. | 1969-1971 | 1.00 - 3.00 |
| Fully embroidered, plastic back, silver border. | 1972 | 0.50 - 1.00 |

## Photography
| | | |
|---|---|---|
| Cut square. | 1912-1933 | 30.00 - 45.00 |
| Tan, wide crimped. | 1934-1935 | 12.50 - 20.00 |
| Tan rough twill, narrow crimped. | 1936-1942 | 12.50 - 20.00 |
| Tan fine twill, narrow crimped. | 1942-1946 | 12.50 - 20.00 |
| Khaki twill, narrow crimped (tripod camera). | 1947-1953 | 7.50 - 15.00 |
| Khaki twill, narrow crimped (camera). | 1954-1960 | 5.00 - 10.00 |
| Fully embroidered, cloth back. | 1961-1971 | 1.00 - 3.00 |
| Fully embroidered, plastic back. | 1972 | 0.50 - 1.00 |
| Computer stitched, bagged. | 1993 | 0.50 - 1.00 |

## Physical Development
| | | |
|---|---|---|
| Cut square (extended thumb). | 1914-1933 | 175.00-250.00 |

| | | |
|---|---|---|
| Cut square (regular thumb). | 1914-1933 | 15.00 - 25.00 |
| Tan, wide crimped. | 1934-1935 | 7.50 - 12.50 |
| Tan rough twill, narrow crimped. | 1936-1942 | 3.00 - 7.50 |
| Tan fine twill, narrow crimped. | 1942-1946 | 10.00 - 17.50 |
| Khaki twill, narrow crimped. | 1947-1952 | 5.00 - 10.00 |

## Pigeon Raising

| | | |
|---|---|---|
| Cut square. | 1913-1933 | 400.00-600.00 |
| Tan, wide crimped. | 1934-1935 | 60.00 - 90.00 |
| Tan rough twill, narrow crimped. | 1936-1942 | 10.00 - 17.50 |
| Tan fine twill, narrow crimped. | 1942-1946 | 20.00 - 30.00 |
| Khaki twill, narrow crimped. | 1947-1960 | 5.00 - 10.00 |
| Khaki twill, rolled edge. | 1961-1968 | 0.50 - 1.00 |
| Fully embroidered, cloth back. | 1969-1971 | 1.00 - 3.00 |
| Fully embroidered, plastic back. | 1972-1980 | 0.50 - 1.00 |

## Pioneering

| | | |
|---|---|---|
| Cut square. | 1912-1933 | 3.00 - 10.00 |
| Tan, wide crimped. | 1934-1935 | 5.00 - 10.00 |
| Tan rough twill, narrow crimped. | 1936-1942 | 3.00 - 7.50 |
| Tan fine twill, narrow crimped. | 1942-1946 | 5.00 - 10.00 |
| Khaki twill, narrow crimped. | 1947-1960 | 1.00 - 3.00 |
| Khaki twill, rolled edge. | 1961-1968 | 0.50 - 1.00 |
| Fully embroidered, cloth back. | 1969-1971 | 1.00 - 3.00 |
| Fully embroidered, plastic back. | 1972 | 0.50 - 1.00 |

## Plant Science

| | | |
|---|---|---|
| Fully embroidered, plastic back. | 1972 | 0.50 - 1.00 |

## Plumbing

| | | |
|---|---|---|
| Cut square. | 1912-1933 | 20.00 - 35.00 |
| Tan, wide crimped. | 1934-1935 | 12.50 - 20.00 |
| Tan rough twill, narrow crimped. | 1936-1942 | 5.00 - 10.00 |
| Tan fine twill, narrow crimped. | 1942-1946 | 12.50 - 17.50 |
| Khaki twill, narrow crimped. | 1947-1960 | 3.00 - 5.00 |
| Khaki twill, rolled edge. | 1961-1968 | 0.50 - 1.00 |
| Fully embroidered, cloth back. | 1969-1971 | 1.00 - 3.00 |
| Fully embroidered, plastic back. | 1972-1992 | 0.50 - 1.00 |
| Computer stitched, bagged. | 1993 | 0.50 - 1.00 |

## Pottery

| | | |
|---|---|---|
| Cut square. | 1928-1933 | 80.00-125.00 |
| Tan, wide crimped. | 1934-1935 | 50.00 - 75.00 |
| Tan rough twill, narrow crimped. | 1936-1942 | 20.00 - 35.00 |
| Tan fine twill, narrow crimped. | 1942-1946 | 40.00 - 60.00 |
| Khaki twill, narrow crimped. | 1947-1960 | 5.00 - 10.00 |
| Khaki twill, rolled edge. | 1961-1968 | 0.50 - 1.00 |
| Fully embroidered, cloth back. | 1969-1971 | 1.00 - 3.00 |
| Fully embroidered, plastic back. | 1972 | 0.50 - 1.00 |

## Poultry Farming/Poultry Keeping

| | | |
|---|---|---|
| Cut square. | 1911-1933 | 35.00 - 60.00 |
| Tan, wide crimped. | 1934-1935 | 25.00 - 40.00 |
| Tan rough twill, narrow crimped. | 1936-1942 | 7.50 - 15.00 |

| | | |
|---|---|---|
| Tan fine twill, narrow crimped. | 1942-1946 | 12.50 - 20.00 |
| Khaki twill, narrow crimped. | 1947-1960 | 5.00 - 10.00 |
| Khaki twill, rolled edge. | 1961-1968 | 0.50 - 1.00 |
| Fully embroidered, cloth back. | 1969-1971 | 1.00 - 3.00 |
| Fully embroidered, plastic back. | 1972-1975 | 0.50 - 1.00 |

## Printing

| | | |
|---|---|---|
| Cut square. | 1912-1933 | 25.00 - 40.00 |
| Tan, wide crimped. | 1934-1935 | 15.00 - 30.00 |
| Tan rough twill, narrow crimped. | 1936-1942 | 10.00 - 15.00 |
| Tan fine twill, narrow crimped. | 1942-1946 | 15.00 - 25.00 |
| Khaki twill, narrow crimped. | 1947-1960 | 3.00 - 5.00 |
| Khaki twill, rolled edge. | 1961-1968 | 0.50 - 1.00 |
| Fully embroidered, cloth back. | 1969-1971 | 1.00 - 3.00 |
| Fully embroidered, plastic back. | 1972-1987 | 0.50 - 1.00 |

## Public Health

| | | |
|---|---|---|
| Cut square. | 1911-1933 | 3.00 - 10.00 |
| Tan, wide crimped. | 1934-1935 | 3.00 - 7.50 |
| Tan rough twill, narrow crimped. | 1936-1942 | 3.00 - 7.50 |
| Tan fine twill, narrow crimped. | 1942-1946 | 5.00 - 10.00 |
| Khaki twill, narrow crimped. | 1947-1960 | 1.00 - 3.00 |
| Khaki twill, rolled edge. | 1961-1968 | 0.50 - 1.00 |
| Fully embroidered, cloth back. | 1969-1971 | 1.00 - 3.00 |
| Fully embroidered, plastic back. | 1972 | 0.50 - 1.00 |
| Computer stitched, bagged. | 1993 | 0.50 - 1.00 |

## Public Speaking

| | | |
|---|---|---|
| Cut square. | 1932-1933 | 175.00-225.00 |
| Tan, wide crimped. | 1934-1935 | 25.00 - 40.00 |
| Tan rough twill, narrow crimped. | 1936-1942 | 10.00 - 15.00 |
| Tan fine twill, narrow crimped. | 1942-1946 | 30.00 - 45.00 |
| Khaki twill, narrow crimped. | 1947-1960 | 3.00 - 5.00 |
| Khaki twill, rolled edge. | 1961-1968 | 0.50 - 1.00 |
| Fully embroidered, cloth back. | 1969-1971 | 1.00 - 3.00 |
| Fully embroidered, plastic back. | 1972-1992 | 0.50 - 1.00 |
| Computer stitched, bagged. | 1993 | 0.50 - 1.00 |

## Pulp & Paper

| | | |
|---|---|---|
| Fully embroidered, plastic back. | 1972 | 0.50 - 1.00 |

## Rabbit Raising

| | | |
|---|---|---|
| Tan rough twill, narrow crimped. | 1936-1942 | 15.00 - 25.00 |
| Tan fine twill, narrow crimped. | 1942-1946 | 15.00 - 25.00 |
| Khaki twill, narrow crimped. | 1947-1960 | 5.00 - 10.00 |
| Khaki twill, rolled edge. | 1961-1968 | 0.50 - 1.00 |
| Fully embroidered, cloth back. | 1969-1971 | 1.00 - 3.00 |
| Fully embroidered, plastic back. | 1972-1993 | 0.50 - 1.00 |

## Radio

| | | |
|---|---|---|
| Tan, wide crimped. | 1934-1935 | 60.00 - 90.00 |
| Tan rough twill, narrow crimped. | 1936-1942 | 12.50 - 17.50 |
| Tan fine twill, narrow crimped. | 1942-1946 | 25.00 - 40.00 |
| Khaki twill, narrow crimped. | 1947-1960 | 5.00 - 10.00 |

| | | |
|---|---|---|
| Khaki twill, rolled edge. | 1961-1968 | 0.50 - 1.00 |
| Fully embroidered, cloth back. | 1969-1971 | 1.00 - 3.00 |
| Fully embroidered, plastic back. | 1972 | 0.50 - 1.00 |

## Railroading

| | | |
|---|---|---|
| Khaki twill, narrow crimped. | 1952-1960 | 5.00 - 10.00 |
| Fully embroidered, cloth back. | 1961-1971 | 1.00 - 3.00 |
| Fully embroidered, plastic back. | 1972 | 0.50 - 1.00 |

## Reading

| | | |
|---|---|---|
| Cut square. | 1929-1933 | 10.00 - 17.50 |
| Tan, wide crimped. | 1934-1935 | 5.00 - 10.00 |
| Tan rough twill, narrow crimped. | 1936-1942 | 3.00 - 7.50 |
| Tan fine twill, narrow crimped. | 1942-1946 | 5.00 - 10.00 |
| Khaki twill, narrow crimped. | 1947-1960 | 1.00 - 3.00 |
| Khaki twill, rolled edge. | 1961-1968 | 0.50 - 1.00 |
| Fully embroidered, cloth back. | 1969-1971 | 1.00 - 3.00 |
| Fully embroidered, plastic back. | 1972 | 0.50 - 1.00 |

## Reptile & Amphibian Study

| | | |
|---|---|---|
| Fully embroidered, plastic back. | 1972 | 0.50 - 1.00 |

## Reptile Study

| | | |
|---|---|---|
| Cut square. | 1926-1933 | 20.00 - 35.00 |
| Tan, wide crimped. | 1934-1935 | 10.00 - 17.50 |
| Tan rough twill, narrow crimped. | 1936-1942 | 5.00 - 10.00 |
| Tan fine twill, narrow crimped. | 1942-1946 | 12.50 - 20.00 |
| Khaki twill, narrow crimped. | 1947-1960 | 3.00 - 5.00 |
| Khaki twill, rolled edge. | 1961-1968 | 0.50 - 1.00 |
| Fully embroidered, cloth back. | 1969-1971 | 1.00 - 3.00 |
| Fully embroidered, plastic back. | 1972 | 0.50 - 1.00 |

## Rifle Shooting

| | | |
|---|---|---|
| Fully embroidered, plastic back. | 1987 | 0.50 - 1.00 |

## Rocks & Minerals

| | | |
|---|---|---|
| Tan rough twill, narrow crimped. | 1937-1942 | 40.00 - 75.00 |
| Tan fine twill, narrow crimped. | 1942-1946 | 75.00 - 100.00 |
| Khaki twill, narrow crimped. | 1947-1953 | 30.00 - 50.00 |

## Rowing

| | | |
|---|---|---|
| Cut square. | 1933-1933 | 100.00 - 150.00 |
| Tan, wide crimped. | 1934-1935 | 12.50 - 20.00 |
| Tan rough twill, narrow crimped. | 1936-1942 | 5.00 - 10.00 |
| Tan fine twill, narrow crimped. | 1942-1946 | 10.00 - 15.00 |
| Khaki twill, narrow crimped (swim suit & white skin). | 1947-1957 | 1.00 - 3.00 |
| Khaki twill, narrow crimped (swim trunks & flesh skin). | 1958-1960 | 3.00 - 5.00 |
| Khaki twill, rolled edge. | 1961-1968 | 0.50 - 1.00 |
| Fully embroidered, cloth back. | 1969-1971 | 1.00 - 3.00 |
| Fully embroidered, plastic back. | 1972 | 0.50 - 1.00 |

## Safety First

| | | |
|---|---|---|
| Cut square (green cross and ring). | 1916-1933 | 30.00 - 50.00 |
| Cut square (white cross and ring). | 1916-1933 | 3.00 - 7.50 |

## Safety

| | | |
|---|---|---|
| Cut square (white cross and green ring). | 1916-1933 | 60.00 - 90.00 |
| Tan, wide crimped. | 1934-1935 | 3.00 - 7.50 |
| Tan rough twill, narrow crimped. | 1936-1942 | 3.00 - 7.50 |
| Tan fine twill, narrow crimped. | 1942-1946 | 5.00 - 10.00 |
| Khaki twill, narrow crimped. | 1947-1960 | 1.00 - 3.00 |
| Fully embroidered, cloth back, green border. | 1961-1969 | 1.00 - 3.00 |
| Fully embroidered, cloth back, silver border. | 1969-1971 | 1.00 - 3.00 |
| Fully embroidered, plastic back, silver border. | 1972 | 0.50 - 1.00 |

## Salesmanship

| | | |
|---|---|---|
| Cut square. | 1927-1933 | 80.00 - 100.00 |
| Tan, wide crimped. | 1934-1935 | 25.00 - 40.00 |
| Tan rough twill, narrow crimped. | 1936-1942 | 10.00 - 20.00 |
| Tan fine twill, narrow crimped. | 1942-1946 | 10.00 - 17.50 |
| Khaki twill, narrow crimped. | 1947-1960 | 5.00 - 10.00 |
| Khaki twill, rolled edge. | 1961-1968 | 0.50 - 1.00 |
| Fully embroidered, cloth back. | 1969-1971 | 1.00 - 3.00 |
| Fully embroidered, plastic back. | 1972 | 0.50 - 1.00 |

## Scholarship

| | | |
|---|---|---|
| Cut square. | 1913-1933 | 5.00 - 15.00 |
| Tan, wide crimped. | 1934-1935 | 7.50 - 12.50 |
| Tan rough twill, narrow crimped. | 1936-1942 | 3.00 - 7.50 |
| Tan fine twill, narrow crimped. | 1942-1946 | 15.00 - 25.00 |
| Khaki twill, narrow crimped. | 1947-1960 | 1.00 - 3.00 |
| Khaki twill, rolled edge. | 1961-1968 | 0.50 - 1.00 |
| Fully embroidered, cloth back. | 1969-1971 | 1.00 - 3.00 |
| Fully embroidered, plastic back. | 1972 | 0.50 - 1.00 |

## Sculpture

| | | |
|---|---|---|
| Cut square. | 1912-1933 | 150.00 - 225.00 |
| Tan, wide crimped. | 1934-1935 | 90.00 - 120.00 |
| Tan rough twill, narrow crimped. | 1936-1942 | 30.00 - 50.00 |
| Tan fine twill, narrow crimped. | 1942-1946 | 40.00 - 60.00 |
| Khaki twill, narrow crimped. | 1947-1960 | 5.00 - 10.00 |
| Khaki twill, rolled edge. | 1961-1968 | 0.50 - 1.00 |
| Fully embroidered, cloth back. | 1969-1971 | 1.00 - 3.00 |
| Fully embroidered, plastic back. | 1972 | 0.50 - 1.00 |

## Seamanship

| | | |
|---|---|---|
| Cut square (black anchor). | 1912-1933 | 750.00 - 1,250.00 |
| Cut square (curved bottom to red anchor). | 1912-1933 | 100.00 - 150.00 |
| Cut square (straight bottom to red anchor). | 1912-1933 | 100.00 - 150.00 |
| Tan, wide crimped. | 1934-1935 | 60.00 - 90.00 |
| Tan rough twill, narrow crimped. | 1936-1942 | 10.00 - 17.50 |
| Tan fine twill, narrow crimped. | 1942-1946 | 30.00 - 45.00 |

| | | |
|---|---|---|
| Khaki twill, narrow crimped. | 1947-1960 | 12.50 - 20.00 |
| Khaki twill, rolled edge. | 1961-1964 | 0.50 - 1.00 |

## Sheep Farming

| | | |
|---|---|---|
| Cut square. | 1928-1933 | 200.00-300.00 |
| Tan, wide crimped. | 1934-1935 | 60.00 - 90.00 |
| Tan rough twill, narrow crimped. | 1936-1942 | 30.00 - 50.00 |
| Tan fine twill, narrow crimped. | 1942-1946 | 40.00 - 60.00 |
| Khaki twill, narrow crimped. | 1947-1960 | 5.00 - 10.00 |
| Khaki twill, rolled edge. | 1961-1968 | 0.50 - 1.00 |
| Fully embroidered, cloth back. | 1969-1971 | 1.00 - 3.00 |
| Fully embroidered, plastic back. | 1972-1975 | 0.50 - 1.00 |

## Shotgun Shooting

| | | |
|---|---|---|
| Fully embroidered, plastic back. | 1987 | 0.50 - 1.00 |

## Signaling

| | | |
|---|---|---|
| Cut square (correct flag colors). | 1911-1933 | 30.00 - 50.00 |
| Cut square (reversed flag colors). | 1911-1933 | 30.00 - 50.00 |
| Tan, wide crimped. | 1934-1935 | 25.00 - 40.00 |
| Tan rough twill, narrow crimped. | 1936-1942 | 12.50 - 20.00 |
| Tan fine twill, narrow crimped. | 1942-1946 | 15.00 - 25.00 |
| Khaki twill, narrow crimped. | 1947-1960 | 5.00 - 10.00 |
| Khaki twill, rolled edge. | 1961-1968 | 0.50 - 1.00 |
| Fully embroidered, cloth back. | 1969-1971 | 1.00 - 3.00 |
| Fully embroidered, plastic back. | 1972-1991 | 0.50 - 1.00 |

## Skating

| | | |
|---|---|---|
| Fully embroidered, plastic back. | 1972 | 0.50 - 1.00 |

## Skiing

| | | |
|---|---|---|
| Tan rough twill, narrow crimped. | 1938-1942 | 40.00 - 75.00 |
| Tan fine twill, narrow crimped. | 1942-1946 | 40.00 - 60.00 |
| Khaki twill, narrow crimped. | 1947-1960 | 5.00 - 10.00 |
| Fully embroidered, cloth back. | 1961-1971 | 1.00 - 3.00 |
| Fully embroidered, plastic back, brown skis. | 1972-1979 | 0.50 - 1.00 |
| Fully embroidered, plastic back, blue skis. | 1980 | 0.50 - 1.00 |

## Small Boat Sailing

| | | |
|---|---|---|
| Fully embroidered, cloth back. | 1964-1971 | 1.00 - 3.00 |
| Fully embroidered, plastic back. | 1972 | 0.50 - 1.00 |

## Small Grains & Cereal Foods/Small Grains

| | | |
|---|---|---|
| Tan rough twill, narrow crimped. | 1936-1942 | 25.00 - 50.00 |
| Tan fine twill, narrow crimped. | 1942-1946 | 40.00 - 60.00 |
| Khaki twill, narrow crimped. | 1947-1960 | 5.00 - 10.00 |
| Fully embroidered, cloth back. | 1961-1971 | 1.00 - 3.00 |
| Fully embroidered, plastic back. | 1972-1975 | 0.50 - 1.00 |

## Soil & Water Conservation

| | | |
|---|---|---|
| Khaki twill, narrow crimped. | 1952-1960 | 3.00 - 5.00 |

| | | |
|---|---|---|
| Fully embroidered, cloth back (vertical rows). | 1961-1969 | 1.00 - 3.00 |
| Fully embroidered, cloth back (horizontal rows). | 1970-1971 | 3.00 - 5.00 |
| Fully embroidered, plastic back. | 1972 | 0.50 - 1.00 |

## Soil Management

| | | |
|---|---|---|
| Cut square. | 1928-1933 | 100.00-175.00 |
| Tan, wide crimped. | 1934-1935 | 60.00 - 90.00 |
| Tan rough twill, narrow crimped. | 1936-1942 | 60.00 - 90.00 |
| Tan fine twill, narrow crimped. | 1942-1946 | 60.00 - 90.00 |
| Khaki twill, narrow crimped. | 1947-1952 | 80.00-120.00 |

## Space Exploration

| | | |
|---|---|---|
| Fully embroidered, cloth back. | 1965-1971 | 1.00 - 3.00 |
| Fully embroidered, plastic back. | 1972 | 0.50 - 1.00 |

## Sports

| | | |
|---|---|---|
| Fully embroidered, plastic back, silver border. | 1972 | 0.50 - 1.00 |

## Stalking

| | | |
|---|---|---|
| Cut square (cougar). | 1912-1933 | 100.00-150.00 |
| Cut square (leaf). | 1912-1933 | 350.00-500.00 |
| Tan, wide crimped. | 1934-1935 | 125.00-175.00 |
| Tan rough twill, narrow crimped. | 1936-1942 | 60.00 - 90.00 |
| Tan fine twill, narrow crimped. | 1942-1946 | 60.00 - 90.00 |
| Khaki twill, narrow crimped. | 1947-1952 | 50.00 - 75.00 |

## Stamp Collecting

| | | |
|---|---|---|
| Cut square. | 1931-1933 | 60.00 - 90.00 |
| Tan, wide crimped. | 1934-1935 | 12.50 - 20.00 |
| Tan rough twill, narrow crimped. | 1936-1942 | 7.50 - 15.00 |
| Tan fine twill, narrow crimped. | 1942-1946 | 10.00 - 20.00 |
| Khaki twill, narrow crimped. | 1947-1960 | 3.00 - 5.00 |
| Khaki twill, rolled edge. | 1961-1968 | 0.50 - 1.00 |
| Fully embroidered, cloth back. | 1969-1971 | 1.00 - 3.00 |
| Fully embroidered, plastic back. | 1972-1992 | 0.50 - 1.00 |
| Computer stitched, bagged. | 1993 | 0.50 - 1.00 |

## Surveying

| | | |
|---|---|---|
| Cut square (2 legs). | 1912-1933 | 60.00 - 90.00 |
| Cut square (3 legs). | 1912-1933 | 60.00 - 90.00 |
| Tan, wide crimped. | 1934-1935 | 35.00 - 50.00 |
| Tan rough twill, narrow crimped. | 1936-1942 | 7.50 - 12.50 |
| Tan fine twill, narrow crimped. | 1942-1946 | 15.00 - 25.00 |
| Khaki twill, narrow crimped. | 1947-1960 | 3.00 - 5.00 |
| Khaki twill, rolled edge. | 1961-1968 | 0.50 - 1.00 |
| Fully embroidered, cloth back. | 1969-1971 | 1.00 - 3.00 |
| Fully embroidered, plastic back. | 1972 | 0.50 - 1.00 |

## Swimming

| | | |
|---|---|---|
| Cut square. | 1911-1933 | 3.00 - 7.50 |
| Tan, wide crimped. | 1934-1935 | 3.00 - 7.50 |

| | | |
|---|---|---|
| Tan rough twill, narrow crimped. | 1936-1942 | 3.00 - 7.50 |
| Tan fine twill, narrow crimped. | 1942-1946 | 5.00 - 10.00 |
| Khaki twill, narrow crimped (swim suit and white skin). | 1947-1957 | 3.00 - 5.00 |
| Khaki twill, narrow crimped (Swim trunks and flesh skin). | 1958-1960 | 1.00 - 3.00 |
| Khaki twill, rolled edge. | 1961-1968 | 0.50 - 1.00 |
| Fully embroidered, cloth back, silver border. | 1969-1971 | 1.00 - 3.00 |
| Fully embroidered, plastic back, silver border. | 1972 | 0.50 - 1.00 |

## Taxidermy
| | | |
|---|---|---|
| Cut square. | 1912-1933 | 100.00-175.00 |
| Tan, wide crimped. | 1934-1935 | 60.00 - 90.00 |
| Tan rough twill, narrow crimped. | 1936-1942 | 60.00 - 90.00 |
| Tan fine twill, narrow crimped. | 1942-1946 | 100.00-150.00 |
| Khaki twill, narrow crimped. | 1947-1953 | 100.00-175.00 |

## Textiles
| | | |
|---|---|---|
| Cut square. | 1924-1933 | 60.00 - 80.00 |
| Tan, wide crimped. | 1934-1935 | 25.00 - 40.00 |
| Tan rough twill, narrow crimped. | 1936-1942 | 7.50 - 15.00 |
| Tan fine twill, narrow crimped. | 1942-1946 | 20.00 - 30.00 |
| Khaki twill, narrow crimped. | 1947-1960 | 5.00 - 10.00 |
| Khaki twill, rolled edge. | 1961-1968 | 0.50 - 1.00 |
| Fully embroidered, cloth back. | 1969-1971 | 1.00 - 3.00 |
| Fully embroidered, plastic back. | 1972 | 0.50 - 1.00 |

## Theater
| | | |
|---|---|---|
| Fully embroidered, plastic back. | 1972 | 0.50 - 1.00 |

## Traffic Safety
| | | |
|---|---|---|
| Fully embroidered, plastic back. | 1972-1992 | 0.50 - 1.00 |
| Computer stitched, bagged. | 1993 | 0.50 - 1.00 |

## Truck Transportation
| | | |
|---|---|---|
| Fully embroidered, plastic back. | 1972 | 0.50 - 1.00 |

## Veterinary Science/Veterinary Medicine
| | | |
|---|---|---|
| Fully embroidered, plastic back. | 1972 | 0.50 - 1.00 |

## Water Skiing
| | | |
|---|---|---|
| Fully embroidered, cloth back. | 1969-1971 | 1.00 - 3.00 |
| Fully embroidered, plastic back. | 1972 | 0.50 - 1.00 |

## Weather
| | | |
|---|---|---|
| Cut square (comet). | 1927-1929 | 200.00-275.00 |
| Cut square (weather vane). | 1929-1933 | 80.00-100.00 |
| Tan, wide crimped. | 1934-1935 | 20.00 - 30.00 |
| Tan rough twill, narrow crimped. | 1936-1942 | 7.50 - 15.00 |
| Tan fine twill, narrow crimped. | 1942-1946 | 15.00 - 25.00 |
| Khaki twill, narrow crimped. | 1947-1960 | 3.00 - 5.00 |
| Khaki twill, rolled edge. | 1961-1968 | 0.50 - 1.00 |

| | | |
|---|---|---|
| Fully embroidered, cloth back. | 1969-1971 | 1.00 - 3.00 |
| Fully embroidered, plastic back. | 1972 | 0.50 - 1.00 |

## Whitewater
| | | |
|---|---|---|
| Fully embroidered, plastic back, black border (error). | 1988 | 0.50 - 1.00 |
| Fully embroidered, plastic back, green border. | 1988-1992 | 0.50 - 1.00 |
| Computer stitched, bagged. | 1993 | 0.50 - 1.00 |

## Wilderness Survival
| | | |
|---|---|---|
| Fully embroidered, plastic back. | 1972 | 0.50 - 1.00 |

## Wildlife Management/Fish & Wildlife Management
| | | |
|---|---|---|
| Khaki twill, narrow crimped. | 1952-1960 | 3.00 - 5.00 |
| Fully embroidered, cloth back. | 1961-1971 | 1.00 - 3.00 |
| Fully embroidered, plastic back. | 1972 | 0.50 - 1.00 |

## Wireless
| | | |
|---|---|---|
| Cut square. | 1919-1933 | 75.00-125.00 |

## Wood Carving
| | | |
|---|---|---|
| Cut square. | 1928-1933 | 3.00 - 7.50 |
| Tan, wide crimped. | 1934-1935 | 7.50 - 12.50 |
| Tan rough twill, narrow crimped. | 1936-1942 | 3.00 - 7.50 |
| Tan fine twill, narrow crimped. | 1942-1946 | 5.00 - 10.00 |
| Khaki twill, narrow crimped. | 1947-1960 | 1.00 - 3.00 |
| Khaki twill, rolled edge. | 1961-1968 | 0.50 - 1.00 |
| Fully embroidered, cloth back. | 1969-1971 | 1.00 - 3.00 |
| Fully embroidered, plastic back. | 1972 | 0.50 - 1.00 |

## Wood Turning
| | | |
|---|---|---|
| Cut square. | 1930-1933 | 60.00 - 90.00 |
| Tan, wide crimped. | 1934-1935 | 30.00 - 40.00 |
| Tan rough twill, narrow crimped. | 1936-1942 | 12.50 - 20.00 |
| Tan fine twill, narrow crimped. | 1942-1946 | 25.00 - 40.00 |
| Khaki twill, narrow crimped. | 1947-1952 | 3.00 - 5.00 |

## Woodwork
| | | |
|---|---|---|
| Cut square. | 1928-1933 | 3.00 - 7.50 |
| Tan, wide crimped. | 1934-1935 | 5.00 - 10.00 |
| Tan rough twill, narrow crimped. | 1936-1942 | 3.00 - 7.50 |
| Tan fine twill, narrow crimped. | 1942-1946 | 5.00 - 10.00 |
| Khaki twill, narrow crimped. | 1947-1952 | 3.00 - 5.00 |
| Khaki twill, narrow crimped (plane). | 1953-1960 | 3.00 - 5.00 |
| Khaki twill, rolled edge. | 1961-1968 | 0.50 - 1.00 |
| Khaki twill, rolled edge. | 1961-1968 | 1.00 - 3.00 |
| Fully embroidered, cloth back. | 1969-1971 | 1.00 - 3.00 |
| Fully embroidered, plastic back. | 1972 | 0.50 - 1.00 |

## World Brotherhood
| | | |
|---|---|---|
| Khaki twill, narrow crimped. | 1952-1960 | 3.00 - 5.00 |
| Fully embroidered, cloth back (world map). | 1961-1968 | 1.00 - 3.00 |

| | | |
|---|---|---|
| Fully embroidered, cloth back (scout sign). | 1969-1971 | 1.00 - 3.00 |
| Fully embroidered, plastic back. | 1972 | 0.50 - 1.00 |

## Zoology

| | | |
|---|---|---|
| Cut square. | 1930-1933 | 125.00-175.00 |
| Tan, wide crimped. | 1934-1935 | 30.00 - 40.00 |
| Tan rough twill, narrow crimped. | 1936-1942 | 10.00 - 20.00 |
| Tan fine twill, narrow crimped. | 1942-1946 | 12.50 - 20.00 |
| Khaki twill, narrow crimped. | 1947-1960 | 5.00 - 10.00 |
| Khaki twill, rolled edge. | 1961-1968 | 0.50 - 1.00 |
| Fully embroidered, cloth back. | 1969-1971 | 1.00 - 3.00 |
| Fully embroidered, plastic back. | 1972 | 0.50 - 1.00 |

# PINBACK BUTTONS

### 1st Bar None
| | | |
|---|---|---|
| FDL outline. 5/8". Fold tab. | 1950-1960 | 4.00 - 6.00 |

### 66th National Encampment G.A.R.
| | | |
|---|---|---|
| Scout facing in campaign hat. | 1931 | 20.00 - 25.00 |

### Anniversary Week, Feb. 7-13
| | | |
|---|---|---|
| Scout bust facing. 7/8". | 1930 | 5.00 - 10.00 |

### Be Prepared
| | | |
|---|---|---|
| On red-white-blue background. 1/2". | 1950-1965 | 5.00 - 7.50 |

### Ben Alexander Says
| | | |
|---|---|---|
| Scott of the Scouts, a Rayart Serial Play. Scout saluting. 7/8". | 1915-1925 | 20.00 - 25.00 |

### Better Uniforming
| | | |
|---|---|---|
| Count on me. FDL. 1-3/16". | 1972 | 2.00 - 3.00 |
| Try it - you'll like it. FDL. 1-3/16". | 1972 | 2.00 - 3.00 |

### Boston Garden Scout Capades
| | | |
|---|---|---|
| Changeable image. 2-1/2". | 1960 | 10.00 - 15.00 |

### Boy Scout Guide
| | | |
|---|---|---|
| First Class emblem. 1-3/4". | 1935-1945 | 10.00 - 15.00 |

### Boy Scout Hosiery
| | | |
|---|---|---|
| Scout kneeling w/ staff looking r. 3/4". | 1915-1920 | 20.00 - 25.00 |

### Boy Scout Jamboree
| | | |
|---|---|---|
| 1-1/4". | 1953 | 3.00 - 5.00 |
| On red-white-blue background, ribbons below. 1-1/4". | 1950 | 10.00 - 15.00 |
| On red-white-blue background. 1-3/4". | 1950 | 10.00 - 15.00 |

### Boy Scout Round Up
| | | |
|---|---|---|
| First Class. Bronco rider. 1-1/4". | 1928 | 10.00 - 15.00 |
| Second Class. Bronco rider. 1-1/4". | 1928 | 10.00 - 15.00 |

### Boy Scout Week
| | | |
|---|---|---|
| June 8-14. Scout stg. saluting. 7/8". | 1915-1925 | 10.00 - 15.00 |

### Boy Scout
| | | |
|---|---|---|
| Scout standing w/ morse signal flags. 1-1/8" shield-shaped fold tab. | 1915-1925 | 25.00 - 35.00 |

### Boy Scouts Anniversary, 1921
| | | |
|---|---|---|
| Ribbon below. 1-1/4". | 1921 | 25.00 - 30.00 |

### Boy Scouts of America 100% Duty
| | | |
|---|---|---|
| 100% Duty 1 Month. Tenderfoot emblem. 7/8". | 1940 | 5.00 - 10.00 |

### Boy Scouts of America 100% Duty
| | | |
|---|---|---|
| tenderfoot emblem. 7/8". | 1940 | 5.00 - 10.00 |

### Boy Scouts of America 25th Anniversary, 1910-1935
| | | |
|---|---|---|
| Scout bugling, Washington D.C. view in distance. 1-1/4". | 1935 | 20.00 - 30.00 |

### Boy Scouts of America, 1936
| | | |
|---|---|---|
| Half-length view of scout stg. r. w/ campaign hat. 1-1/4". | 1936 | 15.00 - 20.00 |

### Boy Scouts of America
| | | |
|---|---|---|
| Red-white-blue background. 1-1/4". | 1950-1960 | 3.00 - 5.00 |
| Red-white-blue background. 1-3/4". | 1950-1960 | 7.50 - 10.00 |

## Boy's Life Fish Derby
Warden. 1-1/2" star-shaped fold tab.    1940-1955    7.50 - 10.00

## Branded 1000 New Scouts
Cowboy on horse w/ lasso.    1935    10.00 - 15.00

## BSA EXPO
1968, I'm on the go!. Road Runner. 2".    1968    3.00 - 5.00

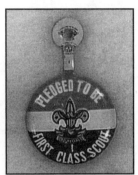

## BSA
Campaign Worker. Tenderfoot emblem in ctr.
  Red-white-blue background. 7/8".    1950-1965    5.00 - 7.50
Campaign Worker. Tenderfoot emblem in ctr.
  Red-white-blue background.
  7/8" w/ fold tab.    1960-1965    2.00 - 4.00
Friend of Scouting.Tenderfoot emblem in ctr.
  Red-white-blue background.
  7/8" w/ fold tab.    1960-1965    2.00 - 4.00
I Gave. (3 letter thicknesses) Tenderfoot
  emblem above. Red-white-blue
  background. 7/8".    1950-1965    5.00 - 7.50
I'll be Invested. Tenderfoot emblem above.
  Red-white-blue background. 7/8".    1950-1965    5.00 - 7.50
I've Invested in Scouting. Tenderfoot
  emblem below. Red-white-blue
  background. 7/8".    1950-1965    5.00 - 7.50
Pledged to be First Class Scout.
  First Class emblem in ctr.
  Red-white-blue background.
  7/8" w/ fold tab.    1960-1965    2.00 - 4.00
Support Scouting. Tenderfoot emblem in ctr.
  Red-white-blue background. 7/8".    1950-1965    5.00 - 7.50
We're Backing Boy Scouts. Tenderfoot
  emblem in ctr. Red-white-blue
  background. 7/8" w/ fold tab.    1960-1965    2.00 - 4.00

We're Backing Boy Scouts. Tenderfoot
  emblem in ctr. Red-white-blue
  background. 7/8".    1950-1965    5.00 - 7.50

## BSA
Aide. 2-1/2".    1960    3.00 - 5.00
Clear w/ slide in name slot. 2-1/2".    1960    3.00 - 5.00
Committee. 2-1/2".    1960    3.00 - 5.00
Director. 2-1/2".    1960    3.00 - 5.00
Judge. 2-1/2".    1960    3.00 - 5.00
Official. 2-1/2".    1960    3.00 - 5.00
Orderly. 2-1/2".    1960    3.00 - 5.00
Participant. 2-1/2".    1960    3.00 - 5.00
Reception. 2-1/2".    1960    3.00 - 5.00
Usher. 2-1/2".    1960    3.00 - 5.00
White space for name to be written. 2-1/2".    1960    3.00 - 5.00

## Bucks County Council
Scouting Booster. 2-1/4".    1936    10.00 - 15.00

## Camden County Boy Scouts
Scout saluting. 7/8".    1920    15.00 - 20.00

## Camp Brereton
St. Louis Council. 2".    1955    7.50 - 10.00
St. Louis Council. 2".    1942    10.00 - 15.00

## Camp Ki-Shau-Wau
First Class emblem. 1".                    1940-1950  10.00 - 15.00

## Camp Migration of '37
B.S.A. and Arrowhead. 1-1/4".        1937       15.00 - 20.00

## Camp Rush of '36
B.S.A. and nugget. 1-1/4".              1936       15.00 - 20.00
Wagon Boss, B.S.A. and nugget. 1-1/4".   1936    20.00 - 25.00

## Catch the Scouting Spirit
                                                 1985        1.00 - 2.00

## Central States Exposition
Scout Service. 2-3/4 x 1-3/4 oval.     1923       20.00 - 25.00
Scout Service. 2-3/4 x 1-3/4 oval.     1924       20.00 - 25.00

## Chicago Boy Scout Camps
Paul Bunyan's Crew. Paul and the
    blue ox. 1-1/4".                             1935       15.00 - 20.00
Paul Bunyan's Crew, Crew Boss. 1-1/4".   1935    15.00 - 20.00
Indian head l. Wrangler. 1-1/4" w/ top
    bar. Fold tab.                              1950-1960  5.00 - 7.50
I'm going to camp. Pine Tree. 7/8".        1933     5.00 - 10.00

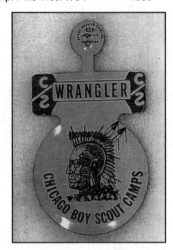

## Court of Honor, Decatur Area No. 121
Advancement. 1-1/4".                   1940-1946  10.00 - 15.00

## Dad Scout
Dan Beard seated talking w/ scout.
    1-1/2".                                     1935-1945  20.00 - 25.00

## Fire Brigade
Fireman's helmet. 1".                  1952-1953  7.50 - 10.00

## GIVE
Boy Scouts of America. Tenderfoot emblem.
    1-1/4".                                     1950-1955  5.00 - 7.50

## Go To Scout Camp
Silhouette of 2 scouts at campfire, scout facing
    as ghost image above. 1-1/4".         1940-1950  10.00 - 15.00

## Golden Jubilee Scout Fair
May 18-19, 1969. 1".                              1968        2.00 - 3.00

## Good Turns for Goodwill
Good Willy character. Zane Trace Council.
2-1/2".                                           1975        2.00 - 4.00

## Heading for the Scouting Exposition
Cartoon Indian Boy. May 17-19,
1956. 2-1/4".                                     1956        5.00 - 7.50

## I am a Scouter
Tenderfoot badge. On red-white-blue,
7/8".                                 1940-1946   5.00 - 7.50

## I Gave
Full length scout walking forward.
1/2 x 1-1/2". Fold tab.              1955-1965    5.00 - 7.50
Tenderfoot emblem in circle. 7/8". Fold tab.   1965-1975   3.00 - 4.00
Tenderfoot emblem. 3/4 x 1". Fold tab.         1965-1975   2.00 - 3.00

## I passed the buck
Liberty Head Dollar. 1-1/4".          1957        12.50 - 17.50

## I Roped One
Cowboy on horse w/ lasso. 1-1/4".     1935        10.00 - 15.00

## I Swing
Troop 1, Lewisboro (NY). 2".          1985        5.00 - 7.50

## I will be at the Scout Camp this Summer
1-1/4".                               1930-1940   7.50 - 12.50

## I'll be invested
At the Scout Circus. 7/8".            1935        5.00 - 7.50
At Scout Camps. 7/8".                 1935        5.00 - 7.50
Boy Scouts of America. Tenderfoot emblem.
1-1/4".                               1940-1946   5.00 - 10.00

## I'm a '49er, B.S.A.
7/8".                                 1949        4.00 - 7.50

## I'm a Camper
Scout by tent and campfire. 7/8".     1940-1946   4.00 - 6.00
Scout by tent and campfire. 1-1/4".   1940-1946   5.00 - 10.00

## I'm a Clean Water Scout
7/8".                                 1970        3.00 - 5.00

## I'm Selling Scouting
Cub, Explorer, and Boy Scout. 1-1/4 x 1-3/4".
Fold tab.                             1950-1965   5.00 - 7.50

## I've Got Mine for '49
S.L.C., B.S.A. Tenderfoot emblem. 7/8".    1949        5.00 - 7.50

## Iver Johnson Boy Scout Bicycle
7/8".    1915-1925  15.00 - 20.00

## Liberty Bell
BSA I'm Joining. 3/4 x 1". Fold tab.    1950-1960   5.00 - 7.50
BSA Pledged. 3/4 x 1". Fold tab.    1950-1960   5.00 - 7.50
I Recruited One BSA. 3/4 x 1". Fold tab.    1950-1960   5.00 - 7.50

## Linen Clad Scout Stocking
    1915-1920  10.00 - 15.00

## Maverick
Bucking calf BSA as brand. 3 background
    color varieties. 1-1/4".    1935        10.00 - 15.00

## Memorial Auditorium
Changeable image. 2-1/2".    1957        10.00 - 15.00

## Merit Badge Exposition
Participant. 1-1/4".    1940-1950   5.00 - 10.00

## National Jamboree, 1935
Scout on horseback.    1935        25.00 - 40.00
Show Me. Scout on horseback. Capitol and
    Washington Monument. 1-1/4".    1935        15.00 - 20.00

## National Jamboree, 1937
I'm Going. Jamboree logo.    1937        15.00 - 25.00

## National Jamboree, 1950
Valley Forge.    1950        15.00 - 20.00
Valley Forge. Red-white-blue background.
    1-1/4".    1950        7.50 - 12.50

## National Jamboree, 1953
I'm Going. Jamboree logo.    1953        15.00 - 20.00
On to the Pacific. tenderfoot emblem.
    1-1/4".    1953        7.50 - 12.50

## National Jamboree, 1957
Boy Scouts Jamboree. White background.
    1-3/4".    1957        7.50 - 12.50

## National Jamboree, 1973
Fishing permit.    1973        5.00 - 7.50
Jamboree '73, B.S.A. 1".    1973        2.00 - 3.00

## National Jamboree, 1977
Orienteering.    1977        2.00 - 3.00

## National Jamboree, 1981
Archery.    1981        2.00 - 3.00
Rifle Shooting.    1981        2.00 - 3.00

## National Jamboree, 1935
Scout w/ bugle, ribbons below.    1935        35.00 - 50.00

## North Shore Area
Boy Scout Monthly Paper Collection.
    1-3/4".    1941-1945  10.00 - 15.00

## Owasippee Lodge
Camp Promotion Information Center.
    2-1/8".    1966        7.50 - 10.00

## Philmont Training Center
3 Color varieties. 1-1/4".    1955-1990   2.00 - 3.00

## Pledged to be
First Class for Scout Circus. First Class
    emblem. 2 background color
    varieties. 1-1/4".    1935-1940  10.00 - 15.00
First Class Scout. Badge on red-white-blue,
    7/8".    1940-1946   3.00 - 5.00
Second Class for Scout Circus. First Class
    emblem. 2 background color
    varieties. 1-1/4".    1935-1940  10.00 - 15.00

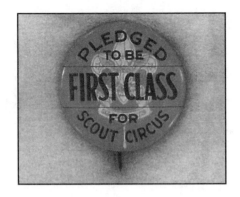

Second Class Scout. Badge on red-white-blue,
7/8".                                   1940-1946   3.00 - 5.00
Tenderfoot Scout. Badge on red-white-blue,
7/8".                                   1940-1946   3.00 - 5.00

## Pledged to pass
Merit Badge Tests for the Scout Circus.
First Class emblem. 2 background color
varieties. 1-1/4".                      1935-1940  10.00 - 15.00
Merit Badge Tests for the Scout Rodeo.
First Class emblem. 2 background color
varieties. 1-1/4".                      1935-1940  10.00 - 15.00
Merit Badge Tests. Tenderfoot badge on
red-white-blue, 7/8".                   1940-1946   3.00 - 5.00

## President W.W. Head Acorn Award
                                        1920-1930  10.00 - 15.00

## Presidential Inauguration, Boy Scout Usher
Brass tag, ribbon below.     1961    75.00-100.00
Brass tag, ribbon below.     1965    75.00-100.00

## Project S.O.A.R.
1-3/4".                      1971     2.00 - 4.00

## Rainbow Council Camp Development Campaign
Scout facing in overseas cap. 2-1/4".  1960-1970   5.00 - 7.50

## Raise a Billion $
Changeable image. 2-1/2".    1969    10.00 - 15.00

## Region Seven Camp Conference
Aurora, Il. Jan. 22-23, 1924. 2-1/8".      1924      20.00 - 25.00

## Region Seven, B.S.A.
Scout signaling, Map w/ WI, IL, IN, MI.
2 x 2-3/4" vertical oval.       1925       30.00 - 40.00

## Roosevelt Pilgrimage
12th. 1-1/4".      1931    10.00 - 15.00
13th. 1-1/4".      1932    10.00 - 15.00
14th. 1-1/4".      1933    10.00 - 15.00
15th. 1-1/4".      1934    10.00 - 15.00
16th. 1-1/4".      1935    10.00 - 15.00
17th. 1-1/4".      1936    10.00 - 15.00
18th. 1-1/4".      1937    10.00 - 15.00
19th. 1-1/4".      1938    10.00 - 15.00
20th. 1-1/4".      1939    10.00 - 15.00
21st. 1-1/4".      1940    10.00 - 15.00
22nd. 1-1/4".      1941    10.00 - 15.00
23rd. 1-1/4".      1942    10.00 - 15.00
24th. 1-1/4".      1943    10.00 - 15.00
25th. 1-1/4".      1944    10.00 - 15.00
26th. 1-1/4".      1945    10.00 - 15.00
27th. 1-1/4".      1946    10.00 - 15.00
28th. 1-1/4".      1947    10.00 - 15.00

Roosevelt Pilgrimage Pinbacks from Sagamore Hill visits.

## Round-Up BSA

| | | |
|---|---|---|
| Cowhand. 1-1/2" star-shaped fold tab. | 1940-1955 | 7.50 - 10.00 |
| I Roped One. 1-1/2" star-shaped fold tab. | 1940-1955 | 7.50 - 10.00 |
| Maverick. 1-1/2" star-shaped fold tab. | 1940-1955 | 7.50 - 10.00 |
| Rancher. 1-1/2" star-shaped fold tab. | 1940-1955 | 7.50 - 10.00 |
| Range Rider. 1-1/2" star-shaped fold tab. | 1940-1955 | 7.50 - 10.00 |

## Round-Up

| | | |
|---|---|---|
| Recruiter. Tenderfoot emblem. 7/8". | 1940-1950 | 7.50 - 10.00 |

## Round-Up, 1948

| | | |
|---|---|---|
| Cowboy on bucking bronco. 1-1/4". | 1948 | 10.00 - 15.00 |

## Round-Up, 1951

| | | |
|---|---|---|
| Cowboy on bucking bronco. 1-1/4". | 1951 | 10.00 - 15.00 |

## Schuylkill County 6th Annual Boy Scout Meet, September 3, 1928

| | | |
|---|---|---|
| Scouts signaling as on handbook cover. | | |
| 1-3/4" multicolored. | 1928 | 25.00 - 35.00 |

## Scout Air Derby

| | | |
|---|---|---|
| 2 Merit Badges. Helicopter. 1-1/4". | 1945-1955 | 7.50 - 12.50 |
| First Class. 5planes in formation | | |
| in clouds. 1-1/4". | 1945-1955 | 7.50 - 12.50 |
| Parachute Jump. 1-1/4". | 1945-1955 | 7.50 - 12.50 |
| Second Class. Racing Plane and finish tower. | | |
| 1-1/4". | 1945-1955 | 7.50 - 12.50 |
| Solo Flight. Plane in clouds. 1-1/4". | 1945-1955 | 7.50 - 12.50 |

## Scout Air Race

| | | |
|---|---|---|
| First Class. 5 planes in formation in clouds. | | |
| 1-1/4". | 1945-1955 | 7.50 - 12.50 |

## Scout Circus

| | | |
|---|---|---|
| Official. Clown. 1-3/4". | 1945-1955 | 10.00 - 15.00 |

## Scout Circus, Cotton Bowl

| | | |
|---|---|---|
| Clown. May 18, 1951. 1-1/4". | 1951 | 10.00 - 15.00 |

## Scout Facing

| | | |
|---|---|---|
| I'll be Invested at the Scout Circus. | | |
| 1-1/4". | 1930-1940 | 10.00 - 15.00 |
| In campaign hat. On blue background. | | |
| 7/8". | 1923-1930 | 5.00 - 7.50 |
| In campaign hat. On blue background. | | |
| Boy Scouts of America 1924 legend. | | |
| 7/8". | 1924 | 10.00 - 15.00 |
| In campaign hat. On blue background. | | |
| Boy Scouts of America 1925 legend. | | |
| 7/8". | 1925 | 10.00 - 15.00 |
| In campaign hat. On blue background. | | |
| Boy Scouts of America 1926 legend. | | |
| 7/8". | 1926 | 10.00 - 15.00 |
| In campaign hat. On blue background. | | |
| Boy Scouts of America legend. 7/8". | 1923-1930 | 5.00 - 7.50 |
| In campaign hat. On blue background. | | |
| Do a Good Turn Daily legend. 7/8". | 1923-1930 | 5.00 - 7.50 |
| In campaign hat. Red-white-blue | | |
| background. 1-1/4". | 1940-1946 | 10.00 - 15.00 |
| Recruit Boy Scouts. 3/4". | 1930-1940 | 10.00 - 15.00 |
| In campaign hat. On red-white-blue | | |
| background. 7/8". | 1940-1946 | 3.00 - 5.00 |
| In overseas cap. On red-white-blue | | |
| background. 7/8". | 1955 | 5.00 - 7.50 |

## Scout Police
2 ribbons below. 7/8".                          1930-1945  10.00 - 15.00

## Scout Profile left
On dark blue background. 7/8".                   1940-1946  5.00 - 7.50
On dark blue background. 1-1/4"                  1940-1946  5.00 - 10.00

## Scout Smiling
Anniversary Week, Feb. 7-13. 7/8".               1920-1930  10.00 - 15.00
Davis Scout Contest. 7/8".                       1920-1930  10.00 - 15.00

## Scout-o-Rama
Investiture Scout. Tenderfoot emblem.
7/8".                                            1948       7.50 - 12.50

## SCOUTS
Half length figure facing. 11/16".               1930-1945  4.00 - 6.00

## Tenderfoot Badge
On red-white-blue background, 3/4".              1940-1946  3.00 - 5.00
On blue background. 5/8".                        1940-1946  5.00 - 7.50

## Tenderfoot emblem and Girl Scout emblem
Feather between. 1".                             1945       7.50 - 10.00

## The Boy Scouts Flag
U.S. Flag. 3/4".                                 1915-1925  10.00 - 15.00

## Troop 31, Hollywood
Historic Trails. Covered wagon. 7/8".     1968        5.00 - 7.50

## Troop Achievement Campaign
Advancement Coup. Feather. 7/8".          1930-1935  10.00 - 15.00
Membership Coup. Feather. 7/8".           1930-1935  10.00 - 15.00

## Wali-Ga-Zhu
Blue Earth. First Class emblem. 1-1/2".   1935       15.00 - 20.00

## We Helped Build our Camps
Camp cabin and sign. 1-1/4".              1940-1950  10.00 - 15.00

# MEDALLIONS

Medallions (tokens) saw their initial use in 1910 with the Excelsior Shoe issues (great advertising!). Groups have used a small pocket piece for various events ever since. They have been extensively cataloged by Rudy Dioszegi in his book *Scouting Exonumia Worldwide*. Second Edition. 1993. The references in this listing come from Dioszegi's book.

## Excelsior Shoe Co.

| | | | |
|---|---|---|---|
| Inverted 1st quote, 2 reins, SCOUT, 12mm date, Co. 4 stars. 33mm, brass. | 1910 | Dio.1910.1A1 | 8.00 - 15.00 |
| Inverted 1st quote, 2 reins, SCOUT, 14mm date, Co. 12mm date, Co. 4 stars. 33mm, brass. | 1910 | Dio.1910.1A2 | 15.00 - 25.00 |
| Inverted 1st quote, 3 reins, SCOUTS, 14mm date, Co. 13mm date, Co. 4 stars. 33mm, brass. | 1910 | Dio.1910.1B1 | 8.00 - 15.00 |
| Inverted 1st quote, 3 reins, SCOUTS, 14mm date, Co. 13mm date, 4 stars. 33mm, brass. | 1910 | Dio.1910.1B2 | 8.00 - 15.00 |
| Inverted 1st quotes, 3 reins, SCOUTS, 15mm date, 4 stars. 33mm, brass. | 1910 | Dio.1910.1B3 | 15.00 - 25.00 |
| Inverted 1st quotes, 3 reins, SCOUTS, 12mm date, 4 stars. 33mm, brass. | 1910 | Dio.1910.1B4 | 8.00 - 15.00 |
| Reversed 1st quotes, 3 reins, SCOUTS, 14mm date, Co. 5 stars. 33mm, brass. | 1910 | Dio.1910.1C | 8.00 - 15.00 |
| Normal quotes, 3 reins, SCOUTS, 13mm date, Co. 5 stars. 33mm, brass. | 1910 | Dio.1910.1D | 15.00 - 25.00 |
| Reversed 1st quote, 3 reins, SCOUTS, 13mm date, Co. 5 stars. 33mm, brass. | 1910 | Dio.1910.1E | 10.00 - 17.50 |
| Reversed 1st quote, 3 reins, SCOUTS, 13mm date, Co. 5 stars. 33mm, brass, thin planchet. | 1910 | Dio.1910.1E1 | 10.00 - 17.00 |

| | | | |
|---|---|---|---|
| Inverted 1st quote, 3 reins, SCOUTS, 12mm date, Co. 5 stars. 33mm, brass. | 1910 | Dio.1910.1F | 8.00 - 15.00 |
| Inverted 1st quote, 3 reins, SCOUTS, 14mm date, Co. 5 stars. 33mm, brass. | 1910 | Dio.1910.1G | 10.00 - 17.50 |
| Inverted 1st quote, 4 stars, 3 reins, SCOUT, 13mm date. 33mm, brass. | 1910 | Dio.1910.2A | 15.00 - 25.00 |
| Inverted 1st quote, 4 stars, 3 reins, SCOUTS, 13mm date. 33mm, brass. | 1910 | Dio.1910.2A1 | 8.00 - 15.00 |
| Normal quotes, 4 stars, 2 reins, SCOUTS, 13mm date. 33mm, brass. | 1910 | Dio.1910.2B | 8.00 - 15.00 |
| Normal quotes, 4 stars, 2 reins, SCOUTS, 15mm date. 33mm, brass. | 1910 | Dio.1910.2B1 | 8.00 - 15.00 |
| Normal quotes, 4 stars, 2 reins, SCOUTS, 15mm date. 33mm, copper. | 1910 | Dio.1910.2B2 | 15.00 - 25.00 |
| Normal quotes, 4 stars, 3 reins, SCOUTS, 15mm date. 33mm, copper. | 1910 | Dio.1910.2C | 8.00 - 15.00 |
| Reversed 1st quote, 5 stars, 3 reins, SCOUTS, 13mm date. 33mm, brass. | 1910 | Dio.1910.2D | 8.00 - 15.00 |
| Normal quotes, 4 stars, 3 reins, SCOUTS, 13mm date. 33mm, brass. | 1910 | Dio.1910.2E | 8.00 - 15.00 |
| Normal quotes, 4 stars, 2 reins, SCOUTS, 13mm date, no maker's name. 33mm, brass. | 1910 | Dio.1910.2E1 | 8.00 - 15.00 |
| Inverted 1st quote, 4 stars, 2 reins, SCOUTS, 13mm date. No reins on right side from hand to horse. 33mm, brass. | 1910 | Dio.1910.2F | 10.00 - 17.50 |
| Inverted 1st quote, 4 stars, 2 reins, SCOUTS, 13mm date. 33mm, brass. | 1910 | Dio.1910.2F1 | 10.00 - 17.50 |
| Normal quotes, 5 stars, 3 reins, SCOUTS, 13mm date. 33mm, copper. | 1910 | Dio.1910.2G | 10.00 - 17.50 |
| Normal quotes, 5 stars, 3 reins, SCOUTS, 13mm date, no maker's name. 33mm, brass. | 1910 | Dio.1910.2H | 15.00 - 25.00 |
| Inverted 1st quote, 5 stars, 3 reins, SCOUTS, 13mm date. 33mm, copper. | 1910 | Dio.1910.2I | 15.00 - 25.00 |
| Inverted 1st quote, 5 stars, 2 reins, SCOUT, 12mm date. 33mm, brass. | 1910 | Dio.1910.2J | 15.00 - 25.00 |
| Normal quote, 4 stars, SCOUT, 13mm date. 33mm, brass. | 1910 | Dio.1910.2K | 10.00 - 17.50 |
| Normal quotes, 2 star, w/ per. 15mm maker. 33mm, brass. | 1910 | Dio.1910.3A | 8.00 - 15.00 |
| Normal quotes, 2 star, w/ per. 15mm maker. Co. as ligature. 33mm, brass. | 1910 | Dio.1910.3A1 | 15.00 - 25.00 |
| Normal quotes, 2 star, w/ per. 15mm maker. Co. as ligature. 33mm, sterling silver. | 1910 | Dio.1910.3B | 8.00 - 15.00 |
| Normal quote, 2 stars, w/ per. 18mm name. 33mm, brass. | 1910 | Dio.1910.3C | 8.00 - 15.00 |
| Normal quotes, 2 stars, w/o per., 18mm name. 33mm, brass. | 1910 | Dio.1910.3C1 | 8.00 - 15.00 |
| Normal quotes, 2 star, w/o per., 18mm name. 33mm, brass. | 1910 | Dio.1910.3C2 | 8.00 - 15.00 |
| Inverted 1st quote, 2 star, w/o per., 18mm name. 33mm, brass. | 1910 | Dio.1910.3D | 8.00 - 15.00 |
| Inverted 2nd quote, 21mm name. 33mm, brass. | 1910 | Dio.1910.3E | 8.00 - 15.00 |
| Inverted 2nd quote, 2 stars, w/o per., 18mm name. 33mm, brass. | 1910 | Dio.1910.3E1 | 8.00 - 15.00 |
| Normal quote, w/o per., 18mm name. 33mm, brass. | 1910 | Dio.1910.3F | 35.00 - 50.00 |
| Normal quote, w/o per., no name. 33mm, copper. | 1910 | Dio.1910.3G | 10.00 - 17.50 |
| Normal quote, 2 star, w/o per., 18mm name. 33mm, copper. | 1910 | Dio.1910.3G1 | 15.00 - 25.00 |
| Inverted 1st quote, no name. 33mm, copper. | 1910 | Dio.1910.3H | 15.00 - 25.00 |
| Reversed 1st quote, no maker's name. 33mm, brass. | 1910 | Dio.1910.3I | 15.00 - 25.00 |
| Inverted 1st quote, 3 stars, w/o per., 18mm name. 33mm, brass. | 1910 | Dio.1910.3J | 15.00 - 25.00 |
| Inverted 1st quote, 3 stars, w/o per., 14mm maker. 33mm, brass. | 1910 | Dio.1910.3K | 15.00 - 25.00 |
| Normal quotes, 2 star, w/ per., 16mm maker. 33mm, brass. | 1910 | Dio.1910.3L | 10.00 - 17.50 |
| Inverted 2nd quote, 2 stars, w/o per., 15mm maker. 33mm, brass. | 1910 | Dio.1910.3M | 10.00 - 17.50 |
| Inverted 2nd quote, 3 stars, w/o per., 18mm maker. 33mm, brass. | 1910 | Dio.1910.3N | 10.00 - 17.50 |
| No quotes, w/ per., 14mm maker. 33mm, brass. | 1910 | Dio.1910.3O | 15.00 - 25.00 |
| No quotes, 2 star, w/o per., 14mm maker. 33mm, brass. | 1910 | Dio.1910.3O1 | 15.00 - 25.00 |

| | | | |
|---|---|---|---|
| Inverted 2nd quote, 3 star, w/o per., 14mm maker. No reins from hand to horse. 33mm, brass. | 1910 | Dio.1910.3P | 15.00 - 25.00 |
| Indian Scout, maker as Whitehead & Hoag. 33mm, brass. | 1910 | Dio.1910.4A | 15.00 - 25.00 |
| Indian Scout, maker as Schwaab. 33mm, brass. | 1910 | Dio.1910.4B | 15.00 - 25.00 |
| Normal quotes, 5 stars, 3 reins, no date, SCOUTS. Maker: SCHWAAB MILWAUKEE in straight line. 33mm, brass. | 1910 | Dio.1910.5A | 10.00 - 17.50 |
| Same as 5a but 33mm and made of copper. | 1910 | Dio.1910.5B | 15.00 - 25.00 |
| Same as 5a but 33mm and made of nickel. | 1910 | Dio.1910.5C | 20.00 - 30.00 |
| Legend reads: The Original Boy Scouts Army Shoe - Munson Last. Normal quotes, 5 stars, 3 reins. Reverse is seal. 33mm, brass. | 1910 | Dio.1910.6A | 10.00 - 17.50 |
| Legend reads: The Original Boy Scouts Army Shoe - Munson Last. Normal quotes, 5 stars, 3 reins. Reverse is seal. 33mm, gilt brass. | 1910 | Dio.1910.6B | 15.00 - 25.00 |
| Obverse same as Type 3 but w/ grass clumps under horse. No beading on rim. 33mm, brass. | 1910 | Dio.1910.7A | 8.00 - 15.00 |
| Obverse same as Type 3 but w/ grass clumps under horse. Beading on obverse rim. 33mm, brass. | 1910 | Dio.1910.7B | 10.00 - 17.50 |
| Obverse same as Type 6, reverse same as Type 2. 33mm, brass. | 1910 | Dio.1910.8 | 15.00 - 25.00 |
| Obverse same as Type 2, less date, reverse same as Type 4. 33mm, brass. | 1910 | Dio.1910.9 | 15.00 - 25.00 |

## Boy Scout Standing w/ staff, holed

| | | | |
|---|---|---|---|
| 32mm, bronze. | 1913 | Dio.1913.1 | 25.00 - 40.00 |

## Every Scout to Save a Soldier/ Weapons for Liberty

| | | | |
|---|---|---|---|
| Kneeling scout holds sword to standing and flag-draped Liberty. 28mm, gold, uniface. | 1917 | Dio.1917.1A | 1,500.00 - 2,000.00 |
| Kneeling scout holds sword to standing and flag-draped Liberty. 28mm, silver, uniface. | 1917 | Dio.1917.1B | 750.00 - 1,000.00 |
| Kneeling scout holds sword to standing and flag-draped Liberty. 28mm, bronze, uniface. | 1917 | Dio.1917.1C | 250.00 - 400.00 |

## Rotary Club, Morris, IL

| | | | |
|---|---|---|---|
| Good Turn Token. Lincoln bust right. 31mm, copper. | 1920 | Dio.1920.1 | 30.00 - 50.00 |

## Boy Scouts, Niagara Falls, NY

| | | | |
|---|---|---|---|
| 32mm, aluminum. | 1923 | Dio.1923.1 | 30.00 - 50.00 |

## Milwaukee Boy Scouts Father and Son Banquet

| | | | |
|---|---|---|---|
| 32mm, bronze, 4 finishes. | 1924 | Dio.1924.1A-D | 30.00 - 50.00 |
| 32mm, copper, 2 finishes. | 1924 | Dio.1924.1E-F | 30.00 - 50.00 |
| 32mm, brass, 2 finishes. | 1924 | Dio.1924.1G-I | 30.00 - 50.00 |
| 32mm, oriode. | 1924 | Dio.1924.1J | 60.00 - 80.00 |
| 32mm, aluminum. | 1924 | Dio.1924.1K | 60.00 - 80.00 |
| 32mm, copper-nickel. | 1924 | Dio.1924.1L | 60.00 - 80.00 |
| 32mm, lead. | 1924 | Dio.1924.1M | 60.00 - 80.00 |

## Boy Scouts of Dallas, TX

| | | | |
|---|---|---|---|
| Service at the Confederate reunion. 36mm, aluminum. | 1925 | Dio.1925.1 | 100.00 - 150.00 |

## Abraham Lincoln Council, IL

| | | | |
|---|---|---|---|
| Lincoln Trail hike. 31mm, bronze. | 1926 | Dio.1926.1 | 30.00 - 50.00 |

## Camp Gifford, Omaha and Covered Wagon Councils

| | | | |
|---|---|---|---|
| Good for 1 cent in trade. 20mm, aluminum. | 1926 | Dio.1926.2 | 20.00 - 30.00 |

Good for 5 cents in trade.
  20mm, aluminum.     1926     Dio.1926.3     20.00 - 30.00

## Kansas City, MO, First National Camporee, Honor Camper

30mm, brass.     1933     Dio.1933.1     60.00 - 80.00

## Salt Lake Council

Do a good turn daily. Steer's skull.
  26mm, brass.     1935     Dio.1935.1     30.00 - 50.00

## Owasippi Scout Camps, Chicago Council

GF 1 cent in merchandise.
  18mm, aluminum.     1936     Dio.1936.1     15.00 - 22.50
GF 5 cents in merchandise.
  20mm, aluminum.     1936     Dio.1936.2     15.00 - 22.50
GF 10 cents in merchandise.
  22mm, aluminum.     1936     Dio.1936.3     15.00 - 22.50
GF 25 cents in merchandise.
  26mm, aluminum.     1936     Dio.1936.4     15.00 - 22.50
GF 5 cents in merchandise.
  20mm, brass.     1936     Dio.1936.5     15.00 - 22.50

## Piase Bird Council, National Scout Jamboree

25mm, brass.     1937     Dio.1937.1     20.00 - 30.00

## Troop 2, Wilkinsburg, PA. 25th Anniv.

36mm, white metal.     1937     Dio.1937.2     30.00 - 50.00

## Manitowoc County Council, National Scout Jamboree

Encased cent.
  35mm, aluminum.     1937     Dio.1937.3     5.00 - 10.00

## Silver Lake Scout Booster, 1937

Encased cent.
  34mm, aluminum.     1937     Dio.1937.4     5.00 - 10.00

## Troop 87, Stroudsburg, PA, Monroe County, the playground of America

58mm, white metal.     1937     Dio.1937.5     10.00 - 17.50

## Gifford Runyon, Troop 17, Anderson, IN

25mm.     1937     Dio.1937.6     15.00 - 25.00

## Nassau County Council, National Scout Jamboree

22mm, copper.     1937     Dio.1937.7     20.00 - 30.00

## Sachem Council, Waltham, watch face, 1937 Jamboree

40mm.     1937     Dio.1937.8     20.00 - 30.00

## World's Fair Greetings, Scout saluting w/ trilon and perispher in background

Elongated Lincoln cent, Indian cent,
  large cent, two-cent piece,
  and various foreign coins
  and tokens.     1939     Dio.1939.1a-1f  20.00 - 35.00
Elongated 1940
  Lincoln cent.     1940     Dio.1940.1     20.00 - 35.00

## Boyce Memorial, Ottawa, IL, Starved Rock Council

39mm, brass.     1941     Dio.1941.1     10.00 - 17.50

## Treasure Island Adventure, District 9

28mm, brass.     1946     Dio.1946.1     20.00 - 30.00

## Treasure Island Adventure, District 8

28mm, brass.     1946     Dio.1946.2     20.00 - 30.00

## Treasure Island Adventure, District 4

28mm, brass.     1946     Dio.1946.3     20.00 - 30.00

## Sauk Paul Bunyan Days

65mm, aluminum.     1949     Dio.1949.1     15.00 - 25.00

## Mysterious Island, District 8

30mm, brass.     1949     Dio.1949.2     15.00 - 25.00

## Region 9, B.S.A. encased Buffalo nickel

39mm, aluminum.          1949      Dio.1949.3      50.00 - 80.00

## National Scout Jamboree

Valley Forge, Official Medal. Washington kneeling.
   Reverse w/ "Hallowed ground" text.
   36mm, bronze.      1950      Dio.1950.1      5.00 - 10.00
Texas Traders, Concho Valley Council.
   Washington kneeling, Texas map
   and bronco rider. 32mm,
   aluminum.          1950      Dio.1950.2      15.00 - 25.00
Bay Shore Council,
   General Electric River Works,
   Lynn, MA. 48mm,
   copper painted red.   1950      Dio.1950.3      15.00 - 25.00
Cleveland Council.,
   Firestone Tire Company.
   65mm, steel,
   2 large holes.      1950      Dio.1950.4      15.00 - 25.00
Bruder Dairy, Cleveland OH.
   Good luck piece.
   32mm, aluminum.      1950      Dio.1950.5      10.00 - 17.50
Camden County Council, NJ.
   Hires Root Beer. 30mm,
   aluminum.          1950      Dio.1950.7      10.00 - 17.50
Washington kneeling,
   scout badge reverse.
   25mm, bronze.      1950      Dio.1950.7      10.00 - 17.50
Troop 33, Pleasant Valley, NY.
   38mm, bronze.      1950      Dio.1950.9      15.00 - 25.00
Badger Council, Kewaskum, WI.
   Lucky Wamoum. 40mm,
   aluminum.          1950      Dio.1950.12     10.00 - 17.50

## Alpha Phi Omega, 25th Anniversary National Convention

28mm, silver.          1950      Dio.1950.6      15.00 - 25.00

## Dodge City Land Rush, District 4, Detroit, MI

33mm, aluminum.          1950      Dio.1950.10     15.00 - 25.00

## Freedom Foundation Get out the Vote Campaign

32mm, silvered plastic.   1952      Dio.1952.1a     2.00-5.00
32mm, golden plastic      1952      Dio.1952.1b     15.00 - 25.00

## Youth of the Scouting World, Society of Medallists issue #46

Eagle breaking chains. Reverse scouts signaling and receiving. 72mm,
   silver.            1952      Dio.1952.2a     150.00 - 200.00
   bronze.            1952      Dio.1952.2b     75.00 - 100.00

Karl Gruppe designed this medal issued by the Society of Medalists to honor scouting.

## Troop 75 Boy Scout Fair

22mm, copper.          1952      Dio.1952.3      10.00 - 17.50

## National Scout Jamboree

Official Medal. Covered Wagon,
   "Forward on Liberty's
   Team" legend. 36mm,
   bronze.            1953      Dio.1953.1      10.00 - 17.50

Region 4, Ohio Sesquicentennial.
   33mm, aluminum.   1953   Dio.1953.2   15.00 - 25.00
Plymouth Auto.
   31mm, bronze.   1953   Dio.1953.3   15.00 - 25.00
Akron Area Council, OH.
   33mm, bronze.   1953   Dio.1953.5   15.00 - 25.00

## Douglas Aircraft, Tenderfoot emblem

51mm, aluminum,
   9mm thick.   1953   Dio.1953.10   15.00 - 25.00

## Boy Scout Jamboree, Los Angeles, CA

Bronco rider. 44mm,
   aluminum.   1953   Dio.1953.4   15.00 - 25.00

## Church of Jesus Christ of Later Day Saints, 40th Anniversary in Scouting

Eagle and Silver Award recognition.
   30mm, pewter.   1953   Dio.1953.6   20.00 - 30.00

## Harvey S. Firestone Award

Scout w/ sapling, town view
   in background. 89mm,
   bronze.   1953   Dio.1953.7   60.00 - 80.00

## Circle B Round-up

36mm, bronze.   1953   Dio.1953.8   15.00 - 25.00

## National Scout Jamboree, Troop 21, Quivera Council, Wichita, KS

70mm, painted aluminum.   1953   Dio.1953.9   10.00 - 15.00

## BSA Fall Round-up

Cabin. Reverse eagle's nest.
   37mm, bronze.   1954   Dio.1954.1   15.00 - 25.00

## Scouting Exposition, Troop 108

40mm, steel.   1954   Dio.1954.2   15.00 - 25.00

## Scouts of Greenville, SC, 9th Annual Camporee

16mm, bronze.   1955   Dio.1955.1   15.00 - 25.00

## San Gabriel Valley Council, CA

I joined 1955; Circus, May 21.
   32mm, aluminum.   1955   Dio.1955.2   15.00 - 25.00

## Detroit Area Council, MI

Governor's Recognition
   Day.   1955   Dio.1955.3   15.00 - 25.00

## John R. Donnell Award, Region 4

Silvered medal set into
   lucite block.   1956   Dio.1956.3   20.00 - 30.00

## National Scout Jamboree

Valley Forge, PA. Official Medal.
   Washington kneeling,
   "Hallowed Ground" text.
   37mm, bronze.   1957   Dio.1957.1   8.00 - 15.00
Scout Tower at Valley Forge.
   32mm, bronze.   1957   Dio.1957.2   10.00 - 17.50
Lucky Penny. 74mm, copper-
   plated pot metal.   1957   Dio.1957.3   15.00 - 25.00
Different die than Official
   Medal, uniface.
   39mm, nickel.   1957   Dio.1957.5   10.00 - 17.50
Lucky Nickel. 74mm,
   nickel-plated pot metal.   1957   Dio.1957.6   15.00 - 25.00
Pennsylvania Railroad
   Good Luck piece.
   34mm, aluminum.   1957   Dio.1957.7   20.00 - 30.00

## Greater Cleveland Council, OH, Baden Powell Centennial Round-up

36mm, golden brass.   1957   Dio.1957.4   8.00 - 15.00

## Safety Good Turn. Set in lucite

47mm, green enameled steel.1958   Dio.1958.1   20.00 - 30.00
50mm, black enameled steel.1958   Dio.1958.3   20.00 - 30.00

## Troop 12, Burbank, CA, Hawaiian Adventure Souvenir

33mm, bronze.   1958   Dio.1958.2   15.00 - 25.00

## Circle 10, BSA

32mm, white plastic.   1959   Dio.1959.1   10.00 - 15.00

## Nassau Camporee, '59, (Nassau County Council, NY?)

43mm, aluminum.   1959   Dio.1959.2   15.00 - 25.00

## National Scout Jamboree, Troop 126, Kewaunee, WI

35mm, aluminum.   1960   Dio.1960.10   10.00 - 17.50

## 50th Anniversary of BSA Founding, Washington D.C.

Scout statue and First Class badge.
   39mm, silver.   1960   Dio.1960.11   20.00 - 30.00

## Rocky Mountain Council, CO, Scout Olympics

105mm, cast pot metal.   1960   Dio.1960.12   10.00 - 17.50

## BSA 50th Anniversary Official Token

For God and Country design.
   Reverse w/ Scout Oath.
   26mm, bronze.   1960   Dio.1960.1a   2.00 - 5.00

For God and Country design.
Reverse w/ Scout Oath.
26mm, gilt bronze.    1960    Dio.1960.1b-c 20.00 - 30.00
For God and Country design.
Reverse w/ Scout Oath.
26mm, chrome-plated,
holed.    1960    Dio.1960.1d    3.00 - 8.00

## BSA 50th Anniversary Medal
For God and Country legend.
Reverse w/ Scout Oath
on plaque within wreath.
63mm, bronze.    1960    Dio.1960.2a-b 10.00 - 17.50

## BSA, unofficial 50th Anniversary Medal
Scout standing. Reverse
First Class badge in rays.
30mm, silver. 7,500 minted
and distributed in
numbered envelopes.    1960    Dio.1960.3a    25.00 - 35.00
Scout standing. Reverse
First Class badge in rays.
30mm, gold. 50 minted and
distributed in
numbered envelopes.    1960    Dio.1960.3b 250.00 - 350.00

## National Scout Jamboree
Official Medal.
36mm, bronze.    1960    Dio.1960.4    3.00 - 8.00
Troop 107, Erie PA.
Copper.    1960    Dio.1960.5    15.00 - 25.00
Tom Charlier, Kewaunee, WI.
Encased cent.
33mm, aluminum.    1960    Dio.1960.7    2.00 - 5.00
Piasa Bird Council, Alton, IL.
51 x 35mm oval, copper. 1960    Dio.1960.9    15.00 - 25.00

## Boy Scouts of America, 1960
Encased cent.
33mm, aluminum.    1960    Dio.1960.6    2.00 - 5.00

## OA Area 7F Conference
Scout badge and arrow.
90mm, bronze.    1960    Dio.1960.8    15.00 - 25.00

## Region Eleven, Exploring Conference, Reed College, Portland, OR
28mm, bronze.    1961    Dio.1961.1    15.00 - 25.00

## Greater New York Council Scouting Exposition
26 x 18mm oval, bronze.    1961    Dio.1961.2    15.00 - 25.00

## Camp Sequassen, Quinnipiac Council, International Camporee
36mm, bronze.    1962    Dio.1962.1    10.00 - 17.50

## Camp Salmem, Slidell, LA, New Orleans Area Council
38mm, bronze.    1963    Dio.1963.1a    5.00 - 10.00
39mm, antiqued silver.    1963    Dio.1963.1b    10.00 - 17.50
39mm, .999 fine silver.    1963    Dio.1963.1c    50.00 - 70.00

## Tenderfoot Emblem stamped into Lincoln cent
Copper. Counterstamp
done much later.    1963    Dio.1963.2    0.50 - 1.00

## AMF Explorer Fitness Program
I passed the Fitness Tests.
39mm, oxidized bronze. 1964    Dio.1964.10    2.00 - 5.00

## National Scout Jamboree
BSA, Kewaunee, WI.
Encased cent. 36mm,
aluminum.    1964    Dio.1964.11    2.00 - 5.00
Valley Forge. Patch design
enamelled, set into lucite.
Staff Service.    1964    Dio.1964.13    15.00 - 25.00

## National Elected Explorer Delegate Conference
36mm, oxidized
silvered bronze.    1964    Dio.1964.14    8.00 - 15.00

## Strengthening America's Heritage, Scout sign partially encircled by stars
Scout Oath on reverse.
65mm, bronze.    1964    Dio.1964.15    8.00 - 15.00

## National Scout Jamboree
Valley Forge, Official Medal.
Washington kneeling.
Reverse w/ Liberty Bell,
log cabin, and arch.
36mm, oxidized bronze. 1964    Dio.1964.1a    3.00 - 8.00
Valley Forge, Official Medal.
36mm, oxidized silver.    1964    Dio.1964.1b    5.00 - 10.00
Continental Dollar copy.
39mm, aluminum.    1964    Dio.1964.2    2.00 - 5.00
Region XI, Bunker Hill Co.
Kellogg, ID.
57mm, cast pot metal.    1964    Dio.1964.3    8.00 - 15.00

## Wonderful World of Scouting, NY World's Fair
35mm, bronze.    1964    Dio.1964.4    2.00 - 5.00

## AMF Explorer Fitness Program
I played Dick Weber. 39mm,
oxidized bronze.    1964    Dio.1964.5    2.00 - 5.00
I beat Dick Weber. 39mm,
oxidized bronze.    1964    Dio.1964.6    5.00 - 10.00

| | | | |
|---|---|---|---|
| I played Ben Hogan. 39mm, oxidized bronze. | 1964 | Dio.1964.7 | 2.00 - 5.00 |
| I beat Ben Hogan. 39mm, oxidized bronze. | 1964 | Dio.1964.8 | 5.00 - 10.00 |
| I qualified for Swim Tests. 39mm, oxidized bronze. | 1964 | Dio.1964.9 | 2.00 - 5.00 |

## Circle Ten Council, TX, Scout Circus

| | | | |
|---|---|---|---|
| 36mm, aluminum. | 1965 | Dio.1965.1 | 8.00 - 15.00 |

## XII World Jamboree, Idaho, USA

| | | | |
|---|---|---|---|
| Scout sign between 2 hemispheres. 35mm, bronze. | 1967 | Dio.1967.1 | 3.00 - 5.00 |

## XII World Jamboree, Idaho, USA

| | | | |
|---|---|---|---|
| 6 scouts marching. 39mm, bronze. | 1967 | Dio.1967.2a | 8.00 - 15.00 |
| 6 scouts marching. 39mm, oxidized bronze. | 1967 | Dio.1967.2b | 8.00 - 15.00 |
| 6 scouts marching. 39mm, oxidized silvered bronze. | 1967 | Dio.1967.2c | 10.00 - 17.50 |
| 6 scouts marching. 39mm, .999 fine silver. | 1967 | Dio.1967.2d | 20.00 - 30.00 |
| Region Eleven Friendship Medal. 35mm, white metal. | 1967 | Dio.1967.3 | 8.00 - 15.00 |
| I am Indian Tea. White plastic. | 1967 | Dio.1967.4 | 8.00 - 15.00 |
| Trans-Atlantic Council, BSA. Heidelberg, Germany. 36mm, bronze. | 1967 | Dio.1967.5 | 10.00 - 15.00 |

## Camp Alexander, Colorado Springs, CO, July 1967, One Fare

| | | | |
|---|---|---|---|
| 24mm, brass. | 1967 | Dio.1967.6 | 2.00 - 5.00 |

## Nassau County Council, NY

| | | | |
|---|---|---|---|
| Teddy Roosevelt face. 45mm, bronzed pot metal, uniface. | 1967 | Dio.1967.7 | 10.00 - 17.50 |

## BSA National Meeting, Pittsburgh, PA

| | | | |
|---|---|---|---|
| US Steel Co. logo. 51mm, steel. | 1967 | Dio.1967.9 | 2.00 - 5.00 |

## Pike's Peak Council, CO, Region 8 Annual Meeting

| | | | |
|---|---|---|---|
| Elongated cent. | 1967 | Dio.1967.10 | 3.00 - 8.00 |
| Elongated dime. | 1967 | Dio.1967.11 | 8.00 - 15.00 |
| Set of elongated cent, nickel, dime, quarter, and half dollar. | 1967 | Dio.1967.12 | 50.00 - 70.00 |

## NOAC, Maka Ina Lodge #350

| | | | |
|---|---|---|---|
| Arrow Head. 44 x 35mm uniface, nickel. | 1967 | Dio.1967.14 | 5.00 - 10.00 |

## BSA, Official Pocket Piece, Scout Law, Scout Oath

| | | | |
|---|---|---|---|
| 39mm, bronze. | 1968 | Dio.1968.1 | 2.00 - 5.00 |

## BSA, Pedro, Good Luck

| | | | |
|---|---|---|---|
| 38mm, bronze. | 1968 | Dio.1968.2 | 2.00 - 5.00 |

## Los Angeles Area Council, CA, Scout-o-Rama

| | | | |
|---|---|---|---|
| 39mm, aluminum. | 1968 | Dio.1968.3 | 5.00 - 10.00 |

## Lewis-Clark Trail Project

| | | | |
|---|---|---|---|
| 35mm, bronze. | 1968 | Dio.1968.9 | 15.00 - 25.00 |

## Chief Green's 20th Anniversary in Scouting, Greater Cleveland Council

| | | | |
|---|---|---|---|
| 32mm, aluminum. | 1968 | Dio.1968.10 | 10.00 - 17.50 |

## National Scout Jamboree

| | | | |
|---|---|---|---|
| Official Medal. Deer, Map of Idaho reverse. 34mm, bronze. | 1969 | Dio.1969.1a | 2.00 - 5.00 |
| 34mm, oxidized silvered bronze. | 1969 | Dio.1969.1b | 3.00 - 8.00 |
| Troop 10, Peninsula Council, VA. 39mm, aluminum, golden color. | 1969 | Dio.1969.3 | 8.00 - 15.00 |
| Troop 70, Mount Rainier Council, WA. 34mm, bronze. | 1969 | Dio.1969.4 | 8.00 - 15.00 |
| Great Northern Railway. 34mm, bronze. | 1969 | Dio.1969.5 | 5.00 - 10.00 |
| Kaiser Aluminum Co. 39mm, aluminum. | 1969 | Dio.1969.6 | 10.00 - 17.50 |
| Washington Wheat Growers Assoc. 36mm, aluminum. | 1969 | Dio.1969.7 | 8.00 - 15.00 |
| Troop 13, Riverside County Council, CA. 34mm, cast pot metal. | 1969 | Dio.1969.8 | 10.00 - 17.50 |
| Troop 13, Riverside County Council, CA. 49mm, cast pot metal. | 1969 | Dio.1969.9 | 10.00 - 17.50 |
| Cleve Coeur Council, IL. 30mm, golden plastic. | 1969 | Dio.1969.17 | 3.00 - 8.00 |

## Calumet Council, IL-IN

| | | | |
|---|---|---|---|
| Peace pipe on scout badge. 39mm, thin aluminum. | 1969 | Dio.1969.10 | 8.00 - 15.00 |

## National Capital Area Council, Admiral Arleigh Burke, Scouter of the Year

| | | | |
|---|---|---|---|
| 39mm, bronze. | 1969 | Dio.1969.11a | 15.00 - 25.00 |
| 39mm, proof bronze. | 1969 | Dio.1969.11b | 10.00 - 17.50 |
| 39mm, .925 silver. | 1969 | Dio.1969.11c | 20.00 - 30.00 |
| 39mm, 18 kt. gold. | 1969 | Dio.1969.11d | 350.00 - 500.00 |

## Pike's Peak Council, CO, Boy Power Award
39mm, aluminum, golden color. 1969    Dio.1969.12a    10.00 - 17.50
39mm, oxidized copper-nickel. 1969     Dio.1969.12b    15.00 - 25.00

## Alpha Phi Omega, 45th Anniversary National Convention
39mm, aluminum.        1970    Dio.1970.6a    5.00 - 10.00
39mm, .999 fine silver. 1970   Dio.1970.6b    8.00 - 15.00

## 13th World Jamboree, Asagai Heights, Nippon, US Contingent
32mm, bronze.          1971    Dio.1971.1a    1.00 - 3.00
32mm, .925 silver.     1971    Dio.1971.1b    20.00 - 30.00

## 13th World Jamboree, Washington Trail Council, PA
35mm, aluminum.        1971    Dio.1971.2     3.00 - 8.00

## 13th World Jamboree, New Orleans Council, LA
39mm, aluminum.        1971    Dio.1971.3a    8.00 - 15.00
39mm, aluminum, colored purple.    1971    Dio.1971.3b    2.00 - 5.00
39mm, aluminum, colored purple, reverse rotated.    1971    Dio.1971.3c    2.00 - 5.00
39mm, bronze.          1971    Dio.1971.3d    10.00 - 17.50
39mm, aluminum, colored blue.    1971    Dio.1971.3e    3.00 - 8.00

## 13th World Jamboree, Philadelphia and Lancaster Councils, PA
39mm, aluminum.        1971    Dio.1971.4     5.00 - 10.00

## 13th World Jamboree
Baden Powell elongated cent. Copper.    1971    Dio.1971.5a    1.00 - 3.00
Baden Powell elongated dime. Copper-nickel, clad.    1971    Dio.1971.5b    1.00 - 3.00

## Boypower/Manpower, Scout Oath
38mm, silvered bronze. 1971    Dio.1971.6a    5.00 - 10.00
38mm, bronze.          1971    Dio.1971.6b    2.00 - 5.00

## Boypower/Manpower, Project SOAR
38mm, bronze.          1971    Dio.1971.7     5.00 - 10.00

## Reynolds Aluminum Company Recycling Project
41mm, olive-colored rubber w/ magnet inside.    1971    Dio.1971.8    5.00 - 10.00

## Lancaster County Council Jamboree Participation Award
41mm, aluminum.        1971    Dio.1971.12    1.00 - 2.00

## Region III Annual Meeting, Pittsburgh, PA
52mm, steel.           1971    Dio.1971.13    5.00 - 10.00

## Lost Lake Scout Reservation, Clinton Valley Council, MI
33mm, bronze.          1971    Dio.1971.14    8.00 - 15.00

## 13th World Jamboree, Troop 412, Ohio
37 x 26mm, bronze, uniface. 1971    Dio.1971.15    10.00 - 17.50

## Salvation Army, New Orleans Area Council Scout Good Turn
39mm, aluminum.        1971    Dio.1971.16a    2.00 - 5.00
39mm, aluminum, golden color.    1971    Dio.1971.16b    2.00 - 5.00

## Blackhawk Council, IL, U.S. Grant Sesquicentennial
44mm, bronze.          1972    Dio.1972.14    8.00 - 15.00

## Salvation Army, New Orleans Area Council, LA, Scout Good Turn
39mm, aluminum.        1972    Dio.1972.19a    2.00 - 5.00
39mm, aluminum, golden color.    1972    Dio.1972.19b    2.00 - 5.00

## Boypower/Manpower, elongated cent
Copper.                1972    Dio.1972.20    2.00 - 5.00

## Spirit of Scouting, Franklin Mint
A Scout is Trustworthy. 39mm, .925 silver.    1972    Dio.1972.1    15.00 - 25.00
A Scout is Loyal. 39mm, .925 silver.    1972    Dio.1972.2    15.00 - 25.00
A Scout is Helpful. 39mm, .925 silver.    1972    Dio.1972.3    15.00 - 25.00
A Scout is Friendly. 39mm, .925 silver.    1972    Dio.1972.4    15.00 - 25.00
A Scout is Courteous. 39mm, .925 silver.    1972    Dio.1972.5    15.00 - 25.00
A Scout is Kind. 39mm, .925 silver.    1972    Dio.1972.6    15.00 - 25.00
A Scout is Obedient. 39mm, .925 silver.    1972    Dio.1972.7    15.00 - 25.00
A Scout is Cheerful. 39mm, .925 silver.    1972    Dio.1972.8    15.00 - 25.00
A Scout is Thrifty. 39mm, .925 silver.    1972    Dio.1972.9    15.00 - 25.00
A Scout is Brave. 39mm, .925 silver.    1972    Dio.1972.10    15.00 - 25.00

A Scout is Clean. 39mm,
.925 silver.         1972     Dio.1972.11    15.00 - 25.00
A Scout is Reverent. 39mm,
.925 silver.         1972     Dio.1972.12    15.00 - 25.00

The Franklin Mint issued this set of twelve images of the Scout Law titled Norman Rockwell's Spirit of Scouting.

## National Scout Jamboree, Farragut, ID, Moraine, PA

Official Medal.
39mm, bronze.       1973     Dio.1973.1a    2.00 - 5.00
39mm, oxidized
    silvered bronze. 1973    Dio.1973.1b    3.00 - 8.00
1937 Jamboree/Lincoln
    Memorial.
    Restrike. 39mm, bronze.1973  Dio.1973.2   1.00 - 2.00
1950 Jamboree Medal, large
    kneeling George Washington.
    Restrike. 39mm, bronze.1973  Dio.1973.3   1.00 - 2.00
1953 Jamboree Medal.
Map of California.
    Restrike. 39mm,
    bronze.          1973     Dio.1973.4     1.00 - 2.00
1957 Jamboree Medal.
    Restrike. 39mm, bronze.1973  Dio.1973.5   1.00 - 2.00
1960 Jamboree Medal.
    Restrike. 39mm, bronze.1973  Dio.1973.6   1.00 - 2.00
1964 Jamboree Medal.
    Restrike. 39mm, bronze.1973  Dio.1973.7   1.00 - 2.00
1967 Jamboree Medal.
    Restrike. 39mm, bronze.1973  Dio.1973.8   1.00 - 2.00

## 1973 National Jamboree, Longs Peak Council, Cheyenne, WY, Troop 101

39mm, bronze.       1973     Dio.1973.10a   5.00 - 10.00
39mm, .999 fine silver.  1973  Dio.1973.10b  20.00 - 30.00

## 1973 National Jamboree East. Troop 44, Brooklyn, CT

47mm, lead.         1973     Dio.1973.11    5.00 - 10.00

## 1973 National Jamboree, Longs Peak Council, WY, Troop 3

39mm, aluminum.     1973     Dio.1973.12    8.00 - 15.00

## Bicentennial Program, GIFT

39mm, bronze.       1973     Dio.1973.13    2.00 - 5.00

Part of a set of ten, the Franklin Mint featured scouting in Norman Rockwell's Fondest Memories.

## Norman Rockwell's Fondest Memories, Franklin Mint

The Big Parade. 2 scouts
    holding American flag.
    50 x 64mm, .925 silver. 1973   Dio.1973.15   25.00 - 40.00

## Salvation Army, New Orleans Area Council, Scout Good Turn

40mm, aluminum.     1973     Dio.1973.17a   2.00 - 5.00
40mm, aluminum,
    golden color.    1973     Dio.1973.17b   2.00 - 5.00

## Tuscarora Council, NC, 50th Anniversary

34mm, copper-nickel.  1973    Dio.1973.18    10.00 - 17.50

## 1973 Jamboree East, Piasa Bird Council, Winchester Western

28mm, bronze.       1973     Dio.1973.19    5.00 - 10.00

## 1973 Jamboree East, Troop 353, Raleigh, NC

34mm, brass.        1973     Dio.1973.20    8.00 - 15.00

## Rockland County Council, NY, 50th Anniversary, Daniel Carter Beard

51mm, bronze.         1974    Dio.1974.1a    10.00 - 17.50
51mm, .925 silver, gilt.  1974  Dio.1974.1b  35.00 - 50.00
51mm, .925 silver.    1974     Dio.1974.1c   20.00 - 30.00

## Scout Oath Series, Wittnauer Mint

The Scout Oath, silver.  1974   Dio.1974.1    15.00 - 25.00

| | | | |
|---|---|---|---|
| On My Honor, silver. | 1974 | Dio.1974.2 | 15.00 - 25.00 |
| I Will Do My Best, silver | 1974 | Dio.1974.3 | 15.00 - 25.00 |
| To Do My Duty To God, silver | 1974 | Dio.1974.4 | 15.00 - 25.00 |
| And My Country, silver | 1974 | Dio.1974.5 | 15.00 - 25.00 |
| To Obey The Scout Law, silver | 1974 | Dio.1974.6 | 15.00 - 25.00 |
| To Help Other People At All TImes, silver | 1974 | Dio.1974.7 | 15.00 - 25.00 |
| To Keep Myself Physically Strong, silver | 1974 | Dio.1974.8 | 15.00 - 25.00 |
| Mentally Awake, silver | 1974 | Dio.1974.9 | 15.00 - 25.00 |
| And Morally Straight, silver | 1974 | Dio.1974.10 | 15.00 - 25.00 |
| Be Prepared, silver | 1974 | Dio.1974.11 | 15.00 - 25.00 |
| Do A Good Turn Daily, silver | 1974 | Dio.1974.12 | 15.00 - 25.00 |

## Troop 44, Brooklyn, CT, 25th Anniversary

| | | | |
|---|---|---|---|
| 39mm, bronze. | 1974 | Dio.1974.14 | 5.00 - 10.00 |

## Bicentennial

Be Prepared for Life.

| | | | |
|---|---|---|---|
| 39mm, bronze. | 1974 | Dio.1974.15 | 2.00 - 50.00 |

## Taconic District, Washington Irving Council, NY, Klondike Derby

| | | | |
|---|---|---|---|
| 47mm, aluminum. | 1974 | Dio.1974.16 | 8.00 - 15.00 |

## National Capital Area Council, Gerald R. Ford, Scouter of the Year

| | | | |
|---|---|---|---|
| 40mm, proof bronze. | 1974 | Dio.1974.17a | 15.00 - 25.00 |
| 40mm, proof silver. | 1974 | Dio.1974.17b | 25.00 - 40.00 |
| 40mm, proof 18kt. gold. | 1974 | Dio.1974.17c | 350.00 - 500.00 |

## Salvation Army, New Orleans Area Council, LA, Scout Good Turn

| | | | |
|---|---|---|---|
| 39mm, aluminum. | 1974 | Dio.1974.18a | 2.00 - 5.00 |
| 39mm, aluminum, golden color. | 1974 | Dio.1974.18b | 2.00 - 5.00 |

## 14th World Jamboree, Troop 3-1, LA-TX

| | | | |
|---|---|---|---|
| 40mm, aluminum, purple color. | 1975 | Dio.1975.1a | 2.00 - 5.00 |
| 40mm, aluminum. | 1975 | Dio.1975.1b | 2.00 - 5.00 |

## Bicentennial

Heritage '76.

| | | | |
|---|---|---|---|
| 40mm, bronze. | 1975 | Dio.1975.2 | 2.00 - 5.00 |

Horizons '76.

| | | | |
|---|---|---|---|
| 40mm, bronze. | 1975 | Dio.1975.3 | 2.00 - 5.00 |

Festival USA.

| | | | |
|---|---|---|---|
| 40mm, bronze. | 1975 | Dio.1975.4 | 2.00 - 5.00 |

## 14th World Jamboree, Scouting/USA, Scout Law

| | | | |
|---|---|---|---|
| 31mm, copper-nickel. | 1975 | Dio.1975.5 | 3.00 - 8.00 |

## Nordjamb '75, You Make the Difference

| | | | |
|---|---|---|---|
| 22mm, brass. | 1975 | Dio.1975.6 | 3.00 - 8.00 |

## Nordjamb '75/New Orleans Area Council Pow Wow

| | | | |
|---|---|---|---|
| 39mm, aluminum, golden color. | 1975 | Dio.1975.7a | 2.00 - 5.00 |
| 39mm, aluminum. | 1975 | Dio.1975.7b | 2.00 - 5.00 |
| 39mm, aluminum, purple color. | 1975 | Dio.1975.7c | 2.00 - 5.00 |
| 39mm, aluminum, orange color. | 1975 | Dio.1975.7d | 2.00 - 5.00 |

## Bi-cent-o-rama, Troop 76

| | | | |
|---|---|---|---|
| 50mm, pot metal, uniface. | 1975 | Dio.1975.8 | 5.00 - 10.00 |

## Arch Monson, Jr. President, Boy Scouts of America, Greetings

| | | | |
|---|---|---|---|
| 40mm, aluminum. | 1975 | Dio.1975.10 | 3.00 - 8.00 |

## OA, NE Region Section 4A

| | | | |
|---|---|---|---|
| 51 x 39mm, brass, uniface. | 1975 | Dio.1975.11 | 5.00 - 10.00 |

## Buffalo Trail Council, TX, America's Bicentennial

| | | | |
|---|---|---|---|
| 39mm, oxidized bronze. | 1976 | Dio.1976.1a | 8.00 - 15.00 |
| 39mm, oxidized brass. | 1976 | Dio.1976.1b | 8.00 - 15.00 |
| 39mm, .925 silver. | 1976 | Dio.1976.1c | 25.00 - 40.00 |

## Concho Valley Council, TX, America's Bicentennial

| | | | |
|---|---|---|---|
| 35mm, copper-nickel. | 1976 | Dio.1976.2 | 8.00 - 15.00 |

## Lancaster, PA, Scout Show

| | | | |
|---|---|---|---|
| 40mm, aluminum. | 1976 | Dio.1976.3 | 5.00 - 10.00 |

## Long Rivers Council, Bicentennial Encampment

| | | | |
|---|---|---|---|
| 35mm, bronze. | 1976 | Dio.1976.4 | 5.00 - 10.00 |

## BSA, National Issue, Bicentennial

| | | | |
|---|---|---|---|
| 64mm, bronze. | 1976 | Dio.1976.5 | 8.00 - 15.00 |

## Arrowhead District, Columbus, OH, Bicentennial Camporal

| | | | |
|---|---|---|---|
| 38mm, tan plastic w/ red lettering. | 1976 | Dio.1976.6 | 2.00 - 5.00 |

## Northwest Suburban Council, IL, 50th Anniversary

| | | | |
|---|---|---|---|
| 43mm, pewter, uniface. Exists plain, as a bolo, or mounted on a block. | 1976 | Dio.1976.7 | 8.00 - 15.00 |

## National Scout Jamboree

| | | | |
|---|---|---|---|
| Official Medal. Moraine State Park, PA. 39mm, bronze. | 1977 | Dio.1977.1a | 2.00 - 5.00 |
| 39mm, oxidized copper-nickel. | 1977 | Dio.1977.1b | 3.00 - 8.00 |
| Azimuth Trail. 33mm, green plastic, white letters. | 1977 | Dio.1977.3 | 2.00 - 5.00 |
| We Found It. 33mm, red plastic, white letters. | 1977 | Dio.1977.4 | 2.00 - 5.00 |
| Northeast Region Pontoon Pass George Cuhaj personal token. 38mm, green plastic, white lettering. | 1977 | Dio.1977.7 | 2.00 - 5.00 |
| Blackhawk Area Council, IL-WI. 49mm, stainless steel. | 1977 | Dio.1977.2a | 5.00 - 10.00 |
| 49mm, copper. | 1977 | Dio.1977.2b | 15.00 - 25.00 |

## Order of the Arrow, BSA

| | | | |
|---|---|---|---|
| 43mm, pewter, uniface. Set into a larger medal or plaque. German in origin. | 1977 | Dio.1977.20 | 8.00 - 15.00 |

## Lancaster-Leganon Council, Long Park, June 1978

| | | | |
|---|---|---|---|
| 33mm, aluminum. | 1978 | Dio.1978.1a | 3.00 - 8.00 |
| 33mm, bronze. | 1978 | Dio.1978.1b | 5.00 - 10.00 |

## General Green Council, NC, 1978 Irish Jamboree

| | | | |
|---|---|---|---|
| Copper. | 1978 | Dio.1978.2 | 3.00 - 8.00 |

## National Order of the Arrow Conference, Ft. Collins, CO

| | | | |
|---|---|---|---|
| Founders Day Award. 32mm, brass. | 1979 | Dio.1979.1 | 5.00 - 10.00 |
| I delivered the Promise, 1979. Scout Badge. 36mm, aluminum. | 1979 | Dio.1979.2 | 3.00 - 8.00 |

## Suanhacky Lodge #49

| | | | |
|---|---|---|---|
| Golden Anniversary Banquet. 42mm, red plastic, gold lettering. | 1979 | Dio.1979.3 | 1.00 - 3.00 |

## National Council Meeting, New Orleans, LA

| | | | |
|---|---|---|---|
| 40mm, aluminum. | 1980 | Dio.1980.1 | 3.00 - 8.00 |

## Suanhacky Lodge #49

| | | | |
|---|---|---|---|
| Lodge Banquet. 42mm, white plastic, red lettering. | 1980 | Dio.1980.3 | 1.00 - 3.00 |
| 50th Anniversary Ordeal, Camp Kernochan. 42mm, Black plastic, gold lettering. | 1980 | Dio.1980.4 | 1.00 - 3.00 |

## Lancaster-Lebanon Council, Long's Park

| | | | |
|---|---|---|---|
| Showman Sam. 36mm, aluminum. | 1980 | Dio.1980.5 | 3.00 - 8.00 |

## Eagle Troop 31, Los Altos, CA

| | | | |
|---|---|---|---|
| Good for $1 in trade. 32mm, brass. | 1980 | Dio.1980.6 | 3.00 - 8.00 |

## 1981 National Scout Jamboree

| | | | |
|---|---|---|---|
| Official Medal, Ft. A.P. Hill, VA. 40mm, copper-nickel, reeded edge. | 1981 | Dio.1981.1 | 2.00 - 5.00 |
| 40mm, copper-nickel, reeded edge. Set into a lucite block. | 1981 | Dio.1981.1b | 5.00 - 10.00 |
| 1937 Jamboree Medal. Restrike. 40mm, copper-nickel, reeded edge. | 1981 | Dio.1981.2 | 1.00 - 2.00 |
| 1950 Jamboree Medal. Restrike. 40mm, copper-nickel, reeded edge. | 1981 | Dio.1981.3 | 1.00 - 2.00 |
| 1953 Jamboree Medal. Restrike. 40mm, copper-nickel, reeded edge. | 1981 | Dio.1981.4 | 1.00 - 2.00 |
| 1957 Jamboree Medal. Restrike. 40mm, copper-nickel, reeded edge. | 1981 | Dio.1981.5 | 1.00 - 2.00 |
| 1960 Jamboree Medal. Restrike. 40mm, copper-nickel, reeded edge. | 1981 | Dio.1981.7 | 1.00 - 2.00 |
| 1964 Jamboree Medal. Restrike. 40mm, copper-nickel, reeded edge. | 1981 | Dio.1981.8 | 1.00 - 2.00 |
| 1969 Jamboree Medal. Restrike. 40mm, copper-nickel, reeded edge. | 1981 | Dio.1981.9 | 1.00 - 2.00 |
| 1973 Jamboree Medal. Restrike. 40mm, copper-nickel, reeded edge. | 1981 | Dio.1981.10 | 1.00 - 2.00 |
| 1977 Jamboree Medal. Restrike. 40mm, copper-nickel, reeded edge. | 1981 | Dio.1981.10 | 1.00 - 2.00 |
| Johnny Appleseed Area Council, OH. 33mm, brass. | 1981 | Dio.1981.11 | 3.00 - 8.00 |

Coin Collecting Merit Badge
Midway Booth. Elongated cent.
Copper.           1981      Dio.1981.12    1.00 - 2.00
Coin Collecting Merit Badge
Midway Booth. Elongated.
Issued on nickel, dime,
quarter, half dollar,
and SBA dollar. Clean
design and cancelled die. 1981   Dio.1981.12b-h 5.00 - 10.00
Inland Empire Council, CA.
Troop 701-702.
34mm, brass.      1981      Dio.1981.13    5.00 - 10.00
Santa Clara County, CA.
Silicon chip attached
to ctr. of disc.
32mm, aluminum.   1981      Dio.1981.14    5.00 - 10.00
George H. Lanier
Council, AL-GA.
59mm, aluminum, cast, uniface. 1981   Dio.1981.15   8.00 - 15.00
Scubapro Snorkel
Swimming Award.
31mm, bronze.     1981      Dio.1981.22    3.00 - 8.00
Orange Council, CA,
Troop 5.
37mm, orange plastic,
raised lettering.  1981     Dio.1981.23    3.00 - 8.00
Displays & Exhibits.
50 x 26mm, aluminum,
uniface.          1981      Dio.1981.25    5.00 - 10.00
Inland Empire Council, CA.
Troop 700-701.
34mm, brass.      1981      Dio.1981.26    5.00 - 10.00
East Central Region. Thanks Plaque
74 x 50mm, bronze, uniface.
Set into a lucite block.  1981   Dio.1981.28   10.00 - 17.50

## Order of the Arrow, BSA

Founders of the Order.
40mm, oxidized bronze. 1981   Dio.1981.16a   2.00 - 8.00
Founders of the Order.
40mm, .925 silver.  1981    Dio.1981.16b   20.00 - 30.00
Treasure Island. 40mm,
oxidized bronze.   1981     Dio.1981.17a   3.00 - 8.00
Treasure Island. 40mm,
.925 silver.       1981     Dio.1981.17b   20.00 - 30.00
Early Ceremony. 40mm,
oxidized bronze.   1981     Dio.1981.18a   3.00 - 8.00
Early Ceremony. 40mm,
.925 silver.       1981     Dio.1981.18b   20.00 - 30.00
The Ordeal. 40mm, oxidized
bronze.            1981     Dio.1981.19a   3.00 - 8.00
The Ordeal. 40mm,
.925 silver.       1981     Dio.1981.19b   20.00 - 30.00

## Order of the Arrow, BSA

OA Fireplace, Brotherhood
Barn. 40mm,
oxidized bronze.   1981     Dio.1981.20a   3.00 - 8.00
OA Fireplace, Brotherhood
Barn. 40mm, .925 silver.1981   Dio.1981.20b   20.00 - 30.00

## Suanhacky Lodge #49

Johannes Knoops, Lodge Chief
personal token.
42mm, white plastic,
red lettering.     1981     Dio.1981.21    2.00 - 5.00

## Robert A. Johnson personal token

28mm, green plastic, gold lettering. 1981 Dio.1981.24   1.00 - 3.00

## National Capital Area Council, Ronald Regan, Scouter of the Year

36mm, proof bronze.  1982   Dio.1982.1     15.00 - 20.00

## Johnny Appleseed Council, OH, Catch that Pepsi Spirit

Scout Badge. 38mm,
bronze, cast.      1982     Dio.1982.10    8.00 - 15.00
Large Tenderfoot Badge.
38mm, bronze, cast. 1982    Dio.1982.11    8.00 - 15.00
Large Second Class Badge.
38mm, bronze, cast. 1982    Dio.1982.12    8.00 - 15.00
Large Star Badge. 38mm,
bronze, cast.      1982     Dio.1982.13    8.00 - 15.00
Large Life Badge. 38mm,
bronze, cast.      1982     Dio.1982.15    8.00 - 15.00
Small Tenderfoot Badge.
38mm, bronze, cast. 1982    Dio.1982.15    8.00 - 15.00
Eagle Scout Award. 38mm,
bronze, cast.      1982     Dio.1982.16    8.00 - 15.00
Small Second Class Award.
38mm, bronze, cast. 1982    Dio.1982.17    8.00 - 15.00
Small First Class Badge.
38mm, bronze, cast. 1982    Dio.1982.18    8.00 - 15.00
Small Star Badge. 38mm,
bronze, cast.      1982     Dio.1982.19    8.00 - 15.00

## First Class Badge counterstruck on Lincoln cent

Copper.            1982     Dio.1982.20    1.00 - 2.00

## 75th Anniversary of Scouting, St. George, Enamelled

50mm, brass.       1982     Dio.1982.22    3.00 - 8.00

## Scouting, 75th Anniversary, MD, ATCA

28mm, white plastic,
green lettering.   1982     Dio.1982.3     1.00 - 3.00

## XV World Jamboree, Troop 605

Elongated cent, copper.  1983   Dio.1983.10   1.00 - 3.00

## Suanhacky Lodge #49, NOAC Delegate

42mm, white plastic,
red lettering.     1983     Dio.1983.11    1.00 - 3.00

## Greater New York Councils, NY, Key to Scouting

| | | | |
|---|---|---|---|
| 55 x 85mm, cast pewter, uniface. | 1983 | Dio.1983.12 | 5.00 - 10.00 |

## Order of the Arrow

| | | | |
|---|---|---|---|
| Ordeal, Brotherhood, Vigil. 40mm, oxidized bronze. | 1983 | Dio.1983.1a | 3.00 - 8.00 |
| Ordeal, Brotherhood, Vigil. 40mm, .925 silver. | 1983 | Dio.1983.1b | 20.00 - 30.00 |
| Lenni Lenape. 40mm, oxidized bronze. | 1983 | Dio.1983.2a | 3.00 - 8.00 |
| Lenni Lenape. 40mm, .925 silver. | 1983 | Dio.1983.2b | 20.00 - 30.00 |
| Carroll A. Edson. 40mm, oxidized bronze. | 1983 | Dio.1983.3a | 3.00 - 5.00 |
| Carroll A. Edson. 40mm, .925 silver. | 1983 | Dio.1983.3b | 20.00 - 30.00 |
| Dr. E. Urner Goodman. 40mm, oxidized bronze. | 1983 | Dio.1983.4a | 3.00 - 8.00 |
| Dr. E. Urner Goodman. 40mm, .925 silver. | 1983 | Dio.1983.4b | 20.00 - 30.00 |
| The Legend. 40mm, oxidized bronze. | 1983 | Dio.1983.5a | 3.00 - 5.00 |
| The Legend. 40mm, .925 silver. | 1983 | Dio.1983.5b | 20.00 - 30.00 |

## Bob Johnson, Scouts on Tokens Society #1

| | | | |
|---|---|---|---|
| 42mm, white plastic, green lettering. | 1983 | Dio.1983.6 | 1.00 - 2.00 |

## NOAC 1983, SE Region, Section 7

| | | | |
|---|---|---|---|
| 29mm, red plastic, gold lettering. | 1983 | Dio.1983.7 | 3.00 - 5.00 |

## Scouting, 1907-1983, MATCA, 16 years

| | | | |
|---|---|---|---|
| 28mm, white plastic, green lettering. | 1983 | Dio.1983.8 | 1.00 - 2.00 |

## Robert A. Johnson, scouting personal token

| | | | |
|---|---|---|---|
| 29mm, green plastic, gold lettering. | 1983 | Dio.1983.9 | 1.00 - 2.00 |

## Scouts on Tokens Society, 1st Anniv.

| | | | |
|---|---|---|---|
| 29mm, white plastic, green lettering. | 1984 | Dio.1984.1 | 1.00 - 2.00 |

## Scouts on Tokens Society

| | | | |
|---|---|---|---|
| Scouting 1984. 29mm, white plastic, green lettering. | 1984 | Dio.1984.2 | 1.00 - 2.00 |

## LDS Scout Encampment, Farragut State Park, ID

| | | | |
|---|---|---|---|
| Elongate cent, copper. | 1984 | Dio.1984.3 | 2.00 - 4.00 |

## National Scout Jamboree, Official Medal

| | | | |
|---|---|---|---|
| 38mm, bronze. | 1985 | Dio.1985.1 | 3.00 - 5.00 |

## Diamond Jubilee, 75th Diamond logo

| | | | |
|---|---|---|---|
| 38mm, cast pewter, uniface. Usually found as a bolo. | 1985 | Dio.1985.10 | 2.00 - 5.00 |

## Camp Sunnen, Cahokia Mound Council

| | | | |
|---|---|---|---|
| 38mm, cast pewter, uniface. Usually found as a bolo. | 1985 | Dio.1985.11 | 2.00 - 5.00 |

## 75th Anniversary Diamond Logo

| | | | |
|---|---|---|---|
| reverse a plain wreath and space for engraved plaque. 76mm, bronze. | 1985 | Dio.1985.12 | 2.00 - 5.00 |

## National Jamboree, South Central Region

| | | | |
|---|---|---|---|
| Youth Staff. 38mm, cast pewter, uniface. Usually found as a bolo. | 1985 | Dio.1985.13 | 5.00 - 10.00 |
| Adult Staff. 38mm, cast pewter, uniface. Usually found as a bolo. | 1985 | Dio.1985.14 | 5.00 - 10.00 |
| Youth Leader. 38mm, cast pewter, uniface. Usually found as a bolo. | 1985 | Dio.1985.15 | 5.00 - 10.00 |
| Adult Leader. 38mm, cast pewter, uniface. Usually found as a bolo. | 1985 | Dio.1985.16 | 5.00 - 10.00 |
| National Jamboree, Orange County, CA. Troops 867-868. 33mm, pewter. | 1985 | Dio.1985.17 | 2.00 - 5.00 |
| West Central Florida Council, Troop 15. TUIT. 39mm, tan plastic, red lettering. | 1985 | Dio.1985.18 | 2.00 - 5.00 |
| Fairfield County Council, CT. Troop 402. 38mm, copper. | 1985 | Dio.1985.19a | 5.00 - 7.50 |
| 38mm, copper-nickel. | 1985 | Dio.1985.19b | 2.00 - 5.00 |
| 38mm, copper, 1/2" thick. | 1985 | Dio.1985.19c | 20.00 - 30.00 |

## Displays and Exhibits

| | | | |
|---|---|---|---|
| 50 x 26mm, aluminum. | 1985 | Dio.1985.23 | 3.00 - 5.00 |

## Jamboree emblem, elongated

| | | | |
|---|---|---|---|
| Cent, copper. | 1985 | Dio.1985.25 | 1.00 - 2.00 |

## Daniel Webster Council, NH

| | | | |
|---|---|---|---|
| 40mm, bronze. | 1985 | Dio.1985.3 | 3.00 - 5.00 |

## Coin Collecting Merit Badge Booth, George Cuhaj personal token

| | | | |
|---|---|---|---|
| 42mm, green plastic, gold letting. | 1985 | Dio.1985.5 | 1.00 - 3.00 |

## Piasa Bird Council, IL

27mm, brass.                1985        Dio.1985.6        5.00 - 10.00

## Footsteps of the Founder, World Scouting 75th Anniversary

37mm, cast pewter,
  uniface. Often encountered
  as a bolo.                1985        Dio.1985.2        3.00 - 5.00

## San Bernadino Coin Club, CA, Salutes Scouting, 22nd Annual Coin Show

32mm, aluminum.             1985        Dio.1985.20       2.00 - 5.00

## Los Altos Eagle Troop 31, Good For $1 in Trade, Salutes 75th Anniversary

32mm, brass.                1985        Dio.1985.21       3.00 - 5.00

## 75th Anniversary, National Medal, Pride in the Past, Footsteps of the Future

38mm, bronze.               1985        Dio.1985.22       3.00 - 5.00

## Boy Scout Saluting

Diamond Jubilee logo.
  Engraved by
  Frank Gasparo.            1985        Dio.1985.24       5.00 - 10.00

## Tenderfoot Badge

38mm, cast pewter,
  high relief, uniface.
  Usually found as a bolo. 1985         Dio.1985.7        3.00 - 7.50

## Catch the Scouting Spirit

38mm, cast pewter, uniface.
  Usually found as a bolo. 1985         Dio.1985.8        3.00 - 7.50

## SOAR for the Better Life

38mm, cast pewter, uniface.
  Usually found as a bolo. 1985         Dio.1985.9        3.00 - 5.00

## 95th ANA Convention, Milwaukee, Coin Collecting Merit Badge Clinic

Encased cent in horseshoe case. 1986   Dio.1986.1        2.00 - 5.00

## Orange County Council, CA

Scout Service Center Dedication.
  38mm, bronze.             1986        Dio.1986.2        7.50 - 10.00

## Camp Tuscarora, Susquenango Council, NY, Robert J. Moppert, Rotary

40mm, .999 fine silver.     1986        Dio.1986.3a       20.00 - 30.00
409mm, oxidized bronze.     1986        Dio.1986.3b       8.00 - 15.00
40mm, proof bronze.         1986        Dio.1986.3c       5.00 - 10.00
40mm, aluminum.             1986        Dio.1986.3d       2.00 - 5.00

## Troop 51, 25th Anniversary

34mm, bronze.               1986        Dio.1986.4        2.00 - 5.00

## Baltimore Area Council, MD, elongated cent

Copper.                     1986        Dio.1986.5        1.00 - 2.00

## EL-KU-TA Lodge #520, UT, elongated cent

Copper.                     1986        Dio.1986.6        1.00 - 2.00

## Wood Badge elongated cent

Copper.                     1986        Dio.1986.7        1.00 - 2.00

## Badge Powell elongated cent

Copper.                     1986        Dio.1986.9        1.00 - 2.00

## Piasa Bird Council

32mm, bronze.               1988        Dio.1988.1        2.00 - 5.00

## National Council Meeting, San Diego, CA

28mm, aluminum.             1988        Dio.1988.2        3.00 - 8.00

## NOAC, Founder's Day Award

Kindle the Flame from Within.
  39mm, aluminum.           1988        Dio.1988.3        3.00 - 8.00

## AH TIC Lodge 50th Anniversary

Alpha Sintered Metals, Ridgeway, PA.
  36mm, steel.              1988        Dio.1988.4        2.00 - 5.00

## Philmont 50th Anniversary

Philmont Grace reverse.
  32mm, bronze.             1988        Dio.1988.5        2.00 - 5.00

## Great Salt Lake Council, UT, International Jamboral

38mm, brass, uniface.       1988        Dio.1988.6        2.00 - 5.00
Official Medal.

Space Shuttle and
  Say No to Drugs
  38mm, bronze.             1989        Dio.1989.1        3.00 - 5.00
BSA High Adventure.
Elongated cent, copper.     1989        Dio.1989.2        1.00 - 2.00
Troop 817.
37mm, black plastic,
  raised letters.           1989        Dio.1989.3        3.00 - 8.00
National Jamboree,
  Displays and Exhibits.
50 x 26mm, aluminum.        1989        Dio.1989.6        3.00 - 8.00

## National Top hands Conference, Orlando, FL, High Adventure
Elongate Cent, copper.    1989    Dio.1989.4    1.00 - 2.00

## Blackhawk Area Council, 1989 Camporee
39mm, aluminum, uniface. 1989    Dio.1989.5    2.00 - 4.00

## Florida Sea Base
High Adventure.
  Elongated cent, copper. 1989    Dio.1989.7    1.00 - 2.00
10th Anniversary.
  29mm, .999 fine silver.  1990    Dio.1990.1    20.00 - 30.00

## Robert E. Lee Council, VA
Appalachian Trail
  elongated cent.
  Copper.    1990    Dio.1990.1    1.00 - 2.00

## Scout Oath elongated cent
Copper.    1990    Dio.1990.2    1.00 - 2.00

## Scout Law elongated cent
Copper.    1990    Dio.1990.3    1.00 - 2.00

## Scout Motto and Slogan elongated cent
Copper.    1990    Dio.1990.4    1.00 - 2.00
Ceremony Competition
  Award Benefactor.
Cast bronze.    1990    Dio.1990.5    100.00 - 150.00
George Cuhaj personal
  token & Vigil name.
42mm, white plastic, red lettering. 1990 Dio.1990.6    2.00 - 5.00
  Founder's Day Medal. Inspired
  to Lead, Dedicated to Serve.
39mm, aluminum.    1990    Dio.1990.9    3.00 - 8.00

## Wood Badge Beads elongated cent
Copper.    1990    Dio.1990.7    1.00 - 2.00

## Great Salt Lake Council, UT, Heritage Jamboral
22mm, gilt brass.    1990    Dio.1990.8    3.00 - 8.00

## Jack Kohler Campership Association, Outstanding Scouter Award of Excellence
57mm, cast bronze, artist proof. 1990    Dio.1990.10  100.00 - 150.00

## Great Salt Lake Council, UT, Heritage Jamboral
38mm, oxidized brass.    1990    Dio.1990.11    2.00 - 5.00

## Baden Powell elongated cent
Copper.    1990    Dio.1990.12    1.00 - 2.00

## WOODBADGE words elongated cent
Copper.    1990    Dio.1990.13    1.00 - 2.00

## Wood Badge axe and log elongated cent
Copper.    1990    Dio.1990.14    1.00 - 2.00

## Motto and Slogan elongated cent, RR maker
Copper.    1990    Dio.1990.15    1.00 - 2.00

## Robert E. Lee Council, VA, Appalachian Trail elongated nickel, dime, quarter, and SBA dollar
1991    Dio.1991.2-5    5.00 - 7.50

## National Top Hands, Nashville, TN
Philmont Arrowhead
  patch on elongated cent.
  Copper.    1991    Dio.1991.6    1.00 - 2.00
Florida Sea Base design
  on elongated cent.
  Copper.    1991    Dio.1991.7    1.00 - 2.00
C.L. Sommers design on
  elongated cent.
  Copper.    1991    Dio.1991.8    1.00 - 2.00

## BSA High Adventure Outdoor Program Seminar, Dallas, TX
Elongated cent, copper.    1991    Dio.1991.9    1.00 - 2.00

## National Top Hands Conference, FB maker
Elongated cent, copper.    1992    Dio.1992.1    1.00 - 2.00

## West Michigan Shore Council, MI, Scouting Rally
Elongated cent, copper.    1992    Dio.1992.2    1.00 - 2.00

## Great Salt Lake Council, UT, Jamboral
22mm, gilt brass.    1992    Dio.1992.3    3.00 - 8.00
22mm, gilt brass.    1992    Dio.1992.4    3.00 - 8.00

## Boy Scout, Motto and Slogan Medal
37mm, bronze.    1992    Dio.1992.7    1.00 - 2.00
National Ceremony
  Events Staff Medal.
  Cast bronze.    1992    Dio.1992.8    100.00-150.00

## Istrouma Area Council, Manchac District, Camporee
20mm, aluminum, yellow color. 1992    Dio.1992.10    2.00 - 3.00

## Great Salt Lake Council, UT, Heritage Medal, CP and UP Railroads
38mm. .999 fine silver.    1993    Dio.1993.1a    20.00 - 30.00

38mm, 24kt. plated
.999 fine silver.       1993       Dio.1993.1b   30.00 - 40.00

## National Jamboree

Official Medal. A bridge to the Future.
A scout is Brave, he says
No to Drugs.
38mm, bronze.          1993       Dio.1993.3    3.00 - 8.00
Coin Collecting Merit Badge Booth.
George Cuhaj personal token.
41mm, red plastic,
gold lettering.        1993       Dio.1993.4    1.00 - 2.00
J.R. Luten personal token.
Black plastic, gold lettering.1993  Dio.1993.5  1.00 - 2.00
Larry Baber personal token.
Green plastic,
gold lettering.        1993       Dio.1993.5    1.00 - 2.00
Thorton Ridder personal token.
Green plastic,
gold lettering.        1993       Dio.1993.6    1.00 - 2.00
Geoffrey Allred personal token.
Blue plastic,
gold lettering.        1993       Dio.1993.7    1.00 - 2.00
Logo elongated cent.
Copper.                1993       Dio.1993.8    1.00 - 2.00
LDS 80th Anniversary in
Scouting.
39mm, aluminum.        1993       Dio.1993.9    2.00 - 5.00
Florida Sea Base Dobloon.
38mm, aluminum,
gold color.            1993       Dio.1993.10   1.00 - 2.00
Troop 414
Elongated cent, copper. 1993      Dio.1993.11   1.00 - 2.00
Pony Express Council, MO-KS.
Elongated cent, copper. 1993      Dio.1993.12   1.00 - 2.00
Central Region, Sub-camp 2.
Initiative Games.
28mm, white plastic,
green lettering.       1993       Dio.1993.13   2.00 - 5.00
Central Region, Sub-camp 3.
Initiative Games.
28mm, white plastic,
red lettering.         1993       Dio.1993.14   2.00 - 5.00
Central Region, Sub-camp 4.
Initiative Games.
28mm, white plastic,
green lettering.       1993       Dio.1993.15   2.00 - 5.00

## Northeast Region, William D. Boyce, Pioneer

Portrait of Boyce. 38mm,
antique bronze, uniface. 1994     Dio.1994.4    7.50 - 10.00

## Utah Heritage, Mining

                       1994       Dio.1994.5    10.00 - 15.00

## Northeast Region, Ernest Thompson Seaton

Portrait of Seaton. 38mm,
antique bronze, uniface. 1995     Dio.1995.1    7.50 - 10.00

## Utah Heritage, Ranching

                       1995       Dio.1995.2    10.00 - 15.00

## EL-KU-TA, Lodge 520, elongated cent, lodge flap design

                       1995       Dio.1995.3    2.00 - 3.00

## Northeast Region, Daniel Carter Beard

Portrait of Beard. 38mm,
antique bronze, uniface. 1996     Dio.1996.1    7.50 - 10.00

## Utah Heritage, Elk

                       1996       Dio.1996.3    10.00 - 15.00

## Utah Heritage, Eagle

                       1996       Dio.1996.4    10.00 - 15.00

## National Scout Jamboree

Official Medal.
Be Prepared for the 21st Century.
Dates of the jamboree in ctr.
on reverse. 38mm,
antique finish and polished
copper-nickel.         1997       Dio.1997.1    4.00 - 6.00
LDS Church 84 Years of Partnership.
Jamboree Logo and
LDS Emblem. 38mm,
brown aluminum.        1997       Dio.1997.2    2.00 - 4.00
Coin Collecting Merit Badge Booth.
Jamboree Emblem modified,
Old and New Coin
Collecting Merit Badges.
38mm, .999 silver
(1 ounce). 20 made.    1997       Dio.1997.3a   75.00 - 100.00
Jamboree Emblem modified,
Old and New Coin
Collecting Merit Badges.
38mm, aluminum,
reeded edge.           1997       Dio.1997.3b   2.00 - 3.00
High Adventure.
Sommers, Philmont,
Florida Sea Base logos.
38mm, aluminum.        1997       Dio.1997.4    2.00 - 3.00
Pontiac-GMC legend.
37mm, pewter.          1997       Dio.1997.5    3.00 - 5.00
High Adventure elongated cent.
Jamboree logo.         1997       Dio.1997.6    1.00 - 2.00
Metalwork, Merit Badge.
Eagle Stamp, NJ 97
flanking. 37mm,
aluminum, handstamped. 1997       Dio.1997.7    4.00 - 5.00
FDL stamped out in disc,
97 Jamboree engraved w/ handtool.
44mm, steel. 60 made.  1997       Dio.1997.8    5.00 - 7.50

## BSA, Official Tenderfoot badge within wreath

Reverse w/ PRESENTED TO
legend. 67mm, bronze.  1960       Dio.U.10      15.00 - 20.00

Recognition for service
 legend, reverse Scout Oath.
  68mm, bronze.        1960      Dio.U.11      15.00 - 20.00

## 5th Annual BSA Vacation Training Camp, Catalina Island, CA

33mm, aluminum.        1960      Dio.U.12      10.00 - 15.00

## Peters Shoe Co. St. Louis, MO, Diamond Brand of Shoes, scout standing w/ staff

32mm, bronze.        1920      Dio.U.2      20.00 - 30.00

## Civic Good Turn, Tenderfoot badge

29mm, silvered brass.    1920    Dio.U.3      25.00 - 40.00

## BSA, Official, Tenderfoot badge within wreath

Reverse black for engraving.
  76mm, bronze.        1960      Dio.U.9      3.00 - 5.00

# POSTCARDS

Postcards have been national supply items since 1912. Two of the more handsome issues are the 1915 set for the points of the Scout Law and the 1920s series for Christmas. In the 1950s a humorous group was made for camps, and finally in the 1960s a humorous selection of note cards was produced. Most camps have cards, and only a small selection are noted here. Real photo cards are more desirable than printed cards.

## 38th Anniversary, Boy Scout Week

Cub, Sea Scout, Air Scout, Explorer,
 and Boy Scout.          1948      5.00 - 7.50

## Christmas

8 scouts hiking right along ridge,
 pine tree left.         1970-1975    3.00 - 5.00

## Alpine Scout Camp, Alpine, NJ, GNYC

Ohrbach Scout Arena.        1970      1.00 - 1.50
Trading Post interior.      1970      1.00 - 1.50
Be A Boy Scout.
 Blue and red recruiting card.   1985    0.25 - 0.50

Camp Alpine Trading Post Interior.

## Boy Scout Jamboree, Howard Chandler Christy painting

Scout w/ Franklin, Madison, Washington,
 and Hamilton in background.    1937    5.00 - 7.50

## Boy Scout Memorial of W.D. Boyce

Statue.                    1960      0.50 - 1.00

## Boy's Life Advertising

Santa at chimney rooftop.    1915-1925  10.00 - 15.00

## Boyce in London fog        1984      0.50 - 1.00

## Broad Creek Memorial Scout Camps

Patrol w/ wagon.            1955      1.00 - 2.00
Troop hiking w/ packs.      1955      1.00 - 2.00

Broad Creek Memorial Camp Card.

Set of ten photos in a card folder sold at
Camp Burton, Allaire, NJ, in 1931.

CHAPEL
CAMP BURTON AT ALLAIRE
MONMOUTH COUNCIL BOY SCOUTS

NATURE TRAIL
CAMP BURTON AT ALLAIRE
MONMOUTH COUNCIL BOY SCOUTS

TENTS - CAMP BURTON AT ALLAIRE
MONMOUTH COUNCIL BOY SCOUTS

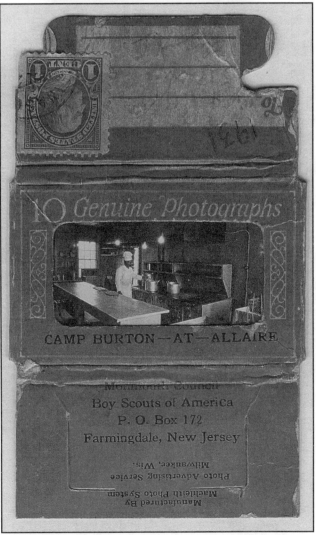

10 Genuine Photographs

CAMP BURTON —AT— ALLAIRE

Monmouth Council
Boy Scouts of America
P. O. Box 172
Farmingdale, New Jersey

Photo Advertising Service
Milwaukee, Wis.

Manufactured By
Maehlith Photo System

EXECUTIVE STAFF
MONMOUTH COUNCIL BOY SCOUTS

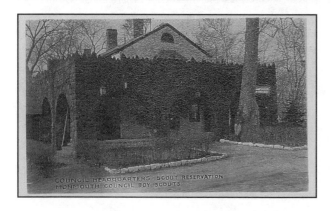

## Brooklyn Scout Camps, Tusten, NY (Ten Mile River Scout Camps)

| | | |
|---|---|---|
| Our Own Delaware 2-1/2 miles of lt. | 1934 | 5.00 - 7.50 |
| Tahlequah Lodge Headquarters. | 1934 | 3.00 - 7.50 |

## Camp Bedford, Adirondack Council, NY

| | | |
|---|---|---|
| Lake and lodge scene. | 1942 | 3.00 - 4.00 |

## Camp Burton at Allaire, Monmouth Council, NJ

| | | |
|---|---|---|
| 10 1-3/4 x 2-3/4" photographic views in mailing folder. | 1931 | 20.00 - 25.00 |

## Camp Manning

| | | |
|---|---|---|
| Mess Call. | 1926 | 10.00 - 12.50 |

## Child Welfare Exhibit, Coliseum, Chicago, IL

| | | |
|---|---|---|
| Scout standing in uniform w/ staff. | 1911 | 15.00 - 20.00 |

## Chippewa Valley Council, WI

| | | |
|---|---|---|
| Council Map and scout's portrait. | 1955 | 3.00 - 5.00 |

## Christmas

| | | |
|---|---|---|
| 3 scouts in forest walking in snow left. 4 line saying and First Class emblem. | 1920-1940 | 7.50 - 12.50 |
| Profile left, in campaign hat and neckerchief. Red Tenderfoot emblem. | 1915-1925 | 10.00 - 15.00 |
| Rural town view. First Class emblem to right. 2 line text. | 1920-1940 | 10.00 - 15.00 |
| Scout bugling in red circle. Be Prepared and 4 line saying. First Class badge. | 1915-1925 | 10.00 - 15.00 |
| Scout in beret dressing Santa. Cub wearing beard. | 1970-1975 | 3.00 - 5.00 |
| Scout Leader striding w/ notecard. Be Prepared and 4 line saying. First Class badge. | 1915-1925 | 10.00 - 15.00 |
| Scout rolling large snowball. | 1915-1925 | 10.00 - 15.00 |
| Scout Saluting. 2 wreaths flanking, folds in half. | 1915-1925 | 10.00 - 15.00 |
| Scout signaling in red circle. Be Prepared and 3 line saying. First Class badge. | 1915-1925 | 10.00 - 15.00 |
| Scout striding in doorway of log cabin. First Class emblem on shield. | 1915-1925 | 10.00 - 15.00 |
| Scout striding, saluting in red circle. Be Prepared and 4 line saying. First Class badge. | 1915-1925 | 10.00 - 15.00 |
| Silhouette of scout bugling and camp scene in pine trees. First Class emblem and 4 line text. | 1915-1925 | 10.00 - 15.00 |
| Scout striding, signaling. Pine trees in background. | | |

| | | |
|---|---|---|
| First Class emblem 5 line text below. | 1920-1940 | 7.50 - 12.50 |
| Star above pine forest scene. First Class emblem in shield. 4 line text below. | 1920-1940 | 7.50 - 12.50 |
| 2 scouts carrying tree to log cabin. 5 line saying and First Class emblem. | 1920-1940 | 7.50 - 12.50 |

## Commercial Colortype Co. Chicago, sepia tone, blue sky

| | | |
|---|---|---|
| Boy Scout Work at a Redpath - Brockway Chautauqua. | 1913 | 15.00 - 20.00 |

## Commercial Colortype Co. Chicago, sepia tone

| | | |
|---|---|---|
| A Learn to Built in 5 Minutes. | 1913 | 15.00 - 20.00 |
| A Letter from Home. | 1913 | 15.00 - 20.00 |
| A Signal Station. | 1913 | 15.00 - 20.00 |
| Basket Carry. | 1913 | 15.00 - 20.00 |
| Carrying the Patient Improved Litter. | 1913 | 15.00 - 20.00 |
| Handling the Patient. | 1913 | 15.00 - 20.00 |
| Kindness to Animals. | 1913 | 15.00 - 20.00 |
| Making Fire by Friction. | 1913 | 15.00 - 20.00 |
| On Parade - A Prize Group of Boy Scouts. | 1913 | 15.00 - 20.00 |
| Sylvester Method - Reviving the Suffocated. | 1913 | 15.00 - 20.00 |
| Typical Scouting Scene. | 1913 | 15.00 - 20.00 |
| Typical Scout. | 1913 | 15.00 - 20.00 |

## Government Postcard

| | | |
|---|---|---|
| Printed w/ merit badge appointment information. | 1930-1940 | 5.00 - 7.50 |

## Headquarters, BSA

| | | |
|---|---|---|
| Hill Top Park, Baltimore, MD. | 1912 | 10.00 - 15.00 |

## Johnston Historical Museum

| | | |
|---|---|---|
| Baden Powell at desk. | 1975 | 1.00 - 2.00 |
| Central exhibition area. | 1975 | 1.00 - 2.00 |

## Johnston National Scout Museum

| | | |
|---|---|---|
| Baden Powell wax figure. | 1965 | 1.00 - 2.00 |
| Interior view, large globe. | 1965 | 1.00 - 2.00 |

## Message from Green Bar Bill at the 1937 World Jamboree

| | | |
|---|---|---|
| Envelope w/ enclosure. | 1937 | 30.00 - 40.00 |

## National Headquarters, North Brunswick, NJ

| | | |
|---|---|---|
| Exterior view. | 1965 | 1.00 - 2.00 |
| MacKenzie Statue close-up. | 1965 | 1.00 - 2.00 |
| MacKenzie Statue and reflecting pool. | 1960 | 3.00 - 4.00 |

A POPULAR SPOT, BROOKLYN SCOUT CAMPS, TUSTEN, N. Y.

Views of Ten Mile River Scout Camp and Baiting Hollow Camp (bottom).

EXPERT SWIMMING AND CANOEING INSTRUCTION IS AVAILABLE AT CAMP BAITING HOLLOW, SUFFOLK COUNTY COUNCIL, BOY SCOUTS OF AMERICA

## National Jamboree

| | | |
|---|---|---|
| Official Card. | 1993 | 0.50 - 1.00 |
| Official Card. | 1985 | 0.50 - 1.00 |
| Official Card. | 1997 | 0.50 - 1.00 |
| Official Card. | 1989 | 0.50 - 1.00 |
| Official Card. | 1964 | 3.00 - 5.00 |
| Official Card. | 1981 | 1.00 - 2.00 |
| Official Card. | 1953 | 5.00 - 7.50 |
| Official Card. | 1960 | 3.00 - 5.00 |
| Official Card. | 1977 | 1.00 - 2.00 |
| Official Card. | 1950 | 5.00 - 7.50 |
| Official Card. | 1969 | 2.00 - 3.00 |
| Official Card. | 1957 | 3.00 - 5.00 |
| Official Card. | 1955 | 1.00 - 2.00 |
| Headquarter Flag area. | 1950 | 2.00 - 4.00 |
| Jamboree East. | 1973 | 1.00 - 2.00 |
| Jamboree West. | 1973 | 1.00 - 2.00 |
| Scout Troop marching on road. | 1950 | 2.00 - 4.00 |
| New 22 cent Boy Scout stamp. Green card. | 1985 | 1.00 - 1.50 |
| New 22 cent Boy Scout stamp. Yellow-orange card. | 1985 | 1.00 - 1.50 |
| SOSSI logo. | 1985 | 1.00 - 1.50 |
| Space shuttle Atlantis launching in sky background. | 1989 | 1.00 - 1.50 |
| Space Shuttle on launch pad. | 1989 | 1.00 - 1.50 |
| Boy's Life Exhibit. | 1969 | 1.00 - 2.00 |

## National Supply Cartoon set, No. 3056

| | | |
|---|---|---|
| Chow's fine, eating like a horse. | 1947 | 3.00 - 5.00 |
| Had a swell time here and will be home soon. | 1947 | 3.00 - 5.00 |
| Just arrived. | 1947 | 3.00 - 5.00 |
| Learn something every day. | 1947 | 3.00 - 5.00 |
| No trouble getting up here. | 1947 | 3.00 - 5.00 |
| Out nightlife. | 1947 | 3.00 - 5.00 |
| Snapshot of the gang. | 1947 | 3.00 - 5.00 |
| This is the life (diving). | 1947 | 3.00 - 5.00 |
| This is the life (fishing). | 1947 | 3.00 - 5.00 |
| Will write later. | 1947 | 3.00 - 5.00 |

## National Supply Cartoon set, No. 3067

| | | |
|---|---|---|
| Craft lodge. | 1956 | 2.00 - 3.00 |
| Food's fine. | 1956 | 2.00 - 3.00 |
| Had a swell time and I'm coming home. | 1956 | 2.00 - 3.00 |
| He says there's a bear in those woods. | 1956 | 2.00 - 3.00 |
| Hello! I just arrived! | 1956 | 2.00 - 3.00 |
| Hi - I've decided to buy that compass! | 1956 | 2.00 - 3.00 |
| I was going to mail you more scout photos, but. | 1956 | 2.00 - 3.00 |
| OK Fred, here's the lake! | 1956 | 2.00 - 3.00 |
| Sure is peaceful here! | 1956 | 2.00 - 3.00 |

## National Supply Cartoon set, No. 3067A

| | | |
|---|---|---|
| Arrived OK, got a wonderful reception. | 1958 | 2.00 - 3.00 |

| | | |
|---|---|---|
| Camp snapshot, have a lot more to show you. | 1958 | 2.00 - 3.00 |
| Every day is full of surprises! | 1958 | 2.00 - 3.00 |
| The food here is 'fit for a king' | 1958 | 2.00 - 3.00 |
| I never had it so good! | 1958 | 2.00 - 3.00 |
| In the afternoon, we go for a long leisurely hike! | 1958 | 2.00 - 3.00 |
| Made friends quickly, lots of help. | 1958 | 2.00 - 3.00 |
| Out night life and don't miss the who-dun-its. | 1958 | 2.00 - 3.00 |
| Too much to do to write! | 1958 | 2.00 - 3.00 |
| Unexpected visitors, will finish writing later! | 1958 | 2.00 - 3.00 |

## National Supply, Rockwell Paintings

| | | |
|---|---|---|
| A Scout is Helpful. | 1993 | 1.00 - 1.50 |
| A Scout is Loyal. | 1993 | 1.00 - 1.50 |
| Breakthrough for Freedom. | 1993 | 1.00 - 1.50 |
| Can't Wait. | 1993 | 1.00 - 1.50 |
| Forward America. | 1993 | 1.00 - 1.50 |
| Growth of a Leader. | 1993 | 1.00 - 1.50 |
| I will do my best. | 1993 | 1.00 - 1.50 |
| On My Honor. | 1993 | 1.00 - 1.50 |
| Our Heritage. | 1993 | 1.00 - 1.50 |
| The right way. | 1993 | 1.00 - 1.50 |
| So much concern. | 1993 | 1.00 - 1.50 |
| We, too, have a job to do. | 1993 | 1.00 - 1.50 |

## National Supply

| | | |
|---|---|---|
| Scout saluting, red-white-blue ribbon below. | 1959 | 2.00 - 4.00 |

## National Supply

| | | |
|---|---|---|
| Scouts seated on lake dock, some swimming. | 1975 | 1.00 - 1.50 |
| 6 scouts swimming. | 1975 | 1.00 - 1.50 |

## NOAC

| | | |
|---|---|---|
| Nani-Ba Zhu Lodge 321. | 1958 | 3.00 - 5.00 |
| Painting of Goodman and Edson. | 1968 | 3.00 - 5.00 |
| Photo of E. Urner Goodman. | 1965 | 3.00 - 5.00 |

## Northwoods Camp, Lake Tomahawk, WI, Milwaukee County Council

| | | |
|---|---|---|
| 5 scouts on Horseback. Real Photo Postcard. | 1929 | 15.00 - 20.00 |
| Canoe at pier. Real Photo Postcard. | 1929 | 15.00 - 20.00 |
| Lake dock scene. Real Photo Postcard. | 1929 | 15.00 - 20.00 |
| Large group learning skill in wooded area. Real Photo Postcard. | 1929 | 15.00 - 20.00 |
| Patrol learning skill in open area. Real Photo Postcard. | 1929 | 15.00 - 20.00 |

PONIL BASE CAMP

RAYADO

Philmont Scout
Ranch views
1950s (left) and
1960s (above).

1990s National Supply
postcards of Rockwell paintings.

| 20. Scouts Study as well as Play. | 1916 | 10.00 - 15.00 |
|---|---|---|
| 21. Scouts Assisting Forestry Commission. | 1916 | 10.00 - 15.00 |
| 22. Decoration Day Duties. | 1916 | 10.00 - 15.00 |
| 23. A Field Wireless Outfit. | 1916 | 10.00 - 15.00 |
| 24. Morning Camp Inspection. | 1916 | 10.00 - 15.00 |
| 25. Each Respects the Other. | 1916 | 10.00 - 15.00 |
| 26. A Prize Crop. | 1916 | 10.00 - 15.00 |
| 27. Outdoor Church at Camp. | 1916 | 10.00 - 15.00 |
| 28. Scout Tilting Contest. | 1916 | 10.00 - 15.00 |
| 29. A Business-like Wireless Station. | 1916 | 10.00 - 15.00 |
| 30. Instruction in Knot Tying. | 1916 | 10.00 - 15.00 |

## Philmont

| I want to go back. | 1980 | 1.00 - 1.50 |
|---|---|---|
| Philmont Grace and Tooth of Time. | 1975 | 1.00 - 1.50 |
| Scouting, Road to Manhood statue. | 1975 | 1.00 - 1.50 |
| Tooth of Time view from Crater Lake. | 1975 | 1.00 - 1.50 |
| Villa Philmonte Trophy Room. | 1975 | 1.00 - 1.50 |
| Camping Headquarters. B/W, full frame. | 1954 | 3.00 - 4.00 |
| Clear Creek Mountain. B/W w/ white border. | 1954 | 3.00 - 4.00 |
| Explorers panning for gold. | 1975 | 1.00 - 1.50 |
| Horse Headquarters. B/W w/ white edge. | 1954 | 3.00 - 4.00 |
| Ponil Base Camp. B/W w/ white edge. | 1954 | 3.00 - 4.00 |
| Rayado. B/W w/ white edge. | 1954 | 3.00 - 4.00 |
| The Stockade. B/W, full frame. | 1954 | 3.00 - 4.00 |
| Tooth of Time. Vertical view through trees. | 1975 | 1.00 - 1.50 |
| Woodbadge Lodge. B/W, full frame. | 1954 | 3.00 - 4.00 |

## Ranaqua Lodge 4, 40th Anniversary

| | 1956 | 5.00 - 7.50 |
|---|---|---|

## Rexcraft Official Bugle Postcard

| Bugle and jobbers listing. | 1928 | 7.50 - 12.50 |
|---|---|---|
| Bugle, box, and bag. | 1928 | 10.00 - 15.00 |

## Schiff Scout Reservation

| East Hall. | 1970 | 1.50 - 2.00 |
|---|---|---|
| Manor House. | 1970 | 1.50 - 2.00 |
| Woodbadge Totem sun dial. | 1970 | 1.50 - 2.00 |

## Scout Exhibit, New York World's Fair

| Indian Dances. | 1964-1965 | 5.00 - 7.50 |
|---|---|---|
| Scout helping family at location map. | 1964-1965 | 5.00 - 7.50 |
| Scouts by Globe. | 1964-1965 | 5.00 - 7.50 |
| Scouts w/ wheelchairs. | 1964-1965 | 5.00 - 7.50 |
| Scouts w/ flags at Unisphere. | 1964-1965 | 5.00 - 7.50 |
| Scouts w/ flags at US Pavilion. | 1964-1965 | 5.00 - 7.50 |
| Set of 6 in packet. | 1964-1965 | 30.00 - 45.00 |

## Scout Gum Co.

| Blazing a trail, No. 4. | 1916 | 10.00 - 15.00 |
|---|---|---|
| Bugle Calls, No. 1. | 1916 | 10.00 - 15.00 |
| Building fire w/o matches, No. 3. | 1916 | 10.00 - 15.00 |

Northwoods Camp, Milwaukee Council, 1927.

## Official Scout Post Cards

| 1. Nautical Scouts Signalling. | 1916 | 10.00 - 15.00 |
|---|---|---|
| 2. A Scout is Thrifty. | 1916 | 10.00 - 15.00 |
| 3. Full Ranks on Sunday. | 1916 | 10.00 - 15.00 |
| 4. A Crew of Nautical Scouts. | 1916 | 10.00 - 15.00 |
| 5. Good Woodcraft. | 1916 | 10.00 - 15.00 |
| 6. Sending Semaphore Signals. | 1916 | 10.00 - 15.00 |
| 7. Weaving a Tent Mattress. | 1916 | 10.00 - 15.00 |
| 8. Genuine First Aid. | 1916 | 10.00 - 15.00 |
| 9. The Lodge by the Lake. | 1916 | 10.00 - 15.00 |
| 10. Bicycle Patrol Awaiting Orders. | 1916 | 10.00 - 15.00 |
| 11. Respect to the Flag; Morning Colors. | 1916 | 10.00 - 15.00 |
| 12. Scout Build Bridges. | 1916 | 10.00 - 15.00 |
| 13. Scout Fire Rescue Squad. | 1916 | 10.00 - 15.00 |
| 14. Wheelbarrow Race at Scout Rally. | 1916 | 10.00 - 15.00 |
| 15. How to Throw a Rope. | 1916 | 10.00 - 15.00 |
| 16. Erecting Camp Wireless. | 1916 | 10.00 - 15.00 |
| 17. Doing a Neighbor a Good Turn. | 1916 | 10.00 - 15.00 |
| 18. Scouts Learn Archery. | 1916 | 10.00 - 15.00 |
| 19. This is the Life. | 1916 | 10.00 - 15.00 |

Greater NY Caramels recruiting cards of Yankees and Mets. The Seaver card is valued at $175.00 - $200.00. Others $15.00 - $20.00.

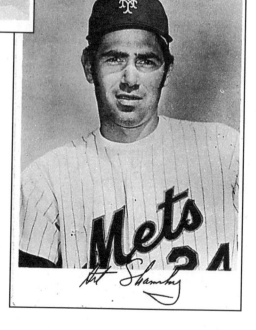

| | | |
|---|---|---|
| The Camp Fire, No. 11. | 1916 | 10.00 - 15.00 |
| First Aid, No. 10. | 1916 | 10.00 - 15.00 |
| Flag Salute, No. 11. | 1916 | 10.00 - 15.00 |
| Hiding a trail. No. 6. | 1916 | 10.00 - 15.00 |
| Loading a canoe, No. 8. | 1916 | 10.00 - 15.00 |
| Signaling, No. 5. | 1916 | 10.00 - 15.00 |
| Swimming, No. 2. | 1916 | 10.00 - 15.00 |
| Toting, No. 9. | 1916 | 10.00 - 15.00 |
| Vaulting a Stream, No. 7. | 1916 | 10.00 - 15.00 |

## Scout Law Series, © Barse & Hopkins

| | | |
|---|---|---|
| Brave. | 1917 | 10.00 - 15.00 |
| Cheerful. | 1917 | 10.00 - 15.00 |
| Clean. | 1917 | 10.00 - 15.00 |
| Courteous. | 1917 | 10.00 - 15.00 |
| Friendly. | 1917 | 10.00 - 15.00 |
| Helpful. | 1917 | 10.00 - 15.00 |
| Kind. | 1917 | 10.00 - 15.00 |
| Loyal. | 1917 | 10.00 - 15.00 |
| Obedient. | 1917 | 10.00 - 15.00 |
| Reverent. | 1917 | 10.00 - 15.00 |
| Scout Law on single card. | 1917 | 10.00 - 15.00 |

Gateway District's High Adventure recruiting postcard.

| | | |
|---|---|---|
| Thrifty. | 1917 | 10.00 - 15.00 |
| Trustworthy. | 1917 | 10.00 - 15.00 |

## Scout Law Series, drawn by S.H.W.

| | | |
|---|---|---|
| Brave. | 1912 | 10.00 - 15.00 |
| Clean. | 1912 | 10.00 - 15.00 |
| Courteous. | 1912 | 10.00 - 15.00 |
| Friendly. | 1912 | 10.00 - 15.00 |
| Helpful. | 1912 | 10.00 - 15.00 |
| Kind. | 1912 | 10.00 - 15.00 |
| Loyal. | 1912 | 10.00 - 15.00 |
| Obedient. | 1912 | 10.00 - 15.00 |
| Reverent. | 1912 | 10.00 - 15.00 |
| Trustworthy. | 1912 | 10.00 - 15.00 |

## Scout Oath, © Barse & Hopkins

| | | |
|---|---|---|
| Oath on single card. | 1917 | 10.00 - 15.00 |

## Scouting - Gateway to Adventure

| | | |
|---|---|---|
| Adirondack Rappelling scene. | | |
| Unit Recruiting back. | 1994 | 0.50 - 1.00 |

## Scouts of the World

| | | |
|---|---|---|
| Boxed set of 111 cards in color. | 1968 | 30.00 - 50.00 |
| Boxed set of 68 cards in color. | 1968 | 50.00 - 75.00 |

## Statue of Black Hawk w/ Scouts

| | | |
|---|---|---|
| | 1958 | 3.00 - 5.00 |

## T.P. & Co. NY, set of 30 views of Scouting Activities, numbered

| | | |
|---|---|---|
| Series No. 252, Official Boy Scout | | |
| Post Card. each. | 1917 | 10.00 - 15.00 |

## T.P. & Co. NY, set of 30 views of Scouting Activities, numbered, deer head logo

| | | |
|---|---|---|
| Series No. 252. Nat. Head, author. | | |
| BSA. each. | 1915 | 10.00 - 15.00 |

## Ten Mile River Scout Camps, Brooklyn Scout Camp

| | | |
|---|---|---|
| Trading Post. | 1930-1940 | 10.00 - 12.50 |

## Ten Mile River Scout Camps, GNYC

| | | |
|---|---|---|
| 6 Views fold-out, map and message area. | 1965 | 3.00 - 4.00 |
| Archery line. | 1970 | 1.00 - 1.50 |
| Camp Keowa Catholic Chapel. | 1970 | 1.00 - 1.50 |
| Camp Keowa Waterfront. | 1974 | 1.00 - 1.50 |
| Campsite scene. | 1970 | 1.00 - 1.50 |
| Canoeing on the Delaware River. | 1970 | 1.00 - 1.50 |
| Down the Delaware, 4 canoes. | 1975 | 1.00 - 1.50 |

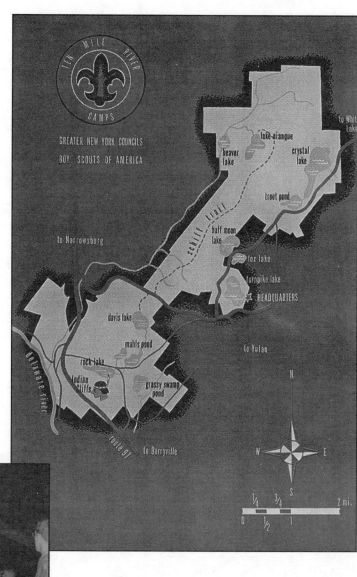

Ten Mile River
postcards of the 1950s.

Indian Village, Ten Mile River Scout Camps.

| | | |
|---|---|---|
| Family Camp cabin. | 1971 | 1.00 - 1.50 |
| Indian Cliffs and Delaware River view. | 1970 | 1.00 - 1.50 |
| Lake sunset. | 1970 | 1.00 - 1.50 |
| Troop 216 at TMR. | 1965 | 3.00 - 5.00 |
| Off on the trail - Horseback riding. | 1970 | 1.00 - 1.50 |
| Ready for a horse ride. | 1970 | 1.00 - 1.50 |
| Rifle and shotgun range. | 1970 | 1.00 - 1.50 |
| Scout receiving OA Legend. | 1970 | 1.00 - 1.50 |
| Stone Arch bridge. | 1970 | 1.00 - 1.50 |
| Sunfish sailing boats on one of the 7 lakes. | 1970 | 1.00 - 1.50 |
| Swimming in one of the 7 lakes. | 1975 | 1.00 - 1.50 |
| Waterfront, E-shaped pier. | 1970 | 1.00 - 1.50 |

## Ten Mile River, Camp Man

| | | |
|---|---|---|
| Canoeing on Crystal Lake. | 1940-1955 | 5.00 - 7.50 |
| Sea Scouts sailing on Crystal Lake. | 1940-1955 | 5.00 - 7.50 |

## The Boy Scout Tree

| | | |
|---|---|---|
| Giant Redwood and scout troop. | 1935 | 2.00 - 3.00 |

## The Scout Law, © BSA    1913    15.00 - 20.00

## The Scout Oath, © BSA    1913    15.00 - 20.00

## W.D. Boyce Memorial, Ottawa, IL

| | | |
|---|---|---|
| Boyce, scout, Big Ben, and Ottawa Memorial. | 1985 | 0.50 - 1.00 |

## We, too, have a job to do

| | | |
|---|---|---|
| Liberty advancing, Boy Scout and Sea Scout flowing. | 1943 | 5.00 - 7.50 |

## World Jamboree, Idaho

| | | |
|---|---|---|
| McDonald's Salute to Scouting. | 1967 | 1.50 - 2.00 |
| US Government Postcard. First Day Cancel. | 1967 | 2.00 - 3.00 |

# SEALS & STICKERS

## 16th Anniversary

| | | |
|---|---|---|
| Scout stg. on rock, pointing r. patrol below looking at landscape. | 1926 | 20.00 - 25.00 |

## 17th Anniversary

| | | |
|---|---|---|
| Scout bandaging girl's arm. | 1927 | 20.00 - 25.00 |

## 18th Anniversary

| | | |
|---|---|---|
| Scout striding w/ Indian looking left and Aviator right. | 1928 | 20.00 - 25.00 |

## 19th Anniversary

| | | |
|---|---|---|
| Scout seated by campfire, pioneer dream scene above. | 1929 | 20.00 - 25.00 |

## 20th Anniversary
Scout w/ staff, globe in background.                    20.00 - 25.00

## 21st Anniversary
Scout striding left.                    1931        5.00 - 7.50

## 21st Annual Meeting
Memphis, TN. Scout striding r. w/ dog.    1931    10.00 - 15.00

## 24th Anniversary
Boy Scout Week. Tenderfoot emblem.
    Blue and red.                    1934        5.00 - 10.00

## 38th Anniversary
  The Scout Citizen at Work
Cub, Sea, Air, Explorer, and Boy Scouts
    standing, flag at l. Boy Scout Week
    at bottom.                    1948    10.00 - 15.00

## 40th Anniversary Crusade,
  Strengthen the Arm of Liberty Seal
2 x 2-7/8".                    1950        5.00 - 7.50

## 50th Anniversary Foil Seal
1-1/4".                    1960        1.00 - 1.25

## Boy Scout Stamps, B.S.A.
Head shot of Boy Scout.
    Sheet of 100 stamps.            1955        5.00 - 7.50

## Boy Scout Week
Scout seated w/ book, Washington image
    in background.                1932    10.00 - 15.00
Scout standing looking l. w/ globe
    in background.                1930    10.00 - 15.00
Scout stg. w/ staff, eagle on
    black background.            1936    10.00 - 15.00
Uncle Sam brushing shoulders of youth
    in suit. Scout camp scene below.    1944    10.00 - 15.00

## Boy's Life Week

| | | |
|---|---|---|
| December 1-7th. Scout at workbench w/ wood horse. | 1934 | 5.00 - 7.50 |
| December 10-16th. Better reading for boys. | 1936 | 5.00 - 7.50 |
| December 9-16th. Better reading for Boys. | 1935 | 5.00 - 7.50 |

## Boy's Life

| | | |
|---|---|---|
| Easier, effective Patrol and troop program. 2 scouts at l. | 1930 | 5.00 - 7.50 |

## Cub Scout Stamps, B.S.A.

| | | |
|---|---|---|
| Head shot of Cub Scout. Sheet of 100 stamps. | 1955 | 5.00 - 7.50 |

## Every Boy in Camp

| | | |
|---|---|---|
| Camp fire scene. | 1928 | 7.50 - 10.00 |

## Every Scout in Camp

| | | |
|---|---|---|
| Scout bugler stg. r., 2 tents l. Black and green. | 1950 | 5.00 - 7.50 |

| | | |
|---|---|---|
| Scout bugler stg. r., 2 tents l. Black and red. | 1950 | 5.00 - 7.50 |

## Every Troop a Camping Troop

| | | |
|---|---|---|
| 2 tents along lake. Black and green. | 1950 | 5.00 - 7.50 |

## Explorers, B.S.A., head shot of Explorer Scout

| | | |
|---|---|---|
| Sheet of 100 stamps. | 1955 | 5.00 - 7.50 |

## Greater New York Councils, Queens, South District

| | | |
|---|---|---|
| Camp promotions sticker. | 1991 | 1.00 - 1.50 |

## Greater New York Councils

| | | |
|---|---|---|
| Sustaining Member sticker. | 1983 | 1.00 - 1.50 |
| Sustaining Member sticker. | 1991 | 1.00 - 1.50 |

## Historic Trails Award Water Decal

| | | |
|---|---|---|
| | 1970 | 2.00 - 3.00 |

## National Jamboree Water Decal

| | | |
|---|---|---|
| Washington kneeling l. | 1964 | 5.00 - 7.50 |
| Washington kneeling l. | 1957 | 5.00 - 7.50 |

## National Jamboree

| | | |
|---|---|---|
| Capitol dome and scout facing. | 1935 | 10.00 - 15.00 |
| On to the Jamboree, 1937. Washington Monument and First Class emblem. Blue sky, dk. blue trees. | 1937 | 10.00 - 15.00 |
| On to the Jamboree, 1937. Washington Monument and First Class emblem. Red-white-blue banner at bottom. | 1937 | 10.00 - 15.00 |
| On to the Jamboree, 1937. Washington Monument. First Class emblem in red-white-blue poster insert. Tents below. | 1937 | 10.00 - 15.00 |
| On to Washington. Scout striding and eagle. 1-3/4 x 2-3/4". | 1935 | 20.00 - 25.00 |

## New York World's Fair and Golden Gate Exposition

| | | |
|---|---|---|
| Boy Scout camp. 1-3/4 x 2-1/2". | 1939 | 20.00 - 25.00 |

## On to the Jamboree, Washington Monument

| | | |
|---|---|---|
| | 1937 | 7.50 - 10.00 |

## Philmont Scout Ranch

| | | |
|---|---|---|
| Pendant shape. green lettering. | 1950 | 5.00 - 7.50 |

## Save our Natural Resources, Project SOAR

| | | |
|---|---|---|
| Sheet of 8 stamps. | 1971 | 2.00 - 3.00 |

## Schiff Scout Reservation

| | | |
|---|---|---|
| Water Decal. | 1970 | 5.00 - 7.50 |

## Scout Anniversary Week, February 8 to 14

| | | |
|---|---|---|
| 2 scouts standing. | 1940 | 5.00 - 7.50 |

## Scout Service Camp, New York World's Fair

| | | |
|---|---|---|
| Blue-orange 3" circle. | 1940 | 15.00 - 20.00 |

## Scouts, too, have a job to do

| | | |
|---|---|---|
| Liberty advancing r. w/ navy and army troops. Scouting Needs Leaders at top. | 1942 | 10.00 - 15.00 |
| Liberty advancing r. w/ navy and army troops. Scouting Needs Money at top. | 1942 | 10.00 - 15.00 |
| Liberty advancing r. w/ navy and army troops. Scouts, too, have a job to do at top. | 1942 | 10.00 - 15.00 |

## Suanhacky Lodge #49, Queens Council, OA
Stag head on red circle.           1973        2.00 - 3.00

## Sustaining Member Window Sticker
                                   1980        2.00 - 3.00

## Tenderfoot Emblem, on red-white-blue square, water decal
                                   1972        2.00 - 3.00

## Tenderfoot Emblem, outline, water decal
                                   1975        1.00 - 2.00

## The Scout Citizen at work
Cub, Sea, Air, Explorer and
   Boy Scouts standing, flag at l.
   Scouting is for All Boys at bottom.   1948    10.00 - 15.00

## W.D. Boyce, BSA, LSA, Seal
                                   1985        0.50 - 1.00

## World Jamboree, Idaho, Seal
                                   1967        1.00 - 2.00

# RELIGIOUS AWARDS - YOUTH

A Scout is Reverent is the title of this 1930 stained glass window in the Catholic Chapel at Camp Kernochan, Ten Mile River Scout Camps, G.N.Y.C.

## Ad Altarre Dei
Roman Catholic Cross, ribbon of
   yellow-white-yellow w/ thin
   red-white-blue-white-red in ctr.
   Back of cross w/ raised
   information for engraving        1950        15.00 - 20.00
Roman Catholic, Cross, yellow-white-yellow
   ribbon w/ red-white-blue-white-red in ctr.
   Back of cross plain.             1980        7.50 - 12.50

## Alpha and Omega
Eastern Orthodox. White cross, orthodox
   cross in red at ctr. lt. blue ribbon w/
   6 thin white stripes.            1980        7.50 - 12.50

## Ararat
Eastern Diocese of the Armenian Church of
   America. Cross, purple ribbon.   1980        7.50 - 12.50

## Compassionate Father
Meher Baba. Mastery in Service on
   pendant, rainbow ribbon.         1980        7.50 - 12.50

## Eternal Light, Ner Tamid

Jewish. Lighted flame, blue-white ribbon.   1980        7.50 - 12.50

## Friends, Spirit of Truth

Religious Society of Friends (Quakers).
  The Light Shines on in the Dark, legend
  on compass. Red-white-blue-red-ribbon.1980        7.50 - 12.50

Scout Religious Medals.

## God and Country

Moravian. Blue enamel on bar,
  white enamel behind lamb w/ banner,
  red-white repeated ribbon.        1980        7.50 - 12.50

## God and Country (Bog I Ojczyzna)

Polish National Catholic Church.
  Red enamel on bar, red-white-red ribbon,
  open book and cross at ctr. of cross.   1980        7.50 - 12.50

## God and Country, Baptist

Cross and open book in blue circle on white
  field, blue ribbon.        1980        7.50 - 12.50

## God and Country, God and Church

Christian Church (Disciples of Christ).
  Red chalice w/ cross in white field,
  blue ribbon.        1980        7.50 - 12.50
Episcopal. Red cross on white field,
  stars in blue 1st quadrant, red ribbon.   1980   7.50 - 12.50
Methodist. Cross and flame on white field,
  blue ribbon.        1980        7.50 - 12.50
Presbyterian. Dove, 2 flames flanking
  priestly vestment, blue ribbon.   1980        7.50 - 12.50
Protestant. Red cross on white field,
  blue ribbon        1980        7.50 - 12.50

## God and Country, God and Life

Episcopal, red cross on white field,
  stars in blue 1st quadrant, red ribbon.   1980   7.50 - 12.50

Protestant. Red cross on white field,
  dark green ribbon.        1980        7.50 - 12.50

## God and Country

First Church of Christ Scientist. Red cross
  in white field, blue ribbon.        1980   7.50 - 12.50
The Salvation Army. Army logo,
  blue ribbon.        1980        7.50 - 12.50

## God is Great

Islamic Council of Scouters. Crescent in
  World Scouting knot, white ribbon.   1980   7.50 - 12.50

## Good Life

Zoroastrian. Flame pyre, white ribbon.   1980   7.50 - 12.50

## Good Servant

Churches of Christ. Cross and 4 hearts,
  red ribbon.        1980        7.50 - 12.50

## In the Name of God

Islamic. Crescents and tracery,
  green ribbon.        1980        7.50 - 12.50

## Light is Life

Eastern Rite, Catholic. Greek letters on
  cross, blue ribbon.        1980        7.50 - 12.50

## Living Faith

Lutheran. P and cross on white
  enamel pendant, red ribbon.        1980   7.50 - 12.50

## Lutheran, God and Church

Lutheran. Heart emblem on white field,
  red ribbon.        1980        7.50 - 12.50

## On My Honor

Church of Jesus Christ of Later-day Saints.
  FDL and Angel, green-yellow ribbon.   1980   7.50 - 12.50

## Pro Deo Et Patria

Lutheran. Red cross on white field,
  blue ribbon        1980 - 85   10.00 - 15.00

## Pius XII

Roman Catholic. Yellow-white ribbon,
  Crossed keys and paper tiara.        1980   7.50 - 12.50

## Religion in Life

Unitarian Universalist. Flame on pedestal,
  white enamel globe around, blue ribbon. 1980   7.50 - 12.50

## Sangha

Buddhist. Ship wheel, rainbow ribbon.   1980   7.50 - 12.50

## St. Mesorib
Armenian Apostolic Church of America,
 Western Prelacy. Red-blue-orange ribbon,
 figure and legend.                1980        7.50 - 12.50

## The New Church, A new Christianity, Open Word
General Church of the New Jerusalem.
 Open book, white-red ribbon.      1980        7.50 - 12.50

## Unity of Mankind
Baha'I. Enameled blue and green globe,
 green-white-green ribbon.         1980        7.50 - 12.50

## Unity, Light of God
Association of Unity Churches. Flower head
 enameled, blue-yellow-blue ribbon.    1980        7.50 - 12.50

## World Community (Liahona-Compass)
Reorganized Church of Jesus Christ of
 Later Day Saints. Peace and family
 within purple enameled cross and globe.
 purple-orange-purple ribbon.      1980        7.50 - 12.50

Beginnings of a pioneering project at camp.

Neighborhood Commissioner square cut khaki.

Scoutmaster cut edge

Scoutmaster rolled edge

# IDENTIFYING UNIT DISTRICT & COUNCIL LEVEL POSITION INSIGNIA, 1913-1970

## LARGE FIRST CLASS DESIGN (77mm)

|  | badge outline | eagle | background |  |
|---|---|---|---|---|
| Scout Commissioner | dark blue | brown | dark blue | 1913-1916 |
| Deputy Scout Comm. | powder blue | brown | powder blue | 1913-1916 |
| Deputy Scout Comm. | dark blue | brown | dark blue | 1916-1919 |
| Asst. Deputy Comm. | powder blue | brown | powder blue | 1916-1919 |
| Troop/Council Comm. | white | brown | white | 1914-1919 |
| National Committee | purple | brown | purple | 1911-1919 |
| National Committee | purple | brown | purple | 1920-1928 |
| Local Councilman | silver | silver | blue | 1920-1928 |
| Scout Master | green | brown | green | 1911-1919 |
| Scout Master | silver | silver | brown | 1920-1928 |
| Asst. Scout Master | gold | gold | brown | 1920-1928 |
| Asst. Scout Master | red | brown | red | 1911-1938 |

## FIRST CLASS DESIGN ENCIRCLED BY A WREATH

|  | wreath | 1st Class background | eagle | 1st Class badge outline |  |
|---|---|---|---|---|---|
| Scout Commissioner | yellow | blue | brown | blue | 1916-1919 |
| Scout/Council Comm. | silver | blue | silver | silver | 1920-1969 |
| Asst. Council Comm. | silver | blue | gold | silver | 1966-1069 |
| Deputy Scout Comm. | gold | blue | silver | silver | 1920-1931 |
| Field/District Comm. | gold | blue | silver | silver | 1931-1969 |
| Asst. Deputy Comm. | gold | blue | gold | silver | 1920-1931 |
| Asst. Field/Dist. Comm. | gold | blue | gold | silver | 1931-1969 |
| Neighborhood Comm. | gold | blue | gold | gold | 1933-1969 |
| Scout Executive | yellow | white | yellow | white | 1917-1919 |
| Scout Executive | silver | red | silver | silver | 1920-1969 |
| Asst. Scout Executive | gold | red | silver | silver | 1920-1969 |
| Field/District Exec. | gold | red | gold | silver | 1920-1969 |
| Asst. Field/Dist. Exec. | gold | red | gold | gold | 1931-1969 |
| Layman | none | blue | gold | gold | 1928-1969 |
| Council President | gold | blue | brown | gold 2 hands | 1966-1969 |
| Council Past President | gold | blue | brown | gold 1 hand | 1966-1969 |

Silver is actually white in most early badges: I.E. Scout Executive is described as silver yet every badge pre-1950s I have ever observed is actually white. Coloration will apply to pins as well as badges. Dates apply only to badges. All badges from 1970 have the position title embroidered in the design.

# POSITION BADGES-LEADERS

## Ambassador
Tenderfoot emblem on fully embroidered
purple, rolled edge. 1989    5.00 - 10.00

## Area Committee
Tenderfoot emblem on dark green twill,
rolled edge. 1973    5.00 - 7.50

## Area President
Tenderfoot emblem on dark green twill,
rolled edge. 1973    5.00 - 7.50

## Assistant Chief Scout Executive
| | | |
|---|---|---|
| Khaki, cut cloth. | 1943-1956 | 250.00-300.00 |
| Khaki cut edge, solid wreath. | 1956-1967 | 175.00-225.00 |
| Khaki, rolled edge. | 1967-1972 | 40.00 - 60.00 |
| Tenderfoot emblem on maroon twill, titled, gray rolled edge. | 1973 | 60.00 - 90.00 |

## Assistant Council Commissioner
| | | |
|---|---|---|
| First Class emblem in white w/ yellow eagle and white wreath. on blue twill, rolled edge. | 1968-1970 | 10.00 - 15.00 |
| Tenderfoot emblem on light blue twill, rolled edge. | 1970-1973 | 5.00 - 7.50 |
| Tenderfoot emblem on red twill, rolled edge. | 1973 | 3.00 - 5.00 |

## Assistant Deputy Scout Commissioner
| | | |
|---|---|---|
| First Class emblem, light blue behind eagle. | 1911 | 1,000.00-1,400.00 |
| Tan cloth. Light blue First Class emblem, brown eagle. | 1915-1920 | 750.00-1,000.00 |
| Tan cloth. Blue First Class emblem w/ silver border, gold eagle, and fine wreath. | 1921-1938 | 400.00 - 800.00 |

## Assistant District Scout Executive
Tenderfoot emblem, solid wreath,
titled, rolled edge. 1973    20.00 - 30.00

## Assistant District (Field) Executive Staff
Tan cloth. Red First Class emblem w/
gold border, eagle, and fine wreath. 1926-1938    20.00 - 30.00

## Assistant District Commissioner
| | | |
|---|---|---|
| First Class emblem in yellow on red background, full wreath, khaki cut cloth. | 1943-1956 | 20.00 - 30.00 |
| First Class emblem in yellow on red background, solid wreath, khaki cut edge. | 1956-1967 | 7.50 - 10.00 |
| First Class emblem, solid wreath, khaki rolled edge. | 1967-1970 | 7.50 - 10.00 |
| Tenderfoot emblem on light blue twill, rolled edge. | 1970-1973 | 5.00 - 7.50 |
| Tenderfoot on red twill, rolled edge. | 1973 | 2.00 - 3.00 |

## Assistant District Scout Executive
| | | |
|---|---|---|
| Fine wreath, Khaki cut cloth. | 1938-1956 | 100.00-125.00 |
| Solid wreath, khaki cut edge. | 1956-1967 | 8.50 - 12.50 |
| Solid wreath, khaki rolled edge. | 1967-1972 | 8.50 - 12.50 |

## Assistant Ranger
| | | |
|---|---|---|
| First Class emblem in yellow w/ yellow eagle and background. Khaki cut edge. | 1956-1967 | 30.00 - 40.00 |
| Tenderfoot emblem in yellow on red twill rolled edge, white title. | 1967-1970 | 7.50 - 10.00 |
| Tenderfoot emblem on red twill, rolled edge. | 1972 | 2.00 - 3.00 |
| Tenderfoot emblem in yellow on red twill rolled edge, yellow title. | 1975 | 5.00 - 7.50 |

## Assistant Scout Executive
| | | |
|---|---|---|
| Tan cloth. Red First Class emblem w/ silver border and eagle, fine gold wreath. | 1921-1938 | 150.00-225.00 |
| Full wreath on khaki cloth. | 1943-1956 | 30.00 - 45.00 |

## Assistant Scoutmaster - Venture
Tan rolled edge. 1989    1.00 - 1.50

Assistant Scoutmaster Patch on square cut wool. Note that there is no central split line in the short crown of the FDL.

## Assistant Scoutmaster

| | | |
|---|---|---|
| First Class badge, red behind eagle. | 1911 | 350.00-450.00 |
| Tan cloth. Red First Class emblem, brown eagle. | 1911-1920 | 200.00-300.00 |
| Tan cloth. Green First Class emblem, gold border, and eagle. | 1921-1934 | 75.00-100.00 |
| First Class badge, red behind eagle, khaki cut cloth. | 1934 | 60.00 - 80.00 |
| First Class emblem in yellow outline on green cut edge twill. | 1938-1966 | 10.00 - 15.00 |
| First Class emblem in yellow outline on green rolled edge twill. | 1966-1972 | 7.50 - 10.00 |
| Tenderfoot emblem on green twill, rolled edge. | 1972-1989 | 1.00 - 2.00 |
| Tenderfoot emblem, fully embroidered green Mylar thread (Trained Leader). | 1972-1989 | 3.00 - 5.00 |
| Tenderfoot emblem on tan twill, rolled edge. | 1989 | 1.00 - 1.50 |

## Assistant Council Commissioner

| | | |
|---|---|---|
| Tenderfoot emblem on red twill, rolled edge. | 1972-1989 | 2.00 - 3.00 |

## Chaplain

| | | |
|---|---|---|
| First Class emblem and crook, within circle, cut tan cloth. | 1931-1940 | 80.00-100.00 |
| First Class emblem and crook, within circle, cut khaki cloth. | 1940-1966 | 80.00-100.00 |
| First Class emblem and crook, within circle, rolled edge. | 1967-1972 | 25.00 - 35.00 |
| Crook, CHAPLAIN, and Tenderfoot emblem in vertical oval, rolled edge. | 1968-1972 | 10.00 - 15.00 |
| Tenderfoot emblem and crook on white twill, dark blue rolled edge border. | 1973 | 4.00 - 5.00 |

## Chartered Organization Representative

| | | |
|---|---|---|
| Tenderfoot emblem on tan twill, rolled edge. | 1989 | 1.00 - 1.50 |

## Chief Scout Executive

| | | |
|---|---|---|
| Tan cloth. Purple First Class emblem w/ silver border, eagle, and fine wreath. | 1921-1923 | 300.00-450.00 |
| Tan cloth. Silver First Class emblem w/ silver border, eagle, and fine wreath. Red-white-blue behind emblem. | 1923-1938 | 175.00-225.00 |
| First Class on white background, w/ white eagle and wreath, red-white-blue ctr. Khaki cut cloth. | 1943-1956 | 150.00-200.00 |
| First Class on white background, w/ white eagle and wreath, red-white-blue ctr. Red-white-blue scroll. Khaki cut edge. | 1956-1969 | 75.00-100.00 |
| First Class on white background, w/ white eagle and wreath, red-white-blue ctr., blue twill scroll. Khaki cut edge. | 1959-1967 | 60.00 - 80.00 |
| First Class on white background, w/ white eagle and wreath, red-white-blue ctr., blue twill scroll. Khaki rolled edge. | 1967-1970 | 50.00 - 75.00 |

| | | |
|---|---|---|
| Tenderfoot emblem on red twill, rolled edge. | 1970-1973 | 30.00 - 50.00 |
| Tenderfoot emblem on maroon twill, rolled edge. | 1973 | 10.00 - 15.00 |

## Chief Scout

| | | |
|---|---|---|
| First Class emblem in white, w/ brown eagle, white wreath. Khaki cut cloth. | 1943-1956 | 100.00-150.00 |
| First Class emblem in white, w/ brown eagle, white wreath. Khaki cut edge. | 1956-1967 | 60.00 - 85.00 |

## Council Commissioner

| | | |
|---|---|---|
| First Class emblem in full wreath on khaki cloth cut. | 1943-1956 | 25.00 - 35.00 |
| First Class emblem in solid wreath, khaki cut edge. | 1956-1967 | 20.00 - 30.00 |
| First Class emblem in solid wreath, khaki rolled edge. | 1967-1970 | 15.00 - 20.00 |
| Tenderfoot emblem on light blue twill, rolled edge. | 1970-1973 | 7.50 - 12.50 |
| Tenderfoot emblem on red twill, rolled edge. | 1973 | 7.50 - 12.50 |

## Council Committee

| | | |
|---|---|---|
| Tenderfoot emblem on light blue twill, rolled edge. | 1973 | 3.00 - 4.00 |

## Council Executive Board

| | | |
|---|---|---|
| Tenderfoot emblem on light blue twill, rolled edge. | 1973 | 3.00 - 4.00 |

## Council Executive Staff

| | | |
|---|---|---|
| Tenderfoot emblem on red twill, rolled edge. | 1973 | 2.00 - 3.00 |

## Council Executive

| | | |
|---|---|---|
| Tenderfoot emblem on red twill, rolled edge. | 1973 | 2.00 - 3.00 |

## Council Past President

| | | |
|---|---|---|
| First Class emblem w/ yellow background, eagle and wreath. Hands point down. Khaki cut edge. | 1956-1967 | 50.00 - 75.00 |
| First Class emblem w/ yellow background, eagle and wreath. Hands point down. Khaki rolled edge. | 1967-1968 | 50.00 - 75.00 |
| First Class emblem w/ brown eagle, yellow background and wreath. Hands point down. Khaki rolled edge. | 1968-1970 | 40.00 - 60.00 |
| Tenderfoot emblem in white on light blue twill, rolled edge. | 1970-1973 | 10.00 - 15.00 |
| Tenderfoot emblem in yellow on light blue twill, rolled edge. | 1973 | 5.00 - 10.00 |
| Tenderfoot emblem on light blue twill, rolled edge. | 1973 | 3.00 - 4.00 |

Adult position badges, 1970-1989.

## Council President

First Class emblem, yellow eagle and
    wreath, blue ctr. Hands pointed out.
    Khaki cut edge.                          1956-1967  50.00 - 75.00
First Class emblem, yellow eagle and wreath,
    blue ctr. Hands pointed out.
    Khaki rolled edge.                       1967-1968  50.00 - 75.00
First Class emblem, brown eagle and yellow
    wreath, blue ctr. Hands pointed out.
    Khaki rolled edge.                       1968-1970  40.00 - 60.00
Tenderfoot emblem in white on light
    blue twill, rolled edge.                 1970-1973  30.00 - 40.00
Tenderfoot emblem in yellow on light
    blue twill, rolled edge.                 1973       10.00 - 15.00
Tenderfoot emblem on light blue twill,
    rolled edge.                             1973        3.00 - 4.00

## Council Vice President

Tenderfoot emblem on light blue twill,
    rolled edge.                             1973        3.00 - 4.00

## Deputy Chief Scout Executive

Tan cloth. Purple First Class emblem
    w/ silver border, eagle, and fine
    silver wreath.                           1920-1923  600.00-800.00
Tan cloth. Silver First Class emblem w/ silver
    border, eagle, and fine silver wreath.
    Red-white-blue behind emblem.            1923-1938  400.00-600.00
Silver First Class emblem w/ silver border,
    eagle, and fine silver wreath.
    Red-white-blue behind emblem.
    Khaki cut cloth.                         1943-1956  100.00-150.00
Silver First Class emblem w/ silver border,
    eagle, and fine gold wreath.
    Red-white-blue behind emblem.
    Khaki cut edge.                          1956-1967  100.00-150.00

## Deputy Scout Commissioner

First Class emblem w/ dark
    blue background.                         1910       600.00-800.00
Tan cloth. Dark blue First Class
    emblem, brown eagle.                     1915-1920  300.00-400.00
Tan cloth. Light blue First Class
    emblem w/ silver border, eagle, and
    fine gold wreath.                        1921-1938  100.00-200.00

## District Executive

Solid wreath, khaki rolled edge.             1967-1970  10.00 - 15.00

## District (Field Scout) Executive

Tan cloth. Red First Class emblem w/ silver
    border and gold eagle, fine gold wreath. 1926-1938  100.00-200.00

## District Chairman

Tenderfoot emblem on light blue twill,
    rolled edge.                             1973        3.00 - 4.00

## District Commissioner

Full wreath, khaki cloth cut.                1943-1956  30.00 - 45.00
Solid wreath, khaki cut edge.                1956-1967  10.00 - 15.00
Solid wreath, khaki rolled edge.             1967-1970   7.50 - 12.50
Tenderfoot emblem on light blue twill,
    title in yellow, rolled edge.            1970-1973   5.00 - 7.50
Tenderfoot emblem on red twill,
    rolled edge.                             1973        2.00 - 3.00

## District Committee

Tenderfoot emblem on light blue twill,
    title in yellow, rolled edge.            1970-1973   5.00 - 7.50
Tenderfoot emblem on light blue twill,
    white title, rolled edge.                1970-1973   3.00 - 4.00

## District Executive Staff

Tenderfoot emblem on maroon twill,
    rolled edge.                             1973        2.00 - 3.00

## District Executive

Fine wreath, khaki cloth cut.                1943-1956  30.00 - 40.00
Solid wreath, khaki cut edge.                1956-1967  15.00 - 25.00
Tenderfoot emblem on maroon twill,
    rolled edge.                             1973        2.00 - 3.00
Tenderfoot emblem on maroon twill.           1973        4.00 - 6.00

## Employee

First Class emblem in bronze w/ red
    background on tan cut cloth.             1926-1940  150.00-200.00
First Class emblem in bronze w/ red
    background on khaki cut cloth.           1940-1956  100.00-140.00
First Class emblem in yellow w/ red
    background on khaki cut edge.            1956-1967  50.00 - 80.00
Tenderfoot emblem on red twill,
    rolled edge.                             1967-1970  30.00 - 40.00
Tenderfoot emblem on red twill, white title,
    rolled edge.                             1970-1975  20.00 - 25.00
Tenderfoot emblem on red twill, yellow title,
    rolled edge.                             1975        4.00 - 7.00

## Institutional Representative

Tenderfoot emblem on light blue twill,
    rolled edge.                             1972-1975   3.00 - 4.00

## International Commissioner

First Class emblem in yellow wreath,
    brown eagle, green ctr.
    Khaki cut cloth.                         1943-1956  400.00-500.00
First Class emblem in yellow wreath,
    brown eagle, green ctr.
    Khaki cut edge.                          1956-1958  80.00-100.00
First Class emblem on white background,
    brown eagle, white wreath.
    Khaki cut edge.                          1958-1967  50.00 - 75.00
First Class emblem on white background,
    eagle, red-white-blue ctr. to wreath.
    Khaki rolled edge.                       1967-1970  50.00 - 75.00

Camp Director Charles M. Heistand welcomes President Franklin Roosevelt on his visit to Camp Man, Ten Mile River Scout Reservation in Narrowsburg, NY (1935).

## International Representative

| | | |
|---|---|---|
| Tenderfoot emblem on fully embroidered purple, rolled edge. | 1989 | 5.00 - 10.00 |

## International Scout Commissioner

| | | |
|---|---|---|
| First Class emblem at ctr. of starburst, 8 clasped hands at 3, 6, 9, and 12 o'clock, golden eagle behind. | 1931-1943 | 1,500.00 - 2,000.00 |

## Lady Scouter

| | | |
|---|---|---|
| Tenderfoot emblem in blue outline on cream square. | 1968 | 10.00 - 15.00 |
| Tenderfoot emblem in yellow outline on navy square. | 1968-1970 | 10.00 - 15.00 |
| Tenderfoot emblem in blue on white square. | 1970-1972 | 10.00 - 15.00 |

## Layman

| | | |
|---|---|---|
| First Class emblem w/ yellow outline and blue background on tan cut cloth. | 1929-1932 | 150.00-200.00 |
| First Class emblem, yellow eagle and background, on khaki cut cloth. | 1932-1938 | 100.00-150.00 |
| First Class emblem, yellow eagle and background, on round khaki cloth. | 1938-1943 | 100.00-150.00 |
| First Class emblem, yellow eagle and background on blue twill. | 1943-1956 | 50.00-100.00 |
| First Class emblem, yellow eagle and background on khaki cut edge. | 1956-1967 | 10.00 - 15.00 |
| First Class emblem, yellow eagle and background on khaki rolled edge. | 1967-1972 | 7.50 - 10.00 |

## Local Council

| | | |
|---|---|---|
| Tan cloth. Blue First Class emblem, silver border, and eagle. | 1921-1928 | 300.00-450.00 |

## Local Councilman

| | | |
|---|---|---|
| First Class emblem, white background, tan cut cloth. | 1921-1928 | 600.00-800.00 |
| First Class emblem in blue, white outline, rolled edge. | 1970-1973 | 50.00 - 75.00 |

## National Committee

| | | |
|---|---|---|
| Tan cloth. Purple First Class emblem, brown eagle. | 1911-1920 | 600.00-800.00 |
| Tan cloth. Purple First Class emblem, silver border, and eagle. | 1921-1930 | 400.00-600.00 |
| Tenderfoot emblem on purple twill, rolled edge. | 1973-1980 | 5.00 - 10.00 |

## National Executive Board, BSA

| | | |
|---|---|---|
| Tenderfoot emblem within wreath. | 1973 | 80.00-100.00 |

## National Executive Board

| | | |
|---|---|---|
| First Class emblem on arrowhead, all within circle. Khaki cut cloth. | 1943-1956 | 250.00-350.00 |
| First Class emblem on arrowhead, all within circle. Khaki cut edge. | 1956-1967 | 200.00-250.00 |
| First Class emblem on arrowhead, khaki twill, gold rolled edge. | 1967-1968 | 80.00-100.00 |
| First Class emblem on arrowhead, khaki twill, purple rolled edge. | 1968-1970 | 80.00-100.00 |
| Tenderfoot emblem in white on purple twill, rolled edge. | 1970-1973 | 5.00 - 10.00 |
| Tenderfoot emblem in yellow on purple twill, rolled edge. | 1973-1980 | 5.00 - 10.00 |
| Tenderfoot emblem on fully embroidered purple, rolled edge. | 1980 | 5.00 - 10.00 |

## National Executive Staff

| | | |
|---|---|---|
| Tenderfoot emblem on red-white-blue ctr. on maroon twill, rolled edge. | 1973 | 10.00 - 15.00 |

## National Field Scout Commissioner

| | | |
|---|---|---|
| Tan cloth. Silver First Class emblem w/ silver border, eagle, and fine gold wreath. Dark blue behind emblem. | 1921-1938 | 600.00-800.00 |

## National Partner Representative

| | | |
|---|---|---|
| Tenderfoot emblem on purple twill, title at top, rolled edge. | 1970-1973 | 60.00 - 80.00 |
| Tenderfoot emblem on purple twill within wreath. title split between top and bottom, rolled edge. | 1973 | 5.00 - 10.00 |

## National Past President

| | | |
|---|---|---|
| First Class emblem on arrowhead, hand below, gavel and axe behind. | 1931-1932 | 500.00-750.00 |
| First Class emblem on arrowhead, star below, gavel and axe behind. | 1932-1943 | 350.00-450.00 |
| Tenderfoot emblem in white on purple twill, rolled edge. | 1970-1973 | 80.00-100.00 |
| Tenderfoot emblem in yellow on purple twill, rolled edge. | 1973 | 40.00 - 50.00 |

## National President

| | | |
|---|---|---|
| First Class emblem on arrowhead, 2 hands below, crossed gavel and axe. | 1931-1932 | 600.00-750.00 |
| First Class emblem on arrowhead, 2 stars flanking, crossed gavel and axe. Brown eagle. | 1932-1943 | 400.00-500.00 |
| First Class emblem on arrowhead, 2 stars flanking, crossed gavel and axe. Golden eagle. | 1943-1958 | 400.00-500.00 |
| First Class emblem in white w/ white eagle and wreath. Khaki cut edge. | 1958-1959 | 100.00-150.00 |
| First Class emblem in white w/ brown eagle and white wreath. Khaki cut edge. | 1959-1968 | 80.00-100.00 |
| Tenderfoot emblem in white on purple twill, rolled edge. | 1970-1972 | 80.00-100.00 |
| Tenderfoot emblem in yellow on purple twill, rolled edge. | 1973 | 10.00 - 15.00 |

## National Scout Commissioner

First Class emblem w/ yellow background
    and wreath, white eagle and powderhorn.
    Tan cut cloth.              1915-1923    700.00 - 900.00
First Class emblem w/ yellow background
    and wreath, white eagle and powderhorn.
    Tan cut cloth.              1923-1937    700.00 - 900.00
First Class emblem w/ white background,
    wreath, eagle and powderhorn.
    Tan cut cloth.              1937-1940    600.00 - 800.00
First Class emblem in yellow w/ yellow
    background, wreath, eagle and powderhorn.
    Khaki cut cloth.            1940-1956    500.00 - 750.00
First Class emblem in white w/ white
    background, wreath, eagle and powderhorn.
    Khaki cut edge.            1956-1958    400.00 - 500.00

## National Staff

Tan cloth. Silver First Class emblem
    w/ silver border, gold eagle,
    and fine wreath. Red-white-blue
    behind emblem.            1931-1938    300.00 - 400.00
First Class emblem on red-white-blue
    background, wreath. khaki cut cloth.   1940-1946    150.00 - 200.00
First Class emblem on red-white-blue
    background, wreath, khaki cut edge.   1956-1967    30.00 - 45.00
First Class emblem on red-white-blue
    background, wreath, rolled edge.      1967-1970    30.00 - 40.00
Tenderfoot emblem in yellow on red
    twill w/ blue in wreath, rolled edge.   1970    5.00 - 10.00

## National Vice President

Tenderfoot emblem in white on purple
    twill, rolled edge.        1970-1972    10.00 - 15.00
Tenderfoot emblem on fully embroidered
    purple, rolled edge.        1980    10.00 - 15.00

## Neighborhood Commissioner

Tan cloth. Blue First Class emblem
    w/ gold border, eagle, and fine wreath.   1932-1938    40.00 - 60.00
Full wreath, khaki cut cloth.      1943-1956    30.00 - 40.00
First Class emblem w/ yellow eagle and
    blue background on khaki cut edge.    1956-1967    20.00 - 25.00
First Class emblem w/ yellow eagle and
    blue background on khaki rolled edge.   1967-1970    10.00 - 15.00
Tenderfoot emblem on blue twill.
    rolled edge.            1970-1972    5.00 - 10.00

## Paraprofessional

Tenderfoot emblem on red twill,
    rolled edge.            1970    2.00 - 3.00

## Physician

Caducesus behind First Class emblem
    in circle, khaki cut cloth.       1931-1956    100.00 - 125.00
Caducesus (yellow) behind First Class
    emblem in circle, cut edge.      1956-1958    60.00 - 80.00

Caducesus (red) behind First Class emblem
    in circle, khaki cut edge.        1958-1966    40.00 - 50.00
Caducesus behind First Class emblem
    on yellow twill, rolled edge.      1967-1970    10.00 - 15.00
Caducesus behind First Class emblem
    in circle, PHYSICIAN, rolled edge.   1970-1972    20.00 - 30.00
Tenderfoot emblem and Caducesus on
    white twill, dark blue rolled edge.   1973    4.00 - 5.00

## Primary Leader

Tenderfoot emblem on green twill,
    rolled edge.            1975-1989    4.00 - 7.00

## Ranger

First Class emblem w/ red background
    and yellow outline. Khaki cut cloth.   1947-1956    40.00 - 60.00
First Class emblem w/ yellow
    background and outline.
    Khaki cut edge.            1956-1967    30.00 - 40.00
First Class emblem w/ yellow
    background and outline.
    Khaki rolled edge.          1967-1970    20.00 - 30.00
Tenderfoot emblem w/ white title on
    red twill. Rolled edge.        1970-1975    10.00 - 15.00
Tenderfoot emblem on red twill.
    Rolled edge.            1973    2.00 - 3.00
Tenderfoot emblem w/ yellow title
    on red twill. Rolled edge.      1975    5.00 - 10.00

## Region Committee

Tenderfoot emblem on wine twill,
    rolled edge.            1973    10.00 - 15.00

## Region President

Tenderfoot emblem on wine twill,
    rolled edge.            1973    10.00 - 15.00

## Regional Scout Executive

Tan cloth. Gold First Class emblem
    w/ gold border, eagle, and fine wreath.
    Red-white-blue behind emblem.    1921-1938    400.00 - 600.00

## Scout Commissioner

Tan cloth, fine yellow wreath. Dark blue
    First Class emblem, brown eagle.    1915-1920    300.00 - 500.00
Tan cloth. Blue First Class emblem w/ silver
    border, eagle, and fine wreath.     1921-1938    250.00 - 400.00

## Scout Executive

Tan cloth, fine yellow wreath.
    White First Class emblem,
    yellow eagle.            1915-1920    400.00 - 600.00
Tan cloth. Red First Class emblem
    w/ silver border and eagle, fine
    silver wreath.            1921-1938    300.00 - 400.00
Wreath, khaki cut cloth.        1943-1956    30.00 - 40.00

| | | |
|---|---|---|
| Khaki cut edge. | 1956-1967 | 20.00 - 30.00 |
| Khaki rolled edge. | 1967-1970 | 15.00 - 25.00 |
| Tenderfoot emblem in white on maroon twill, rolled edge. | 1970-1973 | 10.00 - 15.00 |
| Tenderfoot emblem in yellow on maroon twill, rolled edge. | 1973 | 4.00 - 6.00 |

## Scouting Coordinator

| | | |
|---|---|---|
| Tenderfoot emblem on light blue twill, rolled edge. | 1975 | 4.00 - 7.00 |

## Scoutmaster

| | | |
|---|---|---|
| Green First Class, white stars and motto, 77mm long. | 1910 | 300.00-350.00 |
| Tan cloth. Green First Class emblem, brown eagle. | 1911-1920 | 150.00-200.00 |
| Tan cloth. Green First Class emblem, silver border, and eagle. | 1921-1938 | 100.00-150.00 |
| White outline First Class badge within white circle, cut edge green twill. | 1938-1967 | 25.00 - 35.00 |
| White outline First Class badge within white circle, rolled edge green twill. | 1967-1970 | 20.00 - 25.00 |
| White outline First Class badge within white circle, SCOUTMASTER title, rolled edge. | 1970-1972 | 10.00 - 15.00 |
| Tenderfoot emblem on fully embroidered green Mylar thread (Trained Leader). | 1972-1989 | 3.00 - 5.00 |
| Tenderfoot emblem on green twill, rolled edge. | 1972-1989 | 1.00 - 2.00 |
| Tenderfoot emblem on tan twill, rolled edge. | 1989 | 1.00 - 1.50 |

Scoutmaster badges of the cut edge(left) and rolled edge varieties.

## Special National Field Scout Commissioner

| | | |
|---|---|---|
| Tan cloth. Purple First Class emblem w/ silver border, eagle, and fine gold wreath. Red-white-blue behind emblem. | 1920-1923 | 800.00-1,000.00 |
| Silver First Class emblem within wreath, tan cut cloth. | 1923-1938 | 400.00 - 600.00 |
| Silver First Class emblem, brown eagle, all within wreath, tan cut cloth. | 1923-1938 | 400.00 - 600.00 |

| | | |
|---|---|---|
| First Class emblem on blue background, red-white-blue ctr. of yellow wreath. Khaki cut cloth. | 1940-1956 | 40.00 - 55.00 |
| First Class emblem in white w/ white eagle on purple ctr. Khaki cut edge. | 1956-1961 | 40.00 - 55.00 |
| First Class emblem in white w/ brown eagle on purple ctr. Khaki cut edge. | 1961-1967 | 25.00 - 40.00 |
| First Class emblem in white w/ white eagle on purple ctr. Khaki rolled edge. | 1967-1970 | 20.00 - 30.00 |

## Sponsor Coordinator

| | | |
|---|---|---|
| Tenderfoot emblem on light blue twill, rolled edge. | 1973-1989 | 4.00 - 7.00 |

## Troop Committee

| | | |
|---|---|---|
| First Class emblem in blue on blue twill rolled edge. Yellow title. | 1970-1972 | 5.00 - 8.00 |

## Troop Commissioner

| | | |
|---|---|---|
| Tenderfoot emblem on blue background, silver Mylar border. | 1975-1989 | 7.50 - 10.00 |
| Tenderfoot emblem on blue background, yellow border. | 1975 | 5.00 - 7.50 |

## Troop Committee Chairman

| | | |
|---|---|---|
| Tenderfoot emblem on green twill, rolled edge. | 1973-1989 | 3.00 - 5.00 |
| Tenderfoot emblem on tan twill, rolled edge. | 1989 | 1.00 - 1.50 |

## Troop Committee or Local Council Committee

| | | |
|---|---|---|
| Tan cloth. White First Class emblem, brown eagle. | 1911-1920 | 400.00-600.00 |

## Troop Committee

| | | |
|---|---|---|
| Tan cloth. Blue First Class emblem, gold border, and eagle. | 1921-1938 | 300.00-450.00 |
| Tenderfoot emblem on green twill, rolled edge. | 1973-1989 | 1.00 - 2.00 |
| Tenderfoot emblem on tan twill, rolled edge. | 1989 | 1.00 - 1.50 |

## Unit Commissioner

| | | |
|---|---|---|
| Tenderfoot emblem on ted twill, rolled edge white border. | 1973-1975 | 5.00 - 7.50 |
| Tenderfoot emblem on red twill, yellow rolled edge. | 1975-1989 | 2.00 - 3.00 |
| Tenderfoot emblem on ted twill, rolled edge silver Mylar border. | 1975-1989 | 5.00 - 7.50 |

## Women's Reserve

| | | |
|---|---|---|
| Tenderfoot emblem on white twill, dark blue rolled edge. | 1973-1989 | 4.00 - 5.00 |

# HAT OR COLLAR DEVICES

## Assistant Deputy Commissioner
First Class emblem in silver,
gold eagle, blue enamel background,
gold wreath. 23-25mm.          1920-1938   75.00-100.00

## Assistant Deputy Scout Commissioner
First Class emblem w/
light blue enamel. 40mm.       1917-1919  400.00-600.00

## Assistant Scoutmaster
First Class emblem w/
red enamel. 40mm.              1917-1919  200.00-250.00
First Class emblem in gold w/
green enamel. 23-25mm.         1920-1938   10.00 - 15.00
First Class emblem in gold on
green enameled circle.
Double clutch pin back.        1950-1967   15.00 - 25.00
First Class emblem in gold on
green enameled circle.
Vertical safety pin back.      1950-1967   15.00 - 25.00

Assistant Scoutmaster's hat pin of the 1917–1919 era, with red enamel in the FDL.

## Chaplain
First Class emblem and crook on
blue and white circle.
Double clutch pin back.        1950-1967   60.00 - 80.00

## Deputy Commissioner
First Class emblem in silver,
silver eagle, blue enamel background,
gold wreath. 23-25mm.          1920-1938   75.00-100.00

## Deputy Scout Commissioner
First Class emblem w/ dark blue enamel.
40mm.                          1917-1919  400.00-600.00

## Junior Assistant Scoutmaster
First Class emblem in gold on 3 green
enameled bars. Screw back.     1926-1938   25.00 - 35.00

## Layman
First Class emblem w/ white enamel.
40mm.                          1917-1919  250.00-300.00
First class emblem in gold on
blue enameled circle.          1950-1967   10.00 - 17.50

Layman's collar emblem.

## Local Council Committee
First Class emblem in silver
w/ blue enamel. 23-25mm.       1920-1938   40.00 - 60.00

## National Committee
First Class emblem w/
purple enamel. 40mm.           1917-1919  600.00-800.00
First Class emblem on
white enamel swastika.         1920-1925  500.00-600.00
First Class emblem on silver arrowhead.  1930-1945  150.00-200.00
First Class emblem on silver
arrowhead in circle.           1950-1967   75.00-125.00

## National Council Committee
First Class emblem in silver
w/ purple background. 23-25mm.     1920-1938     75.00-100.00

## National Council Staff
First Class emblem on red-white-blue
background in wreath w/ ribbon.     1950-1967     80.00-100.00

## National Executive Board
First Class emblem on silver
arrowhead in circle.     1950-1967     300.00-400.00

## National Past President
First Class emblem on silver
arrowhead in circle.     1950-1967     400.00-600.00

## Physician
First Class emblem and Caducesus
on blue and white circle.
Double clutch pin back.     1950-1967     150.00-200.00

## Scout Commissioner
First Class emblem in dark blue enamel
in gold wreath. Screw back w/ bent
tabs. 35mm.     1917-1919     600.00-800.00
First Class emblem in silver,
silver eagle, blue enamel background,
silver wreath. 23-25mm.     1920-1938     75.00-100.00

## Scout Executive
First Class emblem in white enamel in
gold wreath. Screw back w/ bent
tabs on back. 35mm.     1917-1919     400.00-500.00

## Scoutmaster
First Class emblem w/ green enamel.
40mm.     1917-1919     200.00-250.00
First Class emblem in silver w/
green enamel. 23-25mm.     1920-1938     10.00 - 15.00
First Class emblem in silver on
green enamel circle.
Double clutch pin back.     1950-1967     15.00 - 25.00
First Class emblem in silver on
green enamel circle. Vertical
safety pin back.     1950-1967     15.00 - 25.00

## Senior Patrol Leader
First Class emblem in silver on 2-1/2
green enameled bars. Screw back.     1921-1933     25.00 - 35.00

First Class emblem in gold on 2-1/2
green enameled bars.     1933-1938     15.00 - 25.00

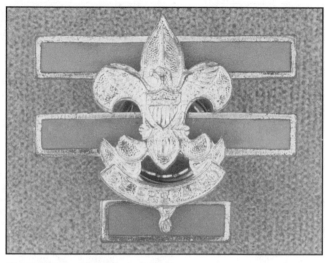

Senior Patrol Leader's hat pin.

## Special National Field Scout Commissioner
First Class emblem in wreath
w/ ribbon.     1950-1967     600.00-750.00

## Troop Committee
First Class emblem in gold w/
blue enamel. 23-25mm.     1920-1938     20.00 - 30.00

## Universal Hat Pin
First class emblem (for campaign hat)     1996     3.00-5.00
Tenderfoot emblem in circle
(for Australian style hat)     1996     3.00-5.00

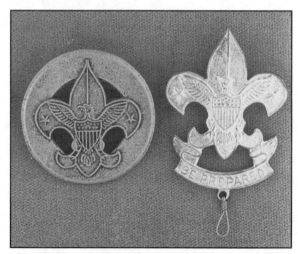

The circular Tenderfoot emblem for the Australian style hat, and the new First Class pin for the Campaign hat.

# HANDBOOKS - LEADERS

Patrol Leader handbooks have been indispens-able references since the 1930s.

References are to Doug Bearce and Chuck Fisk's book *Collecting Scout Literature*.

## Handbook for Patrol Leaders

1st-4th printings. 399 or 408 pgs.
   Scout by campfire on cover,
   dark green background. 1929-1933  F.PL.1.1-4    20.00 - 30.00
5th-12th printings. 562-598 pgs.
   Scout by campfire on cover,
   silver background    1935-1943  F.PL.2.5-12    15.00 - 25.00
13th-18th printings. 444 pgs.
   Scout by campfire on cover,
   silver background.    1944-1949  F.PL.3.13-18   10.00 - 15.00
19th-34th printings. 376-392 pgs.
   Hiking scout w/ patrol
   flag cover.    1950-1965  F.PL.4.19-34    7.50 - 12.50

## Patrol Leader's Handbook, 2nd Edition

4 printings. 217 pgs.
Patrol hiking in wilderness. 1967-1970  F.PL.5.36-39    5.00 - 7.50

## Patrol and Troop Leadership, 7 printings, 128 pgs

Dual green covers, seated
   scouts and 1 standing.  1972-1979  F.PL.6.40-46    5.00 - 7.50

## Official Patrol Leader's Handbook, 3rd Edition

9 printings. 204 pgs.
Action painting and Patrol Leader
   insignia on cover.    1980-1988  F.PL.7.47-55    5.00 - 7.50

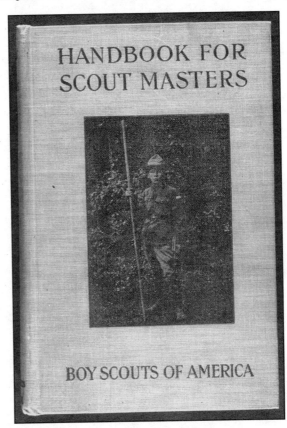

Scoutmaster Handbook, 1915 printing

## Handbook for Scoutmasters

Proof editions (3). 203 or
   161 pgs.    1912-1912  F.SM.1.1-3    150.00 - 200.00
1st Edition. 344, 352, or
   404 pgs. plus ads.
   9 printings.    1913-1919  F.SM.2.4-10   125.00 - 175.00
2nd Edition. 1st printing.
   608 pgs.    1920-1920  F.SM.3.11    100.00 - 135.00
2nd Edition. 2nd printing.
   615 pgs. plus maps.    1920-1921  F.SM.4.12    90.00 - 120.00
2nd Edition. 3rd-6th printings.
   632 pgs.    1922-1924  F.SM.5.13-16   75.00 - 100.00
2nd Edition. 7th-9th printings.
   668 pgs.    1924-1926  F.SM.6.17-19   75.00 - 100.00
2nd Edition.
   10th-15th printings.
   676 pgs.    1926-1930  F.SM.7.20-25   75.00 - 100.00
2nd Edition. 16th-19th printings.
   628 pgs.    1932-1935  F.SM.8.26-29   60.00 - 80.00
3rd Edition, Vol. 1. 13 printings.
   501 or 498 pgs.    1936-1945  F.SM.9a.30-42  40.00 - 60.00
3rd Edition, Vol. 2. 11 printings.
   Between 1142 and
   1164 pgs.    1937-1945  F.SM.9b.43-53  40.00 - 60.00

1950 printing

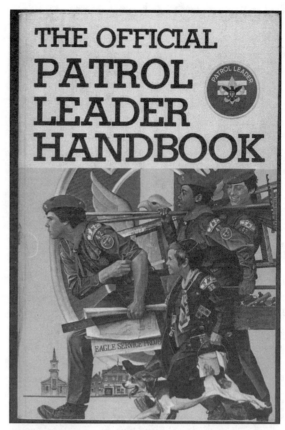

1980 edition

1967 printing

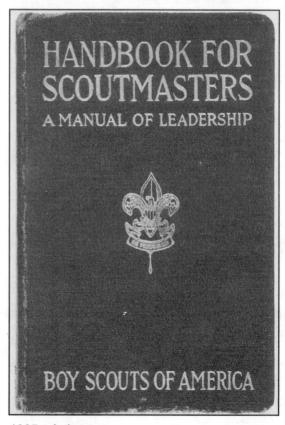

1925 printing

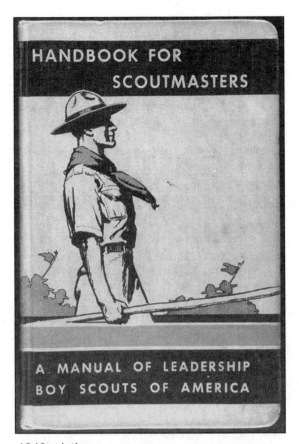

1940 printing

1972 printing

1959 printing

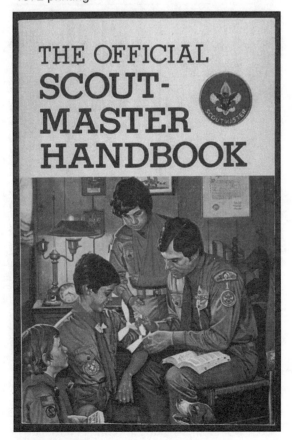

1981 printing

4th edition. 11 printings.
512 pgs.          1947-1957  F.SM.10.54-64 20.00 - 30.00
5th Edition. 1st-6th printings.
509-510 pgs.      1959-1964  F.SM.11.65-71 10.00 - 15.00
5th Edition. 7th-11th printings.
542 pgs.          1965-1970  F.SM.12.72-76 10.00 - 15.00
6th Edition. 9 Printings.
382 pgs.          1972-1980  F.SM.13.77-85  5.00 - 7.50
7th Edition. 9 Printings.
368 pgs.          1981-1990  F.SM.14.86-95  5.00 - 10.00

## How Book of Scouting

1st Edition. 5 printings,
420 pgs.          1927-1931  F.HB.1-5     15.00 - 25.00
2nd Edition.
2 printings, 512 pgs.  1934-1935  F.HB.6-7     15.00 - 25.00
3rd Edition. 2 printings,
627 pgs.          1938-1941  F.HB.8-9     10.00 - 20.00

## Requirement Manual

Annual. Various month
and year printings.  1960-1970  F.RM.1-12    3.00 - 4.00
Single year dates on cover.
                    1971-1979  F.RM.13-21   2.00 - 3.00
Dual year dates on cover.
                    1979-1998  F.RM.22-    2.00 - 3.00

Scout Fieldbooks include in-depth information on camping subjects.

## Scout Field Book

1st Edition. 1st-14th printings.
540 or 552 pgs.    1944-1959  F.FB.1-14    15.00 - 25.00
2nd Edition. 5 printings.
656 pgs.          1967-1972  F.FB.15-19   5.00 - 10.00
2nd Edition title change.
6th-14th printings. 565 pgs.
Two-tone green cover.  1973-1983  F.FB.20-28   5.00 - 10.00
3rd Edition. 630 pgs.
High Adventure cover.  1984      F.FB.29     5.00 - 7.50

## Scouting for Rural Boys, a Manual for Leaders

                    1938      F.RB.1      25.00 - 35.00

## Scouting for the Deaf

                    1970      F.D.1       5.00 - 7.50

## Scouting for the Mentally Handicapped

                    1967      F.MH.1     5.00 - 7.50

## Scouting for the Physically Handicapped

2 printings. 96 pgs.    1971-1979  F.PH.1-2    5.00 - 7.50

## Water Safety program

Every Scout a Swimmer,
1st Edition.         1924      F.WS.1     25.00 - 35.00
Swimming, Water Sports
and Safety, 4th Edition. 1938      F.WS.6     20.00 - 30.00
Swimming and Water
Safety, 2nd Edition.   1927      F.WS.2     20.00 - 30.00
Swimming and Water
Safety, 3rd Edition.
3 printings.        1931-1936  F.WS.3-5   20.00 - 30.00

## Winter Camping

Proof and 1st Edition.  1927      F.WC.1-2   25.00 - 35.00

1967 printing

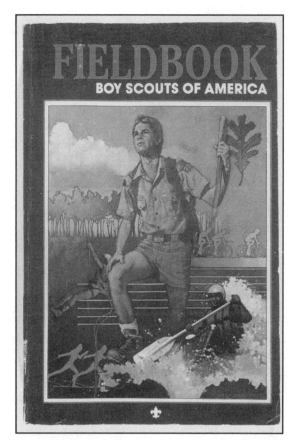

1984 printing

1973 printing

Blazer emblem, 1970s

Queens Council Scout Executive Dennis St. Jean addresses a Gateway District Dinner (1985). Note the bullion pocket patch and stripe tie.

# UNIFORMS - LEADERS

### Bullion embroidered program emblem
| | | |
|---|---|---|
| Boy Scout. | 1971 | 10.00 - 15.00 |

## Blazer
| | | |
|---|---|---|
| Blue w/ removable bullion program emblem. | 1972 | 60.00 - 75.00 |
| Green w/ removable bullion program emblem. | 1971-1977 | 60.00 - 75.00 |

## Breeches
| | | |
|---|---|---|
| Quality olive-drab cotton, laced below the knee. | 1911-1930 | 40.00 - 60.00 |
| Woolen, olive-drab. | 1911-1930 | 50.00 - 75.00 |

1920s scout coat, double pleated, top pockets, belt.

## Coat
| | | |
|---|---|---|
| Light weight olive-drab cotton, 4 pockets, no belt. | 1911-1930 | 30.00 - 50.00 |
| Norfolk design, 2 front pockets and belt. | 1910-1920 | 150.00-175.00 |
| Open collar, 4 pockets and belt. | 1921-1945 | 75.00-125.00 |
| Quality olive-drab cotton cloth, double pleats, belt. | 1911-1930 | 75.00-100.00 |
| Special grade olive-drab wool. | 1911-1930 | 100.00-150.00 |

## Jacket
| | | |
|---|---|---|
| Open collar, no belt. | 1945-1970 | 60.00 - 75.00 |

## Knickers
| | | |
|---|---|---|
| Light weight olive-drab material, buckle below knee. | 1911-1930 | 30.00 - 50.00 |

## Service Star
| | | |
|---|---|---|
| Gold star w/ tenure number, clutch back on blue plastic. | 1956 | 2.00 - 4.00 |
| Gold star w/ tenure number, screwback on blue felt. | 1947-1955 | 2.00 - 4.00 |

1918 Leader uniforms

## Trousers

Full length olive-drab cotton.           1911-1930    40.00 - 60.00

# ADULT RECOGNITIONS

## Scouter's Training Award

First Class emblem on A background.
10 kt. GF on green ribbon w/ 1
thin white stripe.                       1960-1970   15.00 - 20.00
Tenderfoot emblem on A background.
10 kt. GF on green ribbon w/ 1
thin white stripe.                       1960-1970   10.00 - 15.00

Brother Hugh Dymski OFM Conv. proudly displays his Silver Beaver Award with Kenneth Tremaine.

Tenderfoot emblem on A background.
Gilt pendant on green ribbon w/ 1
thin white stripe.                       1960-1970    5.00 - 7.50
Tenderfoot emblem on A background.
10 kt. GF on solid green ribbon.         1960-1970  10.00 - 15.00

Scouter's Training Award (left) and Scouter Key.

## Scouter's Key Award

First Class emblem on key background
10 kt. GF on green ribbon w/ 1
thick white stripe.                      1960-1970   15.00 - 20.00
Tenderfoot emblem on key background.
Gilt pendant on green ribbon
w/ 2 thin white stripes.                 1960-1970    5.00 - 7.50
Tenderfoot emblem on key background.
10 kt. GF on green ribbon w/ 1
thick white stripe.                      1960-1970   10.00 - 15.00

## District Award of Merit

Wood plaque.                             1972          10.00-15.00

## Silver Beaver Award

Type I. Blue-white-blue
pocket ribbon w/ FDL.                    1931-1933  350.00-400.00
Type II. Blue-white-blue
neck ribbon w/ FDL.                      1933-1938  250.00-350.00
Type III. Blue-white-blue neck ribbon.  1938-1950  200.00-250.00
Type IV. Blue-white-blue neck ribbon.   1950-1960  125.00-175.00
Type V. Blue-white-blue neck ribbon.    1960-1970  125.00-175.00
Type VI. Blue-white-blue neck ribbon,
snap-on ribbon.                          1970-1980   50.00 - 75.00
Type VII. Blue-white-blue neck ribbon,
snap-on ribbon.                          1980         35.00 - 50.00

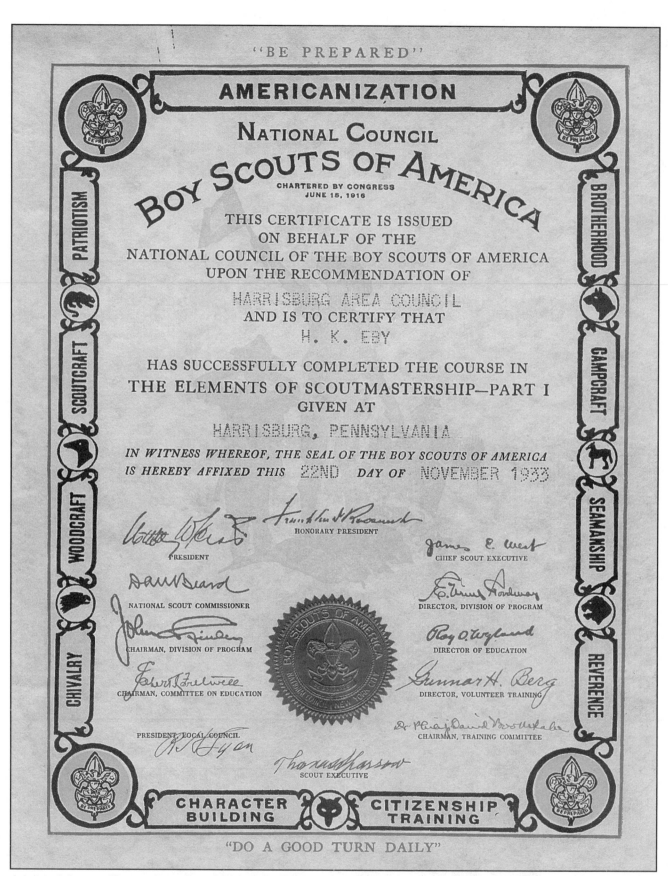

Adult training certificates from the mid-1920s to 1940s were nicely done, value $7.50 - $12.50.

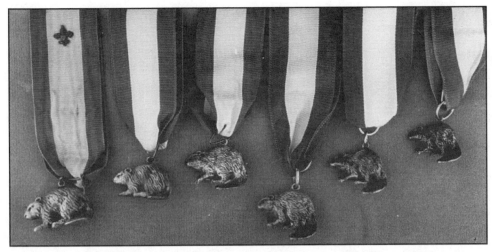

Silver Beaver Award, six major varieties, 1935-1995.

## Silver Fawn

Thin green-white neck ribbon.          1971-1974  300.00-400.00

Silver Fawn Award, early 1970s.

## Silver Antelope Award

| | | |
|---|---|---|
| Type I. Gold-white-gold neck ribbon. | 1955 | 200.00 - 250.00 |
| Type II. Gold-white-gold neck ribbon. | 1970 | 125.00 - 160.00 |
| Type III. Gold-white-gold neck ribbon. Not Silver. | 1980 | 100.00 - 135.00 |

## Silver Buffalo Award

| | | |
|---|---|---|
| Type I. Red-white-red neck ribbon. | 1925 | 800.00-1,000.00 |
| Type II. Red-white-red neck ribbon. | 1955 | 400.00 - 600.00 |
| Type III. Red-white-red neck ribbon. Not Silver. | 1980 | 200.00 - 250.00 |

## Distinguished Eagle Scout Award, Type I

| | | |
|---|---|---|
| 14 kt. Gold eagle on red-white-blue neck ribbon. | 1969-1980 | 300.00 - 400.00 |

## Distinguished Eagle Scout Award, Type II

| | | |
|---|---|---|
| Gold-plated eagle on red-white-blue neck ribbon. | 1980 | 150.00-200.00 |

## Veteran Pin

| | | |
|---|---|---|
| 5 year, BS and V w/ First Class emblem at ctr. 14 kt. gold and enamel. | 1916-1940 | 30.00 - 50.00 |
| 5 year, BS and V w/ First Class emblem at ctr. 10 kt. GF and enamel. | 1916-1940 | 15.00 - 20.00 |
| 5 year, BS and V w/ First Class emblem at ctr. 10 kt. gold and enamel. | 1916-1940 | 25.00 - 40.00 |
| 5 year, Tenderfoot emblem, 5 above. | 1940-1971 | 5.00 - 10.00 |
| 5 year, Tenderfoot emblem, 5 below in blue border. | 1972 | 3.00 - 5.00 |
| 10 year, First Class emblem on XX in enamel circle. 14 kt. GF. | 1916-1940 | 15.00 - 25.00 |
| 10 year, First Class emblem on XX in enamel circle. 14 kt. gold. | 1916-1940 | 30.00 - 50.00 |
| 10 year, Tenderfoot emblem, 10 above. | 1940-1971 | 5.00 - 10.00 |
| 10 year, Tenderfoot emblem, 10 below in blue border. | 1972 | 3.00 - 5.00 |
| 15 year, First Class emblem on XV in circle. | 1925-1940 | 15.00 - 25.00 |
| 15 year, Tenderfoot emblem, 15 above. | 1940-1971 | 5.00 - 10.00 |
| 15 year, Tenderfoot emblem, 15 below in blue border. | 1972 | 3.00-5.00 |
| 20 year, First Class emblem on XX in circle. | 1935 | 15.00 - 25.00 |
| 20 year, Tenderfoot emblem, 20 above. | 1940-1971 | 5.00-10.00 |
| 20 year, Tenderfoot emblem, 20 below in blue border. | 1972 | 3.00-5.00 |
| 25 year, First Class emblem on XXV in circle. | 1935-1940 | 15.00 - 25.00 |
| 25 year, Tenderfoot emblem, 25 above. | 1940-1971 | 7.50-12.50 |
| 25 year, Tenderfoot emblem, 25 below in blue border. | 1972 | 5.00-7.50 |
| 30 year, First Class emblem on XXX in circle. | 1935-1940 | 20.00 - 30.00 |
| 30 year, Tenderfoot emblem, 30 below in blue border | 1972 | 5.00-7.50 |
| 40 year, Tenderfoot emblem, 40 below in blue border | 1972 | 5.00-7.50 |
| 50 year, Tenderfoot emblem, 50 above. | 1960 | 10.00-15.00 |

| | | | |
|---|---|---|---|
| 60 year, Tenderfoot emblem, 60 above. | | 1970 | 10.00-15.00 |
| 75 year, Tenderfoot emblem, 75 above. | | 1985 | 10.00-15.00 |

## Veteran Patches

Five-year veteran patch,
cut khaki material.

| | | |
|---|---|---|
| V. First Class emblem, BS above V below. | 1924-1945 | 10.00-15.00 |
| X. First Class emblem, X behind. | 1925-1945 | 10.00-15.00 |
| XV. First Class emblem, XV behind. | 1925-1945 | 15.00-25.00 |
| XX. First Class emblem, XX behind. | 1930-1945 | 15.00-25.00 |
| XXV. First Class emblem, XXV behind. | 1935-1945 | 15.00-25.00 |
| XXX. First Class emblem, XXX behind. | 1940-1945 | 20.00-30.00 |

## Award Certificates

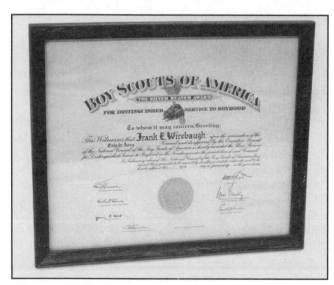

Early Silver Beaver Certificate, 1946.

| | | | |
|---|---|---|---|
| Scoutleaders training award | | | 5.00-10.00 |
| Scouter's key | | | 5.00-10.00 |
| District award of merit | | | 5.00-10.00 |
| Silver Beaver | Type 1 | 1932-1960 | 40.00-60.00 |
| Silver Beaver | Type 2 | 1960-1972 | 10.00-15.00 |
| Silver Beaver | Type 3 | 1972 | 5.00-10.00 |
| Silver Fawn | | 1972-1974 | 20.00-30.00 |
| Silver Antelope | Type 1 | 1960-1972 | 10.00-15.00 |
| Silver Antelope | Type 2 | 1972 | 5.00-10.00 |
| Silver Buffalo | Type 1 | 1925-1960 | 80.00-100.00 |
| Silver Buffalo | Type 2 | 1960-1972 | 50.00-75.00 |
| Silver Buffalo | Type 3 | 1972 | 30.00-50.00 |
| Unawarded Certificate | | | 5.00-15.00 |

# RELIGIOUS AWARDS - ADULT

## Bishop Zielinski Award, open book w/ cross in ctr. of cross

Polish National Catholic Church.

| | | |
|---|---|---|
| Red-white-red neck ribbon. | 1980 | 35.00 - 50.00 |

## David Zeisberger Award, Our Lamb has Conquered Let Us follow Him

Moravian Church in America.

| | | |
|---|---|---|
| Lamb w/ banner, red-white-blue ribbon. | 1980 | 35.00 - 50.00 |

## Distinguished Youth Service Award

Association of Unity Churches.

| | | |
|---|---|---|
| Sunburst, enameled, blue-yellow-blue neck ribbon. | 1980 | 35.00 - 50.00 |

## Faithful Servant Award

Churches of Christ. Cross and 4 hearts,

| | | |
|---|---|---|
| red neck ribbon. | 1980 | 35.00 - 50.00 |

## Friends Award, The Light Shines on in the Dark

Religious Society of Friends (Quakers).

| | | |
|---|---|---|
| Compass, red-white-blue-red-blue-white-red neck ribbon. | 1980 | 35.00 - 50.00 |

## God and Service Award, Life-Family-Church

Presbyterian. Vestment flanked by flames,

| | | |
|---|---|---|
| dove above, pale blue neck ribbon. | 1980 | 35.00 - 50.00 |

Protestant. Red cross on white field,

| | | |
|---|---|---|
| blue neck ribbon. | 1980 | 35.00 - 50.00 |

United Methodist. Flame and Cross,

| | | |
|---|---|---|
| white-red-white neck ribbon. | 1980 | 35.00 - 50.00 |

## Lamb

Lutheran. Lamb, cross on hill,

| | | |
|---|---|---|
| red neck ribbon. | 1980 | 35.00 - 50.00 |

## Prophet Elias Award

Eastern Orthodox. White cross w/ red orthodox cross within. Light blue

| | | |
|---|---|---|
| neck ribbon w/ 6 thin white stripes. | 1980 | 35.00 - 50.00 |

## Religion and Youth Award, flame on lamp, white field

Unitarian Universalist Association.

| | | |
|---|---|---|
| Blue neck ribbon. | 1980 | 35.00 - 50.00 |

## Scouters Award

The Salvation Army emblem.
Red-orange-blue neck ribbon.          1980          35.00 - 50.00

## Shofar

Jewish. Shofar horn and lamp,
multistripe blue-white neck ribbon.          1980          35.00 - 50.00

## St. George

Episcopal. St. George Slaying dragon,
within cross, red neck ribbon.          1980          35.00 - 50.00
Roman Catholic. St. George slaying dragon,
yellow neck ribbon w/ green-red-white-
blue-green thin stripes.          1980          35.00 - 50.00

WWI poster. Actual size 20 x 30". A smaller reproduction exists as do post-cards.

# WORLD WAR SERVICE AWARDS

To assist in the effort on the home front in both World Wars, the Boy Scouts sold bonds for which the U.S. Department of the Treasury awarded a series of medals for each of the five bonds drives (and bars for selling in more than one drive). For the Third Liberty Loan Campaign the scouts were honored with a patriotic poster and an additional medal incentive. Finally, for selling War Savings Stamps, scouts were awarded an Ace medal which featured the torch of the Statue of Liberty.

For World War II efforts scouts were awarded an Eisenhower Waste Paper Campaign medal and two varieties of the McArthur Garden Medal.

## City of Englewood, NJ

For War Service.

|  |  |
|---|---|
| 1918 | 100.00-125.00 |

## Eisenhower Waste Paper Campaign

Eisenhower medal for waster paper collection.

| Plastic pendant from red-white-red ribbon bar. | 1942-1945 | 15.00 - 25.00 |
|---|---|---|

## For Patriotic Service

| Scout planting, crossed flags below. | 1917 | 50.00 - 75.00 |
|---|---|---|

## MacArthur Garden Medal

National Victory Garden Institute MaCarthur Award. Green ribbon. BSA name incuse on back.

| Green ribbon. BSA Name incuse on back. | 1942-1945 | 40.00 - 50.00 |
|---|---|---|
| Red ribbon. BSA Name raised on front. | 1942-1945 | 40.00 - 50.00 |

National Garden Institute MaCarthur Award. Red ribbon. BSA name on front.

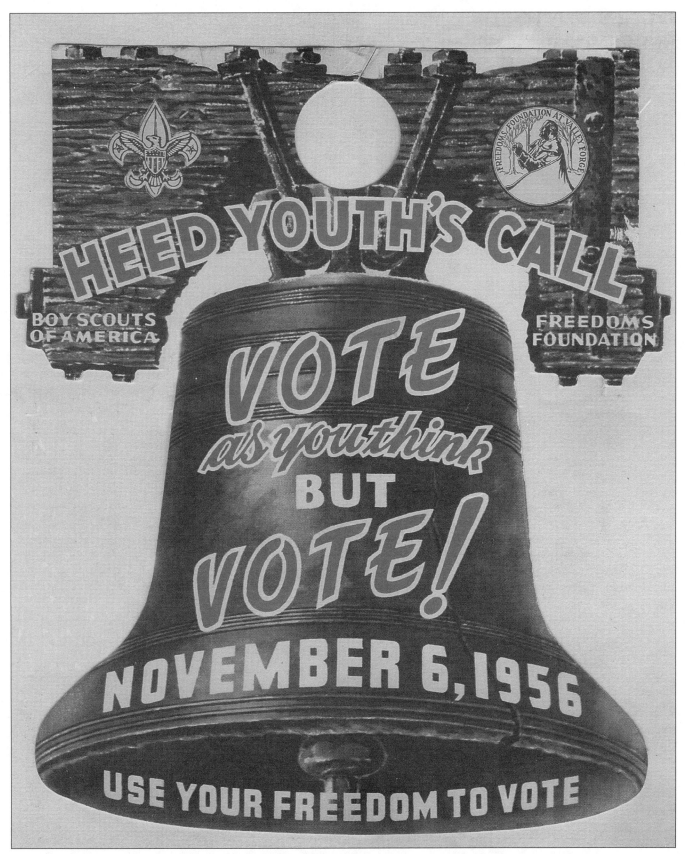

After World War II scouts participated in many community projects. This VOTE reminder door knob hanger is valued from $5.00 - $10.00.

## Treasury Liberty Loan Medal

The U.S. Treasury Department's War Service Medal for selling bonds.

| | | |
|---|---|---|
| June 1917 medal w/ 1 bar. | 1917-1919 | 40.00 - 60.00 |
| June 1917 medal w/ 2 bars. | 1917-1919 | 50.00 - 70.00 |
| June 1917 medal w/ 3 bars. | 1917-1919 | 60.00 - 80.00 |
| June 1917 medal w/ 4 bars. | 1917-1919 | 100.00 - 125.00 |
| June 1917 pendant on blue ribbon. | 1917-1919 | 35.00 - 50.00 |
| October 1917 medal w/ 1 bar. | 1917-1919 | 40.00 - 60.00 |
| October 1917 medal w/ 2 bars. | 1917-1919 | 50.00 - 70.00 |
| October 1917 medal w/ 3 bars. | 1917-1919 | 60.00 - 80.00 |
| October 1917 pendant on blue ribbon. | 1917-1919 | 35.00 - 50.00 |
| April 1918 medal w/ 1 bar. | 1917-1919 | 40.00 - 60.00 |
| April 1918 medal w/ 2 bars. | 1917-1919 | 50.00 - 70.00 |
| April 1918 pendant on blue ribbon. | 1917-1919 | 35.00 - 50.00 |
| October 1918 medal w/ 1 bar. | 1917-1919 | 40.00 - 60.00 |
| October 1918 pendant on blue ribbon. | 1917-1919 | 35.00 - 50.00 |
| May 1919 pendant on blue ribbon. | 1917-1919 | 35.00 - 50.00 |

## War Production Board, Waste Paper Award

| | | |
|---|---|---|
| 1000 above eagle. | 1917-1919 | 20.00 - 30.00 |

## War Savings Stamps Ace Award

| | | |
|---|---|---|
| Statue of Liberty Torch. | 1917-1919 | 60.00 - 80.00 |

Ace Award for selling War Savings Stamps. The medal was awarded for base sales. Bronze, silver, or gold palms were awarded for additional sales.

| | | |
|---|---|---|
| Statue of Liberty Torch. W/ bronze palm. | 1917-1919 | 75.00 - 100.00 |
| Statue of Liberty Torch. W/ bronze and silver palm. | 1917-1919 | 100.00 - 125.00 |
| Statue of Liberty Torch. W/ silver palm. | 1917-1919 | 100.00 - 125.00 |
| Statue of Liberty Torch. W/ gold palm. | 1917-1919 | 250.00 - 350.00 |

Livingston medal for bond sales.

## Every Scout to Save a Soldier/ Weapons for Liberty

| | | | |
|---|---|---|---|
| Kneeling scout holds sword to standing and flag-draped Liberty. 28mm, gold, uniface. | 1917 | Dio.1917.1A | 1,500.00 - 2,000.00 |
| Kneeling scout holds sword to standing and flag-draped Liberty. 28mm, silver, uniface. | 1917 | Dio.1917.1B | 750.00 - 1,000.00 |
| Kneeling scout holds sword to standing and flag-draped Liberty. 28mm, bronze, uniface | 1917 | Dio.1917.1C | 250.00 - 400.00 |

Patrol of Eagle Scouts visits the Statue of Liberty.

# WORLD AND NATIONAL JAMBOREE ITEMS

Both National and World Jamborees are unforgettable lifetime experiences for all who attend. The First National Scout Jamboree in the U.S. was planned for 1935 to honor the 25th Anniversary of the movement, however, an outbreak of polio caused it to be postponed until 1937. After World War II, jamborees resumed in 1950, 1953, 1957, 1960, 1964, 1969, 1973, 1977, 1981, 1985, 1989, 1993, and 1997. The break in the sequence is to have them avoid World Jamboree years and to fall on successive 25th anniversaries. They have been held around the country, but since 1981, all have been at Fort A.P. Hill, Bowling Green, VA. World Jamborees have been held since 1920, with each national scouting organization sending troops of scouts as representatives.

## World Jamboree U.S. Contingent

| | | |
|---|---|---|
| Contingent Medal | 1920 | 1,000.00 - 1,300.00 |
| | 1924 | 2,250.00 - 2,750.00 |
| | 1929 | 350.00 - 450.00 |
| | 1933 | 400.00 - 600.00 |
| Contingent Patch | | |
| | 1920 & 1924 | 350.00 - 450.00 |
| | 1929 | 175.00 - 250.00 |
| | 1933 | 175.00 - 225.00 |
| | 1947 | 80.00 - 120.00 |
| | 1951 | 40.00 - 60.00 |
| | 1955 | 20.00 - 30.00 |
| | 1957 | 20.00 - 30.00 |

## 1935 National Jamboree

| | | |
|---|---|---|
| Identification Card. | 1935 | 15.00 - 25.00 |
| Neckerchief. Boy's, blue, 4" insignia, full square. | 1935 | 100.00-150.00 |
| Neckerchief. Boy's, red, 4" insignia, full square. | 1935 | 100.00-150.00 |
| Neckerchief. Leader, blue, 2" insignia, full square. | 1935 | 100.00-150.00 |
| Neckerchief. Leader, red, 2" insignia, full square. | 1935 | 100.00-150.00 |
| Neckerchief. Staff, purple, 2" insignia, full square. | 1935 | 200.00-250.00 |
| Pennant. Felt. 10-1/2 x 28-3/4". | 1935 | 100.00-125.00 |
| Pocket Patch. Felt copy. Yellow inner and purple-yellow outer circle, red lettering. | 1935 | 3.00 - 5.00 |
| Pocket Patch. Felt, blue inner and purple-gold outer circle, dark red lettering. | 1935 | 100.00-150.00 |
| Pocket Patch. Felt, blue inner circle, purple-gold outer circle, red lettering. | 1935 | 125.00-150.00 |
| Region Shoulder Patch. Felt. | 1935 | 125.00-175.00 |
| Ring, silver. | 1935 | 75.00-100.00 |
| Troop Flag. | 1935 | 750.00-1,000.00 |

## 1937 National Jamboree

Neckerchief, 1937

| | | |
|---|---|---|
| Contest Medal. Red-white-blue ribbon. | 1937 | 250.00-350.00 |
| Identification card w/ RR pass. | 1937 | 15.00 - 25.00 |
| Identification Card. | 1937 | 7.50 - 15.00 |
| Neckerchief. Boy's, 2 blue or red emblems, full square. | 1937 | 90.00-120.00 |
| Neckerchief. Leader's, blue emblem w/ red border, or red emblem w/ blue border. Full square. | 1937 | 150.00-200.00 |
| Newspaper. Full set hardbound. | 1937 | 60.00 - 90.00 |
| Pennant. Felt. 11-1/2 x 29". | 1937 | 90.00-120.00 |
| Pocket Patch, Felt. | 1937 | 60.00 - 90.00 |
| Region Ribbon identification. | 1937 | 100.00-140.00 |
| Stationery. Envelope and letter sheet. | 1937 | 5.00 - 7.50 |
| Troop Flag. | 1937 | 750.00-1,000.00 |

## 1950 National Jamboree

Neckerchief, 1950

| | | |
|---|---|---|
| Identification Card. | 1950 | 10.00 - 15.00 |
| Neckerchief. Rayon-silk material. | 1950 | 30.00 - 50.00 |
| Neckerchief. Cotton, black or brown spur. | 1950 | 25.00 - 40.00 |
| Pennant. Blue felt, 11-1/2 x 29". | 1950 | 20.00 - 30.00 |
| Pocket Patch. Canvas, fine or coarse weave. | 1950 | 30.00 - 40.00 |
| Pocket Patch. Twill. | 1950 | 25.00 - 40.00 |
| Ring. Silver. | 1950 | 30.00 - 40.00 |
| Stationery. Envelope and letter sheet. | 1950 | 4.00 - 7.50 |
| Troop Flag. | 1950 | 300.00-400.00 |

Center emblem of troop flag, 1950

## 1953 National Jamboree

Neckerchief, 1953

| | | |
|---|---|---|
| Identification Card. | 1953 | 7.50 - 10.00 |
| Jacket Patch. Twill. | 1953 | 50.00 - 75.00 |
| Neckerchief. White cotton. | 1953 | 20.00 - 30.00 |
| Pennant. Blue felt, 11 x 28-3/4". | 1953 | 20.00 - 25.00 |
| Pocket Patch. Twill. | 1953 | 20.00 - 30.00 |
| Ring. Silver. | 1953 | 20.00 - 30.00 |
| Troop Flag. | 1953 | 300.00-400.00 |

## 1957 National Jamboree

Neckerchief, 1957

| | | |
|---|---|---|
| Baggage Tag. | 1957 | 5.00 - 10.00 |
| Contest Medal. Red-white-blue ribbon. | 1957 | 100.00-150.00 |
| Jacket Patch. Twill. | 1957 | 40.00 - 65.00 |
| Leather Patch. | 1957 | 30.00 - 45.00 |
| Neckerchief. White cotton. Thin, medium or thick letters. | 1957 | 15.00 - 25.00 |
| Newspaper (full set). | 1957 | 10.00 - 15.00 |
| Pocket Patch. Twill. | 1957 | 15.00 - 20.00 |
| Sardines in can. | 1957 | 15.00 - 25.00 |
| Stationery. Envelope and letter sheet. | 1957 | 3.00 - 5.00 |
| Tie. Silk screen on maroon. | 1957 | 75.00-100.00 |
| Troop Flag. | 1957 | 300.00-400.00 |

## 1960 National Jamboree

| | | |
|---|---|---|
| Area Competition Medal. Gilt. | 1960 | 50.00 - 75.00 |
| Baggage Tag. | 1960 | 7.50 - 12.50 |
| Competition Medal. Gilt Silvered, or bronze. | 1960 | 150.00-175.00 |
| Golden Rule Marble. Blue. | 1960 | 7.50 - 10.00 |
| Jacket Patch. Twill. | 1960 | 25.00 - 35.00 |
| Neckerchief. White cotton. | 1960 | 15.00 - 25.00 |
| Newspaper (full set). | 1960 | 5.00 - 10.00 |
| Pennant. Blue felt. 11 x 29-1/2". | 1960 | 15.00 - 20.00 |
| Pocket Patch. Twill. | 1960 | 12.50 - 17.50 |
| Sardines in can. | 1960 | 15.00 - 25.00 |
| Stationery. Envelope and letter sheet. | 1960 | 3.00 - 5.00 |
| Troop Flag. | 1960 | 300.00-400.00 |

Neckerchief, 1960

## 1964 National Jamboree

Neckerchief, 1964

| | | |
|---|---|---|
| Baggage Tag. | 1964 | 2.00 - 3.00 |
| Jacket Patch. Twill. | 1964 | 15.00 - 20.00 |
| Leather Patch. | 1964 | 15.00 - 20.00 |
| Neckerchief. White cotton. Thin, medium or thick letters. | 1964 | 10.00 - 15.00 |
| Newspaper (full set). | 1964 | 5.00 - 10.00 |
| Pocket Patch. Cloth back. | 1964 | 10.00 - 20.00 |
| Sardine Can. | 1964 | 5.00 - 7.50 |
| Troop Flag. | 1964 | 300.00-400.00 |

## 1969 National Jamboree

| | | |
|---|---|---|
| Jacket Patch. | 1969 | 10.00 - 15.00 |
| Leather Patch. | 1969 | 12.50 - 17.50 |
| Neckerchief. Green and brown on yellow. | 1969 | 10.00 - 15.00 |
| Neckerchief. Souvenir. Red and blue on white cotton. Printed envelope. | 1969 | 5.00 - 7.50 |
| Pennant. 11-1/2 x 28-1/2". | 1969 | 17.50 - 25.00 |
| Pocket Patch. Open or solid bough. | 1969 | 10.00 - 12.50 |
| Stationery. Envelope and letter sheet. | 1969 | 3.00 - 5.00 |
| Troop Flag. | 1969 | 300.00-400.00 |
| Zippo knife. | 1969 | 10.00 - 15.00 |

Neckerchief, green and yellow, 1969

## 1973 National Jamboree

Neckerchief, 1973

| | | |
|---|---|---|
| Baggage Tag. | 1973 | 1.00 - 3.00 |
| Jacket Patch. Clear or green plastic back. | 1973 | 7.50 - 10.00 |
| Jacket Patch. White or yellow woven back. | 1973 | 7.50 - 10.00 |
| Leather Patch. | 1973 | 7.50 - 10.00 |
| Neckerchief. | 1973 | 5.00 - 10.00 |
| Pocket Patch. Twill, clear or green plastic back. | 1973 | 3.00 - 5.00 |
| Pocket Patch. Twill, white or yellow woven back. | 1973 | 5.00 - 7.50 |

| | | |
|---|---|---|
| Sardine Can. | 1973 | 5.00 - 7.50 |
| Stationery. Envelope and letter sheet. | 1973 | 3.00 - 5.00 |
| Troop Flag. | 1973 | 250.00-350.00 |

## 1977 National Jamboree

Neckerchief, 1977

| | | |
|---|---|---|
| Baggage Tag. | 1977 | 1.00 - 3.00 |
| Jacket Patch. Twill. | 1977 | 5.00 - 7.50 |
| Leather Patch. | 1977 | 10.00 - 12.50 |
| Neckerchief. White cotton poly. m/c silk screen. | 1977 | 5.00 - 10.00 |
| Newspaper (full set). | 1977 | 5.00 - 7.50 |
| Pocket Patch. Twill. | 1977 | 3.00 - 5.00 |
| Sardines in can. | 1977 | 7.50 - 10.00 |
| Troop Flag. | 1977 | 200.00-300.00 |

## 1981 National Jamboree

Neckerchief, 1981

| | | |
|---|---|---|
| Baggage Tag. | 1981 | 1.00 - 2.00 |
| Jacket Patch. | 1981 | 5.00 - 7.50 |
| Leather Patch. | 1981 | 4.00 - 6.00 |
| Neckerchief. | 1981 | 4.00 - 6.00 |
| Pocket Patch. | 1981 | 4.00 - 6.00 |
| Troop Flag. | 1981 | 200.00-300.00 |

## 1985 National Jamboree

Neckerchief, 1985

| | | |
|---|---|---|
| Baggage Tag. | 1985 | 0.50 - 1.00 |
| Intaglio Card. | 1985 | 7.50-10.00 |
| Jacket Patch. | 1985 | 7.50 - 10.00 |
| Leather Patch. | 1985 | 5.00 - 7.50 |
| Neckerchief. | 1985 | 4.00 - 6.00 |
| Newspaper (full set). | 1985 | 5.00 - 7.50 |
| Pennant. 9 x 18". | 1985 | 10.00 - 15.00 |
| Pocket Patch. | 1985 | 4.50 - 6.50 |
| Stationery. Envelope and letter sheet. | 1985 | 1.00 - 2.00 |
| Troop Flag. | 1985 | 200.00-300.00 |

Intaglio card given out at the Merit Badge Midway, 1985

## 1989 National Jamboree

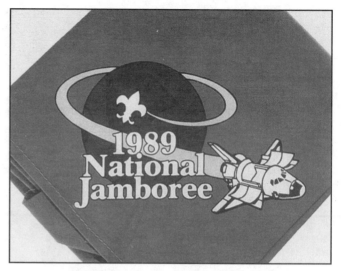

Neckerchief, 1989

| | | |
|---|---|---|
| Baggage Tag. | 1989 | 0.50 - 1.00 |
| Jacket Patch. | 1989 | 7.50 - 10.00 |
| Neckerchief. | 1989 | 4.00 - 6.00 |
| Newspaper (full set). | 1989 | 5.00 - 7.50 |
| Pocket Patch. | 1989 | 5.00 - 7.50 |
| Stationery. Envelope and letter sheet. | 1989 | 0.50 - 1.00 |
| Troop Flag. | 1989 | 200.00-300.00 |

Willard Scott interviews a scout editor at the Jamboree (1989).

## 1993 National Jamboree

Neckerchief, 1993

| | | |
|---|---|---|
| Baggage Tag. | 1993 | 0.50 - 1.00 |
| Jacket Patch. | 1993 | 7.50 - 10.00 |
| Neckerchief. | 1993 | 4.00 - 6.00 |
| Pocket Patch. | 1993 | 4.00 - 6.00 |
| Troop Flag. | 1993 | 200.00-300.00 |

## 1997 National Jamboree

Neckerchief, 1997

| | | |
|---|---|---|
| Jacket Patch. | 1997 | 7.50 - 10.00 |
| Neckerchief. | 1997 | 4.00 - 6.00 |
| Newspaper (full set). | 1997 | 5.00 - 7.50 |
| Pocket Patch. | 1997 | 4.00 - 6.00 |

# SCOUT SERVICE CORPS

## Chicago's Century of Progress Fair
| | | |
|---|---|---|
| Service Unit. Neckerchief. | 1933 | 150.00-200.00 |
| Service Unit. Pocket patch. | 1933 | 200.00-250.00 |

## Gettysburg, 50th Anniversary Reunion
| | | |
|---|---|---|
| Scout Service Medal. | 1913 | 300.00-400.00 |
| Scout Service Patch. | 1913 | 300.00-400.00 |

## International Eucharistic Congress, Philadelphia, PA
| | | |
|---|---|---|
| Scout Service Corps. Neckerchief. | 1976 | 40.00 - 50.00 |
| Scout Service Corps. Pocket patch. | 1976 | 30.00 - 40.00 |

## New York World's Fair

World's Fair neckerchiefs. Above, 1940; below 1964-65.

Linen patch and red cross armband worn by a Service Scout at the Gettysburg veterans' reunion.

| | | |
|---|---|---|
| Service Camp patch. Patch. | 1939 | 30.00 - 45.00 |
| Service Camp. Neckerchief slide, blue-orange Turk's head. | 1939 | 20.00 - 30.00 |
| Service Camp. Neckerchief. | 1940 | 40.00 - 50.00 |
| Service Camp. Neckerchief. | 1939 | 30.00 - 45.00 |
| Service Camp. Patch. | 1940 | 30.00 - 40.00 |
| Service Corps. Neckerchief. | 1964-1965 | 40.00 - 50.00 |
| Service Corps. Pocket patch. | 1964-1965 | 20.00 - 25.00 |
| Service Corps. Metal neckerchief slide. | 1964-1965 | 15.00 - 20.00 |

## Seattle World's Fair

| | | |
|---|---|---|
| Service Scouts. Neckerchief. | 1962 | 40.00 - 60.00 |
| Service Scouts. Patch. | 1962 | 60.00 - 80.00 |

# RESOURCE BOOKS

## Annual Report

| | | |
|---|---|---|
| BSA published. | 1910 | 50.00 - 75.00 |
| BSA published. | 1911 | 50.00 - 75.00 |
| BSA published. | 1912 | 50.00 - 75.00 |
| BSA published. | 1914 | 50.00 - 75.00 |
| BSA published. | 1915 | 50.00 - 75.00 |
| BSA published. | 1916 | 50.00 - 75.00 |
| BSA published. | 1917 | 40.00 - 60.00 |
| BSA published. | 1918 | 40.00 - 60.00 |
| BSA published. | 1919 | 40.00 - 60.00 |
| BSA published. | 1920 | 40.00 - 60.00 |
| BSA published. | 1921 | 40.00 - 60.00 |
| U.S. Gov't Printing Office. | 1921 | 30.00 - 40.00 |
| BSA published. | 1922 | 40.00 - 60.00 |
| U.S. Gov't Printing Office. | 1922 | 30.00 - 40.00 |
| U.S. Gov't Printing Office. | 1923 | 30.00 - 40.00 |
| U.S. Gov't Printing Office. | 1924 | 30.00 - 40.00 |
| U.S. Gov't Printing Office. | 1925 | 25.00 - 35.00 |
| U.S. Gov't Printing Office. | 1926 | 25.00 - 35.00 |
| U.S. Gov't Printing Office. | 1927 | 25.00 - 35.00 |
| U.S. Gov't Printing Office. | 1928 | 25.00 - 35.00 |
| U.S. Gov't Printing Office. | 1929 | 25.00 - 35.00 |
| U.S. Gov't Printing Office. | 1930 | 20.00 - 30.00 |
| U.S. Gov't Printing Office. | 1931 | 20.00 - 30.00 |
| U.S. Gov't Printing Office. | 1932 | 20.00 - 30.00 |
| U.S. Gov't Printing Office. | 1933 | 20.00 - 30.00 |
| U.S. Gov't Printing Office. | 1934 | 20.00 - 30.00 |
| U.S. Gov't Printing Office. | 1935 | 20.00 - 30.00 |
| U.S. Gov't Printing Office. | 1936 | 20.00 - 30.00 |
| U.S. Gov't Printing Office. | 1937 | 20.00 - 30.00 |
| U.S. Gov't Printing Office. | 1938 | 20.00 - 30.00 |
| U.S. Gov't Printing Office. | 1939 | 20.00 - 30.00 |
| U.S. Gov't Printing Office. | 1940 | 20.00 - 30.00 |
| U.S. Gov't Printing Office. | 1941 | 15.00 - 20.00 |
| U.S. Gov't Printing Office. | 1942 | 15.00 - 20.00 |
| U.S. Gov't Printing Office. | 1943 | 15.00 - 20.00 |
| U.S. Gov't Printing Office. | 1944 | 15.00 - 20.00 |
| U.S. Gov't Printing Office. | 1945 | 15.00 - 20.00 |
| U.S. Gov't Printing Office. | 1946 | 15.00 - 20.00 |
| U.S. Gov't Printing Office. | 1947 | 15.00 - 20.00 |
| U.S. Gov't Printing Office. | 1948 | 15.00 - 20.00 |
| U.S. Gov't Printing Office. | 1949 | 15.00 - 20.00 |
| U.S. Gov't Printing Office. | 1950 | 12.50 - 17.50 |
| U.S. Gov't Printing Office. | 1951 | 12.50 - 17.50 |
| U.S. Gov't Printing Office. | 1952 | 12.50 - 17.50 |
| U.S. Gov't Printing Office. | 1953 | 12.50 - 17.50 |
| U.S. Gov't Printing Office. | 1954 | 12.50 - 17.50 |
| U.S. Gov't Printing Office. | 1955 | 12.50 - 17.50 |
| U.S. Gov't Printing Office. | 1956 | 12.50 - 17.50 |
| U.S. Gov't Printing Office. | 1957 | 12.50 - 17.50 |
| U.S. Gov't Printing Office. | 1958 | 12.50 - 17.50 |
| U.S. Gov't Printing Office. | 1959 | 12.50 - 17.50 |
| U.S. Gov't Printing Office. | 1960 | 10.00 - 15.00 |
| U.S. Gov't Printing Office. | 1961 | 10.00 - 15.00 |
| U.S. Gov't Printing Office. | 1962 | 10.00 - 15.00 |
| U.S. Gov't Printing Office. | 1963 | 10.00 - 15.00 |
| U.S. Gov't Printing Office. | 1964 | 10.00 - 15.00 |
| U.S. Gov't Printing Office. | 1965 | 10.00 - 15.00 |
| U.S. Gov't Printing Office. | 1966 | 7.50 - 12.50 |
| U.S. Gov't Printing Office. | 1967 | 7.50 - 12.50 |
| U.S. Gov't Printing Office. | 1968 | 7.50 - 12.50 |
| U.S. Gov't Printing Office. | 1969 | 7.50 - 12.50 |
| U.S. Gov't Printing Office. | 1970 | 7.50 - 12.50 |
| U.S. Gov't Printing Office. | 1971 | 7.50 - 12.50 |
| U.S. Gov't Printing Office. | 1971 | 7.50 - 12.50 |
| U.S. Gov't Printing Office. | 1972 | 7.50 - 12.50 |
| U.S. Gov't Printing Office. | 1973 | 7.50 - 12.50 |
| U.S. Gov't Printing Office. | 1974 | 7.50 - 12.50 |
| U.S. Gov't Printing Office. | 1975 | 7.50 - 12.50 |
| U.S. Gov't Printing Office. | 1976 | 5.00 - 7.50 |
| U.S. Gov't Printing Office. | 1977 | 5.00 - 7.50 |
| U.S. Gov't Printing Office. | 1978 | 5.00 - 7.50 |
| U.S. Gov't Printing Office. | 1979 | 5.00 - 7.50 |
| U.S. Gov't Printing Office. | 1980 | 5.00 - 7.50 |
| U.S. Gov't Printing Office. | 1981 | 5.00 - 7.50 |
| U.S. Gov't Printing Office. | 1982 | 5.00 - 7.50 |
| U.S. Gov't Printing Office. | 1983 | 5.00 - 7.50 |
| U.S. Gov't Printing Office. | 1984 | 5.00 - 7.50 |
| U.S. Gov't Printing Office. | 1985 | 5.00 - 7.50 |
| U.S. Gov't Printing Office. | 1986 | 5.00 - 7.50 |
| U.S. Gov't Printing Office. | 1987 | 5.00 - 7.50 |
| U.S. Gov't Printing Office. | 1988 | 5.00 - 7.50 |
| U.S. Gov't Printing Office. | 1989 | 5.00 - 7.50 |
| U.S. Gov't Printing Office. | 1990 | 5.00 - 7.50 |
| U.S. Gov't Printing Office. | 1991 | 5.00 - 7.50 |
| U.S. Gov't Printing Office. | 1992 | 5.00 - 7.50 |
| U.S. Gov't Printing Office. | 1993 | 5.00 - 7.50 |
| U.S. Gov't Printing Office. | 1994 | 5.00 - 7.50 |
| U.S. Gov't Printing Office. | 1995 | 5.00 - 7.50 |
| U.S. Gov't Printing Office. | 1996 | 5.00 - 7.50 |
| U.S. Gov't Printing Office. | 1997 | 5.00 - 7.50 |

## Boy Scout Diary

| | |
|---|---|
| 1913 | 75.00 - 90.00 |
| 1914 | 60.00 - 75.00 |
| 1915 | 50.00 - 60.00 |
| 1916 | 50.00 - 60.00 |
| 1917 | 50.00 - 60.00 |
| 1918 | 50.00 - 60.00 |
| 1919 | 40.00 - 50.00 |
| 1920 | 40.00 - 50.00 |
| 1921 | 40.00 - 50.00 |
| 1922 | 40.00 - 50.00 |
| 1923 | 30.00 - 40.00 |
| 1924 | 30.00 - 40.00 |
| 1925 | 30.00 - 40.00 |
| 1926 | 30.00 - 40.00 |
| 1927 | 20.00 - 30.00 |
| 1928 | 20.00 - 30.00 |
| 1929 | 20.00 - 30.00 |
| 1930 | 20.00 - 30.00 |
| 1931 | 20.00 - 30.00 |
| 1932 | 15.00 - 25.00 |

| | |
|---|---|
| 1934 | 15.00 - 25.00 |
| 1933 | 15.00 - 25.00 |
| 1935 | 10.00 - 15.00 |
| 1936 | 10.00 - 15.00 |
| 1938 | 10.00 - 15.00 |
| 1937 | 10.00 - 15.00 |
| 1939 | 10.00 - 15.00 |
| 1940 | 7.50 - 10.00 |
| 1941 | 7.50 - 10.00 |
| 1942 | 7.50 - 10.00 |
| 1943 | 7.50 - 10.00 |
| 1944 | 7.50 - 10.00 |
| 1944 | 7.50 - 10.00 |
| 1945 | 7.50 - 10.00 |
| 1946 | 7.50 - 10.00 |
| 1947 | 7.50 - 10.00 |
| 1948 | 5.00 - 7.50 |
| 1949 | 5.00 - 7.50 |
| 1950 | 5.00 - 7.50 |
| 1951 | 5.00 - 7.50 |
| 1952 | 5.00 - 7.50 |
| 1953 | 5.00 - 7.50 |
| 1954 | 5.00 - 7.50 |
| 1955 | 5.00 - 7.50 |
| 1956 | 5.00 - 7.50 |
| 1957 | 5.00 - 7.50 |
| 1958 | 5.00 - 7.50 |
| 1959 | 5.00 - 7.50 |

The Annual Boy Scout Diary was a pocket weekly reminder.

"Camp Fires and Camp Cookery" were part of the leflax binder series published in the late 1920s.

These references are the official BSA numbers.

## Boycraft Booklets for Scout Leaders

| | | | |
|---|---|---|---|
| Building Troop Spirit. | 1923-1926 | A6 | 10.00 - 15.00 |
| Camp Fire Talks on the Scout Law. | 1926 | A21 | 10.00 - 15.00 |
| Camp Fires and Camp Cookery. | unknown | A7 | 10.00 - 15.00 |
| Discipline Without Demerits. | 1922-1926 | A5 | 10.00 - 15.00 |
| First Aid Made Easy. | unknown | A10 | 10.00 - 15.00 |
| The Good Turn Habit. | 1922-1926 | A3 | 10.00 - 15.00 |
| Helpbook for Boy Scouts. | 1926 | A18 | 10.00 - 15.00 |
| Hike Leadership. | 1926 | A19 | 10.00 - 15.00 |
| Hints on the Scout Tests. | 1927 | A22 | 10.00 - 15.00 |
| How to Run a Patrol. | 1922-1926 | A8 | 10.00 - 15.00 |
| How to Run a Troop. | 1924 | A1 | 10.00 - 15.00 |
| Identification of Trees. | unknown | A15 | 10.00 - 15.00 |
| The Job of the Troop Committee. | 1926 | A17 | 10.00 - 15.00 |
| Nature Games. | unknown | A13 | 10.00 - 15.00 |
| Nature Notebook for Scouts. | unknown | CP22 | 25.00 - 40.00 |
| Patrol Leader's Record Book. | unknown | A16 | 10.00 - 15.00 |
| Starting the troop Right. | 1922-1926 | A2 | 10.00 - 15.00 |
| Treasure Island Songbook. | unknown | A20 | 10.00 - 15.00 |
| Troop Ceremonies. | 1926 | A11 | 10.00 - 15.00 |
| The Troop Headquarters. | unknown | A4 | 10.00 - 15.00 |
| Troop Stunts. | 1925 | A12 | 10.00 - 15.00 |
| The Whys and Hows of Scouting. | 1925 | A14 | 10.00 - 15.00 |

## Service Library - Handicrafts Group

| | | | |
|---|---|---|---|
| Craftstrip Braiding Projects. | 1940 | 3169 | 10.00 - 15.00 |
| Leathercraft Methods Booklet. | 1940 | 3167 | 10.00 - 15.00 |
| Metalcraft Methods Booklet. | 1940 | 3168 | 10.00 - 15.00 |
| The Pine Tree Patrol. | 1930 | 3204 | 10.00 - 15.00 |

## Service Library - Plays Group

| | | | |
|---|---|---|---|
| A Strenuous Afternoon. | 1931 | 3175 | 5.00 - 10.00 |
| After Dark - A Boy Scout Comedy. | 1931 | 3150 | 5.00 - 10.00 |
| Be Prepared. | unknown | 3443 | 5.00 - 10.00 |
| Calling Jack's Bluff. | unknown | 3444 | 5.00 - 10.00 |
| Coming Clean - A Boy Scout Comedy. | 1931 | 3154 | 5.00 - 10.00 |
| Father Ex-Officio. | unknown | 3446 | 5.00 - 10.00 |
| The Fourth Musketeer. | 1939 | 3452 | 5.00 - 10.00 |
| Jambomania. | unknown | 3454 | 5.00 - 10.00 |
| Joe's Capture. | 1937 | 3453 | 5.00 - 10.00 |
| Kid's Awakening. | unknown | 3439 | 5.00 - 10.00 |
| The Missing Link. | unknown | 3445 | 5.00 - 10.00 |
| The Scout Circus. | 1934 | 3133 | 5.00 - 10.00 |
| Scout Entertainments. | unknown | 3224 | 5.00 - 10.00 |
| Scout Plays. | 1931 | 3130 | 5.00 - 10.00 |
| Scouts in Camp. | unknown | 3045 | 5.00 - 10.00 |
| Twice A Scout. | 1949 | 3148 | 5.00 - 10.00 |
| The Upper Trail. | unknown | 3447 | 5.00 - 10.00 |

## Service Library - Series A

| | | | |
|---|---|---|---|
| The Adventures of a District Commissioner. | 1933 | 3157 | 10.00 - 15.00 |
| Celebrating Anniversary Week. | 1928 | 3032 | 10.00 - 15.00 |
| Constitution and By-laws of the B.S.A. | 1933 | 3448 | 10.00 - 15.00 |
| Publicity. | 1928 | 3136 | 10.00 - 15.00 |
| Standard Local Council Constitution and By-Laws and District Committee By-Laws. | 1933 | 3736 | 10.00 - 15.00 |
| The Uniform, Badges and Insignia. | 1929 | 3189 | 10.00 - 15.00 |
| Uniform, Badges and Insignia. | 1933 | 3189 | 10.00 - 15.00 |
| Vacation Programs. | 1929 | 3135 | 10.00 - 15.00 |

## Service Library - Series B

| | | | |
|---|---|---|---|
| A Manual of Customs and Drills for Boy Scouts. | 1929 | 3274 | 10.00 - 15.00 |
| After Dark - A Boy Scout Comedy. | 1931 | 3150 | 10.00 - 15.00 |
| Bird Homes and How to Build Them. | 1928 | 3155 | 10.00 - 15.00 |
| Cal Ruggles, Troop Committeeman. | 1930 | 3148 | 10.00 - 15.00 |
| Coming Clean - A Boy Scout Comedy. | 1931 | 3154 | 10.00 - 15.00 |
| First Class Helps. | 1931 | 3021 | 10.00 - 15.00 |
| General Information Bulletin. | 1927 | 3270 | 10.00 - 15.00 |
| The Good Turn Test. | 1928 | 3113 | 10.00 - 15.00 |
| How to Organize a Troop of Boy Scouts. | 1929 | 3389 | 10.00 - 15.00 |
| Indian Handicraft. | 1930 | 3108 | 10.00 - 15.00 |
| Investiture Ceremonies. | 1928 | 3123 | 10.00 - 15.00 |
| Knifecraft. | 1929 | 3186 | 10.00 - 15.00 |
| Meeting Rooms for Troop & Patrol. | 1931 | 3104 | 10.00 - 15.00 |
| Model Airplanes. | 1929 | 3127 | 10.00 - 15.00 |
| The Patrol Method. | 1930 | 3144 | 10.00 - 15.00 |
| Pets. | 1930 | 3140 | 10.00 - 15.00 |
| The Practice of the Oath and Law. | 1928 | 3116 | 10.00 - 15.00 |
| Projects in Leather. | 1930 | 3537 | 10.00 - 15.00 |
| Requirements for the First Class Scout. | 1929 | 3021 | 10.00 - 15.00 |
| Requirements for the Second Class Scout. | 1929 | 3022 | 10.00 - 15.00 |
| Requirements for the Tenderfoot Scout. | 1929 | 3371 | 10.00 - 15.00 |
| Scout Courtesy, Customs and Drills. | 1942 | 3274 | 10.00 - 15.00 |
| Scout Plays. | 1931 | 3130 | 10.00 - 15.00 |
| Scouting with a Handkerchief. | 1927 | 3043 | 10.00 - 15.00 |
| The Scoutmaster and His Troop. | 1929 | 3180 | 10.00 - 15.00 |
| The Scoutmasters' First Six Weeks. | 1930 | 3102 | 10.00 - 15.00 |

| | | | |
|---|---|---|---|
| Second Class Helps. | 1930 | 3022 | 10.00 - 15.00 |
| Tenderfoot Helps. | 1931 | 3371 | 10.00 - 15.00 |
| The Troop Committee. | 1929 | 3080 | 10.00 - 15.00 |
| Troop Meeting Rooms. | 1930 | 3104 | 10.00 - 15.00 |
| Troop Spirit. | 1930 | 3103 | 10.00 - 15.00 |
| Troop Stunts. | 1931 | 3129 | 10.00 - 15.00 |
| The Yucca Patrol Idea. | 1930 | 3138 | 10.00 - 15.00 |

## Service Library - Series D

| | | | |
|---|---|---|---|
| Archery. | 1929 | 3188 | 10.00 - 15.00 |
| Boat Building and Canoe Repair. | unknown | 3145 | 10.00 - 15.00 |
| Boat Building, Canoe Repair and Paddle Making. | 1940 | 3145 | 10.00 - 15.00 |
| The Boy Scout Bird Record Book for Home, Camp and Hike. | 1930 | 3147 | 10.00 - 15.00 |
| Camp Buildings and Scout Shelters. | 1929 | 3441 | 10.00 - 15.00 |
| Camp Fire Helps. | 1930 | 3139 | 10.00 - 15.00 |
| Camp Fires and Camp Cookery. | (none) | 3121 | 10.00 - 15.00 |
| Camp Fires and Cooking. | 1935 | 3121 | 10.00 - 15.00 |
| Commissary, Cooking Gear & Food Cost Accounting. | 1938 | 3703 | 10.00 - 15.00 |
| How to Spin a Rope. | 1930 | 3119 | 10.00 - 15.00 |
| Kites (and Kite Flying). | 1931 | 3146 | 10.00 - 15.00 |
| Making Nature Collections. | unknown | 3198 | 10.00 - 15.00 |
| Minimum Standards for Boy Scout Camps. | 1928 | 3205 | 10.00 - 15.00 |
| Nature Collections. | 1929 | 3198 | 10.00 - 15.00 |
| Totem Poles. | 1929 | 3196 | 10.00 - 15.00 |

## Service Library - Series F

| | | | |
|---|---|---|---|
| The Boy Scout Scheme. | 1929 | 3002 | 10.00 - 15.00 |
| The Father and Son Idea and Scouting. | 1928 | 3137 | 10.00 - 15.00 |
| The Heart of a Boy. | 1928 | 2114 | 10.00 - 15.00 |
| Meeting that Secret Hazard. | 1928 | 3125 | 10.00 - 15.00 |
| Scouting Education. | 1927 | 3156 | 10.00 - 15.00 |
| Scouting in Relation to the Schools. | 1927 | 3176 | 10.00 - 15.00 |
| Service Clubs and Scouting. | 1929 | 3187 | 10.00 - 15.00 |
| True Stories of Real Scouts. | 1931 | 3128 | 10.00 - 15.00 |
| Your Home, Your Boy and Scouting. | unknown | 3158 | 10.00 - 15.00 |

## Service Library - Series Not Assigned

| | | | |
|---|---|---|---|
| Canoeing. | 1931 | 3107 | 10.00 - 15.00 |
| The Rally Book. | 1931 | 3134 | 10.00 - 15.00 |
| The Troop Program and Scout Tenure. Division of Program. | 1934 | | 10.00 - 15.00 |

# CALENDARS

Calendars in the early years of scouting were of a variety of shapes, sizes, and formats. Norman Rockwell designed the calendars until 1976, and since then they have been by Joseph Csatari. The prices are for the largest format, usually 14 x 20", with just the graphic design. Calendars with full year or partial year pads command a premium over just the image. Brown & Bigelow also made several smaller designs, 10 x 14" with removable month pads and a 6 x 8" with a color cover, and month sheets below on separate pages, with additional images and program helps. These smaller ones are somewhat hard to find complete.

The 1945 calendar by Norman Rockwell titled "I Will Do My Best." This is just the front cover from a 6 x 8" calendar. Worth about 1/3 of the price listed for the largest size.

## 1918, The Daily Good Turn

| | | |
|---|---|---|
| Scout w/ suitcase, helping elderly man. Rockwell, N. | 1918 | 50.00 - 75.00 |

## 1925, A Good Scout

| | | |
|---|---|---|
| 2 dogs, scout bandaging smaller dog's leg. Rockwell, N. | 1925 | 50.00 - 75.00 |

## 1926, A Good Turn
Scout seated on floor reading
   to old sailor. Rockwell, N.          1926          50.00 - 75.00

## 1927, Good Friends
Scout kneeling feeding litter of puppies.
   Rockwell, N.          1927          50.00 - 75.00

## 1929, Spirit of America
Boy Scout profile left. Rockwell, N.          1929          50.00 - 75.00

## 1931, Scout Memories
Dan Beard telling story to listening scout.
   Rockwell, N.          1931          40.00 - 60.00

## 1932, A Scout is Loyal
Colonial Patriot w/ outstretched hand,
   scout striding left. Rockwell, N.          1932          40.00 - 60.00

## 1933, An Army of Friendship
Array of 7 International Scouts facing
   forward, saluting. Rockwell, N.          1933          40.00 - 60.00

## 1934, Carry On
Old prospector pointing way to scout
   and dog. Rockwell, N.          1934          40.00 - 60.00

## 1935, On to Washington
1935 National Jamboree, scout striding
   before capitol and eagle in flight.
   Rockwell, N.          1935          40.00 - 60.00

## 1936, The Campfire Story
Scout Leader holding headdress,
   4 scouts and dog around. Rockwell, N.   1936          40.00 - 60.00

## 1937, Scouts of Many Trails
Old Salt w/ globe seated at table
   w/ Sea Scout and Boy Scout.
   Rockwell, N.          1937          40.00 - 60.00

## 1938, America Builds for Tomorrow
Boy Scouts builds bird house w/ 2 Cubs
   and Den Mother. Rockwell, N.          1938          40.00 - 60.00

## 1939, The Scouting Trail
Cub, Boy Scout, and Sea Explorer
   advancing left. In background profiles
   of historical explorers. Rockwell, N.          1939          40.00 - 60.00

## 1940, A Scout is Reverent
Scout and old man kneeling in pew.
   Rockwell, N.          1940          30.00 - 50.00

## 1942, A Scout is Loyal
First Class Scout striding forward holding
   Campaign Hat, Lincoln and Washington
   in background. Rockwell, N.          1942          30.00 - 50.00

## 1943, A Scout is Friendly
Patrol Leader helping immigrant family read.
   Rockwell, N.          1943          30.00 - 50.00

## 1944, We, Too, Have a Job to Do
Facing scout in Campaign Hat, saluting,
   flag in background. Rockwell, N.          1944          30.00 - 50.00

## 1945, I Will Do My Best
First Class Scout holding Campaign Hat,
   giving Scout Sign, before background
   of the Oath. Rockwell, N.          1945          30.00 - 50.00

## 1946, A Guiding Hand
Boy Scout teaching Cub Scout a knot.
   Rockwell, N.          1946          30.00 - 50.00

## 1947, All Together
Scout on high outcrop helps another
   up to the top. Rockwell, N.          1947          30.00 - 50.00

## 1948, Men of Tomorrow
Patrol Portaging 2 canoes, Cub seated
   in corner watching. Rockwell, N.          1948          30.00 - 50.00

## 1949, Friend in Need
Boy Scout patches dog's leg,
   held by Cub Scout. Rockwell, N.          1949          30.00 - 50.00

## 1950, Our Heritage
Boy and Cub Scout striding, looking
   upward at Washington kneeling
   in prayer left. Rockwell, N.          1950          25.00 - 40.00

## 1951, Forward America
Explorer, Cub Scout, Boy Scout,
   Air Scout, and Sea Scout all
   striding left. Rockwell, N.          1951          25.00 - 40.00

## 1952, The Adventure Trail
Boy Scout as Den Chief showing
   arrowheads to 2 intrigued
   Cub Scouts, all under a tree.
   Rockwell, N.          1952          25.00 - 40.00

## 1953, On My Honor
Cub Scout at attention, Boy Scout and
   Explorer giving Scout Sign,
   against background of Scout Oath
   and Liberty Bell. Rockwell, N.          1953          25.00 - 40.00

The 8 x 14-1/2" calendar with monthly pads and program ideas.

## 1954, A Scout is Reverent
Cub, Explorer, and Boy Scout seated
in church pews. Rockwell, N.        1954        25.00 - 40.00

## 1955, The Right Way
Explorer looks on as Boy Scout
shows bird house to 2 Cub Scouts.
Rockwell, N.        1955        25.00 - 40.00

## 1956, The Scoutmaster
Adult standing by campfire as
scouts sleep in tents in background.
Rockwell, N.        1956        30.00 - 50.00

## 1957, High Adventure
Group of Explorers along Philmont
trail, Tooth of Time in distance.
Rockwell, N.        1957        25.00 - 40.00

## 1958, Mighty Proud
Explorer and Mother sharpen up
Tenderfoot uniform on
ex-Cub Scout. Rockwell, N.        1958        25.00 - 40.00

## 1959, Tomorrow's Leader
Boy Scout w/ knapsack and compass
striding, looking right, large
First Class badge and montage
of merit badges in background.
Rockwell, N.        1959        25.00 - 40.00

## 1960, Ever Onward
1910 scout passing Scout Oath Scroll
to 1960 Eagle Scout and Cub Scout.
Rockwell, N.        1960        25.00 - 40.00

## 1961, Homecoming
Dad, Cub Scout greet Boy Scout
w/ backpack and duffle bag.
Rockwell, N.        1961        20.00 - 30.00

## 1962, Pointing the Way
Scoutmaster w/ compass directing
3 scouts. Rockwell, N.        1962        20.00 - 30.00

## 1963, A Good Sign All Over the World
Scottish scout and Boy Scout
Dancing jig, 4 others around,
large globe and Scout Sign in
background. Rockwell, N.        1963        20.00 - 30.00

## 1964, To Keep Myself Physically Strong
Cub Scout measuring Boy Scout's
chest. Rockwell, N.        1964        20.00 - 30.00

## 1965, A Great Moment
Mother pins Eagle Medal on son's chest,
Dad and Scoutmaster look on.
Rockwell, N.        1965        20.00 - 30.00

## 1966, Growth of a Leader
Scoutmaster, Explorer, Boy Scout,
and Cub Scout in profile left,
flag in background. Rockwell, N.        1966        20.00 - 30.00

## 1967, Breakthrough for Freedom
6 international scouts walking
forward w/ arms linked. Rockwell, N.        1967        20.00 - 30.00

## 1969, Behind the Easel
Scouts look on as Rockwell paints
a scene. Rockwell, N.        1969        30.00 - 40.00

## 1970, Come and Get It!
Scouts camping and cooking at lakeside.
Rockwell, N.        1970        20.00 - 30.00

## 1971, America's Manpower Begins with Boypower
2 Cubs, Den Mother, Boy Scout,
and Explorer, back row of Adult
Leaders. Rockwell, N.        1971        10.00 - 15.00

## 1972, Can't Wait
Cub Scout dressing in very loose-fitting
Boy Scout uniform. Rockwell, N.        1972        10.00 - 15.00

## 1973, From Concord to Tranquility
Cub Scout, Boy Scouts, Explorer,
Astronaut, and Colonial Patriot
all salute flag in background.
Rockwell, N.        1973        10.00 - 15.00

## 1974, We Thank Thee, O'Lord
Patrol at camp, Cook by meal,
all bowed in grace. Rockwell, N.        1974        10.00 - 15.00

## 1976, The Spirit of 1976
Cub Scout, Boy Scout, and Explorer
as drummer and flag bearer.
Rockwell, N.        1976        10.00 - 15.00

## 1977
Csatari, J.        1977        7.50 - 12.50

## 1978
Csatari, J.        1978        7.50 - 12.50

## 1979, Eagle Service Project
Csatari, J.                              1979        7.50 - 12.50

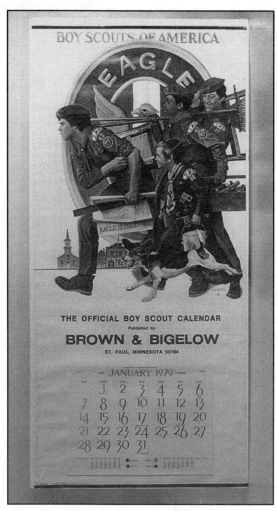

Full size 1979 calendar with full pad of months.

## 1980, The Reunion
Csatari, J.                              1980        7.50 - 12.50

## 1981, After Hours
Csatarii, J.                             1981        7.50 - 12.50

## 1982, Family Camping
Csatari, J.                              1982        7.50 - 12.50

## 1983
Csatari, J.                              1983        7.50 - 12.50

## 1984
Csatari, J.                              1984        7.50 - 12.50

## 1985, The Spirit Lives On, 1910-1985
Csatari, J.                              1985        7.50 - 12.50

## 1986, It's a Boy's Life
Csatari, J.                              1986        7.50 - 12.50

## 1987
Csatari, J.                              1987        7.50 - 12.50

## 1988, Winter Camping
Csatari, J.                              1988        7.50 - 12.50

## 1989, You Can Do It
Csatari, J.                              1989        7.50 - 12.50

## 1990, The Scoutmaster
Csatari, J.                              1990        7.50 - 12.50

## 1991
Csatari, J.                              1991        7.50 - 12.50

## 1992
Csatari, J.                              1992        7.50 - 12.50

## 1993
Csatari, J.                              1993        7.50 - 12.50

## 1994
Csatari, J.                              1994        7.50 - 12.50

## 1995
Csatari, J.                              1995        7.50 - 12.50

## 1996
Csatari, J.                              1996        7.50 - 12.50

## 1997, The Patrol Leader
Csatari, J.                              1997        7.50 - 12.50

# SERIES BOOKS

Inexpensively-produced story books for the youth of the early twentieth century were a way to excite boys to read; they were also a way for publishers to encourage advantage of the scouting movement's vast appeal. Many series titles were produced between 1910 and 1930, some with well-illustrated dust jackets, some with multi-colored paper pasted on cloth covers, and others with multi-colored stamped covers. Collectors today will pay a premium for dust-jacketed books in good condition.

# • MEMBERSHIP CARDS •

he pre-1920 cards are three or four pages with a rivet in the corner. From 1920 through 1942 they
ere tri-fold with various graphic changes. The mid-1940s saw the bi-fold card, and by the 1950s
hey were a single page card without any rank/advancement notations.

# • HANDBOOKS •

Handbooks are what every scout needed and should have used well. The earliest cover in this group is from 1920 (middle row, left). The others represent the major cover designs since then.

# • NECKERCHIEFS •

National Jamboree Neckerchiefs: just one of many popular reminders of a scout's once-in-a-lifetime experience. Pocket patches, baggage tags, rings, and food tickets are some of the other items which use the same general design elements.

# • ACHIEVEMENT MEDALS •

These four medals represent the ultimate in scouting's advancement program. From left: the Eagle (Boy Scout), Quartermaster (Sea Scout), Ranger (Explorer Scout), and Silver Award (Exploring).

The medal at left is a First Aid medal from the 1920s. The center (Knot Tying) and right (a general contest medal) examples were both used in the 1930s and '40s—the solid blue ribbon is a giveaway to their dates of usage.

# • MERIT BADGES •

rom 1911 through the 1930s merit
adges were square cut tan twill (the
wimming badge, center). The nar-
ow border crimped tan twill music
adge (top left) was typical from the
id-1930s to the mid-1940s. The badge for
arm lay-out (top right) shows the fine
an twill used in the early 1940s. In the
960s badges were green twill with a
olled edge (the lifesaving badge). The
oin collecting badge is an example of a
ully-embroidered rolled edge with a plastic back (used since 1972).

# • POSITION PATCHES •

The square
cut cloth patch (Neighborhood
Commisioner; center)[1] was in
an (pre-1939) and later in
khaki (1939-1945). The twill
cut edge was used from 1938-
1956 (Scoutmaster)[2]; from
1956-1966 the embroidered
cut edge was typical (Asst.
District Executive)[3]; the
twill Council Committee
patch[4] has a rolled edge and was
used from 1967-1969. The District Commisioner
patch[5] has an embroidered rolled edge (1967-1969); the 3-
inch twill rolled edge patch[6] (National Executive Staff) was
used from 1970-1989; from 1972-1983 mylar fully embroidered patches were also made for trained volunteers (Asst. Webelos Den Leader)[7].

# • ADULT POSITION PATCHES •

Most of us spend more time in scouting as adults (assisting our children) than we did as youth members. These adult position patches are from 1972-1989. In general, a blue background is for Volunteers, red for Professionals or Commissioners, and purple for National Officers.

# RANK & POSITION PATCHES •

Troop Position, Veteran, and Rank Insignia all experienced changes from cut edge tan[1] (Star and Bugler) to cut edge khaki[2] (Star, SPL, Quartermaster, and Five-year Veteran). These changed to rolled edge khaki twill[3] (Star, Bugler, and Quartermaster) before being replaced in 1972 by oval rank badges and 3-inch rolled edge position patches.

The first official Boy Scout Kodak Camera is from 1928, although the copyright dates are much earlier. The green bellows were replaced with standard black within two years. The carrying case has slots for a belt to pass through.

# • FICTION STORY BOOKS •

Story books have long been a popular way to get youth to read. This particular book is for an age group younger than eleven and has great illustrations.

# • COLLAR & HAT PINS •

From the 1920s through 1969 collar pins were available for adults. This red enameled hat badge at left (1915-1920) was for an Assistant Scoutmaster. The example with the blue enameled background (last used in 1969) was for a Layman (Troop Committeeman).

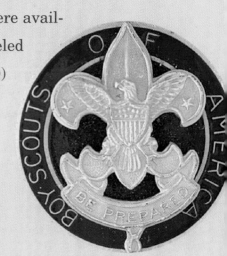

The stories, in general, leave something to be desired by modern-day standards.

## Adventure & Mystery Series for Boys, A.L. Burt

| | | |
|---|---|---|
| The Big Opportunity. | 1934 | 5.00 - 10.00 |

## Ames, Joseph B.

| | | |
|---|---|---|
| Under Boy Scout Colors,<br>(EBL edition) Grosset & Dunlap. | 1917 | 5.00 - 15.00 |

## Boy Scout Life Series

| | | |
|---|---|---|
| The Boy Scout Firefighters, Irving Crump,<br>Barse & Hopkins Publishers. | 1917 | 5.00 - 15.00 |
| The Boy Scout Trailblazers, F.H. Cheley,<br>Barse & Hopkins Publishers. | 1917 | 5.00 - 15.00 |
| The Boy Scout Treasure Hunters,<br>C.H. Lerrigo, Barse & Hopkins<br>Publishers. | 1917 | 5.00 - 15.00 |
| Boy Scouts Afloat, Walter Walden,<br>Barse & Hopkins Publishers. | 1918 | 5.00 - 15.00 |
| Boy Scouts Courageous, Franklin K.<br>Mathiews, Barse & Hopkins Publishers. | 1918 | 5.00 - 15.00 |

| | | |
|---|---|---|
| The Boy Scouts in Africa, Capt. A.P.<br>Corcoran, Barse & Hopkins Publishers. | 1923 | 5.00 - 15.00 |
| The Boy Scouts of Round Table Patrol, C.H.<br>Lerrigo, Barse & Hopkins Publishers. | 1924 | 5.00 - 15.00 |
| The Boy Scouts of the Lighthouse<br>Troop, F. Moulton McLane,<br>Barse & Hopkins Publishers. | 1917 | 5.00 - 15.00 |
| Boy Scouts on the Trail, John Garth,<br>Barse & Hopkins Publishers. | 1920 | 5.00 - 15.00 |
| Boy Scouts to the Rescue, C.H. Lerrigo,<br>Barse & Hopkins Publishers. | 1920 | 5.00 - 15.00 |

## Boy Scout Series, M.A. Donahoue & Co. Publishers

| | | |
|---|---|---|
| Boy Scouts in the Everglades,<br>or The Island in Lost Channel,<br>Fletcher, Mjr. Archibald Lee. | 1913 | 5.00 - 15.00 |

## Boy Scout Series, M.A. Donahue & Co. Publishers

| | | |
|---|---|---|
| Boy Scout's Woodcraft Lesson,<br>or Proving their Mettle in the Field,<br>Fletcher, Mjr. Archibald Lee. | 1913 | 5.00 - 15.00 |

## Boy Scout Series, M.A. Donahue & Co. Publishers

Boy Scouts on a Long Hike, or Two the
  Rescue in the Black Water Swamps,
  Fletcher, Mjr. Archibald Lee.         1913         5.00 - 15.00

## Boy Scout Series, M.A. Donahue & Co., Publishers

Boy Scout Pathfinders, or The Strange
  Hunt for the Beaver Patrol, Fletcher,
  Mjr. Archibald Lee.                   1913         5.00 - 15.00
Boy Scout Rivals, or A Leader of the
  Tenderfoot Patrol, Fletcher,
  Mjr. Archibald Lee.                   1913         5.00 - 15.00
Boy Scouts in Alaska, or The Camp
  on the Glacier, Fletcher,
  Mjr. Archibald Lee.                   1913         5.00 - 15.00
Boy Scouts in the Coal Caverns,
  or The Light in Tunnel Six,
  Fletcher, Mjr. Archibald Lee.         1913         5.00 - 15.00
Boy Scouts on Old Superior, or The Tale
  of the Pictured Rocks, Fletcher,
  Mjr. Archibald Lee.                   1913         5.00 - 15.00
Boy Scouts on the Great Divide,
  or The Ending of the Trail, Fletcher,
  Mjr. Archibald Lee.                   1913         5.00 - 15.00
Boy Scouts' Signal Sender, or When
  Wig Wag Knowledge Paid, Fletcher,
  Mjr. Archibald Lee.                   1913         5.00 - 15.00
Boy Scouts Test of Courage, or
  Winning the Merit Badge, Fletcher,
  Mjr. Archibald Lee.                   1913         5.00 - 15.00

## Boy Scout Series, M.A. Donahue & Co., Publishers

Boy Scouts in Northern Wilds,
  or The Signal from the Hills,
  Fletcher, Mjr. Archibald Lee.         1913         5.00 - 15.00

## Boy Scout Series, W.A. Wilde, Publisher

Boy Scouts at Crater Lake, Eaton, Walter P. 1922    5.00 - 15.00
Boy Scouts at the Grand Canyon,
  Eaton, Walter P.                      1932         5.00 - 10.00
Boy Scouts in Death Valley, Eaton,
  Walter P.                             1939         5.00 - 10.00
Boy Scouts in Glacier Park, Eaton,
  Walter P.                             1918         5.00 - 15.00
Boy Scouts in the Dismal Swamp,
  Eaton, Walter P.                      1913         5.00 - 15.00
Boy Scouts in the White Mountains,
  Eaton, Walter P.                      1914         5.00 - 15.00
Boy Scouts of Berkshire, Eaton, Walter P. 1912      5.00 - 15.00
Boy Scouts of the Wild Cat
  Patrol, Eaton, Walter P.              1915         5.00 - 15.00
Boy Scouts on Green Mountain
  Trail, Eaton, Walter P.               1929         5.00 - 15.00

Boy Scouts on Katahdin, Eaton, Walter P. 1924       5.00 - 15.00
Peanut, Cub Reporter, Eaton, Walter P.   1916       5.00 - 15.00

## Boy Scouts Series, A.L. Chatterton Co.

Boy Scouts in the Black Hills, Victor, Ralph. 1913  5.00 - 15.00
The Boy Scouts in the Canadian Rockies,
  Victor, Ralph.                        1911         5.00 - 15.00
Boy Scouts in the North Woods,
  Victor, Ralph.                        1913         5.00 - 15.00
Boy Scouts on the Yukon, Victor, Ralph.  1912        5.00 - 15.00
The Boy Scouts' Air Craft, Victor, Ralph. 1912      10.00 - 25.00
The Boy Scouts' Canoe Trip, Victor, Ralph. 1911      5.00 - 15.00
The Boy Scouts' Motorcycles, Victor, Ralph. 1911     5.00 - 15.00
The Boy Scouts' Patrol, Victor, Ralph.   1911        5.00 - 15.00

## Boy Scouts Series, Hurst & Co., a still later reprint

Boy Scouts in the Black Hills, Victor, Ralph. 1913  5.00 - 15.00
The Boy Scouts in the Canadian
  Rockies, Victor, Ralph.               1911         5.00 - 15.00
Boy Scouts in the North Woods,
  Victor, Ralph.                        1913         5.00 - 15.00
Boy Scouts on the Yukon, Victor, Ralph.  1912        5.00 - 15.00
The Boy Scouts' Air Craft, Victor, Ralph. 1912      10.00 - 25.00
The Boy Scouts' Canoe Trip, Victor, Ralph. 1911      5.00 - 15.00
The Boy Scouts' Motorcycles, Victor, Ralph. 1911    10.00 - 25.00
The Boy Scouts' Patrol, Victor, Ralph.   1911        5.00 - 15.00

## Boy Scouts Series, Plate and Peck Co. reprint

Boy Scouts in the Black Hills, Victor, Ralph. 1913  5.00 - 15.00
The Boy Scouts in the Canadian
  Rockies, Victor, Ralph.               1911         5.00 - 15.00
Boy Scouts in the North Woods,
  Victor, Ralph.                        1913         5.00 - 15.00
Boy Scouts on the Yukon, Victor, Ralph.  1912        5.00 - 15.00
The Boy Scouts' Motorcycles, Victor, Ralph. 1911    10.00 - 25.00
The Boy Scouts' Air Craft, Victor, Ralph. 1912      10.00 - 25.00
The Boy Scouts' Canoe Trip, Victor, Ralph. 1911      5.00 - 15.00
The Boy Scouts' Patrol, Victor, Ralph.   1911        5.00 - 15.00

## Boys' Life - Pedro Books

Ahead of their Time, G.P. Putnam's Sons.  1968      3.00 - 7.50
Baseball as We Played It,
  G.P. Putnam's Sons.                   1969         3.00 - 7.50
Best Jokes from Boys' Life,
  G.P. Putnam's Sons.                   1970         3.00 - 7.50
Best of Boys Life 1, G.P. Putnam's Sons.  1968       3.00 - 7.50
Great Crime Busters,
  G.P. Putnam's Sons.                   1967         3.00 - 7.50
Great True Adventures,
  G.P. Putnam's Sons.                   1968         3.00 - 7.50
Pedro's Tall Tales, G.P. Putnam's Sons.   1967       3.00 - 7.50
Time Machine to the Rescue,
  Donald Keith, G.P. Putnam's Sons.     1967         3.00 - 7.50

## Boys' Life Editors
Boy's Life Dog Stories, Nelson.    1949    3.00 - 10.00
Boys' Life Adventure Stories, Nelson.    1950    3.00 - 10.00
Boys' Life Book of Scout Stories,
   Doubleday.    1953    3.00 - 10.00
The Boys' Life Treasury, Simon & Schuster. 1958    3.00 - 10.00

## Bronc Burnett Series
Eagle Scout, McCormick, Wilfred,
   G.P. Putnam's Sons.    1952    5.00 - 10.00

## Circling the Globe Series, Arthur Westbrook Co.
Boy Scouts and the Prize Pennant,
   Shaler, Robert.    1914    5.00 - 15.00
Boy Scouts as County Fair Guides,
   Shaler, Robert.    1915    5.00 - 15.00
Boy Scouts as Forest Fire Fighters,
   Shaler, Robert.    1915    5.00 - 15.00
Boy Scouts for City Improvement,
   Shaler, Robert.    1914    5.00 - 15.00
Boy Scouts in the Great Flood,
   Shaler, Robert.    1915    5.00 - 15.00
Boy Scouts with the Red Cross,
   Shaler, Robert.    1915    5.00 - 15.00

## Crowell's Scout Book Series
Along the Mohawk Trail, Fitzhugh,
   Percy, K., Thomas Y. Crowell Co.    1912    5.00 - 15.00
Boy Scouts in a Lumber Camp,
   Otis, James, Thomas Y. Crowell Co.    1913    5.00 - 15.00
Boy Scouts in the Main Woods,
   Otis, James, Thomas Y. Crowell Co.    1911    5.00 - 15.00
For Uncle Sam Boss, or, Boy Scouts at
   Panama, Fitzhugh, Percy, K.,
   Thomas Y. Crowell Co.    1913    5.00 - 15.00
In the Path of LaSalle, or Boy Scouts
   on the Mississippi, Fitzhugh, Percy, K.,
   Thomas Y. Crowell Co.    1914    5.00 - 15.00
Pluck on the Trail, or Boy Scouts
   in the Rockies, Sabin, Edwin L.,
   Thomas Y. Crowell Co.    1912    5.00 - 15.00

## Don Strong Series, D. Appleton & Co.
Don Strong of the Wolf Patrol,
   Heyliger, William.    1916    5.00 - 15.00
Don Strong, American, Heyliger, William.    1920    5.00 - 15.00
Don Strong, Patrol Leader,
   Heyliger, William.    1918    5.00 - 15.00

## Every Boy's Library, Boy Scout Edition
20,000 Leagues Under the Sea, Verne.
   Khaki cover, seal on spine.    1913-1922    5.00 - 10.00
A Gunner Aboard the Yankee, Doubleday.
   Khaki cover, seal on spine.    1913-1922    5.00 - 10.00
A Midshipman in the Pacific, Brady.
   Khaki cover, no seal on spine.    1913-1922    5.00 - 10.00
A Midshipman in the Pacific, Brady.
   Khaki cover, seal on spine.    1913-1922    5.00 - 10.00
Adventures in Beaver Stream Camp,
   Dugmore. Khaki cover, no seal on spine. 1913-1922    5.00 - 10.00
Along the Mohawk Trail, Fitzhugh.
   Color image cover.    1913-1922    5.00 - 10.00
Along the Mohawk Trail, Fitzhugh.
   Khaki cover, seal on spine.    1913-1922    5.00 - 10.00
Animal Heroes, Seton. Color image cover.    1913-1922    5.00 - 10.00
Animal Heroes, Seton. Khaki cover,
   seal on spine.    1913-1922    5.00 - 10.00
Baby Elton, Quarterback, Quirk.
   Khaki cover, seal on spine.    1913-1922    5.00 - 10.00
Baby Elton, Quarterback, Quirk.
   Color image cover.    1913-1922    5.00 - 10.00
Baby Elton, Quarterback, Quirk.
   Khaki cover, no seal on spine.    1913-1922    5.00 - 10.00
Bartley, Freshman Pitcher, Heylinger.
   Khaki cover, seal on spine.    1913-1922    5.00 - 10.00

| | | |
|---|---|---|
| Be Prepared, The Boy Scouts in Florida, Dimock. Khaki cover, seal on spine. | 1913-1922 | 5.00 - 10.00 |
| Billy topsail with Dr. Luke of the Labrador, Duncan. Khaki cover, seal on spine. | 1913-1922 | 5.00 - 10.00 |
| The Biography of a Grizzly, Seton. Khaki cover, seal on spine. | 1913-1922 | 5.00 - 10.00 |
| The Biography of a Grizzly, Seton. Color image cover. | 1913-1922 | 5.00 - 10.00 |
| The Blazed Trail, White. Khaki cover, seal on spine. | 1913-1922 | 5.00 - 10.00 |
| The Blazed Trail, White. Khaki cover, no seal on spine. | 1913-1922 | 5.00 - 10.00 |
| Boat Building and Boating, Beard. Khaki cover, seal on spine. | 1913-1922 | 5.00 - 10.00 |
| The Boy Scouts of bob's Hill, Burton. Khaki cover, seal on spine. | 1913-1922 | 5.00 - 10.00 |
| The Boy Scouts of bob's Hill, Burton. Color image cover. | 1913-1922 | 5.00 - 10.00 |
| The Boy Scouts of the Black Eagle Patrol, Quirk. Khaki cover, seal on spine. | 1913-1922 | 5.00 - 10.00 |
| The Boy Scouts of the Black Eagle Patrol, Quirk. Color image cover. | 1913-1922 | 5.00 - 10.00 |
| The Boy's Book of New Inventions, Maule. Khaki cover, seal on spine. | 1913-1922 | 5.00 - 10.00 |
| Brown Wold, London. Khaki cover, seal on spine. | 1913-1922 | 5.00 - 10.00 |
| Buccaneers and Pirates of Our Coasts, Stockton. Khaki cover, seal on spine. | 1913-1922 | 5.00 - 10.00 |
| Buccaneers and Pirates of Our Coasts, Stockton. Khaki cover, no seal on spine. | 1913-1922 | 5.00 - 10.00 |
| Buccaneers and Pirates of Our Coasts, Stockton. Color image cover. | 1913-1922 | 5.00 - 10.00 |
| Cab and Caboose, Monroe. Khaki cover, no seal on spine. | 1913-1922 | 5.00 - 10.00 |
| Cab and Caboose, Monroe. Khaki cover, seal on spine. | 1913-1922 | 5.00 - 10.00 |
| The Call of the Wild, London. Color image cover. | 1913-1922 | 5.00 - 10.00 |
| The Call of the Wild, London. Khaki cover, seal on spine. | 1913-1922 | 5.00 - 10.00 |
| The Call of the Wild, London. Khaki cover, no seal on spine. | 1913-1922 | 5.00 - 10.00 |
| Cattle ranch to College, Doubleday. Color image cover. | 1913-1922 | 5.00 - 10.00 |
| Cattle ranch to College, Doubleday. Khaki cover, no seal on spine. | 1913-1922 | 5.00 - 10.00 |
| Cattle ranch to College, Doubleday. Khaki cover, seal on spine. | 1913-1922 | 5.00 - 10.00 |
| College Years, Paine. Khaki cover, no seal on spine. | 1913-1922 | 5.00 - 10.00 |
| College Years, Paine. Khaki cover, seal on spine. | 1913-1922 | 5.00 - 10.00 |
| Crooked Trails, Remington. Khaki cover, no seal on spine. | 1913-1922 | 5.00 - 10.00 |
| Crooked Trails, Remington. Khaki cover, seal on spine. | 1913-1922 | 5.00 - 10.00 |
| The Cruise of the Cachelot, Bullen. Khaki cover, no seal on spine. | 1913-1922 | 5.00 - 10.00 |
| The Cruise of the Cachelot, Bullen. Khaki cover, seal on spine. | 1913-1922 | 5.00 - 10.00 |
| The Cruise of the Cachelot, Bullen. Color image cover. | 1913-1922 | 5.00 - 10.00 |
| The Cruise of the Dazzler, London. Color image cover. | 1913-1922 | 5.00 - 10.00 |
| The Cruise of the Dazzler, London. Khaki cover, seal on spine. | 1913-1922 | 5.00 - 10.00 |
| Danny Fists, Camp. Khaki cover, seal on spine. | 1913-1922 | 5.00 - 10.00 |
| Don Strong of the Wolf Patrol, Heyliger. Color image cover. | 1913-1922 | 5.00 - 10.00 |
| Don Strong of the Wolf Patrol, Heyliger. Khaki cover, seal on spine. | 1913-1922 | 5.00 - 10.00 |
| Don Strong, patrol Leader, Heyliger. Color image cover. | 1913-1922 | 5.00 - 10.00 |
| Don Strong, patrol Leader, Heyliger. Khaki cover, seal on spine. | 1913-1922 | 5.00 - 10.00 |
| For the Honor of the School, Barbour. Khaki cover, seal on spine. | 1913-1922 | 5.00 - 10.00 |
| For the Honor of the School, Barbour. Color image cover. | 1913-1922 | 5.00 - 10.00 |
| The Gaunt Gray Wolf, Wallace. Khaki cover, seal on spine. | 1913-1922 | 5.00 - 10.00 |
| Grit-a-Plenty, Wallace. Color image cover. | 1913-1922 | 5.00 - 10.00 |
| Grit-a-Plenty, Wallace. Khaki cover, seal on spine. | 1913-1922 | 5.00 - 10.00 |
| The Guns of Europe, Altsheler. Khaki cover, seal on spine. | 1913-1922 | 5.00 - 10.00 |
| The Half Back, Barbour. Khaki cover, seal on spine. | 1913-1922 | 5.00 - 10.00 |
| The Half Back, Barbour. Color image cover. | 1913-1922 | 5.00 - 10.00 |
| Handbook for Boys, BSA. 11th printing, 1914. Khaki cover, seal on spine. | 1913-1922 | 45.00 - 60.00 |
| Handbook for Boys, BSA. 12th printing, 1915. Khaki cover, seal on spine. | 1913-1922 | 45.00 - 60.00 |
| Handbook for Boys, BSA. 13th printing, 1915. Khaki cover, seal on spine. | 1913-1922 | 45.00 - 60.00 |
| Handbook for Boys, BSA. 13th printing, reprint, 1915. Khaki cover, seal on spine. | 1913-1922 | 45.00 - 60.00 |
| Handbook for Boys, BSA. 14th printing, 1916. Khaki cover, seal on spine. | 1913-1922 | 45.00 - 60.00 |
| Handbook for Boys, BSA. 16th printing, 1917. Khaki cover, seal on spine. | 1913-1922 | 45.00 - 60.00 |
| Handbook for Boys, BSA. 19th printing, 1918. Khaki cover, seal on spine. | 1913-1922 | 45.00 - 60.00 |
| Handbook for Boys, BSA. 20th printing, 1919. Khaki cover, seal on spine. | 1913-1922 | 45.00 - 60.00 |
| Handbook for Boys, BSA. 21st printing, 1919. Khaki cover, seal on spine. | 1913-1922 | 45.00 - 60.00 |
| Handbook for Boys, BSA. 22nd printing, 1920. Khaki cover, seal on spine. | 1913-1922 | 45.00 - 60.00 |
| Handbook for Boys, BSA. 23rd printing, 1921. Khaki cover, seal on spine. | 1913-1922 | 45.00 - 60.00 |
| Handbook for Boys, BSA. 24th printing, 1921. Khaki cover, seal on spine. | 1913-1922 | 45.00 - 60.00 |
| Handbook for Boys, BSA. 28th printing, 1923. Khaki cover, seal on spine. | 1913-1922 | 45.00 - 60.00 |

| | | |
|---|---|---|
| Handicraft for Outdoor Boys, Beard.<br>Khaki cover, seal on spine. | 1913-1922 | 5.00 - 10.00 |
| Horseman of the Plains, Althsheler.<br>Khaki cover, seal on spine. | 1913-1922 | 5.00 - 10.00 |
| Horseman of the Plains, Althsheler.<br>Khaki cover, no seal on spine. | 1913-1922 | 5.00 - 10.00 |
| Horseman of the Plains, Althsheler.<br>Color image cover. | 1913-1922 | 5.00 - 10.00 |
| Jeb Hutton, Connolly. Khaki cover,<br>no seal on spine. | 1913-1922 | 5.00 - 10.00 |
| Jeb Hutton, Connolly. Khaki cover,<br>seal on spine. | 1913-1922 | 5.00 - 10.00 |
| The Jester of St. Timothy's, Pier.<br>Khaki cover, no seal on spine. | 1913-1922 | 5.00 - 10.00 |
| The Jester of St. Timothy's, Pier.<br>Khaki cover, seal on spine. | 1913-1922 | 5.00 - 10.00 |
| Jim Davis, Masefield. Khaki cover,<br>seal on spine. | 1913-1922 | 5.00 - 10.00 |
| Jim Davis, Masefield. Khaki cover,<br>no seal on spine. | 1913-1922 | 5.00 - 10.00 |
| Jim Davis, Masefield. Color image cover. | 1913-1922 | 5.00 - 10.00 |
| Kidnapped, Stevenson. Color image cover. | 1913-1922 | 5.00 - 10.00 |
| Kidnapped, Stevenson.<br>Khaki cover, seal on spine. | 1913-1922 | 5.00 - 10.00 |
| The Last of the Chiefs, Altsheler.<br>Khaki cover, seal on spine. | 1913-1922 | 5.00 - 10.00 |
| The Last of the Chiefs, Altsheler.<br>Color image cover. | 1913-1922 | 5.00 - 10.00 |
| The Last of the Mohicans, Cooper.<br>Khaki cover, seal on spine. | 1913-1922 | 5.00 - 10.00 |
| The Last of the Mohicans, Cooper.<br>Color image cover. | 1913-1922 | 5.00 - 10.00 |
| The Last of the Plainsmen, Grey.<br>Khaki cover, seal on spine. | 1913-1922 | 5.00 - 10.00 |
| The Last of the Plainsmen, Grey.<br>Color image cover. | 1913-1922 | 5.00 - 10.00 |
| Lone Bull's Mistake, Schultz.<br>Color image cover. | 1913-1922 | 5.00 - 10.00 |
| Lone Bull's Mistake, Schultz.<br>Khaki cover, seal on spine. | 1913-1922 | 5.00 - 10.00 |
| The Mutiny of the Flying Spray, Chute.<br>Khaki cover, seal on spine. | 1913-1922 | 5.00 - 10.00 |
| Pete, Cow-Puncher, Ames. Khaki cover,<br>seal on spine. | 1913-1922 | 5.00 - 10.00 |
| Pitching in a Pinch, Mathewson.<br>Khaki cover, seal on spine. | 1913-1922 | 15.00 - 25.00 |
| Pitching in a Pinch, Mathewson.<br>Khaki cover, no seal on spine. | 1913-1922 | 15.00 - 25.00 |
| The Ranch on the Oxhide, Inman.<br>Color image cover. | 1913-1922 | 5.00 - 10.00 |
| The Ranch on the Oxhide, Inman.<br>Khaki cover, seal on spine. | 1913-1922 | 5.00 - 10.00 |
| The Ranch on the Oxhide, Inman.<br>Khaki cover, no seal on spine. | 1913-1922 | 5.00 - 10.00 |
| The Ransom of Red Chief and Other<br>tories for Boys, Henry.<br>Color image cover. | 1913-1922 | 5.00 - 10.00 |
| The Ransom of Red Chief and Other<br>Stories for Boys, Henry.<br>Khaki cover, seal on spine. | 1913-1922 | 5.00 - 10.00 |
| Redney McGaw, McFarland.<br>Khaki cover, seal on spine. | 1913-1922 | 5.00 - 10.00 |
| Redney McGaw, McFarland.<br>Khaki cover, no seal on spine. | 1913-1922 | 5.00 - 10.00 |
| The School Days of Elliot Gray, Jr.,<br>Maynard. Color image cover. | 1913-1922 | 5.00 - 10.00 |
| The School Days of Elliot Gray, Jr.,<br>Maynard. Khaki cover, seal on spine. | 1913-1922 | 5.00 - 10.00 |
| Scouting with Daniel Boone, Tomlinson.<br>Khaki cover, seal on spine. | 1913-1922 | 5.00 - 10.00 |
| Scouting with Daniel Boone, Tomlinson.<br>Color image cover. | 1913-1922 | 5.00 - 10.00 |
| Scouting with Kit Carson, Tominson.<br>Khaki cover, seal on spine. | 1913-1922 | 5.00 - 10.00 |
| Scouting with Kit Carson, Tominson.<br>Color image cover. | 1913-1922 | 5.00 - 10.00 |
| Scouting with General Funston,<br>Tominson. Khaki cover, seal on spine. | 1913-1922 | 5.00 - 10.00 |
| Tecumseh's Young Braves, Tomilson.<br>Khaki cover, no seal on spine. | 1913-1922 | 5.00 - 10.00 |
| Tecumseh's Young Braves, Tomilson.<br>Khaki cover, seal on spine. | 1913-1922 | 5.00 - 10.00 |
| Three Years Behind the Guns, Tisdale.<br>Khaki cover, no seal on spine. | 1913-1922 | 5.00 - 10.00 |
| Three Years Behind the Guns, Tisdale.<br>Khaki cover, seal on spine. | 1913-1922 | 5.00 - 10.00 |
| Through College on Nothing a Year,<br>Gauss. Khaki cover, seal on spine. | 1913-1922 | 5.00 - 10.00 |
| To the Land of the Caribou, Tomlinson.<br>Khaki cover, seal on spine. | 1913-1922 | 5.00 - 10.00 |
| Tom Paulding, Matthews. Khaki cover,<br>seal on spine. | 1913-1922 | 5.00 - 10.00 |
| Tom Paulding, Matthews. Khaki cover,<br>no seal on spine. | 1913-1922 | 5.00 - 10.00 |
| Tom Strong, Washington's Scout, Mason.<br>Khaki cover, seal on spine. | 1913-1922 | 5.00 - 10.00 |
| Tom Strong, Washington's Scout, Mason.<br>Khaki cover, no seal on spine. | 1913-1922 | 5.00 - 10.00 |
| Tommy Remington's Battle, Stevenson.<br>Khaki cover, no seal on spine. | 1913-1922 | 5.00 - 10.00 |
| Tommy Remington's Battle, Stevenson.<br>Khaki cover, seal on spine. | 1913-1922 | 5.00 - 10.00 |
| Treasure Island, Stevenson. Khaki cover,<br>seal on spine. | 1913-1922 | 5.00 - 10.00 |
| Treasure Island, Stevenson. Khaki cover,<br>no seal on spine. | 1913-1922 | 5.00 - 10.00 |
| Under Boy Scout Colors, Ames.<br>Khaki cover, seal on spine. | 1913-1922 | 5.00 - 10.00 |
| Ungava Bob, Wallace. Khaki cover,<br>seal on spine. | 1913-1922 | 5.00 - 10.00 |
| Ungava Bob, Wallace. Color image cover. | 1913-1922 | 5.00 - 10.00 |
| Wells Brothers, the Young Cattle Kings,<br>Adams. Khaki cover, seal on spine. | 1913-1922 | 5.00 - 10.00 |
| Wells Brothers, the Young Cattle Kings,<br>Adams. Khaki cover, no seal on spine. | 1913-1922 | 5.00 - 10.00 |
| White fang, London. Color image cover. | 1913-1922 | 5.00 - 10.00 |
| William of West Point, Johnson.<br>Khaki cover, seal on spine. | 1913-1922 | 5.00 - 10.00 |
| The Wireless Man, Collins.<br>Khaki cover, seal on spine. | 1913-1922 | 5.00 - 10.00 |

| | | |
|---|---|---|
| The Wolf Hunter, Grinnell. Khaki cover, seal on spine. | 1913-1922 | 5.00 - 10.00 |
| The Wrecking Master, Paine. Khaki cover, seal on spine. | 1913-1922 | 5.00 - 10.00 |
| Yankee Ships and Yankee Sailors, Barnes. Khaki cover, no seal on spine. | 1913-1922 | 5.00 - 10.00 |
| Yankee Ships and Yankee Sailors, Barnes. Khaki cover, seal on spine. | 1913-1922 | 5.00 - 10.00 |

## Jerry Hicks Series

| | | |
|---|---|---|
| Jerry Hicks and his Gang, Heyliger, William, Grosset & Dunlap, Publishers. | 1929 | 5.00 - 15.00 |
| Jerry Hicks, Explorer, Heyliger, William, Grosset & Dunlap, Publishers. | 1930 | 5.00 - 15.00 |
| Jerry Hicks, Ghost Hunter, Heyliger, William, Grosset & Dunlap, Publishers. | 1929 | 5.00 - 15.00 |
| Yours Truly, Jerry Hicks, Heyliger, William, Grosset & Dunlap, Publishers. | 1929 | 5.00 - 15.00 |

## Scout and Campfire Players Series

| | | |
|---|---|---|
| Boy Scout Hero, Puller, Edwin, Dennison. | 1916 | 5.00 - 15.00 |

## Sports and Scouts Series, Saalfield Publishing Co.

| | | |
|---|---|---|
| Corley of the Wilderness Trails, Smith, L.K. | 1937 | 5.00 - 10.00 |
| The Hockey Spare, Sherman, H. | 1937 | 5.00 - 10.00 |
| Kelly King at Yale Hall, Strong, Paschal. | 1937 | 5.00 - 10.00 |
| Last Man Out, Sherman, H. | 1937 | 5.00 - 10.00 |
| Phil Burton, Sleuth, Smith, L.K. | 1937 | 5.00 - 10.00 |
| Stan Kent, Captain, Heyliger, W. | 1937 | 5.00 - 10.00 |
| Stan Kent, Freshman Fullback, Heyliger, W. | 1936 | 5.00 - 10.00 |
| Stan Kent, Varsity Man, Heyliger, W. | 1936 | 5.00 - 10.00 |
| Three-Finger Joe, Heyliger, W. | 1937 | 5.00 - 10.00 |
| Tommy of Troop Six, Smith, L.K. | 1937 | 5.00 - 10.00 |
| West Point Five, Lyons, K. | 1937 | 5.00 - 10.00 |
| West Pointers on the Gridiron, Lyons, K. | 1936 | 5.00 - 10.00 |
| The Winged Four, Lyons, K. | 1937 | 5.00 - 10.00 |
| The Winning Point, Sherman, H. | 1936 | 5.00 - 10.00 |

## Sterling Boy Scout Books, Hurst & Co., Publishers

| | | |
|---|---|---|
| Boy Scouts and the Call to Arms, Shaler, Robert. | 1914 | 5.00 - 15.00 |
| Boy Scouts and the Prize Pennant, Shaler, Robert. | 1914 | 5.00 - 15.00 |
| Boy Scouts as County Fair Guides, Shaler, Robert. | 1915 | 5.00 - 15.00 |
| Boy Scouts as Forest Fire Fighters, Shaler, Robert. | 1915 | 5.00 - 15.00 |
| Boy Scouts at Mobilization Camp, Shaler, Robert. | 1914 | 5.00 - 15.00 |
| Boy Scouts for City Improvement, Shaler, Robert. | 1914 | 5.00 - 15.00 |
| Boy Scouts for Home Protection, Shaler, Robert. | 1916 | 5.00 - 15.00 |
| Boy Scouts in the Great Flood, Shaler, Robert. | 1915 | 5.00 - 15.00 |

| | | |
|---|---|---|
| Boy Scouts of Pioneer Camp, Shaler, Robert. | 1914 | 5.00 - 15.00 |
| Boy Scouts of the Field Hospital, Shaler, Robert. | 1915 | 5.00 - 15.00 |
| Boy Scouts of the Flying Squadron, Shaler, Robert. | 1914 | 10.00 - 25.00 |
| Boy Scouts of the Geological Survey, Shaler, Robert. | 1914 | 5.00 - 15.00 |
| Boy Scouts of the Life Saving Crew, Shaler, Robert. | 1914 | 5.00 - 15.00 |
| Boy Scouts of the Naval Reserve, Shaler, Robert. | 1914 | 5.00 - 15.00 |
| Boy Scouts of the Signal Corps, Shaler, Robert. | 1914 | 5.00 - 15.00 |
| Boy Scouts on Picket Duty, Shaler, Robert. | 1914 | 5.00 - 15.00 |
| Boy Scouts on the Roll of Honor, Shaler, Robert. | 1916 | 5.00 - 15.00 |
| Boy Scouts with the Motion Picture Players, Shaler, Robert. | 1916 | 5.00 - 15.00 |
| Boy Scouts with the Red Cross, Shaler, Robert. | 1915 | 5.00 - 15.00 |

## The Aeroplane Boys Series

| | | |
|---|---|---|
| When Scout Meets Scout, or the Aeroplane Spy, Lamar, Ashton, Reilly & Britton. | 1912 | 5.00 - 15.00 |

## The Banner Boy Scouts Series, Cupples & Leon Co.

| | | |
|---|---|---|
| The Banner Boy Scouts Afloat, or The Secret of Cedar Island, Warren, George A. | 1913 | 5.00 - 15.00 |
| The Banner Boy Scouts on a Tour, or The Mystery of Rattlesnake Mountain, Warren, George A. | 1912 | 5.00 - 15.00 |
| The Banner Boy Scouts Snowbound, or A Tour on Skates and Iceboats, Warren, George A. | 1916 | 5.00 - 15.00 |
| The Banner Boy Scouts, or The Struggle for Leadership, Warren, George A. | 1912 | 5.00 - 15.00 |

## The Banner Boy Scouts Series, Saalfield Publishing Co. reprint

| | | |
|---|---|---|
| The Banner Boy Scouts Afloat, or The Secret of Cedar Island, Warren, George A. | 1913 | 5.00 - 15.00 |
| The Banner Boy Scouts on a Tour, or The Mystery of Rattlesnake Mountain, Warren, George A. | 1912 | 5.00 - 15.00 |
| The Banner Boy Scouts Snowbound, or a Tour on Skates and Iceboats, Warren, George A. | 1916 | 5.00 - 15.00 |
| The Banner Boy Scouts, or The Struggle for Leadership, Warren, George A. | 1912 | 5.00 - 15.00 |

## The Banner Boy Scouts Series, World Syndicate Publishing Co. reprint

| | | |
|---|---|---|
| The Banner Boy Scouts Afloat, or The Secret of Cedar Island, Warren, George A. | 1913 | 5.00 - 15.00 |
| The Banner Boy Scouts in the Air, Warren, George A. | 1937 | 5.00 - 10.00 |
| The Banner Boy Scouts Mystery, Warren, George A. | 1937 | 5.00 - 10.00 |
| The Banner Boy Scouts on a Tour, or The Mystery of Rattlesnake Mountain, Warren, George A. | 1912 | 5.00 - 15.00 |
| The Banner Boy Scouts, or The Struggle for Leadership, Warren, George A. | 1912 | 5.00 - 15.00 |
| The Boy Scouts Snowbound, or A Tour on Skates and Iceboats, Warren, George A. | 1916 | 5.00 - 15.00 |

## The Bob Hanson Series

| | | |
|---|---|---|
| Bob Hanson, Eagle Scout, Carter, Russell G., Penn Publishing Co. | 1923 | 5.00 - 15.00 |
| Bob Hanson, First Class Scout, Carter, Russell G., Penn Publishing Co. | 1922 | 5.00 - 15.00 |
| Bob Hanson, Scout, Carter, Russell G., Penn Publishing Co. | 1921 | 5.00 - 15.00 |
| Bob Hanson, Tenderfoot, Carter, Russell G., Penn Publishing Co. | 1921 | 5.00 - 15.00 |

## The Boy Patrol Series, Cassell & Co.

| | | |
|---|---|---|
| The Boy Patrol Around the Council Fire, Ellis, Edward S., reprint. | 1913 | 5.00 - 15.00 |
| The Boy Patrol on Guard, Ellis, Edward S., reprint. | 1913 | 5.00 - 15.00 |

## The Boy Patrol Series, John C. Winston Co.

| | | |
|---|---|---|
| The Boy Patrol on Guard, Ellis, Edward S. | 1913 | 5.00 - 15.00 |
| The Boy Patrol Around the Council Fire, Ellis, Edward S. | 1913 | 5.00 - 15.00 |

## The Boy Scout Explorers Series

| | | |
|---|---|---|
| The Boy Scout Explorers at Emerald Valley, Palmer, Don, Cupples & Leon Co. | 1955 | 5.00 - 10.00 |
| The Boy Scout Explorers at Headless Hollow, Palmer, Don, Cupples & Leon Co. | 1957 | 5.00 - 10.00 |
| The Boy Scout Explorers at Treasure Mountain, Palmer, Don, Cupples & Leon Co. | 1955 | 5.00 - 10.00 |

## The Boy Scout Series, Little, Brown & Co.

| | | |
|---|---|---|
| The Boy Scouts of Lakeville, Quirk, Leslie W. | 1920 | 5.00 - 15.00 |

## The Boy Scout Series, M.A. Donohue & Co.

| | | |
|---|---|---|
| The Boy Scout Camera Club, or The Confession of a Photograph, Ralphson, G. Harvey. | 1913 | 5.00 - 15.00 |
| Boy Scout Electricians, or The Hidden Dynamo, Ralphson, G. Harvey. | 1913 | 5.00 - 15.00 |
| Boy Scouts Beyond the Arctic Circle, or The Lost Expedition, Ralphson, G. Harvey. | 1913 | 5.00 - 15.00 |
| Boy Scouts in a Submarine, or Searching an Ocean Floor, Ralphson, G. Harvey. | 1912 | 10.00 - 25.00 |
| Boy Scouts in an Airship, or The Warning from the Sky, Ralphson, G. Harvey. | 1912 | 10.00 - 25.00 |
| Boy Scouts in California, or The Flag on the Cliff, Ralphson, G. Harvey. | 1913 | 5.00 - 15.00 |
| Boy Scouts in Death Valley, or The City in the Sky, Ralphson, G. Harvey. | 1914 | 5.00 - 15.00 |
| Boy Scouts in Southern Waters, or Spaniard's Treasure Chest, Ralphson, G. Harvey. | 1915 | 5.00 - 15.00 |

Boy Scouts in the Canal Zone, or
    The Plot Against Uncle Sam, Ralphson,
    G. Harvey.                          1911          5.00 - 15.00
Boy Scouts in the North Sea, or
    The Mystery of the U-13, Ralphson,
    G. Harvey.                          1915          5.00 - 15.00
Boy Scouts in the Philippines, or
    The Key to the Treaty Box, Ralphson,
    G. Harvey.                          1911          5.00 - 15.00
Boy Scouts in the Verdun Attack, or
    Perils of the Black Bear Patrol,
    Ralphson, G. Harvey.                1916          5.00 - 15.00
Boy Scouts Mysterious Signal, or
    Perils of the Black-Bear Patrol,
    Ralphson, G. Harvey.                1916          5.00 - 15.00
Boy Scouts on Hudson Bay, or
    The Disappearing Fleet, Ralphson,
    G. Harvey.                          1914          5.00 - 15.00
Boy Scouts on Motorcycles, or
    With the Flying Squadron, Ralphson,
    G. Harvey.                          1912          10.00 - 25.00
Boy Scouts on the Columbia River, or
    Adventures in a Motor Boat,
    Ralphson, G. Harvey.                1912          5.00 - 15.00

Boy Scouts on the Open Plains, or
    The Roundup Not Ordered,
    Ralphson, G. Harvey.                1914          5.00 - 15.00
Boy Scouts Under the Kaiser, or
    The Uhlan's Escape, Ralphson,
    G. Harvey.                          1916          5.00 - 15.00
Boy Scouts Under the Kaiser, or
    The Uhlans in Peril, Ralphson,
    G. Harvey.                          1916          5.00 - 15.00
Boy Scouts With the Cossacks, or
    Poland Recaptured, Ralphson,
    G. Harvey.                          1916          5.00 - 15.00
Boy Scouts in Belgium, or
    Imperiled in a Trap, Ralphson,
    G. Harvey.                          1915          5.00 - 15.00
Boy Scouts in Mexico, or
    On Guard with Uncle Sam, Ralphson,
    G. Harvey.                          1911          5.00 - 15.00
Boy Scouts in the Northwest, or
    Fighting Forest Fires, Ralphson,
    G. Harvey.                          1912          5.00 - 15.00

## The Boy Scout Series, The Century Co.

The Blue Pearl, Scoville, Samuel Jr.    1920          5.00 - 15.00
Boy Scouts in the Wilderness, Scoville,
    Samuel Jr.                          1919          5.00 - 15.00
The Inca Emerald, Scoville, Samuel Jr.  1922          5.00 - 15.00
The Red Diamond, Scoville, Samuel Jr.   1925          5.00 - 15.00
The Snake Blood Ruby, Scoville, Samuel Jr. 1932       5.00 - 10.00

## The Boy Scout Series

The Boy Scouts Afoot in France, or
    With the Red Cross Corps at the Marne. 1917        5.00 - 15.00
The Boy Scouts Along the Susquehanna,
    or The Silver Fox Patrol
    Caught in a Flood.                  1915          5.00 - 15.00
The Boy Scouts at the Battle of Saratoga,
    or The Story of General Bourgone's
    Defeat, Reissue of W.P. Chimpan's
    The Boy Scouts, 1909.               1914          5.00 - 15.00
The Boy Scouts Down in Dixie, or
    The Strange Secret of Alligator Swamp,
    Carter, Herbert A.                  1914          5.00 - 15.00
The Boy Scouts in the Blue Ridge, or
    Marooned Among the Moonshiners,
    Carter, Herbert A.                  1913          5.00 - 15.00
The Boy Scouts in the Maine Woods, or
    The New Test for the Silver Fox Patrol,
    Carter, Herbert A.                  1913          5.00 - 15.00
The Boy Scouts in the Rockies, or
    The Secret of the Hidden Silver Mine,
    Carter, Herbert A.                  1913          5.00 - 15.00
The Boy Scouts of Black Eagle Patrol,
    Quirk, Leslie W., Little, Brown & Co. 1915         5.00 - 15.00
The Boy Scouts on Crusade, Quirk,
    Leslie W., Little, Brown & Co.      1917          5.00 - 15.00
The Boy Scouts on Sturgeon Island, or
    Marooned Among the Gamefish
    Poachers, Carter, Herbert A.        1914          5.00 - 15.00

The Boy Scouts on the Trail, or
Scouting through the Big Game Country,
Carter, Herbert A.                    1913         5.00 - 15.00
The Boy Scouts on War Trails in Belgium,
or Caught Between Hostile Enemies.    1916         5.00 - 15.00
The Boy Scouts through the Big Timber,
or The Search for the Lost Tenderfoot,
Carter, Herbert A.                    1913         5.00 - 15.00
The Boy Scouts' First Campfire, or Scouting
with the Silver Fox Patrol, Carter,
Herbert A.                            1913         5.00 - 15.00

## The Boy Scouts of the Air Series, Reilly & Britton or Reilly & Lee Co.

The Boy Scouts of the Air at Eagle Camp,
Stuart, Gordon.                       1912        10.00 - 25.00
The Boy Scouts of the Air on Flathead
Mountain, Stuart, Gordon.             1912         5.00 - 15.00
The Boy Scouts of the Air on the Great
Lakes, Stuart, Gordon.                1912        10.00 - 25.00
The Boy Scouts of the Air at Greenwood
School, Stuart, Gordon.               1912        10.00 - 25.00
The Boy Scouts of the Air in Indian Land,
Stuart, Gordon.                       1912        10.00 - 25.00

The Boy Scouts of the Air in the
Northern Wilds, Stuart, Gordon.       1912        10.00 - 25.00
The Boy Scouts of the Air in Belgium,
Stuart, Gordon.                       1915        10.00 - 25.00
The Boy Scouts of the Air in the
Lone Star Patrol, Stuart, Gordon.     1916        10.00 - 25.00
The Boy Scouts of the Air on Lost Island,
Stuart, Gordon.                       1917        10.00 - 25.00
The Boy Scouts of the Air on The French
Front, Stuart, Gordon.                1918        10.00 - 25.00
The Boy Scouts of the Air with Pershing,
Stuart, Gordon.                       1919        10.00 - 25.00
The Boy Scouts of the Air at Cape Peril,
Stuart, Gordon.                       1921        10.00 - 15.00
The Boy Scouts of the Air on Bald Crest,
Stuart, Gordon.                       1922        10.00 - 25.00

## The Boy Scouts of Troop Five Series

The Doins of Troop Five, Jenkins, Marshall,
D. Appleton & Co.                     1914         5.00 - 15.00
The Jackal Patrol of Troop Five, Jenkins,
Marshall, D. Appleton & Co.           1915         5.00 - 15.00
Troop Five at Camp, Jenkins, Marshall,
D. Appleton & Co.                     1914         5.00 - 15.00

## The Boy Scouts' Yearbook

Mathiews, Franklin K., D. Appleton & Co.  1915     30.00 - 50.00
Mathiews, Franklin K., D. Appleton & Co.  1916     30.00 - 50.00
Mathiews, Franklin K., D. Appleton & Co.  1917     30.00 - 50.00
Mathiews, Franklin K., D. Appleton & Co.  1918     30.00 - 50.00
Mathiews, Franklin K., D. Appleton & Co.  1919     30.00 - 50.00
Mathiews, Franklin K., D. Appleton & Co.  1920     25.00 - 40.00
Mathiews, Franklin K., D. Appleton & Co.  1921     25.00 - 45.00
Mathiews, Franklin K., D. Appleton & Co.  1922     25.00 - 40.00
Mathiews, Franklin K., D. Appleton & Co.  1923     20.00 - 40.00
Mathiews, Franklin K., D. Appleton & Co.  1924     15.00 - 30.00
Mathiews, Franklin K., D. Appleton & Co.  1925     20.00 - 40.00
Mathiews, Franklin K., D. Appleton & Co.  1925     20.00 - 40.00
Mathiews, Franklin K., D. Appleton & Co.  1926     15.00 - 30.00
Mathiews, Franklin K., D. Appleton & Co.  1927     15.00 - 30.00
Mathiews, Franklin K., D. Appleton & Co.  1928     15.00 - 30.00
Mathiews, Franklin K., D. Appleton & Co.  1929     15.00 - 30.00
Mathiews, Franklin K., D. Appleton & Co.  1930     15.00 - 30.00
Mathiews, Franklin K., D. Appleton & Co.  1931     10.00 - 25.00
Mathiews, Franklin K., D. Appleton & Co.  1932     10.00 - 25.00
Ghost and Mystery Stories, Mathiews,
Franklin K., D. Appleton & Co.        1933         5.00 - 10.00
Stories of Brave Boys and Fearless Men,
Mathiews, Franklin K., D. Appleton & Co. 1934     10.00 - 25.00
Stories About Dogs, Mathiews, Franklin K.,
D. Appleton & Co.                     1935        10.00 - 25.00
Sports Stories, Mathiews, Franklin K.,
D. Appleton & Co.                     1936        10.00 - 25.00
Stories of Daring and Danger, Mathiews,
Franklin K., D. Appleton & Co.        1937        10.00 - 25.00
Fun and Fiction, Mathiews, Franklin K., D.
Appleton & Co.                        1938        10.00 - 25.00

Stories of Daring and Danger, Mathiews,
    Franklin K., D. Appleton & Co.        1939    10.00 - 25.00
Wild Animal Stories, Mathiews, Franklin K.,
    D. Appleton & Co.                     1940    10.00 - 25.00
Patriotic Stories, Mathiews, Franklin K.,
    D. Appleton & Co.                     1941    10.00 - 25.00
Stories of Boy Heroes, Mathiews,
    Franklin K., D. Appleton & Co.        1942    10.00 - 25.00
Stories of Adventure Fliers, Mathiews,
    Franklin K., D. Appleton & Co.        1943    10.00 - 25.00
Stories of Boy Scout Courageous,
    Mathiews, Franklin K., D. Appleton & Co. 1944  10.00 - 25.00
Stories Boys Like Best, Mathiews, Franklin K.,
    D. Appleton & Co.                     1945    10.00 - 25.00

## The Boys' Life Library Books

The Boys' Life Book of World War II
    Stories, Random House.                1965    3.00 - 7.50
The Boys' Life Book of Baseball Stories,
    Windward Books, paperback,
    silver cover.                         1964    1.00 - 4.00
The Boys' Life Book of Baseball Stories,
    Windward Books paperback,
    original cover.                       1964    1.00 - 4.00
The Boys' Life Book of Baseball Stories,
    Random House.                         1964    3.00 - 7.50
The Boys' Life Book of Basketball Stories,
    Random House.                         1966    3.00 - 7.50

The Boys' Life Book of Flying Stories,
    Random House.                         1964    3.00 - 7.50
The Boys' Life Book of Football Stories,
    Windward Books, paperback,
    silver cover.                         1963    1.00 - 4.00
The Boys' Life Book of Football Stories,
    Windward Books, paperback,
    regular cover.                        1963    1.00 - 4.00
The Boys' Life Book of Football Stories,
    Random House.                         1963    3.00 - 7.50
The Boys' Life Book of Horse Stories,
    Random House.                         1963    3.00 - 7.50
The Boys' Life Book of Mystery Stories,
    Random House.                         1963    3.00 - 7.50
The Boys' Life Book of Outer Space Stories,
    Random House.                         1964    3.00 - 7.50
Mutiny in the Time Machine, Donald Keith,
    Random House.                         1963    3.00 - 7.50

## The Buddie Books, Little Brown & Co.

Buddie at Gray Buttes Camp, Ray,
    Anna Chapin.                          1912    5.00 - 15.00
Buddie, The Story of a Boy, Ray,
    Anna Chapin.                          1911    5.00 - 15.00
The Responsibilities of Buddie, Ray,
    Anna Chapin.                          1913    5.00 - 15.00

## The Button Books

The Buttons and the Boy Scouts,
    McCall, Edith S., Benefic Press.      1958    5.00 - 10.00

## The Dan Carter Series, Cupples & Leon

Dan Carter and the Great Carved Face,
    Wirt, Mildred A.                      1952    5.00 - 10.00
Dan Carter and the Haunted Castle,
    Wirt, Mildred A.                      1951    5.00 - 10.00
Dan Carter and the Money Box,
    Wirt, Mildred A.                      1950    5.00 - 10.00
Dan Carter and the River Camp,
    Wirt, Mildred A.                      1949    5.00 - 10.00

## The Fox Patrol Series, The Buzza Co.

The Fox Patrol in the North Woods,
    Gilman, Charles L.                    1912    5.00 - 15.00
The Fox Patrol in the Open,
    Gilman, Charles L.                    1912    5.00 - 15.00
The Fox Patrol on the River,
    Gilman, Charles L.                    1912    5.00 - 15.00

## The Lucky Series, reprint, Whitman Publishing Co.

Lucky, the Boy Scout, Sherwood, Elmer.    1916    5.00 - 10.00
Lucky, the Young Navyman,
    Sherwood, Elmer.                      1917    5.00 - 15.00
Lucky, the Young Soldier,
    Sherwood, Elmer.                      1917    5.00 - 10.00

## The Lucky Series,
## Whitman Publishing Co.

| | | |
|---|---|---|
| Lucky and His Friend Steve, Sherwood, Elmer. | 1922 | 5.00 - 15.00 |
| Lucky and His Travels, Sherwood, Elmer. | 1922 | 5.00 - 10.00 |
| Lucky Finds a Friend, Sherwood, Elmer. | 1920 | 5.00 - 10.00 |
| Lucky on an Important Mission, Sherwood, Elmer. | 1920 | 5.00 - 15.00 |
| Lucky the Boy Scout, Sherwood, Elmer. | 1920 | 5.00 - 10.00 |
| Lucky the Young Volunteer, Sherwood, Elmer. | 1920 | 5.00 - 10.00 |

## The Mark Gilmore Books

| | | |
|---|---|---|
| Mark Gilmore Scout of the Air, Fitzhugh, Percy Keese, Grosset & Dunlap, Publishers. | 1930 | 10.00 - 25.00 |
| Mark Gilmore Speed Flyer, Fitzhugh, Percy Keese, Grosset & Dunlap, Publishers. | 1931 | 5.00 - 15.00 |
| Mark Gilmore's Lucky Landing, Fitzhugh, Percy Keese, Grosset & Dunlap, Publishers. | 1931 | 5.00 - 15.00 |

## The Pee-Wee Harris Books

| | | |
|---|---|---|
| Pee-Wee Harris: Fixer, Fitzhugh, Percy Keese, Grosset & Dunlap, Publishers. | 1924 | 5.00 - 15.00 |
| Pee-Wee Harris Adrift, Fitzhugh, Percy Keese, Grosset & Dunlap, Publishers. | 1922 | 5.00 - 15.00 |
| Pee-Wee Harris and the Sunken Treasure, Fitzhugh, Percy Keese, Grosset & Dunlap, Publishers. | 1927 | 5.00 - 15.00 |
| Pee-Wee Harris F.O.B. Bridgeboro, Fitzhugh, Percy Keese, Grosset & Dunlap, Publishers. | 1923 | 5.00 - 15.00 |
| Pee-Wee Harris in Camp, Fitzhugh, Percy Keese, Grosset & Dunlap, Publishers. | 1922 | 5.00 - 15.00 |
| Pee-Wee Harris in Darkest Africa, Fitzhugh, Percy Keese, Grosset & Dunlap, Publishers. | 1929 | 5.00 - 15.00 |
| Pee-Wee Harris in Luck, Fitzhugh, Percy Keese, Grosset & Dunlap, Publishers. | 1922 | 5.00 - 15.00 |
| Pee-Wee Harris on the Briny Deep, Fitzhugh, Percy Keese, Grosset & Dunlap, Publishers. | 1928 | 5.00 - 15.00 |
| Pee-Wee Harris on the Trail, Fitzhugh, Percy Keese, Whitman reprint. | 1922 | 5.00 - 15.00 |
| Pee-Wee Harris on the Trail, Fitzhugh, Percy Keese, Grosset & Dunlap, Publishers. | 1922 | 5.00 - 15.00 |
| Pee-Wee Harris Turns Detective, Fitzhugh, Percy Keese, Grosset & Dunlap, Publishers. | 1930 | 5.00 - 15.00 |
| Pee-Wee Harris, Fitzhugh, Percy Keese, Grosset & Dunlap, Publishers. | 1922 | 5.00 - 15.00 |
| Pee-Wee Harris: As Good as His Word, Fitzhugh, Percy Keese, Grosset & Dunlap, Publishers. | 1925 | 5.00 - 15.00 |
| Pee-Wee Harris: Mayor for a Day, Fitzhugh, Percy Keese, Grosset & Dunlap, Publishers. | 1926 | 5.00 - 15.00 |

## The Roy Blakeley Books

| | | |
|---|---|---|
| Roy Blakeley in the Haunted Camp, Fitzhugh, Percy Keese, Grosset & Dunlap, Publishers. | 1922 | 5.00 - 15.00 |
| Roy Blakeley on the Mohawk Trail, Fitzhugh, Percy Keese, Grosset & Dunlap, Publishers. | 1925 | 5.00 - 15.00 |
| Roy Blakeley Pathfinder, Fitzhugh, Percy Keese, Grosset & Dunlap, Publishers. | 1920 | 5.00 - 15.00 |
| Roy Blakeley Up in the Air, Fitzhugh, Percy Keese, Grosset & Dunlap, Publishers. | 1931 | 10.00 - 25.00 |
| Roy Blakeley's Adventures in Camp, Fitzhugh, Percy Keese, Grosset & Dunlap, Publishers. | 1920 | 5.00 - 15.00 |
| Roy Blakeley's Bee-Line Hike, Fitzhugh, Percy Keese, Grosset & Dunlap, Publishers. | 1922 | 5.00 - 15.00 |
| Roy Blakeley's Camp on Wheels, Fitzhugh, Percy Keese, Grosset & Dunlap, Publishers. | 1920 | 5.00 - 15.00 |

Roy Blakeley's Elastic Hike, Fitzhugh,
    Percy Keese, Grosset & Dunlap,
    Publishers.                                  1926        5.00 - 15.00
Roy Blakeley's Funny-Bone Hike, Fitzhugh,
    Percy Keese, Grosset & Dunlap,
    Publishers.                                  1922        5.00 - 15.00
Roy Blakeley's Go-As-You-Please Hike,
    Fitzhugh, Percy Keese, Grosset & Dunlap,
    Publishers.                                  1929        5.00 - 15.00
Roy Blakeley's Happy-Go-Lucky Hike,
    Fitzhugh, Percy Keese, Grosset & Dunlap,
    Publishers.                                  1928        5.00 - 15.00
Roy Blakeley's Motor Caravan, Fitzhugh,
    Percy Keese, Grosset & Dunlap,
    Publishers.                                  1921        5.00 - 15.00
Roy Blakeley's Roundabout Hike, Fitzhugh,
    Percy Keese, Grosset & Dunlap,
    Publishers.                                  1926        5.00 - 15.00
Roy Blakeley's Silver Fox Patrol, Fitzhugh,
    Percy Keese, Grosset & Dunlap,
    Publishers.                                  1920        5.00 - 15.00
Roy Blakeley's Tangled Trail, Fitzhugh,
    Percy Keese, Grosset & Dunlap,
    Publishers.                                  1924        5.00 - 15.00
Roy Blakeley's Wild Goose Chase, Fitzhugh,
    Percy Keese, Grosset & Dunlap,
    Publishers.                                  1930        5.00 - 15.00

Roy Blakeley, His Story, Fitzhugh,
    Percy Keese, Grosset & Dunlap,
    Publishers.                                  1920        5.00 - 15.00
Roy Blakeley: Lost, Strayed or Stolen,
    Fitzhugh, Percy Keese, Grosset & Dunlap,
    Publishers.                                  1921        5.00 - 15.00

## The Scout Drake Series, Houghton & Mifflin Co.

Coxwain Drake of the Sea Scouts,
    Hornibrook, Isabel K.                        1920        5.00 - 15.00
Drake and the Adventurers' Cup,
    Hornibrook, Isabel K.                        1922        5.00 - 15.00
Drake of Troop One, Hornibrook,
    Isabel K.                                    1916        5.00 - 15.00
Scout Drake in Wartime, Hornibrook,
    Isabel K.                                    1918        5.00 - 15.00

## The Scout Patrol Series, World Syndicate Publishing Co.

The Scout Patrol Boys and the
    Hunting Lodge Mystery, Wright, Jack.         1933        5.00 - 10.00
The Scout Patrol Boys at Circle U Ranch,
    Wright, Jack.                                1933        5.00 - 10.00
The Scout Patrol Boys Exploring in Yucatan,
    Wright, Jack.                                1933        5.00 - 10.00
The Scout Patrol Boys in the Frozen South,
    Wright, Jack.                                1933        5.00 - 10.00

## The Tad Sheldon Series, Macmillan Co., reprint

Scouts of the Desert, Wilson,
    John Fleming,                                1920        5.00 - 15.00
Tad Sheldon's Fourth of July, More Stories
    of His Patrol, Wilson, John Fleming,         1913        5.00 - 15.00
Tad Sheldon, Boy Scouts, Stories of His
    Patrol, Wilson, John Fleming,                1913        5.00 - 15.00

## The Tad Sheldon Series, Sturgis & Walton Co.

Tad Sheldon's Fourth of July, More Stories
    of His Patrol, Wilson, John Fleming,         1913        5.00 - 15.00
Tad Sheldon, Boy Scouts, Stories of His
    Patrol, Wilson, John Fleming,                1913        5.00 - 15.00

## The Ted Marsh Series, Whitman Publishing Co.

Ted Marsh and His Friend Steve,
    Sherwood, Elmer.                             1920        5.00 - 15.00
Ted Marsh and His Great Adventure,
    Sherwood, Elmer.                             1920        5.00 - 15.00
Ted Marsh on an Important Mission,
    Sherwood, Elmer.                             1920        5.00 - 15.00
Ted Marsh the Boy Scout,
    Sherwood, Elmer.                             1920        5.00 - 15.00
Ted Marsh the Young Volunteer,
    Sherwood, Elmer.                             1920        5.00 - 15.00

## The Westy Martin Books

| | | |
|---|---|---|
| Out West with Westy Martin, A four in one book, Fitzhugh, Percy Keese, Grosset & Dunlap, Publishers. | 1926 | 5.00 - 15.00 |
| Westy Martin in the Land of the Purple Sage, Fitzhugh, Percy Keese, Grosset & Dunlap, Publishers. | 1929 | 5.00 - 15.00 |
| Westy Martin in the Rockies, Fitzhugh, Percy Keese, Grosset & Dunlap, Publishers. | 1924 | 5.00 - 15.00 |
| Westy Martin in the Sierras, Fitzhugh, Percy Keese, Grosset & Dunlap, Publishers. | 1931 | 5.00 - 15.00 |
| Westy Martin in the Yellowstone, Fitzhugh, Percy Keese, Grosset & Dunlap, Publishers. | 1924 | 5.00 - 15.00 |
| Westy Martin on the Mississippi, Fitzhugh, Percy Keese, Grosset & Dunlap, Publishers. | 1930 | 5.00 - 15.00 |
| Westy Martin on the Old Indian Trails, Fitzhugh, Percy Keese, Grosset & Dunlap, Publishers. | 1928 | 5.00 - 15.00 |
| Westy Martin on the Santa Fe Trail, Fitzhugh, Percy Keese, Grosset & Dunlap, Publishers. | 1926 | 5.00 - 15.00 |
| Westy Martin, Fitzhugh, Percy Keese, Grosset & Dunlap, Publishers. | 1924 | 5.00 - 15.00 |

## Tom Slade Books, Grosset & Dunlap, Publishers

| | | |
|---|---|---|
| The Parachute Jumper: A Tom Slade Story, Fitzhugh, Percy Keese | 1930 | 10.00 - 25.00 |
| Tom Slade at Bear Mountain, Fitzhugh, Percy Keese. | 1925 | 5.00 - 15.00 |
| Tom Slade at Black Lake, Fitzhugh, Percy Keese. | 1920 | 5.00 - 15.00 |
| Tom Slade at Haunted Cavern, Fitzhugh, Percy Keese. | 1929 | 5.00 - 15.00 |
| Tom Slade at Shadow Island, Fitzhugh, Percy Keese. | 1927 | 5.00 - 15.00 |
| Tom Slade at Temple Camp, Fitzhugh, Percy Keese. | 1917 | 5.00 - 15.00 |
| Tom Slade in the North Woods, Fitzhugh, Percy Keese. | 1927 | 5.00 - 15.00 |
| Tom Slade on a Transport, Fitzhugh, Percy Keese. | 1918 | 5.00 - 15.00 |
| Tom Slade on Mystery Trail, Fitzhugh, Percy Keese. | 1921 | 5.00 - 15.00 |
| Tom Slade on Overlook Mountain, Fitzhugh, Percy Keese. | 1923 | 5.00 - 15.00 |
| Tom Slade on the River, Fitzhugh, Percy Keese. | 1917 | 5.00 - 15.00 |
| Tom Slade Picks a Winner, Fitzhugh, Percy Keese. | 1924 | 5.00 - 15.00 |
| Tom Slade with the Boys Over There, Fitzhugh, Percy Keese. | 1918 | 5.00 - 15.00 |
| Tom Slade with the Colors, Fitzhugh, Percy Keese. | 1918 | 5.00 - 15.00 |

| | | |
|---|---|---|
| Tom Slade's Double Dare, Fitzhugh, Percy Keese. | 1922 | 5.00 - 15.00 |
| Tom Slade, Boy Scouts of the Moving Pictures, Fitzhugh, Percy Keese. | 1915 | 5.00 - 15.00 |
| Tom Slade, Boy Scouts; reprint of Tom Slade, Boy Scouts of the Moving Pictures, Fitzhugh, Percy Keese. | 1915 | 5.00 - 15.00 |
| Tom Slade, Motorcycle Dispatch Bearer, Fitzhugh, Percy Keese. | 1918 | 10.00 - 25.00 |
| Tom Slade: Forest Ranger, Fitzhugh, Percy Keese. | 1926 | 5.00 - 15.00 |

## Tom Slade Books, Grosset & Dunlap, Publishers

| | | |
|---|---|---|
| Tom Slade with the Flying Corps, Fitzhugh, Percy Keese. | 1919 | 10.00 - 25.00 |

## Tom Slade Books, Whitman

| | | |
|---|---|---|
| Tom Slade at Temple Camp, Fitzhugh, Percy Keese, reprint. | 1917 | 5.00 - 15.00 |
| Tom Slade, Boy Scouts; reprint of Tom Slade, Boy Scouts of the Moving Pictures, Fitzhugh, Percy Keese, reprint. | 1915 | 5.00 - 15.00 |

## Tom Slade Books

| | | |
|---|---|---|
| The Adventures of a Boy Scout, Photoplay edition of Tom Slade. | 1930 | 5.00 - 15.00 |

## Tommy Tip Series, Graham & Matlach Publishers

| | | |
|---|---|---|
| Tommy Tip Top and His Boy Scouts, Stone, Raymond. | 1914 | 5.00 - 15.00 |
| Tommy Tip Top and His Great Show, Stone, Raymond. | 1917 | 5.00 - 15.00 |

# FICTION BOOKS

Because scouting had a great following, many authors tried to tie their stories into the movement, thus creating an instant demand. If readers, or now collectors, see "Boy Scout" in the title, they may want to but it. Sometimes, however, the title only infers a scouting theme, and therefore the contents may not be of interest (so, buyer beware!). Books with strong bindings and dust jackets command a premium, as do color graphics. Books which are written in or have loose pages are less desirable, but are often encountered.

## Ames, G.D.

| | | |
|---|---|---|
| Boy Scout Campfires. | 1920 | 5.00 - 10.00 |

## Ames, Joseph B.

| | | |
|---|---|---|
| Clearport Boys, Century. | 1925 | 5.00 - 10.00 |
| The Flying V Mystery, Century. | 1928 | 7.50 - 12.50 |
| The Mounted Troop, Century. | 1926 | 5.00 - 10.00 |
| Mystery of Ram Island, Century. | 1918 | 5.00 - 10.00 |
| The Secret of Spirit Lake, Century. | 1927 | 5.00 - 10.00 |
| Torrance from Texas, Century. | 1921 | 12.50 - 15.00 |
| Under Boy Scout Colors, Century. | 1917 | 5.00 - 10.00 |

## Balkis, Marjory June

| | | |
|---|---|---|
| The Adventures of Boy Scouting, Vantage Press, Inc. | 1983 | 7.50 - 12.50 |

## Barbour, Ralph Henry

| | | |
|---|---|---|
| All Hands Stand By, D. Appleton Century Co. | 1942 | 5.00 - 10.00 |
| The Mystery of the Rubber Boat, D. Appleton Century Co. | 1943 | 5.00 - 10.00 |

## Barclay, Vera C.

| | | |
|---|---|---|
| Danny the Detective, G. P. Putnam's Sons. | 1918 | 5.00 - 10.00 |

## Barr, Ronald W.

| | | |
|---|---|---|
| Anthology of Lone Scout Verse, Amateur Publications. | 1924 | 25.00 - 35.00 |

## Bear, Gilly

Handsome illustrations popularized scouting books among the public.

| | | |
|---|---|---|
| Billy Boy Scout, Chimney Corner Series, Gabriel Sons. | 1916 | 40.00 - 60.00 |
| The Boy Scout ABC Book, Chimney Corner Series, Gabriel Sons. | 1916 | 40.00 - 60.00 |

## Becker, Bob

| | | |
|---|---|---|
| Land of the Takatu, Reilly & Lee Co. | 1931 | 5.00 - 10.00 |

## Beebe, H.

| | | |
|---|---|---|
| Scouting Serendipities. | 1920 | 5.00 - 10.00 |

## Blake, S.

| | | |
|---|---|---|
| The Honour of the Lions, J.B. Lippincott. | 1920 | 5.00 - 10.00 |

## Bogan, Samuel D.

| | | |
|---|---|---|
| Let the Coyotes Howl: A story of Philmont Scout Ranch, G.P. Putnam's Sons. | 1946 | 15.00 - 25.00 |

## Bonham, Frank

| | | |
|---|---|---|
| Mystery in Little Tokyo, E.P. Dutton & Co. | 1966 | 5.00 - 10.00 |

## Boyton, Fr. Neil, S.J.

| | | |
|---|---|---|
| Cobra Island. | 1922 | 5.00 - 10.00 |

| | | |
|---|---|---|
| On the Sands of Coney. | 1925 | 12.50 - 17.50 |
| Paul in the Scout World. | 1930 | 5.00 - 10.00 |
| Saints for Scouts. | 1930 | 5.00 - 10.00 |
| That Silver Fox Patrol. | 1944 | 5.00 - 10.00 |

## Brandeis, Madeline

| | | |
|---|---|---|
| Jack of the Circus, Reilly & Lee. | 1931 | 5.00 - 10.00 |

## Brereton, Capt. F.S.

| | | |
|---|---|---|
| Tom Stapleton, The Boy Scout, H.M. Caldwell Co. | 1920 | 5.00 - 10.00 |

## Brett, Edna Payson

| | | |
|---|---|---|
| A Merry Scout and other Stories, Rand McNally. | 1922 | 4.00 - 7.50 |

## Brown, Bill

| | | |
|---|---|---|
| Down Memory's Lane Together, Privately Printed. | 1941 | 15.00 - 25.00 |

## Burgess, Thorton W.

| | | |
|---|---|---|
| The Boy Scouts in a Trapper's Camp, Penn Publishing Co. | 1915 | 5.00 - 10.00 |
| The Boy Scouts of Woodcraft Camp, Penn Publishing Co. | 1912 | 5.00 - 15.00 |
| The Boy Scouts on Lost Trail, Penn Publishing Co. | 1914 | 5.00 - 10.00 |
| The Boy Scouts on Swift River, Penn Publishing Co. | 1913 | 5.00 - 10.00 |

## Burritt, Edwin C.

| | | |
|---|---|---|
| The Boy Scout Crusoes, Fleming H. Revell Co. | 1916 | 5.00 - 10.00 |

## Burton, Charles Pierce

| | | |
|---|---|---|
| The Bob's Cave Boys, Henry Holt & Co. | 1905 | 5.00 - 10.00 |
| Bob's Hill Boys in the Everglades, Henry Holt & Co. | 1932 | 5.00 - 10.00 |
| Bob's Hill Boys in Virginia, Henry Holt & Co. | 1939 | 5.00 - 10.00 |
| The Bob's Hill Braves, Henry Holt & Co. | 1912 | 5.00 - 10.00 |
| The Bob's Hill Braves, Henry Holt & Co. | 1910 | 5.00 - 10.00 |
| Bob's Hill Meets the Andes, Henry Holt & Co. | 1938 | 5.00 - 10.00 |
| Bob's Hill on the Air, Henry Holt & Co. | 1934 | 5.00 - 10.00 |
| Bob's Hill Trails, Henry Holt & Co. | 1922 | 5.00 - 10.00 |
| The Boy Scouts of Bob's Hill, Henry Holt & Co. | 1912 | 5.00 - 10.00 |
| Camp Bob's Hill, Henry Holt & Co. | 1915 | 5.00 - 10.00 |
| Raven Patrol of Bob's Hill, Henry Holt & Co. | 1917 | 5.00 - 10.00 |
| The Trail Makers, Henry Holt & Co. | 1919 | 5.00 - 10.00 |
| Treasure Hunters of Bob's Hill, Henry Holt & Co. | 1926 | 5.00 - 10.00 |

## Carey, A.A.

| | | |
|---|---|---|
| Boy Scouts at Sea, Little, Brown & Co. | 1918 | 5.00 - 10.00 |

## Carter, Edward Champe

| | | |
|---|---|---|
| The Lone Scout, Cornhill Co. | 1920 | 5.00 - 10.00 |

## Carter, Russell G.

| | | |
|---|---|---|
| Three Points of Honor, Little, Brown & Co. | 1926 | 5.00 - 10.00 |
| Three Points of Honor, Reprint in tan or yellow covers, Grosset & Dunlap. | 1926 | 5.00 - 10.00 |

## Case, John F.

| | | |
|---|---|---|
| Banners of Scoutcraft, J.B. Lippincott Co. | 1929 | 5.00 - 10.00 |

## Case, Lambert J.

| | | |
|---|---|---|
| Approved Boy Scout Plays, W.H. Baker Co. | 1931 | 12.50 - 17.50 |

## Chaffee, Allen

| | | |
|---|---|---|
| Lost River, or The Adventurers of Two Boys in the Big Woods, reprint of title changed edition, red cover, McLoughlin Bros. | 1937 | 5.00 - 10.00 |
| Lost River, or The Adventurers of Two Boys in the Big Woods, reprint, Title change to Lost! Two Boys Battle with the Elements, McLoughlin Bros. | 1930 | 5.00 - 10.00 |
| Lost River, or The Adventurers of Two Boys in the Big Woods, Milton Bradley Co. | 1920 | 5.00 - 10.00 |

## Cochran, Rice E.

| | | |
|---|---|---|
| Be Prepared: The Life and Illusions of a Scoutmaster, reprint, Avon paperback edition. | 1968 | 5.00 - 10.00 |
| Be Prepared: The Life and Illusions of a Scoutmaster, Sloane Publishing Co. | 1952 | 10.00 - 15.00 |

## Cody, H.A.

| | | |
|---|---|---|
| Rod of the Lone Patrol, Grosset & Dunlap. | 1916 | 5.00 - 10.00 |

## Coe, Roland

| | | |
|---|---|---|
| The Little Scouts in Action, McBride & Co. | 1944 | 5.00 - 10.00 |

## Corcoran, Brewer

| | | |
|---|---|---|
| The Boy Scouts at Camp Lowell, The Page Co. | 1922 | 5.00 - 10.00 |
| The Boy Scouts of Kendallville, The Page Co. | 1918 | 5.00 - 10.00 |
| The Boy Scouts of the Wolf Patrol, The Page Co. | 1918 | 5.00 - 10.00 |

## Davis, Richard Harding

| | | |
|---|---|---|
| The Boy Scout and other Stories for Boys, reprint, Charles Scribners' Sons. | 1924 | 5.00 - 10.00 |
| The Boy Scout and other Stories for Boys, Charles Scribners' Sons. | 1917 | 5.00 - 10.00 |
| The Boy Scout, Charles Scribners' Sons. | 1914 | 5.00 - 10.00 |

## Dimock, A.W.

| | | |
|---|---|---|
| Be Prepared, or the Boy Scouts in Florida, F.A.Stokes Co. | 1919 | 5.00 - 10.00 |

Books of personal experiences and scouting adventures abound, value $5.00 - $12.50 each.

**Eastman Kodak Co.**
Proof Positive, A Kodak Story for Boys. 1912  15.00 - 20.00

**Eastman, Charles A.**
Indian Scout Talks, reprint as Indian
  Scout Craft and Lore, Dover paperback. 1974  5.00 - 10.00
Indian Scout Talks, Little, Brown & Co. 1914  5.00 - 10.00

**Eldred, Warren**
St. Dunstan Boy Scouts, Lathrop,
  Lee & Sheppard Co. 1913  5.00 - 10.00

**English, James W.**
Tailbone Patrol, Holiday House, Inc. 1955  5.00 - 10.00
Tops in Troop 10, Macmillan. 1966  5.00 - 10.00

**Ernst, Clayton**
Blind Trails. 1920  5.00 - 10.00

**Finnemore, John**
Boy Scouts in the Balkans, Macmillan. 1928  5.00 - 10.00
Boy Scouts with the Russians, Macmillan. 1928  5.00 - 10.00
Brother Scouts, Macmillan. 1928  5.00 - 10.00
The Wolf Patrol. A tale of Baden-Powell's
  Boy Scouts, Macmillan. 1928  5.00 - 10.00

**Fitzhugh, Percy Keese**
Harvy Willetts, Grosset & Dunlap,
  Publishers. 1927  5.00 - 10.00
Lefty Leighton, Grosset & Dunlap,
  Publishers. 1929  5.00 - 10.00
Skinny McCord, Grosset & Dunlap,
  Publishers. 1928  5.00 - 10.00
Spiffy Henshaw, Grosset & Dunlap,
  Publishers. 1929  5.00 - 10.00
The Story of Terrible Terry, Grosset &
  Dunlap, Publishers. 1930  5.00 - 10.00
Wigwag Wiegand, Grosset & Dunlap,
  Publishers. 1929  5.00 - 10.00

**Garfield, James B.**
Follow My Leader, Scholastic Book
  Services paperback. 1957  3.00 - 7.50
Follow My Leader, Viking Press. 1957  5.00 - 10.00

**Garis, Howard R.**
Chad of Knob Hill, The Tale of a
  Lone Scout, Little, Brown & Co. 1927  5.00 - 10.00

**Gendron, Val**
Behind the Zuni Masks, Longmans,
  Green & Co. 1958  5.00 - 10.00
Behind the Zuni Masks, Junior Literary
  Guild Book Club edition. 1952  5.00 - 10.00
Behind the Zuni Masks, Junior Literary
  Guild Book Club edition reprint. 1962  5.00 - 10.00

**Gordon, Paul**
The Scout of the Golden Cross, Holt & Co. 1920  5.00 - 10.00

**Hanson, R.O.**
Plays for Boys, Associated Publishers. 1938  10.00 - 15.00

**Hare, Walter Ben**
A Country Boy Scout, Dennison. 1916  5.00 - 10.00

**Heck, B.H.**
Cave-in at Mason's Mine, Scholastic
  Book Services. 1980  5.00 - 10.00

**Hendrick, Edward P.**
The 7th Scout, W.A.Wilde Co. 1938  5.00 - 10.00

**Heyliger, William**
SOS Radio Patrol, Dodd-Meed & Co. 1942  5.00 - 10.00

**Holland, Rupert Sargent**
Blackbeard's Island, The Adventurers of
  Three Boy Scouts in the Sea Islands,
  J.B. Lippincott Co. 1916  5.00 - 10.00
The Boy Scouts of Birch-Bark Island,
  J.B. Lippincott Co. 1911  5.00 - 10.00
The Boy Scouts of Snowshoe Lodge,
  J.B. Lippincott Co. 1915  5.00 - 10.00
The Sea Scouts of Birch-Bark Island,
  J.B. Lippincott Co. 1936  5.00 - 10.00

**Hornibrook, Isabel K.**
A Scout of Today, Houghton & Mifflin Co. 1913  5.00 - 10.00
Lost in the Maine Woods,
  Houghton & Mifflin Co. 1913  5.00 - 10.00

**Houston, Edwin James**
Our Boy Scouts in Camp,
  David McKay, Publisher. 1912  5.00 - 10.00

**Huntington, Edward**
The Forest Pilot, A Story for Boy Scouts,
  Hearst's International Library Co. 1915  10.00 - 15.00

**Hyne, Elizabeth A. Watson**
Little Brothers to the Scouts,
  Rand McNally & Co. 1917  5.00 - 10.00

**Jackson, Jacqueline**
The Paleface Redskins,
  Little, Brown & Co., reissue. 1968  5.00 - 10.00
The Paleface Redskins,
  Little, Brown & Co. 1958  5.00 - 10.00

## Jadberns, Raymond

Three Amateur Scouts,
    J.B. Lippincott Co.                1920        5.00 - 10.00

## Jenkins, Marshall

A Freshman Scout at College,
    D. Appleton & Co.                  1917        5.00 - 10.00
The Norfolk Boy Scouts, D. Appleton & Co.  1916    5.00 - 10.00

## Kantor, MacKinley

Follow Me Boys (Title change after
    Disney Movie), Grosset & Dunlap.   1956        10.00 - 15.00
Follow Me Boys (Title change after
    Disney Movie), Temo Books paperback.  1966     7.50 - 12.50
God and My Country, Reader's Digest
    Condensed Books.                   1954        2.50 - 5.00
God and My Country,
    Bantam Books, paperback.           1954        7.50 - 12.50
God and My Country, World Publishing Co.  1954     10.00 - 15.00

## Keable, R.

African Scout Stories, Macmillan.      1921        5.00 - 10.00

## Keane, Thomas J.

Lubbers Afloat, Dodd, Mead & Co.       1932        5.00 - 10.00

## Kipling, Rudyard

Land and Sea Tales for Scouts and Guides,
    Macmillan & Co.                    1923        5.00 - 10.00
Land and Sea Tales for Scouts and
    Scout Masters, Doubleday,
    Page & Co. reprint.                1926        5.00 - 10.00
Land and Sea Tales for Scouts and
    Scout Masters, Sun Dial Press reprint.  1923   5.00 - 10.00
Land and Sea tales for Scouts and
    Scout Masters, Doubleday,
    Doran & Co., reprint.              1929        5.00 - 10.00

## Kohler, Julilly H.

Razzberry Jamboree, Thomas Y.
    Crowell Co.                        1957        5.00 - 10.00

## Lamb, Marritt

My Scout and Other Poems,
    W.C. Foote Printing Co.            1916        5.00 - 10.00

## LeBretton-Martin, E.

The Boys of the Otter Patrol,
    J.B. Lippincott Co.                1920        5.00 - 10.00
Otters to the Rescue, J.B. Lippincott Co.  1920    5.00 - 10.00

## Lerrigo, Charles Henry

Boy Scouts of Round Table Patrol,
    Barse & Hopkins.                   1924        5.00 - 10.00
Boy Scouts of Round Table Patrol,
    Barse Co. reprint.                 1924        5.00 - 10.00
The Boy Scouts to the Rescue,
    Barse Co. reprint.                 1920        5.00 - 10.00
The Boy Scouts to the Rescue,
    Barse & Hopkins.                   1920        5.00 - 10.00
The Boy Scout Treasure Hunters,
    Barse Co. reprint.                 1917        5.00 - 10.00
The Boy Scout Treasure Hunters,
    Barse & Hopkins.                   1917        5.00 - 10.00
Boy Scouts on Special Service,
    Little, Brown & Co.                1922        5.00 - 10.00
The Merry Men of Robin Hood Patrol,
    Barse & Hopkins.                   1927        5.00 - 10.00

## Lisle, Clifton

A Scout's Honor, Harcourt,
    Brace and Co.                      1921        5.00 - 10.00
Boy Scout Entertainments,
    Penn Publishing Co.                1918        5.00 - 10.00
Saddle Bags, Penn Publishing Co.       1923        5.00 - 10.00
The Treasure of the Chateau,
    Penn Publishing Co.                1929        5.00 - 10.00

## Lone Scout Classics

Lone Scout Press.                      1970        10.00 - 15.00

## Lyons, Kennedy

The Vagabond Scouts or
    The Adventurers of Duncan Dunn,
    Page & Co.                         1931        5.00 - 10.00

## Mathiews, Franklin K.

The Boy Scouts Book of Adventurous
    Youth, D. Appleton - Century Co.   1931        5.00 - 10.00
The Boy Scouts Book of Stories,
    D. Appleton & Co.                  1918        5.00 - 10.00
The Boy Scouts Own Book,
    D. Appleton & Co.                  1929        5.00 - 10.00
The Boy Scouts' Book of Good Turn
    Stories, Charles Scribners' Sons.  1931        5.00 - 10.00
The Boy Scouts Book
    of Campfire Stories, D. Appleton & Co.  1921   10.00 - 15.00
Boy Scouts Courageous, Barse Co.       1918        5.00 - 10.00
Chuckles and Grins, Grosset & Dunlap.  1928        5.00 - 10.00
Coming Through, Grosset & Dunlap.      1927        5.00 - 10.00
Flying High, Grosset & Dunlap.         1930        5.00 - 10.00
Hitting the Trail, Grosset & Dunlap.   1930        5.00 - 10.00
Laugh, Boy Laugh, Grosset & Dunlap.    1930        5.00 - 10.00
The Ransom of Red Chief and other
    O. Henry Stories for Boys,
    Doubleday, Page & Co.              1918        5.00 - 10.00
The Ransom of Red Chief and other
    O. Henry Stories for Boys,
    Grosset & Dunlap reprint.          1918        5.00 - 10.00
Skyward Ho, Grosset & Dunlap.          1930        5.00 - 10.00
Wild Animal Trails, Grosset & Dunlap.  1928        5.00 - 10.00

## Matlock
The Old Scoutmaster's Poems.                1937        5.00 - 10.00

## McCarthy, George T.
Scout Adventures, CYO.                      1930        10.00 - 15.00

## Nendick, V.R.
Jack Corvit, Patrol Leader, or
   Always a Scout, J.B. Lippincott Co.   1920   5.00 - 10.00

## Oakes, Vanya
Hawaiian Treasure, Julian Messner.          1957        10.00 - 15.00

## Park, George F.
Dick Judson, Boy Scout Ranger,
   McBride & Co.                          1916   5.00 - 10.00

## Parker, Capt. Thomas D.
The Cruise of the Deep Sea Scouts,
   W.A. Wilde Co.                         1917   5.00 - 10.00

## Payson, Lt. Howard
The Boy Scouts and the Army Airship,
   Hurst & Co.                            1911   10.00 - 15.00
The Boy Scouts and the Army Airship,
   A.L. Burt Co., pictorial cover reprint.   1911   10.00 - 15.00
The Boy Scouts at the Canadian Border,
   Hurst & Co.                            1918   5.00 - 10.00
The Boy Scouts at the Canadian Border,
   A.L. Burt Co., pictorial cover reprint.   1918   5.00 - 10.00
The Boy Scouts at the Panama Canal,
   A.L. Burt Co., pictorial cover reprint.   1913   5.00 - 10.00
The Boy Scouts at the Panama Canal,
   Hurst & Co.                            1913   5.00 - 10.00
The Boy Scouts at the Panama-Pacific
   Exposition, Hurst & Co.                1915   10.00 - 15.00
The Boy Scouts at the Panama-Pacific
   Exposition, A.L. Burt Co., pictorial
   cover reprint.                         1915   10.00 - 15.00
The Boy Scouts for Uncle Sam,
   Hurst & Co.                            1912   5.00 - 10.00
The Boy Scouts for Uncle Sam,
   A.L. Burt Co., pictorial cover reprint.   1912   5.00 - 10.00
The Boy Scouts of the Eagle Patrol,
   Hurst & Co.                            1911   5.00 - 10.00
The Boy Scouts of the Eagle Patrol,
   A.L. Burt Co., pictorial cover reprint.   1911   5.00 - 10.00
The Boy Scouts on Belgian Battlefields,
   A.L. Burt Co., pictorial cover reprint.   1915   5.00 - 10.00
The Boy Scouts on the Belgian
   Battlefields, Hurst & Co.              1915   5.00 - 10.00
The Boy Scouts on the Range, Hurst & Co.   1911   5.00 - 10.00
The Boy Scouts on the Range,
   A.L. Burt Co., pictorial cover reprint.   1911   5.00 - 10.00
The Boy Scouts Under Fire in Mexico,
   Hurst & Co.                            1914   5.00 - 10.00
The Boy Scouts Under Fire in Mexico,
   A.L. Burt Co., pictorial cover reprint.   1914   5.00 - 10.00
The Boy Scouts under Sealed Orders,
   A.L. Burt Co., pictorial cover reprint.   1916   5.00 - 15.00
The Boy Scouts Under Sealed Orders,
   Hurst & Co.                            1916   5.00 - 10.00
The Boy Scouts with the Allies in
   France, Hurst & Co.                    1915   5.00 - 10.00
The Boy Scouts with the Allies in France,
   A.L. Burt Co., pictorial cover reprint.   1915   5.00 - 10.00
The Boy Scouts' Badge of Courage,
   A.L. Burt Co., pictorial cover reprint.   1917   5.00 - 10.00
The Boy Scouts' Badge of Courage,
   Hurst & Co.                            1917   5.00 - 10.00
The Boy Scouts' Campaign for
   Preparedness, Hurst & Co.              1916   5.00 - 10.00
The Boy Scouts' Campaign for
   Preparedness, A.L. Burt Co.,
   pictorial cover reprint.              1916   5.00 - 10.00
The Boy Scouts' Mountain Camp,
   Hurst & Co.                            1912   5.00 - 10.00
The Boy Scouts' Mountain Camp, A.L.
   Burt Co., pictorial cover reprint.    1912   5.00 - 10.00

## Pier, Arthur Stanwood
The Hilltop Troop, Houghton Mifflin Co.     1919        5.00 - 10.00

## Puller, Edwin
Biff McCarty, The Eagle Scout,
   Abingdon Press.                        1915   5.00 - 10.00

## Reeve, Arthur B.
The Boy Scouts' Craig Kennedy,
   Harper & Brothers.                     1925   5.00 - 10.00

## Reynolds, Dickson and Gerry
Brother Scouts, Thomas Nelson & Sons.   1952   10.00 - 15.00

## Rudd, Stephen
The Mystery of the Missing Eyebrows,
   R.H. Gore Publishing Co.               1921   5.00 - 10.00

## Ruddy, Anna C.
From Tenderfoot to Scout,
   George H. Coran Co.                    1911   5.00 - 10.00

## Savitt, Sam
A Day at the LBJ Ranch, Random House.   1965   10.00 - 15.00

## Schultz, James W.
In the Great Apache Forest,
   The Story of a Lone Boy Scout,
   Houghton-Mifflin Co., green cover.     1920   5.00 - 10.00
In the Great Apache Forest,
   The Story of a Lone Boy Scout,
   Houghton-Mifflin Co., reprint, red cover. 1920   5.00 - 10.00

### Scoville, Samuel, Jr.
The Out-of-Doors Club,
    Sunday School Times Co.                    1919        5.00 - 10.00

### Sherman, Harold, M.
Don Rader, Trail Blazer, Grosset & Dunlap. 1929        5.00 - 10.00

### Slobodkin, L.
Return to the Apple Tree, Macmillan Co.,
    paperback.                                1965        5.00 - 10.00
Return to the Apple Tree, Macmillan Co.      1965        5.00 - 10.00
Space Ship Under the Apple Tree,
    Macmillan Co.                             1952        5.00 - 10.00
Space Ship Under the Apple Tree,
    Macmillan Co. paperback.                  1952        5.00 - 10.00
The Three-Seated Spaceship,
    Macmillan Co. paperback.                  1962        3.00 - 5.00
The Three-Seated Spaceship,
    Macmillan Co.                             1962        10.00 - 15.00

### Smeaton, Douglas and Edwin Baron
Easy Boy Scout Sketches,
    Fitzgerald Publishing Co.                 1938        10.00 - 15.00

### Smith, Leonard K.
Corey Takes the Scout Trail,
    D. Appleton & Co.                         1930        5.00 - 10.00

### So Much Concern
3 Scouts and Explorer plant sapling,
    Rockwell, N.                              1975        5.00 - 10.00

### Stankevich, Boris
Two Green Bars, Doubleday & Co.              1967        5.00 - 10.00

### Sterling, Gray
The Tooth of Time: A Philmont Adventure,
    Marshall Jones Co.                        1955        15.00 - 20.00

### Stevens, C.M.
Uncle Jeremiah at the Panama-Pacific
    Exposition, Hamming-Whitman Co.,
    Publishers.                               1915        10.00 - 25.00

### Strong, P.N.
Behind the Great Smokies.                    1920        5.00 - 10.00

### Thiess, Lewis E.
Flood Mappers Aloft, W.A. Wilde Co.          1937        5.00 - 10.00

### Thurston, Ida, Treadwell
Billy Burns of Troop 5,
    Gleming H. Revell Co.                     1913        5.00 - 10.00

The Scoutmaster of Troop 5,
    Gleming H. Revell Co.                     1912        5.00 - 10.00

### Tull, Jewell Bothwell
Rob Riley - The Making of a Boy Scout,
    Educational Supply Co.                    1916        5.00 - 10.00
Winning of the Bronze Cross,
    Educational Supply Co.                    1915        5.00 - 10.00

### Walden, Walter
The Hidden Islands, Small, Maynard & Co.  1918        5.00 - 10.00

### Wallace, Dillon
Troop One of the Labrador,
    Fleming H. Revell Co.                     1920        5.00 - 10.00

### Wallace, Maude Orita
Peanuts and Pennies, A Musical Play for Boys,
    Raymond A. Hoffman Co.                    1927        10.00 - 15.00

### Webster, Frank V.
The Boy Scouts on Lenox, or
    The Hike Over Big Bear Mountain,
    Cupples & Leon Co.                        1915        10.00 - 17.50

### Wellman, Manly W.
The Sleuth Patrol, Thomas Nelson & Sons. 1947        5.00 - 10.00

### Wodehouse, P.G.
The Swoop, or How Clarence Saved
    England, Seabury Press.                   1979        5.00 - 10.00

# Magazine Scouting Articles

### Boy's Life
| | | |
|---|---|---|
| Any single issue. | 1911-1915 | 40.00 - 60.00 |
| Any single issue. | 1916-1920 | 35.00 - 50.00 |
| Any single issue. | 1921-1930 | 15.00 - 30.00 |
| Any single issue. | 1931-1940 | 8.00 - 15.00 |
| Any single issue. | 1941-1950 | 5.00 - 7.50 |
| Any single issue. | 1951-1960 | 3.00 - 6.00 |
| Any single issue. | 1961-1970 | 2.00 - 3.00 |
| Any single issue. | 1971-1997 | 0.50 - 1.00 |

### Life Magazine
1950, July 24. National Jamboree article.    1950        15.00 - 20.00

### Life
February 5, 1920. The Hero Worshiper
    by N. Rockwell on cover.
    (Dog seated at sleeping scout's feet.)   1920        20.00 - 25.00

## National Geographic Magazine

1956, September. Philmont Scout
    Ranch article.                         1950        5.00 - 7.50

Scouting articles appear in many popular magazines.

## Saturday Evening Post

1960, July 23. National Jamboree article.    1960        7.50 - 10.00

The 25th Anniversary prompted many local newspaper articles.

## Scout Administrator Magazine

Any single issue.                    1935-1950    5.00 - 10.00

## Scouting Magazine

| | | |
|---|---|---|
| Any single issue. | 1916-1920 | 30.00 - 50.00 |
| Any single issue. | 1931-1940 | 10.00 - 20.00 |
| Any single issue. | 1913-1915 | 40.00 - 60.00 |
| Any single issue. | 1941-1950 | 7.50 - 10.00 |
| Any single issue. | 1951-1960 | 3.00 - 6.00 |
| Any single issue. | 1961-1970 | 2.00 - 4.00 |
| Any single issue. | 1971-1997 | 0.50 - 1.00 |
| Any single issue. | 1921-1930 | 20.00 - 30.00 |

## Smithsonian Magazine

1985 Anniversary article.            1985        5.00-7.50

## Texas Monthly

1985 Anniversary article.            1985        5.00-7.50

## Newspaper Articles

Depending on Content.                            1.00-10.00

Even today scouting topics make headlines in local newspapers.

# COMIC BOOKS

## Allen R.S.
Who's Minding the Mint?
    Dell Publishing Co.                    1967        2.00 - 3.00

## Association of American Railroads
Salute to the Boy Scouts.                 1960        4.00 - 5.00

## BSA
Boy Scout Adventure.                      1954        2.00 - 3.00
You Can Be a Scout and a Winner.          1972        2.00 - 3.00

## Coe, Roland
The Little Scouts, #2. Oct.-Dec. 1951.
    Dell Publishing Co.                    1951        2.00 - 3.00
The Little Scouts, #6. Oct.-Dec. 1952.
    Dell Publishing Co.                    1952        2.00 - 3.00

## Coe, Roland
The Little Scouts, #1. July-Sept. 1951.
    Dell Publishing Co.                    1951        2.00 - 3.00
The Little Scouts, #3. Jan.-Mar. 1952.
    Dell Publishing Co.                    1952        2.00 - 3.00
The Little Scouts, #4. Apr.-June 1952.
    Dell Publishing Co.                    1952        2.00 - 3.00
The Little Scouts, #5. July-Sept. 1952.
    Dell Publishing Co.                    1952        2.00 - 3.00

## Crump, Irving
Scouts to the Rescue, Part 1.
    Movie Classics.                        1937        2.00 - 3.00
Scouts to the Rescue, Part 2.
    Movie Classics.                        1937        2.00 - 3.00

## Disney, Walt
Goofy Scoutmaster.                        1962        4.00 - 5.00

## Feldstein, Albert B.
Mad Special, Spring 1971.
    E.C. Publications, Inc.                1971        2.00 - 3.00

## Golden Press Editors
UFO Encounters. Western Publishing Co.    1978        2.00 - 3.00

## Hanna-Barbera Productions
The Flintstones at the Boy Scout Jamboree,
    #18. May 1964. K.K. Publications, Inc
    and Golden Press.                      1964        2.00 - 3.00

## Harvey Publications, Inc.
Devil Kids.                               1978        2.00 - 3.00
Richie Rich Cash.                         1977        2.00 - 3.00
Richie Rich Diamonds.                     1979        2.00 - 3.00
Richie Rich Jackpots.                     1979        2.00 - 3.00
Richie Rich Profits.                      1982        2.00 - 3.00
Richie Rich Success.                      1977        2.00 - 3.00
Spooky Spooktown.                         1975        2.00 - 3.00

## Ketcham, Hank
Dennis the Menace - the Good Scouts,
    #138. May 1975.                        1975        2.00 - 3.00

## Kipling, Rudyard
Jungle Book #83. Classic Comics.          1940        2.00 - 3.00

## McCay, Robert W.
The Life of James E. West, Vol 1, #2.
    March 1942. Pioneer Picture Stories,
    quarterly.                             1942        2.00 - 3.00

## Skeates, Steve and Ralph Reese
The Official Boy Scout Handbook,
    The City Edition; in Crazy Super Special,
    #85. April 1982. Marvel Magazine.     1982        2.00 - 3.00

## Stenzel, Al
Your Flag. BSA.                           1973        2.00 - 3.00

## The Best From Boy's Life Comics
April 1958. Gilberton World-Wide
    Publications.                          1958        2.00 - 3.00
January 1958. Gilberton World-Wide
    Publications.                          1958        2.00 - 3.00
July 1958. Gilberton World-Wide
    Publications.                          1958        2.00 - 3.00
October 1957. Gilberton World-Wide
    Publications.                          1957        2.00 - 3.00
October 1958. Gilberton World-Wide
    Publications.                          1958        2.00 - 3.00

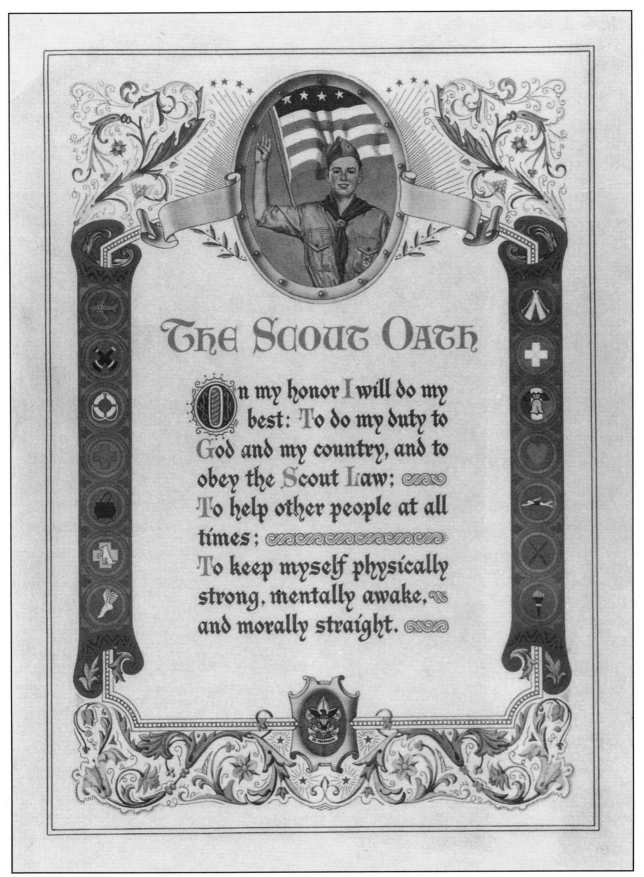

Frameable posters were available in the 1960s, value $10.00 - $15.00.

# MISCELLANEOUS STUFF

Troop 17, Gateway District, Queens Council put on some impressive pioneering displays during the 1980 Queens Day Festival.

## Auto Radiator Cap

| | | |
|---|---|---|
| First Class emblem. | 1920-1930 | 100.00-150.00 |

## Bank

| | | |
|---|---|---|
| Scout and shield w/ r-w-b stripes. Lithographed tin. | 1920 | 20.00 - 30.00 |
| Scout standing w/ staff, 2-part cast iron, painted. | 1920 | 40.00 - 75.00 |
| Scout standing, hands on waist, cast iron, painted. | 1920 | 40.00 - 60.00 |
| Scouts in Camp, boy w/ flag. Mechanical, cast iron, painted. (reproductions exist, $50.) | 1920 | 250.00-350.00 |

## Blotters

| | | |
|---|---|---|
| Scout Law Series-©Brown+Bigelow. | 1916 each | 15.00-20.00 |
| Coke, 2 scouts at Cooler, wholesome refreshment. | | 15.00-25.00 |
| Coke, scout and Cooler - Be Prepared Be Refreshed. | | 15.00-25.00 |

## Bookmark

| | | |
|---|---|---|
| First Class emblem at ctr. | 1950-1960 | 5.00 - 7.50 |
| Tenderfoot emblem at ctr., green enamel background. | 1960-1970 | 2.00 - 3.00 |

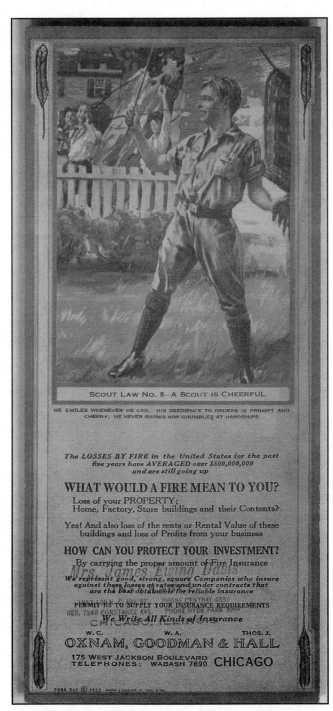

A 1923 ink blotter by Brown & Bigelow from its Scout Law series.

## Camera

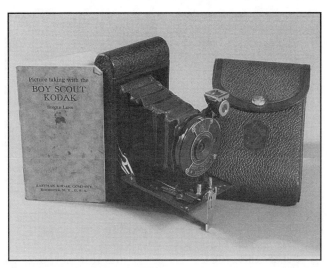

The Boy Scout Kodak (1929)

| | | |
|---|---|---|
| Seneca 2A Boy Scout, or Scout Camera. | 1915 | 50.00 - 75.00 |
| Agfa Ansco Boy Scout Memo Camera. | 1929 | 40.00 - 60.00 |
| Kodak, Boy Scout. Olive green bellows, case, and leather belt pouch. | 1929-1934 | 125.00-200.00 |
| Kodak, Boy Scout Brownie, 120 film. | 1932 | 100.00-125.00 |
| Kodak, Boy Scout Brownie, 620 film. | 1933-1934 | 30.00 - 50.00 |
| Kodak, Boy Scout Black bellows, olive green case, and leather belt pouch. | 1934-1940 | 100.00-150.00 |
| Herco Scout 120. | 1950-1955 | 30.00 - 50.00 |
| Herco Imperial 620 Reflex. | 1955-1960 | 20.00 - 30.00 |
| Official 3-way, 127 film. | 1960-1963 | 10.00 - 15.00 |
| Official Camera, 620 film. | 1960-1963 | 10.00 - 15.00 |
| Official Flash Camera, round attachment, 127 film. | 1961-1963 | 10.00 - 15.00 |
| Official Flash Camera, square attachment, 127 film. | 1963-1965 | 10.00 - 15.00 |
| Lark Flash, built in, 127 film. | 1964-1966 | 10.00 - 15.00 |
| Cubex IV, 127 film. | 1966-1968 | 5.00 - 10.00 |
| Instant Load, 126 cartridge. | 1969-1971 | 5.00 - 10.00 |

## Contest Cup

| | | |
|---|---|---|
| First Class emblem atop 10" high cup w/ wide bottom and fluted top. Silverplate. | 1920-1935 | 50.00 - 75.00 |
| First Class emblem atop 10" high cup, thin base. Silverplate. | 1920-1935 | 50.00 - 75.00 |

## Contest Plaque

| | | |
|---|---|---|
| Fancy brass w/ First Class emblem at top. 9x10". | 1920-1935 | 75.00-100.00 |
| Ornate brass w/ First Class emblem in bottom border. 9x10". | 1920-1935 | 75.00-100.00 |
| Shield shape w/ scout on signal tower and First Class emblem. 9x10. | 1920-1935 | 100.00-125.00 |

## Cuff Links

Cuff links (1914)

| | | |
|---|---|---|
| First Class emblem in oval. Silver. Pair. | 1915-1925 | 125.00-175.00 |
| First Class emblem in oval.<br>  Enameled silver. Pair. | 1915-1925 | 150.00-200.00 |
| Second Class emblem in oval.<br>  Enameled silver. Pair. | 1915-1925 | 125.00-175.00 |
| Second Class emblem in oval. Silver.<br>  Pair. | 1915-1925 | 125.00-175.00 |
| Second Class emblem in oval. Silver.<br>  Pair. | 1915-1925 | 125.00-175.00 |
| Tenderfoot emblem in oval.<br>  Enameled silver. Pair. | 1915-1925 | 125.00-175.00 |
| Tenderfoot emblem in oval. Silver. Pair. | 1915-1925 | 125.00-175.00 |
| Tenderfoot emblem in oval. Silver. Pair. | 1915-1925 | 125.00-175.00 |

## Cup, collapsible

| | | |
|---|---|---|
| First Class emblem on top.<br>  Brass, nickel plated. | 1911-1930 | 30.00 - 45.00 |
| Tenderfoot emblem on top.<br>  Brass, nickel-plated. | 1930-1950 | 15.00 - 20.00 |
| tenderfoot emblem on top. Aluminum. | 1950-1970 | 5.00 - 7.50 |
| Tenderfoot emblem on top. Plastic. | 1960-1980 | 3.00 - 7.50 |

## Figurine, Grossman, Rockwell's

| | | |
|---|---|---|
| A Scout is Helpful. | 1985 | 35.00 - 50.00 |
| Can't Wait. | 1985 | 25.00 - 40.00 |
| Good Turn (1st). | 1985 | 35.00 - 50.00 |
| Good Turn (2nd). | 1985 | 35.00 - 50.00 |
| Physically Strong. | 1985 | 35.00 - 50.00 |
| Scout Memories. | 1985 | 35.00 - 50.00 |

## First Aid Kit

| | | |
|---|---|---|
| Bauer & Black, rounded corners and green,<br>  orange top (if no contents deduct 50%). | 1932 | 40.00 - 60.00 |
| Bauer & Black, rectangular corners and green,<br>  orange top (if no contents deduct 50%). | 1935 | 40.00 - 60.00 |
| Johnson & Johnson, rectangular, green and red<br>  (if no contents deduct 50%). | 1938 | 30.00 - 50.00 |
| Johnson & Johnson, square, removable top<br>  (if no contents deduct 50%). | 1945 | 25.00 - 35.00 |
| Johnson & Johnson, square, flip top<br>  (if no contents deduct 50%). | 1955 | 20.00 - 40.00 |

| | | |
|---|---|---|
| Johnson & Johnson, curved plastic<br>  (if no contents deduct 50%). | 19650 | 10.00 - 15.00 |

## Game

| | | |
|---|---|---|
| The Game of Boy Scouts. Parker Brothers. | 1912 | 40.00 - 60.00 |
| American Boys, a game. Milton Bradley. | 1920 | 75.00-100.00 |
| Boy Scout 10 pins (bowling). | 1920 | 40.00 - 60.00 |
| Boy Scout 5 pins (bowling). | 1920 | 30.00 - 50.00 |
| Boy Scouts in Camp. Cardboard figures<br>  on wood blocks. | 1920 | 75.00-100.00 |
| Sunny Andy Kiddie Kampers. Tin litho. | 1920 | 80.00-120.00 |
| Target Ball (marble shoot). | 1920 | 40.00 - 60.00 |
| Game of Scouting. Parker Brothers. | 1926 | 40.00 - 60.00 |
| The Boy Scout Progress Game. | 1926 | 60.00 - 90.00 |
| Boy Scout Game. Card pick to do action. | 1930 | 30.00 - 40.00 |

## Games

| | | |
|---|---|---|
| Mickey Mouse - The Scout. Cut-out figures<br>  from Post Toasties Box. | 1939 | 40.00 - 60.00 |

## Grave Marker

| | | |
|---|---|---|
| Tenderfoot emblem above palm on square<br>  area for name and dates. Copper-bronze. | 1930-1940 | 75.00-100.00 |

## Greeting Cards

| | | |
|---|---|---|
| Various themes. | 1960-1967 | 2.00 - 3.00 |

Four large-format greeting cards from the 1960s

## Kenner's Bob Scout Doll

| | | |
|---|---|---|
| In uniform w/ box. | 1975 | 55.00 - 75.00 |

## Kenner's Steve Scout Doll

| | | |
|---|---|---|
| In uniform w/ box. | 1975 | 45.00 - 60.00 |

## Kenner's Steve Scout Extras

| | | |
|---|---|---|
| Fire Fighter Gear. | 1975 | 5.00 - 7.50 |
| Metal Detector Gear. | 1975 | 5.00 - 7.50 |

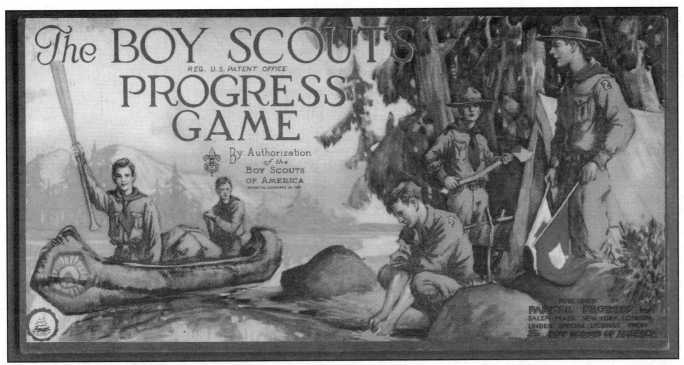

Game board for the 1924 Parker Brothers "The Boy Scouts' Progress Game."

Winchester rifles 1985 tribute lithograph, painted by J. Csatari, value $75.00 - $100.00.

## Lapel Pin, clip on
First Class emblem in oval. Silver.      1915-1925    60.00 - 80.00
Second Class emblem in oval. Silver.     1915-1925   100.00-125.00
Tenderfoot emblem in oval. Silver.       1915-1925   125.00-150.00

## Lapel Pin, long pin

The Stick pin (1914).

First Class emblem in oval. Silver.      1915-1925    60.00 - 80.00
Second Class emblem in oval. Silver.     1915-1925   100.00-125.00
Tenderfoot emblem in oval. Silver.       1915-1925   125.00-150.00

## Light Bulb
First Class emblem in filament.          1935-1940   125.00-150.00

## Morse Flags
Red-white square, 24" muslin.            1911-1930    15.00 - 20.00

## Note Paper
Box of 24 sheets and envelopes,
    First Class emblem.                  1920-1930    20.00 - 30.00
Box of 24 sheets and envelopes,
    Second Class emblem.                 1920-1930    20.00 - 30.00
Box of 24 sheets and envelopes,
    Tenderfoot emblem.                   1920-1930    20.00 - 30.00

## Patrol Flag
Red emblem silkscreened
    on both sides of white muslin,
    11 x 27". 47 different available.    1911-1930    50.00 - 75.00

## Patrol Flags
White w/ red circle. Black embroidered
    animal or figure, B.S.A. below.      1955-1972     7.50 - 15.00
White w/ yellow circle. Black embroidered
    animal or figure, B.S.A. below.      1972-1989     3.00 - 7.50

## Pennant
First Class emblem, BE PREPARED.
    12 x 24" felt.                       1911-1930    25.00 - 30.00
First Class emblem, BE PREPARED.
    9 x 18" felt.                        1911-1930    15.00 - 20.00

## Plaques, Laminated
Official Badges and Insignia.            1940s    30.00-40.00
Grateful Recognition.                    1960s     5.00-10.00
Scoutmaster.                             1960s    10.00-15.00

Laminated plaque, above, identifies scout badges of the 1940s, and below, a 1960s recognition plaque.

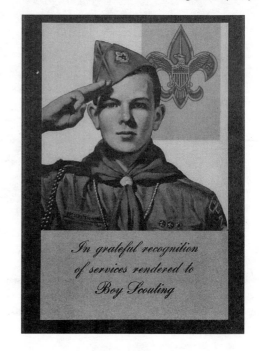

Programs are great local-interest collectibles. This Madison Square Garden, New York, program includes great photographs and advertisements, value $25.00 - $35.00.

## Plate, Gorham China, Rockwell's

Graham China's plate of Rockwell's calendar painting: "Our Heritage"

| A Scout is Loyal. | 1980 | 40.00 - 60.00 |
| Beyond the Easel. | 1980 | 50.00 - 75.00 |
| Campfire Story. | 1980 | 40.00 - 60.00 |
| Good Sign. | 1980 | 40.00 - 60.00 |
| Our Heritage. | 1980 | 40.00 - 60.00 |
| Pointing the Way. | 1980 | 40.00 - 60.00 |
| The Scoutmaster. | 1980 | 60.00 - 80.00 |

## Plate, Grossman China, Rockwell's

| Can't Wait. | 1980 | 40.00 - 60.00 |
| Young Doctor. | 1980 | 40.00 - 60.00 |

## Ring

First Class ring

| First Class emblem incuse in oval top. Spiral design on sides. 10 kt. gold. | 1916-1920 | 100.00-150.00 |
| First Class emblem incuse in oval top. Spiral design on sides. Gold filled. | 1916-1920 | 50.00 - 75.00 |

| First Class emblem incuse in oval top. Spiral design on sides. Sterling silver. | 1916-1920 | 40.00 - 60.00 |
| First Class emblem incuse in oval top. Vertical double loop knot on sides. 10 kt. gold. | 1921-1928 | 100.00-150.00 |
| First Class emblem incuse in oval top. Vertical double loop knot on sides. Gold filled. | 1921-1928 | 60.00 - 75.00 |
| First Class emblem incuse in oval top. Vertical double loop knot on sides. Sterling silver. | 1921-1928 | 40.00 - 60.00 |
| Eagle Scout design on red-white-blue oval field. Vertical double loop knot on side. Sterling silver. | 1925-1932 | 60.00 - 90.00 |
| First Class emblem raised in oval top. Overhand knot on sides. 10 kt. gold. | 1929-1938 | 100.00-150.00 |
| First Class emblem raised in oval top. Overhand knot on sides. Gold filled. | 1929-1949 | 60.00 - 75.00 |
| First Class emblem raised in oval top. Overhand knot on sides. Sterling silver. | 1929-1949 | 40.00 - 60.00 |
| Eagle Scout design on red-white-blue oval field. Vertical double loop knot on side. 10 kt. white gold. | 1930-1932 | 150.00-200.00 |
| Eagle Scout design on red-white-blue oval field. Overhand knot on side. 10 kt. white gold. | 1933-1940 | 150.00-200.00 |
| Eagle Scout design on red-white-blue oval field. Overhand knot on side. Sterling silver. | 1933-1940 | 70.00 - 90.00 |

Early Eagle Scout ring

| Eagle Scout design on red-white-blue oval set on rectangular top. Ribbed edges same as above, blank sides. Sterling silver. | 1937-1957 | 40.00 - 60.00 |
| Life emblem raised on black square. Sterling silver. | 1937-1947 | 20.00 - 25.00 |
| Star emblem raised on black square. Sterling silver. | 1937-1947 | 15.00 - 20.00 |
| Tenderfoot emblem raised on black square. (large emblem). Sterling silver. | 1937-1947 | 10.00 - 15.00 |
| Tenderfoot emblem raised on black square. (small emblem). Sterling silver. | 1937-1947 | 10.00 - 15.00 |
| Eagle Scout design on red-white-blue oval field. Overhand knot on side, rope is continuous. 10 kt. gold. | 1941-1947 | 125.00-175.00 |
| Eagle Scout design on red-white-blue oval field. Overhand knot on side, rope is continuous. 14 kt. gold. | 1941-1947 | 125.00-175.00 |

The Modern Art Foundry in the Steinway section of Queens, New York, is where the life-size statue of R. Tait McKenzie is cast.

Eagle Scout design on red-white-blue oval
field. Overhand knot on side, rope is
continuous. Sterling Silver.          1941-1947   70.00 - 90.00
First Class emblem raised in rectangle top.
Plain sides. Sterling Silver.         1950-1965   10.00 - 15.00
Tenderfoot emblem raised on rectangle top.
Sterling Silver.                      1965-1979   10.00 - 15.00

## Scout Law Statue

Brave, marketed by Scouting Bronzes,      1990    250.00-300.00
Clean, marketed by Scouting Bronzes,      1990    250.00-300.00
Courteous, marketed by Scouting Bronzes.  1990    250.00-300.00
Friendly, marketed by Scouting Bronzes.   1990    250.00-300.00
Helpful, marketed by Scouting Bronzes.    1990    250.00-300.00
Kind, marketed by Scouting Bronzes.       1990    250.00-300.00
Loyal, marketed by Scouting Bronzes.      1990    250.00-300.00
Obedient, marketed by Scouting Bronzes.   1990    250.00-300.00
Reverent, marketed by Scouting Bronzes,   1990    250.00-300.00
Thrifty, marketed by Scouting Bronzes.    1990    250.00-300.00
Trustworthy, marketed by Scouting Bronzes.1990    250.00-300.00

## Scout Statue by R. Tait McKennzie

The McKennzie 11" version first introduced in 1930s.

17" plaster composition, ivory (white)
bronze or copper finishes.            1914        200.00-250.00

11" base metal-plated bronze, silver, or
copper. Scout law on base. Wood or plastic
Bakelite base.                        1930        40.00 - 60.00

## Scout Statue

Daniel C. Beard statue by Scouting Bronzes.

Daniel C. Beard, marketed by
Scouting Bronzes.                     1990        400.00-500.00
Lady Olive Baden-Powell, marketed by
Scouting Bronzes.                     1990        400.00-500.00
Lord R.S.S. Baden Powell, marketed by
Scouting Bronzes.                     1990        400.00-500.00
William Hillcourt, marketed by
Scouting Bronzes.                     1990        400.00-500.00
Baden Powell bust on pedestal, marketed by
Scouting Bronzes.                     1994        175.00-250.00

## Scout's Memory Book

Kodak photo album, leatherette.
7-1/2 x 12" or 12 by 7-1/2".          1920-1930   25.00 - 35.00

## Semaphore Signal Flags

Red-white diagonal 18" square, muslin.   1911-1930   15.00 - 20.00

## Semaphore and Morse Signal Pocket Disc

Rotating discs w/ openings for
   letter and code.                    1916-1930  50.00 - 65.00

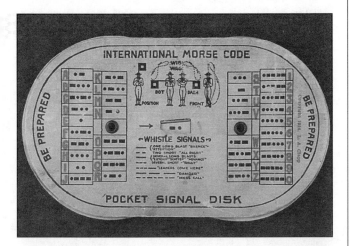

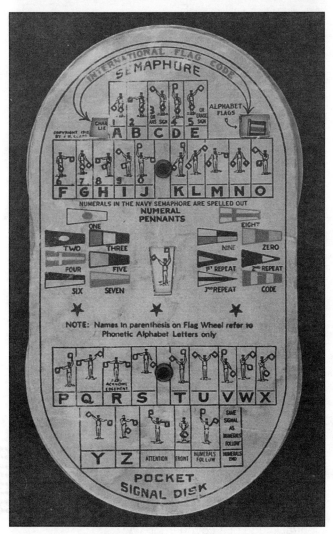

The Pocket Semaphore disc includes helpful graphics on two rotating discs.

## Sheet Music

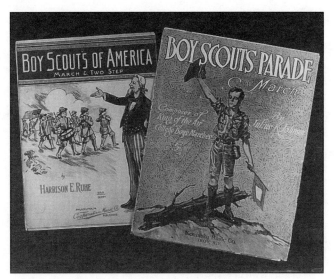

Sheet music scores include contemporary graphics.

| | | |
|---|---|---|
| "The Boy Scouts March" by Herman. | 1911 | 20.00 - 30.00 |
| "A Good Turn" by Murphy. | 1912 | 20.00 - 30.00 |
| "March of the Boy Scouts." | 1912 | 20.00 - 30.00 |
| "March of the Boy Scout" by Grant-Schaefer. | 1913 | 20.00 - 30.00 |
| "Be a Good Scout" by Murphy. | 1914 | 20.00 - 30.00 |
| "The Boy Scout Dream." | 1915 | 20.00 - 30.00 |
| "Boy Scouts of America - A March" by Sousa. | 1916 | 20.00 - 30.00 |
| "Boy Scouts on Parade" by Johnson. | 1917 | 20.00 - 30.00 |
| "Follow Old Glory," American Jr. Boy Scouts. | 1917 | 20.00 - 30.00 |
| "Boy Scouts on Parade" by Martin. | 1920 | 20.00 - 30.00 |
| "Boy Scouts" by Hopkins. | 1920 | 20.00 - 30.00 |
| "Off to Camp by Anthony." | 1921 | 20.00 - 30.00 |
| "A Day with the Boy Scouts" by Rovanger. | 1928 | 20.00 - 30.00 |
| "At a Boy Scout Camp" by Gaul. | 1930 | 10.00 - 15.00 |
| "Boy Scouts March" by Heltman. | 1930 | 20.00 - 30.00 |
| "Youth Pastimes" by Rolfe. | 1930 | 10.00 - 15.00 |
| "Lets all be good Scouts Together" by Penner-Raynor. | 1938 | 20.00 - 30.00 |
| "If He's a Scout" by Waring. | 1940 | 10.00 - 15.00 |
| "Tough-up, Buckle-down." | 1944 | 5.00 - 10.00 |
| "Tomorrow America." | 1949 | 10.00 - 15.00 |
| "The Boy Scout Anthem" by Wright-Mitchell. | 1954 | 10.00 - 15.00 |
| "Be Prepared," dedicated to BSA by Sterns. | 1955 | 5.00 - 10.00 |
| "Onward for God and Country" by Waring-Dolph. | 1955 | 10.00 - 15.00 |

## Signal Set

| | | |
|---|---|---|
| Morse listing on wooden base. | 1916-1930 | 35.00 - 50.00 |
| Morse listing on plastic base. | 1955-1970 | 5.00 - 10.00 |

## Tie Bars

Various events, councils.          1950-1970   5.00 - 7.50

## Tie Chain

Various events, regions, and councils.    1940-1955   5.00 - 15.00

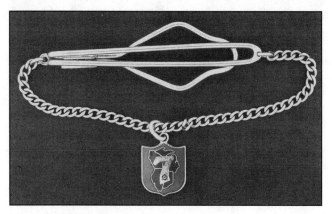

Tie chain from Region 7

## Troop Charter

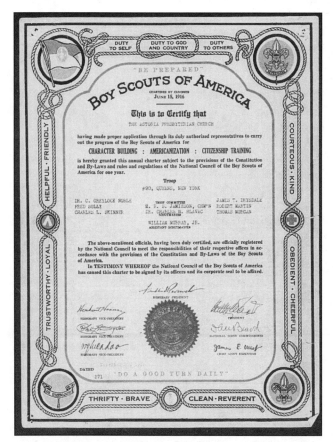

Troop Charters. In the pre-1945 design, the tenure of a unit was included as a large underprint in the central area. (See following pages for more charters.)

Scout Law within rope border.
   Large V underprint in ctr.
   5 year tenured unit.              1925-1945   15.00 - 20.00

Scout Law within rope border.
   Large X underprint in ctr.
   10 year tenured unit.             1925-1945   20.00 - 30.00
Scout Law within rope border.
   Large XV underprint in ctr.
   15 year tenured unit.             1925-1945   20.00 - 30.00
Scout Law within rope border.
   Large XX underprint in ctr.
   20 year tenured unit.             1925-1945   25.00 - 35.00
Scout Law within rope border.
   Large XXV underprint in ctr.
   25 year tenured unit.             1925-1945   25.00 - 35.00
Scout Law within rope border.
   Large XXX underprint in ctr.
   30 year tenured unit.             1925-1945   30.00 - 40.00
Scout Law within rope border.
   no underprint in ctr.             1925-1945   15.00 - 20.00
White, First Class emblem within
   red-white-blue ribbon at top.
   Statue of Liberty in blue at l. corner,
   National Seal in r. corner.       1946-1950   15.00 - 20.00
White, First Class emblem within
   red-white-blue ribbon at top.
   National Seal at bottom ctr.      1950-1965   10.00 - 15.00

## Troop Flag

Central image of a cotton troop flag

First Class emblem at left ctr, red top,
   white bottom. 22 x 36".           1911-1930   50.00 - 75.00

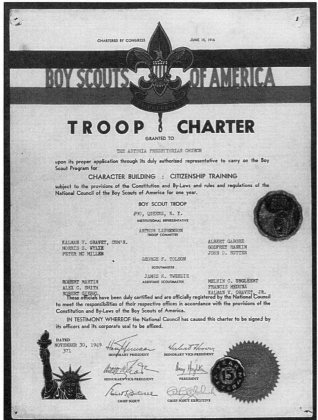

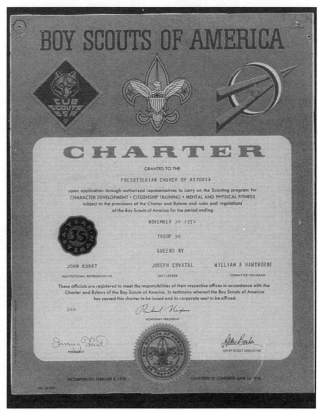

Troop Charters. In the pre-1945 design, the tenure of a unit was included as a large underprint in the central area (top). Later charters include graphics of the era. (1949, 1971)

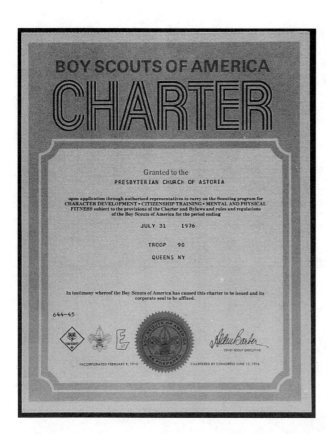

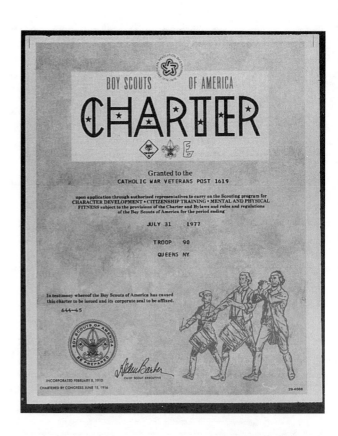

Later charters include graphics of the era. (1976, 1977, 1982, 1990)

| | | |
|---|---|---|
| First Class emblem at ctr, white top, red bottom. Wool. Pennant end. | 1920-1935 | 50.00 - 75.00 |
| First Class emblem at ctr, white top, red bottom. Wool. Square end. | 1925-1950 | 40.00 - 60.00 |
| First Class emblem at ctr, white top, red bottom. Square end. Cotton. | 1950-1970 | 20.00 - 40.00 |
| First Class emblem at ctr. white top, red bottom. Nylon. | 1970 | 15.00 - 30.00 |

## Valentines
| | | |
|---|---|---|
| Various themes. | 1920-1935 | 10.00 - 15.00 |

Scout theme valentine.

## Watch Fob - Leader
| | | |
|---|---|---|
| Assistant Deputy Scout Commissioner, light blue ribbon. | 1915-1925 | 150.00-200.00 |
| Assistant Scoutmaster. | 1915-1925 | 150.00-200.00 |
| Scout Commissioner, dark blue ribbon. | 1915-1925 | 150.00-200.00 |
| Scoutmaster, green ribbon. | 1915-1925 | 150.00-200.00 |
| Troop Committee, Local Council Committee, white ribbon. | 1915-1925 | 150.00-200.00 |

## Watch Fob
| | | |
|---|---|---|
| Scout Signaling. | 1911-1920 | 75.00-100.00 |
| Scout standing w/ rifle. | 1911-1920 | 60.00 - 90.00 |
| Scout w/ cross rifles. | 1911-1920 | 60.00 - 90.00 |
| First Class emblem, gilt. | 1915-1925 | 50.00 - 75.00 |
| First Class Patrol Leader, silver. | 1915-1925 | 150.00-200.00 |

| | | |
|---|---|---|
| Second Class emblem, gilt. | 1915-1925 | 50.00 - 75.00 |
| Second Class Patrol Leader, silver. | 1915-1925 | 150.00-200.00 |
| Tenderfoot emblem, gilt. | 1915-1925 | 50.00 - 75.00 |
| Tenderfoot Patrol Leader, silver. | 1915-1925 | 100.00-150.00 |

## Watch, pocket
| | | |
|---|---|---|
| Radiolite. | 1919-1925 | 100.00-150.00 |
| Reliance, 7 jewel. | 1919-1925 | 100.00-150.00 |
| Waterbury. | 1919-1925 | 100.00-150.00 |
| Ingersoll. | 1934-1940 | 100.00-150.00 |
| Seven Seas. | 1941-1950 | 50.00-100.00 |
| Shipmate. | 1941-1950 | 50.00-100.00 |

## Watch, pocket. Ingersol
| | | |
|---|---|---|
| Hands read: A SCOUT IS. and BE PREPARED. Between Numbers are 12 Law Points. Camp Scene at ctr. Second hand is First Class emblem. | 1920 | 300.00-350.00 |

## Watch, wrist
| | | |
|---|---|---|
| Daynite, nickel-plated. | 1919-1925 | 100.00-150.00 |
| Daynite, silver. | 1919-1925 | 150.00-200.00 |
| Midget Radiolite. Army strap. | 1919-1925 | 100.00-150.00 |
| Headquarters, NYC, First Class emblem on face. | 1930 | 125.00-150.00 |
| Elgin. | 1934-1940 | 100.00-150.00 |
| Ingersoll. | 1934-1940 | 100.00-150.00 |
| New Haven. | 1934-1940 | 100.00-150.00 |
| Sun watch. | 1934-1940 | 75.00-100.00 |
| Imperial. | 1941-1950 | 50.00-100.00 |
| Elgin. | 1944-1950 | 50.00-100.00 |
| New Haven. | 1944-1950 | 50.00-100.00 |
| Timex, shock-proof. | 1955-1965 | 20.00 - 30.00 |

## Whistle
| | | |
|---|---|---|
| Long and round. First Class emblem and BOY SCOUTS OF AMERICA stamped. Brass w/ ring fro lanyard. | 1911-1930 | 20.00 - 30.00 |
| Conventional type, nickel-plated brass. First Class emblem by lip. | 1930-1940 | 10.00 - 15.00 |

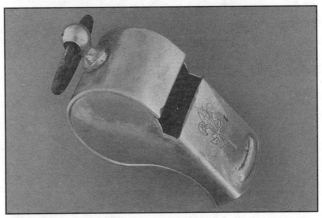

Nickel-plated whistle.

## Wood Composition (pressed)

| | | |
|---|---|---|
| Bookends, rounded shield shape w/ First Class emblem. | 1930-1950 | 20.00 - 30.00 |
| First Class emblem in shield. | 1930-1950 | 10.00 - 15.00 |
| Paperweight, scout and Washington. | 1930-1950 | 10.00 - 15.00 |
| Scout Oath, scout profile left. | 1930-1950 | 10.00 - 15.00 |
| Scout Oath, Tenderfoot emblem at top | 1950 - 1990 | 5.00 - 10.00 |
| Tie rack. First Class emblem in shield, camp scene in background. Metal bar or simulated wood bar to hold ties. | 1930-1950 | 20.00 - 30.00 |
| Trinket box, scout and Washington stg. | | |
| Cub, Tenderfoot. C-A-W design | 1950 - 1960 | 15.00 - 20.00 |
| Law points flanking. | 1930 - 1950 | 15.00 - 25.00 |
| Trinket box, Tenderfoot emblem | 1960 - 1980 | 10.00 - 15.00 |

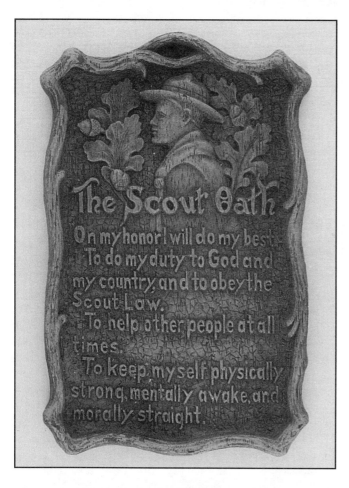

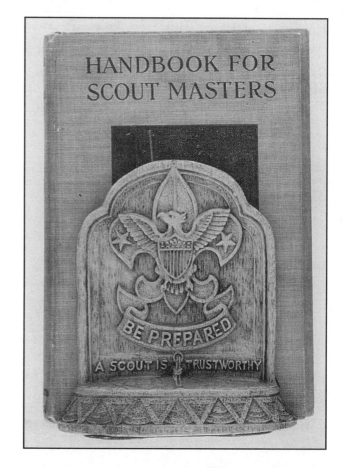

Pressed wood, and later wood composition, plaques, book ends, tie racks, and trinket boxes come in a variety of designs and were made from the 1930s through the 1960s.

# ORDER OF THE ARROW

The Order of the Arrow was founded at the Philadelphia Council summer camp Treasure Island in 1915 by E. Urner Goodman and Carroll A. Edson. It was formed to recognize honor campers. It became an official part of the National Program of the Boy Scouts of America in the 1940s. Within the organization there are Ordeal, Brotherhood, and Vigil Honor members, with a red arrow on white sashes to denote each honor. Each council has a lodge, which acts as part of the council camping committee, and usually each district has a chapter. Lodges have a Lodge Flap, which was developed in the 1950s and worn over the scout's uniform right pocket flap. Lodges are grouped into sections, and sections are grouped into areas. Conferences for sections and areas have their own patches, usually in a circular or other shape, and are worn as temporary uniform insignia. Lodges also have issued neckerchiefs. Lodge items have been cataloged in the *Blue Book*, and only a listing of Lodge names occurs in this book.

Eagle Scout Reidan Cruz as Suanhacky Lodge #49's Chief of the Fire, Ten Mile River Scout Camps, G.N.Y.C.

National Order of the Arrow Conferences have been held on a national basis since the late 1940s and most recently every two years, usually on a major university campus. Lately more than 5,000 Arrowmen gather at these events for training in lodge administration, ceremonies, or Native American dance. Patches exist for participants and staff, and lately many participating lodges make a special flap.

## PINBACK BUTTONS

### National Meeting
Chanute Field, IL. Aug. 1946.
Arrow Point. 2-1/2".                    1946          25.00 - 35.00

## POSITION BADGES - LEADERS

### Chapter Adviser
On light blue background.       1972-1989      2.00 - 3.00

### Lodge Adviser
On light blue background.       1972-1989      2.00 - 3.00

### Lodge Chief
On light blue background.       1972-1976   100.00 - 125.00

## Section Adviser

| | | |
|---|---|---|
| On light blue background. | 1972-1989 | 2.00 - 3.00 |

# ADULT RECOGNITIONS

## Order of the Arrow Distinguished Service Award

| | | |
|---|---|---|
| Silver arrowhead w/ arrow behind. Green neck ribbon. | 1948-1965 | 600.00-800.00 |
| Silver arrowhead w/ arrow behind. White neck ribbon w/ 3 red arrows on each side. | 1966-1980 | 150.00-200.00 |
| Silver arrowhead w/ arrow behind. White neck ribbon w/ 3 red arrows on each side. Rhodium. | 1980 | 50.00 - 75.00 |

# NATIONAL OA CONFERENCES

## Pocket Patch

| | | |
|---|---|---|
| White CTE on red chenille arrowhead. | 1940 | 150.00-200.00 |
| Red on white felt. | 1946 | 150.00-200.00 |
| Red silk screen on white. | 1948 | 100.00-150.00 |
| Green-silver-red embroidery on white twill. | 1950 | 75.00-100.00 |
| Yellow-black-white embroidery on red twill. | 1952 | 75.00-100.00 |
| Yellow-blue-red embroidery on white twill. | 1954 | 50.00 - 75.00 |
| Multicolored embroidery on white twill. | 1956 | 50.00 - 75.00 |
| W/ loop, yellow-red-blue embroidery on white twill arrowhead. | 1958 | 40.00 - 60.00 |
| Red-yellow-black embroidery on white twill shield. | 1961 | 40.00 - 60.00 |
| Multicolored fully-embroidered arrowhead. | 1963 | 25.00 - 40.00 |
| Multicolored embroidery on gray twill shield. | 1965 | 25.00 - 40.00 |
| Multicolored fully-embroidered arrowhead. | 1967 | 25.00 - 40.00 |
| Multicolored fully-embroidered emblem. | 1969 | 20.00 - 30.00 |
| Multicolored fully-embroidered arrowhead. | 1971 | 20.00 - 30.00 |
| Multicolored embroidery on white twill hexagon. | 1973 | 15.00 - 25.00 |
| Participant. | 1975 | 10.00 - 17.50 |
| Participant. | 1977 | 10.00 - 15.00 |
| Participant. | 1979 | 10.00 - 15.00 |
| Participant. | 1981 | 7.50 - 12.50 |
| Participant. | 1983 | 7.50 - 12.50 |
| Participant. | 1986 | 7.50 - 12.50 |
| Participant. | 1988 | 7.50 - 12.50 |
| Participant. | 1990 | 7.50 - 12.50 |
| Participant. | 1992 | 7.50 - 12.50 |
| Participant. | 1994 | 7.50 - 12.50 |
| Participant. | 1996 | 7.50 - 12.50 |
| Participant. | 1998 | 5.00 - 7.50 |

## Pocket Patch, Staff

| | | |
|---|---|---|
| Red embroidery on white. | 1948 | 150.00-200.00 |
| Round. | 1979 | 10.00 - 15.00 |
| Round. | 1981 | 10.00 - 15.00 |
| Round. | 1983 | 10.00 - 15.00 |
| Round. | 1986 | 10.00 - 15.00 |
| Round. | 1988 | 10.00 - 15.00 |
| Round. | 1990 | 10.00 - 15.00 |
| Round. | 1992 | 10.00 - 15.00 |
| Round. | 1994 | 10.00 - 15.00 |
| Round. | 1996 | 10.00 - 15.00 |
| Round. | 1998 | 10.00 - 15.00 |

# SASHES

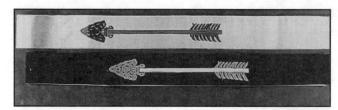

Ordeal Honor Sashes. The red-white is the regular issue and the black-white is a special 1990 75th Anniversary issue.

## Ordeal Sash

| | | |
|---|---|---|
| Red arrow, solid, on white. Wool felt. Arrow sewn on. | 1922-1948 | 35.00 - 50.00 |
| Red arrow sewn on cotton twill. | 1950-1989 | 5.00 - 10.00 |
| Red arrow ironed on cotton twill. | 1987-1990 | 8.00 - 10.00 |
| Black cotton, white embroidered arrow for 75th Anniversary. | 1990 | 75.00-100.00 |

## Brotherhood Sash

| | | |
|---|---|---|
| Red arrow and bars sewn on cotton twill. | 1950-1989 | 10.00 - 15.00 |
| Red Arrow and bars ironed on cotton sash. | 1987-1990 | 10.00 - 15.00 |

## Vigil Sash

| | | |
|---|---|---|
| Red arrow, solid, on white. Wool felt. Arrow sewn on. Large overhanging red triangle added in ctr. | 1922-1948 | 125.00-150.00 |
| Red arrow, detail in point and feathers, on white. Wool felt. Arrow flocked on. Red triangle at ctr. | 1948-1950 | 60.00 - 80.00 |
| Red arrow and bard and triangle sewn on cotton twill. | 1950-1987 | 25.00 - 35.00 |

Why are these scouts smiling? They have just passed their ordeal without flinching.

OA Founders E. Urner Goodman and Carroll A. Edson were popular signers of sashes.

Red arrow and bars and triangle ironed
on cotton twill.                          1987-1990    10.00 - 15.00

## Signed Sash

Edson and Goodman                         1960-1980    30.00 - 50.00

# HANDBOOKS

## Order of the Arrow, Handbook

| | | | |
|---|---|---|---|
| 1950 edition | 1950 printing | Sash cover | 30.00 - 40.00 |
| | 1952 printing | Indian head cover | 30.00 - 40.00 |
| 1961 edition | 1961 printing | Classic Indian cover | 15.00 - 20.00 |
| | 1964 printing | Classic Indian cover | 15.00 - 20.00 |
| 1965 edition | 1965 printing | Gold cover | 20.00 - 25.00 |
| | 1966 printing | Classic Indian cover | 15.00 - 20.00 |
| | 1968 printing | Classic Indian cover | 10.00 - 15.00 |
| | 1970 printing | Classic Indian cover | 10.00 - 15.00 |
| | 1972 printing | Classic Indian cover | 10.00 - 15.00 |
| 1973 edition | 1973 printing | Dancing Indian cover | 10.00 - 15.00 |
| 1975 edition | 1975 printing | Dancing Indian cover | 10.00 - 15.00 |
| | 1975 printing | Silver cover | 15.00 - 20.00 |
| 1977 edition | 1977 printing | MGM Indian cover | 8.00 - 10.00 |
| | 1979 printing | MGM Indian cover | 5.00 - 7.50 |
| | 1981 printing | MGM Indian cover | 5.00 - 7.50 |
| | 1983 printing | MGM Indian cover | 5.00 - 7.50 |
| | 1985 printing | MGM Indian cover | 5.00 - 7.50 |
| | 1986 printing | MGM Indian cover | 5.00 - 7.50 |
| | 1987 printing | MGM Indian cover | 5.00 - 7.50 |
| 1989 edition | 1989 printing | Indian and Scout | 5.00 - 7.50 |
| | 1990 printing | 75th Anniv. cover | 10.00 - 15.00 |

# REFERENCE BOOKS

## Ordeal Ceremony Book

| | | | |
|---|---|---|---|
| 1968 edition | 669 printing | Red & photo | 15.00 - 20.00 |
| | 275 printing | White | 8.00 - 12.00 |
| | 478 printing | Red | 5.00 - 7.50 |
| | 1980 printing | Grey | 2.00 - 4.00 |
| 1980 edition | 1980 printing | Grey | 2.00 - 4.00 |
| | 1990 printing | Grey | 2.00 - 4.00 |

## Brotherhood Ceremony Book

| | | | |
|---|---|---|---|
| 1949 edition | 1964 printing | | 25.00 - 35.00 |
| 1968 edition | 1969 printing | | 15.00 - 20.00 |
| | 1975 printing | White | 8.00 - 12.00 |
| | 1978 printing | Red | 5.00 - 7.50 |
| | 1981 printing | Grey | 2.00 - 4.00 |

## Vigil Ceremony Book

| | | | |
|---|---|---|---|
| 1968 edition | 1969 printing | | 15.00 - 20.00 |
| | 6/73 printing | White | 8.00 - 12.00 |
| | 6/78 printing | Red | 5.00 - 7.50 |
| | 1981 printing | Grey | 2.00 - 4.00 |

## Spirit of the Arrow Book

| | |
|---|---|
| 1972/1976 printing | 5.00 - 7.50 |
| 1981 printing | 3.00 - 5.00 |

## Guide for the Ordeal Book

| | |
|---|---|
| 1981 printing | 5.00 - 7.50 |

## Order of the Arrow

| | | |
|---|---|---|
| National Lodge Constitution & By Laws (ca) 1936 | | 20.00 - 30.00 |
| Local Lodge Manual | 1936 | 20.00 - 30.00 |
| | 1937 | 20.00 - 30.00 |
| | 1939 | 20.00 - 30.00 |
| | 1942 | 20.00 - 30.00 |
| Indian Ritual Costumes | 1936 | 20.00 - 30.00 |

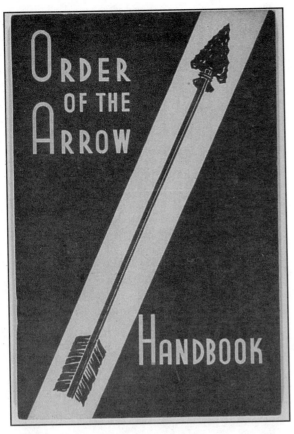

1950

1961-72

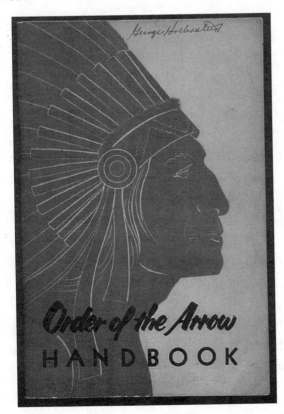

1952

1973-79

OA Handbooks outline the program for the Honor Camper Society.

1977-83

1990

1985-87

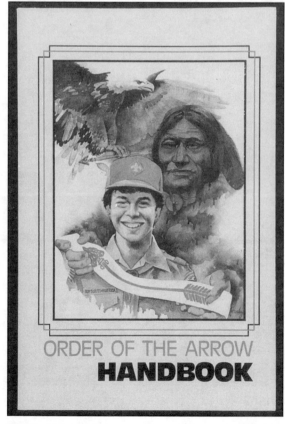

1989

# MISC. STUFF

## Award Medal

| | | |
|---|---|---|
| NOAC 1990 Ceremony Competition. | | 150.00-200.00 |
| NOAC 1992 Ceremony Competition. | | 150.00-200.00 |
| NOAC 1994 Ceremony Competition. | | 150.00-200.00 |

The 1992 National Ceremony Championship Award Medal for the NOAC Ceremony-Events Committee.

## Certificates

| | | |
|---|---|---|
| Standard Lodge. | | 5.00-10.00 |
| Honor Lodge. | | 5.00-10.00 |
| Vigil Honor. | 1930-1960 | 30.00-50.00 |
| Vigil Honor. | 1960-1975 | 15.00-25.00 |
| Vigil Honor. | 1975- | 5.00-10.00 |

## Lodge Totem Pins

| | | |
|---|---|---|
| Sterling silver, arrow w/ chain to animal emblem. | 1940-1960 | 40.00-60.00 |
| Vigil emblem added to animal. | 1940-1960 | 100.00-150.00 |

Lodge Totem Pins were available in the 1950s for civilian wear.

## Membership Cards

| | | |
|---|---|---|
| National Issue. | 1930-1950 | 10.00-15.00 |
| National Issue. | 1950-1965 | 8.00-10.00 |
| National Issue. | 1965-1975 | 4.00-6.00 |
| National Issue. | 1975-1998 | 1.00-2.00 |
| Local Issue. | 1930-1970 | 5.00-10.00 |

## 50th Anniversary Achievement Award

| | | |
|---|---|---|
| | 1965 | 10.00 - 15.00 |

## 60th Anniversary Bicentennial Award

| | | |
|---|---|---|
| | 1976 | 7.50 - 10.00 |

## National Leadership Seminar

| | | |
|---|---|---|
| Participant Patch. | 1975-1989 | 5.00 - 7.50 |
| Staff Patch. | 1975-1989 | 5.00 - 7.50 |

## Pocket Ribbon Drop

| | | |
|---|---|---|
| Silver arrow. | 1960-1970 | 10.00 - 15.00 |
| Non-silver arrow. | 1970 | 5.00 - 7.50 |
| 75th Anniversary, golden turtle. | 1990 | 10.00 - 15.00 |

# LONE SCOUTS OF AMERICA

The Lone Scouts of America was a program developed in 1915 by William D. Boyce and was run out of his Chicago offices until 1925 when the Boy Scouts of America incorporated the program's goals and objectives into their own. The distinctive Native American themes and logo gained the imagination of youth in rural America where groups of one to ten could gather after school for projects. The advancement program was reinforced by a weekly newspaper, which was mailed to all members (by 1925 it was a monthly), that provided opportunity to highlight activities by the rural groups.

This section is referenced to Mitch Reis's book *The History of the Lone Scouts through Memorabilia*.

## RANK BADGES

### First Degree
Indian Brave striding right
w/ arms extended on shield.
5/8". Bronze. Pinback or
lapel clasp.  1916-1928  MR.2.1  40.00 - 60.00

### Second Degree
Campfire within triangle on shield.
11/16". Bronze.  1916-1928  MR.3.1  40.00 - 60.00

### Third Degree
Eagle in flight on shield.
5/8". Nickel silver.  1916-1928  MR.4.1  40.00 - 60.00

### Fourth-Sixth Degree
Totem Pole Lodge. LSA on
scroll, head and hands at
top. Gilt bronze, enamel.  1916-1928  MR.5.1  80.00 - 100.00

### Sagamore Lodge
Indian on horseback within
wreath. Gilt
bronze, enamel.  1917-1928  MR.6.1  100.00 - 125.00

### Membership Pin
Celluloid. 7/8".  1915-1916  MR.1.1  15.00 - 25.00
Arrowhead in circle,
"Lone Scout Do a Useful
Thing Each Day" on arrowhead.
3/4". Bronze.  1916-1921  MR.1.2  20.00 - 30.00
Circle on arrowhead, LSA
monogram at ctr. 3/4".
Bronze.  1921-1935  MR.1.3  20.00 - 30.00
Circle on arrowhead,
LSA monogram. Gilt, red LSA,
blue behind circle.  1921-1935  20.00 - 30.00

Circle on arrowhead. 3/4".
Silver, red LSA monogram,
blue behind circle.  1921-1935  20.00 - 30.00

## POSITION BADGES
### LSD and BSA in red circle
Standing Indian. Full square.  1927-1933  MR.1  25.00 - 40.00

### LSS and BSA in red circle
Standing Indian. Full square.  1933-1950  MR.2  20.00 - 30.00
Standing Indian. Full square.  1950-1970  10.00-15.00
Standing Indian. Rolled edge.  1970-1998  3.00-5.00

LSS and BSA in red circle (full square patch).

### LONE SCOUT BSA and striding Indian
Khaki cloth, red rolled
edge border.  1980-1982  MR.3.1  3.00 - 5.00
Tan cloth, black rolled
edge border.  1985  MR.3.3  3.00 - 5.00
Tan cloth, red rolled
edge border.  1982-1989  MR.3.2  3.00 - 5.00
Tan cloth, tan rolled
edge border.  1990  MR.3.4  1.00 - 2.00

# HANDBOOKS

### The First, or Lone Scout Degree
4 varieties, Indian standing
right w/ arms outstretched. 1915-1918  MR.1.1-4   10.00 - 15.00

### The Second, or Woodcraft Degree
1916-1918   MR.1.5     15.00 - 20.00

### Tepee Lodge Tests, magazine size
1916-1918   MR.1.6     15.00 - 20.00

### Teepe Lodge Book,
### First, Second, and Third Degree
1918-1920   MR.2.1     20.00 - 30.00

### Totem Pole Lodge Book,
### Fourth, Fifth, and Sixth Degree
1918-1920   MR.2.2     20.00 - 30.00

### Sagamore Lodge, Seventh Degree
Lone Scout Record Book.   1918-1920   MR.2.3     20.00 - 30.00

### First Degree,
### Tepee Lodge
1920-1930   MR.3.1     20.00 - 30.00

### Second Degree,
### Tepee Lodge
1920-1930   MR.3.2     20.00 - 30.00

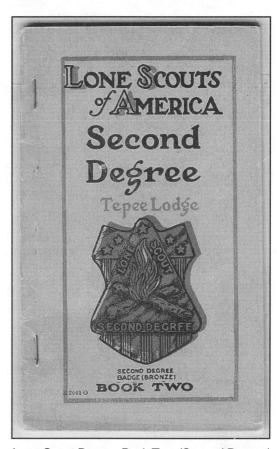

Lone Scout Degree Book Two (Second Degree)

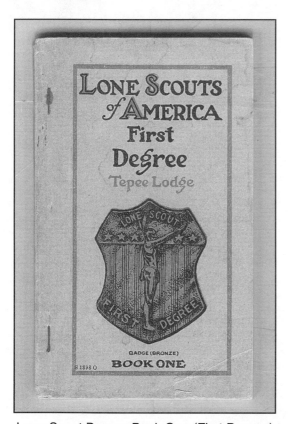

Lone Scout Degree Book One (First Degree)

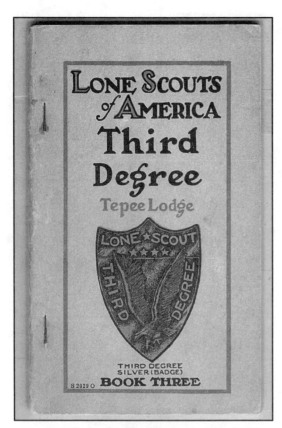

Lone Scout Degree Book Three (Third Degree)

### Third Degree, Tepee Lodge

Varieties on pg. 39 w/ Boyce,
or West (post-1925), as
Chief Totem.                    1920-1930  MR.3.3    20.00 - 30.00

### Fourth Degree, Totem Pole Lodge

Variety on pg. 48 w/ LSA address
at Dearborn Street, or post-1925
w/ BSA at that address.    1920-1930  MR.3.4    20.00 - 30.00

### Fifth Degree, Totem Pole Lodge

Variety w/ or w/o BSA paper
street address label
(post-1925)                     1920-1930  MR.3.5    20.00 - 30.00

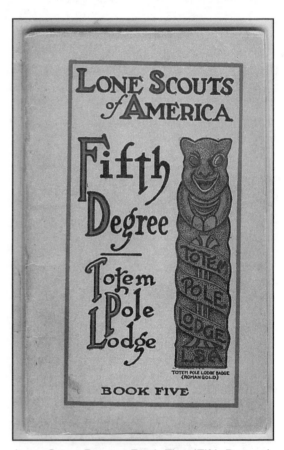

Lone Scout Degree Book Five (Fifth Degree)

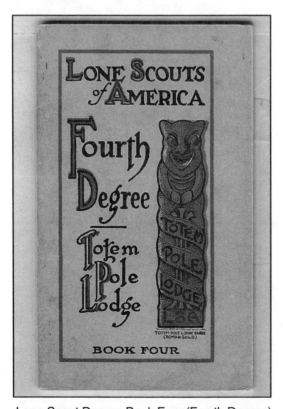

Lone Scout Degree Book Four (Fourth Degree)

## Sixth Degree, Totem Pole Lodge

Variety w/ or w/o BSA address
(post-1925) inside
front cover.                1920-1930  MR.3.6    20.00 - 30.00

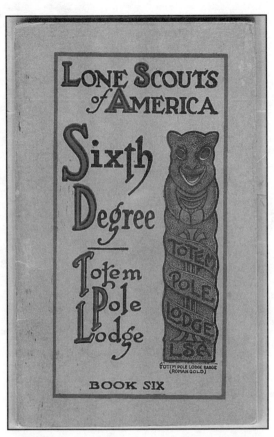

Lone Scout Degree Book Six (Sixth Degree)

## Seventh Degree (Sagamore Lodge)

Woodcraft, Pioneering, and
Camping. Varieties w/ or
w/o BSA address
(post-1925).                1920-1930  MR.3.7    20.00 - 30.00

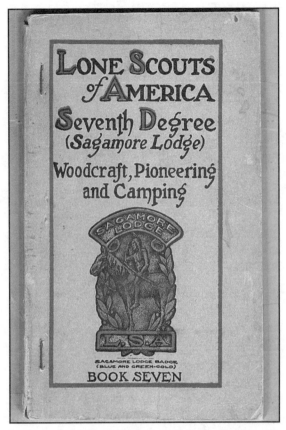

Lone Scout Degree Book Seven (Seventh Degree)

## Lone Scouts of America, Handbook

Indian striding right w/
arms outstretched.          1920-1921  MR.4.1    30.00 - 50.00

## Official Handbook of the
## Lone Scouts of America

2 Indians flanking title,
drawings in 4 corners.
Pg. 22 date is 1921,
2 varieties.                1921-1925  MR.4.2    30.00 - 50.00
2 Indians striding,
flanking title, drawings
in 4 corners. Pg. 22 date
is 1925. 2 varieties.       1925-1927  MR.4.3-4  30.00 - 50.00

# AWARD MEDALS

### Merit Award, First Prize
Gilt, red-blue ribbon.　　　　　1916-1930　MR.1　　　50.00 - 75.00

### Merit Award, Second Prize
Silvered metal,
　red-blue ribbon.　　　　　　 1916-1930　MR.2　　　50.00 - 75.00

### Merit Award, Third Prize
Bronze, red-blue ribbon.　　　 1916-1925　MR.3.1　　50.00 - 75.00

### Merit Award, Third Award,
  Literary Achievement
Bronze, red-blue ribbon.　　　 1925-1930　MR.3.2　　50.00 - 75.00

# POSITION BADGES - LEADERS

### Tribe Captain
Indian bust w/
　headdress, on shield.　　　　1917-1920　MR.1　　　50.00 - 75.00

### Tribe Chief
TRIBE CHIEF and LSA
　monogram below
　Indian bust.　　　　　　　　 1921-1928　MR.2　　　50.00 - 75.00

# COLLAR DEVICES

### LSA within circle
Bronze.　　　　　　　　　　　1917-1921　　　　　　40.00 - 60.00

# MISCELLANEOUS STUFF

### Booster Button
LSA enameled within
　golden wreath, 5/8".　　　　 1920-1930　　　　　　50.00 - 75.00

### Flag
LSA in circle in red,
　blue field.　　　　　　　　　1918-1920　　　　　 100.00 - 150.00

### Key Chain
Indian on horseback,
　within inverted triangle,
　LSA on shield, DAUTED below.
　Bronze or silvered.　　　　　1917-1921　　　　　　80.00 - 100.00

### Lone Scout Ring
LS and XVII on arrowhead
　on top, eagles at sides.
　For the Seventeenth Club.　1917　　　　　　 100.00 - 150.00

## Lone Scout Official Magazine
(weekly 10/1915-12/1920,
　then monthly to 4/1924).　1915-1924　　　　　10.00 - 15.00

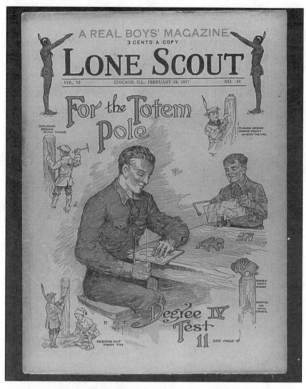

Lone Scout Magazine from 1917

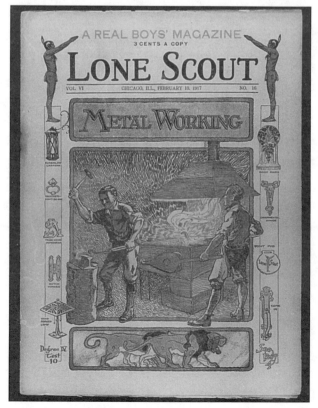

Lone Scout Magazine from 1917

Lone Scout Magazine from 1917

## LSA Helping to Win the War
Bronze 1-5/16" pin. Scene of
   planes above fields and
   glass preservers.     1918          25.00 - 40.00

## LSA monogram
Red felt on blue circle.   1922-1927     50.00 - 75.00
Red felt.                 1922-1927     40.00 - 60.00

## LSC enameled
Gold quill in inkwell. Pinback. 1919-1930     30.00 - 50.00

## Membership Card
4 varieties.              1915-1924     5.00 - 10.00

## Postcard
1918 Lone Scout
   Magazine cover.      1918       10.00 - 20.00
4 paragraph verse, Mac, Fido,
   Slippery Fritz, and Jake.  1918-1920   15.00 - 20.00

## Ring
LSD and BSA w/ Indian
   striding left on round top,
   sides w/ shield and
   First Class badge.    1927-1930    100.00 - 125.00
LSD and BSA w/ Indian striding
   left in oval top, knots at sides.
   Gold filled.         1930-1938    100.00 - 150.00
   Silver             1930-1941    50.00 - 75.00

## Service Bar
LSA on 1 x 5/16" bronze bar.
   6 months membership.  1919-1926    30.00 - 50.00
LSA on gilt 1 x 5/16" bar.
   2 Years Membership.   1919-1926    75.00 - 100.00
LSA on silvered 1 x 5/16" bar.
   1 Year membership.    1919-1926    50.00 - 75.00

## Sweater
LSA monogram in red
   on blue circle.       1917-1921    80.00 - 100.00

## Watch Fob
Indian on horseback within
   inverted triangle,
   LSA on shield, DAUTED below.
   Bronze or silvered,
   on leather strap.     1917-1921    60.00 - 75.00

# SEA SCOUTING/SEA EXPLORING

## RANK BADGES

### Star Scout

| | | |
|---|---|---|
| Blue felt, double knot below. | 1925-1942 | 25.00 - 35.00 |
| Blue felt, single knot below. | 1925-1942 | 25.00 - 35.00 |
| Blue felt, 2 red lines in shield. | 1942-1954 | 10.00 - 15.00 |
| White twill, double knot below | 1925-1942 | 25.00 - 35.00 |
| White twill, single knot below. | 1925-1942 | 25.00 - 35.00 |
| White twill, 2 red lines in shield. | 1942-1954 | 10.00 - 15.00 |

### Life Scout

| | | |
|---|---|---|
| Blue felt, knot under heart. Gold-lettered motto. | 1925-1942 | 25.00 - 35.00 |
| Blue felt, knot in heart. White-lettered motto. | 1942-1950 | 7.50 - 10.00 |
| Blue felt, 2 red stripes. | 1950-1956 | 10.00 - 15.00 |
| White twill, knot under heart. Gold-lettered motto. | 1925-1942 | 25.00 - 35.00 |
| White twill, knot in heart. White-lettered motto. | 1942-1950 | 10.00 - 15.00 |
| White twill, 2 red stripes. | 1950-1956 | 7.50 - 10.00 |

### Eagle Scout

| | | |
|---|---|---|
| Blue felt, no wording. | 1924-1932 | 100.00 - 150.00 |
| Blue felt, full wording in cotton thread. | 1933-1955 | 40.00 - 60.00 |
| Blue felt, full wording in silk thread. | 1933-1955 | 40.00 - 60.00 |
| White twill, no wording. | 1924-1932 | 40.00 - 60.00 |
| White twill, full wording in cotton thread. | 1933-1955 | 40.00 - 60.00 |
| White twill, full wording in silk thread. | 1933-1955 | 100.00 - 150.00 |

Sea Scout Apprentice, Ordinary, and Able patches.

### Sea Scout Apprentice

| | | |
|---|---|---|
| Anchor behind First Class emblem, 1 bar below. | 1924-1949 | 5.00 - 10.00 |

Anchor behind First Class emblem, 1 bar below. — 1924 — 5.00 - 10.00

### Sea Scout Ordinary

| | | |
|---|---|---|
| Anchor behind First Class emblem, 2 bars below. | 1924 | 5.00 - 10.00 |

### Sea Scout Able

| | | |
|---|---|---|
| Anchor behind First Class emblem, 3 bars below. | 1924 | 5.00 - 10.00 |

### Quartermaster Award Patch

| | | |
|---|---|---|
| Anchor behind First Class emblem on compass and ship's wheel. | 1966 | 10.00 - 15.00 |

## RANK MEDALS

### Quartermaster Award Medal

Quartermaster Medal, Sea Scouting's highest honor.

| | | |
|---|---|---|
| Anchor behind First Class emblem on compass and ship's wheel. Blue ribbon w/ diagonal stripe. | 1931-1937 | 500.00 - 750.00 |
| Anchor behind First Class emblem on compass and ship's wheel. Blue ribbon, enamel on silver pendant. | 1937-1969 | 175.00 - 200.00 |

Anchor behind First Class emblem
on compass and ship's wheel.
Blue ribbon, enamel on rhodium
pendant.                                    1969          50.00 - 75.00

# POSITION BADGES

## Assistant Crew Leader
Anchor behind First Class emblem.
1 split chevron behind.                     1949          5.00 - 10.00

## Boatswain
Anchor behind First Class emblem.
2 split and 1 full chevron behind,
star below.                                 1949          5.00 - 10.00

## Boatswain's Mate
Anchor behind First Class emblem.
2 split and 1 full chevron behind.          1949          5.00 - 10.00

## Cabin Boy
Anchor on blue background within
gold oval border. Tan cut cloth.      1924-1935   40.00 - 60.00
Anchor on blue background within
gold oval border. Khaki cut cloth.    1935-1949   20.00 - 30.00

## Crew Leader
Anchor behind First Class emblem.
2 split chevrons behind.                    1949          5.00 - 10.00

## Sea Explorer Purser
Crossed keys behind anchor
and First Class emblem.                     1949          5.00 - 10.00

## Sea Explorer Quartermaster
Anchor behind First Class emblem.           1949          5.00 - 10.00

## Sea Explorer Specialist
Title below anchor and First Class emblem.  1949          5.00 - 10.00

## Sea Explorer Storekeeper
Crossed oars behind open book.              1949          5.00 - 10.00

## Sea Scout Boatswain
Anchor behind First Class emblem.
3 felt chevrons.                      1918-1949   5.00 - 10.00
Anchor behind First Class emblem.
3 twill chevrons.                     1918-1949   5.00 - 10.00

## Sea Scout Boatswain's Mate
Anchor behind First Class emblem.
2 felt chevrons.                      1918-1949   5.00 - 10.00

Anchor behind First Class emblem.
2 twill chevrons.                     1918-1949   5.00 - 10.00

## Sea Scout Bugler
Bugle.                                1941-1949  10.00 - 15.00

## Sea Scout Coxwain
Anchor behind First Class emblem.
1 felt chevron.                       1918-1949   5.00 - 10.00
Anchor behind First Class emblem.
1 twill chevron.                      1918-1949   5.00 - 10.00

## Sea Scout Yeoman
Crossed quills.                       1941-1949  10.00 - 15.00

# HANDBOOKS

## Sea Scouting and Seamanship for Boys
Baden-Powell, Warrington.
The English Sea Scout Manual
used in the U.S.                      1911       100.00 - 150.00

## Cruising for Sea Scouts. Carey, A.A.
3 printings.                          1912-1914  45.00 - 60.00

## Nautical Scouting for Boy Scouts of America
                                      1915        45.00 - 60.00

## The Sea Scout Manual
J.A. Wilder, ed. 5 printings.         1919-1923  45.00 - 65.00

## The Sea Scout Manual
Capt. Felix Riesenberg, ed. 14 printings.   1925-1938  35.00 - 45.00

## The Sea Scout Manual
Carl Langenbacher. 10 printings.
698 pgs. + 10 pg. preface.            1939-1949  25.00 - 35.00

## Sea Explorer Manual, revised edition
640 pgs + 4 pg. foreword.
4-5/8 x 7".                           1950-1963  15.00 - 20.00

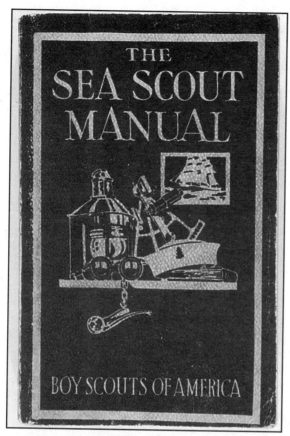

Sea Scout Manual, 1930s edition

Sea Exploring Manual, 1980s

## Sea Exploring Manual

442 pgs. 5-3/8 x 8".                     1966-1976    7.50 - 12.50

# UNIFORMS

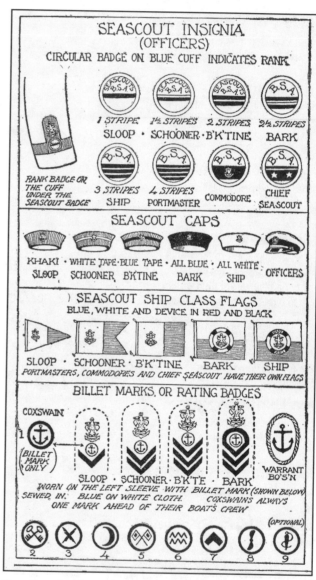

Sea Scout officers insignia chart from 1920s equipment catalog

## BSA in blue felt circle

Sweater patch.                            1924-1941   15.00 - 20.00

## Community Strip
Blue on white twill or white on blue felt.   1924   3.00 - 5.00

White on blue or blue on white Council Shoulder Patches.

## Council Strip
Blue on white twill on blue felt.   5.00-10.00

## Flagship Fleet Rating
Anchor behind First Class emblem at ctr.,
    red and blue fully-embroidered
    background patch.   1941-1947   10.00 - 15.00

## Flagship Flotilla Rating
Anchor behind First Class emblem at ctr.,
    red and blue fully-embroidered
    background patch.   1941-1947   10.00 - 15.00

## Flagship Squadron Rating
Anchor behind First Class emblem
    at ctr., red and blue
    fully-embroidered background patch.   1941-1947   10.00 - 15.00

## Long Cruise
Sailing ship in circle.   1924   5.00 - 10.00
Red or white arc.   1924   2.00 - 3.00

## National Fleet Rating
Anchor behind First Class emblem
    at ctr., blue fully-embroidered patch.   1939-1940   10.00 - 15.00

## Qualified Seaman Pin
   1960   5.00 - 7.50

## Regional Flotilla Rating
Anchor behind First Class emblem
    at ctr., blue fully-embroidered patch.   1939-1940   10.00 - 15.00

## Sea Explorer Medallion
Anchor behind First Class emblem
    on cut edge blue felt.   1949   5.00 - 10.00

Anchor behind First Class emblem
    on rolled edge blue twill.   1949   5.00 - 10.00
Anchor behind First Class emblem
    on rolled edge white twill.   1949   5.00 - 10.00

## Small-Boat Handler Pin
Pin bar.   1960   5.00 - 7.50

## State Strip
Blue on white twill or white on blue felt.   1924   3.00 - 5.00

## Sweater Patch
BSA in FDL on anchor, SEA SCOUTS
    around. White on blue felt.   1918-1924   20.00 - 30.00

## Unit Numerals, 0-9
Solid embroidery, white on blue,
    blue on white, black on white.   1960   1.00 - 2.00

# KNIVES

## Ulster Knife Co.
Sea Scout emblem in
    shield-shaped shield,
    4-1/8" bone handle, sheep
    foot and marlin spike.   1936-1940   175.00 - 225.00

# PINBACK BUTTONS

## Sea Scout Facing
On red-white-blue background. 3/4".   1950-1965   10.00 - 15.00
On red-white-blue background. 1-1/4".   1950-1965   15.00-20.00

# MEDALLIONS

## Sea Scouting 75th Anniversary
Cast pewter, uniface.   1987   15.00 - 25.00

# POSITION BADGES - LEADERS

## Committee Chairman
Anchor behind First Class emblem
    in diamond rope border.   1941-1949   10.00 - 15.00

## Committeeman
Anchor behind First Class emblem
    in oval rope border.   1941-1949   10.00 - 15.00

## Local Chairman
Anchor behind First Class emblem
    within rope diamond. 2 stars below.   1949   10.00 - 15.00

## Local Committee Member
Anchor behind First Class emblem
   within rope oval. 2 stars below.   1949   10.00 - 15.00

## Local Council Staff
Anchor behind First Class emblem.
   2 stars below.   1949   10.00 - 15.00

## Local Officer Rating Strip
2 stars.   1941-1949   5.00 - 10.00

## National Professional Staff
Anchor behind First Class emblem.
   4 stars below.   1949   10.00 - 15.00

## Regional/National Chairman
Anchor behind First Class emblem
   within rope diamond. 4 stars below.   1949   20.00 - 30.00

## Regional/National Committee Member
Anchor behind First Class emblem
   within rope oval. 4 stars below.   1949   10.00 - 15.00

## Regional/National Officer Rating Strip
4 stars.   1941-1949   5.00 - 10.00

## Sea Scout
Anchor behind First Class emblem.
   1 stripe below.   1918-1941   20.00 - 25.00
Star patch to be added to
   Universal emblem.   1941-1949   5.00 - 10.00

## Sea Explorer Mate
Anchor behind First Class emblem.
   1 star below.   1949   5.00 - 10.00

## Sea Explorer Skipper
Anchor behind First Class emblem.
   Star and bar below.   1949   5.00 - 10.00

## Sea Scout Universal Emblem
Anchor behind First Class emblem.   1941-1949   5.00 - 10.00

## Ship Committee
Anchor behind First Class emblem,
   all within rope oval.
   1-1/2 stripes below.   1918-1941   20.00 - 25.00

## Ship Committee Chairman
Anchor behind First Class emblem,
   all within rope diamond.
   1-1/2 stripes below.   1918-1941   20.00 - 25.00
Anchor behind First Class emblem
   within rope diamond. 1 star below.   1949   10.00 - 15.00

## Ship Committee Member
Anchor behind First Class emblem
   within rope oval. 1 star below.   1949   10.00 - 15.00

## Ship Officer Rating Strip
1 star.   1941-1949   5.00 - 10.00

# HANDBOOKS - LEADERS

## Handbook for Crew Leaders
First Edition. 2 printings.   1941-1942   20.00 - 30.00
Second Edition. 1 printing.   1946   20.00 - 30.00

## Handbook for Skippers
First Edition, Menninger,
   W.C. 3 printings. 280 pgs.   1932-1936   40.00 - 60.00
Second Edition. 5 printings. 400-440 pgs.
   (5th printing 314 pgs.)   1939-1947   20.00 - 30.00
Third Edition. 224 pgs.   1971   10.00 - 15.00

# UNIFORMS - LEADERS

## Seabadge Pin
Trident behind anchor
   behind First Class emblem.   1970   10.00 - 15.00

## Seabadge Pin
Trident within wreath.   1970   15.00 - 20.00

## Blazer
Bullion-embroidered
   program emblem for Blazer
First Class badge and anchor.   1971   10.00 -15.00

# ADULT RECOGNITIONS

## Skipper's Key Training Award
Anchor behind First Class emblem
   on training award pendant.
   10 kt. GF, solid blue ribbon.   1941   25.00 - 40.00
Anchor behind First Class emblem
   on training award pendant.
   10 kt. GF, blue-white ribbon.   1941   25.00 - 40.00

# MISCELLANEOUS STUFF

## Ship Flag
Wool, red top, blue bottom,
   Sea Scout emblem in ctr.   1950-1970   35.00 - 50.00

# ROVER SCOUTING

## UNIFORMS

### ROVER SCOUT on circle below Tenderfoot badge
Squat crown. Cut edge.                 1935-1954 40.00 - 50.00

### ROVER SCOUT on circle below Tenderfoot badge
Tall crown w/ ctr. line. Cut edge.     1935-1954 40.00 - 50.00

### ROVER SCOUT on circle below Tenderfoot badge
Tan cut cloth.                         1935-1954  75.00 - 100.00

# SENIOR SCOUT OUTFIT

## POSITION BADGES

### Senior Scout Outfit Assistant Crew Leader
1 bar behind white universal emblem,
cut edge blue twill.                   1945-1949  20.00 - 30.00

### Senior Scout Outfit Crew Leader
2 bars behind white universal emblem,
cut edge blue twill.                   1945-1949  20.00 - 30.00

### Senior Scout Outfit Deputy Senior Crew Leader
2-1/2 bars behind white universal emblem,
cut edge blue twill.                   1945-1949  20.00 - 30.00

### Senior Scout Outfit Universal Emblem
White C-A-W on gold FDL, white border
on blue cut edge twill.                1945-1949  10.00 - 15.00

# SENIOR SCOUTING

## RANK BADGES

### Explorer Medallion
BSA at top, EXPLORER SCOUT legend below.
   Tenderfoot emblem at ctr.
   Senior Scout titles added
   around this central badge.          1935-1949  10.00 - 15.00

### Explorer First Honors
2 green bars on tan cut cloth.       1935-1949  25.00 - 40.00

### Explorer Second Honors
3 green bars on tan cut cloth.       1935-1949  25.00 - 40.00

### Senior Scout title
| | | |
|---|---|---|
| Airman. On air scout blue twill. | 1943-1949 | 150.00 - 200.00 |
| Artisan. On explorer green twill. | 1935-1949 | 30.00 - 45.00 |
| Artisan. On scout green twill. | 1935-1949 | 15.00 - 25.00 |
| Artisan. On sea scout blue felt. | 1935-1949 | 40.00 - 60.00 |
| Artisan. On sea scout blue felt. | 1935-1949 | 40.00 - 60.00 |
| Artist. On explorer green twill. | 1935-1949 | 30.00 - 45.00 |
| Artist. On scout green twill. | 1935-1949 | 15.00 - 25.00 |
| Artist. On sea scout blue felt. | 1935-1949 | 40.00 - 60.00 |
| Citizen. On explorer green twill. | 1935-1949 | 30.00 - 45.00 |
| Citizen. On scout green twill. | 1935-1949 | 15.00 - 25.00 |
| Citizen. On sea scout blue felt. | 1935-1949 | 40.00 - 60.00 |
| Conservationist. On explorer green twill. | 1935-1949 | 30.00 - 45.00 |
| Conservationist. On scout green twill. | 1935-1949 | 15.00 - 25.00 |
| Conservationist. On sea scout blue felt. | 1935-1949 | 40.00 - 60.00 |
| Craftsman. On explorer green twill. | 1935-1949 | 30.00 - 45.00 |
| Craftsman. On scout green twill. | 1935-1949 | 15.00 - 25.00 |
| Craftsman. On sea scout blue felt. | 1935-1949 | 40.00 - 60.00 |
| Dairyman. On explorer green twill. | 1942-1949 | 30.00 - 45.00 |
| Dairyman. On scout green twill. | 1942-1949 | 15.00 - 25.00 |
| Farm Manager. On explorer green twill. | 1942-1949 | 30.00 - 45.00 |
| Farm Manager. On scout green twill. | 1942-1949 | 15.00 - 25.00 |
| Gardener. On explorer green twill. | 1942-1949 | 30.00 - 45.00 |
| Gardener. On scout green twill. | 1942-1949 | 15.00 - 25.00 |
| Journalist. On explorer green twill. | 1935-1949 | 30.00 - 45.00 |
| Journalist. On scout green twill. | 1935-1949 | 15.00 - 25.00 |
| Journalist. On sea scout blue felt. | 1935-1949 | 40.00 - 60.00 |
| Livestockman. On explorer green twill. | 1942-1949 | 30.00 - 45.00 |
| Livestockman. On scout green twill. | 1942-1949 | 15.00 - 25.00 |
| Naturalist. On explorer green twill. | 1935-1949 | 30.00 - 45.00 |
| Naturalist. On scout green twill. | 1935-1949 | 15.00 - 25.00 |
| Naturalist. On sea scout blue felt. | 1935-1949 | 40.00 - 60.00 |
| Poultryman. On explorer green twill. | 1942-1949 | 30.00 - 45.00 |
| Poultryman. On scout green twill. | 1942-1949 | 15.00 - 25.00 |
| Radioman. On explorer green twill. | 1935-1949 | 30.00 - 45.00 |
| Radioman. On scout green twill. | 1935-1949 | 15.00 - 25.00 |
| Radioman. On sea scout blue felt. | 1935-1949 | 40.00 - 60.00 |
| Seaman. On explorer green twill. | 1935-1949 | 30.00 - 45.00 |
| Seaman. On scout green twill. | 1935-1949 | 15.00 - 25.00 |
| Seaman. On sea scout blue felt. | 1935-1949 | 40.00 - 60.00 |
| Sportsman. On explorer green twill. | 1935-1949 | 30.00 - 45.00 |
| Sportsman. On scout green twill. | 1935-1949 | 15.00 - 25.00 |
| Sportsman. On sea scout blue felt. | 1935-1949 | 40.00 - 60.00 |
| Woodsman. On explorer green twill. | 1935-1949 | 30.00 - 45.00 |
| Woodsman. On scout green twill. | 1935-1949 | 15.00 - 25.00 |
| Woodsman. On sea scout blue felt. | 1935-1949 | 40.00 - 60.00 |

## RANK & POSITION BADGES

### Explorer Patrol Leader
1 green chevron on tan cut cloth.    1935-1949  25.00 - 40.00

### Explorer Patrol Leader w/ First Honors
2 green chevrons on tan cut cloth.   1935-1949  25.00 - 40.00

### Explorer Patrol Leader w/ Second Honors
3 green chevrons on tan cut cloth.   1935-1949  25.00 - 40.00

## POSITION BADGES

### Senior Scout Outfit Senior Crew Leader
3 bars behind white universal emblem,
   cut edge blue twill.              1935-1949  20.00 - 30.00

## HANDBOOKS

### Adventuring for Senior Scouts
### W.H. Hurt, ed.
Proof ed. and all printings.
Hardcover w/ Senior and Sea Scout.   1938-1939  25.00 - 35.00
Tan cover w/ Senior, Sea Scout,
   and Air Scout.                    1945-1946  20.00 - 30.00

### Adventuring for Senior Scouts
### W.H. Hurt, ed.
Revised second printing.
   In 1944 w/ red cover.             1942-1944  15.00 - 20.00

# UNIFORMS

## Senior Scout Hat Patch
White C.A.W. on gold outline FDL.
  Red twill.                          1935-1949  10.00 - 15.00

## SENIOR SCOUT legend about Tenderfoot emblem, red twill, gold border, cut edge
                                      1935       10.00 - 15.00

# POSITION BADGES - LEADERS

## Advisor, BOY SCOUTS OF AMERICA EXPLORERS legend
8-pointed star behind First Class emblem.
  White on green twill, cut edge.     1935-1949  10.00 - 15.00

## Assistant Advisor, BOY SCOUTS OF AMERICA EXPLORERS legend
8-pointed star behind First Class emblem.
  Gold on green twill, cut edge.      1935-1949  10.00 - 15.00

# MISCELLANEOUS STUFF

## Senior Scout Unit Local Standard Patch
Fully embroidered, red-blue background.   1935-1949  10.00 - 15.00

## Senior Scout Unit National Standard Patch
Fully embroidered, red-blue background.   1935-1949  10.00 - 15.00

## Senior Scout Unit Regional Standard Patch
Fully embroidered, red-blue background.   1935-1949  10.00 - 15.00

# EMERGENCY SERVICE CORPS & EXPLORING

## POSITION BADGES

### Emergency Service Apprentice
Lightning bolt on First Class
emblem all on red felt.                1941-1949  15.00 - 20.00

### Emergency Service Corps
Lightning bolt and life ring on FDL,
EMERGENCY SERVICE CORPS legend.
Red felt, black legend.              1941-1948  15.00 - 20.00

### Emergency Service Explorer
Lightning bolt and life ring on FDL,
EMERGENCY SERVICE EXPLORER
legend. Red felt, black legend.        1949-1957  15.00 - 20.00

## UNIFORMS

### Emergency Service Apprentice Emblem
On oval red cloth patch, elastic armband.   1941-1948 10.00 - 15.00

### Emergency Service Apprentice Emblem
On red cloth armband.                1941-1948 20.00 - 25.00

### Emergency Service Emblem
On khaki armband.                    1939-1948 20.00 - 30.00

### Emergency Service Emblem
On oval red patch, elastic strap armband.   1939-1948 10.00 - 15.00

### Emergency Service Emblem
On red armband.                      1939-1948 20.00 - 30.00

### Emergency Service Explorer Emblem
Black legend on oval red
patch on elastic armband.           1949-1957 10.00 - 15.00

### Emergency Service Explorer Emblem
Black legend on red armband.        1949-1957 15.00 - 20.00

### Emergency Service in Training
Oval red cloth patch, elastic armband.
Lightning bolt through BSA.          1949-1957  10.00 - 15.00

### Emergency Service in Training
Red cloth armband.
Lightning bolt through BSA. 1949-1957          10.00 - 15.00

### Emergency Service
READY armband, legend and
Circle V emblem.
Oval patch, elastic armband.1958-1969          10.00 - 15.00

### Emergency Service
Large E in oval patch, elastic armband.   1969   5.00 - 10.00

# AIR SCOUTING/AIR EXPLORING

## RANK BADGES

### Air Scout Apprentice
Single-engine plane w/ AIR SCOUT
and FDL below.     1942-1949  25.00 - 40.00

### Air Scout Observer
Twin-engine plane w/ AIR SCOUT
and FDL below.     1942-1949  25.00 - 40.00

### Air Scout Craftsman
Tri-motor plane w/ AIR SCOUT
and FDL below.     1942-1949  25.00 - 40.00

### Air Scout Ace
Four-motor plane w/ AIR SCOUT
and FDL below.     1942-1949  25.00 - 40.00

### Air Explorer Apprentice
Single-engine plane, AIR EXPLORER
and FDL below.     1949-1954  15.00 - 25.00
Single-engine plane above FDL.   1954-1966  10.00 - 15.00

### Air Explorer Observer
Twin-engine plane, AIR EXPLORER
and FDL below.     1949-1954  15.00 - 25.00
Twin-engine plane above FDL.   1954-1966  10.00 - 15.00

### Air Explorer Craftsman
Tri-motor plane, AIR EXPLORER
and FDL below.     1949-1954  15.00 - 25.00
Tri-motor plane above FDL.   1954-1966  10.00 - 15.00

### Air Explorer Ace
Four-motor plane, AIR EXPLORER
and FDL below.     1949-1954  15.00 - 25.00

### Tenderfoot Air Scout Candidate
Twin-blade prop. in blue on tan
or khaki cut twill.   1942-1949  20.00 - 30.00

### Second Class Air Scout Candidate
Triple-blade prop. in blue on tan
or khaki cut twill.   1942-1949  20.00 - 30.00

### First Class Air Scout Candidate
Four-blade prop. in blue on tan
or khaki cut twill.   1942-1949  20.00 - 30.00

### Specialist Rating
Ace Airman.     1947-1949  10.00 - 15.00

Ace Builder.   1947-1949  10.00 - 15.00
Ace Communicator.   1947-1949  10.00 - 15.00
Ace Mechanic.   1947-1949  10.00 - 15.00
Ace Navigator.   1947-1949  10.00 - 15.00
Ace Outdoorsman.   1947-1949  10.00 - 15.00
Craftsman Airman.   1947-1949  10.00 - 15.00
Craftsman Builder.   1947-1949  10.00 - 15.00
Craftsman Communicator.   1947-1949  10.00 - 15.00
Craftsman Mechanic.   1947-1949  10.00 - 15.00
Craftsman Navigator.   1947-1949  10.00 - 15.00
Craftsman Outdoorsman.   1947-1949  10.00 - 15.00
Observer Airman.   1947-1949  10.00 - 15.00
Observer Builder.   1947-1949  10.00 - 15.00
Observer Communicator.   1947-1949  10.00 - 15.00
Observer Mechanic.   1947-1949  10.00 - 15.00
Observer Navigator.   1947-1949  10.00 - 15.00
Observer Outdoorsman.   1947-1949  10.00 - 15.00

## Pin
Advanced Aeronautics and wings
w/ Circle V at ctr.   1959-1966  15.00 - 20.00
Basic Aeronautics and wings
w/ Circle V at ctr.   1959-1966  15.00 - 20.00

## Skills Rating Strip
Aviation.   1949-1958  10.00 - 15.00
Communications.   1949-1958  10.00 - 15.00
Construction.   1954-1966  10.00 - 15.00
Craft.   1949-1958  10.00 - 15.00
Emergency.   1949-1958  10.00 - 15.00
Mechanics.   1954-1966  10.00 - 15.00
Navigation.   1949-1958  10.00 - 15.00
Outdoor.   1949-1958  10.00 - 15.00
Physical Fitness.   1949-1958  10.00 - 15.00
Seamanship.   1949-1958  10.00 - 15.00
Vocational Exploration.   1949-1958  10.00 - 15.00
Weather.   1954-1966  10.00 - 15.00

## RANK MEDALS

### Air Scout Ace
Wings upstretched from four-motor plane,
Tenderfoot emblem at bottom,
compass as frame, wide blue ribbon
w/ thin red edging.   1942-1949  1,200-1,500

### Air Explorer Ace Medal
Wings upstretched, four-motor plane
and Tenderfoot emblem below,

Air Scouting's Ace Medal.

compass in back, red-blue-red ribbon
of equal widths.                    1949-1954  1,200-1,500

# POSITION BADGES

### Air Explorer Deputy Senior Crew Leader
Tenderfoot emblem above 3 blue bars
    within rectangle, gold wings.    1949-1966  15.00 - 20.00

### Air Explorer Secretary
Tenderfoot emblem above crossed
    blue quills within rectangle, gold wings.  1949-1966  15.00 - 20.00

### Air Explorer Senior Crew Leader
Tenderfoot emblem above 3 blue bars
    within rectangle, silver wings,
    blue circle at ctr. back.        1949-1966  15.00 - 20.00

### Air Exploring Universal emblem
E and FDL at ctr. of wings,
    on blue twill rectangle.         1969       5.00 - 10.00

### Airport Management
E and FDL at ctr. of wings, title below,
    on blue twill rectangle.         1969       5.00 - 10.00

### Air Scout Assistant Flight Pilot
Tenderfoot emblem above blue rectangle
    w/ 1 gold bar, gold wings at sides.   1942-1949  25.00 - 40.00
Tenderfoot emblem above rectangle
    w/ 1 blue bar, gold wings at sides.   1942-1949  25.00 - 40.00

### Air Scout Assistant Squadron Pilot
Tenderfoot emblem above blue rectangle
    w/ 2-1/2 blue bars, gold wings at sides.  1942-1949  25.00 - 40.00
Tenderfoot emblem above rectangle
    w/ 2-1/2 blue bars, gold wings at sides.  1942-1949  25.00 - 40.00

### Air Scout Flight Pilot
Tenderfoot emblem above blue
    rectangle w/ 2 silver bars,
    silver wings at sides.           1942-1949  25.00 - 40.00
Tenderfoot emblem above rectangle
    w/ 2 blue bars, gold wings at sides.   1942-1949  25.00 - 40.00

### Air Scout Medallion
Universal emblem within light blue twill,
    dark blue rolled edge border.    1942-1949  40.00 - 50.00

### Air Scout Scribe
Crossed blue quills on light blue cut twill.  1942-1949  15.00 - 20.00

### Air Scout Squadron Pilot
Tenderfoot emblem above blue rectangle
    w/ 2-1/2 silver bars,
    silver wings at sides.           1942-1949  25.00 - 40.00
Tenderfoot emblem above rectangle
    w/ 2-1/2 blue bars,
    silver wings at sides.           1942-1949  25.00 - 40.00

### Flight Attendant
E and FDL at ctr. of wings, title below,
    on blue twill rectangle.         1969       5.00 - 10.00

### Ground Support
E and FDL at ctr. of wings, title below,
    on blue twill rectangle.         1969       5.00 - 10.00

### Mechanic
E and FDL at ctr. of wings, title below,
    on blue twill rectangle.         1969       5.00 - 10.00

### Private Pilot
E and FDL at ctr. of wings, title below,
    on blue twill rectangle.         1969       5.00 - 10.00

### Student Pilot
E and FDL at ctr. of wings, title below,
    on blue twill rectangle.         1969       5.00 - 10.00

# HANDBOOKS

### Air Scout Manual
H. W. Hunt, Lorne W. Barclay,
    ed. 2 pre-proof editions.        1942       50.00 - 60.00

Air Scout Manual (1942-43)

## Air Scout Manual
H. W. Hunt, Lorne
    W. Barclay, ed. 6 printings.        1942-1943 40.00 - 60.00

## Air Explorer Manual
Ted S. Holstein, ed. Proof
    edition and 5 printings.        1951-1958 20.00 - 30.00

# UNIFORMS

## Air Explorer Jacket Patch
Tenderfoot emblem at ctr. of
    wings on blue twill.        1969        10.00 - 15.00

## Air Scout Universal Wings (type 1)
Tenderfoot emblem w/ silver wings.    1942-1949 40.00 - 50.00

## Air Explorer Universal Wings
Tenderfoot emblem at ctr. of extended
    silver wings, wings dip at ctr.    1949-1966 15.00 - 20.00

## Air Scout Hat Patch
Gold Tenderfoot emblem on silver wings.    1942-1949 15.00 - 20.00

## Community Strip
Dark blue embroidery on light blue twill.    1942-1949 10.00 - 15.00

## Community Strip
Brown on dark green twill.    1949-1958        5.00 - 10.00

## Explorers Universal Badge
White C-A-W in gold outline,
    FDL on blue twill.        1949-1958 10.00 - 15.00
White C-A-W in gold outline,
    FDL on dark green twill.        1949-1958 10.00 - 15.00
White C-A-W in gold outline,
    FDL on red twill.        1949-1958 10.00 - 15.00

## Merit Badge Sash
Wide light blue (3 across).        1946-1957 30.00 - 50.00

## Squadron Numerals, 0-9
Royal blue embroidery on light blue felt.    1942-1949    5.00 - 10.00

## State Strip
Dark blue embroidery on light blue twill.    1942-1949 10.00 - 15.00

# MERIT BADGES

## Aerodynamics
Blue border and background.        1942-1952 75.00 - 150.00

## Aeronautics
Blue border and background.        1942-1952 75.00 - 150.00

## Airplane Design
Blue border and background.        1942-1952 75.00 - 150.00

## Airplane Structure
Blue border and background.        1942-1952 75.00 - 150.00

# POSITION BADGES - LEADERS

## Air Scout Assistant Squadron Leader
Tenderfoot emblem w/ gold wings,
    small circle behind at ctr.        1942-1949 40.00 - 50.00

## Air Scout Squadron Leader
Tenderfoot emblem w/ silver wings,
    small circle behind at ctr.        1942-1949 40.00 - 50.00

# COLLAR DEVICES

## Advisor
C-A-W on blue enamel compass.        1950        60.00 - 80.00

## Assistant Advisor
Gold C-A-W on blue enamel.        1950        100.00 - 120.00

Two Chicago Explorers meet author C.R. Olsen. Note the Eagle and Contest Medals on the center Explorer, and the Eagle and Silver Award Medals on the right Explorer. The OA Sash is a Brotherhood flocked felt variety.

# EXPLORER SCOUTING

## RANK BADGES

### Explorer Scout Apprentice
 Tenderfoot badge
 at top of empty compass
EXPLORER SCOUT below. Dark green twill. 1944-1949  15.00 - 20.00

### Explorer Scout Frontiersman
 Tenderfoot badge at top of
 compass w/ teepee within
EXPLORER SCOUT below. Dark green twill. 1935-1949  15.00 - 20.00

### Explorer Scout Woodsman
 Tenderfoot badge at top
 of compass w/ pine tree within
EXPLORER SCOUT below. Dark green twill. 1944-1949  15.00 - 20.00

### Explorer Scout Ranger Badge
 Tenderfoot badge at top of compass
 w/ powderhorn within
EXPLORER SCOUT below. Dark green twill. 1944-1949  40.00 - 60.00

## Explorer Bronze Award
Bronze C-A-W and white FDL on blue twill. 1949-1958 15.00 - 25.00
Bronze C-A-W and white FDL
    on dark green twill.          1949-1958 15.00 - 25.00

## Explorer Gold Award
Gold C-A-W and white FDL on blue twill. 1949-1958 15.00 - 25.00
Gold C-A-W and white FDL
    on dark green twill.          1949-1958 15.00 - 25.00

## Explorer Silver Award
Eagle in flight left on compass,
    red-white-blue background.    1949-1958 50.00 - 75.00
Silver C-A-W and white FDL on blue twill. 1949-1958 15.00 - 25.00
Silver C-A-W and white FDL.
    Dark green twill.          1944-1958 15.00 - 25.00

## Skills Rating Strip
Aviation.             1949-1958 10.00 - 15.00
Communications.      1949-1958 10.00 - 15.00
Craft.              1949-1958 10.00 - 15.00
Emergency.         1949-1958 10.00 - 15.00
Navigation.        1949-1958 10.00 - 15.00
Outdoor.           1949-1958 10.00 - 15.00
Physical Fitness.     1949-1958 10.00 - 15.00
Seamanship.        1949-1958 10.00 - 15.00
Vocational Exploration.  1949-1958 10.00 - 15.00

## Star Scout
Dark green C/E, coarse twill.    1958-1969  5.00 - 7.00

# RANK MEDALS

## Explorer Scout Ranger Medal
Powderhorn in ctr. of compass,
    Tenderfoot emblem above.
        Green-white-green ribbon.    1944-1949 500.00 - 750.00

Explorer Program's Ranger Award.

## Bronze Award
Bronze C-A-W on red-orange ribbon.    1949-1959 200.00 - 250.00

## Gold Award
Gold C-A-W on red-orange ribbon.    1949-1959 400.00 - 500.00

## Silver Award, type I
Silver C-A-W on red-orange ribbon.    1949-1959  1,000 - 1,400

Explorer Program's Silver Award (type I).

## Silver Award, type II
Eagle in flight left on compass,
    Tenderfoot emblem below.
    White ribbon w/thin
    red-white-blue stripe.          1954-1959 200.00 - 275.00

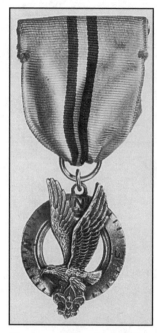

Explorer Program's Sil-
ver Award (type II).

# POSITION BADGES

## Explorer Assistant Crew Leader
1 white bar behind white C-A-W
    and gold FDL. Cut edge green twill.    1949-1958 10.00 - 15.00
1 white bar behind white C-A-W
    and gold FDL. Cut edge blue twill.    1944-1960 10.00 - 15.00
1 white bar behind white C-A-W
    and gold FDL. Cut edge
    green twill w/ border.                1944-1960 10.00 - 15.00

## Explorer Crew Leader
2 white bars behind white C-A-W
    and gold FDL. Cut edge blue twill.    1949-1958 10.00 - 15.00
2 white bars behind white C-A-W
    and gold FDL. Cut edge green twill.   1949-1958 10.00 - 15.00
2 white bars behind white C-A-W
    and gold FDL. Cut edge green twill
    w/ border.                            1944-1960 10.00 - 15.00

## Explorer Deputy Senior Crew Leader
3 white bars behind white C-A-W
    and gold FDL. Cut edge blue twill.    1949-1958 25.00 - 40.00
3 white bars behind white C-A-W
    and gold FDL. Cut edge dark green twill. 1944-1960 25.00 - 40.00
3 white bars behind white C-A-W
    and gold FDL. Cut edge dark
    green twill w/ border.                1944-1960 25.00 - 40.00

## Explorer Post Secretary
Crossed quills behind white C-A-W
    w/ gold FDL. Cut edge blue twill.     1949-1958 40.00 - 60.00
Crossed quills behind white C-A-W
    w/ gold FDL. Cut edge dark green twill. 1949-1958 40.00 - 60.00
Crossed quills behind white C-A-W
    w/ gold FDL. Cut edge dark
    green twill w/ border.                1944-1960 40.00 - 60.00

## Explorer Scout Assistant Crew Leader
1 bar behind Explorer Scout emblem,
    gold on green cut cloth twill.        1935-1949 40.00 - 60.00

## Explorer Scout Assistant Post Guide
2-1/2 bars behind Explorer Scout emblem,
    gold on green cut cloth twill.        1935-1949 40.00 - 60.00

## Explorer Scout Crew Leader
2 bars behind Explorer Scout emblem,
    gold on green cut cloth twill.        1935-1949 40.00 - 60.00

## Explorer Scout Post Guide
3 bars behind Explorer Scout emblem,
    gold on green cut cloth twill.        1935-1949 40.00 - 60.00

## Explorer Scout Post Secretary
Crossed quills behind Explorer Scout
    emblem, gold on green cut cloth twill. 1935-1949 50.00 - 75.00

## Explorer Senior Crew Leader
White C-A-W and gold FDL.
    Cut edge blue twill.                  1949-1958 25.00 - 40.00
White C-A-W and gold FDL.
    Cut edge dark green twill.            1949-1958 25.00 - 40.00

Exciting High Adventures continue to be made available to older scouts.

Explorer Scout Manual, 1946-1947

Explorer Manual, 1950-1952

# HANDBOOKS

### Explorer Scout Manual
Carl D. Lane. 382 pgs. 2 printings.        1946-1947 20.00 - 30.00

### Explorer Manual
Ted S. Holstein, ed. 330 pgs.
3 printings.                               1950-1952 15.00 - 20.00
Ted S. Holstein, ed. 380 pgs.
4/54 printing.                             1954      10.00 - 15.00
Ted S. Holstein, ed. 386 pgs. + 14pgs.
5 printings.                               1954-1958 10.00-15.00

### Exploring
Ted S. Holstein, ed. 317 pgs. 3 printings.   1958-1966  7.50 - 10.00

Exploring Handbook, 1960s

### Medical Exploring
2 printings.                               1973-1980  5.00 - 10.00

A Region 7 executive and four happy Explorers celebrate receiving Eagle or Silver Awards. Note the placement on the sleeve of the Universal Emblem, a National Standard Post Award, the Emergency Service Patch, and rating strips.

# UNIFORMS

## Community Strip
Brown on dark green twill.                1949-1958   5.00 - 10.00

## Council Strip, green and brown
New York City/Brooklyn.                    1945-1955  35.00 - 50.00

## Explorers Hat Patch
Tenderfoot badge on dark green twill.     1949-1958   7.50 - 10.00
C-A-W design on red twill.                1949-1958   8.00-12.50
Circle-V design on green twill.           1960-1967   5.00-10.00

## Explorers Universal Badge
White C-A-W in gold outline,
    FDL on blue twill.                    1949-1958  10.00 - 15.00

Explorers Universal Badge

Explorer "Overseas" Cap with the C-A-W or Circle V design.

White C-A-W in gold outline,
  FDL on dark green twill.          1949-1958  10.00 - 15.00
White C-A-W in gold outline,
  FDL on red twill.                 1949-1958  10.00 - 15.00

## Hat patch
BSA and EXPLORER SCOUT on compass,
  star behind Tenderfoot emblem.    1935-1949 10.00 - 15.00

## Merit Badge Sash
Wide, dark green (3 across).        1949-1958  5.00 - 10.00

## Service star
Gold star w/ tenure number,
  screwback on red felt.            1947-1955  3.00 - 5.00
Gold star w/ tenure number,
  clutch back on red plastic.       1956       1.00 - 1.50

## State Strip, green and brown
| | | |
|---|---|---|
| CALIF. | 1945-1955 | 20.00-30.00 |
| GA. | 1945-1955 | 20.00-30.00 |
| ILL. | 1945-1955 | 20.00-30.00 |
| IOWA. | 1945-1955 | 20.00-30.00 |
| LA. | 1945-1955 | 25.00-35.00 |
| MASS. | 1945-1955 | 20.00-30.00 |
| MD. | 1945-1955 | 25.00-35.00 |
| MICH. | 1945-1955 | 20.00-30.00 |
| MINN. | 1945-1955 | 25.00-35.00 |
| MO. | 1945-1955 | 20.00-30.00 |
| MONT. | 1945-1955 | 20.00-30.00 |
| N.H. | 1945-1955 | 25.00-35.00 |
| N.J. | 1945-1955 | 20.00-30.00 |
| N.Y. | 1945-1955 | 20.00-30.00 |
| OHIO. | 1945-1955 | 20.00-30.00 |
| OKLA. | 1945-1955 | 20.00-30.00 |
| PA. | 1945-1955 | 20.00-30.00 |
| S. DAK. | 1945-1955 | 25.00-35.00 |
| TEXAS. | 1945-1955 | 20.00-30.00 |
| UTAH. | 1945-1955 | 20.00-30.00 |
| WASH. | 1945-1955 | 20.00-30.00 |
| WIS. | 1945-1955 | 20.00-30.00 |

## Unit numeral
Green twill
  w/ brown embroidery.              1950       1.00 - 2.00

## Unit Numerals
Green felt w/ brown embroidery.     1935-1949  3.00 - 5.00

## Explorer Scout and BSA around compass w/ 8-pointed star behind Tenderfoot badge
Dark green twill.                   1935-1949 10.00 - 15.00

# PINBACK BUTTONS

## National Jamboree, 1950
Red River Valley Post 22. 2-1/4".   1950      10.00 - 15.00

## Region Seven Explorer Delegate
C-A-W emblem. 4".                   1961      15.00 - 20.00

# POSITION BADGES - LEADERS

## Explorer Post Advisor
White C-A-W and FDL on dark green twill.  1949-1958 10.00 - 15.00

## Explorer Post Assistant Advisor
Gold C-A-W and FDL on dark green twill.   1949-1958 10.00 - 15.00

## Explorer Scout Advisor
BOY SCOUTS OF AMERICA and
  EXPLORERS legend around
  First Class emblem on 8-pointed
  star, white on dark green twill.  1935-1949 10.00 - 15.00

## Explorer Scout Assistant Advisor
BOY SCOUTS OF AMERICA and
  EXPLORERS legend around
  First Class emblem on 8-pointed
  star, gold on dark green twill.   1935-1949 10.00 - 15.00

# COLLAR DEVICES

## Advisor
C-A-W on green enamel.　　　　1950　　60.00 - 80.00

## Assistant Advisor
Gold C-A-W on green enamel.　　1950　　60.00 - 80.00

# UNIFORMS - LEADERS

## Bullion-embroidered program emblem for Blazer
Explorer, E.　　　　　　　　1971　　15.00 - 20.00

# AWARD MEDALS

## Contest Medal
Bronze C-A-W within wreath,
　　red-blue ribbon.　　　　1949-1958　20.00 - 30.00
Gold C-A-W within wreath,
　　red-blue ribbon.　　　　1949-1958　20.00 - 30.00
Silver C-A-W within wreath,
　　red-blue ribbon.　　　　1949-1958　20.00 - 30.00

# MISCELLANEOUS STUFF

## Explorer Unit Local Standard Patch
Blue and red, fully embroidered.　1949-1958　5.00 - 10.00

## Explorer Unit National Standard Patch
Blue and red, fully embroidered.　1949-1958　5.00 - 10.00

## Explorer Unit Regional Standard Patch
Blue and red, fully embroidered.　1949-1958　5.00 - 10.00

## Explorer Unit Standard Patch
Blue and red, fully embroidered.　1949-1958　5.00 - 10.00

## Post Flag
Wool, red top,
　　blue bottom, C-A-W in ctr.　　1950-1958　30.00 - 50.00

Central C-A-W design from a Post Flag.

Cotton, red top, blue bottom,
　　Circle V emblem in ctr.　　1959-1968　20.00 - 30.00
Nylon, red top, blue bottom,
　　E emblem in ctr.　　　　1969　　15.00 - 25.00

# KNIVES

## Camillus
Exploring E emblem on green handle,
　　2-1/2", spear, file, and scissors. 1987-1990E.2　25.00 - 30.00

# MEDALLIONS

## Explorer, "E" You Make the Difference
Elongated cent. Copper.　　1992　　Dio.1992.9　1.00 - 1.50

# HIGH ADVENTURE BASE - PHILMONT

## Arrowhead Patch, Staff
| | | |
|---|---|---|
| Cloth back. | 1960-1967 | 25.00 - 35.00 |
| Plastic back. | 1970-1997 | 25.00 - 35.00 |

## Arrowhead Patch
| | | |
|---|---|---|
| Cloth back. | 1960-1967 | 12.50 - 17.50 |
| Plastic back. | 1970-1997 | 10.00 - 15.00 |

## BSA's 50th Anniversary Patch
| | | |
|---|---|---|
| | 1960 | 40.00 - 50.00 |

## Bull Patch
| | | |
|---|---|---|
| Black felt (men). | 1940 | 5.00 - 7.50 |
| White felt (women). | 1940 | 5.00 - 7.50 |

## Burro Race Patch
| | | |
|---|---|---|
| White twill. | 1970-1975 | 10.00 - 15.00 |

## Camp Uracca Patch
| | | |
|---|---|---|
| Yellow twill. | 1969 | 10.00 - 17.50 |

## Commissary Staff Patch
| | | |
|---|---|---|
| Brown twill. | 1950-1955 | 20.00 - 25.00 |

## Field Sports Patch
| | | |
|---|---|---|
| Square. | 1950-1955 | 100.00 - 125.00 |

## Field Sports Tournament
| | | |
|---|---|---|
| Rectangle. | 1980-1995 | 10.00 - 15.00 |

## Kit Carson Men
| | | |
|---|---|---|
| Blue twill. | 1968 | 15.00 - 20.00 |

## Kit Carson Trek
| | | |
|---|---|---|
| Blue twill. | 1974 | 15.00 - 20.00 |

## National Explorer Elected Leader
| | | |
|---|---|---|
| Shield shape. | 1956 | 40.00 - 60.00 |

## Nature Award
| | | |
|---|---|---|
| Leather Indian head. | 1950-1955 | 20.00 - 25.00 |

## OA Indian Seminar
| | | |
|---|---|---|
| | 1974 | 30.00 - 40.00 |

## OA Trek
| | | |
|---|---|---|
| Pocket patch. | 1985 | 10.00 - 15.00 |
| Pocket patch. | 1989 | 15.00 - 20.00 |

## Orienteering Patch
| | | |
|---|---|---|
| Red twill. | 1970-1975 | 17.50 - 22.50 |

## Philmont
| | | |
|---|---|---|
| Tooth of Time belt buckle, bronze. | 1960-1998 | 7.50 - 12.50 |
| Bull in oval belt buckle, bronze. | 1970-1998 | 7.50 - 12.50 |
| Tooth of Time belt buckle, silver. | 1970-1998 | 75.00 - 125.00 |

## Philmont 2" Patch Segments
| | | |
|---|---|---|
| Camper. | 1941-1950 | 10.00 - 15.00 |
| Conservationist. | 1941-1950 | 10.00 - 15.00 |
| Horseman. | 1941-1950 | 10.00 - 15.00 |
| Mountain Man patch. Rifle. | 1941-1950 | 20.00 - 30.00 |
| Naturalist. | 1941-1950 | 10.00 - 15.00 |
| Sportsman. | 1941-1950 | 10.00 - 15.00 |
| Woodman. | 1941-1950 | 10.00 - 15.00 |

## Philmont 2" Patch
| | | |
|---|---|---|
| P brand, landscape background. | 1941-1950 | 15.00 - 20.00 |

## Philmont 2" Universal Patch Segment
| | | |
|---|---|---|
| Staff. | 1941-1950 | 30.00 - 50.00 |

## Philmont Director Patch
| | | |
|---|---|---|
| | 1940-1950 | 100.00 - 125.00 |

## Philmont Ranger
| | | |
|---|---|---|
| Back patch. | 1980-1995 | 15.00 - 20.00 |

## Philmont's 35th Anniversary patch
| | | |
|---|---|---|
| Light blue twill. | 1973-1974 | 15.00 - 20.00 |

## Philmont
| | | |
|---|---|---|
| 30th Anniversary. | 1971 | 40.00 - 50.00 |
| 40th Anniversary. | 1981 | 7.50 - 12.50 |
| 50th Anniversary. | 1988 | 2.50 - 5.00 |

## Philturn Patch
| | | |
|---|---|---|
| Type I. PT brand, plain background. | 1938 | 225.00 - 275.00 |
| Type II. PT brand, landscape background. | 1940 | 125.00 - 175.00 |

## Rayado Program
| | | |
|---|---|---|
| Gray twill. | 1975-1990 | 10.00 - 15.00 |

## Seatonb Library & Museum
| | | |
|---|---|---|
| Blue twill. | 1975-1990 | 4.00 - 5.00 |

## Training Center
Handicraft.
|  |  |  |
|---|---|---|
| Stamped leather skin shape. |  | 175.00 - 225.00 |
| JLT patch. | 1960-1967 | 40.00 - 60.00 |
| 3" round, yellow twill. | 1969-1970 | 10.00 - 12.50 |
| 2-3/4" round, yellow twill. | 1970-1971 | 7.50 - 10.00 |
| 3" round, orange twill. | 1970-1971 | 4.00 - 5.00 |
| Staff patch. | 1970-1971 | 20.00 - 30.00 |
| National Catholic Conf. | 1974-1996 | 10.00 - 15.00 |
| 25th Anniversary, orange twill. | 1975 | 20.00 - 25.00 |

## USA - Bicentennial
| | | |
|---|---|---|
| Flag over Tooth of Time. | 1976 | 10.00 - 15.00 |

# HIGH ADVENTURE BASE - FLORIDA SEA BASE

## Florida High Adventure
| | |
|---|---|
| Bahamas. | 3.00 - 5.00 |
| Sailing. | 3.00 - 5.00 |

## Florida Sea Base
| | |
|---|---|
| Adult patch, w/ red border. | 60.00 - 80.00 |
| Pocket patch, 10th Anniversary. | 100.00 - 125.00 |
| Round participant patch. Blue. | 25.00 - 35.00 |
| Staff patch, 3-1/2" blue border. | 100.00 - 130.00 |
| Weekend Course, 3" white border. | 50.00 - 60.00 |

# HIGH ADVENTURE BASE - C.H. SOMMERS

## Charles L. Sommers Canoe Base
| | |
|---|---|
| Jacket patch. | 20.00 - 30.00 |
| Pocket patch, felt. | 50.00 - 75.00 |
| W/ loop. | 10.00 - 15.00 |
| W/o loop. | 10.00 - 15.00 |

## Les Voyageurs
| | |
|---|---|
| Staff. | 125.00 - 175.00 |

## Region Ten BSA Wilderness Canoe Trails
| | |
|---|---|
| 73mm round twill. | 40.00 - 55.00 |
| 78mm Round twill, w/ loop. | 25.00 - 35.00 |

## Sommers Canoe Base
| | |
|---|---|
| Pocket patch. | 10.00 - 15.00 |
| Voyageur Historic Trails pocket patch. | 10.00 - 15.00 |

# HIGH ADVENTURE BASE - N. WISCONSIN

## Explorer Canoe Base
| | |
|---|---|
| Minor varieties. | 20.00 - 30.00 |

## Northern Wisconsin High Adventure
| | |
|---|---|
| Back patch. | 15.00 - 25.00 |
| Pocket patch. | 7.50 - 10.00 |

## Northern Wisconsin National Canoe Base
| | |
|---|---|
| Back patch. | 25.00 - 35.00 |
| Pocket patch. | 10.00 - 15.00 |
| Winter Expedition. | 15.00 - 25.00 |

## Region 7 Base
| | |
|---|---|
| Pocket patch, 30th anniversary. | 25.00 - 35.00 |
| Pocket patch. | 10.00 - 15.00 |

## Region 7 Canoe Base
| | |
|---|---|
| Pocket patch. | 10.00 - 15.00 |

## Region 7 Explorer Base
| | |
|---|---|
| Pocket patch. | 10.00 - 15.00 |

## Region 7 Explorer Canoe Base
| | |
|---|---|
| Pocket patch. | 10.00 - 15.00 |

## Region 7 Scout Landing
| | |
|---|---|
| Cut edge. | 60.00 - 80.00 |

## Region 7 Scout Landing Segments
| | |
|---|---|
| Camper. | 50.00 - 75.00 |
| Leader. | 50.00 - 75.00 |
| Portageur. | 100.00 - 150.00 |
| Voyageur. | 100.00 - 150.00 |

# HIGH ADVENTURE BASE - LAND BTWN LAKES

## Back Patch
17.50 - 22.50

## Crew Patch
10.00 - 15.00

## Pocket Patch
7.50 - 12.50

# HIGH ADVENTURE BASE - MAINE

## Maine High Adventure Base

| | |
|---|---|
| Back patch. | 15.00 - 20.00 |
| Pocket patch, 10th anniversary. | 10.00 - 15.00 |
| Pocket patch. | 15.00 - 25.00 |

## Maine High Adventure Base

| | |
|---|---|
| St. Croix. | 80.00 - 100.00 |

## Maine National High Adventure Area

| | |
|---|---|
| Back patch. | 25.00 - 35.00 |
| Pocket patch. | 20.00 - 30.00 |

## Matagamon, BSA

| | |
|---|---|
| Pocket patch. | 35.00 - 45.00 |

# SCHIFF SCOUT RESERVATION

## BSA 50th Anniversary

| | | |
|---|---|---|
| Pocket patch. | 1960 | 75.00 - 100.00 |

## Schiff Scout Reservation

| | |
|---|---|
| Cut edge green khaki. | 25.00 - 30.00 |
| Shield, rolled edge, cloth back. | 5.00 - 7.50 |
| Shield, rolled edge, plastic back. | 4.00 - 6.00 |
| Square cut khaki cloth. | 30.00 - 50.00 |

## Shield Design

| | |
|---|---|
| National Conservation Instructor Camp. | 15.00 - 20.00 |
| National Conservation Instructor Training Camp. | 30.00 - 40.00 |
| National Jr. Leader Instructor Training Camp. 2 lines. | 30.00 - 40.00 |
| National Junior Leader Instruction Camp. | 15.00 - 20.00 |
| National Junior Leader Instructor Training Camp. 3 lines. | 30.00 - 40.00 |

# NATIONAL CAMP SCHOOL

## National Camp School

| | |
|---|---|
| Handicrafts. | 200.00 - 225.00 |
| Jacket patch, rolled edge khaki. | 10.00 - 15.00 |
| Jacket patch, rolled edge tan. | 10.00 - 15.00 |
| Pocket patch, cut edge khaki. | 10.00 - 15.00 |
| Pocket patch, cut khaki. | 30.00 - 40.00 |
| Pocket patch, rolled edge khaki. | 7.50 - 10.00 |
| Pocket patch, rolled edge tan. | 7.50 - 10.00 |

# REGIONS (12)

## Region 1

| | |
|---|---|
| Large 1, States of CT, NH, VT, MA, RI, ME. VT has wavy lines. White felt. | 60.00 - 80.00 |
| Large 1, States of CT, NH, VT, MA, RI, ME. White felt. | 30.00 - 40.00 |
| Large 1, States of CT, NH, VT, MA, RI, ME. White twill, cut edge. | 15.00 - 25.00 |
| Large 1, States of CT, NH, VT, MA, RI, ME. White twill, rolled edge. | 10.00 - 15.00 |
| Large 1, States of CT, NH, VT, MA, RI, ME. White twill, rolled edge. Boypower Team. | 7.50 - 10.00 |

## Region 10

| | |
|---|---|
| Large-faced Paul Bunyan, solid embroidered ctr. Cut edge white twill. | 100.00 - 125.00 |
| Paul Bunyan in circle, name below. Rolled edge white twill. | 10.00 - 15.00 |
| Paul Bunyan in circle, name below. Rolled edge white twill. | 10.00 - 15.00 |
| Paul Bunyan in circle, Region 10 above, name below. Rolled edge white twill. | 10.00 - 15.00 |

## Region 11

| | |
|---|---|
| Dome-shaped, NOR'WESTERS large and ax. Cut edge. | 40.00 - 60.00 |
| Dome-shaped, NOR'WESTERS large and ax. Rolled edge. | 20.00 - 25.00 |
| Dome-shaped, NOR'WESTERS small and ax. Rolled edge. | 10.00 - 15.00 |
| States OR, WA, ID, MT. listed. Red felt. | 100.00 - 130.00 |

## Region 12

| | |
|---|---|
| Blue felt, 3-1/2" w/ sunset over water. Silk screened. | 125.00 - 150.00 |
| Blue felt, 3-1/2" w/ sunset over water. Silk screened. 12 added in design. | 120.00 - 140.00 |
| Felt 3" w/ wagon wheel and state outlines. | 90.00 - 120.00 |
| Large 12 and white bull's head on white felt. | 130.00 - 160.00 |
| Twill, Bull's head on wagon wheel. Cut edge. | 20.00 - 30.00 |
| Twill, Bull's head on wagon wheel. Rolled edge. | 10.00 - 15.00 |

## Region 2

| | |
|---|---|
| Dome shaped, Statue of Liberty and NY, NJ names, cut edge. | 20.00 - 30.00 |
| Dome shaped, Statue of Liberty and NY, NJ, PR names, cut edge. | 15.00 - 25.00 |
| Dome shaped, Statue of Liberty and NY, NJ, PR names, rolled edge. | 10.00 - 15.00 |
| Dome shaped, Statue of Liberty and NY, NJ, PR, VI names, rolled edge. | 7.50 - 10.00 |
| Oval w/ large 2, NY and NJ flanking. | 75.00 - 125.00 |
| Round 3" blue twill, embroidered 2 and states of NY and NJ. | 25.00 - 35.00 |
| Round 3" gray twill, embroidered 2 and states of NY and NJ. | 30.00 - 45.00 |

## Region 3

| | |
|---|---|
| Band. 1950 Jamboree. | 100.00 - 150.00 |
| Round 3", scout sign on red twill cut edge. | 15.00 - 20.00 |
| Round 3", scout sign on white twill cut edge. | 10.00 - 15.00 |

## Region 4

| | |
|---|---|
| Red Twill, states of OH, KY, WV, and spacecraft. Rolled edge. | 7.50 - 10.00 |
| Red Twill, states of OH, KY, WV. Green 4. | 20.00 - 30.00 |
| Red Twill, states of OH, KY, WV. Lime green 4. | 17.50 - 25.00 |
| Red Twill, states of OH, KY, WV. Rolled edge. | 10.00 - 15.00 |
| Yellow felt, states of OH, KY, and WV. | 100.00 - 140.00 |

## Region 5

| | |
|---|---|
| Acorn and large 5 in 3" green felt. | 80.00 - 125.00 |
| Green felt circle w/ yellow V and arrow. | 75.00 - 100.00 |

| | |
|---|---|
| Shield w/ V and arrow. R-W-B background. Cut edge. | 20.00 - 25.00 |
| Shield w/ V and arrow. R-W-B background. Rolled edge. | 10.00 - 15.00 |

## Region 6

| | |
|---|---|
| White felt, states of NC, SC, GA, FL. | 40.00 - 60.00 |
| White twill, states of NC, SC, GA, FL Rolled edge. | 10.00 - 15.00 |
| White twill, states of NC, SC, GA, FL. Cut edge. | 20.00 - 30.00 |

## Region 7

| | |
|---|---|
| Shield, large 7 and states WI, MI, IN, IL. Cut edge. | 15.00 - 20.00 |
| Shield, large 7 and states WI, MI, IN, IL. Rolled edge. | 10.00 - 15.00 |

## Region 8

| | |
|---|---|
| GCW on red felt 4" w/ bronco rider. Great Central West. | 100.00 - 130.00 |
| Round 2-7/8" cowboy on beige twill. | 75.00 - 100.00 |
| Round 3" bronco and rider on beige twill. | 30.00 - 40.00 |
| Round 3" bronco and rider on blue twill. | 50.00 - 75.00 |
| Round 3" bronco and rider on flesh twill. | 25.00 - 35.00 |
| Tear drop, bronco rider l. | 15.00 - 25.00 |

## Region 9

| | |
|---|---|
| Golden 3" felt, bison and 9. | 75.00 - 100.00 |
| Round 2" bison and 9 on golden twill. | 60.00 - 80.00 |
| Round 2-1/2" bison and 9 on golden twill. | 60.00 - 80.00 |
| Star and 9 in shield w/ feathers below. | 25.00 - 35.00 |
| Star, 9 and bison in shield w/ feathers below. | 20.00 - 25.00 |
| Star, 9 and bison in shield w/ feathers below. Solid embroidery. | 7.50 - 12.50 |

 268

Daniel Beard in his famous buckskin outfit. Note the autograph in the upper right hand corner.

# BOOKS BY THE U.S. FOUNDERS

## Daniel Carter Beard

| | | |
|---|---|---|
| American Boy's Book of Birds and Brownies of the Woods. Lippincott. | 1923 | 10.00 - 15.00 |
| American Boy's Book of Bugs, Butterflies and Beetles. Lippincott. | 1915 | 10.00 - 15.00 |
| American Boy's Book of Signs, Signals and Symbols. Lippincott. | 1918 | 10.00 - 15.00 |
| American Boy's Book of Wild Animals. Lippincott. | 1921 | 10.00 - 15.00 |
| American Boy's Handbook of Camplore and Woodcraft. Lippincott. | 1920 | 10.00 - 15.00 |
| American Boy's Handybook: What to Do and How to Do It. Scribners. | 1882 | 75.00 - 100.00 |
| American Boy's Handybook: What to Do and How to Do It. Reprint. Nonpariel Book. | 1983 | 10.00 - 15.00 |
| Animal book and Campfire Stories. Moffat, enlarged edition. | 1910 | 15.00 - 25.00 |
| Animal book and Campfire Stories. Moffat. | 1907 | 15.00 - 25.00 |
| Black Wolf Pack. Scribners | 1922 | 10.00 - 15.00 |
| Boat Building and Boating. Scribners. | 1911 | 10.00 - 15.00 |
| Boy Heroes of Today, Brewer, Warren and Putnam. | 1932 | 10.00 - 15.00 |
| Boy Pioneers of the Buckskin Men. | 1911 | 10.00 - 15.00 |
| Boy Pioneers: Sons of Daniel Boone. Scribners. | 1909 | 40.00 - 60.00 |
| The Buckskin Book and Buckskin Calendar. | 1911 | 20.00 - 30.00 |
| Buckskin Book for Buckskin Men and Boys, Lippincott. | 1925 | 20.00 - 30.00 |
| Camp Hints for Hike and Bike. U.S. Rubber Co. | 1916 | 10.00 - 15.00 |
| Dan Beard Talks to Scouts (books and record set.) Garden City. | 1940 | 50.00 - 75.00 |
| Do It Yourself, Lippincott. | 1925 | 10.00 - 15.00 |
| Fair Weather Ideas. Scribners. | 1904 | 20.00 - 25.00 |
| For Playground, Field and Forest: The Outdoor Handybook. Scribners. | 1900 | 40.00 - 50.00 |
| Handicraft for Outdoor Boys. Grosset and Dunlap. | 1913 | 10.00 - 15.00 |
| Hardly a Man is Now Alive. Doubleday. | 1939 | 20.00 - 30.00 |
| How to Make a Totem Bookcase. Lippincott. | 1921 | 5.00 - 10.00 |
| Jack of All trades: New Ideas for American Boys. Scribners. | 1900 | 40.00 - 50.00 |
| Moonblight and Six Feet of Romance. Websterm. | 1892 | 10.00 - 15.00 |
| Outdoor games for All Seasons: American Boy's Book of Sport. Scribners. | 1906 | 40.00 - 50.00 |
| Shelters, Shacks and Shanties. Scribners. | 1914 | 10.00 - 15.00 |
| Wisdom of the Woods, Lippincott | 1926 | 10.00 - 15.00 |

## Ernest Thompson Seton.

| | | |
|---|---|---|
| Animal Heroes. Scribners. | 1905 | 10.00 - 15.00 |
| Animals (Selections from Life Histories) The Nature Library. Doubleday. | 1926 | 10.00 - 15.00 |
| Animals Worth Knowing (Selections from Life Histories) The Little Nature Library. Doubleday. | 1928 | 10.00 - 15.00 |
| Arctic Prairies. Scribners. | 1911 | 10.00 - 15.00 |
| Bannertail: The Story of a Grey Squirrel. Scribners. | 1922 | 10.00 - 15.00 |
| Billy the Dog that Made Good. Hodder. | 1930 | 10.00 - 15.00 |
| The Biography of a Grizzly. Century. | 1900 | 10.00 - 15.00 |
| Biography of a Silver Fox. Century. | 1909 | 10.00 - 15.00 |
| Biography of an Arctic Fox. Appleton-Century. | 1937 | 10.00 - 15.00 |
| The Birch Bark Roll combined with Handbook for Boys. Doubleday, Page & Co. | 1910 | 300.00 - 400.00 |
| The Birch Bark Roll combined with Scouting for Boys. Doubleday, Page & Co. | | 300.00 - 400.00 |
| The Birch Bark Roll of the Woodcraft Indians. Doubleday. | 1906 | 150.00 - 200.00 |
| The Birch Bark Roll of the Woodcraft Indians. Doubleday. | 1908 | 150.00 - 200.00 |
| The Birch Bark Roll: 19th through 30th editions, Doubleday or A.S. Barnes. | 1920-1940 | 40.00 - 60.00 |
| The Birch Bark Roll: Manual of the Woodcraft Indians. Doubleday. | 1915 | 40.00 - 60.00 |
| The Birch Bark Roll: The American Boy Scout. Doubleday, Page & Co. | 1910 | 150.00 - 200.00 |
| The Birch Bark Roll: The Book of Woodcraft and Indian Lore. Doubleday. | 1912 | 50.00 - 75.00 |
| The Birch Bark Roll: The Book of Woodcraft and Indian Lore. Doubleday. | 1915 | 50.00 - 75.00 |
| The Birch Bark Roll: Woodcraft Boys, Woodcraft Girls, How to Begin. Woodcraft Headquarters. | 1915 | 40.00 - 60.00 |
| The Birch Bark Roll: Woodcraft manual for Boys. Doubleday. | 1917 | 40.00 - 60.00 |
| The Birch Bark Roll: Woodcraft Manual for Boys. Doubleday. | 1918 | 40.00 - 60.00 |
| The Birch Bark Roll: Woodcraft manual for Girls. Doubleday. | 1916 | 40.00 - 60.00 |
| The Birch Bark Roll: Woodcraft Manual for Girls. Doubleday. | 1918 | 40.00 - 60.00 |

Birch Bark Rolls. American Woodcraft.
7 monthly installments in
Ladies Home Journal. 1902.
Curtis Publishing Co. 1902 100.00 - 150.00
Birch Bark Rolls. How to Play Indian.
Curtis Publishing Co. 1903 30.00 - 40.00
Birch Bark Rolls. Laws of the
Seton Indians. 1905 30.00 - 40.00
Birch Bark Rolls. Laws of the
Seton Indians. Seaton. 1906 30.00 - 40.00
Birch Bark Rolls. Laws of the Seton
Indians. Association Press. 1905 30.00 - 40.00
Birch Bark Rolls. The Red Book, or
How to Play Indian. Seaton. 1904 30.00 - 40.00
Birds of Manitoba. Foster. 1892 20.00 - 30.00
Blazes on the Trail (three pamphlets).
Little Peego Press. 1928 30.00 - 45.00
Brownie Wigwam.
Woodcraft League. 1921 20.00 - 30.00
Buffalo Wind. Private. 1937 200.00 - 300.00
Chink and Other Stories. Hodder. 1927 10.00 - 15.00
Cute Cyote and Other
Stories. Hodder. 1930 10.00 - 15.00
Fauna of Manitoba. British Assoc.
Handbook. 1909 10.00 - 15.00
Foam the Razorback. Hodder. 1927 10.00 - 15.00
The Forester's Manual. Doubleday. 1912 10.00 - 15.00
Gospel of the Redman. Doubleday. 1926 10.00 - 15.00
Great Historic Animals. Scribners. 1937 10.00 - 15.00
How Boys Can Form a Band of Indians.
Curtis. 1903 10.00 - 15.00
How to Catch Wolves. Oneida
Community. 1884 40.00 - 50.00
How to Make a Real Indian.
Teepee. Curtis. 1903 10.00 - 15.00
Johnny Bear and Other
Stories. Hodder. 1927 10.00 - 15.00
Johnny Bear; Lobo and Other Stories.
Scribners. 1935 10.00 - 15.00
Katug the Snow Child. Blackwell. 1927 10.00 - 15.00
Krag and Johnny Bear. Scribners. 1902 15.00 - 20.00
Krag, the Kootenay Ram and Other Stories.
University of London Press. 1929 10.00 - 15.00
The Laws and Honors of the Little
Lodge of Woodcraft. Cheyenne. 1919 25.00 - 35.00
Legend of the White Reindeer.
Constable. 1915 10.00 - 15.00
Library of Pioneering and Woodcraft.
Matching set re-issue of: Rolf in the
Woods, Wild Animal Ways, Two Little
Davages, Book of Woodcraft and
Indian Lore, Woodland Tales, Wild
Animals at Home. 50.00 - 75.00
Lives of Game Animals.
4 vols. Doubleday. 1925-28 40.00 - 75.00
Lives of the Hunted. Scribners. 1901 15.00 - 20.00
Lobo and Other Stories. Hodder. 1927 10.00 - 15.00
Lobo, Rag, and Vixen. Scribners. 1899 20.00 - 30.00

Lobo; Bingo; The Pacing Mustang. State. 1930 10.00 - 15.00
Mainly About Wolves. Methuen. 1937 10.00 - 15.00
Manual of the Brownies.
Woodcraft League. 1922 20.00 - 30.00
Monarch, the big Bear of Tallac.
Scribners. 1904 10.00 - 15.00
The Natural History of the Ten
Commandments. Scribners. 1907 10.00 - 15.00
Old Silver Grizzle. Hodder. 1927 10.00 - 15.00
Pictographs of the Southwest.
Cedar Rapids. 1937 50.00 - 75.00
Preacher of Cedar Mountain.
Doubleday. 1917 10.00 - 15.00
Raggylug and other Stories.
Hodder. 1927 10.00 - 15.00
The Red Lodge. Private. 1912 50.00 - 75.00
Rolf in the Woods. Doubleday. 1911 10.00 - 15.00
Santana, The Hero Dog of France.
Phoenix Press. 1945 150.00 - 200.00
Sign Talk. Doubleday. 1918 10.00 - 15.00
The Slum Cat. Constable. 1915 10.00 - 15.00
Studies in Art Anatomy of Animals.
Macmillan. 1896 20.00 - 30.00
The Ten Commandments in the
Animal World. Doubleday reprint
of Scribners. 1907 10.00 - 15.00
Trail of an Artist Naturalist.
Scribners. 1940 20.00 - 30.00
Trail of the Sandhill Stag. Scribners. 1899 20.00 - 30.00
Twelve Pictures of Wild Animals.
Scribners. 1901 25.00 - 35.00
Two Little Savages. Doubleday. 1903 15.00 - 20.00
War Dance and the Fire-Fly Dance.
Doubleday. 1910 10.00 - 15.00
The Wild Animal Play for Children.
Doubleday & Curtis. 10.00 - 15.00
Wild Animal Ways. Doubleday. 1916 10.00 - 15.00
Wild Animals at Home. Doubleday. 1913 10.00 - 15.00
Wild Animals I Have Known.
Scribners. 1898 20.00 - 30.00
Woodland Tales. Doubleday. 1921 20.00 - 30.00
Woodmyth and Fable. Century. 1905 10.00 - 15.00

## James E. West

The 1993 Scout Jamboree Book. G.P.
Putnam's Sons. 1933 20.00 - 25.00
The Boy Scout's Book of True Adventure.
G.P. Putnam's Sons. 1931 10.00 - 15.00
The Boys' Book of Honor.
F.H. Revell Co. 1934 10.00 - 15.00
He-Who-Sees-In-The-Dark: The Boys'
Story of Frederick Burnham, the
American Scout. Brewer, Warren &
Putnam. 1932 10.00 - 15.00
Lone Scout of the Sky: The
Story of Charles A. Lindbergh.
J.C. Winston, Co. 1928 7.50 - 12.50

Books by the U.S. Founders    271

| | | |
|---|---|---|
| Lone Scout of the Sky: The Story of Charles A. Lindbergh. BSA. | 1927 | 15.00 - 20.00 |
| Lone Scout of the Sky: The Story of Charles A. Lindbergh. Trade. edition (orange covers), J.C. Winston, Co. | 1928 | 7.50 - 12.50 |
| Making the Most of Yourself. D. Appleton-Century Co. | 1941 | 15.00 - 20.00 |
| The Scout Jamboree Book. G.P. Putnam's Sons. | 1930 | 15.00 - 20.00 |
| Thirty Years of Service: Tributes to James E. West. Carey Press. | 1941 | 20.00 - 25.00 |

## William Hillcourt, Gordon Lynn pseudonym

| | | |
|---|---|---|
| Golden Book of Camping and Camp Crafts, A Golden Hobby Book. Golden Press. | 1964 | 5.00 - 10.00 |
| Golden Book of Camping and Campcrafts. Golden Press. | 1959 | 5.00 - 10.00 |

## William Hillcourt, R.D. Bezucha pseudonym

| | | |
|---|---|---|
| Golden Anniversary Book of Scouting. Golden Press. | 1960 | 15.00 - 20.00 |

## William Hillcourt, Robert Brent pseudonym

| | | |
|---|---|---|
| Golden Book of Chemistry Experiments. Golden Press. | 1960 | 5.00 - 10.00 |

## William Hillcourt

| | | |
|---|---|---|
| The 1933 Scout Jamboree Book. G.P. Putnam's Sons. | 1933 | 10.00 - 15.00 |
| All Out for Scouting - Plan of Action. BSA. | 1975 | 10.00 - 15.00 |
| Baden Powell - The Two Lives of a Hero. G.P. Putnam's Sons. | 1964 | 15.00 - 20.00 |
| The Boy Campers. Warren & Putnam. | 1931 | 10.00 - 15.00 |
| Boy Scout Handbook. 6th edition. BSA. | 1959 | 10.00 - 15.00 |
| Boy Scout Handbook. 7th edition. BSA. | 1965 | 5.00 - 10.00 |
| Field Book of Nature Activities and Conservation. G.P. Putnam's Sons. | 1961 | 10.00 - 15.00 |
| Field Book of Nature Activities and Hobbies. G.P. Putnam's Sons. | 1970 | 5.00 - 10.00 |
| Field Book of Nature Activities. G.P. Putnam's Sons. | 1950 | 10.00 - 15.00 |
| Fun with Nature Hobbies. G.P. Putnam's Sons. | 1970 | 5.00 - 10.00 |
| Golden Book of Camping. Golden Press. | 1971 | 5.00 - 10.00 |
| Golden Book of Fitness for Boys. Golden Press. | 1967 | 5.00 - 10.00 |
| Golden Book of Fitness for Girls. Golden Press. | 1967 | 5.00 - 10.00 |
| Guildebook for Gilwell One Scoutmastership Wood Badge. | 1988 | 20.00 - 25.00 |
| Handbook for Patrol Leaders, Silver Jubilee Edition. BSA. | 1935 | 15.00 - 25.00 |
| Handbook for Patrol Leaders. 1st edition. BSA. | 1929 | 15.00 - 20.00 |
| Handbook for Patrol Leaders. 2nd edition. BSA. | 1947 | 10.00 - 15.00 |
| Handbook for Patrol Leaders. Golden Jubilee edition. BSA. | 1979 | 5.00 - 10.00 |
| Handbook for Scoutmasters, 2 volume edition. BSA. | 1936-37 | 30.00 - 40.00 |
| Handbook for Scoutmasters, 4th edition. BSA. | 1947 | 10.00 - 15.00 |
| Norman Rockwell's World of Scouting. H.N. Abrams. | 1977 | 15.00 - 20.00 |
| Official Boy Scout Handbook. 9th edition. BSA. | 1979 | 5.00 - 10.00 |
| Official Patrol Leader Handbook. 3rd edition. BSA. | 1980 | 5.00 - 10.00 |
| Outdoor Things to Do. Golden Press. | 1975 | 5.00 - 10.00 |
| Scout Field Book. BSA. | 1944 | 20.00 - 30.00 |

# SCOUTING FOUNDERS AND FAMOUS PEOPLE

## R.S.S. Baden Powell

General Cigarette card.

| | |
|---|---|
| Scout Cigarette card. | 10.00 - 15.00 |
| Autograph on card. | 75.00 - 100.00 |
| Autograph on letter. | 100.00 - 150.00 |
| Autograph on photo. | 150.00 - 200.00 |

## E.T. Seaton

| | |
|---|---|
| Autograph on card. | 75.00 - 100.00 |
| Autograph on letter. | 100.00 - 150.00 |
| Autograph on photo. | 150.00 - 200.00 |

## D.C. Beard

| | |
|---|---|
| Autograph on card. | 75.00 - 100.00 |
| Autograph on letter. | 100.00 - 150.00 |
| Autograph on photo. | 150.00 - 200.00 |

## J.C. West

| | |
|---|---|
| Autograph on card. | 20.00 - 30.00 |

| | |
|---|---|
| Autograph on letter. | 25.00 - 40.00 |
| Autograph on photo. | 25.00 - 40.00 |

## Paul Siple (Antarctic Scout)

| | |
|---|---|
| Autograph on card. | 10.00 - 15.00 |
| Autograph on letter. | 20.00 - 30.00 |
| Autograph on photo. | 25.00 - 35.00 |

## W. Hillcourt

| | |
|---|---|
| Autograph on card. | 5.00 - 10.00 |
| Autograph on letter. | 10.00 - 15.00 |
| Autograph on photo. | 15.00 - 20.00 |
| Autograph in handbook (1979 ed.). | 25.00 - 40.00 |

## C.H. Livingstone

| | |
|---|---|
| BSA, letter autographed content. | 20.00 - 30.00 |

COLIN H. LIVINGSTONE, President
NATIONAL COUNCIL
AMERICAN NATIONAL BANK BUILDING
WASHINGTON, D.C.

HEADQUARTERS—EXECUTIVE
AND ADMINISTRATIVE
200 FIFTH AVENUE
NEW YORK CITY

**BOY SCOUTS OF AMERICA**
INCORPORATED BY
SPECIAL ACT OF CONGRESS

Aug. 15, 1917.

Mr. James J. Hackett,
   500 W. 41st Street,
   NEW YORK CITY.

Dear Sir:

        I wish to thank you very much for your letter of
the 14th instant and your courtesy in returning to me a
letter from my young son Kenneth, who is now at our summer home on the St. John River, New Brunswick, Canada, and
which was lost by me on 34th Street, New York, while passing from the Waldorf to a taxicab.   The letter had been
brought to me from Washington with some other mail and had
slipped out of a larger envelope which contained it.  This
explains why you found it where you did and bearing the
Canadian stamps.  I appreciate your courtesy very much
and hope sometime it will be in my power to do you a return favor.   I am enclosing herewith the postage which
you used, in connection with the forwarding of the letter
to me.

        I am also sending you, under separate cover, a

Letter from President Colin Livingstone, 1917

copy of the Boy Scout hand-book, an organization
with which you perhaps have been in some way con-
nected and, of which, I happen to be the national
president.

                    Sincerely yours,

                                        President.

L-M

# DR. PAUL A. SIPLE

Dr. Paul A. Siple, explorer and military geographer, is perhaps best known for his explorations in the polar regions. He is the Scientific Advisor of Army Research Office.

Dr. Siple began his polar activities over thirty years ago when he was selected out of 60,000 candidates, as a Boy Scout representative to accompany Admiral Byrd on his first expedition to Little America. On this first trip, he served as dog driver, naturalist, and made a biological collection for the American Museum of Natural History. Since then, Dr. Siple has made six separate trips to Antarctica and in this period wintered over four times. He attained the rank of Eagle Scout in 1923 and earned 61 Merit Badges.

In December 1957, he returned from having served as the Station Scientific Leader at the IGY Geographic South Pole Station where he and seventeen companions spent the first year of occupation at one of the earth's poles, carrying out their scientific program despite record low temperatures of −102.1 degrees fahrenheit.

Dr. Siple has been the recipient of many honors for his polar, scientific, and military work. Notable among these are honorary academic degrees, distinguished civilian and military service medals, Boy Scout Silver Buffalo Award, Congressional Polar Medals, highest awards from leading Geographic Societies and many other distinguished organizations. He is one of the foremost authors on polar scientific papers and books. His first book, "A Boy Scout With Byrd" was published in 1931. He also has numerous patents on protective clothing and articles used in frigid climates.

Paul Siple was popular on the speaker circuit for 35 years. This is a page from a 1960 dinner program of Region 10.

# Council Listing

| Council Name | Council # | State | Yr.S | Yr.E |
|---|---|---|---|---|
| Alabama-Florida | 003 | AL | 1963 | |
| Birmingham Area | 002 | AL | 1915 | 1996 |
| Black Warrior | 006 | AL | 1922 | |
| Central Alabama | 002 | AL | 1996 | |
| Choccolocco | 001 | AL | 1921 | |
| Mobile Area | 004 | AL | 1927 | |
| Tennessee Valley | 659 | AL | 1934 | |
| Tukabatchee Area | 005 | AL | 1947 | |
| Midnight Sun | 696 | AK | 1960 | |
| Southeast Alaska | 608 | AK | 1955 | |
| Western Alaska | 610 | AK | 1955 | |
| Catalina | 011 | AZ | 1922 | |
| Copper | 009 | AZ | 1962 | 1977 |
| Desert Trails | 029 | AZ | 1959 | 1992 |
| Grand Canyon | 010 | AZ | 1993 | |
| Grand Canyon | 012 | AZ | 1944 | 1993 |
| Theodore Roosevelt | 010 | AZ | 1962 | 1993 |
| De Soto Area | 013 | AR | 1924 | |
| Eastern Arkansas Area | 015 | AR | 1935 | |
| Ouachita Area | 014 | AR | 1925 | |
| Quapaw Area | 018 | AR | 1927 | |
| Westark Area | 016 | AR | 1937 | |
| Canal Zone | 801 | | | 1979 |
| Alameda | 022 | CA | 1917 | |
| Buttes Area | 647 | CA | 1924 | 1992 |
| California Inland Empire | 045 | CA | 1973 | |
| Desert Pacific | 049 | CA | 1992 | |
| Forty Niner | 052 | CA | 1957 | |
| Golden Empire | 047 | CA | 1937 | |
| Grayback | 024 | CA | 1952 | 1974 |
| Great Western | 051 | CA | 1972 | 1985 |
| Long Beach Area | 032 | CA | 1943 | |

| Council Name | Council # | State | Yr.S | Yr.E |
|---|---|---|---|---|
| Los Angeles Area | 033 | CA | 1921 | |
| Los Padres | 053 | CA | 1993 | |
| Marin | 035 | CA | 1923 | |
| Mayfield County | 999 | CA | 1988 | |
| Mission | 053 | CA | 1929 | 1993 |
| Monterey Bay | 025 | CA | 1934 | |
| Mount Diablo | 023 | CA | 1951 | 1992 |
| Mount Diablo-Silverado | 023 | CA | 1992 | |
| Mount Larsen Area | 036 | CA | 1924 | 1992 |
| Mount Whitney Area | 054 | CA | 1929 | 1992 |
| Old Baldy | 043 | CA | 1922 | |
| Orange County | 039 | CA | 1973 | |
| Pacific Skyline | 031 | CA | | |
| Piedmont | 042 | CA | 1921 | |
| Redwood | 044 | CA | 1923 | 1992 |
| Redwood Empire | 041 | CA | 1992 | |
| Riverside County | 045 | CA | 1921 | 1972 |
| San Diego County | 049 | CA | 1921 | 1993 |
| San Francisco Bay Area | 028 | CA | 1965 | |
| San Gabriel Valley | 040 | CA | 1951 | |
| San Mateo County | 020 | CA | 1934 | 1993 |
| Santa Clara County | 055 | CA | 1935 | |
| Santa Lucia Area | 056 | CA | 1939 | 1993 |
| Sequoia | 027 | CA | 1925 | |
| Silverado Area | 038 | CA | 1923 | 1992 |
| Sonoma-Mendocino | 041 | CA | 1944 | 1992 |
| Southern Sierra | 030 | CA | 1966 | |
| Stanford Area | 031 | CA | 1941 | 1993 |
| Ventura County | 057 | CA | 1921 | |
| Verdugo Hills | 058 | CA | 1922 | |
| Western Los Angeles County | 051 | CA | | |
| Yosemite Area | 059 | CA | 1937 | |
| Denver Area | 061 | CO | 1921 | |
| Longs Peak | 062 | CO | 1929 | |

| Council Name | Council # | State | Yr.S | Yr.E |
|---|---|---|---|---|
| Pikes Peak | 060 | CO | 1925 | |
| Rocky Mountain | 063 | CO | 1925 | |
| Western Colorado | 064 | CO | 1942 | |
| Connecticut Rivers | 066 | CT | | |
| Fairfield County | 068 | CT | 1973 | |
| Greenwich | 067 | CT | 1922 | |
| Housatonic | 069 | CT | 1922 | |
| Indian Trails | 073 | CT | 1971 | |
| Long Rivers | 066 | CT | 1973 | |
| Quinnipiac | 074 | CT | 1935 | |
| Del-Mar-Va | 081 | DE | 1937 | |
| Direct Service | 800 | | 1967 | |
| D S Argentina | 800 | | | 1967 |
| D S Egypt | 800 | | | 1967 |
| D S Guatemala | 800 | | | 1967 |
| D S Hong Kong | 800 | | | 1967 |
| D S Indonesia | 800 | | | 1967 |
| D S Kenya | 800 | | | 1967 |
| D S Pakistan | 800 | | | 1967 |
| D S Panama | 800 | | | 1967 |
| D S Saudi Arabia | 800 | | | 1967 |
| D S Singapore | 800 | | | 1967 |
| D S Venezuela | 800 | | | 1967 |
| Central Florida | 083 | FL | 1922 | |
| Gulf Coast | 773 | FL | 1939 | |
| Gulf Ridge | 086 | FL | 1939 | |
| Gulf Stream | 085 | FL | 1937 | |
| North Florida | 087 | FL | 1939 | |
| Pinellas Area | 089 | FL | 1935 | 1978 |
| South Florida | 084 | FL | 1945 | |
| Southwest Florida | 088 | FL | 1967 | |
| Sunny Land | 724 | FL | 1926 | 1995 |
| Suwannee River Area | 664 | FL | 1925 | |
| West Central Florida | 089 | FL | 1978 | |

| Council Name | Council # | State | Yr.S | Yr.E |
|---|---|---|---|---|
| Alapha Area | 098 | GA | 1960 | |
| Atlanta Area | 092 | GA | 1921 | |
| Central Georgia | 096 | GA | 1923 | |
| Chattahoochee | 091 | GA | 1964 | |
| Chehaw | 097 | GA | 1985 | |
| Coastal Empire | 099 | GA | 1942 | |
| Flint River | 095 | GA | 1930 | |
| Georgia-Carolina | 093 | GA | 1941 | |
| George H. Lanier | 094 | GA | 1950 | 1989 |
| Northeast Georgia | 101 | GA | 1935 | |
| Northwest Georgia | 100 | GA | 1934 | |
| Okefenokee Area | 758 | GA | 1926 | |
| Southwest Georgia | 097 | GA | | 1985 |
| Transatlantic (Germany) | 802 | | 1959 | |
| Aloha | 104 | HI | 1957 | |
| Maui County | 102 | HI | 1941 | |
| Grand Teaton | 107 | ID | 1993 | |
| Idaho Panhandle | 110 | ID | 1929 | 1992 |
| Lewis-Clark | 108 | ID | 1946 | 1992 |
| Ore-Ida | 106 | ID | 1935 | |
| Snake River Area | 111 | ID | 1985 | |
| Snake River | 111 | ID | 1924 | |
| Tendoy Area | 109 | ID | 1934 | 1993 |
| Teaton Peaks | 107 | ID | 1925 | 1993 |
| Abraham Lincoln | 144 | IL | 1925 | |
| Arrowhead | 117 | IL | 1934 | 1991 |
| Blackhawk Area | 660 | IL | 1935 | |
| Cahokia Mound | 128 | IL | 1925 | 1990 |
| Chicago Area | 118 | IL | 1921 | |
| Chief Shabbona | 735 | IL | 1934 | 1968 |
| Des Plaines Valley | 147 | IL | | |
| Du Page Area | 148 | IL | 1929 | 1992 |
| Egyptian | 120 | IL | 1941 | 1994 |
| Illiana | 117 | IL | 1991 | |

| Council Name | Council # | State | Yr.S | Yr.E |
|---|---|---|---|---|
| Lincoln Trails | 121 | IL | 1939 | |
| Northeast Illinois | 129 | IL | 1971 | |
| Northwest Suburban | 751 | IL | 1926 | |
| Okaw Valley | 116 | IL | 1965 | |
| Piankeshaw | 739 | IL | 1926 | 1991 |
| Piasa Bird | 112 | IL | 1930 | 1990 |
| Prairie | 125 | IL | 1941 | 1993 |
| Prairielands | 117 | IL | | 1991 |
| Rainbow | 702 | IL | 1926 | |
| Saukee Area | 141 | IL | 1935 | 1993 |
| Thatcher Woods Area | 136 | IL | 1941 | 1993 |
| Three Fires | 127 | IL | | 1968 |
| Trails West | 112 | IL | 1991 | |
| Two Rivers | 127 | IL | 1968 | 1992 |
| Two Rivers-Dupage Area | 127 | IL | 1992 | |
| W D Boyce | 138 | IL | 1973 | |
| West Suburban | 147 | IL | 1921 | 1993 |
| Anthony Wayne Area | 157 | IN | 1925 | |
| Buffalo Trace | 156 | IN | 1955 | |
| Calumet | 152 | IN | 1966 | |
| Crossroads Of America | 160 | IN | 1972 | |
| George Rogers Clark Area | 143 | IN | 1927 | 1993 |
| Hoosier Trails | 145 | IN | 1973 | |
| La Salle | 165 | IN | | 1973 |
| Northern Indiana | 165 | IN | 1973 | 1990 |
| Pioneer Trails | 155 | IN | 1935 | 1973 |
| Sagamore | 162 | IN | 1973 | |
| Wabash Valley | 166 | IN | 1934 | |
| Hawkeye Area | 172 | IA | 1953 | |
| Illowa | 133 | IA | 1967 | |
| Mid-Iowa | 177 | IA | 1970 | |
| Mississippi Valley | 171 | IA | 1937 | 1964 |
| Northeast Iowa | 178 | IA | 1935 | |
| Prairie Gold Area | 179 | IA | | |

| Council Name | Council # | State | Yr.S | Yr.E |
|---|---|---|---|---|
| Southeast Iowa | 171 | IA | 1969 | 1993 |
| Winnebago | 173 | IA | 1939 | |
| Far East (Japan) | 803 | | 1961 | |
| Coronado Area | 192 | KS | 1939 | |
| Jayhawk Area | 197 | KS | 1929 | |
| Kanza | 190 | KS | 1946 | |
| Kaw | 191 | KS | 1929 | 1974 |
| Quivira | 198 | KS | 1940 | |
| Santa Fe Trail | 194 | KS | 1946 | |
| Audubon | 200 | KY | 1952 | 1994 |
| Blue Grass | 204 | KY | 1928 | |
| Four Rivers | 207 | KY | 1940 | 1994 |
| Lincoln Heritage | 205 | KY | 1993 | |
| Lonesome Pine | 203 | KY | 1934 | 1979 |
| Many Waters | 200 | KY | 1994 | |
| Old Kentucky Home | 205 | KY | 1953 | 1993 |
| Shawnee Trails | 200 | KY | | 1993 |
| Attakapas | 208 | LA | 1938 | |
| Calcasieu Area | 209 | LA | 1930 | |
| Evangeline Area | 212 | LA | 1924 | |
| Istrouma Area | 211 | LA | 1925 | |
| New Orleans Area | 214 | LA | 1927 | |
| Norwela | 215 | LA | 1923 | |
| Ouachita Valley | 213 | LA | 1925 | |
| Katahdin Area | 216 | ME | 1929 | |
| Pine Tree | 218 | ME | 1933 | |
| Baltimore Area | 220 | MD | 1925 | |
| Mason-Dixon | 221 | MD | 1956 | |
| National Capital Area | 082 | MD | | |
| Potomac | 757 | MD | 1937 | |
| Algonquin | 241 | MA | 1925 | |
| Annawon | 225 | MA | 1930 | |
| Boston | 227 | MA | 1921 | 1980 |
| Boston Minuteman | 227 | MA | 1993 | |

| Council Name | Council # | State | Yr.S | Yr.E |
|---|---|---|---|---|
| Cambridge | 229 | MA | 1919 | |
| Cape Cod & Islands | 224 | MA | 1981 | |
| Great Trails | 243 | MA | 1968 | |
| Greater Boston | 227 | MA | 1980 | 1993 |
| Greater Lowell | 238 | MA | 1929 | |
| Lone Tree | 749 | MA | 1926 | 1993 |
| Massachusetts Bay Federation | 850 | MA | 1976 | 1980 |
| Minuteman | 240 | MA | 1959 | 1993 |
| Moby Dick | 245 | MA | 1972 | |
| Mohegan | 254 | MA | 1955 | |
| Monadnock | 232 | MA | 1924 | 1993 |
| Nashua Valley | 230 | MA | 1964 | |
| North Bay | 236 | MA | 1966 | 1993 |
| North Essex | 712 | MA | 1925 | 1993 |
| Norumbega | 246 | MA | 1918 | |
| Old Colony | 249 | MA | 1969 | |
| Pioneer Valley | 234 | MA | 1961 | |
| Yankee Clipper | 236 | MA | 1993 | |
| Blue Water | 277 | MI | 1939 | |
| Chief Okemos | 271 | MI | 1932 | |
| Clinton Valley | 276 | MI | 1937 | |
| Detroit Area | 262 | MI | 1926 | |
| Gerald R. Ford | 266 | MI | 1975 | |
| Grand Valley | 266 | MI | 1936 | 1975 |
| Great Sauk Trail | 255 | MI | | 1993 |
| Hiawathaland | 261 | MI | 1945 | |
| Lake Huron Area | 265 | MI | 1971 | |
| Land O'Lakes | 269 | MI | 1971 | 1993 |
| Land O'Lakes-Wolverine | 255 | MI | 1993 | |
| Scenic Trails | 274 | MI | 1939 | |
| Southwest Michigan | 270 | MI | 1973 | |
| Tall Pine | 264 | MI | 1937 | |
| Timber Trails | 275 | MI | 1944 | 1975 |
| West Michigan Shores | 266 | MI | 1995 | |

| Council Name | Council # | State | Yr.S | Yr.E |
|---|---|---|---|---|
| Wolverine | 255 | MI | 1973 | 1993 |
| Central Minnesota | 296 | MN | 1926 | |
| Gamehaven | 299 | MN | 1925 | |
| Headwaters Area | 290 | MN | 1922 | 1994 |
| Indianhead | 295 | MN | 1954 | |
| Lake Superior | 286 | MN | 1959 | 1994 |
| Twin Valley | 283 | MN | 1969 | |
| Viking | 283 | MN | 1951 | |
| Voyageurs Area | 286 | MN | 1994 | |
| Andrew Jackson | 303 | MS | 1937 | |
| Choctaw Area | 302 | MS | 1935 | |
| Delta Area | 300 | MS | 1924 | 1993 |
| Pine Burr Area | 304 | MS | 1935 | |
| Pushmataha Area | 691 | MS | 1936 | |
| Yocona Area | 748 | MS | 1926 | |
| Great Rivers | 653 | MO | 1951 | |
| Greater St.Louis Area | 312 | MO | 1994 | |
| Heart of America | 307 | MO | 1974 | |
| Mo-Kan Area | 306 | MO | 1929 | 1994 |
| Ozark Trails | 306 | MO | 1994 | |
| Ozarks | 308 | MO | 1965 | 1994 |
| Pony Express | 311 | MO | 1932 | |
| St. Louis Area | 312 | MO | 1911 | 1994 |
| Southeast Missouri | 305 | MO | 1930 | 1993 |
| Montana | 315 | MT | 1973 | |
| Yellowstone Valley | 318 | MT | 1928 | 1993 |
| Cornhusker | 324 | NE | 1929 | |
| Mid-America | 326 | NE | 1964 | |
| Overland Trails | 322 | NE | 1954 | |
| Tri Trails | 323 | NE | 1954 | 1994 |
| Wyo-Braska Area | 325 | NE | 1936 | 1974 |
| Boulder Dam Area | 328 | NV | 1944 | |
| Nevada Area | 329 | NV | 1929 | |
| Daniel Webster | 330 | NH | 1929 | |

| Council Name | Council # | State | Yr.S | Yr.E |
|---|---|---|---|---|
| Aheka | 354 | NJ | 1939 | 1972 |
| Atlantic Area | 331 | NJ | 1926 | 1992 |
| Bayonne | 332 | NJ | 1918 | 1993 |
| Bergen County | 350 | NJ | 1969 | |
| Burlington County | 690 | NJ | 1925 | |
| Canden County | 335 | NJ | 1921 | |
| Essex | 336 | NJ | 1975 | |
| George Washington | 362 | NJ | 1937 | |
| Hudson-Hamilton | 348 | NJ | 1968 | 1993 |
| Hudson Liberty | 348 | NJ | 1993 | |
| Jersey Shore | 341 | NJ | 1991 | |
| Middlesex | 344 | NJ | 1929 | 1969 |
| Monmouth | 347 | NJ | 1928 | |
| Morris-Sussex Area | 343 | NJ | 1936 | |
| Ocean County | 341 | NJ | 1940 | 1992 |
| Passaic Valley | 353 | NJ | 1973 | |
| Ridgewood-Glen Rock | 359 | NJ | 1922 | |
| Southern New Jersey | 334 | NJ | 1967 | |
| Tamarack | 333 | NJ | 1935 | 1985 |
| Thomas Edison | 352 | NJ | 1969 | |
| Union | 338 | NJ | 1928 | 1980 |
| Watchung Area | 358 | NJ | 1926 | |
| Conquistador | 413 | NM | 1952 | |
| Great Southwest Area | 412 | NM | 1982 | |
| Great Southwest | 412 | NM | 1976 | 1982 |
| Adirondack | 394 | NY | 1927 | |
| Allegheny Highlands | 382 | NY | 1973 | |
| Baden Powell | 381 | NY | 1975 | |
| Bronx Valley | 370 | NY | 1923 | 1958 |
| Cayuga County | 366 | NY | 1924 | |
| Chautauqua County | 382 | NY | 1942 | 1973 |
| Dutchess County | 374 | NY | 1919 | 1995 |
| Finger Lakes | 391 | NY | 1924 | |
| Five Rivers | 375 | NY | 1990 | |

| Council Name | Council # | State | Yr.S | Yr.E |
|---|---|---|---|---|
| General Herkimer | 400 | NY | 1934 | |
| General Sullivan | 779 | NY | 1927 | 1992 |
| Genesee | 667 | NY | 1925 | 1994 |
| Governor Clinton | 364 | NY | 1971 | 1990 |
| Greater New York | 640 | NY | 1936 | |
| G N Y Bronx | 642 | NY | 1915 | |
| G N Y Brooklyn | 641 | NY | 1911 | |
| G N Y Manhattan | 643 | NY | 1918 | |
| G N Y Queens | 644 | NY | 1915 | |
| G N Y Staten Island | 645 | NY | 1928 | |
| Greater Niagara Frontier | 380 | NY | 1965 | |
| Hiawatha | 373 | NY | 1969 | |
| Hudson-Delaware | 392 | NY | 1957 | 1995 |
| Hudson Valley | 392 | NY | 1995 | |
| Iroquois | 395 | NY | 1969 | 1981 |
| Iroquios Trail | 376 | NY | | |
| Jefferson Lewis | 408 | NY | 1932 | 1982 |
| Land of the Oneidas | 395 | NY | 1982 | |
| Lewiston Trail | 385 | NY | 1937 | 1994 |
| Mohican | 378 | NY | 1927 | |
| Nassau County | 386 | NY | 1916 | |
| Otetiana | 397 | NY | 1943 | |
| Otschodela | 393 | NY | 1927 | |
| Rip Van Winkle | 405 | NY | 1950 | |
| Rockland County | 683 | NY | 1924 | 1995 |
| St. Lawrence | 403 | NY | 1938 | 1982 |
| Saratoga County | 684 | NY | 1924 | 1990 |
| Schenectady County | 399 | NY | 1924 | 1991 |
| Seaway Valley | 403 | NY | 1982 | |
| Seneca | 750 | NY | 1929 | 1975 |
| Sir William Johnson | 377 | NY | 1937 | 1990 |
| Steuben Area | 402 | NY | 1931 | 1991 |
| Suffolk County | 404 | NY | 1919 | |
| Sullivan Trail | 375 | NY | 1947 | 1991 |

| Council Name | Council # | State | Yr.S | Yr.E |
|---|---|---|---|---|
| Susquenango | 368 | NY | 1925 | |
| Twin Rivers | 364 | NY | 1990 | |
| Upper Mohawk | 406 | NY | 1937 | 1981 |
| Westchester Putnam | 388 | NY | 1974 | |
| Cape Fear Area | 425 | NC | 1930 | |
| Central North Carolina | 416 | NC | 1937 | |
| Cherokee | 417 | NC | 1923 | 1994 |
| Daniel Boone | 414 | NC | 1925 | |
| East Carolina | 426 | NC | 1932 | |
| General Greene | 418 | NC | 1947 | 1991 |
| Mecklenburg County | 415 | NC | 1942 | |
| Occoneechee | 421 | NC | 1929 | |
| Old Hickory | 427 | NC | 1942 | |
| Old North State | 070 | NC | 1992 | |
| Piedmont | 420 | NC | 1924 | |
| Tuscarora | 424 | NC | 1923 | |
| Uwharrie | 419 | NC | 1992 | 1991 |
| Northern Lights | 429 | ND | 1974 | |
| Red River Valley | 429 | ND | 1925 | 1973 |
| Black Swamp Area | 449 | OH | 1992 | |
| Buckeye | 436 | OH | 1958 | |
| Central Ohio | 441 | OH | 1930 | 1993 |
| Chief Logan | 464 | OH | 1994 | 1993 |
| Columbiana | 455 | OH | 1953 | 1991 |
| Dan Beard | 438 | OH | 1956 | |
| Firelands Area | 458 | OH | 1925 | 1993 |
| Fort Steuben Area | 459 | OH | 1929 | 1991 |
| Great Trail | 433 | OH | 1970 | |
| Greater Cleveland | 440 | OH | 1929 | |
| Greater Western Reserve | 463 | OH | 1993 | |
| Harding Area | 443 | OH | 1926 | 1993 |
| Heart of Ohio | 450 | OH | | |
| Johnny Appleseed Area | 453 | OH | 1926 | 1993 |
| Licking County | 451 | OH | 1922 | 1987 |

| Council Name | Council # | State | Yr.S | Yr.E |
|---|---|---|---|---|
| Mahoning Valley | 466 | OH | 1927 | 1993 |
| Miami Valley | 444 | OH | 1949 | |
| Mound Builder's Area | 454 | OH | 1932 | 1985 |
| Muskingum Valley | 467 | OH | 1957 | |
| Northeast Ohio | 463 | OH | 1929 | 1993 |
| Put-Han-Sen Area | 449 | OH | 1930 | 1991 |
| Scioto Area | 457 | OH | 1931 | 1993 |
| Shawnee | 452 | OH | 1926 | 1991 |
| Simon Kenton | 441 | OH | | |
| Tecumseh | 439 | OH | 1929 | |
| Toledo Area | 460 | OH | 1928 | |
| Western Reserve | 461 | OH | 1948 | 1993 |
| Arbuckle Area | 468 | OK | 1945 | |
| Black Beaver | 471 | OK | 1930 | |
| Cherokee Area Oklahoma | 469 | OK | 1925 | |
| Eastern Oklahoma | 478 | OK | 1948 | 1983 |
| Great Salt Plains | 474 | OK | 1927 | |
| Indian Nations | 488 | OK | 1957 | |
| Last Frontier | 480 | OK | 1939 | |
| Will Rogers | 473 | OK | 1948 | |
| Cascade Area | 493 | OR | 1926 | 1992 |
| Cascade Pacific | 492 | OR | 1993 | |
| Columbia Pacific | 492 | OR | 1965 | 1992 |
| Creater Lake | 491 | OR | 1925 | |
| Modoc Area | 494 | OR | 1936 | 1993 |
| Oregon Trail | 697 | OR | 1944 | |
| Panama Canal | 801 | | | 1987 |
| Allegheny Trails | 527 | PA | 1967 | 1993 |
| Bucks County | 777 | PA | 1927 | |
| Bucktail | 509 | PA | 1930 | |
| Chief Cornplanter | 538 | PA | 1953 | |
| Chester County | 539 | PA | 1919 | |
| Columbia-Montour | 504 | PA | 1931 | |
| East Valley Area | 530 | PA | 1973 | 1993 |

| Council Name | Council # | State | Yr.S | Yr.E |
|---|---|---|---|---|
| Elk Lick | 499 | PA | 1947 | 1973 |
| Forest Lakes | 501 | PA | 1962 | 1990 |
| French Creek | 532 | PA | 1972 | |
| Greater Pittsburgh | 527 | PA | 1993 | |
| Hawk Mountain | 528 | PA | 1971 | |
| Juniata Valley | 497 | PA | 1929 | |
| Keystone Area | 515 | PA | 1948 | |
| Lancaster County | 519 | PA | 1924 | 1970 |
| Lancaster-Lebanon | 524 | PA | 1995 | |
| Lebanon County | 650 | PA | 1924 | 1970 |
| Minsi Trails | 502 | PA | 1968 | |
| Moraine Trails | 500 | PA | 1973 | |
| Northeastern Pennsylvania | 501 | PA | 1990 | |
| Penn Mountains | 522 | PA | 1969 | 1990 |
| Penn's Woods | 508 | PA | 1970 | |
| Pennsylvania Dutch | 524 | PA | | 1995 |
| Philadelphia | 525 | PA | 1914 | 1996 |
| Susquehanna | 553 | PA | 1974 | |
| Susquehanna Valley Area | 533 | PA | 1927 | 1974 |
| Valley Forge | 507 | PA | 1936 | 1996 |
| Washington Trails | 511 | PA | 1944 | 1972 |
| Westmoreland-Fayette | 512 | PA | 1937 | |
| York Adams Area | 544 | PA | 1931 | |
| Puerto Rico | 661 | | | |
| Narragansett | 546 | RI | 1930 | |
| Blue Ridge | 551 | SC | 1932 | |
| Central South Carolina | 553 | SC | 1929 | 1978 |
| Coastal Carolina | 550 | SC | 1941 | |
| Indian Waters | 553 | SC | 1978 | |
| Palmetto Area | 549 | SC | 1935 | |
| Pee Dee Area | 552 | SC | 1928 | |
| Black Hills Area | 695 | SD | 1930 | |
| Pheasant | 693 | SD | 1942 | 1978 |
| Sioux | 733 | SD | 1927 | |

| Council Name | Council # | State | Yr.S | Yr.E |
|---|---|---|---|---|
| Cherokee Area | 556 | TN | 1943 | |
| Chickasaw | 558 | TN | 1925 | |
| Great Smoky Mountain | 557 | TN | 1943 | |
| Middle Tennessee | 560 | TN | 1949 | |
| Sequoyah | 713 | TN | 1931 | |
| West Tennessee Area | 559 | TN | 1939 | |
| Adobe Walls | 569 | TX | 1938 | 1987 |
| Alamo Area | 583 | TX | 1925 | |
| Bay Area | 574 | TX | 1937 | |
| Buffalo Trail | 567 | TX | 1923 | |
| Caddo Area | 584 | TX | 1936 | |
| Capitol Area | 564 | TX | 1934 | |
| Chisholm Trail | 561 | TX | 1926 | |
| Circle Ten | 571 | TX | 1928 | |
| Comanche Trail | 479 | TX | 1932 | |
| Concho Valley | 741 | TX | 1926 | |
| East Texas Area | 585 | TX | 1931 | |
| Golden Spread | 562 | TX | 1987 | |
| Gulf Coast Texas | 577 | TX | 1929 | |
| Heart O'Texas | 662 | TX | 1929 | |
| Llano Estacado | 562 | TX | 1939 | 1987 |
| Longhorn | 582 | TX | 1948 | |
| Netseo Trails | 580 | TX | 1955 | |
| Northwest Texas | 587 | TX | 1937 | |
| Rio Grande | 775 | TX | 1947 | |
| Sam Houston Area | 576 | TX | 1936 | |
| South Plains | 694 | TX | 1925 | |
| Texoma Valley | 566 | TX | 1966 | 1993 |
| Three Rivers | 578 | TX | 1970 | |
| Yucca | 573 | TX | 1937 | |
| Cache Valley | 588 | UT | 1924 | 1992 |
| Great Salt Lake | 590 | UT | 1951 | |
| Lake Bonneville | 589 | UT | 1951 | 1992 |
| Trapper Trails | 589 | UT | 1992 | |

| Council Name | Council # | State | Yr.S | Yr.E |
|---|---|---|---|---|
| Utah National Parks | 591 | UT | 1936 | |
| Virgin Islands | 410 | | | |
| Green Mountain | 592 | VT | 1972 | |
| Blue Ridge Mountains | 599 | VA | 1972 | |
| Colonial Virginia | 595 | VA | 1992 | |
| Old Dominion Area | 601 | VA | 1927 | 1992 |
| Peninsula | 595 | VA | 1929 | 1992 |
| Robert E. Lee | 602 | VA | 1953 | |
| Shenandoah Area | 598 | VA | 1928 | |
| Stonewall Jackson Area | 763 | VA | 1927 | |
| Tidewater | 596 | VA | 1935 | |
| Blue Mountain | 604 | WA | 1923 | |
| Chief Seattle | 609 | WA | 1954 | |
| Evergreen Area | 606 | WA | 1941 | 1993 |
| Fort Simcoe | 614 | WA | 1954 | 1992 |
| Grand Columbia | 614 | WA | 1992 | |
| Inland Empire Washington | 611 | WA | 1931 | 1987 |
| Island Northwest | 611 | WA | 1987 | |
| Mount Baker Area | 603 | WA | 1929 | |
| Mount Rainier | 612 | WA | 1948 | 1993 |
| North Central Washington | 613 | WA | 1924 | 1992 |
| Olympic Area | 605 | WA | | 1974 |
| Pacific Harbors | 612 | WA | 1993 | |
| Tumwater Area | 737 | WA | 1934 | 1993 |
| Twin Harbors Area | 607 | WA | 1930 | 1993 |
| Allohak | 618 | WV | 1990 | |
| Appalachian | 701 | WV | 1956 | 1991 |
| Buckskin | 617 | WV | 1949 | |
| Central West Virginia | 616 | WV | 1941 | 1990 |
| Chief Cornstalk | 756 | WV | 1954 | 1990 |
| Kootaga Area | 618 | WV | 1933 | 1990 |
| Mountaineer Area | 615 | WV | 1928 | |
| National Trail | 619 | WV | 1966 | 1991 |
| Ohio River Valley | 619 | WV | 1991 | |

| Council Name | Council # | State | Yr.S | Yr.E |
|---|---|---|---|---|
| Tri-State Area | 672 | WV | 1935 | |
| Bay Lakes | 635 | WI | 1973 | |
| Chippewa Valley | 637 | WI | 1928 | |
| Four Lakes | 628 | WI | 1929 | |
| Gateway Area | 624 | WI | 1925 | |
| Milwaukee County | 629 | WI | 1929 | |
| Potawatomi Area | 651 | WI | 1931 | |
| Samoset | 627 | WI | 1930 | |
| Sinnissippi | 626 | WI | 1966 | |
| Southeast Wisconsin | 634 | WI | 1972 | |
| Central Wyoming | 638 | WY | 1929 | |
| Jim Bridger | 639 | WY | 1946 | 1992 |

The author's vigil fire, 1985.

# Lodge Listings

| No. | Lodge Name | Yr. | Council | ST | Notes |
|---|---|---|---|---|---|
| 001 | Unami | 1915 | Philadelphia | PA | Absorbed 8 in 1924. |
| 002 | Trenton | 1919 | Trenton-Mercer | NJ | Rechartered in 1920s. Changed name. |
| 002 | Sanhican | 1920s | George Washington | NJ | |
| 003 | Pamunkey | 1919 | Richmond | VA | Rechartered in 1945. Changed name. |
| 003 | Nawakwa | 1945 | Robert E. Lee | VA | |
| 004 | Ranachqua | 1920 | Bronx | NY | |
| 005 | Indiandale | 1921 | Daniel Boone | PA | Changed name in 1920. |
| 005 | Minsi | 1922 | Daniel Boone | PA | Merged 1971 with 125 to form 5. |
| 005 | Kittatinny | 1971 | Hawk Mountain | PA | |
| 006 | Umpah | 1921 | Westmoreland-Fayette | PA | Rechartered in 1939. |
| 006 | Wagion | 1939 | Westmoreland-Fayette | PA | |
| 007 | Moqua | 1922 | Chicago | IL | Merged 1929 with 13, 21, 23, and 25 to form 7. |
| 007 | Owasippe | 1929 | Chicago | IL | From merger of 7, 13, 21, 23, and 25. |
| 008 | Unalactigo | 1921 | Philadephia Camp Biddle | PA | Absorbed into 1 in 1924. |
| 008 | Mascoutens | 1972 | Southeast Wisconsin | WI | From merger of 153 and 524. |
| 009 | Cowaw | 1922 | Raritan | NJ | Merged 1969 with 287 to form 9. |
| 009 | Narraticong | 1969 | Thomas E. Edison | NJ | From merger of 9 and 287. |
| 010 | Wawonaissa | 1921 | Central Union | NJ | Disbanded 1922. |
| 010 | Sassacus | 1972 | Indian Trails | CT | From merger of 297 and 388. Merged 1995 with 59. |
| 010 | Tschitani | 1995 | Connecticut Rivers | CT | From merger with 59. |
| 011 | Susquehannock | 1922 | Keystone Area | PA | |
| 012 | Nentico | 1922 | Baltimore Area | MD | |
| 013 | Wakay | 1922 | Chicago | IL | Merged 1929 with 7, 21, 23, and 25 to form 7. |
| 013 | Wiatava | 1973 | Orange County | CA | From merger of 298 and 430. |
| 014 | Pamrapaugh | 1921 | Bayonne | NJ | Merged 1993 with 37 to form 14. |
| 014 | Mantowagan | 1993 | Hudson-Liberty | NJ | |
| 015 | Chappegat | 1923 | Siwanoy | NY | Merged 1957 with 47 to form 15. |
| 015 | Mide | 1957 | Hutchinson River | NY | Merged 1973 with 246 to form 15. |
| 015 | Ktemaque | 1973 | Westchester-Putnam | NY | |
| 016 | Tonkawampus | 1924 | Viking | MN | |

| No. | Lodge Name | Yr. | Council | ST | Notes |
|-----|-----------|-----|---------|----|----|
| 017 | Cuyahoga | 1924 | Greater Cleveland | OH | Disbanded 1920s. Rechartered 1950s. |
| 018 | Wyona | 1925 | Columbia-Montour | PA | |
| 019 | Buffalo | 1925 | Schenectady County | NY | Changed name in 1920s. |
| 019 | Sisilija | 1925 | Schenectady County | NY | Merged 1991 with 181 to form 19. |
| 019 | Ganienkeh | 1992 | Twin Rivers | NY | |
| 020 | Unalachtigo | 1925 | Del-Mar-Va | DE | Disbanded prior to 1936. |
| 020 | Nentego | 1957 | Del-Mar-Va | DE | |
| 021 | Sqechnaxen | 1922 | Chicago | IL | Changed name in 1920s. |
| 021 | Checaugau | 1922 | Chicago | IL | Merged 1929 with 7, 13, 23, and 25 to form 7. |
| 021 | Wulakamike | 1973 | Crossroads Of America | IN | From merger of 222, 308, and 512. |
| 022 | Octoraro | 1926 | Chester County | PA | |
| 023 | Blackhawk | 1922 | Chicago | IL | Merged 1929 with 7, 13, 21, and 25 to form 7. |
| 023 | Wenasa Quenhotan | 1973 | W.D. Boyce | IL | From merger of 63, 143, and 191. |
| 024 | Shu-Shu-Gah | 1925? | GNY Brooklyn | NY | |
| 025 | Garrison | 1922 | Chicago | IL | Merged 1929 with 7, 13, 21, and 23 to form 7. |
| 025 | Nacha Tindey | 1975 | West Michigan Shores | MI | From merger of 79 and 401. |
| 026 | Blue Ox | 1927 | Gamehaven | MN | Absorbed 1946 part of 144. Disbanded 1950. Rechartered 1953. |
| 027 | Mohawks | 1927 | Columbia | NY | Disbanded prior to 1936. Absorbed 1944 into 181. |
| 027 | Pa-Hin | 1976 | Northern Lights | ND | From merger of 52, 176, 183, and 371. |
| 028 | Mohican | 1927 | Green | NY | Rechartered 1947 after previously disbanding. Changed name to Half Moon. |
| 028 | Half Moon | 1927 | Rip Van Winkle | NY | |
| 029 | Chippewa | 1927 | Clinton Valley | MI | |
| 030 | Winingus | 1927 | General Sullivan | PA | Merged 1992 with 186 to form 30. |
| 030 | Tkaen Dod | 1993 | Five Rivers | NY | |
| 031 | Chemahgwa | 1927 | Central Minnesota | MN | Rechartered 1945 after previously disbanding. Changed name to Naguonabe. |
| 031 | Naguonabe | 1927 | Central Minnesota | MN | |
| 032 | Kitchawonk | 1927 | Yonkers | NY | Rechartered 1942 after previously disbanding. Changed name to Tahawus. |
| 032 | Tahawus | 1927 | Yonkers | NY | Absorbed 1955 into 246. |

| No. | Lodge Name | Yr. | Council | ST | Notes |
|-----|-----------|-----|---------|----|-------|
| 032 | Kishkakon | 1991 | West | IL | From merger 1991 of 94 and 126. |
| 033 | Ajapeu | 1927 | Bucks County | PA | |
| 034 | Gonlix | 1928 | Madison County | NY | Merged 1968 with 500 to form 34. |
| 034 | Ko Mosh I Oni | 1968 | Iroquois | NY | Merged 1981 with 465 to form 34. |
| 034 | Ona Yote | 1982 | Land Of The Oneidas | NY | |
| 035 | Wichita | 1928 | Northwest Texas | TX | |
| 036 | Mitigwa | 1928 | Beaumont Area | TX | Changed name in 1950. |
| 036 | Meche | 1928 | Trinity-Neches | TX | Merged 1970 with 62 to form 578. |
| 037 | Achtu | 1928 | Hudson | NJ | Merged 1969 with 440 to form 37. |
| 037 | Elauwit | 1969 | Hudson-Hamilton | NJ | Merged 1993 with 14 to form 14. |
| 037 | Ka-Ti Missi Sipi | 1995 | Mississippi Valley | IL | From merger 1995 of 80 and 136. |
| 038 | Shaubena | 1928 | Wigwam | IL | Absorbed 45 in 1938. Changed name in 1941. |
| 038 | Inali | 1928 | Prairie | IL | Merged 1994 with 170 to form 38. |
| 038 | Konepaka Ketiwa | 1994 | Illowa | IA | |
| 039 | Swatara | 1928 | Lebanon County | PA | Merged 1972 with 519 to form 39. |
| 039 | Wunita Gokhos | 1972 | Lancaster-Lebanon | PA | |
| 040 | Ma-Ka-Ja-Wan | 1929 | Northest Illinois | IL | Absorbed 248 in 1969 and 215 in 1971. |
| 041 | Natokiokan | 1929 | Du Page Area | IL | Merged 1995 with 106 to form 41. |
| 041 | Lawaneu Allanque | 1995 | Three Fires | IL | |
| 042 | Osage | 1929 | Ozark Area | MO | Merged 1995 with 91 to form 42. |
| 042 | Wah-Sha-She | 1995 | Ozark Trails | MO | |
| 043 | Delmont | 1929 | Valley Forge | PA | |
| 044 | Pohopoco | 1929 | Lehigh County | PA | Merged 1969 with 58 and 476 to form 44. |
| 044 | Witauchsoman | 1969 | Minsi Trails | PA | |
| 045 | Pokawachne | 1929 | Kewanee Area | IL | Absorbed by 38 in 1938. |
| 045 | Tiwahe | 1992 | Pacific | CA | From merger of 436 and part of 532. |
| 046 | Eriez | 1929 | Washington Trail | PA | Merged 1972 with 251 and 256 to form 46. |
| 046 | Langundowi | 1972 | French Creek | PA | |
| 047 | Hanigus | 1930 | Bronx Valley | NY | Merged 1957 with 15 to form 15. |
| 047 | Amangi Nacha | 1993 | Golden Empire | CA | From merger 1993 of 354, 395, and 485. |
| 048 | Wakpominee | 1930 | Mohican | NY | |
| 049 | Suanhacky | 1930 | GNY Queens | NY | |

| No. | Lodge Name | Yr. | Council | ST | Notes |
|-----|-----------|-----|---------|-----|-------|
| 050 | Cherokee | 1930 | Birmingham Area | AL | |
| 051 | Shawnee | 1930 | Greater St.Louis Area | MO | |
| 052 | Chan-O-Wapi | 1930 | Missouri Valley | ND | Merged 1976 with 176, 183, and 371 to form 27. |
| 052 | Moswetuset | 1994 | Boston Minuteman | MA | From merger 1994 of 195 and 261. |
| 053 | Mini Ska | 1930 | Cedar Valley | MN | Changed name after 1955. |
| 053 | Wapaha | 1930 | Cedar Valley | MN | Merged 1969 with 69 to form 53. |
| 053 | Midewiwin | 1969 | Twin Valley | MN | Changed name in 1975. |
| 053 | Wahpekute | 1969 | Twin Valley | MN | |
| 054 | Allemakewink | 1930 | Morris Sussex Area | NJ | |
| 055 | Waukheon | 1930 | Piankeshaw | IL | Merged 1994 with 92 to form 55. |
| 055 | Illini | 1994 | Prairielands | IL | |
| 056 | Okiciyapi | 1930 | Texoma Valley | TX | Disbanded 1930s. Reorganized 1949. Merged 1994 with 101 to form 101 |
| 056 | Wapashuwi | 1995 | Greater Western Reserve | OH | From merger of 114, 368, and 396. |
| 057 | Kuwewanik | 1931 | Allegheny | PA | Merged 1966 with 242 to form 57. |
| 057 | Kiasutha | 1967 | Allegheny Trails | PA | Merged 1993 with 67 to form 57. |
| 057 | Enda Lechauhanne | 1993 | Greater Pittsburgh | PA | |
| 058 | Kittatinny | 1931 | Delaware Valley | PA | Rechartered 1948 after previously disbanding. |
| 058 | Ah-Pace | 1931 | Delaware Valley | PA | Merged 1969 with 44 and 476 to form 44. |
| 058 | Ut-In Selica | 1994 | Mount Diablo-Silverado | CA | From merger of 263 and 468. |
| 059 | Wahquimacut | 1931 | Middlesex | CT | Rechartered 1957 after previously disbanding. |
| 059 | Kiehtan | 1931 | Middlesex County | CT | Merged 1973 with 217, 234, 491, and 558 to form 59. |
| 059 | Eluwak | 1973 | Long Rivers | CT | Merged 1995 with 10 to form 10. |
| 060 | Aina Topa Hutsi | 1931 | Alamo Area | TX | |
| 061 | Shaginappi | 1932 | Badger | WI | Merged 1974 with 73, 194, 233, 244, and 501 to form 61. |
| 061 | Awase | 1974 | Bay Lakes | WI | |
| 062 | Sioux | 1932 | Sabine Area | TX | Merged 1970 with 36 to form 578. |
| 062 | Talligewi | 1995 | Lincoln Heritage | KY | From merger 1995 of 65 and 123. |
| 063 | Potawatomie | 1932 | Corn Belt | IL | Merged 1973 with 143 and 191 to form 23. |
| 063 | Ohlone | 1995 | Pacific Skyline | CA | From merger 1995 of 207 and 528. |

| No. | Lodge Name | Yr. | Council | ST | Notes |
|-----|-----------|-----|---------|----|----|
| 064 | Skanondo | 1932 | Hudson-Delaware | NY | Merged 1995 with 443 and 444 to form ???. |
| 065 | Tseyedin | 1932 | George Rogers Clark | IN | Merged 1994 with 123 to form 62. |
| 065 | Tecumseh | 1996 | Simon Kenton | OH | From merger of 93, 109, and 350. |
| 066 | Yah-Tah-Ney-Si-Kess | 1933 | Northern New Mexico | NM | Changed name in 1962. |
| 066 | Yah-Tah-Hey-Si-Kess | 1933 | Great Southwest Area | NM | |
| 067 | Anicus | 1933 | East Boroughs | PA | Merged 1973 with 130 to form 67. |
| 067 | Tanacharison | 1973 | East Valley Area | PA | Merged 1993 with 57. |
| 068 | Watchung | 1933 | Watchung Area | NJ | Changed name in 1939. |
| 068 | Miquin | 1933 | Watchung Area | NJ | Absorbed 431 in 1980. |
| 069 | Tribe Of Mazasha | 1933 | Minnesota Valley Area | MN | Changed name in 1944. |
| 069 | Mazasha | 1933 | Minnesota Valley Area | MN | Merged 1969 with 53 to form 53. |
| 070 | Tali Taktaki | 1933 | General Greene | NC | Merged 1992 with 208 to form 70. |
| 070 | Keyauwee | 1992 | Old North State | NC | Merged 1994 with 163 to form 70. |
| 070 | Tsoiatsi Tsogali'i | 1995 | Old North State | NC | |
| 071 | Ohowa | 1933 | Monmouth-Ocean | NJ | Reorganized 1950 after previous lapse. Changed name. |
| 071 | Na-Tasi-Hi | 1951 | Monmouth | NJ | Changed name in 1953. |
| 071 | Na-Tsi-Hi | 1951 | Monmouth | NJ | |
| 072 | Tejas | 1934 | East Texas Area | TX | |
| 073 | Ay-Ashe | 1934 | Manitowoc | WI | Changed name in 1937. |
| 073 | Sinawa | 1934 | Waumegesako | WI | Merged 1974 with 61, 194, 233, 244, and 501 to form 61. |
| 074 | Timmeu | 1934 | Northest Iowa | IA | |
| 075 | Miami | 1935 | Anthony Wayne Area | IN | Changed name in 1938. |
| 075 | Kiskakon | 1935 | Anthony Wayne Area | IN | Absorbed 1973 half of 142. |
| 076 | Hunnikick | 1935 | Burlington County | NJ | |
| 077 | Lekau | 1935 | Camden County | NJ | |
| 078 | Antelope | 1935 | Eastern New Mexico | NM | Changed name after 1955. |
| 078 | Kwahadi | 1935 | Conquistador | NM | |
| 079 | Jibshe-Wanagan | 1935 | Grand Valley | MI | Merged 1975 with 401 to form 25. |
| 080 | Silver Tomahawk | 1935 | Southeast Iowa | IA | Merged 1995 with 136 to form 37. |
| 081 | Mannaseh | 1935 | Mississippi Valley | IL | Merged 1966 with 115 to form 81. |
| 081 | Taleka | 1966 | Okaw Valley | IL | |
| 082 | Man-A-Hattin | 1936 | GNY Manhattan | NY | |

| No. | Lodge Name | Yr. | Council | ST | Notes |
|---|---|---|---|---|---|
| 083 | Allogagan | 1936 | Valley | MA | Absorbed 277 in 1960. |
| 084 | Tamarack | 1936 | Tamarack | NJ | Changed name in 1950. |
| 084 | Wakanta | 1936 | Tamarack | NJ | Disbanded 1986. Absorbed by 178 and 484. |
| 085 | Kiondashama | 1936 | Tampa Bay | FL | Changed name in 1938. |
| 085 | Seminole | 1936 | Gulf Ridge | FL | |
| 086 | Wiccopee | 1936 | Hendrick-Hudson | NY | Merged 1951 with 246 to form 246. |
| 087 | Bob White | 1936 | Georgia-Carolina | GA | |
| 088 | Munhacke | 1936 | Portage Trails | MI | Merged 1973 with 332 to form 88. |
| 088 | Allohak | 1973 | Wolverine | MI | Merged 1994 with 206 to form 88. |
| 088 | Manitous | 1995 | Great Sauk Trail | MI | |
| 089 | Kepayshowink | 1936 | Saginaw Bay Area | MI | Absorbed 214 in 1961. Merged 1972 with 469 to form 89. |
| 089 | Mischigonong | 1972 | Lake Huron Area | MI | |
| 090 | Canalino | 1936 | Mission | CA | Merged 1996 with 304 to form 90. |
| 090 | Chumash | 1996 | Los Padres | CA | |
| 091 | Nik-Ka-Ga-Hah | 1936 | Mo-Kan | MO | Merged 1995 with 42 to form 42. |
| 092 | Illini | 1936 | Arrowhead | IL | Merged 1994 with 55 to form 55. |
| 093 | Katinonkwat | 1936 | Central Ohio | OH | Absorbed 420 in 1987. Merged 1996 with 109 and 350 to form 65. |
| 094 | Blackhawk | 1936 | Piasa Bird | IL | Merged 1990 with 126 to form 32. |
| 094 | Tatanka-Anpetu-Wi | 1994 | Overland Trails | NE | From merger 1994 of 510 and 517. |
| 095 | Ty-Ohni | 1936 | Otetiana | NY | |
| 096 | Tesomas | 1936 | Samoset | WI | Changed name in 1939. |
| 096 | Tom Kita Chara | 1936 | Samoset | WI | |
| 097 | Cha-Pa | 1936 | Southwest Iowa | IA | Merged 1965 with 445 to form 97. |
| 097 | Kit-Ke-Hak-O-Kut | 1965 | Mid-America | NE | |
| 098 | Navajo | 1937 | Old Baldy | CA | |
| 099 | Te Jas | 1937 | Capitol Area | TX | Changed name in 1940. |
| 099 | Tonkawa | 1937 | Capitol Area | TX | |
| 100 | Jonito-Otora | 1937 | Southeast Missouri | MO | Rechartered 1956 after previously disbanding with a name change. |
| 100 | Anpetu-we | 1937 | Southeast Missouri | MO | Absorbed 240 in 1994. Merged 1995 with 51 to form ???. |
| 101 | Mikanakawa | 1937 | Circle Ten | TX | Absorbed 209 in 1948. Merged with 56 in 1994. |
| 102 | Mirimichi | 1937 | Mount Whitney | CA | Merged 1994 with 548 to form 195. |

| No. | Lodge Name | Yr. | Council | ST | Notes |
|-----|-----------|-----|---------|-----|-------|
| 103 | Juniata | 1937 | Juniata Valley | PA | Changed name in 1941. |
| 103 | Monaken | 1937 | Juniata Valley | PA | |
| 104 | Occoneechee | 1937 | Occoneechee | NC | |
| 105 | Tetonwana | 1937 | Sioux | SD | Absorbed 460 in 1978. |
| 106 | Wiyapunit | 1938 | Aurora Area | IL | Merged 1968 with 120 to form 106. |
| 106 | Kishagamie | 1968 | Kedeka Area | IL | Merged 1971 with 279 to form 106. |
| 106 | Glikhikan | 1971 | Two Rivers | IL | Merged 1995 with 41 to form 41. |
| 107 | Kon-Kon-Tu | 1938 | South Jersey | NJ | Merged 1967 with 411 to form 107. |
| 107 | Apatukwe | 1967 | Southern New Jersey | NJ | |
| 108 | Mesquakie | 1938 | Wapsipinicon Area | IA | Changed name in 1943. |
| 108 | Wakosha | 1938 | Wapsipinicon Area | IA | Merged 1972 with 473 to form 108. |
| 108 | Sac-N-Fox | 1972 | Winnebago | IA | |
| 109 | Shawnee | 1938 | Scioto Area | OH | Changed name in 1939. Merged 1996 with 93 and 350 to form 65. |
| 109 | Scioto | 1938 | Scioto Area | OH | Changed name in 1950. |
| 109 | Shawnee | 1938 | Scioto Area | OH | |
| 110 | Nisaki | 1938 | Pokagon | IN | Changed name before 1940. |
| 110 | Pokagon | 1938 | Pokagon Trails | IN | Absorbed 122 in 1944. Merged 1965 with 189 to form 110. |
| 110 | Michigamea | 1965 | Calumet | IN | Absorbed 352 in 1972. |
| 111 | Wa-Hi-Nasa | 1938 | Middle Tennessee | TN | |
| 112 | Aquehongian | 1938 | GNY Staten Island | NY | |
| 113 | Wihinipa Hinsa | 1938 | Bay Area | TX | |
| 114 | Stigwandish | 1938 | Northeast Ohio | OH | Merged 1995 with 368 and 396 to form 56. |
| 115 | Ellini | 1938 | Kaskaskia | IL | Changed name in 1938. |
| 115 | Cascasquia | 1938 | Kaskaskia | IL | Merged 1966 with 81 to form 81. |
| 116 | Cherokee | 1938 | Pee Dee Area | SC | Name not accepted; Lodge 50 had name. |
| 116 | Santee | 1938 | Pee Dee Area | SC | Rechartered 1953 after previously disbanding twice. |
| 117 | Croatan | 1938 | East Carolina | NC | |
| 118 | Wahissa | 1938 | Old Hickory | NC | |
| 119 | Toma Chi-Chi | 1938 | Costal Empire | GA | |
| 120 | Chief Shabbona | 1938 | Chief Shabbona | IL | Changed name in 1963. |
| 120 | Ne Con Che Moka | 1938 | Chief Shabbona | IL | Merged 1968 with 106 to form 106. |

| No. | Lodge Name | Yr. | Council | ST | Notes |
|-----|-----------|-----|---------|-----|-------|
| 120 | Gosh Wha Gono | 1982 | Seaway Valley | NY | From merger of 461 and 357. |
| 121 | Wyandota | 1938 | Harding Area | OH | Merged 1996 with 205 and 513 to form 619. |
| 122 | Potawattomi | 1938 | Potawattomi Trails | IL | Absorbed by 110 in 1944. |
| 123 | Zit-Kala-Sha | 1938 | Old Kentucky Home | KY | Merged 1995 with 65 to form 62. |
| 124 | Noquochoke | 1938 | Massasoit | MA | Merged 1972 with 509 to form 124. |
| 124 | Neemat | 1972 | Moby Dick | MA | |
| 125 | Memeu | 1938 | Appalachian Trail | PA | Merged 1971 with 5 to form 5. |
| 126 | Cahokia | 1938 | Cahokia Mound | IL | Merged 1991 with 94 to form 32. |
| 127 | Tahquitz | 1938 | Riverside County | CA | Merged 1973 with 478 to form 127. |
| 127 | Cahuilla | 1973 | California Inland Empire | CA | Absorbed 380 in 1976. |
| 128 | Kickapoo | 1938 | Wabash Valley | IN | |
| 129 | Broad-Winged Hawk | 1938 | Atlanta Area | GA | Changed name in 1950. |
| 129 | Egwa Tawa Dee | 1938 | Atlanta Area | GA | |
| 130 | Sagamore | 1938 | Monongahela Valley | PA | Merged 1971 with 497 to form 130. |
| 130 | Scarouady | 1938 | Mon-Yough | PA | Merged 1973 with 67 to form 67. |
| 131 | Kahagon | 1938 | Cambridge | MA | |
| 132 | Illinek | 1938 | Abraham Lincoln | IL | |
| 133 | Ma-Nu | 1938 | Last Frontier | OK | |
| 134 | Tsali | 1938 | Daniel Boone | NC | |
| 135 | Achunanchi | 1938 | Choccolocco | AL | |
| 136 | Maheengun | 1938 | Saukee Area | IL | Merged 1995 with 80 to form 37. |
| 137 | Coloneh | 1938 | San Houston | TX | Name corrected in 1950. |
| 137 | Colonneh | 1938 | San Houston Area | TX | |
| 138 | Yaqui | 1938 | Tulsa | OK | Merged 1957 with 154 to form 138. |
| 138 | Daw-zu | 1957 | Indian Nations | OK | Changed name in 1959. |
| 138 | Ta Tsu Hwa | 1957 | Indian Nations | OK | Absorbed 320 in 1973. Absorbed 328 in 1983. |
| 139 | Ah-tic | 1938 | Bucktail | PA | |
| 140 | Blackhawk | 1939 | Blackhawk Area | IL | Changed name in 1941. Merged 1970 with 227 to form 140. |
| 140 | Ma-Ka-Tai-Me-She-Kia-Kiak | 1939 | Blackhawk Area | IL | |
| 140 | Wulapeju | 1970 | Blackhawk Area | IL | |
| 141 | Tatanka | 1939 | Buffalo Trail | TX | |

| No. | Lodge Name | Yr. | Council | ST | Notes |
|---|---|---|---|---|---|
| 142 | Papakitchie | 1939 | Pioneer Trails | IN | Half merged 1973 with 182 and 452 to form 573. |
| 143 | Kinebo | 1939 | Starved Rock Area | IL | Changed name in 1950. |
| 143 | Nee-Schoock | 1939 | Starved Rock Area | IL | Merged 1973 with 63 and 191 to form 23. |
| 144 | Tsun-Ga'Ni | 1939 | South Central Minnesota Area | MN | Part absorbed by 26 and 257 in 1946. |
| 145 | Nachenum | 1939 | Mound Builders Area | OH | Merged 1985 with 462 to form 145. |
| 145 | Ku-Ni-Eh | 1985 | Dan Beard | OH | |
| 146 | Tichora | 1939 | Four Lakes | WI | |
| 147 | Tamegonit | 1939 | Heart Of America | MO | Absorbed Tribe of Micosay in 1973. |
| 148 | Inola | 1939 | Will Rogers | OK | Absorbed 283 in 1948. |
| 149 | Caddo | 1939 | Norwela | LA | |
| 150 | Nakona | 1939 | South Plains | TX | |
| 151 | Marnoc | 1939 | Great Trail | OH | |
| 152 | Indian Drum | 1939 | Scenic Trails | MI | |
| 153 | Oh-Da-Ko-Ta | 1939 | Kenosha County | WI | Merged 1972 with 524 to form 8. |
| 154 | Checote | 1939 | Creek Nation | OK | Merged 1957 with 138 to form 138. |
| 155 | Nipperine | 1939 | Northern Kentucky | KY | Rechartered 1953 after previously disbanding. Changed name. |
| 155 | Michikinaqua | 1939 | Northern Kentucky | KY | Absorbed into 462 in 1956. |
| 155 | Nisqually | 1995 | Pacific Harbors | WA | From merger 1995 with 285, 348, and 392. |
| 156 | Northwoods Circle | 1939 | Copper Country Area | MI | Merged 1945 with 198 and 250 to form 156. |
| 156 | Ag-Im | 1945 | Hiawathaland | MI | |
| 157 | Delevan | 1939 | West Suburban | IL | Changed name in 1948. |
| 157 | Leekwinai | 1939 | West Suburban | IL | Merged 1994 with 334 to form 246. |
| 158 | Winnepurkit | 1939 | Bay Shore | MA | Absorbed by 505 in 1965. |
| 158 | Nanepashemet | 1993 | Yankee Clipper | MA | From merger 1993 with 490, 505, and 539. |
| 159 | Ganosote | 1939 | Buffalo Area | NY | Merged 1966 with 284 to form 159. |
| 159 | Ho-De-No-Sau-Nee | 1966 | Greater Niagara Frontier | NY | |
| 160 | Quapaw | 1939 | Quapaw Area | AR | |
| 161 | Ne-Pah-Win | 1939 | Piedmont Area | VA | Changed name after 1955. |
| 161 | Koo Koo Ku Hoo | 1939 | Piedmont Area | VA | Merged 1972 with 456 to form 161. |
| 161 | Tutelo | 1972 | Blue Ridge Mountains | VA | |

| No. | Lodge Name | Yr. | Council | ST | Notes |
|---|---|---|---|---|---|
| 162 | Mi-Gi-Si O-Paw-Gan | 1939 | Detroit Area | MI | |
| 163 | Tslagi | 1939 | Cherokee | NC | Changed spelling of name 1987. |
| 163 | Tsalagi | 1939 | Cherokee | NC | Merged 1994 with 70 to form 70. |
| 164 | Doog Gni Tuocs | 1939 | Old Colony | MA | Changed name before 1951. |
| 164 | Manomet | 1939 | Old Colony | MA | Merged 1969 with 518 to form 164. |
| 164 | Tisquantum | 1969 | Old Colony | MA | |
| 165 | Chautauqua | 1939 | Chautauqua | NY | Absorbed 187 in 1942. Merged 1973 with 455 to form 165. |
| 165 | Ho-Nan-Ne-Ho-Ont | 1973 | Allegheny Highlands | NY | Absorbed 547 in 1975. |
| 166 | Calcasieu | 1939 | Calcasieu | LA | Recharted 1952 after previously disbanding. Changed name. |
| 166 | Quelqueshoe | 1939 | Calcasieu | LA | |
| 167 | Woapink | 1939 | Ambraw Wabash | IL | Disbanded 1955 when council divided. |
| 167 | Woapink | 1957 | Lincoln Trails | IL | |
| 168 | Unalachtigo | 1939 | Pioneer Trails | PA | Merged 1973 with 419 to form 168. |
| 168 | Kuskitannee | 1973 | Moraine Trails | PA | |
| 169 | Pushmataha | 1939 | Pushmataha Area | MS | Changed name between 1943 and 1951. |
| 169 | Watonala | 1939 | Pushmataha Area | MS | |
| 170 | Khu-Ku-Koo-Huu | 1939 | Moline Area | IL | Merged 1959 with 504 to form 170. |
| 170 | Wisaka | 1959 | Sac N Fox | IL | Merged 1967 with 313 to form 170. |
| 170 | Muc-Kis-Sou | 1967 | Illowa | IA | Merged 1994 with 38 to form 38. |
| 171 | Nasupa Tanka | 1939 | BlackHills Area | SD | Rechartered 1955 after previously disbanding. Changed name. |
| 171 | Crazy Horse | 1939 | Black Hills Area | SD | Changed name in 1982. |
| 171 | Tashunka Witco | 1939 | Black Hills Area | SD | Changed spelling of name in 1984. |
| 171 | Tasunka Witco | 1939 | Black Hills Area | SD | Changed name in 1988. |
| 171 | Crazy Horse | 1939 | Black Hills Area | SD | |
| 172 | Kiamesha | 1940 | Susquenango | NY | Changed name prior to 1950. |
| 172 | Otahnagon | 1940 | Susquenango | NY | |
| 173 | Ojibwa | 1940 | Harrison Trails | IN | Merged 1973 with 269 and 425 to form 173. |
| 173 | Takachsin | 1973 | Sagamore | IN | |
| 174 | Nagadjiwanang | 1940 | Gitche Gumee | WI | Absorbed 1959 by 526. |
| 175 | Lakota | 1940 | Northwest Suburban | IL | |
| 176 | Minniduta | 1940 | Red River Valley | ND | Merged 1976 with 52, 183, and 371 to form 27. |

| No. | Lodge Name | Yr. | Council | ST | Notes |
|-----|-----------|-----|---------|----|-------|
| 177 | Victorio | 1940 | Cochise | AZ | Absorbed by 494 in 1965. |
| 178 | Mohican | 1940 | Robert Treat | NJ | Merged 1976 with 362 and 515 to form 178. |
| 178 | Meechgalanne | 1976 | Essex | NJ | Absorbed part of 84 in 1985. |
| 179 | Alabama | 1940 | Montgomery | AL | Changed name in 1949. |
| 179 | Alabamu | 1940 | Tukabatchee Area | AL | |
| 180 | Chickagami | 1940 | Blue Water | MI | |
| 181 | Mahikan | 1940 | Fort Orange | NY | Merged 1963 with 267 to form 181. |
| 181 | Nischa-Nimat | 1963 | Governor Clinton | NY | Merged 1990 with 268 and 418 to form 181. |
| 181 | Ganienkeh | 1990 | Twin Rivers | NY | Merged 1991 with 19 to form 19. |
| 182 | Lone Wolf | 1940 | St. Joseph Valley | IN | Merged 1952 with 314 to form 182. |
| 182 | White Beaver | 1952 | Tri-Valley | IN | Merged 1972 with part of 142 and 452 to form 573. |
| 183 | Chatoka | 1940 | Great Plains Area | ND | Merged 1976 with 52, 176, and 371 to form 27. |
| 184 | Sequoyah | 1940 | Sequoyah | TN | |
| 185 | Atta Kulla Kulla | 1940 | Blue Ridge | SC | |
| 186 | Wakanda | 1940 | Steuben Area | NY | Merged 1990 with 394 to form 186. |
| 186 | Tkaen Dod | 1990 | Five Rivers | NY | Merged 1993 with 30 to form 30. |
| 187 | Sah-Dah-Gey-Ah | 1940 | Lake Shore | NY | Absorbed by 165 in 1942. |
| 188 | Iti Bapishe Iti Hollo | 1940 | Central North Carolina | NC | |
| 189 | Oposa Achomawi | 1940 | Sauk Trails | IN | Merged 1965 with 110 to form 110. |
| 190 | Wisawanik | 1940 | Arbuckle Area | OK | |
| 191 | Kashapiwigamak | 1940 | Creve Coeur | IL | Merged 1973 with 63 and 143 to form 23. |
| 191 | Lowwapaneu | 1991 | Northeastern Pennsylvania | PA | From merger of 223 and 542 in 1991. |
| 192 | Shawnee | 1941 | Canadian Valley Araea | OK | Absorbed by 133 in 1949. |
| 193 | Choctaw | 1941 | Choctaw Area | MS | Changed name after 1955. |
| 193 | Ashwanchi Kinta | 1941 | Choctaw Area | MS | |
| 194 | Chequah | 1941 | Nicolet Area | WI | Merged 1974 with 61, 73, 233, 244, and 501 to form 61. |
| 194 | Orca | 1994 | Redwood Empire | CA | From 1994 merger of 262 and 537. |
| 195 | Ma-Ta-Cam | 1941 | Greater Boston | MA | No records exist that 195 ever charted under this name. |
| 195 | King Philip | 1941 | Greater Boston | MA | Absorbed 370 in 1965. Merged 1993 with 261 to form 52. |

| No. | Lodge Name | Yr. | Council | ST | Notes |
|---|---|---|---|---|---|
| 195 | Tah Heetch | 1995 | Sequoia | CA | From merger of 102 and 548 in 1995. |
| 196 | Little Bear | 1941 | Headwaters Area | MN | Recharted 1953 after previously disbanding. Changed name. |
| 196 | Mesabi | 1941 | Headwaters Area | MN | Merged 1995 with 526 to form 196. |
| 196 | Ka'Niss Ma'Ingan | 1995 | Voyageurs | MN | |
| 197 | Waupecan | 1941 | Rainbow | IL | |
| 198 | Ottawa | 1941 | Iron Range | MI | Merged 1945 with 156 and 250 to form 156. |
| 199 | Wahinkto | 1941 | Concho Valley | TX | |
| 200 | Echockotee | 1941 | North Florida | FL | |
| 201 | Kootaga | 1941 | Kootaga Area | WV | Merged 1990 with 527 to form 618. |
| 201 | White Horse | 1996 | Shawnee Trails | KY | From merger of 367 and 499 in 1996. |
| 202 | Chicksa | 1941 | Yocona Area | MS | |
| 203 | Wakazoo | 1941 | Fruit Belt Area | MI | Merged 1973 with 315 and 373 to form 373. |
| 204 | Chattahoochee | 1941 | Chattahoochee | GA | Absorbed 333 in 1963. Absorbed 273 in 1990. |
| 205 | Hilo-Hos-Kula | 1941 | Firelands Area | OH | Rechartered 1955 after previously disbanding. Changed name. |
| 205 | Notowacy | 1941 | Firelands Area | OH | Inactive 1960–71 then rechartered. Merged 1996 with 121 and 513 to form 619. |
| 206 | Teetonkah | 1941 | Land O Lakes | MI | Merged 1994 with 88 to form 88. |
| 207 | Stanford | 1941 | Stanford Area | CA | Changed name c.1948. |
| 207 | Stanford-Oljato | 1941 | Stanford Area | CA | Merged 1995 with 528 to form 63. |
| 208 | Uwharrie | 1941 | Uwharrie | NC | Merged 1992 with 70 to form 70. |
| 209 | Texoma | 1941 | Red River Valley | TX | Absorbed by 101 in 1947. |
| 210 | Blaknik | 1941 | Logan-Boone-Mingo | WV | Changed name in 1954. |
| 210 | Adjudimo | 1941 | Chief Cornstalk | WV | Merged 1993 with 416 and 475 to form 617. |
| 211 | Pamola | 1941 | Katahdin | ME | Rechartered 1955 after disbanding in 1951. |
| 212 | So-Aka-Gha-Gwa | 1941 | White River | IN | Merged 1974 with 290 to form 212. |
| 212 | Nischa Chuppecat | 1974 | Hoosier Trails | IN | |
| 213 | Thunderbird | 1941 | Great Salt Plains | OK | Changed name in 1948. |
| 213 | Coyote | 1941 | Great Salt Plains | OK | Changed name after 1955. |
| 213 | Ah-Ska | 1941 | Great Salt Plains | OK | |
| 214 | Gimogash | 1942 | Summer Trails | MI | Changed name after 1947. |

| No. | Lodge Name | Yr. | Council | ST | Notes |
|-----|-----------|-----|---------|----|----|
| 214 | Tom-Tom | 1942 | Summer Trails | MI | Changed name back before 1953. |
| 214 | Gimogash | 1942 | Summer Trails | MI | Inactive. Absorbed by 89 in 1961. |
| 215 | Noo-Ti-Mis Oh'ke | 1942 | Oak Plain | IL | Absorbed by 40 in 1972. |
| 216 | Metab | 1942 | Lake Of The Ozarks | MO | Merged 1972 with 426 to form 216. |
| 216 | Nampa-Tsi | 1972 | Great Rivers | MO | |
| 217 | Mattatuck | 1942 | Mattatuck | CT | Merged 1973 with 59, 234, 491, and 558 to form 59. |
| 218 | Cuwe | 1942 | Tall Pine | MI | |
| 219 | Calusa | 1942 | Sunny Land | FL | Disbanded 1956. Rechartered 1961 as 552. |
| 220 | Passaconaway | 1942 | Daniel Webster | NH | |
| 221 | Muscogee | 1942 | Indian Waters | SC | |
| 222 | Kikthawenund | 1942 | Kikthawenund | IN | Merged 1973 with 308 and 512 to form 21. |
| 223 | Acahela | 1942 | Wyoming Valley | PA | Merged 1969 with 316 to form 223. |
| 223 | Gischigin | 1969 | Penn Mountains | PA | Changed name in 1985. |
| 223 | Acahela | 1969 | Penn Mountains | PA | |
| 224 | Cowikee | 1942 | Alabama-Florida | AL | |
| 225 | Tamet | 1942 | Crescent Bay Area | CA | Merged 1972 with 228 to form 566. |
| 226 | Potawatomi | 1942 | State Line | WI | Changed name in 1942. |
| 226 | Ka'Katowi Meshe-Ka | 1942 | State Line | WI | Changed name around 1950. |
| 226 | Maunguzet | 1942 | State Line | WI | Changed name sometime after 1955. |
| 226 | Manquzet | 1942 | State Line | WI | Merged 1965 with 302 to form 226. |
| 226 | Chemokemon | 1965 | Sinnissippi | WI | |
| 227 | Wetassa | 1942 | U.S. Grant | IL | Merged 1970 with 140 to form 140. |
| 228 | Walika | 1942 | San Fernando Valley | CA | Merged 1972 with 225 to form 566. |
| 229 | Chippewa | 1943 | Okefenokee Area | GA | Changed name in 1943. |
| 229 | Chawtaw | 1943 | Okefenokee Area | GA | Changed name around 1950. |
| 229 | Pilthlako | 1943 | Okefenokee Area | GA | |
| 230 | Pelissippi | 1943 | Great Smokey Mountains | TN | |
| 231 | Mikano | 1943 | Milwaukee County | WI | |
| 232 | Akela Wahinapay | 1943 | Caddo Area | TX | |
| 233 | Wa-Zi-Ya-Ta | 1943 | Valley | WI | Merged 1974 with 61, 73, 194, 244, and 501 to form 61. |
| 234 | Keemosahbee | 1943 | Keemosahbee | CT | Merged 1968 with 471 to form 234. |

| No. | Lodge Name | Yr. | Council | ST | Notes |
|-----|-----------|-----|---------|----|----|
| 234 | Wihungen | 1968 | Nathan Hale | CT | Merged 1973 with 59, 217, 491, and 558 to form 59. |
| 235 | Ittawamba | 1943 | West Tennessee Area | TN | |
| 236 | Un A Li'yi | 1943 | Coastal Carolina | SC | |
| 237 | Aal-Pa-Tah | 1943 | Gulf Stream | FL | |
| 238 | Meshepeske | 1943 | Shawnee | OH | Changed name in 1950. |
| 238 | Ketchikeniqua | 1943 | Shawnee | OH | Merged 1994 with 382 to form 449. |
| 239 | Suriarco | 1943 | Suwanee River Area | FL | Changed name in 1948. |
| 239 | Semialachee | 1943 | Suwanee River Area | FL | |
| 240 | Ney-A-Ti | 1943 | Egyptian | IL | Absorbed by 100 in 1994. |
| 241 | Tomahawk | 1943 | Lonesome Pine | KY | Changed name sometime after 1955. |
| 241 | Tomahaken | 19?? | Lonesome Pine | KY | Absorbed by 480 in 1979. |
| 242 | Chimalus | 1943 | Washington Greene | PA | Merged 1967 with 57 to form 57. |
| 243 | Mowogo | 1943 | Northeast Georgia | GA | |
| 244 | Day Noomp | 1943 | Twin Lakes | WI | Merged 1974 with 61, 73, 194, 233, and 501 to form 61. |
| 245 | Tulpe | 1943 | Annawon | MA | |
| 246 | Wakoda | 1943 | Fennimore Cooper | NY | Merged 1951 with 86 to form 246. |
| 246 | Apachedotte | 1951 | Washington Irving | NY | Merged 1955 with 32 to form 246. |
| 246 | Horicon | 1955 | Washington Irving | NY | Merged 1973 with 15 to form 15. |
| 246 | Pachsegink | 1994 | Des Plaines Valley | IL | From merger of 157 and 334 in 1994. |
| 247 | Tahgajute | 1943 | Cayuga County | NY | |
| 248 | Wabaningo | 1943 | Evanston | IL | Absorbed by 40 in 1969. |
| 249 | Spe-Le-Yei | 1943 | Verdugo Hills | CA | |
| 250 | Minnewasco | 1943 | Chippewa Area | MI | Merged 1945 with 156 and 198 to form 156. |
| 251 | Hoh-Squa-Sa-Gah-Da | 1943 | Mercer Country | PA | Merged 1972 with 46 and 256 to form 46. |
| 252 | Siwinis | 1944 | Los Angeles Area | CA | |
| 253 | Tsisqan | 1944 | Oregon Trail | OR | |
| 254 | Comanche | 1944 | Ouachita Valley | LA | |
| 255 | Cornplanter | 1944 | Warren County | PA | Rechartered about 1954 after possibly disbanding. Changed name about 1954. |
| 255 | Chief Cornplanter | 1944 | Chief Cornplanter | PA | Changed name in 1960. |
| 255 | Gyantwachia | 1960 | Chief Cornplanter | PA | |
| 256 | Deer Rock | 1944 | Colonel Drake | PA | Changed name after 1955. |

| No. | Lodge Name | Yr. | Council | ST | Notes |
|-----|-----------|-----|---------|-----|-------|
| 256 | Skanondo Inyan | 1944 | Colonel Drake | PA | Merged 1972 with 46 and 251 to form 46. |
| 257 | Agaming | 1944 | Indianhead | MN | Absorbed part of 144 in 1946. |
| 258 | Shenandoah | 1944 | Stonewall Jackson Area | VA | |
| 259 | Cole Snass Lamatai | 1944 | Cascade Area | OR | Merged 1994 with 442 to form 442. |
| 260 | Sebooney Okasucca | 1944 | Andrew Jackson | MS | |
| 261 | Missituck | 1944 | Fellsland | MA | Merged 1958 with 447 and 496 to form 261. |
| 261 | Taskiagi | 1958 | Minuteman | MA | Merged 1994 with 195 to form 52. |
| 262 | Mow-A-Toc | 1944 | Redwood Area | CA | Merged 1994 with 537 to form 194. |
| 263 | Swegedaigea | 1944 | Silverado Area | CA | Merged 1993 with 468 to form 58. |
| 264 | Attakapas | 1944 | Attakapas | LA | Changed name in 1949. |
| 264 | Osouiga | 1944 | Attakapas | LA | Changed name in 1952. |
| 264 | Ouxouiga | 1944 | Attakapas | LA | |
| 265 | O-Shot-Caw | 1944 | South Florida | FL | |
| 266 | Thunder City | 1944 | Ore-Ida | ID | Changed name in 1959. |
| 266 | In-Mut-Too-Yah-Lat-Lat | 1944 | Ore-Ida | ID | Merged 1967 with 365 to form 266. |
| 266 | Tukarica | 1968 | Ore-Ida | ID | |
| 267 | Mohawk | 1944 | Uncle San | NY | Merged 1963 with 181 to form 181. |
| 268 | Ta-Oun-Ya-Wat-Ha | 1944 | Saratoga County | NY | Merged 1990 with 181 and 418 to form 181. |
| 269 | Akonequa | 1944 | Meshingomeshia | IN | Changed name around 1950. |
| 269 | Me-She-Kin-No-Quah | 1944 | Meshingomeshia | IN | Merged 1973 with 173 and 425 to form 173. |
| 270 | Skyuka | 1944 | Palmetto Area | SC | |
| 271 | Madockawanda | 1944 | Pine Tree | ME | |
| 272 | Wewanoma | 1944 | Rio Grande | TX | |
| 273 | Wehadkee | 1944 | George H. Lanier | GA | Disbanded 1965. Rechartered 1972. Absorbed by 204 in 1990. |
| 274 | Wangunks | 1944 | Central Connecticut | CT | Absorbed by 369 in 1978. |
| 275 | Monachgeu | 1944 | William Penn | PA | Rechartered 1954 after previously disbanding. Changed name in 1954. |
| 275 | Hopocan | 1944 | William Penn | PA | Merged 1971 with 347 and 441 to form 275. |
| 275 | Nachamawat | 1971 | Penn's Woods | PA | |
| 276 | Shenshawpotoo | 1944 | Shenandoah Area | VA | |
| 277 | Nonotuck | 1944 | Holyoke Area | MA | Changed name in 1950. |

| No. | Lodge Name | Yr. | Council | ST | Notes |
|-----|-----------|-----|---------|----|----|
| 277 | Apinakwi Pita | 1944 | Mount Tom | MA | Absorbed by 83 in 1960. |
| 278 | Yo-Se-Mite | 1944 | Yosemite Area | CA | |
| 279 | Nawakwa | 1944 | Elgin area | IL | Changed name before 1953. |
| 279 | Consoke | 1944 | Fox River Valley | IL | Merged 1971 with 106 to form 106. |
| 280 | Wag-O-Shad | 1944 | Potawatomi | WI | |
| 281 | Black Beaver | 1945 | Black Beaver | OK | Changed name prior to 1960. |
| 281 | Sekettummaqua | 1945 | Black Beaver | OK | |
| 282 | Royaneh | 1945 | San Francisco | CA | Merged 1965 with 375 to form 282. |
| 282 | Achewon Nimat | 1965 | San Francisco Bay Area | CA | |
| 283 | Cimeroon | 1945 | Cimarron Valley Area | OK | Absorbed by 148 in 1948. |
| 284 | Tuscarora | 1945 | Niagara Frontier | NY | Merged 1966 with 159 to form 159. |
| 285 | Kcumkum | 1945 | Twin Harbors Area | WA | Merged 1994 with 348 and 392 to form 155. |
| 286 | Iaopogh | 1945 | Ridgewood-Glen Rock | NJ | |
| 287 | Kit-Chee-Ke-Ma | 1945 | Middlesex | NJ | Changed name in 1948. |
| 287 | Sakawawin | 1945 | Middlesex | NJ | Merged 1970 with 9 to form 9. |
| 288 | Washita | 1945 | Cherokee Area | OK | |
| 289 | Papoukewis | 1945 | Fort Steuben Area | OH | Merged 1993 with 323 to form 36. |
| 290 | Wazi Yata | 1945 | Hoosier Hills Area | IN | Merged 1974 with 212 to form 212. |
| 291 | Topa Topa | 1945 | Ventura County | CA | |
| 292 | Tarhe | 1945 | Tecumseh | OH | |
| 293 | Chickamauga | 1945 | Cherokee Area | TN | Rechartered 1957 after previously disbanding. Changed name. |
| 293 | Talidandaganu' | 1945 | Cherokee Area | TN | |
| 294 | Kamargo | 1945 | General Herkimer | NY | |
| 295 | Otena | 1945 | Comanche Trail | TX | |
| 296 | Nayawin Rar | 1945 | Tuscarora | NC | |
| 297 | Uncas | 1945 | Eastern Connecticut | CT | Merged 1972 with 388 to form 10. |
| 298 | Gorgonia | 1945 | Orange Empire Area | CA | Changed name about 1948. |
| 298 | San Gorgonio | 1945 | Orange Empire Area | CA | Merged 1972 with 430 to form 13. |
| 299 | Nez Perce | 1945 | Vigilante | MT | Merged 1974 with 300, 361, and 390 to form 300. |
| 300 | Peta | 1945 | North Central Montana | MT | Merged 1974 with 299, 361, and 390 to form 300. |
| 300 | Apoxky Aio | 1974 | Montana | MT | |
| 301 | Moskwa | 1945 | Fort Simcoe Area | WA | Merged 1992 with 335 to form 614. |

| No. | Lodge Name | Yr. | Council | ST | Notes |
|-----|-----------|-----|---------|-----|-------|
| 302 | Koshkonong | 1945 | Indian Trails | WI | Merged 1965 with 226 to form 226. |
| 303 | Yowlumne | 1945 | Southern Sierra | CA | |
| 304 | Cayucos | 1945 | Santa Lucia Area | CA | Rechartered after previously disbanding. Changed name after 1955. |
| 304 | Miwok | 1945 | Santa Lucia Area | CA | Rechartered 1962 after disbanding. Changed name. |
| 304 | Chumash | 1945 | Santa Lucia Area | CA | Merged 1996 with 90 to form 90. |
| 305 | Kelcema | 1945 | Evergreen Area | WA | Merged 1995 with 325 to form 338. |
| 306 | Michi-Kina-Kwa | 1945 | Fort Hamilton | OH | Absorbed by 462 in 1959. |
| 307 | Karankawa | 1945 | Gulf Coast | TX | |
| 308 | Wahpinachi | 1945 | Whitewater Valley | IN | Merged 1973 with 222 and 512 to form 21. |
| 309 | Tsutsusid | 1945 | Wachusett | MA | Merged 1964 with 319 to form 309. |
| 309 | Quanopin | 1964 | Nashua Valley | MA | Merged 1994 with 329 to form 309. |
| 309 | Grand Monadnock | 1994 | Nashua Valley | MA | |
| 310 | Kaskanampo | 1945 | Tennesse Valley | AL | |
| 311 | Koo Ben Sho | 1945 | Idaho Pan Handle | ID | Changed name in 1962. |
| 311 | Sel Koo Sho | 1945 | Idaho Pan Handle | ID | Merged 1994 with 415 to form 311. |
| 311 | Es Kaielgu | 1994 | Inland Northwest | WA | |
| 312 | Sinawava | 1945 | Boulder Dam Area | NV | Disbanded 1950. Changed name when rechartered in 1955. |
| 312 | Nebagamon | 1945 | Boulder Dam Area | NV | |
| 313 | Bison | 1945 | Buffalo Bill | IA | Disbanded 1952. Changed name when rechartered in 1955. |
| 313 | Golden Eagle | 1945 | Buffalo Bill Area | IA | Absorbed 376 in 1959. Merged 1967 with 170 to form 170. |
| 313 | Tankiteke | 1973 | Fairfield County | CT | From merger of 389, 408, and 521 in 1973. |
| 314 | Mishawaka | 1945 | Mishawaka | IN | Merged 1952 with 182 to form 182. |
| 315 | Mandoka | 1945 | Nottawa Trails | MI | Merged 1973 with 203 and 373 to form 373. |
| 316 | Quekolis | 1945 | Anthracite | PA | Merged 1969 with 223 to form 223. |
| 317 | Guneukitschik | 1945 | Mason-Dixon | MD | |
| 318 | Waguli | 1945 | Northwest Georgia | GA | |
| 319 | Watatic | 1945 | Fitchburg Area | MA | Merged 1964 with 309 to form 309. |
| 320 | Oskihoma | 1945 | Choctaw Area | OK | Changed name in 1956. |
| 320 | Oklahoma | 1945 | Choctaw Area | OK | Changed name in 1966. |
| 320 | Oskihoma | 1945 | Choctaw Area | OK | Absorbed by 138 in 1973. |

| No. | Lodge Name | Yr. | Council | ST | Notes |
|-----|-----------|-----|---------|----|----|
| 321 | Nani-Ba-Zhu | 1945 | Kanza | KS | |
| 322 | White Fang | 1945 | Mobile Area | AL | Changed name in 1957. |
| 322 | Woa Cholena | 1945 | Mobile Area | AL | Changed name in 1958. |
| 322 | War Eagle | 1945 | Mobile Area | AL | Changed name in 19??. |
| 322 | Woa Cholena | 1945 | Mobile Area | AL | |
| 323 | Arrowhead | 1945 | Nationa Trail | WV | Merged 1993 with 289 to form 36. |
| 324 | Thundering Spring | 1945 | Flint River | GA | Changed name in 1952. |
| 324 | Ini-to | 1945 | Flint River | GA | |
| 325 | Quilshan | 1945 | Mount Baker Area | WA | Merged 1995 with 305 to form 338. |
| 326 | Tipisa | 1946 | Central Florida | FL | |
| 327 | Huaco | 1946 | Heart O'Texas | TX | |
| 328 | Ya Ha Klack Go | 1946 | Muskogee Area | OK | Rechartered after 1955 and after previously disbanding. Changed name. |
| 328 | Nanomihistiim | 1946 | Eastern Oklahoma | OK | Changed name in 1975. |
| 328 | Ni-U-Kon-Sha | 1946 | Eastern Oklahoma | OK | Absorbed by 138 in 1983. |
| 329 | Nikiwigi | 1946 | Monadnock | MA | Merged 1994 with 309 to form 309. |
| 330 | Kotso | 1946 | Chisholm Trail | TX | |
| 331 | Klahican | 1946 | Cape Fear Area | NC | |
| 332 | Tecumseh | 1946 | Wolverine Area | MI | Merged 1973 with 88 to form 88. |
| 333 | Hiawassee | 1946 | West Georgia | GA | Absorbed by 204 in 1963. |
| 333 | Wahunsenakah | 1996 | Colonial Virginia | VA | From merger of 463 and 483 in 1996. |
| 334 | Shin-Go-Beek | 1946 | Thatcher Woods Area | IL | Merged 1994 with 157 to form 246. |
| 335 | Ump Quah | 1946 | North Central Washington | WA | Merged 1992 with 301 to form 614. |
| 336 | Wa-La-Moot-Kin | 1946 | Blue Mountain | WA | |
| 337 | Otyokwa | 1946 | Chippewa Valley | WI | |
| 338 | Nisjaw | 1946 | Three G Counties | AZ | Disbanded 1947. Rechartered 1961 as 551. |
| 338 | Sikhis Mox Lamonti | 1995 | Mount Baker Area | WA | From merger of 305 and 325 in 1995. |
| 339 | Genesee | 1946 | Genesee | NY | Changed name in 1948. |
| 339 | Tana Wis Qua | 1946 | Genesee | NY | Changed name in 1952. |
| 339 | Amo'chk | 1946 | Genesee | NY | Merged 1994 with 409 to form 339. |
| 339 | Ashokwahta | 1995 | Iroquois Trail | NY | |
| 340 | Timuquan | 1946 | West Central Florida | FL | |
| 341 | Chief Lone Wolf | 1946 | Adobe Walls Area | TX | Merged 1987 with 486 to form 486. |

| No. | Lodge Name | Yr. | Council | ST | Notes |
|---|---|---|---|---|---|
| 341 | Japeechen | 1992 | Jersey Shore | NJ | From merger with 423 and 535 in 1992. |
| 342 | Stanislaus | 1946 | San-Joaquin-Calaveras | CA | Changed name in 1948. |
| 342 | Sumi | 1946 | Forty-Niner | CA | |
| 343 | Wapsu Achtu | 1946 | Susquehanna Valley | PA | Merged 1975 with 384 to form 343. |
| 343 | Woapeu Sisilija | 1975 | Susquehanna | PA | |
| 344 | Golden Tomahawk | 1946 | Iowa River Valley | IA | Merged 1952 with 467 to form 467. |
| 345 | White Panther | 1946 | Delta Area | MS | Changed name in 1956. |
| 345 | Koi Hatachie | 1946 | Delta Area | MS | Merged 1995 with 406 to form 558. |
| 346 | Wiyaka | 1946 | Nevada Area | NV | Changed name in 1961. |
| 346 | Tannu | 1946 | Nevada Area | NV | |
| 347 | Wisawanik | 1946 | Blair Bedford Area | PA | Changed name in 1946. |
| 347 | Wopsononock | 1946 | Blair Bedford Area | PA | Merged 1971 with 275 and 441 to form 275. |
| 348 | Tahoma | 1946 | Mount Rainier | WA | Merged 1994 with 285 and 392 to form 155. |
| 349 | Blue Heron | 1946 | Tidewater | VA | |
| 350 | Maka-Ina | 1946 | Chief Logan | OH | Merged 1996 with 93 and 109 to form 65. |
| 351 | Wisie Hal'a Con | 1946 | Long Trail | VT | Merged 1973 with 398 to form 351. |
| 351 | Ajapeu | 1973 | Green Mountain | VT | |
| 352 | Zhingwak | 1946 | Twin City | IN | Absorbed by 110 in 1972. |
| 353 | Immokalee | 1947 | Southwest Georgia | GA | |
| 354 | Mayi | 1947 | Golden Empire | CA | Absorbed 511 in 1979. Merged 1993 with 395 and 485 to form 47. |
| 355 | Nanuk | 1947 | Western Alaska | AK | |
| 356 | Tatokainyanka | 1947 | Central Wyoming | WY | |
| 357 | Adirondack | 1947 | Jefferson-Lewis | NY | Merged 1982 with 461 to form 120. |
| 358 | Echeconnee | 1947 | Central Georgia | GA | |
| 359 | Aheka | 1947 | Aheka | NJ | Merged 1974 with 449 to form 359. |
| 359 | Aquaninoncke | 1974 | Passaic Valley | NJ | |
| 360 | Shinnecock | 1947 | Suffolk County | NY | |
| 361 | Wilgus | 1947 | Western Montana | MT | Merged 1974 with 299, 300, and 390 to form 300. |
| 362 | Ken-Etiwa-Pec | 1947 | Orange Mountain | NJ | Merged 1976 with 178 and 515 to form 178. |
| 363 | Shoshoni | 1947 | Snake River Valley Area | ID | Rechartered 1954 after previously disbanding. Changed name. |

| No. | Lodge Name | Yr. | Council | ST | Notes |
|-----|-----------|-----|---------|-----|-------|
| 363 | Ma I Shu | 1947 | Snake River Area | ID | |
| 364 | Loon | 1947 | Adirondack | NY | |
| 365 | Lemonti Lemooto | 1947 | Mountainview | ID | Merged 1967 with 266 to form 266. |
| 366 | Wazhazee | 1947 | Ouachita Area | AR | |
| 367 | Wapiti | 1947 | Audubon | KY | Absorbed 405 in 1959. Merged 1996 with 499 to form 201. |
| 368 | Tapawingo | 1947 | Western Reserve | OH | Merged 1995 with 114 and 396 to form 56. |
| 369 | Chi Sigma | 1947 | Quinnipiac | CT | Changed name in 1954. |
| 369 | Arcoon | 1947 | Quinnipiac | CT | Absorbed 274 in 1978. |
| 370 | Massasoit | 1947 | Quincy | MA | Rechartered 1959 after previously disbanding. Changed name. |
| 370 | Moswetuset | 1947 | Quincy | MA | Absorbed by 195 in 1965. |
| 371 | Thunderbird | 1947 | Lake Agassiz | ND | Merged 1976 with 52, 176, and 183 to form 27. |
| 372 | Mandan | 1948 | Santa Fe Trail | KS | |
| 373 | Carcajou | 1948 | Southwest Michigan | MI | Merged 1973 with 203 and 315 to form 373. |
| 373 | Nacha-Mawat | 1973 | Southwest Michigan | MI | |
| 374 | Gab-Shi-Win-Gi-Ji-Kess | 1948 | Chief Okemos | MI | |
| 375 | Machek N'Gult | 1948 | Oakland Area | CA | Merged 1965 with 282 to form 282. |
| 376 | A-Me-Qua | 1948 | Mesquakie Area | IA | Absorbed by 313 in 1959. |
| 377 | Sipp-O | 1948 | Buckeye | OH | Absorbed 472 in 1992. |
| 378 | Gila | 1948 | Yucca | TX | |
| 379 | Kaweah | 1948 | Alameda | CA | |
| 380 | Ho-Mita-Koda | 1948 | Redland Area | CA | Rechartered 1955 after previously disbanding. Changed name. |
| 380 | A-Tsa | 1948 | Grayback | CA | Rechartered 1955 after previously disbanding. Absorbed by 127 in 1976. |
| 381 | Braves of Decorah | 1948 | Gateway Area | WI | Changed name in 1995. |
| 381 | Ni-Sanak-Tani | 1948 | Gateway Area | WI | |
| 382 | Eagle Creek | 1948 | Put-Han-Sen Area | OH | Merged 1994 with 238 to form 449. |
| 383 | Tahosa | 1948 | Denver Area | CO | |
| 384 | Tiadaghton | 1948 | West Branch | PA | Merged 1975 with 343 to form 343. |
| 385 | Yustaga | 1948 | Gulf Coast | FL | |
| 386 | Tuckahoe | 1948 | York Adams Area | PA | |
| 387 | Pike's Peak | 1948 | Pikes Peak | CO | Changed name in 1953. |

| No. | Lodge Name | Yr. | Council | ST | Notes |
|-----|------------|-----|---------|----|----|
| 387 | Ha-Kin-Skay-A-Ki | 1948 | Pikes Peak | CO | |
| 388 | Samson Occum | 1948 | Pequot | CT | Merged 1972 with 297 to form 10. |
| 389 | Mauwehu | 1948 | Mauwehu | CT | Merged 1972 with 408 and 521 to form 313. |
| 390 | Nitapokaiyo | 1948 | Yellowstone Valley | MT | Changed name in 1964. |
| 390 | Amangi Mos | 1948 | Yellowstone Valley | MT | Merged 1974 with 299, 300, and 361 to form 300. |
| 391 | Chiriqui | 1948 | Panama Canal | CZ | Absorbed by 555 in 1987. |
| 392 | Tillicum | 1948 | Tumwater Area | WA | Merged 1994 with 285 and 348 to form 155. |
| 393 | Abake-Mi-Sa-Na-KI | 1948 | Cape Cod | MA | |
| 394 | Seneca | 1948 | Sullivan Trail | NY | Merged 1990 with 186 to form 186. |
| 395 | Tribe of La Porte | 1948 | Buttres Area | CA | Changed name in 1950. |
| 395 | Kowaunkamish | 1948 | Buttes Area | CA | Merged 1993 with 354 and 485 to form 47. |
| 396 | Nea-To-Ka | 1948 | Mahoning Valley | OH | Rechartered 1953 after previously disbanding. Changed name. |
| 396 | Mahoning | 1948 | Mahoning Valley | OH | Changed name in 1957. |
| 396 | Neatoka | 1948 | Mahoning Valley | OH | Merged 1995 with 114 and 368 to form 56. |
| 397 | Chilantakoba | 1948 | New Orleans | LA | |
| 398 | Memphremagog | 1948 | Green Mountain | VT | Merged 1964 with 493 to form 398. |
| 398 | Nianque | 1964 | Ethan Allen | VT | Merged 1973 with 351 to form 351. |
| 399 | A-Booik-Paa-Gun | 1948 | De Soto Area | AR | |
| 400 | Quetzal | 1948 | Lewis-Clark | ID | Changed name in 1954. |
| 400 | Wawookia | 1948 | Lewis-Clark | ID | Merged 1995 with 311 to form ???. |
| 401 | Nakida-Naou | 1948 | Timber Trails | MI | Merged 1975 with 79 to form 25. |
| 402 | Onteroraus | 1948 | Otschodela | NY | |
| 403 | Red Feather | 1948 | Wyo-Braska Area | ME | Changed name in 1955. |
| 403 | Wiyaka Luta | 1948 | Wyo-Braska Area | Me | Absorbed by 464 in 1975. |
| 404 | Ti'ak | 1949 | Pine Burr Area | MS | |
| 405 | Land of Big Caves | 1949 | Mammoth Cave | KY | Changed name in 1950. |
| 405 | Walah Elemamekhaki | 1949 | Mammoth Cave | KY | Absorbed by 367 in 1959. |
| 406 | Chickasah | 1949 | Chickasaw | TN | Merged 1995 with 345 to form 558. |
| 407 | Novando Ikeu | 1949 | Tendoy Area | ID | Merged 1994 with 544 to form 407. |
| 407 | Shunkah Mahneetu | 1994 | Grand Teton | ID | |

| No. | Lodge Name | Yr. | Council | ST | Notes |
|---|---|---|---|---|---|
| 408 | Chief Pomperaug | 1949 | Pomperaug | CT | Merged 1972 with 389 and 521 to form 313. |
| 409 | Tuighaunock | 1949 | Lewiston Trail | NY | Merged 1994 with 339 to form 339. |
| 410 | Aola | 1949 | Oswego County | NY | Merged 1968 with 516 to form 410. |
| 410 | Nischa Nitis | 1968 | Hiawatha | NY | |
| 411 | Unalachtigo | 1949 | Gloucester-Salem | NJ | Changed name in 195?. |
| 411 | Unilachtego | 1949 | Gloucester-Salem | NJ | Merged 1967 with 107 to form 107. |
| 412 | Buckskin | 1949 | Nassau County | NY | |
| 413 | Hi'lo Ha Chy'a-la | 1949 | Eastern Arkansas Area | AR | |
| 414 | Musketahquid | 1949 | Norumbega | MA | |
| 415 | Lemolloillahee | 1949 | Island Empire | WA | Merged 1993 with 311 to form 311. |
| 416 | Wolf | 1949 | South West Virginia | WV | Changed name in 195?. |
| 416 | Hytone | 1949 | Appalachian | WV | Merged 1993 with 210 and 475 to form 617. |
| 417 | Finger Lakes | 1949 | Finger Lakes | NY | Changed name in 195?. |
| 417 | Ganeodiyo | 1949 | Finger Lakes | NY | |
| 418 | Nick Stoner | 1949 | Sir William Johnson | NY | Changed name in 1953. |
| 418 | Thay-En-Da-Ne-Gea | 1949 | Sir William Johnson | NY | Merged 1990 with 181 and 268 to form 181. |
| 419 | Packanke | 1949 | Lawrence County | PA | Merged 1973 with 168 to form 168. |
| 420 | Kaniengehaga | 1949 | Licking County | OH | Absorbed by 93 in 1987. |
| 421 | Mazama | 1949 | Crater Lake | OR | Merged 1994 with 437 to form 491. |
| 422 | Acorn | 1949 | South Indiana | IN | Changed name in 1953. |
| 422 | Kiondaga | 1949 | Buffalo Trace | IN | Absorbed part of 167 in 1955. |
| 423 | Gitche Gumee | 1949 | Atlantic Area | NJ | Merged 1992 with 535 to form 341. |
| 424 | Amochol | 1949 | Zane Trace | OH | Changed name after 1952. |
| 424 | Netawatamass | 1949 | Muskingum Valley | OH | Absorbed 448 in 1956. Changed name in 1975. |
| 424 | Netawatwees | 1949 | Muskinggum Valley | OH | |
| 425 | Chippewa | 1949 | Three Rivers | IN | Changed name in 1952. |
| 425 | Tipicon | 1949 | Three Rivers | IN | Merged 1973 with 173 and 269 to form 173. |
| 426 | Po-E-Mo | 1950 | Great Rivers | MO | Merged 1972 with 216 to form 216. |
| 427 | Achewon Netopalis | 1949 | Greenwich | CT | |
| 428 | Loquanne Allangwh | 1950 | Ne Tse O | TX | |
| 429 | Dzie-Hauk Tonga | 1950 | Jayhawk Area | KS | |

| No. | Lodge Name | Yr. | Council | ST | Notes |
|-----|-----------|-----|---------|----|----|
| 430 | Ahwahnee | 1950 | North Orange | CA | Merged 1973 with 298 to form 13. |
| 431 | Witauchsundin | 1950 | Union | NJ | Absorbed by 68 in 1980. |
| 432 | Wipala Wiki | 1950 | Grand Canyon | AZ | Absorbed 503 in 1992. |
| 433 | Mi-Ni-Ci-No | 1950 | Sekan Area | KS | Absorbed by 458 in 1973. |
| 434 | Cherokee | 1950 | Coronado Area | KS | Changed name in 1951. |
| 434 | Kidi-Kidish | 1950 | Coronado Area | KS | |
| 435 | Mischa Mokwa | 1950 | Cumberland | KY | Absorbed by 480 in 1962. |
| 436 | Ashie | 1950 | San Diego County | CA | Merged 1992 with part of 532 to form 45. |
| 437 | Makualla | 1950 | Modoc Area | OR | Merged 1994 with 421 to form 491. |
| 438 | Wahpeton | 1950 | Prairie Gold Area | IA | Merged 1973 with 474 to form 438. |
| 438 | Miniconjou | 1973 | Prairie Gold Area | IA | |
| 439 | Miwok | 1950 | Santa Clara County | CA | Disbanded in 1952. Rechartered in 1964. |
| 440 | Chinchewunska | 1950 | Alexander Hamilton | NJ | Merged 1969 with 37 to form 37. |
| 441 | Amadahi | 1950 | Admiral Robert E. Perry | PA | Merged 1969 with 275 and 347 to form 275. |
| 442 | Hyas Chuck Kah Sun Klatawa | 1950 | Portland Area | OR | Changed name in 1960. |
| 442 | Skyloo | 1950 | Columbia Pacific | OR | Merged 1994 with 259 to form 442. |
| 442 | Wauna La-Mon 'Tay | 1994 | Cascade Pacific | OR | |
| 443 | Nooteeming | 1950 | Dutchess County | NY | Merged 1995 with 64 and 443 to form ???. |
| 444 | Munsi | 1950 | Rockland County | NY | Merged 1995 with 64 and 444 to form ???. |
| 445 | Pohawk | 1950 | Covered Wagon | NE | Merged 1964 with 97 to form 97. |
| 446 | Cuauhtli | 1951 | Direct Service | MX | Disbanded 1971. Absorbed by 555. |
| 447 | Souhegan | 1951 | Quannapowitt | MA | Merged 1958 with 261 and 496 to form 261. |
| 448 | Wapagoklos | 1951 | Tomakawk | OH | Absorbed by 424 in 1956. |
| 449 | Minisi | 1951 | Alhtaha | NJ | Merged 1974 with 359 to form 359. |
| 449 | Mawat Woakus | 1994 | Black Swamp Area | OH | From merger of 238 and 382 in 1994. |
| 450 | Mitigwa | 1951 | Mid-Iowa | IA | Absorbed 453 in 1969. |
| 451 | Wannalancit | 1951 | Greater Lowell | MA | |
| 452 | She-Sheeb | 1951 | Pottawattomie | IN | Merged 1972 with half of 142 and 182 to form 573. |
| 453 | Winnebago | 1951 | South Iowa Area | IA | Changed name after 1955. |
| 453 | Bo-Qui | 1951 | Southern Iowa Area | IA | Absorbed by 450 in 1969. |

| No. | Lodge Name | Yr. | Council | ST | Notes |
|-----|-----------|-----|---------|-----|-------|
| 454 | Kamehameha | 1951 | Kilauea | HI | Merged 1972 with 557 and 565 to form 567. |
| 455 | Allegewi | 1951 | Elk Lick | PA | Merged 1973 with 165 to form 165. |
| 456 | Powhatan | 1951 | Blue Ridge | VA | Merged 1972 with 161 to form 161. |
| 457 | Thal-Coo-Zyo | 1951 | Tri-State Area | WV | |
| 458 | Hi-Cha-Ko-Lo | 1951 | Quivira | KS | |
| 459 | Catawba | 1951 | Mecklenburg County | NC | |
| 460 | Iyatonka | 1951 | Pheasant | SD | Absorbed by 105 in 1978. |
| 461 | Manatoanna | 1951 | St. Lawrence | NY | Merged 1982 with 257 to form 120. |
| 462 | Ku-Ni-Eh | 1951 | Dan Beard | OH | Absorbed 155 in 1956. Absorbed 306 in 1959. Merged 1985 with 145 to form 145. |
| 463 | Kecoughtan | 1951 | Peninsula | VA | Merged 1995 with 483 to form 333. |
| 464 | Kola | 1951 | Longs Peak | CO | Absorbed 403 in 1973. |
| 465 | Yahnundasis | 1951 | Upper Mohawk | NY | Merged 1981 with 34 to form 34. |
| 466 | Hungteetsepoppi | 1951 | Piedmont | CA | |
| 467 | Black Crescent | 1952 | Waubeek Area | IA | Merged 1952 with 344 to form 467. |
| 467 | Cho-Gun-Mun-A-Nock | 1952 | Hawkeye Area | IA | |
| 468 | Oo Yum Buli | 1952 | Mount Diablo | CA | Merged 1993 with 263 to form 58. |
| 469 | Tittabawasink | 1952 | Paul Bunyan | MI | Merged 1972 with 89 to form 89. |
| 470 | Amanquemack | 1952 | National Capital Area | MD | Changed name in 1954. |
| 470 | Amangamek-Wipit | 1952 | National Capital Area | MD | |
| 471 | Woapalane | 1952 | Bristol | CT | Merged 1967 with 234 to form 234. |
| 472 | Scaroyadii | 1952 | Columbiana | OH | Absorbed by 377 in 1992. |
| 473 | Aiaouez | 1952 | Winnebago | IA | Merged 1972 with 108 to form 108. |
| 474 | Ta | 1952 | Sergeant Floyd | IA | Rechartered 1958 after previously disbanding. Changed name. |
| 474 | War Eagle | 1952 | Sergeant Floyd | IA | Merged 1973 with 438 to form 438. |
| 475 | Wachu Menetopolis | 1952 | Buckskin | MV | Merged 1993 with 210 and 416 to form 617. |
| 476 | Tunkhannock | 1952 | Bethlehem Area | PA | Merged 1969 with 44 and 58 to form 44. |
| 477 | Ah Wa Ge | 1952 | Tioughnioga | NY | Merged 1975 with 546 to form 477. |
| 477 | Gajuka | 1975 | Baden-Powell | NY | |
| 478 | Wisumahi | 1952 | Arrowhead Area | CA | Merged 1973 with 127 to form 127. |
| 479 | Istrouma | 1952 | Istrouma Area | LA | Changed name in 1953. |
| 479 | Quinipissa | 1952 | Istrouma Area | LA | |

| No. | Lodge Name | Yr. | Council | ST | Notes |
|-----|-----------|-----|---------|----|----|
| 480 | Kawida | 1952 | Blue Grass | KY | Absorbed 435 in 1962. Absorbed 241 in 1979. |
| 481 | Aracoma | 1952 | Black Warrior | AL | |
| 482 | Black Eagle | 1952 | Transatlantic | GE | |
| 483 | Chanco | 1952 | Old Dominion Area | VA | Merged 1995 with 463 to form 333. |
| 484 | Oratam | 1952 | Bergen | NJ | Absorbed part of 84 in 1985. |
| 485 | Tehama | 1952 | Mount Lassen Area | CA | Merged 1993 with 354 and 395 to form 47. |
| 486 | Palo Duro | 1952 | Llano Estacado | TX | Merged 1987 with 341 to form 486. |
| 486 | Nischa Achowalogen | 1987 | Golden Spread | TX | |
| 487 | Taunkacoo | 1953 | Algonquin | MA | |
| 488 | Ta Tanka | 1953 | San Gabriel Valley | CA | |
| 489 | Nishkin Halupa A Pe Lachi | 1953 | Longhorn | TX | |
| 490 | Shingebis | 1953 | North Essex | MA | Merged 1993 with 505 and 539 to form 158. |
| 491 | Tunxis | 1953 | Tunxis | CT | Merged 1973 with 59, 217 234, and 558 to form 59. |
| 491 | Lo La 'Qam Geela | 1994 | Crater Lake | OR | From merger of 431 and 437 in 1994. |
| 492 | Golden Sun | 1953 | Cornhusker | NE | |
| 493 | Kola | 1953 | Calvin Coolidge | VT | Changed name in 19??. |
| 493 | Nicaweegee | 1953 | Calvin Coolidge | VT | Merged 1964 with 398 to form 398. |
| 494 | Papago | 1953 | Catalina | AZ | Absorbed 177 in 1965. |
| 495 | Miami | 1953 | Miami Valley | OH | |
| 496 | Menetomi | 1953 | Sachem | MA | Merged 1958 with 261 and 447 to form 261. |
| 497 | Shingis | 1953 | Yohogania | PA | Merged 1971 with 130 to form 130. |
| 498 | Hinode Goya | 1953 | Far East | JP | Absorbed 538 in 1965. Changed name in 1975. |
| 498 | Ikunuhkatsi | 1953 | Far East | JP | Changed name in 1985. |
| 498 | Achpateuny | 1953 | Far East | JP | |
| 499 | White Feather | 1953 | Four Rivers | KY | Merged 1996 with 367 to form 201. |
| 500 | Ona Yote Kaonaga | 1953 | Fort Stanwix | NY | Merged 1968 with 34 to form 34. |
| 501 | Wolverine | 1953 | Kettle Moraine | WI | Merged 1973 with 61, 73, 194, 233, and 244 to form 61. |
| 502 | T'Kope Kwiskwis | 1954 | Chief Seattle | WA | Absorbed 530 in 1975. |
| 503 | Chee Dodge | 1954 | Grand Canyon | AZ | Absorbed by 432 in 1992. |
| 504 | Saukenuk | 1954 | Fort Armstrong Area | IL | Merged 1959 with 170 to form 170. |

| No. | Lodge Name | Yr. | Council | ST | Notes |
|-----|-----------|-----|---------|----|----|
| 505 | Amiskwi | 1954 | North Bay | MA | Merged 1993 with 490 and 539 to form 158. |
| 506 | Yokahu | 1954 | Puerto Rico | PR | |
| 507 | Penain Sew Netami | 1954 | Berkshire | MA | Merged 1968 with 556 to form 507. |
| 507 | Memsochet | 1968 | Great Trails | MA | |
| 508 | Tu-Cubin-Noonie | 1954 | Utah Nationa Park | UT | |
| 509 | Agawam | 1954 | Cacholot | MA | Merged 1972 with 124 to form 124. |
| 510 | Three Arrows | 1955 | Tri Trails | NE | Merged 1994 with 517 to form 94. |
| 511 | Canaku | 1955 | Tahoe Area | CA | Absorbed by 354 in 1970. |
| 512 | Wah-Pe-Kah-Me-Kunk | 1955 | Delaware County | IN | Merged 1973 with 222 and 308 to form 21. |
| 513 | Lou Ott | 1955 | Johnny Appleseed | OH | Merged 1996 with 121 and 205 to form 619. |
| 514 | Choa | 1955 | Cache Valley | UT | Changed name in 1955. |
| 514 | Twoa-Ba-Cha | 1955 | Cache Valley | UT | Merged 1996 with 529 and 561 to form 535. |
| 515 | Oleleu | 1955 | Eagle Rock | NJ | Merged 1976 with 178 and 362 to form178. |
| 516 | Onondaga | 1955 | Onondaga | NY | Merged 1968 with 410 to form 410. |
| 517 | We-U-Shi | 1955 | Overland Trails | NE | Merged 1994 with 510 to form 94. |
| 518 | Tisqauntum | 1956 | Squanto | MA | Merged 1969 with 164 to form 164. |
| 519 | Minqua | 1956 | Lancaster County | PA | Merged 1972 with 39 to form 39. |
| 520 | El-Ku-Ta | 1956 | Great Salt Lake | UT | |
| 521 | Ponus | 1956 | Alfred W. Dater | CT | Merged 1972 with 389 and 408 to form 313. |
| 522 | Wa-Be-Wa-Wa | 1957 | Toledo Area | OH | Changed name in 1973 |
| 522 | Tindeuchen | 1957 | Toledo Area | OH | |
| 523 | Kootz | 1957 | Southeast Alaska | AK | |
| 524 | Chippecotton | 1957 | Racine County | WI | Merged 1972 with 153 to form 8. |
| 525 | Pachachoag | 1957 | Mohegan | MA | Changed name in 1959. |
| 525 | Pachachaug | 1957 | Mohegan | MA | |
| 526 | Nahak | 1957 | Lake Superior | MN | Merged 1995 with 196 to form 196. |
| 527 | Buckongehannon | 1957 | Central West Virginia | WV | Merged 1990 with 201 to form 618. |
| 528 | Pomponio | 1957 | San Mateo County | CA | Merged 1995 with 207 to form 63. |
| 529 | Tatanka | 1957 | Jim Bridger | WY | Merged 1996 with 514 and 561 to form 535. |
| 530 | Mox Kar-Po | 1957 | Olympic Area | WA | Absorbed by 502 in 1975. |

| No. | Lodge Name | Yr. | Council | ST | Notes |
|-----|-----------|-----|---------|-----|-------|
| 531 | Esselen | 1957 | Monterey Bay Area | CA | |
| 532 | Pang | 1957 | Desert Trails | AZ | Part merged with 436 to form 45 in 1992. Part absorbed by 432 in 1992. |
| 533 | Talako | 1958 | Marin | CA | |
| 534 | Wincheck | 1958 | Narragansett | RI | |
| 535 | Schiwa'pew Names | 1958 | Ocean County | NJ | Merged 1992 with 423 to form 341. |
| 535 | Awaxawee Awachia | 1996 | Trapper Trails | UT | From merger of 514, 529, and 561 in 1996. |
| 536 | Tupwee Gudas Gov Youchiquot Soovep | 1958 | Rocky Mountain | CO | From 1973–93 used abbr. of Tupwee on insignia. |
| 537 | Cabrosha | 1959 | Sonoma Mendocino | CA | Merged 1993 with 262 to form 194. |
| 538 | Baluga | 1959 | Philipine Islands | PI | Absorbed by 498 in 1965. |
| 539 | Passaquo | 1959 | Lone Tree | MA | Merged 1993 with 490 and 505 to form 158. |
| 540 | Ahtuhquog | 1959 | Potomac | MD | |
| 541 | Mic-O-Say | 1959 | Western Colorado | CO | |
| 542 | Kiminschi | 1960 | Mid Valley | PA | Merged 1962 with 543 to form 542. |
| 542 | Amad'ahi | 1962 | Forest Lakes | PA | Merged 1991 with 223 to form 191. |
| 543 | Monsey | 1960 | Dan Beard | PA | Merged 1962 with 542 to form 542. |
| 544 | Ha-Wo-Wo-He-Que'-Nah | 1960 | Teton Peaks | ID | Merged 1994 with 407 to form 407. |
| 545 | Alapaha | 1960 | Alapaha Area | GA | |
| 546 | Chi Sigma | 1960 | Louis Agassiz Fuertes | NY | Merged 1975 with 477 to form 477. |
| 547 | Ga-Goh'-Sa | 1960 | Seneca | NY | Merged 1975 with 165 to form 165. |
| 548 | Sha-Cha-Quoi | 1961 | Sequoia | CA | Merged 1994 with 102 to form 195. |
| 549 | Toontuk | 1961 | Midnight Sun | AK | |
| 550 | Menawngihella | 1961 | Mountaineer Area | WV | |
| 551 | Na-Ko-Na | 1961 | Copper | AZ | Changed name in 19??. |
| 551 | Saldo | 1961 | Copper | AZ | Absorbed by 432 in 1977. |
| 552 | Eckale Yakanen | 1961 | Sunny Land | FL | Rechartered 1961 after disbanding in 1955 as 219. Absorbed by 564 in 1995. |
| 553 | Paugassett | 1961 | Housatonic | CT | |
| 554 | He-Dia | 1962 | Maui County | HI | Changed name in 1963 |
| 554 | Haleakala | 1962 | Maui County | HI | Changed name in 1964. |
| 554 | Maluhia | 1962 | Maui County | HI | |
| 555 | Gamenowinink | 1962 | Direct Service | TX | Absorbed 446 in 1971 Absorbed 391 in 1987. |

| No. | Lodge Name | Yr. | Council | ST | Notes |
|---|---|---|---|---|---|
| 556 | Metacomet | 1962 | Hampshire-Franklin | MA | Merged 1968 with 507 to form 507. |
| 557 | Pupukea | 1962 | Aloha | HI | Merged 1972 with 454 and 565 to form 567. |
| 558 | Wipunquoak | 1964 | Charter Oak | CT | Merged 1973 with 59, 217, 234, and 491 to form 59. |
| 558 | Ahoalan-Nachpikin | 1995 | Chickasaw | YN | From merger of 345 and 406 in 1995. |
| 559 | Wachtschu Mawachpo | 1964 | Westark Area | AR | |
| 560 | Eswau Huppeday | 1964 | Piedmont Area | NC | |
| 561 | Oala Ishadalakalish | 1966 | Lake Bonneville | UT | Merged 1996 with 514 and 529 to form 535. |
| 562 | Arawak | 1966 | Virgin Islands | VI | |
| 563 | Atchafalaya | 1966 | Evangeline Area | LA | |
| 564 | Osceola | 1968 | Southwest Florida | FL | Absorbed 552 in 1995. |
| 565 | Achsin | 1970 | Chamorro | GM | Merged 1973 with 454 and 557 to form 567. |
| 566 | Malibu | 1972 | Great Western | CA | From merger of 225 and 228 in 1972. |
| 567 | Mokupuni O Lawelawe | 1972 | Aloha | HI | From merger of 454, 557, and 565 in 1972. Changed name in 1986. |
| 567 | Na Mokupuni O Lawelawe | 1972 | Aloha | HI | |
| 573 | Sakima | 1973 | LaSalle | IN | From merger of 182, half of 142, and 452 in 1973. |
| 578 | Hasinai | 1970 | Three Rivers | TX | From merger of 36 and 62 in 1970. |
| 614 | Tataliya | 1992 | Grand Columbia | WA | From merger of 301 and 335 in 1992. |
| 617 | Chi-Hoota-Wei | 1993 | Buckskin | WV | From merger of 210, 416, and 475 in 1993. |
| 618 | Nendawen | 1990 | Allohak Area | WV | From merger of 201 and 527 in 1990. |
| 619 | Portage | 1996 | Heart of Ohio | OH | From merger of 121, 205, and 513 in 1996. |

# REFERENCE BOOKS

In the past 20 years collectors have begun to combine their interests and publish specialized guidebooks, many of which are listed below.

*An Aid to Collecting Council Shoulder Patches with Valuation Guide*, 1998
  Franck, Hook, Ellis and Jones

*The Blue Book, Standard Order of the Arrow Insignia Catalog*
  American Scouting Historical Society

*The Boy Scouts of America During World War I and II*
  Mitch Reis

*BSA National Jamboree Shoulder Insignia, A History in Color*

*The Camp Book, A Listing of B.S.A. Camps*
  Dave Minnihan and Bob Sherman

*Charles L. Sommers High Adventure Base Patch Guide*
  Robert Hannah

*Collecting Boy Scout Literature, A Collector's Guide to Boy Scout Fiction and Non-Fiction*
  Chuck Fisk and Doug Bearce

*Collecting Boy Scout Rank Badges*
  Paul Myers

*Collecting Deputy Scout, District Commissioner Badges and Pins*
  Paul Myers

*Collecting Scout Leader Pins*
  Paul Myers

*Collecting the Original 12 Regions*
  Paul Myers

*A Complete Guide to Scouting Collectibles with Value*, 1992
  Rolland J. Sayers

*A Comprehensive Guide to the Eagle Scout Award*
  Terry Grove

*First Flaps*
  Morley, Topkis, and Gould

*Green Khaki Crimped Edge Merit Badges, 1947–1960*
  Fred Duersch, Jr.

*A Guide to CSP Collecting*
  Prince Watkins

*A Guide to Dating Boy Scouts of America Badges, Uniforms and Insignia*
  Mitch Reis

*The History of the Lone Scouts through Memorabilia*
  Mitch Reis

*A History of the Order of the Arrow through Insignia, Arapaho II*, 1993
  Hoogeveen, Briethaupt and Leubitz

*Insignia Guide: Florida Sea Base*
  Hannah and Petersen

*Merit Badge Price Guide*
  Chris Jensen

*National Jamboree Memorabilia Guide Book*, 1995
  Chris Jensen, Jim Ellis

*The OA Price Guide*
  Farnsworth and J. Groves

*Order of the Arrow Conclave Handbooks*, Vols. 1 & 2
  Dingwerth and Jensen

*Order of the Arrow Price Guide*, 1996
  Greg Baechtle

*Patch Collector's Handbook*
  Myers and Bearce

*Patrol Yell - The Guide for Collecting Patrol Medallions*
  Richard Shields

*Philmont Insignia*
  John Williams

*Red and White Council Shoulder Strips*
  Art Hyman and Rob Kutz

*Region 7 Canoe Base*
  Chuck McBride

*Scouting Exonumnia Worldwide*
  Rudy Dioszegi

*Scouting History through Memorabilia: the Bernie Miller Collection*, Vols. 1 & 2
  Roy More

*Senior Scouting Collectibles*
  Jim Clough

# GLOSSARY OF COMMONLY USED TERMS

**Bar mount:** a solid bar onto which the pin is attached (rather than a pin attached directly to device)

**BSA:** Boy Scouts of America

**B-W-R:** Blue-White-Red colors in a patch or ribbon

**C-A-W or C.A.W:** Compass-Anchor-Wings combined design of the Explorer Division

**Chenille:** fuzzy style of patch, like a school varsity letter

**Cloth back:** patch with plain back

**Community Strip:** single line arc with town name

**Clutch back:** pin or collar device with pin on back and detachable circular squeeze wing

**Crude clasp:** safety style pin with only a bent metal fastener; usually found on rank pins

**CSP:** Council Shoulder Patch

**Cut edge:** patch edge where cloth is just cut

**FDL:** Fleur-de-lis; the scout emblem

**Felt:** usually a base material which is embroidered with a design

**Flap:** a patch in the shape of a button-down pocket flap; worn on the right pocket flap, identifies OA Lodge membership

**Folded pin:** plain bent wire

**Full square:** a pre-1940 neckerchief which is a large full square of cloth

**Gauze back:** patch with gauze material on back

**Green and Brown:** Community, State, or Council Strip of brown lettering on green twill (Explorers)(1945–55)

**Jacket Patch:** a large 6-10" patch made for the back of a jacket

**JSP:** Jamboree Council Shoulder Patch

**Khaki and Red:** Community, State, or Council Patch with red lettering on khaki twill (1935–1950)

**Leather Patch:** made for back packs

**LSA:** Lone Scouts of America (1915–1925 name)

**LSD:** Lone Scout Division (post-1925 name, after inclusion into BSA)

**LSS:** Lone Scout Service (post-1925 name, after inclusion into BSA)

**National:** The National Council, currently in Irvine, TX; formerly New York City and North Brunswick, NJ

**N/C:** neckerchief

**NESA:** National Eagle Scout Association

**NOAC:** National Order of the Arrow Conference

**NSJ:** National Scout Jamboree

**OA:** Order of the Arrow

**Plastic back:** patch with plastic coating on back

**Pocket Patch:** a 2-4" patch usually worn on the right pocket

**Red and White:** Community, State, or Council Patch with white lettering on red twill. (1950–1972)

**Region:** From 1921–1972 the local councils were divided into twelve regional groupings; there are now six

**Rolled edge:** patch edge where cloth is embroidered over

**R-W-B:** Red-White-Blue colors in a patch or ribbon

**Safety clasp:** pin fits into locking housing

**Safety pin clasp:** standard style safety pin; usually found on rank pins

**Screw back:** pin or collar device with screw post on back and detachable circular, hexagon, or florate

**Solid:** a fully-embroidered patch

**State Strip:** single line small arc with state name or abbreviation

**Twill:** rough or smooth; a cotton base material for a patch with rib-like design which slants left or right

**WJ:** World Jamboree

**Yellow and Blue:** Community, State, or Council Patch with yellow lettering on blue (Cubs) (1930–1950)

# WHERE TO BUY AND SELL STUFF

The following is a listing of individuals and organizations that have recently produced a printed scouting fixed price list or mail bid auction catalog. The listing of a company does not in any way mean an endorsement by the author or the publisher. If you are interested in buying scouting items from, or selling scouting items to, any of these firms you should request a sample of their product (include $1.00 for postage) and compare their terms of sale or purchase.

Brush Creek Trading Co.
(John Pleasants) P.O. Box 296, Staley, NC 27355

The Carolina Trader
(Richard Shields) P.O. Box 769, Monroe, NC 28111

Grand Teton Scout Museum,
(Bill Gomm) P.O. Box 3, Shelly, ID 83274

Hasty's Auction,
P.O. Box 1786, Anderson, IN 46014

Heart o'Texas Trader
(John C. Williams) P.O. Box 23374, Waco, TX 76702

Looking for Something?
(Darrel & Janice Wessinger) 177 Sandy Bank Dr., Lexington, SC 29072

Pacific Skyline Council, BSA (TOR Auction)

The Patch Connection,
P.O. Box 1248, Summerville, SC 29484

Rolland J. Sayers,
P.O. Box 629, Brevard, NC 28712

Santa Clara County Council, BSA (TOR Auction)

The Scout Patch Auction
(Roy More) 2484 Dundee, Ann Arbor, MI 48103

Scout Patch Network
(Gene Cobb) 2097 Highway 1153, Oakdale, LA 71463

Scout Stuff
(Chris Jensen) P.O. Box 1841, Easley, SC 29641

Scouting Collectibles
(Doug Bearce) P.O. Box 4742, Salem, OR 97302

The Stevensons
(Jim & Bea Stevenson) 316 Sage Lane, Euless, TX 76039

The Trading Post
(Peter Bielak) 5516 Trent St. Somerset, Washington, DC 20815

# COLLECTOR ORGANIZATIONS

These organizations publish newsletters of interest to collectors (price shown is annual dues):

American Scouting Historical Society
c/o Bill Topkis, 2580 Silver Cloud Court, Park City, UT 84060

American Scouting Traders Association
P.O. Box 21013, San Francisco, CA 94121

National Scouting Collectors Society ($12)
c/o Mrs. Billie Lee, 806 E. Scott, St. Tuscola, FL 61953

Scout and Stamps Society International ($15)
c/o Corresponding Secretary
Kenneth A. Shuker, 20 Cedar Lane, Cornwall, NY 12518

The Scouter's Journal ($18)
P.O. Box 4100, Shawnee Mission, KS 66204

Scouting Memorabilia ($5)
P.O. Box 1121, Manchester, NH 03105

World Scout Sealers ($4)
Murray Fried, 25 Gildner St. Kitchener, Ontario, Canada N2H 6M4

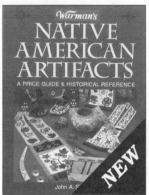